The One Voice of
James Dickey

The One Voice of

James Dickey

His Letters and Life, 1970–1997

Edited with Commentary
by Gordon Van Ness

University of Missouri Press
Columbia and London

University of Missouri Press, Columbia, Missouri 65201
Printed and bound in the United States of America
5 4 3 2 1   09 08 07 06 05

Library of Congress Cataloging-in-Publication Data

Dickey, James.
    The one voice of James Dickey : his letters and life, 1970–1997 / edited with commentary
by Gordon Van Ness.
        p. cm.
    Summary: "The second volume of the letters and life of James Dickey. This volume
chronicles Dickey's career from the publication of *Deliverance* through his poetic experimentation in *The Eye Beaters, Blood, Victory, Madness, Buckhead and Mercy* and *Puella*.
Includes correspondence with Saul Bellow, Arthur Schlesinger, and Robert Penn Warren"
—Provided by publisher.
    Includes index.
    ISBN 0-8262-1572-6 (alk. paper)
    1. Dickey, James—Correspondence. 2. Authors, American—20th century—
Correspondence.   I. Van Ness, Gordon, 1950– II. Title.
    PS3554.I32Z48 2005
    811'.54—dc22
                                                                                    2005002500

♾™ This paper meets the requirements of the
American National Standard for Permanence of Paper
for Printed Library Materials, Z39.48, 1984.

Designer: Jennifer Cropp
Typesetter: Crane Composition, Inc.
Printer and binder: Thomson-Shore, Inc.
Typefaces: Minion, Galliard, LTZapfino

The University of Missouri Press gratefully acknowledges the generous assistance of Eugene
Davidson in the publication of this volume.

For Lara

Blood into light

Is possible: . . .
        surviving   reviving, and wearing well
    For this sundown, and not any other,
            In the one depth

Without levels, deepening for us.

James Dickey, "Deborah as Scion"

Contents

"Don't give away *anything* to the target. He's not just going to sit there and let you shoot him. If he's got any notion you're around, he'll gain altitude, he'll lose. He'll turn all sorts of ways. He's going to jink and he's going to jank. So be ready. Be one ahead of him. Always. Every second. Think like he does. *Be* him. . . . And you'll live. So will your pilot. And like the kids say when they play 'Put Your Right Foot In' on skates at the birthday party, that's what it's all about."

Crux

Life and poetry at the best levels, are, so to speak, interchangeable.

Letter to James Wright

The poet tries to make a kind of order, . . . it would not be possible except for the divine *disorder* of human experience.

Self-Interviews

A man cannot pay as much attention to himself as I do without living in Hell all the time.

Sorties

Why is the sense of starting over so important to me.

Sorties

My lies seemed better, more and more like truth.

Deliverance

My life belongs to the world. I will do what I can.

"The Strength of Fields"

Splinter uncontrollably whole.

"The Eagle's Mile"

Who has told you what discoveries
There are, along the stressed blank
Of a median line? From it, nothing

Can finally fall. Like a spellbinder's pass
A tense placid principle continues

Over it, and when you follow you have the drift,

The balance of many compass needles
Verging to the pole.

"Basics"

Acknowledgments

Clichés of acknowledgment are sometimes accurate. This book simply would not have been possible without the assistance and generosity of many people.

Stephen Enniss and the exemplary staff in Special Collections at Emory University accommodated my visits and promptly acted on my copying requests. I am particularly grateful to Linda Matthews and Kathy Shoemaker, whose knowledge of the extensive James Dickey Papers facilitated my efforts. Joyce Pair allowed me use of personal letters and photographs and critiqued sections of the manuscript; this book is immeasurably better as a consequence. As the founding editor of the *James Dickey Newsletter*, she first believed in my research when I was a graduate student at the University of South Carolina and has continued to provide sound guidance and editorial counsel. Don Greiner, one of the finest professors I ever had, graciously answered my many questions about the "power lunches" he and Ben Franklin had with Dickey. He shared memories and photographs, and his generosity made clearer Dickey's own.

Henry Hart offered me access to materials he used for his biography of Dickey; my research is better because of his own extensive efforts. David Havird and Gary Kerley made available copies of letters Dickey exchanged with them. William Mills kindly allowed me use of photographs he took. Throughout my long study of James Dickey, William Frank believed.

Florence Southall and Tammy Hines of the Reference and Interlibrary Loan Departments, respectively, of the Longwood University Library were indispensable in obtaining difficult-to-secure articles and essays. I am grateful for their efforts.

Lisa Seamster explained to me how computers can print from disks, and Bianca Conn provided duplicating help whenever I needed it, which was often. Without their assistance, the manuscript of this book would still be in my own "cave of making."

Both David Cordle, Dean of the College of Arts and Sciences, and Norm Bregman, Provost and Academic Vice President, supported faculty grants and my sabbatical, which hastened the completion of this project. Their support of pure research is commendable and deeply appreciated.

Beverly Jarrett, Director and Editor-in-Chief of the University of Missouri Press, remains a fervent believer that James Dickey was one of the greatest poets in twentieth-century American literature. That she staunchly supported and defended the 868-page manuscript I sent her, never asking me to cut its length, awes me. Jane Lago remains the best editor I know; I cannot write a sentence without considering what she is likely to say.

Matthew J. Bruccoli, Literary Personal Representative of the Estate of James Dickey, granted permission to publish unprinted letters. His knowledge of literary copyright and his promotion of authorship command my respect. Correspondence previously published is used by permission of Alfred A. Knopf, a division of Random House, Inc.

The following libraries granted permission to publish from their holdings:

James Dickey Papers, Special Collections, Robert W. Woodruff Library, Emory University

John Berryman Papers and James Wright Papers, Manuscripts Division, University of Minnesota Libraries

Milne Special Collections and Archives, University of New Hampshire Library

Willard and Margaret Thorp Papers, Manuscript Division, Department of Rare Books and Special Collections, Princeton University Library

Harry Ransom Humanities Research Center, University of Texas at Austin

James Dickey Papers, Department of Special Collections, Washington University Libraries

Yale Collection of American Literature, Beinecke Rare Book and Manuscript Library, Yale University

I am thankful for my children, Courteney, Gordon, and Ian, whose presence in this world enriches my life and brings me home. Their bright passion, striving for height, holds, and holds me. They are part of all of it—part of flowing stone, the wave's infinite glittering, the glacier's millennial inch—and remind me of the words of Rainer Maria Rilke: "*Wandelt sich rasch die Welt / wie Wolkengestalten, / alles Vollendete fällt / heim zum Uralten.*"

Editorial Note

James Dickey was a prolific letter writer. He wrote artists and scholars, editors and media executives, friends and former students, businessmen and politicians, actors and directors, athletes and admirers. He once even wrote the pope. He understood that correspondence, properly used, might open up new opportunities. "Try to get out at least three or four letters a day. Or five," he wrote in *Sorties*. "Five would be better. There is no telling what that extra letter might bring into being." Critics frequently condemned such statements as self-centered and self-serving, but that is too simplistic. Dickey consciously cultivated his career, attempting without apology to advance himself and his poetic beliefs by engaging in literary politics. He understood the odds any American poet faced, regardless of his or her talent, and he believed that his poems did not exist if they were not published and read. Yet his correspondence is more than self-aggrandizement. It constitutes a statement of identity, of who he essentially was, and in so doing reveals not only his deep love for literature and his far-ranging intelligence but also his astonishing generosity. He frequently nominated writers for fellowships or grants, for example; he arranged readings for them or coordinated efforts for their membership in prestigious literary organizations, such as the American Academy of Arts and Letters. As poetry editor for *Esquire,* moreover, he deliberately attempted whenever possible to publish and promote poets whose work he deemed important regardless of their literary reputation or the state of current fads. Dickey would often include in his correspondence a copy of his most recent book or a signed typescript of a work in progress. Late in his life, he wrote old friends and acquaintances, reestablishing personal connections or thanking them for their presence in his life or their creative influence in the world. Dickey's letters, in other words, reveal a munificent personality, selfless and sensitive, and at odds with the swaggering poet-outdoorsman that constituted his public persona.

Speaking at the memorial service held at the University of South Carolina to honor Dickey, Pat Conroy declared of his former teacher and mentor, "He tried to live a hundred lives and succeeded in living 95 of them. No American life has been so restless in the pursuit of expertise in so many fields. A whole city of men lived in that vivid, restless country behind James Dickey's trans-fixing eyes." The statement suggests that in his search for experience and self-identity, Dickey lost the fundamental sense of who he was. Dickey's own comments support such a contention. In *Sorties* he wrote, "I have self-dramatized myself out of myself, into something else. What was that other I have left?" The letters, however, disprove that assertion. They reveal a multi-talented writer whose broad interests, deep imagination, and psychological needs necessitated that he continually remake the past and revitalize the pre-sent. He believed that the only excuse for getting older was that one also got better, and he was determined to enter totally into the inexplicable fullness and wonder of life. To accomplish this, he assumed many roles. If he did not always live up to the experiences his persona promoted, he nevertheless re-membered to write down what a man vitally alive should do and be. He altered what he said and how he said it depending on the audience, but his was always only one voice.

Because the amount of Dickey's correspondence is so large, any volume of letters must necessarily limit itself. I have selected not only those letters that best reveal the development of his literary career and his conscious efforts to shape and chart its course but also, and just as important, those that portray his other interests and that depict the various aspects of his personality. The letters do not provide a systematic or comprehensive biography of Dickey's life, though they yield a general sense of his comings, goings, and doings. To facilitate a larger understanding and to place his life and art in perspective, I have included an overview of each decade. These prose sections depict the "lay of the literary land" in which Dickey discerned himself and suggest the psychological needs that determined his course of action in the literary mis-sion to which he devoted himself.

The letters are reproduced here without emendations; there are no silent deletions or revisions. Spelling and punctuation, including the absence of punc-tuation, have been preserved exactly, because how a writer writes, the appear-ance of his words on a page, makes a statement. I have minimized the number of footnotes, including them only when necessary to provide clarification or an explanation beyond those provided by the introductions to each section; the more footnotes, the fewer the number of letters a volume may contain.

I have given each letter an identifying heading, thus:

Recipient   **Description and location of letter**
Assigned date (if needed)   **Assigned place of writing (if needed)**

The return address and date are transcribed exactly as they appear on the document, but the address of the recipient has not been included. The following abbreviations are used in the description rubric:

CC   carbon copy
RTL   revised typed letter
RTLS   revised typed letter signed
TL   typed letter unsigned
TLS   typed letter signed

Throughout his life James Dickey believed himself variously at war—against his parents, opposing football teams, the Japanese, social restraints and conventions, suspect poets, and the New York literary establishment. Most of all, however, he was at war with himself, with the coward he believed he essentially was, and with time, the Great Enemy, which inexorably debilitated and depleted and thereby defeated what he innately needed to be, a hero or savior of some kind. He believed in the power of dreams to defeat time, frequently citing a line by the French poet Gérard de Nerval to the effect that the dream was a second life. Dickey was not afraid to die—he understood the nature of existence despite a kind of Romantic longing for the Platonic—but he was afraid of being alone. At the end of his life, he always seemed to want—to need—friends by his side. Christopher Dickey remembers that when his father was hospitalized just before he died, "the whole team of people who had come together for him in the previous months and years was on the scene." One of these close friends was Ward Briggs, a colleague from the University of South Carolina, who had immediately recognized how weak Dickey was when he visited the hospital. A few weeks previously, after a night in which Briggs had slept over at Dickey's house, Dickey had told him of a dream he had had. He was at North Fulton High School and had scored three touchdowns, including the game-winner, and then had had a date with the most beautiful girl in Georgia. He was with her in a convertible, the top down and bathed in moonlight. All things on all sides were exactly right, but he could not be happy, he told the girl, because it was all a dream. She had said to him, "It's all real within the dream, Jim. It's all real in the dream." Briggs now remembered this and took Dickey's hand. "It's all real within the dream," he said, and Dickey smiled. "I know it is," he said.

Rest easy, Jim. The thing itself, this dream, is over.

The One Voice of
James Dickey

Angels Nine

For James Dickey, writing was always a statement of identity, revealing variations of himself that he emotionally or psychologically needed to project and promote. His poetry and fiction, therefore, properly read, reflect his complex personality and provide a sense of its development. Dickey himself admitted as much in *Self-Interviews,* published in 1970: "I have never been able to dissociate the poem from the poet, and I hope I never will. I really don't believe in Eliot's theory of autotelic art, in which the poem has nothing to do with the man who wrote it. I think that's the most absolute rubbish!"[1] His correspondence is no different; it portrays who Dickey essentially was, his one voice. As he wrote in an unpublished letter to Donald Hall dated February 10, 1963, "It's good to do new things, as you are doing, but it is also good to remember that a writer has one main stream running through him and a lot of tributaries that feed into it (also a lot of sumps and stagnant water), and that the work has force and truth only in that current, as it must flow."[2] Dickey's work had force and truth precisely because he recognized that "one main stream" and flowed with it. It was who he was.

Dickey loved rivers and streams, oceans, lakes, swimming pools—any body of water. His son Christopher, recognizing this fact, related in his memoir, "Wherever we went he was drawn to them, and if we could, we lived near them, and if we could not, he sought them out."[3] It is as if water for Dickey held within it a secret promise, another life, as if its various forms, motions, and locations identified him. It is not surprising, therefore, that in his letter to Hall, who was then struggling to write poetry distinctive in subject and style and who had recently sent Dickey a group of poems for comment (Dickey best liked one entitled "The Swamp"), he should utilize the image of flowing water to epitomize not only the writer but also the process by which he wrote.

1. *Self-Interviews* (Garden City, N.Y.: Doubleday, 1970), 24.
2. Hall's correspondence is in the Milne Special Collection and Archives, University of New Hampshire Library, Durham.
3. *Summer of Deliverance: A Memoir of Father and Son* (New York: Simon and Schuster, 1998), 128.

Yet Dickey also loved, and was literarily drawn to, the air. If his 1970 best-selling novel, *Deliverance*, focuses on water (specifically, a canoe trip by four ordinary suburbanites down the Cahulawassee River), his 1987 work, *Alnilam*, a massive novel of 682 pages that required more than thirty years to complete after its conceptualization in the fifties, centers on the air. In an interview following its publication, he declared, "What I wanted to do with the book more than anything else was to restore to the human being the sense of *bodily* flight. I mean, men have only been able to do this for less than a hundred years, to get way up there in the element that they *breathe*, you know, to sustain life, to get up in it."[4] Air seemed to compel Dickey's attention, to insist on its intimate connection to human life and its simultaneous otherness. In a poem entitled "Air," first printed in 1985 and later a section of a longer work published as "Immortals" in *The Whole Motion*, Dickey wrote:

> Air, much greater than the sea—
> . . . .
>   unpeopled, wearing the high lucidity
> Of vigil. Maybe one day the mere surface
>   Of the earth will feel you.

He concluded with what for him was the quality that made the element so important:

>   The air glitters
> All the outside, and keeps carrying
>   You from within.

Water was personal and either redemptive or destructive; air was omnipresent and mystical.

Dickey's entrance into World War II immersed him in that element which would transfix his imagination. He was a P-61 navigator, part of the 418th Night Fighter Squadron stationed in the Philippine Islands, then in the process of being turned from a defensive unit into a squadron whose sorties would be primarily offensive, flying intruder missions to bomb and strafe. The P-61 "Black Widow" was a two-man plane prized for its maneuverability, reliable

---

4. Bob Gingher, "James Dickey Talks about Story behind *Alnilam*," in *The Voiced Connections of James Dickey*, ed. Ron Baughman (Columbia: University of South Carolina Press, 1989), 263–68.

performance above thirty-five thousand feet, state-of-the-art radar equipment, and weaponry, which included 20 mm cannon and four .50 caliber machine guns. Dickey participated in thirty-eight combat missions, earning five bronze stars while centered in what he would call in his poem "The Performance" "the great, untrustworthy air / He flew in each night, when it darkened." The role of navigator required him to determine the plane's astronomical position, and he became so intrigued with pinpointing location that, years afterward, at his second home at Litchfield Plantation on Pawleys Island, he daily used his collection of more than a dozen sextants to determine his exact place in the world, utilizing thick volumes of navigational tables and a satellite-synchronized global positioning system to check his calculations. Later poems, such as "The Firebombing," "Falling," "The Lord in the Air," and "Reunioning Dialogue," among others, as well as *Sorties,* his book of journal entries and critical essays, and his final novel, *To the White Sea,* all attest to Dickey's abiding interest in air. In a sense his career was an extended aerial combat mission, for war colored his view of life. His letters, the flight "transmissions" he made from the altitudes and locations at which he found himself, reflect the heights he achieved and the lows he suffered as he endeavored to chart and steer his course.

Dickey's correspondence during the forties and fifties, when he had first undertaken his artistic mission, clearly reveals feelings of inadequacy. He believed that his athletic and academic accomplishments at North Fulton High School, as well as during his subsequent year at Darlington High, which he attended to prepare for college, had disappointed both his father and his mother and that he remained a failure to them. Nothing that he had done or that he would do would render him noteworthy. Even his military achievements, respectable in themselves, seemed insignificant to him, especially when compared to the feats of the pulp fiction heroes he idolized during his adolescence, the idealized pilots of *War Birds* and *Flying Aces* who courageously outmaneuvered and attacked enemy pilots. Exaggerated stories that he later related to friends of daring aerial combat derived from these early fantasies; they satisfied his psychological need to feel heroic. That need also underlies other fabrications he created that rendered him larger than life: that he might have played professional football, that he was an expert outdoorsman and an accomplished hunter, that he was a proficient guitarist who once gave lessons to earn money and who played at small "dark" Atlanta clubs. Indeed, Dickey demanded that he not only be the best but also the *acknowledged* best. His fictions reflect a complex personality who protected his vulnerability by directly confronting the world with a pose of male bravado, a poet-action figure who just happened to be sensitive. They also enabled Dickey to project the truth as he envisioned it to be. "Lying," he asserted in *Self-Interviews*, "with luck sublimely, is what the creative man does," arguing that "art is a lie which makes us see the truth, or which makes truth better than it is."[5]

Throughout his career, Dickey continually re-created himself, enlarging or embellishing aspects of his personality. In poems that he wrote, in readings that he gave, in classes that he taught, and in conversations with other artists, he offered versions of himself necessitated by his desire to remake the past and vitalize the present. He altered what he said and how he said it depending on his audience. Like the speaker's mother in his poem "Buckdancer's Choice," who warbles "all day . . . / The thousand variations of one song; . . . Through stratum after stratum of a tone / Proclaiming what choices there are," he enlarged his identity to include Dickey the Celestial Navigator, Dickey the Father, Dickey the Political Strategist, Dickey the Southern Redneck, Dickey the Poet, all personae he willingly assumed to explore himself. Despite the variations, however, he always knew who he was. As his career soared, and as it later fell, seeming near the end of his life to fade entirely off the literary radar screen, his was always one voice.

In the unparalleled glamour following the publication of *Deliverance*, Dickey soared beyond anything he might have imagined when, as a six-year-old boy, he had composed a five-page autobiography, "The Life of James Dickey," characterizing himself as a combat pilot and illustrating the book with crayoned pictures of airplanes. In the early seventies, Dickey seemed to be flying at "angels nine," nine thousand feet in the language of World War II aviators, at the apogee of literary and financial success. Reflecting on the novel's publication, Matthew J. Bruccoli, a colleague at the University of South Carolina who became his close friend and literary executor, stated: "It was a very good and a very bad experience for Jim. It gave him an enlarged readership, but with the money he made from it, he began living too well and stopped working as hard as he had. I'm not saying he was corrupted, but the spur wasn't there anymore."[6] Popular and critical interest in *Deliverance*, for which Dickey received a $5,000 advance, had increased when *Atlantic Monthly* in its February 1970 issue printed an excerpt of the novel, entitled "Two Days in September." Houghton Mifflin published the book in March with a first printing of 50,000 copies, a high number for an author whose previous books

---

5. *Self-Interviews*, 32.
6. William W. Starr, "'Deliverance' Lifted Dickey into a Prominence He Never Managed to Match," *The State*, June 30, 2002, pp. E1–2.

were either collections of poetry or critical books about poetry, the largest printing of which had been 7,500 copies. By July 21, *Deliverance* had sold 67,000 hardback copies and become a best seller. The paperback, published by Dell, was released in April 1971. By its eighth printing in June 1973, sales had reached 1,800,000 copies. Dickey seemed baffled by the response. Despite claims for the novel, he considered himself primarily a poet, but the financial windfall overwhelmed him. "All this is very strange," he wrote on April 13, 1970, to Jonathan Williams, a poet and founder of the Jargon Society, a small press specializing in poetry, art, photography, and fine printing, "to someone who is use [*sic*] to counting his literary earnings at the rate of fifty cents a line, doled out on that basis from <u>The Kenyon Review</u>."[7] He reiterated the same point to Willie Morris, an editor at *Harper's,* in an unpublished letter dated May 20: "All this is kind of strange to me, though very gratifying, as you may imagine."[8] Dickey earned approximately $20,000 in paperback rights and $17,500 from the Literary Guild rights in 1970. The following year royalties totaled $45,000.[9]

The success of *Deliverance* changed Dickey's literary reputation, making him one of the country's best-known writers, but the fame arrived at a price; in gaining such height, he lost his poetic bearings. He even appears to have been aware of the danger, writing Ken McCormick, his editor at Doubleday, in an unpublished letter dated April 8, 1970: "I <u>do</u> want you to know that I am battling hard to keep our book [*The Eye-Beaters, Blood, Victory, Madness, Buckhead and Mercy*] from being swamped by the attention paid to <u>De-liverance</u>, just as I have always fought to keep poetry itself from being ignored in the attention paid to the novel, generally."[10] He expressed the same sentiment the following month to Donald Hall, who worried that Dickey would now abandon his poetry. In an unpublished letter dated May 22, he thanked Hall for "the things you say about <u>Deliverance</u>, and about the poetry. No; have no fear, I will not 'go down for (on?) poetry.' Poetry is the center and the basis of everything I do, whether this is criticism, novel-writing, or even writing the advertising copy I used to do. So, if and when poetry goes for me, so will everything else, so far as the written word is concerned. So I will hang on to that before everything else." Dickey's letters, however, clearly indicate that

7. *Crux: The Letters of James Dickey,* ed. Matthew J. Bruccoli and Judith Baughman (New York: Knopf, 1999), 327.

8. The letter is in the James Dickey Papers, Special Collections Department, Robert W. Woodruff Library, Emory University, Atlanta (hereafter cited as Dickey Papers).

9. Henry Hart, *James Dickey: The World as a Lie* (New York: Picador, 2000), 455.

10. The letter is in the Dickey Papers.

he became increasingly caught up by and involved in the publicity and fanfare, interviews and television appearances, surrounding both the publication of the novel and the subsequent filming of the movie, for which he wrote the script and in which he played a small part.

Dickey worked on the novel throughout 1969, attempting to revise diction he believed too poetic for the narrator, Ed Gentry, the vice president of an advertising agency. In a 1976 interview he reflected on this concern with language:

> *Deliverance* was originally written in a very heavily charged prose, somewhat reminiscent of James Agee. But it was too juicy. It distracted from the narrative thrust, which is the main thing that the story has going for it. So I spent two or three drafts taking that quality out. I wanted a kind of unobtrusively remarkable observation that wouldn't call attention to itself. That's why I made the narrator an art director. He's a guy who *would* see things like this; a writer would perform all kinds of cakewalks to be brilliant stylistically, which would have interfered with the narrative drive of the story.[11]

Jacques de Spoelberch, Dickey's editor at Houghton Mifflin, pressed for the revision of certain scenes. His efforts enhanced the novel's tight, at moments lyrical, flow, though reviewers nevertheless questioned the language. Evan S. Connell, for example, who reviewed *Deliverance* in the March 22, 1970, *New York Times Book Review,* noted that "it is just barely possible to accept the voice of a domesticated American businessman narrating such a horror story," adding, "the story is told in the past tense, yet it is full of absolutely remembered dialogue." Despite this reservation, Connell began the front-page review with unmitigated praise: "*Deliverance* is James Dickey's first novel and it is bad news for the competition." Reviews in *Newsweek, Time,* and *Life* were similarly good. Yet critics generally failed to regard the novel as significant, largely discerning instead an adventure story. Benjamin DeMott was typical when he dismissed the book as "entertaining, shoot'em-up mindlessness" and an "emptily rhetorical horse-opera played in canoes."[12] Only later did critics properly understand the novel's mythic underpinnings and its significance in the development of American literature.

At Vanderbilt, Dickey had immersed himself in reading anthropologists

---

11. Franklin Ashley, "James Dickey: The Art of Poetry XX," *Paris Review* 65–68 (Spring 1976): 52–88 (quotation at 77).

12. Connell, "*Deliverance*," *New York Times Book Review,* March 22, 1970, pp. 1, 23; DeMott, "The 'More Life' School and James Dickey," *Saturday Review,* March 28, 1970, pp. 25–26, 38.

and mythologists, such as Jane Harrison, W. H. R. Rivers, and Franz Boas. In a 1949 issue of *Kenyon Review,* he read Stanley Edgar Hymen's discussion of several books involving ritual and myth, including Joseph Campbell's *The Hero with a Thousand Faces,* in which Hyman quotes Van Gennep's "Rites of Passage" as involving "a separation from the world, a penetration to a source of power, and a life-enhancing return"; the review provided Dickey with the narrative framework of *Deliverance.* Ed Gentry returns home not with a golden fleece or a beautiful princess but rather with a treasure both more intangible and more transcendent. "And so it ended," Gentry thinks, "except in my mind, which changed the events more deeply into what they were, into what they meant to me alone." He understands what only he possesses: "The river underlies, in one way or another, everything I do."[13]

Van Gennep's "Rites of Passage" also yielded Dickey a lens by which to view his own journey from home to college, from training bases to war zone, and from Pacific combat to peacetime Atlanta. Life, he now perceived, was always a conflict against what Campbell had termed "the dragon forces" arrayed against him.[14] At Clemson the struggle had been against opposing linemen; later, it involved the Japanese. Later still, during the sixties, Dickey had engaged the New York literati whose cultural preferences he believed were antithetical to what poetry could deliver. Moreover, if he now gleaned the pattern of his life more clearly than before, he also understood various aspects of his personality, for in crafting the four suburbanites, Dickey also consciously depicted himself.[15] He admitted to John West, an English professor at Appalachian State University, in an unpublished letter dated October 20, 1972: "you could say either that the four main characters are <u>more or less</u> based on people I knew—and still know. But it would probably be even more true to say that they are all aspects of myself. For example, I was an art director like Ed, a kind of survival nut and archer like Lewis, a guitarist like Drew and a weakling like Bobby."[16] With each character, however, the similarities went beyond such a simple generality, a fact Dickey indirectly acknowledged in his journals: "I am Lewis; every word is true."[17]

---

13. *Deliverance* (Boston: Houghton Mifflin, 1970), 280, 281.

14. Campbell, *The Hero with a Thousand Faces* (Princeton: Princeton University Press, 1973), 69.

15. Keen Butterworth argues compellingly that the four main characters reflect aspects of Freudian psychology. See "The Savage Mind: James Dickey's *Deliverance*," *Southern Literary Journal* 28.2 (Spring 1996): 69–78.

16. The letter is in the Dickey Papers.

17. *Sorties* (Garden City, N.Y.: Doubleday, 1971), 75.

As he exchanged a series of letters with Spoelberch discussing revision, Dickey inexplicably worried that some harm would befall either the manuscript or himself. On August 5, 1969, for example, he wrote a seventeen-page unpublished missive detailing proposed alterations throughout the typescript. "I have completed working on the book," he declared, "as you will see when I give you the manuscript in Boston next week. This letter is in the nature of a safety device in the unlikely event that something happens to the manuscript on the airplane or somewhere between here and Boston." The next day he wrote a shorter letter with additional changes he wished to make, asserting that "this is a precaution: it has to do with the unlikely eventuality that I, my wife, my family, vanish without a trace—or, maybe more to the point—without a trace of the manuscript."[18] Later he would express a similar concern regarding *The Zodiac,* when in 1973 he instructed Stewart Richardson, his editor at Doubleday, not only about revisions he wanted to include but also about how the book-length poem should be marketed if anything should happen to him. It is unclear why Dickey felt threatened. Certainly, he courted the attention, but while he was always cognizant of chance occurrences, in *The Eye-Beaters, Blood, Victory, Madness, Buckhead and Mercy,* published in 1970, and in *Sorties,* published in 1971, he also seemed particularly concerned with the debilitating effects of aging and disease.

The Eye-Beaters presented poems that were more socially conscious, less focused on self, and that reveal a preoccupation with mortality. The titles of these new poems, such as "Diabetes," "Mercy," "Venom," "Knock," and "Madness," reflect the loss of afflatus and affirmation characteristic of Dickey's early volumes; they posit only doubt and uncertainty, the individual confronting unstoppable forces. The narrator in "The Cancer Match," for example, realizes

> I don't have all the time
> In the world, but I have all night.
> I have space for me and my house,
>   And I have cancer and whiskey.

Forty-seven years old, Dickey worried about his health. Entries in *Sorties* reinforce the sense of concern. The journal opens, "You cannot feel your own blood run. You can feel the pulse, but not what the pulse does: not what the pulse is for," and becomes more pointed: "The sadness of middle

18. Both letters are in the Dickey Papers.

age is absolutely unfathomable; there is no bottom to it. Everything you do is sad."[19]

As the decade progressed, so did his despair, deepened not only by declining health and the loss of physical abilities but also by the deaths of his father and mother as well as his wife, Maxine. In his 1979 essay, "The Energized Man," Dickey continued to voice an anguish predicated on the effects of aging: "We somehow lead ourselves to believe that the moments of youth—ah, youth, indeed!—were those times when our faculties responded and we loved and hated violently, spent sleepless nights, conceived great projects, and lived in a world of purpose which could not have existed without us. We persuade ourselves that, yes, it was nice, but it was a long time ago, and we should turn to other things: things like . . . well, comfort."[20] Dickey seemed to be waging a war against time itself, what he had called in an early poem, "The Leap," "that eternal process / Most obsessively wrong with the world."

In the April 8, 1970, letter to Ken McCormick, Dickey declared that he was selling as many copies of *The Eye-Beaters* as he was of *Deliverance* and that he hoped sales would soon top ten thousand copies, helped by his readings at Young Harris College on April 2 and Oklahoma State University on April 4. Although sales of the poetry collection did reach the hoped-for number in late May, *The Eye-Beaters* could never attain the novel's popular success. Dickey also informed McCormick that sales of *Deliverance* were approaching one hundred thousand copies, an inflated figure since Houghton Mifflin's initial printing on March 23 had totaled fifty thousand. The exaggeration resulted partly from Dickey's competitiveness, his need to be the best at everything he attempted. *Deliverance* was competing against Erich Segal's *Love Story*, Mario Puzo's *The Godfather*, and John Fowles's *The French Lieutenant's Woman*. The boasting, however, was also partly an effort to overcome feelings of inadequacy by projecting a confident superiority. He always needed his voice, in a sense, to be the loudest, the most acknowledged, and because literary success was defined by sales, he misled others to promote himself. The novel reached number three on the *New York Times* best-seller list in early June before sales slackened.

Dickey's competitiveness led to friction with John Boorman, whom Warner Brothers had hired to direct the movie version of *Deliverance*. Initially, the company wanted Roman Polanski, whom Dickey considered a mood director

---

19. *Sorties*, 1, 55.
20. *The Imagination as Glory: The Poetry of James Dickey*, ed. Bruce Weigl and T. R. Hummer (Urbana and Chicago: University of Chicago Press, 1984), 163.

lacking the ability to depict action well. He also worried that the recent murders of Polanski's wife, Sharon Tate, and their unborn child would hinder his
abilities. Dickey favored Sam Peckinpah, whose recent film, *The Wild Bunch,*
he admired for its treatment of violence within a civilized setting. The doomed
gunslingers resembled the doomed adventurers in *Deliverance.* The selection
of Boorman, however, excited him. Boorman's film *Hell in the Pacific* had
portrayed a single Japanese soldier and a lone American fighter isolated on a
Philippine island where they engage in combat to the death. The movie reminded him of his own experiences in the Pacific during World War II, which
Deliverance indirectly re-created, and imparted to the action a philosophical,
even existential dimension that reduced life to its essential elements.

Dickey had written the screenplay, disregarding sample scripts Warner
Brothers had sent, including that for *Clockwork Orange.* He used as examples
instead treatments written by James Agee. Warner Brothers approved the script
on August 20, but Boorman immediately proposed alterations that substan-
tively changed the novel's opening and closing scenes and revised the dialogue. At the center of the disagreement was the question of who controlled
the script, which is to say, what the film's emphasis would be. To enhance the
action, Boorman wanted to place the four suburbanites on the river as
quickly as possible; by contrast, Dickey insisted on preserving the novel's
mythical structure, the circular movement that would effectively render
Deliverance a contemporary representation of the *Odyssey.* He believed "the
hero with a thousand faces to be," he wrote Boorman on January 18, 1971,
"the most powerful theme in all of literature, all of mythology." Despite attempts at accommodation, Dickey concluded that Boorman lacked artistic
vision, and Boorman believed Dickey was cinematically shortsighted and
would remain intrusive; as a consequence, Boorman assumed complete charge
of the screenplay. Dickey, who had been informed in December that John
Calley of Warner Brothers would only accept a script by the director, nevertheless insisted that he alone receive screenwriting credit. While Boorman
later claimed that "In fact, I wrote the script; it wasn't he who actually drafted
it,"[21] the Credit Arbitration Committee determined in Dickey's favor. Dickey's
efforts to influence the selection of actors and musicians, however, were in-
effectual. Not only was Jon Voigt selected to play Ed Gentry despite Dickey's
attempt to use a cast with no star, but also Dickey was unable to fulfill a
promise to Mike Russo and Ron Brentano that they would play the music for
"Dueling Banjos." Final defeat came when Boorman asked Dickey to leave

21. Hart, *Dickey,* 475.

Clayton, Georgia, where the movie was being shot, because he was interfering with the director and the actors.

Dickey never forgave Boorman's alteration of his script and the treatment he received. Ten years later, he published the original draft of the screenplay and attempted to provide the author's perspective. "Since the writer of screenplays," he wrote in "Bare Bones: Afterword to a Film," "is quite literally not limited by anything, he is free to visualize in ideal terms the story as he would like to see it: that is, *his* ideals as they have always existed in connection with the story, or as they develop from instant to instant as he works." Against this ideality, however, is the reality he confronts:

> The director, first, then the actors, then the technicians and other functionaries set things up to be filmed in a way which is congruent with the director's version of the dramatic and scenic possibilities of the story and whether or not this is consistent with the writer's is strictly immaterial, irrelevant, and in the end something of an embarrassment, at least to the writer. Details are changed, whole sequences are changed, dialogue is altered or improvised until, though something which resembles the original idea of the story remains, the texture, the field of nuance, the details, characterizations, dramatic buildup and resolution as originally conceived, are lost; nothing but the bones are left.[22]

Dickey's adolescent insecurities and his participation in the Second World War led not only to his conviction that life itself was warfare, a Darwinian struggle for dominance, but also to a conceptualization of himself as a hero whose efforts must save society. He needed to overcome whatever forces opposed him, and he needed to be the best at whatever he attempted. As his accomplishments grew and the number of literary prizes he won increased, however, Dickey required even greater recognition in order to feel successful— higher reading fees, more prestigious awards, greater sales, new accomplishments. Advised by friends not to become involved with the filming of *Deliverance,* simply to take the money and run, he nevertheless decided both to write the script and to act in the movie because he wanted to protect the novel's integrity and to assure himself additional acclaim. That he failed to win control of the screenplay and that he was asked to leave the film's set because he interfered with Boorman's directing and the actors' performances suggest the degree to which Dickey committed himself to the conflict with Hollywood and to which he decidedly lost.

22. *Night Hurdling* (Columbia, S.C., and Bloomfield Hills, Mich.: Bruccoli Clark, 1983), 82–86.

Throughout the filming, editing, and promotion of *Deliverance,* Dickey conveyed to his friends none of the disagreements with Boorman; to have done so would have suggested to others that he was not flying at "angels nine" or that his voice was not in command. Despite his blustery, public-performing persona, he was an uncertain, feeling-his-way poet. In an unpublished letter to John Malek dated February 2, 1971, for example, he declared, "I must participate in the filming of my book, Deliverance, this spring, for I did the screen play, and am responsible for it to a certain extent"; to Helen Sorrells on May 17, he asserted, "I will probably have to come out to Hollywood a few more times in connection with the cutting, editing, publicity, and so on connected with the film of Deliverance"; and to Theodore Weiss on January 17, 1972, he proclaimed, "what a film we have got! John Boorman, my director, and I finished the final editing in Los Angeles last month, and it is really some film, I can tell you!" When the movie appeared, Dickey exuded genuine excitement for what he now viewed as *his* movie, and he exaggerated his participation in the project. Apologizing to Charles Gaines for the delay in writing, he wrote in an unpublished letter dated January 20, 1972, "We spent the spring and summer up in the mountains of north Georgia with Warner Brothers filming the movie version of Deliverance, and since then I have been running all over the country doing editing, publicity, and whatever else they are continually having me do with the film. . . . It is some film, too, I can tell you! I don't believe the American public is going to believe what it sees coming up on that Panavision screen. In fact, some of the scenes are so terrifying that even I can't bear to look at them, and I wrote the screenplay!"[23] Unable to control or at times even participate in the filming of the movie, he nevertheless contrived to appear to be doing so.

Dickey consciously manipulated situations in order to promote himself, but the dichotomy between reality and appearance confused friends and distanced artists and later contributed to the decline of his career when critics seemed unable to see through the public persona he had fashioned. Tales he had created to glamorize or mythologize himself—which is to say, the stories he invented to bolster his vulnerable self-image, such as his combat accomplishments, his exaggerated hunting exploits, and his football, track, and tennis prowess—outwardly spoke of a writer who was merely boasting. His identity threatened, however, Dickey created fictions to protect himself and accentuate aspects of his personality. Reviews of *Self-Interviews,* for example, published

---

23. The letters to Malek, Weiss, and Gaines are in the Dickey Papers. The letter to Sorells is included herein.

the same year as *Deliverance*, which examined the development of his own career and the intent of many of his early poems, noted the book's basic self-centeredness, lack of profundity, and linguistic simplicity. James Aronson complained that the "gee-whiz tone of the whole still leaves one wondering," and Richard Calhoun noted that Dickey's commentary offered so little one considers unexpected, as if the reader encounters "the public Dickey speaking on the level of good conversation" and not "the voice of the inner man."[24]

The disparity that developed between Dickey's basic self and the image he needed to portray, an image that appeared more and more manipulative and manipulated, increasingly affected critics' views of his works. Dickey, moreover, distinguished who he was and what he said or even wrote depending on the situation or conflict as well as on his audience. For example, his son Kevin nearly fell into a chasm while crossing a rope bridge during the filming of *Deliverance*, after which Kevin claimed his father "basically jerked me off the set, saying, 'You're coming with me. Do you realize you scared the hell out of me?'"[25] But Dickey recounted the incident differently. In his essay "Delights of the Edge," he celebrated such daring, the deliberate courting of risk, where mutilation, paralysis, and death are real possibilities. At those moments, he asserted, "you don't really know what on earth you *will* do, can do, or what some blind agency outside your control will cause you to do. That is when the void can be danced with."[26] There was always, in other words, a vital distinction between the real world and the ideal. Words for Dickey were Possibility; they provided an illusion that sustained him by creating a truth that was more real than facts, allowing him a needed sense of self regardless of its effect on others.

Such illusions never became delusions. Yet his inability to control the film presentation of *Deliverance* affected his sensibilities and led to self-imposed demands for heightened recognition just as his creative endeavors were becoming more experimental and provocative. Reviews of *Sorties* were disappointing, particularly since he had anticipated a positive critical reception. He had exchanged considerable correspondence with Stewart Richardson to select journal entries and essays and met with the editor for three days in September 1971. Dickey had also declined to serve as a poetry judge for the National Book Awards, fearing that it might jeopardize the book's chances in the

24. Aronson, "*Self-Interviews*," *Antioch Review* 30 (Fall/Winter 1970–1971): 463–64; Calhoun, "'His Reason Argues with His Invention': James Dickey's *Self-Interviews* and *The Eye-Beaters*," *South Carolina Review* 3 (June 1971): 9–16 (quotation at 11).

25. Hart, *Dickey*, 485.

26. *Night Hurdling*, 169.

Arts and Letters category, which was won by Charles Rosen's *The Classical Style: Hayden, Mozart, Beethoven.* He then discovered that *The Eye-Beaters* had failed the previous year to make the short list for the National Book Award, though he consoled himself that the same was true of Robert Lowell's *Notebooks* and John Berryman's *Love and Fame. The Eye-Beaters* was also overlooked for the Pulitzer. The only significant award accorded Dickey in 1971 came from another country; in late November he flew with wife, Maxine, and son Kevin to accept France's Prix Médicis for the best non-French novel of the year.

Doubleday published *Sorties* on December 10, 1971. Two-thirds of the book consists of journal entries, many of which Dickey intended to be inflammatory. Despite labeling the journals "a catchall," in which "I am not likely to say anything scandalous or private," he proceeded in the next entry to declare masturbation "one of the most profound forms of self-communication and even self-communion." Often Dickey appeared deliberately to criticize and condemn other writers: Galway Kinnell was "very limited, and very monotonous"; Richard Wilbur, "tiresome"; and John Berryman, "a timid little academic who stays drunk all the time . . . tortures his poems up, deliberately misspells words, [and] wrenches the syntax around in various ways that are easy enough to do." Anne Sexton, Anne Stevenson, and Adrienne Rich, moreover, all had "a rather studied way of avoiding any kind of rhetorical statement" in their effort to say "something quirky and offhand." Sylvia Plath's poems exhibited "hysterical intelligence," and Donald Hall was "bad, awfully bad, and funnily bad." Dickey, however, was not entirely condemnatory. The Russian poet Yevgeny Yevtushenko, he declared, had "a true *seeming* spontaneity." The work of Luis Cernuda and Vicente Aleixandre "explore[s] their own segment of reality, and . . . is very good indeed." Reviewers generally believed that in *Sorties* Dickey had ventured upon a self-charted ego trip that promoted his memories and literary opinions as important postmodern criticism. The large egocentric presence in his essays, like that in his controversial poetry readings when Dickey was obviously intoxicated, merely increased the perception that he seriously considered only himself, a perception best exemplified in an entry where Dickey states, "It seems to me that I am the bearer of some kind of immortal message to humankind. What is this message? I don't know, but it exists."[27]

Other entries in *Sorties* center on masks and poses, the persona a writer assumes. At times Dickey seemed to assert that he remained his essential self,

27. *Sorties,* 54.

free from such deviation or deception, while revealing his continuing self-hatred: "one feels so damn sorry for writers, the poor posers. People like Hemingway and Yeats spend their whole lives trying to make good a pose because they despise themselves. They put infinite time and energy into trying to make themselves come true, when they know that it's all a damn lie, anyway." Yet as one of the posers who "despise themselves," he also asserted, "I have self-dramatized myself out of myself, into something else," and admitted, "I am a haunted artist like the others. I know what the monsters know, and shall know more." Dickey also addressed the relationship between the poet and his persona in his essay "The Self as Agent," where he argued that the "I" in a poem is more than the ordinary self; it is the agent who enables the poet to discover his poem and thereby vitalize an aspect of himself. Because the poet is a varied personality, he remains "capable of inventing or of bringing to light out of himself a very large number of I-figures to serve in different poems, none of them obliged to act in conformity with the others."[28] Although he did not provide any psychological justification for this theory, the view is consistent with Dickey's need to transcend socially dictated standards and validate a self that continually needs enlargement.

Dickey's concern with his own identity, his Self, appears in other essays in *Sorties,* such as "The Son, the Cave, and the Burning Bush," "Metaphor as Pure Adventure," and "Spinning the Crystal Ball." Each begins with Dickey as an informing presence on the American literary scene, commenting in the first essay as a middle-aged poet on an anthology of fifty-four new writers entitled *The Young American Poets* and lecturing in the others as consultant to the Library of Congress on, respectively, the poet's search for metaphors of discovery and the present movements in and future course of American poetry. Unlike his critical stance in "The Suspect in Poetry," or his reviews of other poets, however, Dickey here clearly makes himself the critical center. For example, in "The Son, the Cave, and the Burning Bush," he considers the prospect that young poets might fulfill the redemptive potential of poetry, declaring, "For a middle-aged poet like myself this promise takes on a particularly acute anguish of hope." The concern here is with his own emotional reaction. When he then adds, "The aging process almost always brings to the poet the secret conviction that he has settled for too little, that he has paid too much attention to the 'limitations' that his contemporaries have assured him he has, as well as to literary tradition and the past," the lack of first person never mitigates the sense that Dickey is referring to himself, particularly when

28. Ibid., 104, 74, 73, 161.

one remembers his preoccupation in *Sorties* with aging and death and with his stated concern for the "forms" of poetry.[29]

"Metaphor as Pure Adventure" and "Spinning the Crystal Ball" also place Dickey at the center of the criticism. The former opens by establishing the poet's inward exploration: "The longer I continue to write, the more it seems to me that the most exciting thing about poetry is its sense of imminent and practical discovery." The essay presents what he conceives poetry to be, what he favors or opposes, and how he believes the mind operates in relating items. When he asserts that the poem is "a kind of action in which, if the poet can participate *enough,* other people cannot help participating as well," Dickey not only offers his own understanding of poetic effect but establishes his Self as essential to the process. "Spinning the Crystal Ball" more explicitly declares his involvement, stating that the lecture "will be partly about what I think will happen in American poetry and what I *hope* will happen." At the conclusion Dickey expands the perspective to include everyone: "That is what we want: to be gathered together once more, to be able to enter in, to participate in experience, to possess our lives." Such an almost Whitmanesque extension, however, proceeds from Dickey himself, for he then asserts: "I think that the new poetry will be a poetry of the dazzlingly simple statement." This poetry, if attained, will reveal a new, intimate aspect of Self, one more vital and enhanced than any currently known. It will share in the forces and processes that govern the universe. "We have one self that is conditioned, all right," Dickey asserts, "But there is another self . . . that connects most readily with the flow of rivers and the light from the sun; it is in this second (or first) and infinitely older being that we can be transfigured by eyes and recreated by flesh."[30] Dickey's criticism exposes this possibility; the poetry, he hopes, will actualize it. The lecture, simply stated, posits Dickey the poet as spokesman and seer, not surprising perhaps, for he believed himself under attack on a number of fronts: by film directors who lacked artistic vision, by critics and reviewers who failed to comprehend the fact that poetic experimentation mandated new forms, and by New York intellectuals and literati who embraced poetry he considered suspect. That he viewed himself at war is evidenced by an unpublished letter dated October 9, 1970, to Christopher Sinclair-Stevenson of Hamish Hamilton, his British publisher, who had informed him that sales of *Deliverance* were going "extremely well." While obviously pleased, Dickey remained concerned about the critical reception of *The*

29. Ibid., 166.
30. Ibid., 172, 173, 189, 204.

Eye-Beaters, pleading, "for God's sake, <u>do</u> get Vernon Scannell or Dennis En-
right or somebody over there who <u>likes</u> my poetry to review the poetry book
when it comes out. A lot of people over there apparently dislike my verse
rather violently, and we'll need something to redress the balance!"[31]

In the fifties and sixties, Dickey had struggled to win in a literary field
dominated first by modernists and then by beats and confessionals. He had
gained the advantage, risen, and commanded the artistic skies, but such distinction only required that he achieve greater successes. As he wrote in his
poem "The Cancer Match," first published in the June 1969 issue of *Poetry*
and included in *The Eye-Beaters:*

Tonight we are going
Good   better and better   we are going
To win, and not only win but win
Big, win big.

For Dickey, each "win" had to be bigger than the last.

With his psychological need for increasing recognition, Dickey actively
began to solicit honorary degrees. When Austin Briggs at Hamilton College
in New York asked Dickey to contribute to a volume honoring its alumnus
Ezra Pound in order to fund a lectureship in Pound's name, Dickey declined
in an unpublished letter dated August 17, 1970, citing commitments regarding *Deliverance.* He added, "Although I myself would probably not be able to
take the Pound Lectureship were it offered to me, I would like for you to
count me in as far as making recommendations for it is concerned." In correspondence dated November 2, he then informed Briggs, "I have held off ac-
cepting honorary degrees, but I would surely accept one from Ezra Pound's
old college. . . . I am kind of touchy about this subject. I have turned down a
good many degrees from schools that did not seem to me to have the proper
literary associations yours does." As Wesleyan College in Georgia and the College of Charleston in South Carolina did, Hamilton agreed to Dickey's request;
a year later Moravian College also gave him an honorary degree. Dickey continued to invite such honors throughout the seventies and into the eighties,
often making it a condition for a reading or an address. When Pitzer College,
for example, asked him to speak at the tenth anniversary commencement in
1975, he responded to its president, Robert Atwell, on September 11, 1972: "But
I would like also the guarantee of an honorary degree." During the summer of

---

31. The letter to Sinclair-Stevenson is in the Dickey Papers.

1981 he pressured James Kilroy, chairman of the English department at Vanderbilt University: "I cannot for the life of me understand why Vanderbilt, my old university, has not seen fit to confer an honorary degree on me. Though I realize this may sound fatuous, it is a matter of some concern to me. I have six others, but in all the time since the first one Vanderbilt did not come forward." Kilroy responded simply that Vanderbilt traditionally did not confer honorary degrees. Typical of Dickey's correspondence regarding speaking fees and commencement addresses is an unpublished letter dated January 15, 1975, to David Larrabee, director of New Hampshire Technical Institute, who had written and invited him to participate in commencement exercises: "My fee for such events is $3500 plus all first-class expenses. I know this is high, and it is deliberately so, not because I am particularly mercenary, but because these days, time is of much more importance to me than money, and it takes a good deal of money to justify my expenditure of time and energy in doing such things." Dickey then added: "Also, should I participate in your exercises, I would like to receive an honorary degree from your institution."[32] By 1993 he had acquired more than a dozen doctorates.

Dickey's drinking progressively worsened; he often appeared completely intoxicated during poetry readings or while teaching his classes at the University of South Carolina. His wife, Maxine, had also begun drinking heavily, as if in resolution to the question of leaving her marriage. Her husband behaved outrageously, conducting extramarital affairs with, among others, Amy Burk, a single mother acting in Brendan Behan's *Borstal Boy* on Broadway whom he had met at an *Esquire* party; Mary Cantwell, the managing editor at *Mademoiselle;* Rosemary Daniell, who had taken his poetry writing workshop; and Paula Goff, a former student who became his secretary.[33] As she increased her drinking, Maxine gained weight, which increased her health problems and eventually led to her death in 1976. Dickey at times admitted his own problem with alcohol, declaring baldly in *Sorties:* "I have been drunk, more or less, for about the last twenty-five years. Everything I remember is colored at least to some extent by alcohol."[34] Soliciting submissions as poetry editor at *Esquire,* he wrote John Berryman on January 20, 1971, in an unpublished letter: "we should get together, because, as they say on the pro football games on Sunday afternoon, the clock is running. I know all about the alco-

32. The letters to Briggs, Atwell, Kilroy, and Larrabee are all in the Dickey Papers.
33. For discussion of these relationships, see Hart, *James Dickey;* Mary Cantwell, *Speaking with Strangers* (Boston: Houghton Mifflin, 1998); and Rosemary Daniell, *Fatal Flowers: On Sin, Sex, and Suicide in the Deep South* (New York: Holt, Rinehart, and Winston, 1980).
34. *Sorties,* 84.

holic situation, though my own condition is further compounded by dia-betes."[35] Shared physical debilities or poetic sensibilities generated such confes-sion and created a genuine need within Dickey for camaraderie and kinship.

Yet efforts to establish such kinship were sometimes feigned, letters that flattered the recipient to convey a sympathetic sensibility and secure a favor-able impression, as Dickey had done with Ezra Pound and Wallace Stevens, or to create sympathy for or interest in himself, as had happened with James Wright. Exaggerated stories and demands for honorary doctorates as well as correspondence that endeavored to manipulate suggest an uncertain, emo-tionally insecure poet seeking to bolster his literary reputation, assuage his ego, and confirm a self-identity. The actions suggest, too, a writer who has lost his artistic bearings and is searching not so much for poetic transcendence as for navigational landmarks. Dickey had not lost the sense of his mission, of who he was, his essential voice, and where he wanted to go, but personal set-backs and literary turbulence had endangered his success, and he struggled to regain control by searching for others who had experienced such difficulty.

This affinity extended to writers other than Berryman, including James Wright and Stanley Burnshaw. In an unpublished letter to Wright dated Sep-tember 13, 1971, he eagerly agreed to introduce his friend at a New York read-ing of his poetry, stating, "there is no other American poet that I would prefer to introduce, and that's the truth," and alluded to the "very moving phone call" they recently shared.[36] Wright had written him earlier to praise the pub-lication of *The Eye-Beaters*, and Dickey had responded on March 16, 1970, thanking Wright for his "wonderful, life-giving letters":

> I am so happy that you like the new book, for it is really not very much like any
> of the others. . . . It seems to me that the great lesson of Picasso is that he never
> allowed himself to be trapped in a single style, as so many of our young and
> not-so-young American poets have done. . . . You have convinced me that I
> have made at least part of the right move, though while I was writing the book
> I was quite prepared to have critics say that this book was "disappointing," that
> it "represented a retrogression," and so on. As I say, I was quite ready for that. I
> hoped that there would be a few people who were not mystified but interested
> in what I was attempting to do. But your letter! All I can say is thanks, and with
> great humbleness.

35. The letter is in the John Berryman Papers, Manuscripts Division, University of Min-nesota Libraries, Minneapolis.

36. The letter is in the James Wright Papers, Manuscripts Division, University of Minnesota Libraries, Minneapolis.

Berryman's suicide on January 7, 1972, stunned Dickey, and though he had once called Berryman "a poet so preoccupied with poetic effects as to be totally in their thrall,"[37] he nevertheless felt the loss. Robert Lowell had recently suffered another manic-depressive breakdown (he would die five years later); when Ezra Pound died in a Venice hospital on November 1, Dickey was almost overwhelmed, conscious as he was of Pound's influence on his own poetry and of their meeting and correspondence during the fifties. Commenting on Pound's death, he told *The State* newspaper in Columbia: "Pound was a monolith, a great writer," who "did more for the human imagination, did more for the cause of imaginative delight and personal power, than anyone of our time." Later, in a 1982 essay, he detailed Pound's importance. Pound's love for all he believed excellent in the world, while often resulting in heavy-handed assertions that proselytize, also provided what for Dickey was most important—"startling, isolated shocks of possibility: conjunctions of words that opened up my own rather unbookish but very word-sensitive mentality to what I might come upon in my own memory and set forth with a corresponding imaginative forthrightness." Pound's desire for a highly relevant, individualized experience guaranteed both by the self and by the culture led Dickey to conclude: "A sense of the consequentiality of things, actions, men, ideas and civilizations is what we most want, and what we most sorely lack. Pound was on the right side of the question."[38]

Although Dickey at times often criticized, even excoriated, writers in his own essays and reviews, he paradoxically praised them at other times in his correspondence, flattering their work and declaring that their approach to life generally and to poetry specifically set them apart from others. He did so to avoid confrontations—he claimed to be essentially a coward—and to ingratiate himself politically. Yet in the early seventies, with his career seeming to stall and his health in decline, Dickey genuinely sought shared sensibilities. If his personal behavior appeared callous and self-destructive, it was a measure of how off-course his mission had become, his voice muffled by circumstances that increasingly seemed to frustrate and overwhelm him, causing him to act erratically.

In 1972, for example, Dickey proposed taking Glenn Helgeland to Bull Island off the South Carolina coast for a hunting trip. Helgeland, editor of *Archery World,* wanted Dickey as the central figure of a magazine article, believing

---

37. *Babel to Byzantium: Poets and Poetry Now* (New York: Farrar, Straus and Giroux, 1968), 198.
38. "American Poet Ezra Pound Dies," *The State,* November 2, 1972, pp. A1, 7; "The Water-Bug's Mittens: Ezra Pound: What We Can Use," in *Night Hurdling,* 29–46.

Dickey's projection of himself as a southern outdoorsman whose daring and bravado had included stalking wild boar and deer and even, on at least one memorable occasion, hunting rattlesnake with blow darts. Yet on Bull Island, the only arrows Helgeland saw Dickey shooting targeted a makeshift bull's-eye. He spent most of the hunt drinking, having purchased two six-packs of beer and a fifth each of gin and whiskey. On December 18, Dickey met with old Atlanta friends, the group about which he had reminisced in his 1969 poem "Looking for the Buckhead Boys," who had decided to bestow on him their first award for the most distinguished and successful member. In the poem, the persona searches for those close friends who had made his childhood meaningful and memorable. "If I can find them," he thinks,

> even one,
> I'm home. And if I can find him   catch him in or around
> Buckhead, I'll never die; it's like my youth will walk
> Inside me like a king.

The group had invited him to speak at its annual reunion, held at Saccone's restaurant in Atlanta. Dickey began drinking heavily upon his arrival. Conversations with those he had grown up with and known at North Fulton High School led him to realize quickly how different he was in interests, sensibilities, and intellect; other than his high school friend Bill Barnwell, Dickey felt forlorn, alone, and alienated. His drinking increased, and his speech to the Buckhead boys was slurred and incoherent.[39]

Despite conduct that suggested emotional problems and deep feelings of inadequacy, Dickey's finances remained remarkable. In 1972 his royalties and advances totaled more than $120,000; together with his teaching salary, among the highest at the University of South Carolina, and his reading fees, his gross income exceeded $200,000. On November 2, moreover, his agent Theron Raines had negotiated a $150,000 contract for Dickey to write a screenplay for *Amos Berry*, a novel by Allan Seager, whose biography of Theodore Roethke had been championed by Dickey. Elliott Kastner, the producer, promised to sign a director and secure a distribution contract by January 31, 1973. Although both Armitage Watkins, Seager's agent, and Seager's widow raised financial roadblocks, Dickey persisted with the project, sending an outline for a screenplay to Charles Fries, a Hollywood producer interested in acquiring the film rights.

39. Hart, *Dickey*, 516–18.

Clearly, Dickey's career, despite poor reviews, erratic behavior, and marital difficulties, remained, at least financially, at "angel's nine."

As the Watergate scandal broke upon and transfixed the American public in 1973, however, Dickey's problems became exacerbated by additional concerns and distractions. Warner Brothers was sued by Arthur Smith, who claimed copyright infringement regarding "Dueling Banjos" (Smith eventually won), and temporarily Dickey became involved in the legal maneuverings and proceedings, though he was not summoned to testify. He undertook an extensive reading tour, informing friends the hectic schedule reduced his legal expenses. In truth, Dickey "barnstormed" partly because he judged himself by his economic success and partly because he simply needed diversions from his problems. During late winter and spring 1973, he gave poetry readings at Washington and Lee University, Appalachian State, Elon College, Atlantic Christian College, Tulane University, St. Mark's, Morris Harvey College, and Seminole Junior College. Maxine had driven to the airport when her husband was to return from Washington and Lee, but Dickey missed his flight. Maxine waited. When he finally arrived in Columbia, he exited the plane "falling-down drunk." In his reminiscence of that period, Christopher Dickey relates:

> At the dinner table in Columbia that night, she'd tried to talk to him about the drinking. About the way he was living and acting. And he'd started to quote one of Lewis's speeches in *Deliverance*. Whenever he started re-enacting *Deliverance,* you know you'd lost him. "It is a question of SURVIVAL!" he'd shout, nostrils flaring, face reddening. He'd play out the whole scene. "Law? Hah! What law? Do you see any law around here?"
>
> My mother told me there was another woman, or women. She told me again she was going to leave him. And I just listened. I felt as if there were a huge wave of misery bearing down on us.[40]

Maxine repeatedly threatened to leave her husband, but repeatedly recanted. The marriage had become dysfunctional; yet observers concluded that she had become accustomed to the privileges Dickey's fame and fortune provided and he had become dependent on her organizational skills and her ability to manage the household.

Dickey's drinking problems led to an interest in and concerns about diabetes and blindness, both of which he would later incorporate into his 1987 novel *Alnilam.* Henry Hart argues that Dickey was attracted to diabetes be-

40. *Summer of Deliverance,* 191–92.

cause "he associated it with blindness, drinking, and the prophetic insight of seers" and that he imagined himself a diabetic in order to write a poem on the disease.[41] In "Diabetes," which appeared in the June 1969 issue of *Poetry,* the persona worries over the alcohol necessary to ignite his "tongue / Of flame":

> One night I thirsted like a prince
> > Then like a king
> Then like an empire like a world
> On fire.

The doctor advises "needles moderation / And exercise," and, at least initially, the speaker complies, believing he has discovered "A livable death at last." Yet the persona realizes that he is losing his creativity, his ability to enter into and transfix the world. After an injection of insulin, he thinks:

> > My blood is clear
> For a time. Is it too clear? Heat waves are rising
> Without birds. But something is gone from me.

He then understands that the body's knowledge of medical books is not everything: "everything is how / Much glory is in it." With that recognition, he asks his companion to open a beer.

Dickey's correspondence, however, does not clarify whether he actually believed himself to have the disease. He had informed Stanley Burnshaw in a letter dated July 10, 1969, that "I've just been to yet another doctor," who, following a two-day series of tests and examinations, had concluded that he did not have diabetes: "His 'explanation' was that the California doctor examined me when I was twenty pounds or so over my present weight, and some conditions sometimes, he says, bring out 'diabetes-like' symptoms. And so it goes."[42] Yet in subsequent letters to Willard Thorp, John Berryman, Richard Howard, and others, Dickey continued to state that he suffered from the disease, a mask that enabled him not only to garner sympathy and concern but also to create a new, imaginatively conceived and enabling self.

Dickey's interest in and need for masks found a new outlet when, on a trip to Boone, North Carolina, he allowed William Dunlap, an art professor at

---

41. Hart, *Dickey,* 415.
42. *The One Voice of James Dickey: His Letters and Life, 1942–1969,* ed. Gordon Van Ness (Columbia: University of Missouri Press, 2003), 468–69.

Appalachian State who was also a painter and sculptor, to apply plaster to his face to make a mold. After the mold was removed, Dickey inadvertently rubbed his eyes before he had completely washed his face. Some dry plaster caused minor alkaline burns. He could distinguish light and dark, but objects remained blurred when he attempted to focus. Dunlap immediately drove Dickey to the emergency room of the local hospital, where the attending physician allayed Dickey's fear of blindness. Because Dickey continued to worry, however, Dunlap subsequently drove him to an eye clinic, which determined that his eyes had recovered. *Esquire* exaggerated the incident when it printed the opening chapter of *Alnilam,* entitled "Cahill Is Blind," in its February 1976 issue:

> It was in sitting for the composition of this aluminum life mask [shown on the magazine's cover] that poet James Dickey was temporarily blinded. Sculptor William Dunlap, artist in residence at Appalachian State University, was forming the plaster cast when calcium seeped through to Mr. Dickey's eyes and produced an alkaline burn that scalded the corneas. The poet was raced from Boone, North Carolina, to Johnson City, Tennessee, for medical treatment that saved his vision. The experience, which left him sightless for several hours, contributed to the store of feeling from which the poet's second novel proceeds.[43]

As with the diabetes, Dickey embellished his imagined blindness, using the uncertainty of his blurred vision, which resembled that of a newborn, to bring heightened attention to himself. He purchased several masks from Dunlap to decorate his house.

W. H. Auden's death in Vienna from a heart attack on September 28, 1973, contributed to Dickey's growing sense of mortality. He was particularly affected by the deaths of those of his own generation, including Delmore Schwartz, Theodore Roethke, Randall Jarrell, Winfield Townley Scott, and John Berryman. His classroom teaching provided Dickey the necessary psychological ballast to counter the depression he experienced from these deaths. During his years as Carolina Professor of English at the University of South Carolina, he taught two courses each semester unless he was on sabbatical: verse composition and a seminar in twentieth-century American and British poetry. In the former, he required his students during the fall semester to write specific verse forms, one each week, including the sonnet, villanelle, lyric, and ballad, as well as poems utilizing epigrammatic couplets, blank

43. "Cahill Is Blind," *Esquire,* February 1976, p. 67.

verse, and satire. In the spring, students wrote a poem in free verse and then revised it each week for the remainder of the semester. His seminar on American and British poetry (he alternated the focus each semester) was not a literary survey in the usual sense of a chronological study of selected poets who represent "the tradition" but rather a systematic analysis of the nature of the artistic impulse and the conditions under which it thrives, beginning with the prehistoric cave paintings in Lascaux, France, and Altamira, Spain. The origin of the creative impulse, he asserted in his lectures, lay in man's religious nature, which flourished even amid his brutal and terrifying life, his living like an animal in the depths of caves. That religious nature manifested itself in a fascination with the objects and the animals he worshipped, particularly the latter's strength, speed, or skill, and in a tendency to distort or accentuate features such as the horns of a buffalo. Dickey viewed this characteristic as early evidence of the human need not simply to imitate but to create—"man's delight in tinkering and playing with things," as he phrased it. Man, then, was a defective animal; when he boasted, man pictured himself by referencing the animal world, a tendency that stressed the child within as a source of genius and the Jungian urge to tap into the collective memory that is the lifeblood of the past.

Dickey's focus on the beauty and mystery of this Paleolithic art largely derived from his own readings, including Henry Miller's travelogue *The Colossus of Maroussi*, in which Miller journeys through Greece and in doing so celebrates his friend Katsimbalis, who lives a life of immediacy and close connection to the world around him. "There is something colossal about any human figure when that individual becomes truly and thoroughly human," Miller wrote. "Walking with him through the streets of Amaroussion I had the feeling that I was walking the earth in a totally new way. The earth became more intimate, more alive, more promising. He spoke frequently of the past, it is true, not as something dead and forgotten, however, but rather as something which we carry within us, something which fructifies the present and makes the future inviting." Dickey, who carried his own past and explored it in poetry and fiction, also identified with the storytelling abilities of Katsimbalis, whose exaggerated tales, Miller asserts, invigorated life. "Certainly in those endless and seemingly fabulous stories . . . there must have been a good element of fancy and distortion, yet even if truth were occasionally sacrificed to reality the man behind the story only succeeded thereby in revealing more faithfully and thoroughly his human image." Because he was a "virtuoso who played only his own compositions," Miller declares, Katsimbalis therefore had "the right to alter them as he pleased."[44] Dickey's fabrications were no less important. Lying was what the creative man did.

In his class Dickey encouraged students to cast a wide net in their readings, urging them to examine J. B. Priestley's *The History of Mankind: Prehistory,* Herbert Read's *Icon and Idea,* André Malroux's *Man's Fate,* Stanley Edgar Hyman's *The Promised End,* and Joseph Campbell's *The Hero with a Thousand Faces.* Subsequent lectures explored not only Greek and Roman cultures and the efforts of Homer and Virgil, respectively, to present their times (the Greek mind wanted to know, he declared; the Roman mind thought it already did), but also the struggles of Dante and Milton to portray visually a prevailing cosmology. Dickey led into the twentieth century by stressing the dissolution of traditional myths and symbols and the often ill-fated struggle by modern poets to respond to this bankruptcy, centering on such figures as Tolstoy, Auden, Marx, D. H. Lawrence, Durrell, Whitman, Eliot, and Joyce before discussing the metaphysical and symbolist poets. The final third of the semester, ten class periods, dealt with individual poets Dickey variously selected, beginning with Emily Dickinson and including, for example, Frederick Tuckerman, Joseph Stickney, E. A. Robinson, Robert Frost, Edgar Lee Masters, Vachel Lindsay, Wallace Stevens, Robinson Jeffers, and Hart Crane. Better known or critically respected poets, such as William Carlos Williams, Randall Jarrell, and even Theodore Roethke, whom he had labeled in an essay "the greatest American poet," were absent from his discussion.[45]

Dickey's father died on March 12, 1974. Although he had asserted in *Self-Interviews* that "my father and I have always been very close," his attitude was better characterized by his statement in *Sorties:* "I am appalled by the thinness of my father's experience. It has been monotonous, tiresome, and valueless because he has been essentially, passive [*sic*]."[46] He had imagined his father's death in poems such as "The Hospital Window" and "Approaching Prayer," in which Eugene Dickey assumes an elevated or messianic stature, but his reaction was now muted. At his father's request, Dickey played on his guitar the Baptist hymn "Just a Closer Walk with Thee," which he had learned as a child before abandoning Christianity; by the time he finished the second chorus, Eugene had died. Christopher Dickey remembers that "barely a ripple had passed through the family. Or, at least, none that I could feel. My father had built such a screen of contempt around his own father that he barely talked

44. Henry Miller, *The Colossus of Maroussi* (New York: New Directions, 1958), 238, 239, 240.
45. See Ken Autrey's extended discussion, "James Dickey's American Poetry Course: A Recollection," *James Dickey Newsletter* 4.2 (Spring 1988): 2–8.
46. *Self-Interviews,* 26; *Sorties,* 68.

about him in life and seemed to forget about him in death. No reason he ever gave me could tell me why. . . . He was no more missed than a piece of furniture that had been moved to storage."[47] Dickey's relationship with his father, complex when he was a child, had become one of adult indifference, Christopher implied, with the coming of literary and financial success. Yet Dickey's response to his father's death, more reserved than indifferent—he kissed Eugene on the head and left the hospital with the mother of an Atlanta friend, Ashley Walker, who talked to him about her diabetic blindness—lay more in his fundamental paralysis when confronting death than in any view of his father as a weak-willed tyrant.

Dickey's success continued the same year when Hollywood producers Malcolm Stuart and Charles Fries offered Dickey $40,000 to write a screenplay for NBC based on Jack London's *Call of the Wild,* the last film version of which had been made in the thirties. London's novel portrayed the conflict between the wilderness and civilization that *Deliverance* had featured; like London, moreover, Dickey romanticized nature while admitting its stark brutality. However, Dickey's effort initially resulted in a script NBC executives considered too unpolished; Stuart wrote a five-page letter on December 20 requesting revisions. Two months later Dickey submitted his revisions, informing Stuart that he considered the script complete and advising him to begin production. The television adaptation, which aired on May 19, 1976, straightforwardly depicted London's characters and ideas and revealed little imaginative creation. With Maxine and Christopher, Dickey flew to California to watch the "premier," an advance screening. Christopher, then twenty-three and married with a four-year-old son, remembered afterward: "I don't think any of us knew what to say. Even as a TV movie it was mediocre. But there was no way to tell that to Jim Dickey."[48] Dickey reveled in the new attention; in his letters his voice exudes confidence. Hollywood money reinforced his sense of success.

That financial success continued. During the fall of 1974 Dickey involved himself in the promotion of *Jericho: The South Beheld,* a coffee-table book so large (sixteen and one-half by thirteen inches) and so heavy (seven pounds) that he later claimed if one did not have a coffee table, the book would serve as one. Christopher describes this time:

> Jim Dickey was more famous than ever. But there were so many works in progress, and only the worst of them seemed to get done. We had entered the

---

47. *Summer of Deliverance,* 209.
48. Ibid., 197.

era of James Dickey coffee-table books, lavishly illustrated overpriced tomes published by the same company that did *The Progressive Farmer* and *Southern Living* magazines. They were marketed by junk mail like trinkets from the Franklin Mint. The first was *Jericho: The South Beheld,* with tempera illustrations that were Southern-sentimental knockoffs of Andrew Wyeth, and the books got worse after that.

The booze and bluster were carrying over into everything my father wrote, everything he did. The obsessions of the poetry—the whole voice of it— changed. Ecstasy and creation gave way to masturbation and menstruation.[49]

Over the previous two years, Dickey had worked intermittently on *Jericho,* a collaborative effort with Hubert Shuptrine, whose 101 watercolor paintings accompanied, though not necessarily followed, the imaginative journey Dickey's prose depicts in the book's 168 pages. As with his poetry and fiction, Dickey's plot was both picaresque and mythic, bestowing his imagination with "pure spirit" in its creative journey and asking his readers "to hover, to swoop, to enter into the veer of the land and rivers, to zigzag over the landscape of people, to live the trembling of the Web of custom and family." Like the mythic Dedalus, Dickey's spirit is to transcend geographic locales, specific custom and lore, and particular individuals, such as a potter gardening, a hitchhiker playing bluegrass, and a black man fishing, to achieve a mystic wholeness of vision that reveals the truth of the South, not its "magnolia-and-moonlight" stereotype. Although some critics suggested that Dickey's model was Stephen Dedalus in James Joyce's *Portrait of the Artist as a Young Man,* who counsels his soul to soar above the restraints of nationality, language, and religion, it is also clear that Dickey's vision, the series of epiphanies he presents, is voiced in a more popularly accessible medium and therefore directed at a more profitable marketplace.

Oxmoor House, the publisher, extensively promoted the book, announcing that its printing required twenty-eight carloads (one million pounds) of paper and thirty-one miles of cloth. Critics quickly pounced on what they perceived as Dickey's commercialism. Eli Evan's review in the *New York Times* typified the criticism when he wrote that "the poet decided to give himself over to the Alabama Chamber of Commerce."[50] Other critics suggested that Dickey failed to utilize the principal source of what had been his poetic power, specifically, his own artistic control of the transcendent experience. In the introduction to *Jericho,* he had asked the reader to become a "beholder,"

49. Ibid., 198.
50. "The South the South Sees," *New York Times Book Review,* February 9, 1975, pp. 4–5.

someone who can "enter into objects and people and places with the sense of these things entering into him." While this approach succeeds in an early poem entitled "The Beholders," published in the December 1, 1962, issue of *New Yorker*, by fusing the personae with their surroundings, the implication in *Jericho* is that Dickey himself cannot impart the needed energy or transcendence, particularly when he asks the reader to provide the imaginative vision requisite for such a fusion of inner and outer states: "You, reader, must open up until you reach the point . . . of sensing your locality pour into you simultaneously through every sense." Dickey additionally eliminated, it was claimed, the need for the creative lie, the very means by which he had previously provided transcendence and thereby given the reader, for example, a sheep-child ("The Sheep Child"), two young lovers in the mist around their wrecked motorcycle ("May Day Sermon"), a stewardess who lives only as she prepares to die ("Falling"), and blind children who attempt to see the origins of the race ("The Eye-Beaters"). In *Jericho*, Dickey took additional stories and simply asked readers to view them in a heightened manner, an approach that reviewers argued merely accommodated the readership of *Southern Living*. That, however, was precisely Dickey's intent. He had always understood that poetry, or poetic prose, might release a new or insufficiently realized part of men and women, might free them or make them more inclusive. In publishing a coffee-table book, he was simply targeting a wider, less scholarly audience, an advertising strategy that coincidentally would also earn him more money.

Initially Oxmoor had ordered a printing of 5,000 copies, but because *Southern Living* had undertaken a lavish advertising campaign, 20,000 copies had been ordered by December 8, 1973. The publisher then revised its plans again, ordering a first printing of 150,000 copies and setting up a $100,000 two-month book promotion tour for both Dickey and Shuptrine that featured television, radio, and press interviews as well as autograph sessions. Stops included Birmingham, Houston, New Orleans, Dallas, Atlanta, Columbia, Charlotte, Greenville, Richmond, and Nashville. To guarantee the widest possible market, the two artists were also booked for appearances on the *Today Show*, Johnny Carson's *Tonight Show*, and the *Merv Griffin Show*. Dickey canceled all his October classes to accommodate the tour without consulting William Nolte, who chaired the English department and who subsequently placed him on unpaid leave. In October 1974 *Jericho* sold 100,000 copies at a list price of forty dollars. In an unpublished letter dated November 31, Dickey inquired whether the book might not be worthy of a review in the *New York Times*, asking, "should not this huge sales volume entitle Jericho to a place on your best-seller list?"[51] The book continued to sell after January 1, 1975, when the price rose to sixty dollars a copy. Dickey had received a $25,000 advance. Because his royalty agreement stipulated one dollar per copy, he garnered approximately $150,000 from sales after earning back the advance.[52]

After concluding the promotional tour, Dickey seemed to withdraw into his self-made "cave of making," the room in his home by Lake Katherine where he wrote, determined to complete the most ambitious project he had ever attempted, *The Zodiac*. Totaling sixty-two pages when published in 1976 and divided into twelve sections, the single poem, he later declared, was the effort by which his poetic reputation would rise or fall.[53] In its sprawling format and split-line technique, it resembles such previous efforts as "Falling" and "May Day Sermon," yet Dickey's use of a translated text that he then re-creates, his gradual merging of perspectives, and his transformation of a traditional Christian myth into a personal and universal mythology that comments on the nature of art and the artist all render *The Zodiac* unique. At its heart *The Zodiac* is a quest for the single redeeming poem that unites the poet with the constellations, with the star-beasts of "God's scrambled zoo." Discussing the poem in the preface to *The Central Motion*, Dickey stated:

> I sought to deal with risks, and take them, and to have my spokesman exemplify the conviction that the poet must go all-out for his vision, his angle, as it presents itself *at that moment*. A good deal of *The Zodiac* is the self-hypnotized yammering and assertiveness of a drunk, but a drunk who would not be able to achieve his occasionally clear and perhaps deep focus on matters of concern to him unless he had had his inhibitions broken down—or through—by the dangerous means he employs, for he insists on nothing less than a personal connection between an exalted and/or intoxicated state, the starry universe, the condition he calls Time, and words. Taking off from Hendrik Marsman's respectable and ambitious poem and re-inventing almost everything in it, I tried to present a number of states of mind in which the cosmos changes moment to moment in a single consciousness, from a display of miracles to a delusional nightmare—the horrors of delirium tremens—and then back, all changes being parts of its encounter with that hugely mortal beast, the universe, and the smaller, mega-billion-miled Forms, the animals that comprise some of it, in their stark, hinting, and timorous patterns.[54]

51. The letter is in the Dickey Papers.
52. Hart, *Dickey,* 348–49.
53. Francis Skipp, "James Dickey's *The Zodiac:* The Heart of the Matter," *Concerning Poetry* 14.1 (Spring 1981): 1–10.
54. *The Central Motion: Poems, 1968–1979* (Middletown, Conn.: Wesleyan University Press, 1983), v–vi.

Marsman's poem "De Dierenriem," translated from the Dutch by A. J. Barnouw as "The Zodiac," was published in the spring 1949 issue of *Sewanee Review* while Dickey was attending Vanderbilt. Reprinted the following year in Barnouw's anthology, *Coming After: An Anthology from the Low Countries,* the translation served as the narrative basis for Dickey's longer effort. In a 1979 interview Dickey described the poem as a "sublimated narrative" and asserted that its subject was "The kind of half-mad, half-drunken afflatus that gets into a poet, or a certain kind of poet, when he believes that he can write the ultimate poem."[55] To find it, the drunken poet must glean from the external world the vision necessary to make his words "lie for glory," a vision that effaces the boundaries between the poet's inner world and the outer world of natural phenomena and that requires the Zodiac poet to rise above the pain of his personal and creative failures. A resurrection must occur, and appropriately *The Zodiac* spans a three-day period. Because the Zodiac poet only intermittently escapes his alcoholism, he pleads, "Oh God you rocky landscape give me, Give / Me drop by drop / desert water at least." The redemptive vision comes: "A face-up flash. Triangular eyesight," but he cannot pen the universe

> That poetry has never really found,
> Undecipherable as God's bad, Heavenly sketches,
> Involving fortress and flower, vine and wine and bone,
>
> And shall vibrate through the western world
> So long as the hand can hold its island
> Of blazing paper, and bleed for its images:
> Make what it can of what is:
>
> So long as the spirit hurls on space
> The star-beasts of intellect and madness.

Although he achieves the connection he desires, the poet ironically fails in the final object of his quest; he cannot write the ultimate poem: "the virgin sheet becomes / More and more his, more and more another mistake." The myth he writes recedes even as he grasps it; truth, Dickey insists, resides in flux. Because he believed controversy and excitement about a forthcoming publication would increase sales, Dickey in correspondence claimed the poem would rival Eliot's *The Waste Land* as a major cultural work.

55. Ron McFarland, "An Interview with James Dickey," in *Voiced Connections,* ed. Baughman, 173–86.

Reviewers were unimpressed. Poet Turner Cassidy considered the resemblance to Barnouw's translation too close, declaring Dickey's re-creation a "compromise" of what the poet obviously intended as "his artistic testament with the hint of plagiarism," and Thomas Lask simply termed the poem a failure, noting "its clotted lines and convoluted ideas" and berating Dickey for trying to make his verse "virile." Robert Penn Warren, Dickey's close friend, cited a vaguely defined structural principle in the opening half of the work and "some sort of structural blockage" in the concluding two sections, adding, however, that the bold imagery as well as varied rhythms "redeems all." Although later critics were less condemnatory, labeling the work a flawed masterpiece, they frequently misread it. Dave Smith, for example, argued that the poem occurs over a single day, and Francis Skipp asserted that its divisions relate to the zodiac.[56]

Although *The Zodiac* was discussed as serious poetry, critics noted Dickey's interest in a specialized market. The poem's working manuscript was sectioned and bound in special-edition volumes; these Bruccoli Clark collectors' editions were then sold by private subscription at $400 apiece. Other specialty volumes in the seventies, including *The Owl King* (Red Angel Press, 1977), *The Enemy from Eden* (Lord Jim Press, 1978), *In Pursuit of the Grey Soul* (Bruccoli Clark Press, 1978), and *Head-Deep in Strange Sounds* (Palaemon Press, 1979), only seemed to confirm for critics Dickey's decline, as did the publication in 1977 of another coffee-table book, *God's Images*. Amid the disdain, Dickey himself became defensive, writing Dave Smith on November 17, 1980, that *The Zodiac* "of <u>course</u> is a failure; there is no way that any poem which attempts to be a projection of booziness and confusion is ever going to be the kind of hand-fitted-together sort of 'success' that, say, <u>The Waste Land</u> is."

Like the poem's protagonist, Dickey had returned to his native land following his service in World War II; that Marsman himself had died during the conflict only heightened the emotional appeal. Moreover, Dickey's return to the South in 1968, his use of sextants to locate himself among the stars, and his alcoholic self-destructiveness (the same reason he later became interested in the movie *Leaving Las Vegas*) all contributed to his interest in Marsman's poem. Because *The Zodiac* centers on poetic inspiration and divine commu-

56. Cassidy, "Double Dutch: *The Strength of Fields* and *The Zodiac*," *Parnassus* 8 (1980): 177–93; Lask, "Serene and Star-Crazed," *New York Times*, January 22, 1977, p. 19; Warren, "A Poem about the Ambition of Poetry: *The Zodiac*," *New York Times Book Review*, November 14, 1976, p. 8; Smith, "The Strength of James Dickey," *Poetry* 137 (March 1982): 349–58; Skipp, "James Dickey's *The Zodiac*."

nication, however, critical efforts to portray the work as overtly confessional are overstated. Henry Hart in his biography, *James Dickey: The World as a Lie,* for example, asserts, "Dickey transformed Marsman's hero into an image of his own drunken, garrulous self, careening between sublimity and bathos." Yet the statement fails to consider Dickey's abhorrence of self-dramatized poetry; his interest in translation, or what he sometimes referred to as "double-tongue"; and his belief that the poem is a fiction in which the persona "is correspondingly conditioned far more by the demands of the poem as a formal linguistic structure than by those of the literal incident upon which it may be based."[57] Dickey's art, however, did imitate his life. Drinking continued to hinder his creativity and, now, endanger his life. While on sabbatical in September 1975, he crashed his 1968 Jaguar into a utility pole after leaving one of his favorite bars.

During his trip to Hollywood in August 1974 to work on *Call of the Wild,* Dickey had proposed to Charles Fries another movie idea. Conscious of the proclivity in both himself and his recently deceased father toward cowardice, he imagined a character's difficult but, finally, triumphant struggle to overcome his fear. The proposed movie would dramatize the struggle of a man discovering his own heroism. The epigraph Dickey eventually selected for the screenplay derived from John Berryman: "A man can live his whole life in this society, and never know whether he is a coward or not." The outline for the new film, originally entitled "Crownfire" and later "Gene Bullard," introduced Sheriff Bullard, whose first name reflects that of Dickey's father, as a former athlete who shuns violence and checks for parking violations while driving a "meter maid" vehicle for the small North Carolina town of Ellijah, the town Dickey used in his 1962 poem "On the Coosawatee." Supported by a tough young woman, Beth Culclashure, whose last name resembles the maiden name of Paula Culclasure Goff, he confronts an assortment of local criminals, including Joby, the son of deeply religious Baptist parents who were killed in an automobile wreck when he was eighteen; Makens, a sadist who has committed several bizarre sex crimes; Leon, a comically moronic ex-convict; and Jimbo, a forty-five-year-old escaped convict whose name reflects Dickey's own. Fries was interested, and Dickey undertook writing the script.

In Hollywood again in March 1976 after a rough cut of *Call of the Wild* had been completed, Dickey once more endeavored to generate interest in "Gene Bullard," which had languished at several film companies. He delivered an emotionally charged summary of the script that so mesmerized Gary MacElwaine,

---

57. Hart, *Dickey,* 551; Dickey, "The Self as Agent," in *Sorties,* 155.

an executive at Warner Brothers, that he consented to produce it. Dickey's Hollywood agent, Robert Littman, arranged for his client to receive $40,000 for the first draft of the screenplay, $20,000 for revisions, $35,000 for another draft if Warner Brothers decided to produce the movie, and a $30,000 bonus in addition to royalties if Dickey received sole screen credit. On May 25, Littman informed Dickey that he had also formalized a deal with Columbia Pictures for another proposed film, "The Spell." In the prospectus Dickey characterized the plot as an examination of "the interaction between politics and religion, especially as it evidences itself in the South." The story featured a character much like Joel Cahill in *Alnilam*, Joshua Daniels, minister of a small rural congregation who is "a spell-binder, that is, he can cast the spell over people, over his congregations, and over just about anybody he chooses to cast it upon." In the synopsis Dickey further characterized Daniels: "He does not talk about sin, but of salvation, and his version of salvation includes the element of joy: joy in nature, joy in sex, joy even in drink, but essentially joy in existence." Daniels, who boards in the house of Hannah Crewes, a widow, desires to unify everyone under a single idea; his obsession spills over into despotic politics.[58]

By autumn, however, Dickey had become frustrated with the continual changes demanded by Warner Brothers for each draft he submitted, not only refusing to make any more revisions but also demanding the final payment stipulated by his contract. In stern, straightforward language, he wrote Fries in an unpublished letter dated October 1:

> I put a whole summer's work into the revisions you suggested. If that is not the fulfillment of a contract to write a screenplay, I do not know where to find it. And still no forthcoming of the contracted payment. Now I am absolutely dumbfounded at the request to make additional changes without the slightest indication of the monies for work I have spent a year in doing. . . . I am bewildered by all of this, but I can categorically guarantee that I will not touch the script of <u>Gene Bullard</u> again until I have received payment for the first draft. I'd as soon drop the whole project rather than proceed on this basis.[59]

Both "Gene Bullard" and "The Spell" languished, despite efforts by Fries, and Dickey abandoned the projects, frustrated with Hollywood practices and procedures even as he remained attracted to the financial incentives.

58. "Prospectus for film THE SPELL" and "Synopsis for Projected Movie to Be Called *THE SPELL*," Dickey Papers.
59. This letter is in the Dickey Papers.

In mid-October 1976 Dickey's wife, Maxine, suffered a hemorrhage of the blood vessels surrounding her esophagus, the bleeding caused by damage from years of drinking. She lost half her blood. Despite being stabilized by doctors and kept in intensive care, she hemorrhaged again and died on October 27. Later Dickey would describe her initial collapse to his son Christopher. "She *exploded* in my *arms*," he said, imitating her voice and pretending to throw up blood, "Buckets of it." Then amid tears of drunken grief, he declared, "Thirty years I was married to that woman. THIRTY YEARS. And I killed her."[60] Without Maxine's support and her managerial skills, Dickey floundered. Dedicated to her husband's career, Maxine had provided stability by organizing schedules, directing activities, entertaining literary figures, and raising children. In short, she had enabled Dickey to have not only a literary career but a successful one. For her gravestone, he chose two lines from "Damelus' 'Song to Diaphenia'" by the sixteenth-century English poet Henry Constable—"I do love thee as each flower / Loves the sunne's life-giving power"—a tribute that acknowledged his dependency. In the weeks following her burial, Dickey appeared rootless and apathetic, often drinking excessively to assuage his grief. He told the *National Observer* on December 4: "I've thought about my death a lot. Once I thought I wanted to die by violence—get killed by a grizzly, maybe. But now I think I'd prefer to die by water, by drowning not with others but alone. Just slip beneath it all." Asked if he believed in an afterlife, he simply responded "No. I saw Maxine lying there, and it could have just been a dead dog in the road."[61] He blamed his own actions for the alcoholism that had killed his wife.

On December 30 at the courthouse in Columbia, South Carolina, Dickey married Deborah Dodson, a twenty-five-year-old graduate student who had enrolled that fall semester in his verse composition course. As they climbed the courthouse steps, Deborah said, "This is the last chance to back out," to which he replied, "I ain't gonna take it, and you ain't gonna get it."[62] Dickey informed friends and family as well as the press that Deborah had restored him, and temporarily he gave up drinking. Her presence in what he called "the new life" emotionally elevated him, heightening his sensitivity to the physical world and quickening his intuitive responses. As would soon become apparent, she also revealed to him previously unseen creative possibilities and

60. *Summer of Deliverance*, 203.

61. Paul Hendrickson, "Poet James Dickey: Now He's the 'Top Cat,'" *National Observer*, December 4, 1976, p. 24.

62. Franklin Ashley, "Happy: For Newly Widowed Poet James Dickey, Deliverance Is a Bride Named Debbie," *People*, January 17, 1977, pp. 28, 30.

guided him in directions that had remained undiscovered or unexplored. Deborah's youth and sensibilities inspired him, making his 1982 poetry collection, *Puella,* possible. In many ways she became his muse, a mythical deliverer whose physical appearance, Dickey told friends, reminded him of Robin Jarecki, the young and gifted woman with whom he had had an affair and whose tragic death in 1967 had inspired Dickey to undertake a long poem entitled "The Indian Maiden." In a 1982 interview Dickey remarked on Deborah's effect on *Puella,* which was inspired, he asserted, "by the mystery of her existence, of her radiation, her mysterious radiation." He wanted the public, he then declared, to perceive him not simply as an image of vitality or strength but as one possessing "above all a passionate and involved male tenderness."[63]

In the commencement address Dickey delivered in December 1995 at the University of South Carolina, he commented on his marriages and specifically on Deborah's influence: "I married, and thirty years after that my wife died. I married again, to a young woman who loved the poetry of John Donne and showed me that I had never read it in depth before. I came especially to like some lines of his about waking up with someone you love. You can be sure that the love-relation is a true one when there is no apprehension present, no fear in it; fear of betrayal, of being lied to, fear that the other person will cease to love you, fear of anything." Then he read those lines from Donne's "The Good Morrow":

And now good morrow to our waking souls,
Which watch not one another out of fear;
For love, all love of other sights controls,
And makes one little room, an everywhere.[64]

Yet Dickey's relationship with Deborah was also troubled. Her addiction to drugs and her various arrests became media news, and rumors of her physical and verbal abuse of Dickey also circulated. In interviews Dickey frequently deflected questions about separation and divorce. Reynolds Price in a tribute to Dickey following the latter's death called the poet's domestic situation "tragic."[65] Because of the turbulence, Christopher and Kevin Dickey retreated from almost all contact with their father.

---

63. L. Elisabeth Beattie, "James Dickey Rides Again," *Carolina Lifestyle* 1 (May 1982): 42–46; rpt. in *Voiced Connections,* ed. Baughman, 187–92.

64. "The Weather of the Valley—Reflections on the Soul and Its Making," commencement address, University of South Carolina, December 18, 1995, Dickey Papers.

65. "James Dickey, XL," *New York Times Book Review,* March 23, 1997, p. 31.

Dickey was not by nature inclined to involve himself in politics. During the Vietnam conflict, he had assiduously avoided participating in popular protests—unlike, for example, Robert Lowell and Robert Bly—nor did he issue any tracts, make any statements, or write any poems in support of or in opposition to the war. Although opponents labeled him conservative, for Dickey poetry was all that mattered. He did, however, cultivate his relationship with Jimmy Carter during Carter's campaign for the presidency. They had met during the Atlanta premier of *Deliverance,* and Carter had later invited Dickey to become Georgia's poet laureate, an honor Dickey declined because he was living in South Carolina. In an unpublished letter dated August 4, 1976, he reintroduced himself and delivered an inspirational message that promoted agrarian values and idealism:

> The clue to our national and international salvation lies not in a futile yearning for a nebulous "unity," but in an emphasis on diversity, or the right—and eventual glory, given the right government—of differences. The South is not the East and the East is not the Pacific Northwest, nor is any one of these Alaska or Hawaii. What we should seek, as a political organ, is a reaffirmation of the principal differences, both local and individual. . . . I would like very much, Jimmy, to see an emphasis, under your Presidency, on the diversity of peoples that we have in this country, and a fertile cross-fertilization of different kinds of groups, mores, fashions, and all of the diversity that gives richness to life.

Carter responded with a note thanking Dickey for his comments on diversity. In subsequent letters over the next several months, Dickey offered Carter advice on his campaign and on the televised debates.

The correspondence eventually led to Carter's request that Dickey write an inaugural poem. Dickey responded with "The Strength of Fields," which he read at the inaugural concert on January 19, 1977. He later told the *Christian Science Monitor* that, as in *Deliverance,* he had based the poem on Van Gennep's "Rites of Passage." After winning the election, Carter had returned to his hometown of Plains, Georgia: "I cast Jimmy Carter in his withdrawal from Washington and his return to his roots, his hometown, in the role of a mythical hero, and that is always the same. It doesn't make any difference if it's Theseus or Perseus or any one else."[66] Carter's victory over Gerald Ford, though narrow, seemed to promise a new beginning, a new hope, for a nation that had surrendered to cynicism and despair following Vietnam and Watergate.

66. Diana Loercher, "Georgia Poet Who Cast Carter as a Mythical Hero," *Christian Science Monitor,* October 5, 1977, p. 19.

Nixon's resignation had symbolized the final defeat. Carter's humility, his sense of moral wholeness, appeared to many Americans a national deliverance that began with the organization of a five-day People's Inaugural celebration. Six hundred Iowa farmers and their families, 106 Minnesota square dancers, twenty-six Crow Indians, and an assemblage of Irish musicians, bluegrass groups, country singers, Hollywood celebrities, and Georgia working folk joined one million other Americans in Washington to herald the new day promised by Carter. "How to penetrate and find the source," Dickey's speaker asks in "The Strength of Fields," "Of the power you always had." The poem's quiet, dignified, and uplifting conclusion seemed appropriate when Dickey read it at the Folger Theatre.

>   Lord, let me shake
> With purpose. Wild hope can always spring
> From tended strength. Everything is in that.
>   That and nothing but kindness. More kindness, dear Lord
> Of the renewing green.   That is where it all has to start:
>   With the simplest things. More kindness will do nothing less
>   Than save every sleeping one
>   And night-walking one
>
>   Of us.
>   My life belongs to the world. I will do what I can.

Dickey's presence, however, was not without controversy, for the perceived racist and sexist attitudes his personae portrayed appeared at odds with the tone of the inauguration. Denise Levertov publicly attacked Dickey's attitudes, including his support of American involvement in southeast Asia. Yet many felt the poem epitomized the country's yearning and concurred with Dickey's belief that "We can all be saved / By a secret blooming."

Shortly after the inauguration, Carter asked Dickey to represent the United States at a ceremony opening the Franklin and Jefferson exhibit at Mexico City's National Museum of Anthropology. Honored, Dickey agreed, and flew with Deborah to begin his ambassadorial duties on April 14, attending receptions, discussing *Deliverance,* lecturing on modern poetry, conferring with dignitaries, and sightseeing. Before an audience that included Mexico's president, José López Portillo, he celebrated the spirit of friendship and cultural cooperation between the neighboring countries. He also met with Octavio Paz, whose acquaintance he had first made as poetry consultant and whom he believed to be not only Mexico's finest poet but also deserving of the Nobel Prize for Literature. Later he would re-create some of Paz's poetry, including "Mexican Valley," which he included with other translations as part of *The Strength of Fields* and published in a specialty edition in 1979 entitled *Head-Deep in Strange Sounds*.

Following his return from Mexico, Dickey continued to send Carter political advice, and in a long letter dated July 16, 1979, he analyzed the latter's energy speech. Carter had addressed a nation crippled by the oil crisis and confronted with a severe shortage. Dickey's analysis disparaged Carter's rhetorical strategies and urged him to uplift the country by gathering up its "great resources of intellectual and spiritual power," "a kind of hidden treasure: enormous, full of power and light and certainty and even a fierce and renewing kind of joy: above all, a sense of going-toward rather than escaping-from. It is a great deal better to lead people toward a goal, a kind of just city, a 'city of the sun,' than it is to attempt to intimidate a nation of sluggards and timorous wastrels into acting for its own good." Presenting his vision of this "city of the sun," Dickey in effect seemed to be instructing Carter, outlining its conditions and promising its reality if Carter would, as E. M. Forster had written, "only connect," a phrase Dickey used as an epigraph in his 1967 poem "Power and Light."

Attracted by the spotlight of national politics, Dickey continued his correspondence with and pledges of support for the Carters, including sending Christmas cards. The Carters, in turn, invited the Dickeys in January 1980 to participate in a White House reception honoring American poets. Louise Glück, Simon Ortiz, David Ignatow, Theodore Weiss, Philip Levine, Maxine Kumin, Stanley Kunitz, and Richard Eberhart attended. So, too, did James Wright, physically diminished by a debilitating cancer that would within four months bring his death. After Wright had greeted him and explained his medical condition, Dickey suddenly grew angry and left, bewildering Wright and angering his wife, Anne. Dickey's own health problems, a malfunctioning esophagus that would soon require major surgery, and his shocked recognition of what he told David Wagoner in a April 21, 1980, letter of Wright's "hoarse, diminished and obviously dying ghost,"[67] turned sadness and grief into anger at life's processes and physical limitations. Unlike Theodore Roethke, who understood, as he wrote in the title poem of his last poetry collection, *The Far Field*, "The pure serene of memory in one man,— / A ripple widening from a single stone / Winding around the waters of the world,"

67. Hart, *Dickey*, 584.

Dickey never truly accommodated himself to time and its attendant diminishment.

Carter's campaign never contacted Dickey during the 1980 reelection efforts. Undeterred, Dickey proffered his counsel, writing Carter a week before the election: "Since I haven't heard from Jody Powell, and since time is getting short, I thought I had better send you what thoughts I have on the points you might want to emphasize in your debate with Reagan." He urged Carter to have a simple, widely applicable metaphor that would catch up the public and describe his position, suggesting the image of driving defensively. Americans, however, had wearied of Carter's liberal humanitarian ideals and his inability to solve the Iranian hostage crisis. In rhetoric that Dickey surely must have admired, Ronald Reagan projected himself as a mythmaker, a leader who could energize the country and lead it to the "city of the sun." His victory at the polls largely signaled an end to Dickey's participation in politics; his correspondence with Carter noticeably diminished following Carter's defeat.

Dickey continued to work on his projects during the late seventies, including *God's Images*, a new coffee-table book, and several screenplays, one of which, "The Sentence," involved a professor at a southern university coping with arrest and incarceration and was based on his 1975 crash into a utility pole. "The Breath" was a dramatic presentation of a hunt for one man by another. Quentin Dodson, the protagonist, whose last name parallels Deborah's maiden name, resembles Julian Glass, the main character in "The Casting," Dickey's unfinished first novel, in his voyeurism and perversity, and in some ways anticipates Muldrow in his last novel, *To the White Sea*, in his inability to understand reality. "The Buzzer," another proposed screenplay, explored life as a competitive game. The single-page prospectus presents an unnamed protagonist, an outstanding basketball star, sensitive and withdrawn, idealistic, who leads his team to the championship game but surrenders the chance to win because he is disgusted by the moblike vulgarity of the sport. His final action, throwing the ball down and walking off the court, repudiates the profession he represents.

Reviews of *God's Images*, published in 1977, were mixed, and later critics compared it unfavorably to *Jericho*. Less ambitious in size, though not in artistic intent, it contains fifty-three prose poems that not so much reinterpret as represent particular biblical texts from individual perspectives. Etchings by Marvin Hayes accompany Dickey's interior imagery. Oxmoor House, anticipating controversy from the book's unusual perspectives, established an advisory board of biblical scholars, both Jewish and Christian, to assure that the portrayals were faithful to scriptural materials. GraceAnne DeCandido, reviewing the book for *Library Journal*, considered Dickey's text "oddly secular," stating that it lacked "palpable spirituality" because emphasis shifts from God to the figures that present the biblical story, characters moreover that are "predominantly masculine." Noting the absence of Judith, Esther, and Mary Magdalene from the portrayals and declaring that Ruth and Mary are only "shadow and symbol," DeCandido believed *God's Images* narrowed the Bible to "the worldly visions of two men."[68] Her review, however, ignored Dickey's own statement in the book's foreword:

> To an artist such as Marvin Hayes, or to a poet, such as I hold myself to be, these images have unfolded in us by means of the arts we practice. These are *our* images of *God's Images*. . . . Hayes and I do not wish to supersede or in any way substitute our interpretations of the Bible for yours. These are crucial to you, and therefore vital and living. We should like to think, though, we may be able to give an added dimension to your own inner Bible and enrich your personal kingdom of God, there where it lies forever . . . within you.

Failing to allow Dickey the choice of his material, DeCandido nevertheless reflected a problem Dickey's personal projection of male bravado caused him. His career suffered because, in depicting himself with masculine boisterousness, he opened himself to charges of political incorrectness, a problem he would recognize and attempt to counter in *Puella*.

In their critical study Richard Calhoun and Robert Hill viewed *God's Images* as more academic than *Jericho* because within Dickey's text lie the voices of Milton and Blake as well as the translators of the King James Bible, not simply certain past and present southern poets. While the book lacks any unifying theme, they argued that Dickey reworked the images in his own poetic idiom and that in attempting to recover the common, unrecognized culture of his readers, he actualized the biblical images that "lie buried and live in us." The book therefore is more than a mere commercial enterprise. Jane Martin-Bowers, however, considered the book a decided retreat from Dickey's previous efforts. Dickey, she argued, believing that his interpretation of readers' personal images would engender a heightened understanding of each biblical story, had relied not on his own creativity but on preexisting text. Consequently, the fusion of the readers' own state with the larger Kingdom of God lies with the audience, not the poet. Dickey, in other words, had avoided his creative responsibilities.[69]

68. "God's Images: The Bible—A New Vision," *Library Journal* 103 (January 15, 1978): 154.
69. Calhoun and Hill, *James Dickey* (Boston: Twayne, 1983), 107–8; Martin-Bowers, "Jericho and God's Images: The Old Dickey Theme," in *The Imagination as Glory*, ed. Weigl and Hummer, 143–51.

Dickey, despite the negative reviews his work was now regularly receiving, endeavored to broaden his artistic capabilities with his first children's book, *Tucky the Hunter*, published in 1978 and named for and written about his grandson, James Tuckerman Dickey. In his notebooks from the fifties, Dickey had cited the need to explore creatively, to cast a wide artistic net: "To write (poetry) in ways that are difficult for you and alien to you is one of the major tools of exploration one can have. Cocteau: 'Learn what you can do and then don't do it.' You can write any kind of poetry in any form. To assume the mask the poem requires."[70] In good children's poetry, words and illustrations, taken together, constitute an integrated, complex work, with each aspect complementing the other, so that the book's format and layout are, finally, a coherent aesthetic, psychological, and intellectual presentation. However, while the pastel sketches by Marie Angel in *Tucky the Hunter* delicately cohere with Dickey's text rather than confront it, the plot itself is simplistic and the protagonist's adventure mostly static. Reviews were largely negative, offering no substantive analysis and often revealing only the most general knowledge of Dickey's poetic themes. The poem celebrates the imagination of Dickey's grandson, what John Logue in his review called his "oneness with the animal kingdom and his popgun," but the anonymous critic for *Kirkus Review*, comparing the book to other works by noted authors of children's literature, including Maurice Sendak and A. A. Milne, labeled the verses "forgettable."[71] With Dickey's poems appearing less and less frequently in prestigious magazines and journals, reviewers were now greeting his books with indifference or hostility.

Dickey's mother, Maibelle, the woman responsible for his idealization of women, died of cancer on June 10, 1977, in the house at 166 W. Wesley where he grew up. His sister, Maibelle, wailed during the funeral, and when Dickey, who had been drinking, tried to comfort her, she continued to cry loudly and ultimately fainted. Overwhelmed by memories, he abruptly resolved to abandon alcohol. Because he refused to acknowledge his alcoholism, however, he dismissed all treatment for withdrawal, as he had following Maxine's death. Walking on Williams Street in Atlanta, he suffered a seizure, severely bit his tongue, and nearly bled to death. In the hospital he suffered another seizure and again bit his tongue.

God's Images had recently received an auspicious reception at the American

70. *Striking In: The Early Notebooks of James Dickey*, ed. Gordon Van Ness (Columbia: University of Missouri Press, 1996), 129.

71. J. D. Logue, "Books about the South," *Southern Living* 14 (January 1979): 68; "*Tucky the Hunter*," *Kirkus Review* 46 (August 15, 1978): 917.

Booksellers Association Convention in San Francisco, news that heartened Dickey. Sales were brisk, although they never approached those of *Jericho,* and were quickened when the book was nominated on April 10, 1978, for the Carey-Thomas Award, which *Jericho* had won for the most significant publishing event in 1974. In many ways the book constituted an act of atonement. In the foreword he had honored Maxine: "She was all her life a devoted dweller in the Bible, and now, through the flowering tomb, she resides among the superhuman reality of God's images. God bless you, my good girl, bride of the first night, and now in the first light." Dickey was never a Christian; for him, the universe and its creative forces were God. Yet he liked the rituals of the church and the stories, language, and images of the Bible. When Deborah asked for a formal wedding at St. Joseph's, a Roman Catholic Church in Columbia, Dickey acquiesced. Matthew Bruccoli was the best man.

Dickey continued to stay busy. On sabbatical for the 1978 winter and spring terms, he undertook numerous readings in Washington State; taught classes at George Mason University in Fairfax, Virginia, for John Gardner, who was ailing; and on March 6, 1978, attended a Library of Congress reunion with twelve former poetry consultants. Daniel Boorstin, the current librarian, as well as Howard Nemerov, Elizabeth Bishop, Stanley Kunitz, Daniel Hoffman, and Stephen Spender convened to discuss past problems and offer possible solutions. Dickey bemoaned the absence of poetry on cassette and video and spoke about the program of taped readings he had initiated. Later the poets read to an audience of more than one thousand people for two and a half hours.

Robert Lowell had died in a New York taxi on September 12, 1977. Dickey had spent years trying to best Lowell but now sent his second wife, Elizabeth Hardwick (whom Lowell was visiting after leaving his third wife, Caroline Blackwood, in England), a telegram, saying, "All we can do for him is to love him forever." On February 9, 1979, his early mentor Allen Tate died. Once more confronted with his inability to counter time's relentless debilitation, what in *The Zodiac* he called "the thing that eats," Dickey commented to a Columbia reporter on Tate's large presence. Tate left, he declared, citing from Tate's poem "Aeneas in Washington," "a mind imperishable if time is." "Allen was the very last of his kind," Dickey asserted, "the critic, essayist, the personal scholar, and finally the poet. He had a strong sense of values, those classical values. He believed that the imagination, cultural cohesion, the sense of meaning something instead of nothing, are the qualities which define us. He was a marvelous, brilliant man."[72]

72. William W. Starr, "Literary Giant Allen Tate Dies," *The State,* February 10, 1979, p. A15.

When Dickey was invited to deliver the fifth annual Ezra Pound lecture on April 26, 1979, at the University of Idaho, he accepted, partly for the attention he received, partly for the opportunity to honor Pound's originality, and partly because the recent deaths of friends and family had reinforced his growing sense of mortality and the need to do and say things of consequence. Since his years at North Fulton High School, Dickey had always needed to confront whatever opposed him with a fierce counterthrust that would establish his own superiority, whether this meant hitting a fullback harder than he had been hit or writing a review that unflinchingly challenged poets he believed suspect. Now, however, he seemed unable to reconcile himself to death, with the result that he often dropped any public posing. Before the lecture, Dickey talked with Ron McFarland, a local poet, about a variety of subjects, including his latest work, *The Zodiac*, and his public persona. His tone was honest and straightforward, at times even humble, admitting that he had been of only average ability in football and indifferent in advertising. When McFarland suggested that the "real James Dickey" might lie concealed by "a self-created and media-assisted mask," Dickey replied: "I suppose anybody would have a tendency to do that, would partially invent or would partially have invented for him a kind of persona. You don't know which the real one is. The person himself would be the least qualified to answer that." When McFarland inquired whether he had ever had his self-confidence shaken, Dickey answered, "I've never had it when it was not shaken. But if you let all that bother you, you just can't write, you won't try anything." McFarland also noted the sadness and terror of middle age in *Sorties*. Dickey responded, "It's even worse now that I've lived through it than I said it was." He believed that the only excuse for getting older was the achievement of a "mastery of something that you would not without those years have been able to have in that degree." That experience, he declared, had made Ezra Pound an "oracle": "He had known all those people, he had done all those things, and had accumulated, maybe not wisdom, but a lot of things that were worth passing on."[73]

Dickey realized his own reputation was in decline. Astute to both publishing realities and literary politics, to the need for continued sales and awards as well as public relations and gamesmanship that could bury worthy poets and elevate suspect ones, he attempted to dominate the air in which he moved. His sense of competition and his psychological need to win required him to achieve ever higher measures of success. He also needed to prove himself by

73. "An Interview with James Dickey," *Slackwater Review* 3 (Winter 1979–1980): 17–20; rpt. in *Voiced Connections*, ed. Baughman, 173–86.

continual experimentation in form and technique, a belief partly responsible for his efforts in fiction, screenplays, children's poetry, translation, and coffee-table books. Experimentation, however, entailed risk. In the same interview with McFarland, he declared, "You should always be prepared to make a fool of yourself," and added, "I think the business of playing out there at the edge of consciousness where you're trying to push things out a bit beyond where they were before you made the attempt, that's the thing that interests me." He had declared the same idea in *Sorties* when, commenting on the tendency of Anne Sexton, Adrienne Rich, and others to avoid rhetorical statement, he wrote: "anyone who courts sublimity has to run the risk of looking ridiculous."[74]

Increasingly, critics viewed Dickey's creative efforts as failures. No one, not even Dickey himself, viewed him as flying at "angels nine." In presenting himself as a football and track star, as a decorated combat pilot who had flown more than one hundred missions, as an expert archer, competent hunter, and guitar enthusiast, Dickey had lost his poetic bearings. The lonely, self-watchful search for a unique subject matter and manner that had characterized his extended missions in the fifties and sixties, including his use of early notebooks to record and explore his literary reflections, his travels in Europe on *Sewanee Review* and Guggenheim Fellowships, and his years in business when "I was selling my soul to the devil all day and trying to buy it back at night,"[75] had in the decade after *Deliverance* yielded to the rewards of literary success. Money and popular acclaim had brought complacency. Sorties into new creative skies, such as translations and children's poetry, lacked the determined pursuit characteristic of his early motion. Other efforts, the screenplays and coffee-table books, seemed undertaken only for quick-and-easy financial gain, even as they generated a larger or different audience. Dickey had, it appeared, abandoned his immaculateness of purpose.

Dickey had been upset when *The Zodiac* did not win the Pulitzer Prize for Poetry in 1976. In 1979, he asked Doubleday to move the scheduled 1980 publication date of his new collection, *The Strength of Fields,* to 1979, believing that the Pulitzer committee that year favored him. Richard Howard chaired the committee, and because Dickey had helped Howard win the prize in 1970, Dickey thought Howard would return the favor. James Applewhite and Helen Vendler also sat on the committee, the former a poet whose values Dickey believed similar to his own and the latter a critic whom, though she

74. *Sorties,* 52–53.
75. *Self-Interviews,* 44.

had supported Lowell when she and Dickey both served on the 1977 Pulitzer committee (Dickey had favored Nemerov, who eventually won), he had flattered in a July 14, 1977, letter. Despite the maneuvering, *The Strength of Fields* did not win; the prize was awarded to Donald Justice's *Selected Poems*. Neither the Pulitzer judges nor the critics were impressed with Dickey's collection, whose title evoked a softer resiliency than his earlier "virile" poems. Apart from a section of translations that Dickey labeled "Head-Deep in Strange Sounds: Free-Flight Improvisations from the UnEnglish," the volume contained only thirteen poems, all but one of which had previously been published. Two poems, moreover—"Root-Light, or the Lawyer's Daughter" and "Drums Where I Live"—had appeared in *New Yorker* a full decade earlier. Calhoun and Hill concluded that the book was "mostly just a collection," one that was not "particularly fresh" and that constituted "a gathering of forces,"[76] which was to say, merely a roundup of previous poetic methods.

Dickey's books were also going out of print: *Self-Interviews* in 1973, *The Eye-Beaters* in 1977, and *Sorties* in 1978. He felt disappointed that *God's Images* had not been as commercially successful as *Jericho* and that *Tucky the Hunter* had not sold as many copies as *God's Images*. On May 28, 1979, he submitted a poem, "A Saying of Farewell—Homage to Nordahl Grieg," to Howard Moss at *New Yorker*, acknowledging his long absence from the magazine. Moss rejected it as he did another poem Dickey submitted several months later, "For the Running of the New York Marathon." *New Yorker*, moreover, allowed its first-read contract with Dickey to lapse, paying him the $2,705.29 that his account had accrued.[77] At the end of the seventies Dickey appeared to reviewers and critics alike to be nosediving off the literary radar, unable to determine a new direction for himself and limited to reworking old techniques and materials.

What was not apparent in 1979 was the literary transformation that was already underway but would not achieve distinct force for three more years. That force had tentatively manifested itself when Dickey published "Pine: Taste, Touch, and Sight" in the June 1969 issue of *Poetry* and when a two-part poem containing "Sound" and "Smell" appeared in *New Yorker* the same month. The full poem, which he included (though without the subtitles) in his 1970 collection, *The Eye-Beaters, Blood, Victory, Madness, Buckhead and Mercy*, was singled out for praise by reviewers who, as they would with *The Zodiac* and *The Strength of Fields*, generally disliked the volume, citing the feeble, clotted,

76. *James Dickey*, 102.
77. Hart, *Dickey*, 604.

or bathetic qualities of the remaining poems. Dickey, however, failed to pursue this distinctive new technique largely because he became involved with, first, the completion of his novel *Deliverance* and, later, its filming.

In 1982 *Puella* became the book in which Dickey finally accomplished his late poetic style, a motion that strove to synthesize or perhaps transcend two distinctive types of poetry—on the one hand, "Magic Language," poems whose words play among themselves, illuminating one another, and, while referring to nature or existence, shimmer off the backdrop of the external world as a secondary necessity; on the other hand, "literal" poetry, which centers itself in ordinary reality not to invent or impose but to discover a real unity in the world.[78] These late poems, which "Pine" first anticipates, were flights launched to reveal what new linguistic territory he might still explore and, if possible, claim; their mission, in effect, was to attack language itself in an effort to make it offer up correspondences, complicity, an extralinguistic kinship of the mind. Beginning with the appearance of "The Surround" in the July 1980 issue of *Atlantic,* they regularly saw print. Five poems appeared in the March 1981 issue of *Poetry* and won the Levinson Prize; "The Lyric Beasts" and "Tapestry and Sail" appeared later that year in *Paris Review* and *Lone Star Review,* respectively. After *The Eye-Beaters* and two derivative collections, volumes that he acknowledged as his central motion and that critics generally condemned, Dickey's final attack on language, his progressive effort to apprehend existence from perspectives utterly outside himself, was decidedly underway.

The direction, he believed, was finally clear; he had only again to notice the little things and to connect in this new language, and both the poetry and the world itself would be exalted. No longer would he feel alienated; no longer would he live in fragments. While the public did not esteem poets very much, he knew they were masters of a superior secret. In the title poem of his last collection, *The Eagle's Mile,* a poem whose epigraph from Blake, "The Emmet's Inch and Eagle's Mile," suggests the full equality of experience, he urged Supreme Court Justice William Douglas, following his death, to "power-hang in it all now, for all / The whole thing is worth." With such a flight plan, Douglas might "Splinter uncontrollably whole," might fully enter the world and be everything. Using words, Dickey intended to lead the way, flowing in the current that was his one voice.

78. "The G.I. Can of Beets, the Fox in the Wave, and the Hammers over Open Ground," keynote address, South Atlantic Modern Language Association, Atlanta, Georgia, 1982; rpt. in *Night Hurdling,* 230–42.

To: Mrs. Rose Valenstein[1]   CC, Emory University

4620 Lelia's Court
Lake Katherine
Columbia, S.C. 29206
January 2, 1970

Dear Mrs. Valenstein:

I have conferred with Mr. Auden, and have confirmed with him the awarding of the 1969 Pulitzer Prize for Poetry to Richard Howard's book Untitled Subjects. I talked this over very carefully with Mr. Auden by phone, and since you have told me, as he has, that Mrs. Hayden's opinion is the same as ours, we can consider this a unanimous choice. You asked us to make a statement about Mr. Howard's book, and about the two other books we have chosen for mention, Lenore Marshall's Latest Will and Julia Randall's Adam's Dream, and I will now attempt to make such a statement for your use.

The jury felt that Richard Howard's Untitled Subjects is a consistently interesting, varied, and intelligent book of poems, with little of the sense of the thrown-together that characterizes most books of poems; that is, we felt that the book has a wholeness of purpose, of imagination, and of poetic integrity lacking in most of the others we read. It is a civilized and fascinating achievement.

Julia Randall's Adam's Dream is a modest but deeply imaginative book. Miss Randall makes no great claims, nor does she burden the reader with excessive sentiment or with untidy confession. She is lucid, and her poems mean exactly what they say. The jury felt that Adam's Dream was a modest but probably permanently valuable achievement.

The jury felt that Lenore Marshall's Latest Will contained some startlingly original and profound work. Though we felt that Miss Marshall's achievement is somewhat uneven, we also agreed that her quality of imaginative excitement raises her above the level of all but one or two of the books we considered.

Please let me know if there is anything more required of me, or of the other members of the jury. And please see, also, that Mr. Auden and Mrs. Hayden are paid the honoraria we agreed upon, and as soon as possible. I will send copies of this letter to them, but if you wish to call them by phone prior to their reception of the letter, it might be of advantage.

I shall be in New York the 7th, 8th and 9th of this month, staying at the St.

---

1. Administrative assistant to the Pulitzer prizes.

Moritz, so, if you can, give me a call there, and maybe we can get together, albeit briefly.

I have enjoyed this work very much. Thank you for asking me to do it.

Sincerely yours,

To: Larry M. Klingman[2]   **CC, Emory University**

4620 Lelia's Court
Lake Katherine
Columbia, S.C. 29206
January 21, 1970

Dear Larry:

Very good. Sorry I haven't answered sooner, but as usual I have been traveling, and haven't had a chance to answer any correspondence at all. Yours is the first, and it should be. First of all, a little talk about projects other than <u>our</u> project. How is Croner coming along with the film? Have you seen any of it yet? I hear rumors that he thinks he has enough material to make an hour film rather than a half hour film, and naturally I think that's what he should do, if he can swing it with the various Bosses. We took an awful lot of stuff, and I think it can be more interestingly put together if we have a little bit more leisure to show, say, longer sequences of each of the things we plan to use. So I'd like to know something about this, what the possibilities are, and what the procedures are. Next, I'd like you to check out somebody for me. This is a guy named Len Richmond and he lives at 1158 North Fuller Avenue, Hollywood, California 90046. He has just made a kind of interesting experimental 16mm, 10 minute film about a poem of mine, and he looks like an interesting young film-maker. But he is very shy, and I'd like to know something about him, because he wants to do some other things of mine. He wants to show these in underground film houses, and, since I've never had any experience with such, I'd like to know more about the guy who is making the proposal, because I can't get him to tell me much through the mails. You can go about this your own way, or not go about it, if you don't want to do it. But I have an idea this fellow might be useful to us in some way. But that shall be as you wish.

2. Director who helped make Stanley Croner's Encyclopedia Britannica documentary on Dickey entitled *Lord Let Me Die, But Not Die Out*. Dickey wanted to produce a film version of his essay "Barnstorming for Poetry."

As to the film that we are thinking about making, I have in mind something that would go like this (and understand that this letter is not in any sense a treatment or even a full synopsis of the story, but is just something to let you know what I have roughly projected). The story would concern a man in early middle age, possibly divorced, who, something like Wallace Stevens, writes poetry in his spare time. Unlike Stevens, he is in some kind of technical capacity, perhaps a consulting engineer, researcher, or something of that sort. His approach to poetry is one of extreme intellectual preciseness; in fact, we may even have him call his one book of poems Structures. He has, as his primary interest in poetry, the practice of the craft as intellectual discipline, or, as Mr. Eliot calls it, a "superior amusement." Somewhat to his surprise, a venerable poetry magazine, something like Poetry in Chicago, writes to him that there is a good deal of interest in his work among the schools, and that they would like to sponsor a kind of reading tour for him, if he is agreeable. The letter from the magazine outlines what would be expected of him, what he would be paid, how he would make his travels around the circuit, and so on. Since he is along, and, though he would not admit this, rather lonely, he decides to take it on, perhaps during a vacation which he has previously planned to spend at an engineering or other scientific conference. The story would then take him to, say, Chicago to meet the sponsors for his trip, then to his first reading, his second, and so on. What we would want to show would be the increasing involvement of this poet with other people, with language, poetry, political movements, and so on, which he had previously rather prided himself on being detached from. A great deal of this could be very funny, because the nature of the material will allow us to take him to any school, any local, any kind of climate, that we wanted to. We could set him down among any kind of people we wished to, from the driest academics to the wildest revolutionaries. We could really say something about the youth of today, I believe, and we could also say a good deal about the middle age vested interest type of person, such as our poet-engineer. We could have a lot of extremely cogent, humorous, and sad encounters, and the permutations and combinations, the possibilities for these, are almost countless. And believe me, I have seen them all. Anyway, there is what I now think we should do, in its very broadest outlines. The details of course will require some juggling, and I will want you and Steve to be in on these, and work them out with me very closely.

That's enough for this time, I guess. Let me know what you think of this very preliminary accounting of what we might want to do, and we can go forward on the basis of what we decide. Please feel free to add any and all thoughts you have, and if we can get together on these, I will incorporate them into the next run-through.

All yours,

To: Ken McCormick   CC, Emory University

4620 Lelia's Court
Lake Katherine
Columbia, S.C. 29206
January 28, 1970

Dear Ken:

I, of course, can't speak for you and the other Doubleday people, but I can certainly tell you that I was absolutely delighted with the meeting. I can't think of anything that I should have said or brought up that I didn't think of then, so I must depend on you to tell me if there is any other information you need from me, any traveling you want me to do, or whatever. Theron was just as happy about the meeting as I was, as he has told me several times since then. Unfortunately, I went off without my number one copy of the book. Maxine said you have this on hand, and will send it down. Again, I appreciate it.

And that is wonderful news about the second edition of the book in paperback before publication.[3] By the way, how is this determined? I mean, do you decide you need another edition on the basis of prepublication sales to stores, or what? I have never been connected with a book operation this big, and, compared to Wesleyan, this is a whole new dimension of things, a new orbit.

I can't make this the long letter I would like to be able to do, but I just wish to thank you for your very great kindness to myself and to Theron. The whole thing felt like an awfully good occasion for all of us, and you deserve entire credit for setting the stage for what we did. I think it is going to pay off, and probably very large, too.

I've forgotten the date of the National Book Award, but I will come, if you think our cause can be served thereby. I believe you told me that it takes place on March 4th. I have a reading at Coker College in Heartsville, S.C., on the 3rd of March, but I can almost certainly come up the next day for the big do-

---

3. McCormick, Dickey's editor at Doubleday, had informed him that after an initial edition of 5,000 copies, an additional 10,000 copies of *The Eye-Beaters* had been printed.

ings that night. But again, I am not sure that you <u>said</u> the 4th, and would appreciate your catching me up on this a bit.

As to the book of essays and journals, I indeed <u>do</u> want you and Sandy to pick out the excerpts from the journals and weave them into the text in a way you think effective. Frankly, this never would have occurred to me, but it is an arrangement which is better than what <u>did</u>, in fact, occur to me, which was simply to print the essays in the first part of the book and have a section too comprised of journal entries. I would be very much interested to see what Sandy and you do with this; what kind of arrangement you finally decide is best. I myself am so close to the events described in the journal, that I would be less good at picking the entries than you and Sandy would. So, let me know how you plan to work the thing, and I will be guided accordingly. As I say, a good many of the entries are so personal that I am afraid—literally <u>afraid</u>—to publish them. Also, the notations to myself about guitar strings, and so on, I am afraid would not be awfully interesting to anyone other than a guitar player, and of my particular kind. But, if you can make a case for some of these, I might surely be persuaded.

My best to Sandy, and to all those in the Great Common Effort.

All yours,

To: John Guest[4]   **CC, Emory University**

4620 Lelia's Court
Lake Katherine
Columbia, S.C. 29206
January 30, 1970

Dear John Guest:

It was kind indeed of you to write me about <u>Deliverance</u>. I am very happy that you are so favorable to it, for I remember your previous kindness in writing about the novel when it was announced. I quite understand why Longman had to bow out of the bidding for the book, though, in view of your letters to me, I have a particular and personal kind of regret that we couldn't get together. My agent over here, though, wanted the British company that we finally went with to handle the poetry, the novels, and some other things too, and Hamish Hamilton seemed to have the right combination for us. So

---

4. Editor at Longmans, Green and Co. in England who was interested in publishing *Deliverance* in Britain. The company declined to proceed in the bidding after deciding to reduce drastically its already small poetry list, which Guest believed would be unfair to Dickey.

<u>Deliverance</u> will appear with Hamilton, as soon as a few other decisions can be made.

But, really, my reason for writing this is not to tell you of my publishing plans, but simply to record my appreciation for your kindness in telling me your feelings about my novel. I doubt very seriously whether I will ever write another, so the reaction to this one is doubly important to me. When you say that the book is "intensely visual," I am especially pleased, for my whole purpose in writing <u>Deliverance</u> was to show how a man can have a certain kind of reawakening in middle age, or indeed at any other time. Though this particular reawakening includes a most terrible kind of violence, that is really not the necessary ingredient. The river, the experiences in the woods, and the other things, are also factors in this kind of rebirth, and I am glad that someone else has seen that this is the case. But it's very exciting, isn't it? I read it over again, and when I tell you that I couldn't put it down, you see that I have at long last satisfied my own standards for the book.

Meanwhile, my very best to you and Longmans.

Sincerely yours,

To: Edgar K. Sheldon[5]   CC, Emory University

                                                4620 Lelia's Court
                                                Lake Katherine
                                                Columbia, S.C. 29206
                                                February 2, 1970

Dear Mr. Sheldon:

Thank you for your latest letter. I am sorry Gwendolyn Brooks has declined to be one of the judges, and twice as sorry that Kenneth Rexroth, whom I detest and who detests me even more, is going to be one of the judges. However, I will stick with you, and we will see if we can't come up with some decent kind of winner.

No, I don't know where Jack Gilbert, that strange night-creature, is. I haven't seen him since San Francisco about eight or ten years ago, and I have no idea in the world—literally, in the world, for he travels a lot—he is.

Well, I guess the next thing to do would be for you to get the material to me, so that I can have a look at it. You have your own procedures, and I will

5. Public relations director for Hallmark Cards who had invited Dickey to judge the company's poetry contest.

follow these in any way you desire me to, insofar as it is possible for me to do so.

Please remember me to those at Hallmark Cards I have been corresponding with, particularly Webster Schott. Tell him that I liked his piece on Auden enormously. I had dinner with Auden a couple of weeks ago, and the man is just as Webster says he is.

Sincerely yours,

To: Stewart Richardson   CC, Emory University

4620 Lelia's Court
Lake Katherine
Columbia, S.C. 29206
February 4, 1970

Dear Sandy:

Thank you so very much for your wonderful letter. I am very happy indeed that you like Deliverance, and have been kind enough to write to me about it. It is an awfully exciting book, and is very easy to read, I think. The things I like most about the book, myself, are that it is both simple and imaginative, without straining for either of these qualities. I won't go on and on about my own work in this immodest fashion, but will just thank you once more for your remarks.

I'm also very happy that you like the journal. I think it has some awfully good reflections in it, though I am not sure how many people would be interested in my deliberations about the thickness of the aluminum walls of the kinds of arrows I use, or my passionate self-debate over guitar strings and the qualities of silk and steel strings and those of metal strings. I will be completely beholden to you if you can make some kind of readable book for me. Your ideas on format are much better than my own thus far, and I am entirely delighted to place myself completely in your hands on the matter.

As to my continuing work on the journal itself, I haven't done much more than what you have. But some days I do almost nothing else but sit down and make entries on my little 20th century machine for my secretary to transcribe. I have an idea that I will soon be getting into another one of those periods, and will rattle off another fifty or a hundred pages of the journal in just a few days. As must surely be obvious, I have plenty of opinions on everything. I or somebody else just needs to write them down, that's all.

As I said to Ken in another letter, I need to know whether you wish me to come up to New York around the time of the publication of our book. I am holding out the time for this, but I would like to be advised as to whether it will be desirable for me to come, and if so, what you would like me to do, and so on. Please <u>do</u> let me know about this as soon as you can reasonably do so, and I will be guided accordingly.

But what I <u>really</u> want to say is what a damn good time I always have with you. You are the kind of man and editor that I most cotton to. What you advise me to do has never turned out to be wrong yet, and I don't expect that you will make many mistakes in dealing with my work. As I say, that is the kind of editor to have. Thank you very much for the work you are doing on the Essays and Journal. I am not sure that my working title of <u>Assertions</u> is as good as we could come up with. If you think of anyother titles you like better, please let me know. I am sure we can do better than <u>Assertions</u>, but that is, I guess, all right as a <u>working</u> title. I have never been very good at titles, anyway, and must depend on you here as elsewhere.

My very best to all, and I'll see you soon.

All yours,

To: Philip Rahv[6]   CC, Emory University

4620 Lelia's Court
Lake Katherine
Columbia, S.C. 29206
February 11, 1970

Dear Philip:

Yes, I can easily let you have the piece on Ginsberg by June. I have a good many notes on it already, and I think it will be pretty good, by the time I finish it.

I haven't time for a long letter, but thought I would just send you this note by way of reassurance about the article. I'm just as glad, too, that it will come out in the fall, for I have two books of my own this spring, and it somehow did not seem quite right for me to be bringing out my own books and at the same time—that is, the <u>same</u> time—attacking another writer. I don't mind doing that at all, if there is a kind of decent interval between the time my own

6. Prominent critic and cofounder of *Partisan Review* who was then editor of *Modern Occasions*. The essay Dickey discusses never appeared. In a June 17 letter to Rahv, Dickey apologized for the delay, attributing it to travel requested by Houghton Mifflin to promote *Deliverance*.

books come out and the article on Ginsberg. I am going to try to expand the remarks I have on Ginsberg into a whole attack on the <u>kind</u> of audience that goes to hear him read, reads his works, imitates his style, or no-style, and so on: that is on the whole <u>climate</u> that has created him and his like.

Again, thanks so much for your wonderful hospitality to me. Do you ever get to New York? I must be in and out of there a good deal in the next few months, and if you had any business down there while I was in town, we could have dinner together or something. I'd like that, believe me.

All yours,

To: Brent Ashabranner   CC, Emory University

4620 Lelia's Court
Lake Katherine
Columbia, S.C. 29206
February 11, 1970

Dear Mr. Ashabranner:

Thank you very much for your long and very cordial letter of January 31st concerning the symposium on space and poetry which you are projecting. I don't know at this time whether it will be possible for me to come out there next fall, but my spirit, such as it is, is certainly with you. I might conceivably be able to write the paper you mentioned, if my schedule lessens a little bit, but right now I am run absolutely headless by the various things I have taken on. I have four books coming out in 1970, and have to spend most of my time with factors that they bring up: with making personal appearances, receiving prizes of whatever kind, doing promotional work, appearing on TV shows, and the like. I have done a good deal of this kind of thing before, but then it was only in connection with books of poetry and literary criticism. Now I have a novel coming out March 23rd, and that is, as they say, another ball game. I have never been in one quite like it.

I think your letter is extremely interesting, and I like also the other material you sent. As to September, I don't know whether I will be available or not. My novel comes out in England at that time, and I must go over there to help in the send-off.

Let me ask you a couple of practical questions, if I may. You speak of "an appropriate honorarium." What, exactly, would this be? Also, how long would I be expected to stay? A couple of summers ago, I was at the University of Colorado, at the annual Writers' Conference, and enjoyed it very much indeed. I love that country out there, and have always wanted to visit Aspen, at whatever time of year. An old friend of mine, Jonathan Williams, has some kind of connection with your Institute, and he is always urging me to come out there and visit him, which, sadly, I have not been able to do.

Let me get to a couple of your questions, briefly. You asked why so few poets have written anything about space, and I am not sure why this is so. The whole effort to get beyond the earth-environment is fascinating to me, as you may have noticed. I think that the reason writers, particularly the better ones, don't write about space, and the new type of exploration, is that they don't know anything about the technical part of it, and don't want to learn, for various reasons of their own. Again, the task of the writer in our time seems to have devolved into a kind of last-ditch effort to preserve the individual sensibility against excessive mechanization, computers, and so on. Among some of my friends, praising the astronauts is a little bit like praising Genghis Khan. The technician is looked on as the enemy, more and more as time passes. The so called science fiction writers like Vonnegut and Bradbury are not writers of any degree of talent; it seems to me that this kind of science fiction is about all they could do. I am not downgrading the genre of science fiction, but only suggesting that it has not as yet turned out or attracted a writer of any durable merit.

You asked me as to whether any astronaut is likely to produce a work of the quality of Night Flight. I very much doubt it, though when I was down at the astronaut complex before Wally Schirra's lift-off, I spent a good deal of time with a good many of the astronauts, and their main source of dissatisfaction with themselves is that no one of them has the verbal skill or the imagination to tell of the wonders that they alone are beholding. This worries them a good deal, some more than others; but it worries all of them to a degree that I would not have believed, unless they had told me. I found all of them, particularly Armstrong and Lovell, very intelligent fellows, who worry to some extent about the loss of their essential humanity that so much "programming" of their minds and bodies is likely to occasion.

You asked me if I would go to the moon, were I given a chance, and I can give you an unconditional yes on that. If it were ever possible for me to go, I would do it. One loses one's life, on earth, in so many ignoble ways, that I would consider it a privilege or even an honor to die in such a way as a death like that would turn out to be: in some kind of absolute galactic loneliness, in some kind of aloneness that no other men have ever been in. And, my Lord, how expensive, too!

Let me know if you get this letter all right, and maybe we can plan this thing out some more. But <u>do</u> know that I am very much interested in your project, and my participation in it will depend on my being available, and engaged in a time-sequence which has not already been pre-empted. I'd like to come, believe me.

My best to you, your Institute, to Colorado, and to Aspen. Let me hear from you again when you have a chance.

Sincerely yours,

To: Ken McCormick   CC, Emory University

4620 Lelia's Court
Lake Katherine
Columbia, S.C. 29206
March 11, 1970

Dear Ken:

Maxine and I had a fine time up there with you, and look forward to seeing you again in about ten days, when the big bash for <u>Deliverance</u> takes place at the St. Regis. Maxine and my little boy will come up with me, and probably my mother-in-law also. They will stay just through the party and maybe one extra day, and I will stay the whole week, as I did this time. Any kind of publicity business you want me to do, I will be very happy to do.

Meanwhile, I am staggered by Doubleday's distribution system. I was at the Airport Bookstore at La Guardia preparing to come back down here, and they had several copies of the new book there: my God, you surely couldn't miss <u>that</u> cover!

Some of the first reviews are just beginning to come in, and they surely do look good. Richard Howard tells methat he has a new long article about me in this week's <u>Nation</u>, and there are some others pending, too. It is very important to me that our book does not get swallowed up in the general publicity over <u>Deliverance</u>, as it is also important to me that poetry itself does not get swallowed up in the greater sales and greater publicity of the novel at large. I am fighting hard to get the recognition for our book that it surely deserves to have, if any poetry I have ever written deserves to have any. For example, the speech I did before the Booksellers Association the other day, or whatever it was, contained a complete reading of "Giving a Son to the Sea," which was very well received. A number of the correspondents wanted to get hold of the book the poem appeared in, and so on. So—everything seems to be okay from that standpoint. Both trips ran our money supply down a little, and since you and Doubleday kindly offered to help us out a little here, I enclose an itemized list by Maxine as to what our expenditures and expenses were for the two trips. Let me know what you think of this, and I will be guided accordingly.

I will come up on Sunday, and probably Maxine and Kevin will too, although I may come from Charlotte and they from Columbia. At any rate, we will be in on March 22nd, all staying at the St. Moritz, as usual. I surely do hope we can get together a good deal while I am up there, for there is a good deal to talk about, not only in connection with our current book, but having to do with the two we are bringing out. I'll hope to have some more journal entries for you by that time. We ought to have a good time arranging the criticism book, for I believe it will be a format not yet seen on these shores.

Maxine and I do thank you enormously for your very great kindness to us while we were there. We'll look forward with a very great deal of warmth to seeing you in about ten days. Wonderful news about your baby. That makes a great deal of difference to us; makes us very happy. Our love to all in your home.

All yours,

To: Peter F. Neumeyer   CC, Emory University

4620 Lelia's Court
Lake Katherine
Columbia, S.C. 29206
March 16, 1970

Dear Peter:

Thank you very, very much for your letter of March 1st. It has been a long time since I have had a letter from another writer which seemed to me to be so life-giving. Your remarks about Rilke are very interesting, and help me to understand that strange poet better than I had previously been able to do. He seems to have such a strong identification with other forms of life—even with inanimate matter—that it is often difficult for a person like myself, who is always so conscious of his <u>own</u> identity to understand exactly what is going on. I guess the difference between his attitude and mine is that we <u>merge</u> with things differently. He seems to be able to <u>become</u> the other thing, while I am very conscious of the fact that <u>I am also involved in the merging</u>, and that I am giving something to the thing I am merging with as well as getting something back from it. Please excuse all this mysterious and cloudy talk; I can only hope that you have at least some idea of what I am talking about.

Your reference to Edwin Muir is nothing less than uncanny. Yes indeed, I

<u>do</u> know his work, and if there has been any one person I would acknowledge as being an influence on my own work, it would be him. I don't have anything like his diction, or his mythic concerns, but there is something about the way the man <u>takes</u> the world that I am very sympathetic toward. It is too bad that Muir did not have a great gift of phrase, for his <u>situations</u> are fascinating, even if his style is not. He is a very great man to me; I wish I could have known him. But, in a way, I guess I do, through his poems. That is the only real way of knowing, anyway.

I can't make this the long letter I would like to, for I must get on yet another airplane. The real purpose of <u>this</u> communication, though, is to invite you to a party in New York on the 23rd of this month, when my novel, <u>Deliverance</u>, is coming out. If you can make it into the city, the party will be from five to seven at the St. Regis Hotel. I hope very much you can come in, for I would love to see you. Anyway, let me know if you can come, and I will be guided by what you tell me.

About Louis Simpson, I just don't know. I think he is a man of talent—that is, of <u>some</u> talent—but these wild pronouncements he makes simply seem to me to indicate that he is incapable of reviewing judiciously or fairly. I saw a review of his about John Unterecker's <u>Biography of Hart Crane</u> which was simply appalling. It was not so much that it was appallingly bad, which it certainly was, but that it was appallingly <u>arrogant</u> in its badness. When a man of Simpson's ordinariness of mind talks about Crane and his supposed inability to get his ideas straight, and so on, one simply wants to kick Simpson's ass. Crane, though uneducated by university standards or other ordinary standards, had one of the most vivid, incisive, volatile and above all <u>original</u> minds that have ever been concerned with poetry. I cannot see how anyone, even Simpson, could fail to see this. But a kind of planned obtuseness seems to be becoming more and more part of his critical "equipment" and it will simply result in his being laughed at by anyone who takes the time and trouble to <u>read</u> the things that Louis purports to review. I won't go on and on, for I consider Simpson a friend of mine. It is simply disheartening to see him do these things to other writers, but more importantly to himself. I expect he knows pretty much how I feel about all this, so I don't think it will be necessary for you to tell him. I expect also, that you are as dismayed as I am.

But, to come back to happier things, please <u>do</u> come into the city, and to the party, if you possibly can. And if you can make it, make your presence known to me. I would love to see you, I can tell you.

Thanks so much for your long, detailed letter. It is moving, and, to me, permanent.

Sincerely,

To: Paul Schlueter

4620 Lelia's Court
Lake Katherine
Columbia, S.C. 29206
March 16, 1970

Dear Mr. Schlueter:

Thanks for your very great kindness in sending your review of <u>Deliverance</u>. Believe me, I will be looking forward with great interest to seeing it come out in <u>The Christian Century</u>. This is, as far as I know, the first review of the book; or at least it is the first one I have seen, though I have had letters from the critics who are reviewing it for <u>Playboy</u>, <u>The New York Times</u>, <u>Bookworld</u>, <u>Time</u>, <u>Life</u>, <u>Look</u>, and some other places. I haven't seen any of these others, as I say, and so yours is the first. Believe me, if the others are as perceptive as yours I shall be very happy over the press that the book receives. It is evidently going to get a good deal of attention, and naturally I am interested to see what will be said of it. Meanwhile, the Hollywood people have been in touch with me, and it looks as though Roman Polanski will be directing the film, for which I am doing the screenplay. Your perceptive remarks about the "flatness" of the characters are very well taken. Originally the book was four or five times longer than it is in its present form. I had complete dossiers on each of the men on the trip, long accounts of their background, and so on. All this would have taken care of any objections about my not focusing sufficiently on the characters. But it held up the flow of the narrative to such an extent that I spent a couple of years taking out most of the stuff I had so laboriously put in. I like the book a lot better this way; the other way, it sounded too much like too many other books I have read, where the author earnestly attempts to give you his characters in the "round," and succeeds in boring everybody half to death, including himself. No, I don't think this book, as I finally conceived it, needed much of that. After all, with the exception of the narrator and Lewis, the fellows in the boat don't really know very much about each other, to begin with. There is no need to concentrate on a great deal of introspective and/or historical comment as pertains to them. As I see it—and as you saw it—the main interest of the story is in the narrative <u>thrust</u>, and nothing should interfere with that. Perhaps this is the after-the-fact rationalizing, but I don't think it is. I reread the book again the other day, and I'm quite satisfied with it.

And I'm very happy indeed that you like it, too, and have been kind enough to send along your review. Would it be possible for you to send me a copy of <u>The Christian Century</u>, or perhaps just a cutting of the review when it appears there? I would surely appreciate it very much.

Meantime, my very best to you. If you like, tell me something of yourself, and how life is, up there in Evansville. But that shall be as you wish.

Sincerely yours,

To: James Wright   TLS, University of Minnesota

4620 Lelia's Court
Lake Katherine
Columbia, S.C. 29206
March 16, 1970

Dear Jim:

It has been years, literally, since I have received one of your wonderful, life-giving letters, and this is the best of all. I am so happy that you like the new book, for it is really not very much like any of the others. One reviewer said that I seemed to be groping for a new style, which is in part true. I thought it was a departure from other things I have written, as it certainly is, for better or worse, but I also thought I had got hold of something quite exciting in a couple of places. I had not hoped that it would receive anything like the response that you have given it, and this is marvelously gratifying to me, I can tell you. It seems to me that the great lesson of Picasso is that he never allowed himself to be trapped in a single style, as so many of our young and not-so-young American poets have done. Anyway, I wanted to move out of what had already been successful for me, if anything has, and do something a little different, and maybe, eventually, a lot different. You have convinced me that I have made at least part of the right move, though while I was writing the book I was quite prepared to have critics say that this book was "disappointing," that it "represented a retrogression," and so on. As I say, I was quite ready for that. I hoped that there would be a few people who were not mystified but interested in what I was attempting to do. But your letter! All I can say is thanks, and with great humbleness.

Maxine, Chris, Kevin, my mother-in-law, and all manner of other people will be coming up to New York on the 22nd for the big party in connection with the publication of my novel, Deliverance, on the 23rd of this month. Surely you have received an invitation to the party at the St. Regis from five to seven on the evening of the 23rd, but if by chance you have not received it, this letter is an invitation. Please do come. Chris will be there, and he very much wants to see you. You are a kind of hero of the imagination and spirit to him, as you are to me.

I'll close now, hoping to see you on the 23rd. If you can't make the party, I'll be at the St. Moritz from the Sunday just before the party to the following one, so please call me, and we'll try to get together. I would like that a lot, believe me.

My best to you, my old friend.

All yours,
Jim D.

To: Virginia Kirkland Blackwood   CC, Emory University

4620 Lelia's Court
Lake Katherine
Columbia, S.C. 29206
April 8, 1970

Dear Virginia:

Of <u>course</u> I remember you. You have a very special place in my mind, for, as nearly as I can remember, the sight of you and some other girls—but especially you, playing on the old jungle gym in that kindergarten across the street from E. River School, with your skirt tucked up like bloomers, was the first really sexual vision I ever had, in the mortal life. I felt something come over me like the sun coming out from behind a cloud, and have never really been the same since. No wonder I called you out for a Special Delivery Letter! Though, I must assure you, I called out Peggy Stewart plenty of times too, as the other fellows did. But mainly it was you who sent me.

I don't know exactly how to comment on the second paragraph of your letter, having to do with divorce, the Mafia, the brink of insanity, and so on. All this sounds very fascinating indeed, but I am not, really, in the business of dealing with other people's books. It is hard enough for me to write my own. I don't know exactly how to advise you in how to proceed, though I expect, since you are relatively inexperienced in writing, that it would be a good idea for you to get <u>somebody's</u> advise. I wish I could help you myself, but I am so caught up in movie scripts, new novels, new books of poems, books of literary criticism, and so on, that I could not possibly spare the time, though, needless to say, I would love to see you, and to get some further idea of the kind of book you want to write. Is it a novel, or example? Or some kind of documentary?

And, sure, I'd like to get together with you face to face after all these years, if you will promise to tuck up your skirt again and swing upside down from the bar: I mean the <u>exercise</u> bar! I don't know as yet when we might be able to do this, but will be able to let you know a little more later, if you'd like.

Meanwhile, my very best to you.

In memory,

To: Barry Beckerman[7]　　　　　　　　　　　　**CC, Emory University**

4620 Lelia's Court
Lake Katherine
Columbia, S.C. 29206
April 8, 1970

Dear Barry:

I am very sorry that we didn't have a chance to get together in New York, but I quite understand the impossibility of your making it to the big city at that time. I have had an awful lot of trouble, myself, traveling from place to place during the air strike, and have been looking for excuses not to make the trips I had contracted for, because of the trouble in the air terminals, and so on.

By the time you get this, the book will be number seven on the best seller list, barely three weeks after its publication. We are approaching the hundred thousand mark now in sales, and the whole affair looks, quite frankly, phenomenal. The reviews have all been great, ranging from <u>The Christian Century</u> to <u>Playboy</u>. We've had the cover of the book section of <u>The New York Times</u>, of <u>The Washington Post</u>, and the Chicago <u>Book Week</u>, several others, and so on. We've had awfully good notices in <u>News Week</u>, <u>Time</u>, and <u>Life</u>. There are lots more to come. So there will be a great deal of notoriety attached to the book, which, I think, will be very good for the film as well.

I would like very much to come out there, but the trouble is, right now, that the publisher is tearing me up with so many publicity appearances having to do with the book that I would be very hard pressed to make the time to come out there even for a day. I might be able to come out for a couple of days in May, though I have just been asked to make the Phi Beta Kappa address at Harvard, which is the same occasion as when Emerson delivered the American Scholar address. That is rather rarefied company for me to be running

---

7. Beckerman, with whom Dickey initially discussed producing *Deliverance*, wanted Dickey to fly to California to discuss directors, actors, film sites, shooting schedules, and other concerns.

in, and I must put virtually the whole month of May into writing the address. There are a lot of things like that pending, and, as I say, I am being pushed pretty hard. But I might be able to come out in May, so that we can sit down and talk some of this out. From what you say in your letter, you'd like to get some notion from me as to which film maker I would prefer. I'd like to know how we stand with Polanski. I have seen only a couple of his things, but I think they are very good, and I think he might possibly be the perfect choice for this film. I am a little troubled, however, by a couple of things in connection with him. One is that he is not an American, much less a southerner, and might have some trouble understanding some of the nuances that we ought to avail ourselves of in connection with the locale. The other is that, because of what happened to his wife, he might possibly suffer some kind of psychological trauma in making a movie that deals so obviously with violence and bloodshed. I don't know Polanski, of course, and so could not say in advance what effect dealing with these matters would have on him. But aside from these two considerations I can see no block at all to his directing, if he wants to. I am still also thinking of Sam Peckinpah, if he is free, and if you would like to have him. Please keep me informed as to the progress in these areas, either by letter or, more advantageously, by phone. We really ought to talk a little bit more before we go any further with this.

As to your inquire about my feelings concerning the screenplay, I think probably it would be best for me to write the whole thing through and give you the draft, for your comment, emendations, and so on. That is the way I had planned to do it. However, if we can fix fairly early on a director, I would also consider working with him on the screenplay. Again I would have to consult with my agent on this matter, and be advised by him. But from _my_ point of view, if I found a director I liked, I would be very happy to work with him on the screenplay. I know very little about the actual _mechanics_ of film scripts, though I have some ideas I think would be very good. But, since it cost so much money to make movies, I would be guided by your particular wishes in this matter, if they did not create a situation in which it was impossible for me to work at all. But, believe me, I anticipate nothing like that.

I think it _would_ be better if we fired back and forth a few more letters than we have done to date, have a few more phone calls, and so on. I am in and out most of the time, but, if you could let me know when you'd like to call, or when you'd like to write, I could make myself available, in one way or another.

Well; we're going to make ourselves a film. A real one.

All yours,

To: Charles Gaines   **CC, Emory University**

4620 Lelia's Court
Lake Katherine
Columbia, S.C. 29206
April 10, 1970

Dear Charles:

Awfully good to hear from you once more, and to learn that you like
Deliverance. The book has jumped onto the best seller list two weeks after
publication. It is now seventh, will be fifth the next week, and, so the computers tell us, first after that for an indefinite period. This is a strange kind of ball
game for someone who has been publishing poetry in the literary quarterlies
for the last twenty years at fifty cents a line. Warner Brothers is doing the
movie version, with myself writing the screenplay and Norman Polanski directing. They paid us an absurdly high figure for it, and the paperback people
doubled that. All in all, the book has already made my family well off, even
rich, for the rest of our lives, and will provide for our grandchildren too, or so
it looks. And we haven't even had a single royalty payment yet! We are just
past the hundred thousand mark in sales now, and computations tell us that
the book is running well ahead of Portnoy's Complaint at a similar time. As I
say, it is very strange. I record all these statistics, though, only to tell you that
I would rather have your letter about the book than all of these other things,
including the money, put together. I won't go on and on about this, but will
simply record how I feel, and end it there.

I haven't any plans to be up your way in the future, for most of my traveling time is going to have to go into the movie, into personal appearances having to do with the book, autograph parties, TV shows, and the like. All of this
is very tiring, and in none of it do I find the expectation of delight and friendship that I would have if I were allowed to visit with you and Patricia, way up
there in New Hampshire. Well, God willing, that will come later.

Meanwhile, I just gave you a glowing recommendation to the McDowell
Colony—I think it was, or was it Breadloaf?—and I hope very much you will
get what you want out of those people. I myself have only been in one such
place. This was Yaddo, up at Saratoga Springs, New York, where I roomed
with Phil Roth during the time he was first drafting Portnoy. He used to come
in the place where I worked a couple or three times a day while I was sitting
around not working but playing the guitar, and read me what he had written
that morning, doubling up with laughter, and assuring me that, if I were
Jewish, I would think it twice as funny as I did, which in point of fact I didn't

think it was: that is, I didn't think it was funny, especially, even though I am a redneck southerner. Anyway, I have a very pleasant memory of Yaddo, and I imagine that the McDowell Colony—or whatever—would be very similar. The atmosphere is very relaxed, and there are some good companions, though some of the people take themselves a bit seriously.

Now let me extend an invitation to you. We are settled at Columbia now, have a glorious house on a lake, are within a few minutes of an excellent field archery range, a great wildlife section, the ocean, beaches, and all such things, and you could come down here and stay with us whenever you would like to do so. Just let me know, and I will make arrangements to be here myself, amongst all this traveling.

My very best to you, and to Patricia and your children. Hang in there!

All yours,

To: Hayden Carruth   CC, Emory University

4620 Lelia's Court
Lake Katherine
Columbia, S.C. 29206
May 4, 1970

Dear Hayden:

Very good to hear from you again, and to have the anthology that you have edited. No, I don't have any plans to come up to Crow's Mark at Johnson, Vermont, although I must admit that the locale sounds fascinating, judging from the names. I hope you are well up there, and are doing your thing, which is one of the best things going on in the literary scene. I always look for your poems, and I know of no better literary criticism being written any-where. I thought <u>Appendix A</u> was an awfully good book, and the book on Camus is one of my favorite books of its kind, but, since there aren't any other books of its kind, it has to be an <u>especial</u> favorite.

Now let me come to the point about your anthology. I think it surely should be a commercial success, despite the enormous number of anthologies being published these days. You must understand, however, that I deplore the inclu-sion of so many rotten poets, most of them of the Ginsberg-Ferlinghetti ilk. I cannot for the life of me see why a man of your discrimination feels called upon to include these people who, no matter what their final place is in his-tory, will find it in the history of sociology rather than poetry. Therefore, I must say that I cannot in all good conscience give you a quotation which embodies my feelings about your anthology, and have these feelings be entirely favorable. This is painful to me, as it must be to you. And I will add one further thing. I think so highly of you that I will give you a quotation if you ask for it under these circumstances. That is, if you ask me for a quotation knowing that I have serious and grave misgivings about your anthology, I will make up something favorable. Doubtless this is not the first time such has gone on. But it is certainly the first time that I have offered to do it. Almost all plugs for books come from friends or acquaintances of the authors or the anthologists. There is nothing new in this, and doubtless almost all of the opinions expressed on book jackets and in publicity quotes are to some extent falsifications of the writer's true feelings. Myself, I place my regard for a man and his work above any quoted opinion of mine. As I say, then, if you still want a quotation from me, knowing how I feel about your book, I will give you one. If you want it, ask me, and don't draw back under some kind of false feelings—or true feelings—of integrity. My own integrity is quite well satisfied by my unburdening myself to you in this manner. But I did think I should let you know how I feel before giving you the quote. So let me hear from you on this. Perhaps I'm making too much of the whole thing, but for some reason I thought I should tell you all this.

As for quotations on your own work—either in poetry or in criticism—I have no qualifications at all, of any kind.

The acquaintance of mine that you mention is, I think, not a man named Philip Horton, but a young politically-minded guy from Atlanta named Jerry Horton. If his name indeed was Philip Horton, I don't know him; but if it was Jerry Horton I quite agree that he is an extraordinary young fellow. Jerry Horton is very bright, and is crazy about politics and poetry. The last time I saw him he was taking on a good deal of weight, and already looked like the politician he so desperately wants to become.

Do keep in touch with me, if you like. And let me know what I must do about your anthology.

My very best to you, and to your writings.

All yours,

To: James Wright   **TLS, University of Minnesota**

4620 Lelia's Court
Lake Katherine
Columbia, S.C.
May 11, 1970

Dear Jim:

Please forgive my not answering your letter immediately, but I have been doing so much traveling in connection with the promotion of <u>Deliverance</u> that I just haven't been home either to receive mail or to answer it. I am back, now, for the month of May, and hasten to answer.

First thank you so very much for your letter, and for the things you say about the new poems. If I can run down a copy of the <u>New Yorker</u> where "Root-light" appeared, I will have it Xeroxed for you and send it on. I have about half a new manuscript, and the poem will be in that, whenever it chances to appear. I haven't written any poetry, now, for about eight months or a year, and it feels very strange indeed to do nothing but travel and not write. I have taken the month of May off, for I must somehow contrive to write the Phi Beta Kappa poem for Commencement at Harvard next month. I am told that this is the same occasion on which Emerson delivered the American Scholar Address, which, you may imagine, filled me with a sense of total inadequacy! Nevertheless, I am pushing ahead with what I think is a rather interesting idea, whether or not I can bring it off. This is to take a man's entire lifework—in this case, Trumbull Stickney, an old Harvard man, minor poet and a corpse at the age of twenty nine—and go through it laboriously time after time, picking out some lines that have meant a great deal to me personally. Then we take these lines and phrases and write a poem out of them illustrative of what the phrases evoke in <u>me</u>, personally. The whole question of poetic imagery is so fascinating that I hope to get some of this fascination into the poem. For example, when I say "tree" there will flash up in the mind's eye of anyone within earshot a different tree for each person. When Stickney says "the burned season shone" you and I are going to see different burning seasons, and different shinings. So the poem is actually going to be about Stickney's imagery's effect on me, and therefore will be about poetry, and therefore will be about my life more than about Stickney's life. All this may sound rather vague at this stage, but it is yielding some rather interesting stuff, I think. I hope I can get it done by June 9th, which is the target date for Harvard graduation, and probably for a huge riot in which poets will be stoned to death like St. Stephen—or not like St. Stephen.

Also, the Apollo Eleven boys want me to come up to New York and read at a program for them on the 1st of June, which I plan to do. I will try to contrive to spend a couple of days in New York, and maybe you and Annie can go out to dinner together with me. I would sure like that, you can believe.

By the way, I taught your entire lifework yesterday in an hour and a half class, and I got a finer and deeper response to your work than to that of any other poet—English or American, great or small—than I have taught this year. These kids are really crazy about the stuff, I can tell you.

Love to Annie, and to everything surrounding you. Even to Old Bob, who has tried his God-damnedest to make an enemy out of me, but will never succeed. He is a good man with no talent, and he ought to be content with that. He is killing himself trying to be a "great writer and great literary influence." Terribly sad. But I have good memories of Bob, and when can one ever have too many of those?

Love,

Jim D.

To: Jay Deiss   **CC, Emory University**

4620 Lelia's Court
Lake Katherine
Columbia, S.C. 29206
May 18, 1970

Dear Jay:

Thank you so very much for your note on the poetry interview over WGBH, and for the things you say about <u>Deliverance</u>. The book is now third on all the best seller lists, and my editor tells me that this weekend or, at the very latest, next, it will be second, and thereafter, in a couple or more weeks I suppose, first. All this is very bewildering to me, though gratifying, as you may suppose. But the best effect of the publication of <u>Deliverance</u> is that it has restored my connections with many friends all over the world, including old Air Force buddies, and so on, whom I thought I had lost forever.

I am just so damned terribly sorry to hear about Casy. He was, though I did not know him as well as I would have liked to do, very close to me, as far as <u>my</u> feeling was concerned. He got me interested in the guitar in a way I had not been before, and, since I knew him, I have been playing steadily all this time. I feel very much like Casy is, in a way, in my hands, and one person cannot give another a greater gift. I have never understood the way the world works, the way the universe works, and the way chance works. But when the lightning killed Casy, that seems to me to make out a very good case for the malevolence of the entire design of things. I know how you must feel, and I sympathize with you as much as one man may do with another. Yes, and more than that too.

I shall certainly get hold of your <u>Roman Years of Margaret Fuller</u> and read it carefully. Anything that concerns my friends in Positano concerns me, you may very well be sure. I look back on those days with an affection which one can only have when looking back on the Lost Paradise, and I can hardly believe that I was ever in such a gentle, generous and carefree atmosphere. I want to go back there, for at least a little while, but I also dread going back, because, like most human beings, I believe that you <u>can</u> relive the past, recapture it, become immortal, not age, not die. But if I went back there, I know that the first persons I would be looking for would be you and Casy, and just a few, close, intimate friends. The fact that none of you would be there, most likely, would tear me to pieces, despite the amount of loving that I do for Positano, its location, and its people. Perhaps we will all go back there together when we die, and all will be as it was.

All yours,

To: Paul Bowles   **CC, Emory University**

4620 Lelia's Court
Lake Katherine
Columbia, S.C. 29206
May 20, 1970

Dear Paul Bowles:

Thank you very much for taking the trouble to write, for I hadn't really expected that you would do so. Yes, I inquired about you from Dan Halpern,[8] for you are one of my favorite writers, and are probably my favorite composer of all the new fellows. By the way, Ned Rorem was down here in Columbia a couple of weeks ago in connection with a festival of the arts that I put on here at the University, and he spoke of your work as though you were a kind of new messiah of music. He is really very knowledgeable about music and musicians, and I was delighted to hear his high opinion of your work. I have only the one record that was put out about fifteen or twenty years ago, but it surely

---

8. Editor of *Antaeus.*

has some beautiful stuff on it. Are you writing some new music? You may be sure I will try my best to get hold of your <u>A Picnic Cantata</u>, and will ransack the record magazines to see if I can find anything else.

Meanwhile, are you writing some new things? I have read almost everything you have written, beginning with <u>The Sheltering Sky</u>, which as I remember came out when I was going to Vanderbilt. You have a very great gift, and it must be a terrific pleasure for you to sit down at the writing desk whenever you do so.

If you'll let me know, I'll send you a copy of my book <u>Deliverance</u>; I'd like very much to do so.

Do you know my old friends Alec Waugh and his wife? They have been going to Tangier for years and years and years, and must be pretty well known among the English-speaking folks down there. Alec has recently married the lady he has been keeping company with for a good many years, and he tells me that he now <u>lives</u> in Tangier. I don't have his address, but you could probably find out from other people, as Alec gets around a good deal socially, and probably any of the people in the British Consulate could tell you where he lives, if you don't know already. He is a very sweet old party, and it is absolutely impossible not to be crazy about him.

How do the prospects look for Dan's magazine? If you see him, please tell him to send me a copy of the opening issue, for he has got me interested in the damn thing. Surely an international kind of journal like that is sorely needed. To my knowledge there hasn't been any such since the demise of <u>Botteghe Oscure</u>, which I—probably among many others—miss sorely. You used to publish a good deal with them, as I remember. My former poetry publisher, Wesleyan, recently sent me a complete file of the magazine, and I have been reading through it slowly, issue by issue. If Dan's magazine is half way as good as <u>Botteghe Oscure</u>, he is doing everybody a real service.

I can't make this a long letter, for I must get on yet another airplane. But I did want to let you know how much I appreciate your taking the trouble to write. Let me hear from you again, from that far, exotic place, whenever you have a moment, or have the inclination.

Meanwhile, my very best to you.

Sincerely yours,

To: Hayden Carruth   **CC, Emory University**

4620 Lelia's Court
Lake Katherine
Columbia, S.C. 29206
May 20, 1970

Dear Hayden:

   Thanks enormously for your long, full and friendly letter from Crow's
Mark. I felt like a dog, as they say, about my rather aloof reply to your asking
me for a quotation in connection with your anthology. Thank you for being
so understanding. Would it be possible for you to have me say something like
"There is an astonishing amount of good poetry here?" Or something like
that? I wouldn't mind giving you a quotation at all if I could find something
to say which would stress the qualities of the book I <u>do</u> like without intimat-
ing that I like everything. Couldn't we do something on the order of suggesting that I have gotten a good deal of enjoyment out of the book, have found
some new poems and poets I didn't know about previously, and so on? That
would get everybody out, with honor satisfied on all sides.

   I know something about your personal situation from Henry Rago and
others, and my conscience has been bugging me a good deal over the matter
of your anthology, because I respect and like your work so much, and because
I know that you are usually fairly strapped financially. So, if you can figure
out something for me to say that meets the conditions I've just been talking
about, you can use a quotation from me if you like. It really <u>is</u> a good anthology, with an awful lot of good poetry in it, as well as some bad.

   Have you ever thought to collect your reviews and other criticism? My two
critical books—and now a third that is coming out in the fall—are almost all
composed of reviews and pieces I did on commission for one magazine or
another. If I can collect <u>my</u> reviews, why can't you collect yours, which are so
much better? Also, it seems to me that you have done even more reviewing
than I have, so you would have a lot more material to work with. I remember
especially your estimate of Ted Hughes a few years ago in <u>Poetry</u>, and if that
isn't telling it like it is, I have never heard it told like it is. That was an intelligent murder, and absolutely and completely deserved. The English critics are
always whooping it up over Hughes, who to me is a very predictable kind of
pseudo-energetic D. H. Lawrence-type British phony. The reason the British
like him so much is that he has at least a <u>symbolence</u> of energy, amongst so
much great intellectuality. Anyway, your review of him was first rate, and it is
not the only good hatchet job you've done, or by any means, I hope, the last.
You also praise very well, and that is the surest mark of a good critic.

And how about collecting your poems, too? It seems to me that now would be a very good time for a large edition. Tell me what you think of all this; I'm eager to know.

Thank you very much for the things you say about my own work, and particularly about the last poem of mine in the <u>Virginia Quarterly</u>.[9] All those things were such a long time ago, but I believe I could get in a Stearman right now and take it off, and go anywhere I wanted to in it, and set it down again more or less safely. As you may know, I have a novel that is now topping the best seller lists, and my editors are already after me to write another. I don't think I will, but if I decide to do so, I believe I might write something about those old Stearman days, when flying <u>meant</u> something, and one actually did have the sensation of one's body being carried through the air, rather than being blasted through it.

When you have a chance, write again and tell me what your life is like. Someone said to me once that you had some kind of place-phobia, and I would like to know about this, and if it is possible for you to tell me. But that shall be as you wish.

All yours,

To: Willard Thorp   TLS, Princeton University

4620 Lelia's Court
Lake Katherine
Columbia, S.C. 29206
May 22, 1970

Dear Willard:

Thank you very much for your communication of a couple of weeks ago. I have got Bob Taylor into direct contact with my agent, Theron Raines, for any financial transaction that I engage in must be handled by him. I am quite sure that Mr. Taylor and Theron will be able to work out some equitable arrangement, though I have not as yet had time to hear from Theron. But you may be assured that I would like very much to have the drafts and the other material concerning <u>Deliverance</u> at Princeton. I have always loved the school, though I have only been there a few times. The literary associations—of Scott Fitzgerald, of Edmund Wilson, of John Peale Bishop, of yourself, of Dick Blackmur— have always been a constant inspiration to me, and so I would very much

9. "Camden Town" was published in the spring 1970 issue.

enjoy the knowledge that what very likely is going to be my only novel will be cloistered in those particular hallowed halls.

I am terribly sorry to hear about Margaret. Isn't there some kind of central-brain surgery that they can do with a new kind of freezing-technique to alleviate Parkinson's disease? As you can see, I'm certainly no doctor, but medical discoveries get so thoroughly publicized these days that I, like the rest of the American public, can hardly avoid hearing a good deal of discussion of "new discoveries" in medicine these days. Anyway, I hope there will be some way for her to enjoy her life, and to come home. And arthritis for you! I hope it is not in your hands, for one of the chief pleasures in memory for me is in hearing you play the organ in Houston, and hearing you play Charles Ives at your home in Princeton. My God, anybody who can play Charles Ives' music surely ought not to have arthritis! As for myself, getting in on the current infirmity sweepstakes, I have just been informed that, whether I knew it or not, I am a diabetic. And how about that? My doctor is very literary, and before he told me the melancholy news, he had—poor soul!—looked up all the illustrious literary people who were diabetics, and divided these into two categories: those who took care of themselves, as for example H. G. Wells, who lived until the age of 83, and those who did not take care of themselves, and so consequently—of course!—died young, such as Dylan Thomas and Bredan Behan. Well, that is a dilemma indeed! I am still debating this, meanwhile drinking a little forbidden bourbon to help me decide.

But, no matter what the medicos say, the end is not yet. There is an awful lot to be done, and we are trying to move on it as well as may be done. I must go up to Harvard and deliver the Phi Beta Kappa poem on June 9th. Since this is the same occasion on which Emerson delivered the American Scholar Address, I am naturally a little shaky, but will do the best I can, which is of course the best I might be expected to do anyway. I was also elected to the American Academy of Arts and Sciences yesterday, which is bewildering indeed, in the company of all those people you see written up all the time in Life and Look and Newsweek.

I hope to get up through there this summer some time, and will try and stop off to see you. It would be great. You can believe.

All yours,

Jim

P.S. And could you tell me if Bink Noll is still around there? What shape is he in? And Ted Weiss?

To: Richard Howard   **CC, Emory University**

4620 Lelia's Court
Lake Katherine
Columbia, S.C. 29206
June 17, 1970

Dear Richard:

Thank you so much for your June 11th letter, which I am awfully happy to have. No, I most emphatically did not find your Nation piece disappointing. The contrary was true: it seems to me one of the most favorable and penetrating things yet written on anything I have done. I might have expected this of you, for you have written so much about my work elsewhere, but you surely seemed to understand the wave length that the new book is tuned on, and, though there have been a good many reviews, none have been so close to the mark as yours. I can only thank you once more for this, and move on to wherever I am going from here.

Most interesting news about your editorship of the New American Review, and the new poetry series that Braziller is going to do under your editorship. I don't know very much about Chester Kallman's work, though I haven't read much that I've liked by him, but I do like Charles Simic very much, and once wrote him one of the few fan letters that I have ever sent to anyone. And of course Eleanor Taylor is one of the really good women poets in the country; quite possibly the best now writing.

Meanwhile, I, too, have become an editor, and in rather a curious place. Esquire is starting a poetry program, and I am, God save the mark, their editor. Why I took this on I can't quite say, though it is most likely for some such reason as that which prompts me to serve on committees, nominating boards, and so on: if I don't do it, some bad guy will do it. After all, I was the chairman of the board that voted you the Pulitzer Prize, and God knows who would have got it if _____ (fill in blank) had been on it! So many things like this are the luck of the draw, and I would rather have my hand on the deck than somebody else's I could think of. Anyway, I would like to ask you for a short poem or two, if you think you will have anything ready in a couple of months. I think I should have something from you, something maybe from Jim Wright, maybe something from Archie Ammons, something from Wendell Barry, and so on. Do you have any suggestions as to the really good writers now? I am not up on the very latest fellows, and so, were it left to me alone, I would probably go with people like Bill Stafford, whose work I know best. But I would surely welcome suggestions from you, since you are, as they say, on the scene.

Good to know that Sandy is writing again. I had no notion of his monumental depressions, as you call them, but then I see so very little of him that it would be impossible for me <u>to</u> know. But it is good to know that he is feeling better, and getting back to work. As to your own hyperventilation attacks, I am concerned, naturally. But since you tell me that you can control them and that there is no real danger in them or surrounding them, I am not so worried as I might be. My God, how mortal and fragile we all are. my own diabetes seems to be all right, or at least it hasn't found a way to bother me yet other than mentally. But that is a plenty bad way, as you may know. Christ, the damn curious disease has made such a hypochondriac of me that I can hardly walk to the door without feeling some new pain, probably having something to do with sugar and a regulatory system I had no notion, four years ago, that I even had—well, I won't go into all that. You, like everybody else, has his own troubles. But I did want to let you know that I am all right, only very rushed, what with doing the screenplay of <u>Deliverance</u>, bringing out two more books in the fall, writing some new things, traveling around a bit, the considerations of a new grandchild—a boy—and a good many other things—that I simply have not had time to write anybody. But now, home for a few days, I can get off some mail to those who really matter, foremost of which is yourself, as always.

My very best to you, and to Sandy. I will be looking for what you both write. Take care of yourself, Dick. I will try to do the same, down here in my own hot, sandy, South Carolina way.

All yours,

To: Ken McCormick   **CC, Emory University**

                                                     4620 Lelia's Court
                                                     Lake Katherine
                                                     Columbia, S.C. 29206
                                                     June 29, 1970

Dear Ken:

Thank you very much for your June 23rd letter. Tony has sent along his final suggestions about the translations that I have already done, and they look fine to me. Doubtless he is in touch with Kate Medina, and we are moving along all right so far. I shall have the other six done in a couple of weeks, and will send them on either to Kate or to Tony. I am enjoying doing these renditions very much, and may include several of them in my next volume, which should be ready in about a year. I have about half a manuscript now, and am working on some new things whenever I can get time from the labor on the screenplay of <u>Deliverance</u> and some other projects I have to do.

As to some of the things you mentioned in your most recent letters. Sure, I am always very happy indeed to get any books that you want to send along to me. And you may be assured that if I find one I like particularly I will give you a jacket quote for it. Of course I haven't time to read them all, but if anything looks good I usually give it a go. If anything happens as a result of these readings, I will let you know right away. But, as I say, I <u>am</u> always very happy to have these books, and delighted that you take the trouble to send them to me.

As to the business with Wesleyan: I saw Will Lockwood at Hollins last week, and asked him about it. As I thought I had remembered, Wesleyan has a kind of set fee for such anthology or other uses, and has its own reason for having the fee what it is. I would have felt a little embarrassed, particularly since Wesleyan has always treated me so well, at asking my old publisher—a small one—to come down on what they consider is a fair fee in favor of my new publisher, a very large house indeed. I'm sure you can understand this. Anyway, I think it is important that we keep the best possible relationships with Wesleyan, for we may want to ask favors of them concerning material that I have published with them in four books.

I'm very happy you liked the Encyclopaedia Britannica film. It runs forty minutes, and the total footage we took over a three week period ran to some 25 hours. I think Stan Croner did a good job, though, as is bound to be the case, it is questionable as to whether he did the best conceivable job. But I think the film is good in its way, and I believe it will be awfully good for our purposes. I thought the "Buckhead Boys" sounded good, and the other poem too. In all, we have the advantage of provoking in people that instinct that usually <u>is</u> provoked when a writer gets a certain amount of publicity "the wish on the part of the reader to have the <u>latest</u> book that this particular author has written."

I have just come back from Hollins, and I must have signed at least one hundred of our book. The <u>availability</u> of the book as determined by the Doubleday procedures, is astonishing to me. Wesleyan was certainly never like this! I had a nice conversation with Lockwood about this in Roanoke, and he quite readily and even cheerfully admitted—which he was certainly not willing to do before—that I really <u>do</u> need a large outfit like Doubleday. But, as I say, I must have signed at least a hundred copies there, and people keep sending them to me from all over for signatures. So the book is getting around, as we hoped it would do.

Thank you also for enclosing the inserter for bookshops. It should be effective.

From the standpoint of publishing, since we are bringing out three books within, say, a year or year and a half, what would be your advice as to when we should publish another book of poems? As I said earlier, I have about half a manuscript now, and could very easily furnish the rest of it in six or eight months, if I can make time to complete the ones I'm already working on. It will make a difference to me as to how I conceive the book, so, if you would give me some idea as to when we might want to publish it. I could, for example, take on a number of long-range poetry projects if I knew I were going to have a lot more time than I had originally conceived. Give me a tentative schedule as to this, and I will go ahead as you think fit. Either way would be all right with me. Bear in mind, though, that I want to bring the Indian Maiden out separately, since it will be so very long. There are some relatively long poems in the new manuscript, but Indian Maiden is likely to be pretty nearly book-length. There is no rush on either book, though I want to bring out Slowly Toward Hercules before the Indian Maiden, and this is a definite wish, insofar as I am concerned. So we will really be spacing out two books instead of one.

My very best to you, Ken. You are the editor I have always wanted, and you have never been wrong on anything you advise me to do. Maxwell Perkins never did so well by Thomas Wolfe, even, and believe me, I know it, and appreciate it.

Meanwhile, my best to Barbara, to Sandy, and to all those I know up there. And please do let me have the jacket samples of Self-Interviews as soon as you have printed a few.

I will most likely be in New York during the very last part of the summer, and you may be sure I will let you know in plenty of time for us to get together, if you're in town. I'd like that, believe me.

All yours,

P.S. I spoke a couple of weeks ago at the meeting of the American Booksellers Association in Washington. I was the last speaker, which I understand is the best position to be in, and talked about twenty minutes. Ostensibly I was supposed to be there to talk about and read from Deliverance, but I also read a couple of poems from our book, and the response to these was warm indeed.

To: David Willson   **CC, Emory University**

4620 Lelia's Court
Lake Katherine
Columbia, S.C. 29206
July 9, 1970

Dear Mr. Willson:

   Thank you indeed for taking the trouble to write and correct the places in Deliverance where I was wrong, or half-wrong, anyway, in my references to various guitar players. You must remember, though, that Ed Gentry, the man who is making available all this information in the novel, is really not a guitar player himself; he just remembers the few names that he has heard Drew use, and very well might have been confused—as, indeed, Drew himself might have been confused—as to which players are blind or not. I guess I might better have put in Lemon Jefferson or Willie McTell or Blind Blake, just to make sure that Drew, and after him, Ed, were sort of authorities on guitar players, but I didn't think I needed to be this exact. As a matter of fact, the reference to Brownie McGhee is just such a mistake that Ed, misreading Drew, who might himself have been wrong about it, might have been responsible for. After all, like I say, Ed is no professional in these matters, and it might cast a certain suspicion on his character if he were presented as such. I quite agree with you on Dave Van Ronk, but again the question of too much expertise comes in to the characterization of these men. But thank you anyway for writing to me as you have done. If you have another chance, write me and tell me something of yourself. You are evidently something of an expert in guitar playing your-self, and folks of that nature I respond to readily, I can tell you. What do you think of Mike Russo? I may get him to do the guitar track for the film version of Deliverance, which I am now readying.

   All best, and I shall be looking forward to hearing from you. But that shall be as you wish.

                                        Sincerely yours,

4620 Lelia's Court
Lake Katherine
Columbia, S.C. 29206
July 14, 1970

Dear Phillip:

Here is the long-promised piece, which I hope you will like. Perhaps it is a bit unfair, but I don't think so. Anyway, it says what I have been wanting to say for a good long time, and if people don't like it, well that's just too bad. I remember your telling me, when you first asked me to do the essay, that you wanted something to stir up snakes, and this will sure accomplish that end, I am quite sure. Meanwhile, I have read some other things of Dickstein's, and am happy to report that I disagree with him in his estimates of other writers—like the ludicrous Donald Barthelme—fully as much as I do with his opinions on Ginsberg. He is evidently one of these people who can see no virtue in any writing or writer unless one or the other is "new." He is always talking about the "new" this and the "new" that and the "new" the other. Very tiresome, I think.

If you decide to run this, when will it run? Of course I'll be looking forward very much to seeing it when it comes out, and will depend on your letting me know when this is to be.

One other thing. I don't really have any wish to become embroiled in some kind of long exchange of letters with Dickstein, with anyone else who writes in, or indeed anyone at all. I must make this more or less a proviso here. I won't have time to answer any letters, either in print or out of it. If any come in, as a result of the publication of the piece, just forward them on here to me. But I really can't take on a public feud over these opinions. What I have wanted to say about Ginsberg, his audience and the rest, I have said in the essay, and don't wish to add anything to these remarks, defend any of the, or take up any further points pertaining to the material. I'm sure you will understand this. Maybe it is just as well that Dickstein be allowed to have the last word if he's of a mind to write a letter, which naturally he will be. After all, there should be some occasions in which the attacking letter-writer has the last say, instead of giving it invariably to the original essayist!

Again, thanks so much for the things you say about <u>Deliverance</u>. I am bewildered by the success of it, and hope to be so for some time to come. I now plan to get back to poetry, and probably will stay there, bringing out maybe another book of essays next spring. By the way, can I have clearance to print this essay in the forthcoming book? I'd appreciate your telling me how you stand on this?

　　With every best wish, and hoping to see you again soon, I remain

Sincerely yours,

To: Gordon Lish[10]　　　　　　　　　　　　　　　　**CC, Emory University**

4620 Lelia's Court
Lake Katherine
Columbia, S.C. 29206
July 15, 1970

Dear Gordon:

　　I haven't time to look up my last letter to you, but if I haven't already, I want to tell you now that I will be in New York—for the Today Show on the 20th and the Cavett Show on the evening of the 22nd—from Sunday afternoon until the following Saturday: from the 19th to the 25th, I guess it is. I will be, as usual, at the St. Moritz, and will hope to hear from you there. I have a good many ideas about our first issue, and want to talk them over with you. Mainly, though, I have got hold of a remarkable young—or I guess he's young, anyway—poet from California by the name of Jesse Shields, and I want to know what you think of him. He is apparently a very curious kind of a recluse, for he doesn't seen to want to talk about himself, but the stuff he has sent me is absolutely dazzling.

　　The other thing is that I am absolutely bowled over by your sending along the poem of Helen Sorrells. If there is any one writer that I think I can personally take complete responsibility for it is Helen Sorrells. She was a member of my writing class when I taught in California, at San Fernando Valley State College. She is now between 60 and 65, I should judge. You should have seen the first stuff that she turned in! But, all during that year, she began to see the light, little by little, and to write some interesting and original things. I haven't seen any of her recent work except what you send me. I like this a lot, and, if you can come up with an address for her, would like to get in touch. I may have her address around somewhere, but I am not sure that I do, after all this moving around. Anyway, Helen Sorrells has got the seeds of grace, I believe. But what an extraordinary coincidence that it should be <u>her</u> whose work you were struck by, and have sent along! Well, good things can happen, every once in a while: to you, to Helen Sorrells, to me, to <u>Esquire</u>.

---

10. Editor of *Esquire*.

Please <u>do</u> let me hear from you in New York, and we'll have lunch again, or something. And I do indeed want you to come down here and stay with us for a few days. It is very pleasant, though hot. We have a lake, a speed boat, and some other things you might enjoy fooling around with. Anyway, I'll see you in a few days in New York, and we'll talk it all out.

Meanwhile, my best as always.

All yours,

P.S. By the way, would you be kind enough to do me a favor? The last time I was there I promised a lady named Mary Cantwell—or at least I think the first name is Mary, and am sure the last name is Cantwell—at <u>Mademoiselle</u> Magazine that I would come by and pose for a couple of pictures, as she suggested, since <u>Mademoiselle</u> is running part of <u>Self-Interviews</u>. Would you call her and tell her the dates that I'm to be in New York, and where I'm staying? I feel as though I owe people there the courtesy of doing what they suggested and I agreed to, though, as I say, this must be done belatedly.

To: John Calley

CC, Emory University
4620 Lelia's Court
Lake Katherine
Columbia, S.C. 29206

August 6, 1970

Dear John:

Here is the first draft of the screenplay, as promised. Get back to me on it as soon as you have read it through. I think it turned out very well, myself. It was great fun to do, and, since the novel is conceived scenically anyway, it was comparatively easy to translate it over into visual terms. It may be that I have gone into too much detail in places; I can't of course know what you will think of this. I read through the scripts that Barry Beckerman sent along, and it seemed to me that they were pretty thin. I had much rather try to do a James Agee-type script, and perhaps put in too much rather than too little. Anyway, you will tell me what you think. This is, as the agreement has it, a first draft. Doubtless there will be some changes suggested, perhaps by you and almost certainly by whatever director we select. Nevertheless, this screenplay is essentially what I want to do, and when I thought I had come up with a good shot or camera angle, I said so. This is for the director to accept or reject, as he sees fit. As you will notice, I have changed the ending and several other of the parts to include material that is not in the novel. But I have stuck pretty closely with the story, for I think that any changes we make should be in the interests of making a better film of our material, and not simply to change for the sake of changing. I pondered this story, its characters and scenes and implications for eight years, and I have everything fitted into place exactly as I want it. So, if the dialogue in the book seemed right, I included it in the screenplay. As you will see, I have shortened down the narrative after the men come off the river, and have taken care of everything that it took me two or three scenes to resolve in the book, in one scene on the riverbank, as I have it in the script. The end is changed completely, though the implications are the same.

The next step, then, I guess, is up to you. Let me know what you wish me to do after you've read this carefully. I say carefully, knowing you will do so without my saying it, because I have worked the script out very carefully, and anyone reading through it too quickly will chance missing a great deal that I have tried to do.

I am now planning to stay in Columbia for most of the rest of the summer. Playboy is doing what they call a profile on me, and the interviewer is coming down here to stay with us for about a week, and I am planning to take him over into north Georgia and show him some of these rivers. Other than that, and a trip to England for a week around the tenth of September for the British publication of Deliverance, I will be here, and could even come out to the coast, should you deem it necessary or advisable. Again, I will wait to hear from you on this.

One more thing: several magazines—Esquire, McCall's, Atlantic, and a couple of others—wish to publish parts of the screenplay. I told them I would consult with you on this, and see what you said about it. We can publish with any or all of them, or not, as you say. I have no wish to infringe on our original contract, but since my agent, Theron Raines, takes care of all this for me, and since he is out of the country right now, I am not quite sure what the contract does say about matters of this sort. It might be good publicity for us; on the other hand, it might not. Let me know, and I will swing with what you want to do.

My best to Barry Beckerman, and to yourself. But if you think it would be a good idea for me to come out there at some time before the beginning of school here—September 16th—please let me know, so that I can make plans accordingly, and save the time required from whatever else might impend.

Sincerely yours,

To: William Heyen

CC, Emory University
4620 Lelia's Court
Lake Katherine
Columbia, S.C. 29206

August 11, 1970

Dear Bill:

Thank you very much for your recent letter, and for the comments on the Cromie show and the Cavett show. Those are strange occasions, as you no doubt know from your own experience. There is a time-slot, and you are supposed to do <u>something</u> within it. Most things that are done on such programs are eminently forgettable; one sees them and they flush right out of ones system. That is what they are designed for. However, when you get on a show of that type <u>yourself</u>, you feel that, with great luck, it can be otherwise. Maybe something you say will <u>matter</u>, in some way or other, to someone, somewhere. Anyway, I am very happy that you like what I did, for there is no sanction for assuming that this will happen.

You have my sincere word that I will do my best to come to Brockport, if it can be arranged at all. My main commitment, right now, is to the film version of <u>Deliverance</u>, which is one of the two major productions that Warner Brothers are going to do this year. That may be important from Warner Brothers standpoint, but from mine it is important in the sense that this is very likely going to be the only film that I will ever do, and so it <u>has</u> to be right. I expect there will be a great deal of agony connected with the making of the film, but when has the artist ever had anything else? But you can be assured that I will do my dead level best, as they say in South Carolina, to come up there to Brockport. This is not because of Brockport, or because of the money—which I certainly don't need—but because of you, and your own qualifications, talent, and integrity as a writer. I am not one to gush, but you are one of the good people writing now. Morality is in your criticism, and that is the only factor that can give criticism the dignity and the <u>weight</u> that makes it matter beyond the latest throwaway review. I won't go on and on, but will close now. Let me know what Brockport can pay me, and I will take this up with my agent. My usual fee is $3,500, but I might be able to come down at least <u>somewhat</u> from that, in this particular case. But, as I say, let me know what the traffic will bear, and I will be guided accordingly.

Hang in there, buddy. You have got the true right thing in what you put down on the page, and when can we ever have enough of that!

Sincerely yours,

To: Peter Neumeyer

CC, Emory University
4620 Lelia's Court
Lake Katherine
Columbia, S.C. 29206

August 13, 1970

Dear Peter:

What a <u>damned</u> nice thing to do: that sending along of the John Davidson book. I read through it with delight. It is not the Davidson that I admire the most—<u>that Davidson</u> is lost even to the literary histories, and is known only to me—but it is Davidson, and is the Davidson that led me into reading the <u>other</u> Davidson. Strange thing, that! I think the turning point in the early part of my so called career was in reading a long poem of John Davidsons' called "Ballad in Blank Verse of the Making of a Poet." Davidson came from Oban, a grim, Calvinistic town on the coast in the west of Scotland, and the poem is a rather lurid account of how he divested himself of his Calvinistic upbringing, and struck out for London to live or die as a poet. It is not a very good poem, but it is the kind of poem that a young poet—though Baptist, not Calvinist—<u>should</u> read, and at right that time in in his life. And I still remember the last line of the poem as expressing the kind of attitude that I myself attach most value to, even after all these years:

Men to know and women to love are waiting everywhere.

I haven't time to answer your long, information-packed and insightful letter, as I never have been able to do, and never will be able to do. Believe me, it is a very great grace for me to receive a letter of yours. But I am much beset, these days, and you will understand why I cannot reciprocate in kind. But you must also know how very grateful I am for your letters, and for your extreme kindness—that kind of <u>personalized</u> kindness that is the best kindness of all—in sending along the Davidson book. I don't have very many <u>old</u> books, and so this one is doubly precious to me. I won't go on and on in this maudlin vein, but will just close out by thanking you once more. And please <u>do</u> keep in touch. I hope that one day we will meet. Yes indeed; I surely do.

All yours,

To: Peter Bird Martin[11]

CC, Emory University
4620 Lelia's Court
Lake Katherine
Columbia, S.C. 29206

September 3, 1970

Dear Peter:

Well, that is <u>some</u> review, I can tell you! Especially from a lady! It was very nice indeed to read, and even nicer than that for you to send it on. I have duly turned it over to Maxine, who has a couple of boxes of clippings, publicity, and other things in regard to <u>Deliverance</u>, though God knows what will happen to all the stuff. I suppose it will be put into a scrapbook, but I can't really be sure, and must one day get round to asking Maxine about it. But we are especially glad to have <u>this</u> one, I can surely tell you!

We are going to England for the British publication of <u>Deliverance</u> on September 10, and I must stop back by New York for something called the David Frost Show on the seventeenth. Maxine and Kevin will probably come back to Columbia, but <u>I</u> will be in the city through the eighteenth, which, if I read the calendar aright, means that I might be able to drop by for one of the famous Friday afternoons. If at all possible, I will surely try to, you can believe me.

Meanwhile, <u>Playboy</u> has sent a young, enthusiastic fellow to do what Hefner calls a "profile" on me. He spent the better part of a week here in Columbia and in Atlanta and in north Georgia with me. I took him on one of the rivers up there, and the damn thing nearly did us both in. It was spectacular, sad, thrilling, fun, and exhausting. I kept shaking my head in disbelief, and saying to myself and to Jeff Norman, which is the young fellow's name, "I seem to have read all this before, somewhere." I got my left eye almost knocked out of my head when we fell out of the canoe on one particularly rough stretch, and I can still hardly walk from all the rock-bruises I got. Jeff fared a little better, but only a little. After we got back to the city, like Ed and Louis and Bobby, we sat around and discussed the title of the article that he is supposed to write for <u>Playboy</u>. We took five hours to go from a little place called Leaf, Georgia, to View, and we worked out an article-title called "From Leaf to View, Or, Tippy, Canoue and Dickey Too." None of us has any idea of how it is going to come out, but I for one look forward to it with great fear and pleasure. It is supposed to run in the January issue.

Also, Larry called up and is coming by this Friday to interview me about

11. Senior editor of Time/Life's press, cinema, theater, and show business sections.

something <u>else</u> for <u>Playboy</u>. He tells me that this is a great break for him, and that he is very much looking forward to working with <u>Playboy</u>, getting more assignments, and so on. I have very little idea as to what he wants to do, but we will welcome him here, as usual.

We'll be staying at the St. Moritz from September fifteenth to the eighteenth or nineteenth, so give us a call there. Maybe we can get together for dinner, or at least a drink. I'd like that, believe me.

All yours,

To: Willie Morris

CC, Emory University
4620 Lelia's Court
Lake Katherine
Columbia, S.C. 29206

September 30, 1970

Dear Willie:

We don't get the David Frost Show here, but my reports from Atlanta were that the show was as good as you and I thought it was, even if they didn't give us as much time as we thought they would. Several people called over from Atlanta, where the show ran in the morning rather than late at night, and said, with apparently very real enthusiasm, that it was one of the best such shows that they had seen. Maybe one of these days I will get to see it myself. By the way, did <u>you</u> see it?

Since I've been home, I've had a kind of breakdown, or something. I guess it was the exhaustion of the England trip, the few days in New York, and so on, plus a lot of drinking. Anyway, I went into sort of a short coma, and have had to be going back and forth to doctors ever since. Apparently my diabetes is worse than I or anybody else thought, and I have to check in at the clinic a couple of times a week and have a lot of blood tests, and so on. Anyway, my doctor said that under no circumstances can I take on any more work, any more travel, or anything that entails stress at this time, so I guess I won't be able to go over and cover the fight for you after all, though as you know, I wanted to do so, and was greatly looking forward to it, particularly since it is taking place in my home town. But I would like to get back on my feet, so that I can possibly dissipate some more later on, preferably with you, and preferably in New York. I am awfully sorry that I can't take on the quarry thing, because it might be a really explosive situation over there, not only with the fight itself, but with Governor Maddox and so on. I hope I am telling you this early enough for you to get another man to go down there. I envy him, whoever he is, for you know I would do it if it were at all possible, but right now it doesn't look as though it is.

Please remember me with great affection to Muriel. I agree. It was a great evening, and I'll be back. This I promise.

All yours,

To: Stewart Richardson

CC, Emory University
4620 Lelia's Court
Lake Katherine
Columbia, S.C. 29206

September 30, 1970

Dear Sandy:

Yes, it was great; I always relish those occasions, I can tell you. I am told that the Frost show was very good, though we don't get it here in Columbia, and I have to rely on my spies in Atlanta where the show comes on in the morning rather than at night, and in New York. Did you or anybody you know happen to see it, by the way? Willie Morris and I were on, and as I remember, feeling unusually sober that evening. It was one of the good such shows that I have either been in or witnessed lately. Anyway, it ought to sell some books.

I called you the other day, but you were out and I gave the message to your secretary. I am one of the nominators for the National Book Awards, and they sent me the list in the various categories. They left our poetry book off, which, since it was published in February, is clearly eligible. I called up the secretary of the man I got the letter from, whose name is John Frantz, and gave her hell about this, and she promised to send out a supplement with our book on it in a few days. This should be forthcoming tomorrow or the next day, as I judge. But you should <u>lean</u> on the National Book Committee people about this. John Frantz is the guy directly responsible, but you could also talk to Peter Jennison, who is a real big shot in that outfit. But the point is to get the book <u>on</u>, which they should have done in the first place. The way the juries are shaping up, I stand a very good chance of being the first double winner in the history of the award, and we don't want to miss this because of an oversight by some secretary. Please get on this right away, if you haven't done so already for it is important.

I talked to Theron a long time about the possibility of bringing the next novel to you. In fact, it was Theron who brought up the idea in the first place, so he is already favorable to doing so. That's all I know as far as right now is concerned. I think that it is quite possible that we can work something out, though the novel is at least three to five years away, depending on how much time I can get to work on it. I have a lot of notes now, but that is about all. But I am far enough along to know that it can be worked out, and if it is as good as I think it can be, it will be very good indeed. But that's all to be done, and it will be a lot of work and a lot of frustration. But I am settled on doing it. The problem is simply to find time to do it.

Meanwhile, I have another batch of journal entries and will send them on to you when I get them typed up. Again, do you think it would be feasible to include the screen play of Deliverance, which in some ways is different from the book, in this miscellaneous collection of ours? After all, we already have literary essays and journal entries. Maybe we would want to put the screen play in too. What do you think?

All yours,

To: Larry Dubois[12]

CC, Emory University
4620 Lelia's Court
Lake Katherine
Columbia, S.C. 29206

October 12, 1970

Dear Larry:

Thank you for your letter, and please forgive me for waiting so long to answer, but I have been crazy busy, as you might know. I finally got the director I wanted for the film version of Deliverance. His name is John Borman—no kin to either Frank or Martin—and he's an Irishman who has two very good film credits over here. One of them is Point Blank, with Lee Marvin, and the

---

12. Writer for *Time* magazine whose article on Dickey, entitled "The Poet as Journalist," was published in the December 13, 1968, issue.

other, also with Marvin is <u>Hell in the Pacific</u>, which you may also have seen. There are only two people in the movie, Marvin and the Japanese actor Mifune, and its a World War II story about Marvin and an enemy Japanese alone together on an island. I saw these, and when Calley told me that Borman wanted to do the film I immediately got in touch with him, and he said he had read the book already three times and would break his contract with MGM, where he is now halfway through a film for them, in order to be able to do <u>Deliverance</u>. Anyway, its all set now, and we'll start filming in the spring. I want you to come down and get in on some of these good times, for film-making is such a social thing, and the studios always have a big budget which they expect the directors, actors, personnel and hangers-on to squander; that is just part of the scene. I'll let you know when all this business is going to start, and will suggest a time and place to get together.

I think your enthusiasm and excitement about the writing that you are doing on your <u>own</u> are simply glorious, Larry. What a time this is for you! You have talent, you have a beautiful girl, you have a lot of assignments, word of your ability is beginning to get around, and the whole thing is <u>there.</u> I won't go on and on in this immoderate vein, but will just call attention once more to what you already know: good things can happen.

Keep me posted about when your article in <u>Playboy</u> is going to appear. Jeff Norman, the fellow who is doing the profile on me for the January issue, writes me that the project is going well. I gave him a hunting bow, and he has gone ape, as they say, over the subject of bow hunting. In fact, it looks as though he's going to get to go hunting this year and I'm not! I went into the Congaree swamp the other day, just looking around. I can usually find my way around in hilly country, but in swamps and flatlands where there are very few landmarks except curiously shaped trees, I get confused. I got lost about fifty times, and I saw the biggest water moccasin, I can guarantee, that has ever lived on this planet. He must have been eight feet long, and a big, fat, heavy monster he was too. I sat on the bank and watched him for about forty-five minutes, with my mouth hanging open in astonishment at what God hath wrought. He turned to me once and opened his mouth, and it looked like the white gates of hell itself. In fact, it was!

Keep in touch, my old friend.

All yours,

To: Larry Lieberman

CC, Emory University
4620 Lelia's Court
Lake Katherine
Columbia, S.C. 29206

October 12, 1970

Dear Larry:

Thank you for the good letter. I was allowed two recommendations for Guggenheims this year, and had I known that you were going to apply, you would certainly have been one of them. However, they have already gone in, so I can't work with you from the standpoint of <u>my</u> initiating your nomination. However, that is not so important anyway. Yu can surely be absolutely certain that I will back your play for the fellowship in any way that I can. If you have any forms, or things like that, that you want me to fill out, please send them to me and I will do so right away. Meanwhile, I will write to Dean Alpert and make that recommendation also.

I like the new poems a lot. They are awfully good, Larry, as you certainly know. I also like your "Description of Project," for it sounds like something very much worth doing, and, knowing you, I'm quite positive that they will get done, whether you get these fellowships or not.

I'd like to know a little more about the book on modern poets that you're writing. I have read a good many such books lately, and most of them are rather disappointing. It is not that they are not thorough, or not very kind to my own work, but that they seem academic and going-through-the-motions criticism that I have read so much of—and doubtless written a good deal of—in the years that I have been on the poetry scene. What it needed is a truly and brilliantly <u>biased</u> book: one with the stamp of a strong personality on it. I am convinced that you can supply this, and so I'd like to know exactly what your situation is in regard to your plans for the particular book.

It is also good to know that you are going to work with John Palmer. This business of being a <u>regular</u> poetry reviewer can be good and it can be bad, according to who the reviewer is. You have a serious and good and very exciting chance of being a real <u>power</u> on the scene, a real taste-maker and mover and shaker of the poetic firmament. This is a position of a good deal of authority, and I am very happy that you have taken it. It will be hard work, but when did Larry Lieberman ever draw back from <u>that</u>?

Yes, indeed, I'll be there Monday, November 2, and stay with you through the fourth. As soon as I have my reservations, I'll let you know when to meet me. I don't have a very good idea about distances between Chicago and Urbana, but I had a lot rather ride down with you, and talk along the way, than sweat out one of those little local air lines, especially in cold weather. I have sat for so many hours around so many airports waiting for the aircraft of such air lines that I would surely welcome <u>not</u> having to do it on this occasion.

Things continue well here, though very hectic. I finally have the director for the film version of <u>Deliverance</u> that I want. His name is John Borman, and he's a Dubliner. I talked to him for about a half hour on the phone yesterday, and he canceled out a contract with MGM in order to be able to do <u>Deliverance</u>. I met with Sam Peckinpah, who directed <u>The Wild Bunch</u>, in London, but I'm not at all sorry that I turned him down, though I liked him very much. I also requested that Roman Polanski be taken off the picture, for he is essentially a mood director, and does not handle an action line at all well. Borman does. The pictures of his that I have seen—<u>Point Blank</u>, with Lee Marvin and <u>Hell in the Pacific</u>, with Marvin and the Japanese actor Mifune—have exactly the ingredients I want, mainly action with a philosophical dimension. Peckinpah tries for this, but achieves it only intermittently. Roman's score is very high, I think. Anyway, he's going to do it.

Meanwhile, <u>Self-Interviews</u>, is due out the seventh of November; I'll see that you get a copy when I get the box of copies that Doubleday is supposed to send me. I think you'll like the book, though it is rather naive in places. The naivete, though, is really the best thing about it. It is not one of these carefully considered, over written books, but sounds exactly like talk, which in fact it is. It was taken off tapes, and I did very little editing on it. Since you have written about so many of the same things in connection with my work, I think it will be interesting to you to have a look at it. Anyway, as I say, I'll get the book to you in a week or so. I have another critical book building up in which I'm going to mix essays with entries from a kind of undated journal that I've been keeping for the last couple of years. I think I'll probably call the whole thing <u>Assertions</u>, with maybe a subtitle reading "Essays and Journals," or something like that. I'm getting the book together now, and it seems pretty good. I <u>want it to be good</u>, for it is probably the last critical book I'll do, at least for a long time. I'm starting on another novel which I like a lot so far, though I don't understand it completely. The working title is <u>The Field of Dogs</u> and its about a blind man and also about the early days of training in the Air Force for World War II. Strange book, but very exciting, at least to me. I haven't got very far with it yet, but am beginning to see what can be done with the material, if I can do it. Am also translating twelve poems of Yevtushenko for a volume Doubleday is doing. My Russian is not much, but I have the help of a very knowledgeable young fellow in Russian studies at Harvard, and he is helping me very much indeed. I like some of the translations pretty good. Yevtushenko's knock-about enthusiastic style is just what I need to be working with right now, for my poetry, such of it as I have written in the last few weeks has gotten awfully solemn, and I want to open it up some to joy and recklessness. I don't know whether I'll publish any of these solemn ones or not, though one or two of them are, I think, pretty good. I have about half of a new manuscript, and should bring out another volume of poetry about fall of '71, though I am not absolutely sure that this will be the case. It will depend on how much of my time is committed to the film, and how much time I can get to work on poems. I am trying out a couple of new directions, mainly in connection with metrical innovations, and some of these are promising, although some of them are dead, flat failures. But the exploratory sense of language is strong in my make-up, and is what I like most about writing poetry to begin with.

My love to all in your house. See you soon.

All yours,

To: Richard Howard   CC, Emory University
                                                4620 Lelia's Court
                                                Lake Katherine
                                                Columbia, S.C. 29206

                                                October 19, 1970

Dear Dick:

Thank you very much for your last two letters, but I am worried about Sandy and you, as maybe you are not, or needn't be. Both of you are such precious people to me that these dim, subterranean rumblings of—what shall I say?—disaffiliation, or something, are deeply disturbing to me. They are disturbing in the ways in which things are disturbing which one can, at one's particular remove, do nothing at all about. I know that your life with Sandy is intensely private, and a person like myself, married for twenty-two years, with two children and a grandchild, cannot really presume to know anything, really, of the circumstances that are disturbing you. Please do know, that I understand as fully as it is possible for a person like myself to understand, but more importantly, I sympathize, whatever may befall.

I am much indebted to you for the quotation from Jimmy Merrill to the effect that after forty, the lid comes off. How damn true that is! People do not understand, actually, the desperation that begins to settle on one at this time of life. Erotic experience comes to seem, not only the best of answers to the Void, but the only one. If people—wives, lovers—would grant us this very obvious fact and let us go our way and do our thing when the body and the mind most demand that it be done, things would be very much easier all around, and we would no longer live in the world of phoniness that we now inhabit. I won't get on the soapbox about this, but believe me, I understand what you mean when you talk about getting around more.

Self-Interviews is out, at least in the twelve-volume version of the complimentary copy box I've been sent, and I'll get one of them to you in the next few days. Meanwhile, you might ask the Times if you can review it for them, but even if they send you a copy, I'll send you one too. Get one free, get another one free!

Meanwhile, I've sent on your snake swallower poem to the people at Esquire. I've accepted it, but since I'm new to this business of editing for Esquire, I don't know whether Harold Hays will accept my acceptance or not. Anyway, I'll let you know. There shouldn't be any trouble about printing the poem—and very handsomely too—but I don't know yet, so I'll have to inform you when the Powers up there let me know. But it's a damn good poem, in a crazy kind of Yeatsian mode which is kind of beyond Yeats, both fore and aft, by which I mean it's in the nineteenth century and also in the present and future. I like it a lot, and also the other stuff. I am so damned glad that we got the Pulitzer for you! As I may have said earlier, Auden was for it, and all I had to do as chairman was to say, OK! Phyllis McGinley was in the hospital with some kind of bathtub accident at the time, so I don't really know if she was ever consulted or not. But it wouldn't have made any difference, for we were for you, and we got it! Thank God.

Your project having to do with printing, say, a poem of mine and an earlier poem is very interesting. My God, what will editors think up! I pondered this for awhile, and I think that I have come up with something that might be pretty good. Why don't you print my poem "The Sheep Child" with the lines from Christopher Smart's "Jubilate Agno" beginning, "For I will consider my cat, Jeoffry"? That might provide a pretty lively kind of essay for somebody! The lines I allude to are printed in Auden and Norman Holmes Pearson's anthology, Poets of the English Language, put out by Viking. They are on page 564 and run through 567. A great deal could be said about the relationship of men and animals, and many other lighter and darker things by an astute commentator. Anyway, since you ask me, that's my choice. Let me know what you think. As to all these lectureships you are either now fulfilling or planning to fulfill, I think they are all great. I would like to get into your Princeton class myself! The business in Kyoto is fascinating, and it might be a great thing for you to do. I was there about two and a half years ago, and liked Kyoto very much, and the university as well. What's the name of it? Do-Shisha? Something like that? Anyway, it's a very good school, and Kyoto is still one of the greatly beautiful cities of the earth. As to how much you might like <u>living</u> there for a period of time, is maybe another thing. It could be great. A couple of American poets live there. One of them is Cid Corman, and another one teaches at the university: a very good woman poet named Edith Shiffert. There is a kind of colony of American poets there.

I must close now. Please remember me to Sandy, and buoy him up any way you can. I know what hard times are like, believe me.

All yours,

To: James Wright   TLS, University of Minnesota

4620 Lelia's Court
Columbia, S.C. 29206
October 19, 1970

Dear Jimbo:

Thanks so much for the poems. I think we should publish them both, but, new in this job, I must first try them out on the various other editors of <u>Esquire</u> before I can give you a final acceptance. There is some strange kind of editorial policy there, and I must get on to what people expect me to do, how I am expected to operate, in order to be able to publish good poetry like yours. But you were the first one I solicited from, and that should carry some weight, with the <u>Esquire</u> editors as it does with me. But <u>do</u> know that I like the poems very much, especially the one about Bologna, and will print it if I am allowed to.

Things are very hectic with us here, particularly in regard to the filming of <u>Deliverance</u>. I finally got the director I want, an Irishman named John Borman, who did a couple of Lee Marvin films over here, <u>Hell in the Pacific</u>, with the Japanese actor Mifune, and a crime film called <u>Point Blank</u>, which had a kind of mindless and very sinister energy about it. Anyway, he's going to do it, and we are going to spend all spring and the early part of next fall in doing it <u>right</u>.

I haven't time for one of our old, life-giving letters—my God, how much those meant to me at a time when I <u>needed</u> them!—but will just close off now to get this in the mail.

Incidentally, my new book, <u>Self-Interviews</u>, should be available now, though the publication date is November 7th. See if you can get it in one of the Doubleday stores around there. If you can't, I'll send you one of my complimentary copies. It's a strange book, and somebody like Bob will be sure to think of it as being very immodest and self-revelatory in the wrong sense. But it is about my life and my poetry in the same way that <u>anybody's</u> book can be about his life and his poetry. We all have lives, and some of us have poetry as well. Anyway, get hold of it and tell me what you think.

I am moving ahead slowly on a few new poems, and on another novel. I like the novel, but I don't know what it's about yet. Well, I guess you write novels to find out what they're about. Anyway, there doesn't seem to be any other way for me.

Maxine and I send love. We had a visit from Chris and his wife, Susan, and my grandson, who is named after me. He is a lot more beautiful than I am, and, really, he is more beautiful than anybody I know except you and me and Annie and W.C. Fields and Wallace Beery. And <u>that's</u> beautiful!

Please remember me to all those I know up there, including John Hollander and Les Mansfield, if he's still there in the French Department at Hunter, and if you know him. Incidentally, if you don't know him, you should meet him. He knows more about modern French literature than anybody in the world, and you would <u>love</u> him. He's a great friend of Jackson Matthews too.

All yours,
Jim

To: William Heyen

CC, Emory University
4620 Lelia's Court
Lake Katherine
Columbia, S.C. 29206

October 21, 1970

Dear Bill:

Thanks very much for the letter, and for the things you say in it. I also much enjoyed the telephone conversation. It turns out that I could come in December, after all. So, if you want to set the date up for the 3rd and 4th of December, that would be fine with me. I <u>do</u> depend on you for one thing, though, Bill, if things get <u>too</u> unsettled up there at your school, please let me know, for I don't really want to come into some place or situation where I could contribute, by whatever means, to an unrest in which somebody could get hurt. The word has in some way got around that I am a political reactionary, when, in point of fact, I have no political feelings one way or the other, except a dislike of violence and coercion. In these days when there are so many pretexts for violence on campus, I might quite easily be another one such, and I don't want to contribute to that kind of atmosphere either at your school or any other. So let me know, quite honestly, when the time approaches for me to come up there, as to whether such a situation is likely. I'll trust you implicitly on this, and will be guided by what you say.

I wrote Berryman and asked him for some poems for Esquire, and I may get together with him later on. I have always felt that I could do something for John, for he seems to listen to what I say. But maybe nothing can be done. Anyway, I want to try. He always seems so desperately lonely, and needs to have somebody to talk to.

Well, things are shaping up, let me know what date you actually do decide on, if you've already shifted from the December suggestion. I'll have to get all of this into my calendar, which is filling up awfully fast, to be able to come at all.

My very best to you. Keep in touch, and we'll gradually get the thing worked out.

All yours,

To: John Berryman   TLS, University of Minnesota

4620 Lelia's Court
Columbia, S.C. 29206
October 21, 1970

Dear John:

I am supposed to go up to Brockport to read for Bill Heyen, and have consequently been in touch with him. He told me that you were there recently and wanted to get in touch with me for some reason, and I wanted to let you know where I am, on the possibility that Bill might not have known my address, or forgotten it, or something. But anyway, I wanted also to get some more poems from you for Esquire. For some reason, Harold Hays didn't want to publish the two that Gordon Lish and I suggested that Esquire publish, so, if you want to send some more, I can have another try. I was crazy about the two that didn't make it with Hays, and I can't for the life of me see what his objection to them was. But, since he's the editor and I'm only the poetry editor—and new at that—there is nothing I can do except get some more poems from you and try to ram them through. Anyway, if you want to send some stuff down here, I would sure be glad to look at it.

It has been a long time since we have written back and forth about Bhain Campbell and those other people and other matters of the period when I was working in advertising in Atlanta. I remember the correspondence with a great deal of affection; I was looking through some of your old letters the other day, and the whole feeling of that time came back. I won't go on and on, but just will let you know that I remembered those things, those letters.

If you have a moment, write and let me know what your life is like, these days. And if there is anything I can do, anyway I could get us together for a long-delayed meeting, please let me know, and I'll do it. I have to travel around some this winter and spring, but most of my time will be taken up with the film version of my novel, <u>Deliverance</u>, which is going to be pretty demanding, from what the people at Warner Brothers tell me. Anyway, though, I <u>will</u> be traveling, and could probably come through Minneapolis, or wherever you happen to be at the time. Why don't we give a reading together, come to think of it? I don't usually like to read with other people, but I could sure make an exception in your case, I can tell you.

Anyway, the very best from me to you. In this case, there has never been anything else to send, and I'll settle for that.

All yours,
James Dickey

To: Charles Simic

CC, Emory University
4620 Lelia's Court
Columbia, S.C. 29206

October 21, 1970

Dear Charlie:

Thank you very much for sending the poems along. <u>Esquire</u> has only had a poetry department for a few weeks; our first issue with poetry in it will be the January number. I am not sure of exactly what attitude the other editors are going to take toward what I want to do. Hays, the big, big, BIG editor turned down some stuff of John Berryman's that I wanted to print. I don't know whether he will pass on your poems or not; we'll have to see. Anyway, I'm recommending a couple of these, and Hays will let me know what he thinks of them in a week or so. But from <u>my</u> standpoint, I am very glad indeed to have these. As I told you in one of the few fan letters I have ever written in my whole entire life, I liked the book you sent to me earlier. You are very good indeed, Charlie, and I think will be even better as you grow older. You are not nearly so indebted to the Bly school of things as you seem to think you are, from what I can tell in the poems themselves. That is a very thin vein, that kind of American landscape surrealism, and I think probably you will do more dramatic things later on. But the basic stuff, you really have, and plenty of it. I won't go on and on, but will just close with a friendly handshake, hoping to see more poems later on, whenever you see fit to send them. Send your things here to me at South Carolina; they needn't go through New York at all.

Sincerely yours,

To: Thomas E. Gaddis   CC, Emory University
                                                          4620 Lelia's Court
                                                          Columbia, S.C. 29206

October 26, 1970

Dear Tom:

Thank you so much for your letter of a month or so ago, and for sending along your absolutely horrendous book, Killer. I read the whole thing in a couple of sittings. My God, what a monster that guy was! And yet you can see how he got that way, too. If you want to use some such quotation as that and attribute it to me for publicity, you surely may. I found the book truly fascinating, and this is partly because it is so fascinatingly and horribly true.

Thank you very much indeed for the kind things you say about Deliverance. The fact that the sodomy scene was done as it was—that is with one guy providing the physical means to coerce the victim—is meant to suggest the possibility that these men have had some kind of prison experience that you document so well in your book. No one knows this about the men in Deliverance, and no one is meant to know it; it is only a kind of possibility. Personally, I think they were probably escaped convicts, but I don't know either!

Please remember me to all those up there that I remember. My very best to you, and best wishes for the success of your book.

All yours,

To: Wendell Berry

CC, Emory University
4620 Lelia's Court
Columbia, S.C. 29206

October 28, 1970

Dear Wendell:

Thank you very much for your new poems. Since I have just become poetry editor of <u>Esquire</u>, and since I have had some bad luck getting the poems
into the magazine that I most wanted to get in, I can't guarantee that the
magazine will print these. Berryman, for example, was turned down in, as
they used to say, no uncertain terms. But I have hopes for these, and have sent
them on to the Powers up there with my strongest recommendation. That is
all I can do, and we'll just have to see if Hays goes for them, or if he wants to
have some new pronouncement by the Black Panthers in place of the work of
a fine poet, such as yourself.

Meanwhile, I have your two new books. The thing about negroes is very
impressive, very sad, and very true, and the new poems are fine. You are one
of the few writers in the world who has a true sense of the land, and that is a
very, very important thing, especially as the land disappears. My own youngest boy is going into the sea, to live there, to research there, and, as a father
<u>would</u> think, probably to die there. But it is important to have a sense of <u>place</u>
and to have a sense of relating to the world and to the universe as it was made
by something other than men. Of all the poets of my time, you have this the
most. If the <u>Esquire</u> editors permit it, it will be a very great pleasure and a
very great privilege to print your poems. The sense of living in the world
comes out of them strangely and strongly. As the German Ernst Junger says,
"It is like a ray of reality."

Let me hear from you whenever you have a chance. We will sit down and
play those guitars together one of these days, I can promise you.

All yours,

To: Peter Neumeyer

CC, Emory University
4620 Lelia's Court
Columbia, S.C. 29206

November 2, 1970

Dear Peter:

Again, I am remiss, but please forgive me, for I have been sore beset. The
only thing that I can say about success, and the great American success

syndrome is that it is superior to obscurity and failure. Still, it has its perils, as I would be, not only the first to tell you, but <u>before</u> the first to tell you. Anyway, I have rarely been here, and so have not been able to answer any mail at all except a few business notes, and the like. But I <u>do</u> want to keep the lines of communication open, particularly to such as you, who would have written to me about the poems regardless of any of the rest of this falderal. One of these days I am going to be able to sit down and work out some new poems, though God knows when this will be. Maybe next summer, if all goes well. I have about half of a new manuscript of poetry, but I also have some very ambitious things that are going to take a good deal of time, meditation, experimentation, and so on, in order to realize themselves, and I just don't know when I will be able to do it. But, for the poet, all things resolve into a dream of the future, when he will get out of his material what he is convinced is there to be got. Poems are stacking up in huge bales of paper, but the laborious Dickey process is not being brought to bear on them, sadly enough.

I do have a new book out, though, which deals with some of the poems that I have already written. Perhaps it will be thought immodest; I don't know, but since this is the great age of the <u>interview</u>, it seemed to me that I might as well interview myself, because I have been interviewed by so many other people. The new book is called <u>Self-Interviews</u>, and if you like, I will send along a copy, although the actual publication date is the 7th of November. Let me know if you want one of these, and I'll send it along. It is kind of a naive book, but the naivete in this age of so much professionalism and self-protection, seems to me the best thing about it. Anyway, have a look, and let me know what you think.

Again, as always, I haven't time for a long letter. But you are one of my people. You declared yourself in on this count whether you know it or not, and now you are stuck with it. I hope this is not distasteful to you, because the clock is running.

All yours,

To: Wes Taft   CC, Emory University

4620 Lelia's Court
Columbia, S.C. 29206
November 2, 1970

Dear Wes:

Yes, indeed, it's good to be in touch again. I've played the film over for a couple of dozen people, and all of them think that the landscape photography is superb. It is. I have seldom seen such beautiful color cinema. Mike doesn't get a chance to play very much, though. Just a little bit at the very beginning, and you might be interested to know that I grabbed up my D-28 and played the film through three or four times to figure out what kind of double-thumbing stuff he's doing in that opening section. My God, what an instrumentalist he is! I haven't got it yet, but if you will leave the film with me a little longer, I'll get it, or, as they say, a reasonable facsimile thereof.

Meanwhile, please keep Ron Brentano in sight, for I may be able to get him in on the movie too. My film director, John Borman, is coming in from Dublin this evening, and we will talk all this out, as we see fit. I will tell him that I have recommended Mike to do the film music, and, if he wants to get Ron in on the scene in the filling station with the albino boy, I will have Ron do the sound-track for this section of the film. But, as they say, this is all subject to the review of Borman. He may have something entirely different in mind; I don't know yet. I don't know if it's necessary for me to write Ron or not; it might be better just if you walked across, one evening, and told him what I have in mind, without holding out any promises. But do give him to understand that he is my choice for this film work, if the director goes for my suggestion.

I like your poem, "The Indians" very much indeed, and if my encouragement to keep on writing will make you keep on writing, then I enclose all of it that this letter will hold.

Thanks also for the review of Mike's record from the September 3rd "Rolling Stone." John Cunnick, whoever he is, is very charitable toward Mike, but he doesn't really understand where Mike's true contribution lies. Mike is a very good twelve-string player, but there are better ones, and it could even be argued that Mike's indebtedness to Leadbelly is something that keeps him from being the truly creative twelve-string player that he might, with his technique, be. But there is no one else who can do what Mike does on the six-string, in pieces like "Flat-top Fling" and "Don't Get Mad at Me, Boys, if Your Buggy Don't Ride Like Mine," or that extraordinary double-thumbing thing he does in his version of "Maple on the Hill." There is not a single other guitarist in the world who can match the stuff that Mike does, and John Cunnick ought to have that much knowledge of the guitar; that much, that is to enable him to know what exactly is going on when Mike plays the six-string.

Anyway, we will try to use both Russo and Brentano, not only because they would be the best instrumentalists for the film, but as a kind of tribute of my own to the old days in the Pacific Northwest, never to come again.

I would love to accept your invitation to visit with you out there, and if there is any necessity for me to be in the Pacific Northwest, I will surely let you know, come and stay with you, bring my typewriter and guitar, play some music and talk about some poetry. Yes, and write some too. I'd like that a lot.

Meanwhile, at your leisure, let me know what life is like for you these days. You are really a very fine writer indeed. The poem is good, and the prose of the letter is more than good. I like to look after a young fellow like you, way off in space, as you are from me. Let me know what satisfactions there are, if you have time and the right mind for it <u>at</u> the time. But that shall be as you wish.

All yours,

To: Dave Evans

CC, Emory University
4620 Lelia's Court
Columbia, S.C. 29206

November 23, 1970

Dear Dave:

Yes, the $3,300 for my trip out there will be fine. I am much beholden to you and to John Little for working so hard and so diligently to get the price up, but I <u>insist</u> on having as much as Al Capp, the famous conservative journalist, gets! I am very much looking forward to coming up there, to be with you again, and the rest of it. As to where I go first, and all of those matters of protocol, I will leave those matters to you and John to settle the most satisfactorily you can do among yourselves. I am perfectly amenable to doing it any way that you and John decide it should be done.

By the way, does either one of your weather-bound colleges give honorary degrees? I have sworn to my wife that I would accept one this year, after a good many refusals. Those things make me rather queasy, and especially so since I sat down with Bill Buckley last year and he leafed through about fifty or sixty of them that he had. My wife is bound and determined that I shall have one, so see your big honchos out there, and see if you can rustle us something like that for me, either at your university or John's. I could even deliver the graduation address, which I guarantee will be controversial, if not absolutely resounding. I won't lean on you about this, but will simply ask you if any such thing is possible, and will be guided by your counsel in the matter.

So the thing is all set, then. Just let me know when you want me to come, when I am to travel from this point to that point, what I am to do when I get there, and so on.

Meanwhile, I am delighted that you are continuing to work on your poems, and I will be looking in various periodicals for their appearance.

As for Arkansas, I think it might be all right for you. Jim Whitehead and Bill Harrison are there, and they are two good men and good writers. The town is not much, but the company is very good indeed, and it looks as though the University is developing a very good creative writing program. So, if you decide to go down there, please let me know. I'll do anything you like in the way of recommendations, advice, and the like.

Let me know, again, how things shape up as they do.

All yours,

To: David Buzzard

CC, Emory University
4620 Lelia's Court
Columbia, S.C. 29206

December 4, 1970

Dear David Buzzard:

Well, I'll just be damned if I believe there is anybody named David Buzzard! But, if there is, I am quite prepared to entertain the notion that it might as well be you! Anyway, thank you indeed for your comments on the poems, and about my novel, Deliverance.

Let me get right to your questions:

1. I think of the cliff which Ed Gentry scales as being between 175 and 200 feet high. As the passage dealing with this event makes more or less clear through Ed's feels, his physical situation, and so on, the cliff begins as a rather steep slant and then becomes more vertical toward the top, where Ed nearly falls off, and then breaks into a kind of little canyon that he uses to ascend the rest of the way. Neither Ed Gentry, Lewis, nor I know whether it would be possible to reach its top by another route. You'll remember that at one point Ed considers trying to do this, but can find no way to get back down from the position he is currently on. The point is that one would not be able to get up another way from anywhere along the river where the men find themselves. Ed is satisfied about this in his mind, and that is why he tries it at the place he does. Also, this is a gauge to enable him to tell his particular spacial relationships to the men in his party below him.

2. I am not crazy about the eye on the novel's cover, myself. It is supposed to be Ed's eye looking out through the pine needles as he lies in wait for the man with the rifle. It may, as you say, also represent Ed's fear of his deed being discovered, but the other meaning is the primary one. Or at least that was the intention, anyway.

3. You are very perceptive to note the same name being used for Lucas

Gentry in "On the Coosawattee" and Ed Gentry in <u>Deliverance</u>. I did run up on a country family on a canoe trip up in north Georgia named Gentry. The boy's name was really, if I remember correctly, Ira Gentry, but I just changed it to Lucas for the poem, and took the name for my protagonist in the novel just because I thought it would, well, be a good name for him to have.

4. My brother, as I wrote about him in the poem "The String" was named Eugene Dickey. He died when he was six years old of what was then called "brain fever," but which was almost certainly meningitis. Yes, I have an older sister, Maibelle, who is about 59 or 60, and a brother, Tom, two years younger than I am which would make him about 46. Yes, I was raised up north of Atlanta, not in the city proper, but in what was then called the "County": that is, Fulton County. I went to North Fulton County High School.

5. I admire Theodore Roethke very much indeed. But there is no stylistic affinity between my work and his at all. I think he is the best <u>kind</u> of poet for American poetry to have, especially right now. He deals with eternal objects and eternal feeling, and does not throw the sop of temporality or headline-mongering at the audience. For that reason, he will be around a long time. But his work has no relationship at all to mine. He is essentially a meditative poet, and I am rather, I guess, more of a dramatic poet. That is, I deal in <u>incidents</u>, and feelings about them, where Roethke deals mainly about feelings and thoughts occasioned by, say, landscape, seascape, and so on. But he surely is a wonderful poet. As for other writers, you seem to assume that there is some kind of influence of Roethke working on my poetry, but I assure you that there is none at all. The main injunction that I have to myself, when I admire a writer as much as I do him, is to say to myself, "go thou and do otherwise." I don't want to do Roethke's thing; I want to do my thing. The more I like a writer, the less likely he is to be influential on what I write. I think that I belong more to the European tradition than to the English. The best poets I know are little-known modern French poets like Louis Emié, Lucien Becker, and André Frénaud. I read French, as well as other foreign languages, indifferently, but with the greatest excitement, and I read them all the time.

6. I don't know <u>what</u> you should know about me that has not appeared in print. My God, how could I answer <u>that</u>? I don't even know what you have seen in print! But I just have had a new book come out last week from Doubleday called <u>Self-Interviews</u>, and that would answer a great many of your questions, in one way or another, I am sure. Why not get hold of that, read it, send it down here for me to autograph, and ask questions pertaining to the answers I give in the book? That might be more helpful to you than anything else that either you or I could think of. But that shall be as you wish.

Again, thank you very much for the things you say about my poetry, and about <u>Deliverance</u>. We will film the novel this spring, and I hope you will like that, too.

Sincerely yours,

To: Robert Penn Warren   **TLS, Emory University**

4620 Lelia's Court
Columbia, S.C. 29206
14 December, 1970

Dear Red:

Thank you so very much for your note. It was wonderful to see you again after much too long a time, and to meet with Eleanor again also. Maxine was crazy about you both, and I was happy that she had the opportunity of getting together with you. Well, the end is not yet, and we'll get together lots of times more, or so I certainly hope.

It was fun out there at Stafford's place, wasn't it? Bill is so awfully low-key that he sometimes just sits at social functions—including some he himself gives—and stares off into the crowds or groups of other people in a kind of silent wonder. He is terribly shy, but a good person and—or at least <u>I</u> think— a fine writer as well. We're printing something of his in <u>Esquire</u> that I think is pretty good: the "New Jefferson Letters."

By the way, if you have anything you'd like to show us for <u>Esquire</u>, please just send it on to me at this address, and I'll see that the other editors get it right away. I don't think that you could write anything that I wouldn't want, myself, to print, but sometimes Hays and Gordon Lish and some of the others veto what I recommend. But anyway, if you'd like to try, <u>I'll</u> sure as hell try, I can tell you.

I can't make this the long letter I'd like to, but will just close now to get it in the mail. Please <u>do</u> keep in touch, and let's try to meet again soon. I'll need some advice on a novel I'm trying to get straight in my head, and on a new long poem I've been thinking about for years.

Congratulations again on the medal—or Medal.

All yours,

Jim

I'll look for your Melville book. As I may not have told you, I did my Master's thesis—or Thesis—on Melville's poetry, and remember using your article in a <u>Kenyon Review</u> article of that time. I hope you didn't lose a finger to the Maldive Shark. I almost lost all ten of mine, typing about him.

To: John Boorman   CC, Emory University
                                              4620 Lelia's Court
                                              Columbia, S.C. 29206

December 29, 1970

Dear John:

I have both your long, good letter, and the copy of the screen play which you sent. I have gone over both very carefully. In a situation of this kind, there are two possible reactions. One of these is to take issue with the whole con-ception of the thing that has been presented. I am very happy to report that I have no such major objections to what you have done. On the contrary, I think it is very good indeed: that you have condensed, cut, added, in a manner that does enhance the story and make it possible for film. The other kind of objection, which is bound to occur in a case of this sort, is merely an argument over details, and here I have a few to offer you. But the big thing is that I feel quite willing to go along with what you want to do. Believe me, when you say that you want the screen play to be good, I concur completely. The version of the screen play, treatment, or whatever you would want to call it, that I offered you and Calley was intended to do exactly what it did do. Of course it was too long. If I have one working principle as a writer it is to write long: one can always take out, but one can not always put in. I wrote it with more details and more elaboration than any movie could possibly have. As you say, it was up to you to take this and make it something that we could work with. This you have done. I am lost in admiration for the manner in which you have done it. In other words, if we film the story as you have it, we will have the strange and magnificent movie that we should have: that I am convinced is in the story itself. As to the matter of listing the screen play cred-its as a collaboration of myself and you, that is quite all right with me, partic-ularly since I have your assurance about the money part of it. There is no one else's name that I would more care to have bracketed with mine. You are the director that I want for the film; surely I must have made that clear by now. I met with Sam Peckinpah in London before I ever heard your name at all, and I figured I could do better. I have, in fact, done better, and we are going to make a hell of a movie. I will go with you right down the line on what you want to do. As you say in your letter, it is my novel, but it is your film. I con-cur in this completely. Believe me, I know it is your film, and am happy to have it so. Any remarks that I may make are in the area of doing what you want so much to do: that is, make a good film. Let it be understood at this time that in any decision concerning the film version of Deliverance, you shall have the final say. If you want to take my advice on a point, of course I would be happy to see it happen, for I, too, want to see the film that I am convinced this can be. But, if you reject the advice, that is your prerogative. As I say, you must understand this, as I do.

Now as to details. First of all, the stuff about the archery range that you have used to introduce the characters is all right with me. I know of only one range which has a highway running by it such as you describe. It is the Cub Run Archery Range in Virginia. I also know, however, a range in Los Angeles in which one can walk along a high ridge and have as a background enormous mills and factories. This is at Pacoima, a tough district of the San Fernando Valley, where the range is in a kind of public park where there are a lot of Mexicans sitting around having family picnics and so on. To get the effect you want, we might have the shooting done up on one of these ridges—that is, if the range still exists as it did four or five years ago—and see Lewis and Ed against this background of mills and factories, instead of against a superhighway, as you suggest. The only thing about it is that the vegetation out there is clearly not southern vegetation, and we might have to compensate for that in some way. I just thought I would offer this as a suggestion, for, as I say, I don't know of a range that has the condition of being hedged about by highways, such as the range you subscribe.

I don't find in your version of the script anything to suggest that they are going up into the woods in the spring time, and this will be very evident in the film. We need a little additional dialogue, most probably between Drew and Lewis, to indicate that they are going to be hunting in exactly the wrong season of the year. This could be done very easily. Drew could say something like, "You're not supposed to hunt deer in the spring, Lewis." Lewis could say something like, "They're just as much deer in the spring as they are any other time. There are no forest rangers up where we're going." As I say, this could be ironed out, but it should be in the film all the same.

Now, about the conversation in the car going up. You've taken out almost all of Lewis's "survival" talk, and I think some of this should be put back in. The subject is one of paramount importance to people these days, and we should have a better voicing of it than we do. It needn't be more than twenty or thirty seconds of dialogue, but we should come down on this point much harder than we are presently doing. Incidentally, your added dialogue on Lewis's part about going crazy is excellent; I wish I had thought of it in time to put it in the novel myself!

Now, we come, I'm afraid, to what amounts to a basic disagreement, which is the end. I have tried your version of the ending out on a number of people, and their reaction was uniform: don't do it. I will give you my reasons for feeling the same way. First of all, you have made the girl from the studio a good deal more important than she actually is to the story. It is almost as though the part were being built up for an ingenue, or something. The last thing we need here is some kind of Disneyesque subliminal dream-imagery for the end of the film. What you have done in the tent scene, the prelude to the appearance of the owl, is fine; I like it. But the ending plainly won't do. First of all, as I have said, the girl is really not that important to the film. I had just as soon drop her out of it altogether rather than have the film end with a commitment to making her one of the central figures of the story, which she plainly is not. Then, as you have it, there is no reason for Ed and Dean and Martha and Lewis to be looking out over the lake. We would have to account for their being there, other than simply having them there to provide a pretty tableau for the ending of our picture. It is not that kind of story, and I doubt very much whether any story is that kind of story. If you want to keep the girl, we should have whatever is to happen between happen in the office, rather than some kind of nude swimming scene. Personally I would like to see such a scene because I like naked girls, though naked men much less well, but it is not functional at all. It is far too Hollywoodish, and that is the last thing we want to do here. The scene should be in the office, and the girl should just be indicated as a pleasant part of the furniture, of the functioning of the business. When you have her come back in the little scene where she appears and Ed is working, you lead the audience to believe that she is just as important as she ever was to him, that she represents all the promise that his life has never attained, and the rest, when the very opposite of this is the fact. It is misleading to have Ed so shook up on seeing her again; instead, he should dismiss her or indicate to her in some manner that he no longer has the same feelings about her: that her fantasy life has been destroyed, if you want to put it that strongly. But to have him this much impressed on seeing her again, and then have this nude swimming scene where they swim off blissfully, two subliminal angels, into the sunset and disappear into the lake, watched by the family tableau of Ed, plus Lewis, is not what we want to do here, John. I don't know what scene you might suggest as an alternative, but I am very much against this one. The one I had originally seems a good deal better, though I may sound immodest in saying so. I hope you will think about this very deeply and strongly. If you don't agree with me, we will do the thing as you wish to do it, as I have said. But it is against my every instinct both to make the girl that important and to end the film as you have written it.

A couple of things more. You tell me that Calley and the people at Warners were not willing to undertake the film as I wrote it. It was never intended on my part that the film should be made in this manner. I merely wanted to furnish you something to work from, to convert the story into the kind of movie you wanted to make, in your style, and in your way. This should have been apparent to Calley. Again, it's not Calley's business to tell you things of this nature and not tell me. This surely comes as a complete surprise to me. How can you possibly account for this? Calley should be dealing with me directly on matters that concern me and my participation in the film.

Again, you say that Warners was not willing to undertake the film on my script. That is all right, for we now have your script. But if he rejects mine, how can he possibly accept yours, which for page after page after page is a literal transcription of mine? In other words, though you have shortened the script and added a few scenes, why would Calley not reject this, which is so similar to the former one? You must keep me abreast of these developments, John, for I have no means of knowing them without you. Calley is strangely uncommunicative, so I have no one else but you to depend on. The last conversation I had with him, he told me that they were going to talk to Nicholson, but I have heard no news at all. When do we start to cast this thing? What do we do now? When will you be over here again?

Otherwise, I don't think there are any problems, except for making the film. I must tell you that the people I know in Hollywood advised me, almost to a man, to take the money and run, and let Warners do whatever they want to with the film: make it, shelve it, or whatever. I have chosen not to do this. I want to see the film made, I have the director I want, and I have a great belief in the film possibilities of the story. My son, Chris, is the first graduate in film from the University of Virginia, and I want him to have the experience of being around where this movie is made; it will be invaluable for him in his future work. But I need to know a lot more about what we are getting ready to do than I do know. I have the spring term off, so I can give you as much time as you like. But I must know when the time-period is going to start. When people ask me about this, I say that we will start the film when the leaves get back on the trees. That was something you and I discussed, and that is fine with me. There will be more water in the rivers then, which is an added plus, but can you give me some exact timetable? My calendar is filling up rapidly, and I will need to save the time to work with you, to be in north Georgia, and so on. So, when you know, let me know! And how about casting? Has any decision at all been made about this? I have heard nothing from Calley except the brief conversation about the possibility of Nicholson. Again, I need to be informed about these matters.

Meanwhile, Lewis—the <u>real</u>, fabulous Lewis—has been in the mountains for practically the whole time since we last saw you. He says he has some fantastic new locations, that he has found a place in Alabama with the cliff and the rapids exactly as the novel has them, he has a <u>lot</u> more maps, and he wants to take another trip or two with you and me—and maybe crazy Charlie Wiggin in his Land Rover—and look over some of these other locations. Can you come over here and do some of this, or are you content with what we have already unearthed? Again, I need to hold out the time, I want to hold out the time, but I must know when the time <u>is</u>.

We have no serious problems at all at this juncture, I want to reiterate. It is inevitable that you and I would disagree on certain details. You must know how fond I am of you, John, how much I want you to do this picture, and how highly I esteem your talent. What we want is a film that satisfies uss both, and I will contribute to that end as well as it is given to me to do. You have my word.

All yours,

To: Selden Rodman
Ca. early January 1971

CC, Emory University
4620 Lelia's Court
Columbia, S.C. 29206

Dear Selden:

Thank you indeed for sending along this material, which I hope I am returning in time, before you leave for South America. I'm sorry I didn't have time to make the good many comments that your provocative remarks call for—there is scarcely a judgment you make that couldn't profitably be talked about—but I have been in and out of Columbia—mostly out—that I only just got to read your foreword and afterword yesterday, and in a few minutes I must get on yet another airplane and go up to Yale and decide about this year's Bollingen winner.

But generally I think that your interpretation of what has happened and is happening in American poetry is very well done. As I told you before I also think that your inclusion of people like Ginsberg, a person whose importance, if any, is quite clearly sociological rather than poetic, is a mistake. So is the inclusion of freaks like McClure. But the worst trouble, at least from <u>my</u> point of view, is the space you give to an innocuous song-writer like Zimmerman (or "Dylan," as he calls himself). "Lyric poet," indeed! They are all right as <u>songs</u>, song-lyrics, I suppose, but as <u>poetry</u>—as Sam Goldwyn said once, "Include me out."

All these opinions are of course, quite personal, and I have no real objection to the general tendencies in poetry that you describe. My quarrel would be over individual writers and their significance. You are very good on Lowell, though I don't think much attention should be paid to Stanley Kunitz, a nice man but no poet. Berryman is so synthetic and ersatz that I can't read him at all. Jarrell is far better than any of these, and to accuse him of "intellectualism" simply (I imagine) because he <u>was</u> an intellectual (and of the best type, too, incidentally) seems very odd to me, for his poetry is anything but intellectual.

The section you were kind enough to write on my work I liked very much, though I am not really sure why you have chosen to bracket me with Sylvia Plath, a writer whom I thoroughly detest. For contrast, maybe? Anyway, it's all right. But you mistake the intent of my work when you speak of it as having the effect of making life bearable "or even enjoyable." This sounds as though I were attempting to provide a palliative for obvious and real evils, or even trying to operate out of an ostrich head-burying position, or something. None of this is the case. I want to open the human being up to the possibilities of his own joy, delight and ecstasy, which are things far more intense and meaningful than mere "enjoyment." Being fully alive, as Lawrence says, is really all we want. I think it is still possible to achieve this state, and to write about it.

But again, thank you for sending your words along. They will be good for American poetry, as your poems and articles and anthologies always have been.

Have a good trip, and let me know when you get back. We'll play some tennis.

All yours,

To: Robert Penn Warren   TLS, Yale University

4620 Lelia's Court
Columbia, S.C. 29206
January 15, 1971

Dear Red:

After I got home from New Haven I found your letter to me. It is awfully good to have it, just as it was good to see you in New Haven, though all too briefly. Don't worry about not having any new poems to offer <u>Esquire</u> at <u>this</u> date. The project is conceived as a long-lasting one, and there will be plenty of time to print what you write in the future, whenever you wish to send us something.

I wish I had more time to talk to you about the Melville book. He is certainly a mystery to me. As I said at the party, I don't believe I know of any poet who has written such distinguished <u>lines</u> and such downright bad ones, frequently on the same page. I think it was Eliot who said of Hardy that Hardy had genius but no talent. Something of this is what I feel in connection with Melville himself, and particularly about the poetry. But you have said all this better than I can do, and I thank you very much for your selection and your introduction, which is certainly the best writing on Melville's poetry that has been done. I haven't read it <u>all</u>, of course, but I surely did read what existed up till the time, twenty years ago, when I wrote my master's thesis on the subject. It is not my impression that Melville's poetry has been much written about since then, though of course it may have been, for all I know.

Again, it was a delight to see you and Eleanor last week, and is a continuing delight to remember it. Maxine sends love, and so do I. And please tell Eleanor that I <u>will</u> bring my guitar the next time we get together.

By the way, you say that you are leaving in June and won't be back until the fall of '72. Are you going back to Italy? I do hope so. We used to live at Positano, down on the Amalfi coast between Sorrento and Amalfi, about eight or nine years ago, and haven't been back since. But I surely do love that place over there. It is on all counts the land of <u>my</u> heart's desire, I can tell you.

All yours,
Jim

To: James Wright   TLS, University of Minnesota

4620 Lelia's Court
Columbia, S.C. 29206
January 15, 1971

Dear Jim:

Please forgive me for waiting so long to answer your wonderful letter of December 21st, which came as the finest Christmas present I have ever received in all my 48 years. I am very happy that you liked the comment that I made for publicity for the jacket of your <u>Collected Poems</u>, and you can know that I meant every word of it. It was just a question of saying something that was right <u>enough</u>, out of all of the good things I might have said.

The things that you say of my own work are very sustaining to me, I can tell you. I am very happy that you like it as well as you do, that it has meant as much as it has to you, for the things you say make me very happy that I spent the time, time that I might have spent living and doing other supposedly necessary things, in trying to compose these poems. It costs me blood to write, as you above anybody else knows. I am very happy that someone of your eminence thinks as highly of my work as you do. I won't go on and on in this effusive way, but will simply thank you once more, as warmly as I know how.

I get all kinds of disturbing reports about Robert Bly, and if he continues to do some of the things he has done in regard to me, I am going to have to confront him in some manner, either through lawyers or through a personal encounter of some sort. One simply cannot allow someone to go about in public meeting after public meeting, at reading after reading on college after college calling one a racist, a fascist, a nazi, a nigger-hater, a toady of the government, and so on. This is quite clearly slanderous, and if you have any contact with Bob, you may tell him that I am not going to put up with it any longer. I will either come after him myself, or I will have lawyers deal with it. I have consulted a couple, and they say that if I can prove that he is saying in public the things about me that he definitely is saying, I can take him for all he's worth. I doubt if he has much to be taken for, but if he continues as he is doing now, I will surely ruin him. You can tell him this and let him be guided by whatever conscience he may have. Or perhaps I shouldn't depend on that! It is not that all this is disturbing to me, but that the laws of this country are set against the kind of character assassination that he is bent on doing. I am sorry for Bob; a life spent in envy of another person, in spite and frustration, is not an enviable life. But neither is a life of being consistently slandered and lied-about in public. He even goes around telling people that he has heard me read and say these things: things like "tell that nigger down in the front row to get me a mint julep or I won't read." Now can you imagine my possibly saying that, or anything remotely resembling it? I think Bob should be in a straightjacket, and I am either going to put him there, or in jail, or in the poor house, or in the hospital. As I say, I won't put up with this any more, and if you see him, you can tell him exactly that.

I don't mean to take up this letter with talk about such unpleasant matters, but you can surely see how I might be concerned about them. I wanted this letter, though, to be simply a letter of thanks for your letter and for the things you say in it. You are a very precious friend to me, Jim, and I don't think these things can ever be said too often. I am very happy I said what I did about your book; I mean it all, you can well believe.

Love to Annie, and to all those who visit that good house of yours. With one exception!

All yours,
Jim

P.S. I thought your poem looked awfully good in Esquire. Give us a little more time—a couple of months, maybe—and we'll do some more of yours. The response to that one has been extraordinarily good.

To: John Boorman   CC, Emory University
                                                          4620 Lelia's Court
                                                        Columbia, S.C. 29206

                                                          January 18, 1971

Dear John:

Well, that is a wonderful letter, wonderful news. I expect that by the time this reaches you, you will be closeted with Ashly and Calley about the budget. You know a great deal more about that end of film-making than I do, but I am quite sure that you will get what you want from them. From the little contact I have had with Calley, he seems <u>most</u> eager to make this movie, as it is well that he should be! Anyway, just keep me posted as to what transpires, and I'll swing with you, anyway <u>you</u> swing. What we want to remember is that the best thing that we can possibly do for the film is to bring both our best creative and critical efforts to bear on it. Our degree of agreement about the overall feel of the movie and its details is surely heartening to me, but we must never concede a point, one to the other, that we think is merely being given away for the sake of friendship. As you say, we <u>should</u> be very critical as well as enthusiastic, and if we can mix these two qualities and play them back and forth between us, we will have the nearest earthly creatures can ever get to a perfect working environment.

I was in Atlanta with Lewis two weekends ago, and he had a number of fanatical canoeists over to his house showing films of all different kinds of locations. The gorge Lewis must have mentioned to you is on the Little River in northern Alabama, and some of the films taken by these canoe maniacs of that location <u>do</u> look awfully good. When you come over, maybe we could spend a day or two in Atlanta with these fellows, looking over some of this footage. I think it would be better to do that than to go up to the location itself. We should be able to determine from the film whether a trip up to that area is necessary or advisable.

I am very happy that we are going to change the ending. I won't dwell on the former ending, but will simply look forward to seeing what you have done in the way of making a new one. As you know, I am much against making so very much, much of the girl in the studio. Her function in the film, if we decide to include her at all, should be the same as it was in the novel: simply to serve as a focus of the unfulfilled feeling about Ed's life. We may be able to do this in another way, but if we use the girl as this kind of symbol, we should not make a major part of the film revolve around her. The point is that his vague longings, which formerly had nothing better than a strange young girl to focus on, have received a new focus, not in sex but in violence and in the discovery on Ed's part that, if called upon, he can do these terrible, bloody, things, and get away with it. This is not to be seen as any kind of <u>substitute</u> sexual longing at all, but is merely meant to show that a sense of unfulfillment which gravitated, under Ed's ordinary, day-to-day circumstances, to sex, as such things will, have actually found a much more powerful and positive medium than his erstwhile sexual preoccupation.

Now to another of your points. You say that you think it somewhat "devalues the piece to direct the audience's concern to 'will they be found out.'" I don't think we need to dwell unduly on this, but it must be remembered that there surely <u>would</u> be some apprehension on the part of Ed and the others as to this happening. There should, quite legitimately, be <u>some</u> sort of explanation on their part as to what has happened, and I don't object at all to a slight heightening of effect on the part of the film as to whether they <u>will</u> be found out. It should be borne in mind that the deception following the murders is as much a part of Ed's "deliverance" as the actual climbing of the cliff, the shooting of the man with the rifle, and so on. In other words, it would be most effective if we could show what the book tries to show: that he can not only do these things, but do what is probably even <u>harder</u> to do: get away with it, give a plausible explanation, and trick society into his way of thinking, so that it, too, "delivers" him.

As to the matter of anticlimax, I am not adverse to having the film a <u>little</u> bit anticlimactic, though certainly I agree that we should not drag this out. What I had in mind is a situation where Ed and the others are shown in their ordinary-life conditions, the trip to the river and down the river, and a return, showing Ed—perhaps briefly—in both his office and home situations, as the book has them. This will give the story a kind of circular movement which I think is quite desirable. That is, the change is <u>inner</u>: everybody else thinks that he is the same man, and he doesn't do anything to disabuse them of this notion.

Meantime, let me suggest a couple of alternatives in keeping with your recent feeling that "the film must end very quickly after they leave Aintry." If you wanted to cut the film off at a dramatic moment which would sum up the whole action, Ed's transfiguration, and the rest, we might very well end it just after Bobby leaves in Lewis's car and Ed is standing beside the overturned canoe, on the river bank. The end might very well come when he stoops down and takes a double handful of the river up to his lips and drinks it. That itself might be "deliverance" enough. If we want to do that, we could come in close on his face as he drinks, and make a kind of similar shot with which you open the film, in your version of the script. That might work out fine, here is the symbolic gesture. But again, I think we should show him, however briefly, getting back into his life. This has the added advantage of showing his new relationship to Martha, and I hope we can get back in some of the business about her taking care of his wound, and so on. That is good, practical, man-woman, man-wife love, and is as good as I can do in the way of showing that a new kind of quiet, honest, un-frustrated thing is taking place between them. We would not have to be insistent about this, but it could make a very effective little sequence, and show the things that I think should be shown at this point in the film; that is, the very end.

What I really have in mind for the whole story, both in the novel and the film is an updated version of Van Gennep's Rites de Passage: "a separation from the world, a penetration to some source of power, and life-enhancing return." This blueprint for "the hero with a thousand faces" is a very powerful adjunct to this story. Deliverance illustrates this for our time just as surely as the Odyssey did for its, or any other work at any other time which employs this theme. For my money, it is the most powerful theme in all of literature, all of mythology, and, if you couple it with my other favorite theme, that of the hunted becoming the hunter, well, you really have something. It follows, though, that if we follow the Rites de Passage, we must in some measure show the return, and, as I say, I am for doing this, though we may very well do it very briefly indeed.

Back to the river bank. If you still would like to cut the action off, end the film, and so on just shortly after they get off the river, I have a couple more ideas in relation to the scene at the river bank by the canoe that I have been talking about. If we have a couple of very effective shots of the digging up of the graveyard across the river, this would get us out of the necessity of having to show the actual dam, since we are showing the effects of damming up the river in a more dramatic way than a public ceremony could afford us. So we get the inundation prefigured in the graveyard scene, and we can surely imply the deliverance as Ed stands by the river and ceremonially drinks from it.

Another possibility, if we should decide to end the film on this note, is to have Ed drink from the river and turn away. The camera could then zoom in on the hull of the canoe, and then very close in on a certain portion of it, and there, sure enough, is a bullet hole. We could then see Ed working his way up through the kudzu, and leave to the audience whether this will ever be noticed or not.

Or we could show the bullet holes and show Ed turning away and walking about half way through the kudzu back to his car. He might then turn, as though an afterthought—we don't know whether he has noticed the bullet holes himself or not—go down to the canoe, take it by the bow-rope and start to drag it laboriously up through the vegetation. <u>That</u> might be the ending.

Again, I don't know how these things will strike you; I am only throwing them out as suggestions, just to see what you think of them.

To answer a couple of questions in your former letter. You asked whether or not the first body, the one buried under the ferns, might not surface when the area was inundated. I'm quite sure it would not. However, your question brings up an additional little bit of action that might be effective at this point. Lewis might suggest that the four of them drag a dead tree over the grave as additional protection. This wouldn't take but a moment or so, and it would surely knock out any possibility that the body would ever rise.

As to the story being set, now, in the spring of the year, and the relation of this to the football game, and so on, we can mend that very easily indeed. For "pro game" we can just say "ball game": there are, to be sure, "ball games" in <u>every</u> season in America: baseball games, basketball games, and so on.

There are some small errors of diction in some of the dialogue you have supplied; some of them are not really American expressions, such as "fuck-all," which I associate, personally, with Australia, but must surely be current in England. An American audience would not know what this means: that it means, so to speak, nothing. Other little things, like Drew saying as they pass under the bridge, "spooky kid," are not really examples of how southern people speak. The word "kid" has never really caught on in the South. I would suggest that Drew say something with a kind of resigned shrug, like, "Well, he sure can play the banjo, anyway."

But these are very small points indeed, and can easily be changed, if you feel they should be. What we must do, just as soon as you come back to Columbia, is to sit down with your very latest version of the script—I hope you will bring me a Xerox of this—and go over it, quite literally page by page, and word by word. We are now at the stage where we are not trying to get <u>approximately</u> what we want, but <u>exactly</u> what we want, and are within very exciting striking distance of this. So <u>do</u> keep me posted about your plans, and we will make us—well, one <u>hell</u> of a movie.

We are ready at this end. Lewis is ready, Crazy Charlie is ready with his Land Rover, the new bunch of fellows, the canoe maniacs, are all ready, and we have plenty of help, which ever way you want to use it. Surely <u>I</u> am ready, I can tell you. I have finished teaching until next September and can be available as much as you desire me to.

Please remember me to Charles, and to your as-yet-unmet family. Everything looks exceedingly good to me at this time. Your letter is the greatest boost I have had in quite a long time.

It now looks as though <u>Deliverance</u> is a solid bet to win both the National Book Award and Pulitzer Prize over here, and if that happens it will be an additional boost to the film. The paperback comes out in March, and that will help, too.

All yours,

P.S.: When you come over, could you or Charles bring me a couple of those Swedish compasses like Charles had when we were up in north Georgia together? I would surely appreciate it very much indeed. A couple of those things, and I would <u>never</u> get lost. Not in <u>this</u> world, anyway!

To: Ken McCormick   **CC, Emory University**
4620 Lelia's Court
Columbia, S.C. 29206

January 29, 1971

Dear Ken:

Thank you so very much for your unfailing kindness in sending down the <u>Pushkin</u> book and the others, and for sending along also the very welcome news that <u>Self-Interviews</u> is in a second edition, and that we are now printed up to 8,500. That is quite heartening.

A couple of things here that you might not know about. Some company out on the West Coast sent me a very handsome tape recording machine on condition that I would record a cassett for broadcast on the West Coast. They ask me to talk, not about <u>Deliverance</u>, but about <u>Self-Interviews</u>, and I think I made quite a good tape for their use. I am waiting now to hear from them as to how the tape will be employed. But it certainly can't hurt us, I'm quite sure of that. The other thing may amuse you. A friend of ours in the Department of International Studies goes to Taiwan every year. This time he brought back pirated copies of <u>Deliverance</u>, done on that kind of thin rice-paper they use over there, but he also brought back a copy of <u>Self-Interviews</u>, and I take it as a good sign that the Taiwanese think enough of a book of that sort to pirate it as well as a better known book like <u>Deliverance</u>. Certainly does make an odd-looking piece of book-making, I can tell you.

I wait to hear from you on the contract for the novel, the various papers to lawyers, and the rest of it. My operation is getting so complicated now that I just turn everything over to Maxine, who in turn has her fingers, supposedly, on the pulses of all these other people, agents, and so on.

I'm sorry our poetry book didn't get on the final list for the NBA, but I was told by one of the poetry judges that the attention paid to <u>Deliverance</u>, the fact that it is a leading contender in its category, and the fact that I had won the award before, all conspired to take the book off the list, which shouldn't have been the case. Maybe we'll have better luck with the Pulitzer, because the poetry list for the NBA this year is so weak that I think the judges would be quite justified in abstaining from giving the prize this year. You might notice also that neither John Berryman's <u>Love and Fame</u> nor Robert Lowell's <u>Note-books</u>, which he considers his major work, are on the list either. The whole list is taken up with pip-squeaks, and I think that not much attention will be paid to whatever results from it.

I'll be back in New York on March 8th—an easy date to remember, for it is the date of the Cassius Clay-Joe Frazier fight, for a reading at the Poetry Center, and will try to make a couple of days on either side of that date so that you and I and Sandy and maybe Theron can get together and talk about whatever we need to talk about. But mostly, it would just be very good to see you. I am still elated over the news concerning Sally. I guess she is back at work now, and that must be fine for her too.

One more thing. Tony Kahn, my Russian expert at Harvard, has written and asked me for a statement about my particular relationship to the Yevtushenko renderings that I did. I went ahead and complied with this, and you may want to get Tony's response, as well as my remarks, from either Tony or Kate Medina. I'd like to know how these remarks, and those of the other translators, are going to be fitted into the book, the introduction, or wherever they <u>are</u> going to be fitted.

Things are very good with us here, though most of my time now is taken up with script revisions, "additional dialogue," and the like, in connection with the film version of <u>Deliverance</u>. John Calley, production chief at Warners, called the other night and told me that the two leading candidates for the main roles in the film are Jack Nicholson as Ed Gentry, the narrator, and Robert Redford as Lewis. None of this is official, but that is a pretty good pair, don't you think.

Again, my best to you, to Sandy, and to all those I know at Doubleday.

All yours,

To: Eileen Glancy

CC, Emory University
4620 Lelia's Court
Columbia, S.C. 29206

February 3, 1971

Dear Mrs. Glancy:

Very good indeed to hear from you. I saw your bibliography in <u>Twentieth Century Literature,</u> and was very pleased with it. You did the best job on the subject that has yet been done, and I am very happy that the project turned out as well for you as it seems to have done; surely it was very good for <u>me</u>!

And now you are going to update the bibliography. That would be fine, and I hope you will send the whole thing to me when you have finished it. You ask for permission to quote passages from the criticism and also some lines from a number of poems which you list. Yes, indeed, you certainly <u>do</u> have my permission to quote these just as you wish. I ask only that you send me a copy of what you write, so I can see what has been done with the material. Otherwise, no problem at all.

You ask about my new book, due out the latter part of the summer. It is a book of new essays interspersed with entries from a kind of undated journal that I have been keeping more or less intermittently, on audio tape for the past year or so. We are just working out the format now, and I think it will be rather an interesting book, when we've done with it. Doubleday is going to publish it, but the exact publication date has not been set, at this time. It should be in August or September, or maybe even as late as October; as I say, I will let you know when the Doubleday people tell <u>me</u>.

And thank you also for your comments on <u>Deliverance</u>. I am very happy you like it, and I hope you will also like the film version which we are going to make this spring, just as soon as the leaves get back on the trees.

Please <u>do</u> keep in touch, for you have more information on me and my work than <u>I</u> have, and I can't lose track of <u>that</u> kind of source of knowledge!

Sincerely yours,

To: Robert Bly

CC, Emory University
4620 Lelia's Court
Columbia, S.C. 29206

February 8, 1971

Dear Robert:

Jim Wright called me the other day about a letter I had written to him, and said he had been in touch with you about the subject of the letter. I simply cannot understand why you have conducted yourself—and, apparently still are conducting yourself—in this manner. The most disturbing stories come to me from all over, from students, from teachers, from people who come to hear you read and talk to you. Now let me make my position very plain at the outset. I do not object to anything you want to say about my writings, or even any of the absurd interpretations that you insist on putting on them. What I do object to is your campaign of bald-faced lies about me, my attitude toward minority groups, my politics, and things of that nature. I will stand behind anything I have ever gone on record as saying; that is, things that are facts. What I object to, and what I will do something about if it continues is your paranoic habit of fabricating stories about me and giving them out to audiences as though they were the truth. One boy called me, for example, from some place in Arizona or New Mexico, and told me that you had told an audience that you had <u>heard</u> me read, and say "tell that nigger down there in the first row to get me a mint julep or I won't read." You have never heard me read anywhere, since that time in NYU. Again, let me put this to you very, very directly. If I get one more report from anywhere that you have said anything of this nature, I am going to take you to court. If you have money for lawyers' fees, fine. I would very much like to get this on public record, in a court of law. After all, you leave behind you when you do these reprehensible, disgusting, and dishonest things, not only tapes of the various performances, but hundreds of witnesses at each college. It would not be difficult to gather all the evidence I need to make a case against you that would stand up in any court in this country, and I will do just that. Be guided by this as you may, but I will put you on the line against the laws of this land, if you continue this. And that's the truth.

Sincerely yours,

To: Thomas Hart

CC, Emory University
4620 Lelia's Court
Columbia, S.C. 29206

March 6, 1971

Dear Tom Hart:

My God, good things can happen! It was so <u>very</u> kind of you to write, to send along the orders, and the rest. As a result of <u>Deliverance</u> and certain other things I've written, I hear from one of the "old boys" once and a while. All of the letters have been sad ones except yours; most of the fellows on those shipping orders you were kind enough to send along are dead. About half of the fellows listed there were in my squadron, the 418th, and the rest, I imagine, were in yours. I have been often haunted by the fact that I used Darden Armstrong's name in the poem I wrote about him, for it occurred to me much after the fact—after the poem had been anthologized in about a hundred different places—that it might be that the Armstrong family and Jim Lally's family might have got hold of the information through the poem that their sons were beheaded when the Air Force may have seen fit to conceal this fact from them. I have never received any communications from either family, and so I hope they don't read poetry anthologies.

It is wonderful of you to fill me in on all the details of the fellows I remember very poignantly from those good and bad days. Sure, I remember George Aubill very well. I liked him quite a good deal. Actually, I was in a class or two ahead of you at Hammer Field. I was held over as an instructor, and so didn't go out with the fellows I went through training with. Gene Wick and Bob Davis were in my class, who were killed by running into a mountain on one of those tracking flights we used for practice. The fellows, like Galloway, Paul Fridley, and the others that I ended up in the 418th with were either the class immediately after mine or the second class after mine. Anyway, they were very good fellows, and I wish them all the luck there is, whatever they may be. I used to talk to Don Armstrong about his family difficulties, and I remember he told me he and his wife spent their wedding night in an automobile, for some reason. I had heard, vaguely, some of the things about Don and his wife, particularly his wife, that you repeat, but it is good to have the much more complete run-down that you have provided me with. I don't know exactly how to take all this, but it surely does move me very much indeed, I can tell you.

I have been racking my brains trying to remember you, and I <u>think</u> I have a hazy mental picture, but my mental picture might not be you at all. But it certainly was very handsome of you to write, and in such detail too! Let me hear from you again whenever you wish to communicate, for I am always very pleased and gratified to hear from one of those who have ridden the dark wind with me, and come back. I wish I could hear from the others too, but that is not to be, at least in this life.

Again, Tom, thank you so very much. I am very much gratified and very much moved by what you have done.

All yours,

To: Stewart Richardson

CC, Emory University
4620 Lelia's Court
Columbia, S.C. 29206

March 22, 1971

Dear Sandy:

It was great to see you and Ken, and I'm very sorry that we didn't have more time to talk. But there will be other times, which I look forward to very much, you may very well believe.

I had a couple of ideas for the title for our critical and notebook-entry book, and I send them along to you. These are, I think—at least some of them—better than Assertions, which sounds a shade too militant, I believe. What I want is a title that will give some kind of notion of the two kinds of material to be found in the book: that is, the essays and the journal entries. Why couldn't we call it something like Sorties, or Sorties and Returns? I also thought of calling it Forays, but I think Sorties is better, because less aggressive. After all, a foray is a raid for the purpose of taking spoils, whereas a sortie is a mission which comes out of a defended position, or an aircraft flight against an enemy. I thought also of your double-word kind of title and we could call it, if we wanted to, as you suggested, Assertions and Flights, but this is not quite right because, if you use the word "flights," we ought to have some other word in the title that plays off against that: that is, something that was most emphatically, not a flight, indeed the opposite of it. I thought, also, that we might call it Penetrations, but that seems to be a title which assumes a little too much on the part of the author. If we had something like Penetrations and Flights, it might be better. Nonetheless, I think Sorties or Sorties and Returns is about the best I have been able to do so far. Let me know what you think of this, and I will be guided accordingly.

By the way, I have a lot more journal entries, but I don't know where your copy of the journals leaves off. If you will tell me the last page you have, I will send to you all the pages after that, and that should do the job up to the point where I now am.

I heard from John Boorman day before yesterday, and he says that Marlon Brando is definitely going to play Lewis in the film version of <u>Deliverance</u>. I certainly hope so, for that would bring Nicholson in, and after that the rest would be easy, provided we don't get Brando's and Nicholson's heads bashed in on some of those rocks up in north Georgia, which is quite easy to do.

I haven't time for a long letter, but will close with best wishes for you and Sally and Ken. I'll be back in the city in a few weeks, and we'll get together again.

I don't really have much of an idea about what Maxine and my accountant, Stith, and Theron and you-all are working out on this contract, plus commentary by my lawyer, Kirk Finlay. Surely we should get the whole thing straightened out before too long, but, since I've never done this before, I can't really say. I'll try to push everybody along at approximately the same rate, and we should get it worked out on <u>some</u> kind of basis pretty soon. I sure hope so. It's hard enough for me to write the stuff, much less look after all the legalistic and financial business connected with it. But it will all be all right, I'm quite sure.

Thanks so very much for your comments on the Moyers article. I have had a good deal of mail on it, but nothing which pleased me nearly so much as the things you said at dinner.

Warmly,

To: Joyce Carol Oates

CC, Emory University
4620 Lelia's Court
Columbia, S.C. 29206

March 22, 1971

Dear Mrs. Oates:

I cannot tell you how very much gratified and much moved I am to receive your new book and the dedication you were so gracious as to inscribe in it. I have received a good deal of mail lately, as you may imagine, but nothing I have gotten has given me nearly the gratification—nor the occasion for gratitude—that your book has done. Sending it to me was a kind human act, and when can there ever be enough of them?

I read through the poems too, and found much to admire. It seems to me that, despite all the Anne Sextons and the Adrienne Riches, that there has been very little real womanly sensibility in American poetry. Many are called but few—well, very few women can or do write like women. Your poems of love-making are very beautiful indeed, and I hope there will be a lot more of them. A man cannot really understand how a woman feels about these things, as a woman cannot understand how a man feels, but with poetry like yours the man can come a lot closer to understanding them than he otherwise would have been able to do, in his blundering, mortal way.

Again, thank you for your poems, your book, and your inscription. It was wonderful of you to send them all to me.

Sincerely yours,

To: James E. Coleman, Jr.   CC, Emory University
                                                  4620 Lelia's Court
                                                  Columbia, S.C. 29206

                                                  March 24, 1971

Dear Jim:

Thank you so very much for writing to me as you have done, and from so very deep in the past, too! I'll return your book, signed, in a couplee of days, but I did want to get this note off to you to tell you how grateful I am for your communication.

I haven't seen any of the "Buckhead boys" in a long time, though, on impulse, I did go by and see Richard Lamb a few years ago. He is very fat and very happy, and I was delighted to see him, but there is always a certain amount of <u>embarrassment</u> on these occasions, and he and I both felt it, though we drank a couple of stiff shots of Jack Daniels, and things seemed to be better. But they will never be what they were when we were boys, and as I think back on those times I am filled with enormous nostalgia for the decent fellows we were in those days, though God knows, as boys we were certainly not any angels. But I remember the long afternoons when we used to go skating down on River Road, the afternoons always organized by Jack Emerson, when we played football until we could hardly see the ball in the air any longer, and the rest. That is not the worst way to grow up, and I remember Jack and you and Richard Lamb and Dick Harris, and the others, before we got into the <u>organized</u> phase of sports at North Fulton with a great deal of affection and nostalgia. You, I remember as more or less the best of all of us, and I am delighted at your success in your chosen profession. When the war came along, all those days went with them, and all we can do now is remember. But what I remember is very good indeed, and it is fine to hear from you. Myself, I'm a grandfather now. My oldest boy, Chris, is going to be, next year, the first graduate in film-making from the University of Virginia, which is a strange prospect for his father, I can tell you. I did the screen play for the film version of Deliverance, and Chris helped me out a good deal with it, so maybe he can jump off this particular springboard into a full-time career in film-making, though I can tell you that this is my only venture into that rather precarious but very exciting realm.

I won't go on and on, but will just thank you again for your letter. So many of us are dead now, Jim. It is good to think of you, the best, the most honest and courageous and the straightest of us all, as being the success that you are. And you can surely understand—you have my word—that in my travels, if I come through Dallas, I will surely look you up, and maybe we could have dinner, a couple of drinks, and so on. I would like very much to meet your family, to see what your operation is like, these days. I like Texas, myself, very much. My first teaching job, at Rice University, was there, and I was stationed at Waco after I came back from Korea for a few months. I go in and out of Texas a good deal, and the University of Texas has a good many of my papers, correspondence, and all that sort of necrophilia. Anyway, believe me, I will not only let you know when I am coming to Dallas, but will do my best to make an excuse to come to Dallas, so we can get together once more. From my point of view, it would surely be something to look forward to. And I will do just that.

All yours,

To: George I. Kline   CC, Emory University
                                                       4620 Lelia's Court
                                                       Columbia, S.C. 29206

April 14, 1971

Dear Mr. Kline:

Thank you very much for your letter in regard to my review of Bill Moyers' book.[13] "The incredible boredom of American life" is something that we all feel in various ways, and I suspect it is engendered by the monotony of the way most men and women earn their living, and the monotony in which most

13. "Listening to America," New York Times Book Review, March 14, 1971, pp. 2, 37.

households spend their time. I doubt if there is very much to be done about this, if we are to continue the way of life we have cast ourselves upon. Thus, my despair being of a much less practical kind than Moyers'.

I don't necessarily mean that it would be less boring to live in another country, although I myself think that it is. I also think that the best way to live in America is to flout its values and enjoy its money. Maybe times will change; I don't know. It is better for me to live in America, because I can earn a living as a poet and a writer here that I could not possibly earn anywhere else. And some things about American life I like very much indeed: its very real freedom of choice, for example. The things I don't like stem from a kind of combination of feverish anxiety and crushing ennui, which combination is probably what Walker Percey was talking about when he called the feeling the malaise.

Again, thank you very much for your letter. I care about these things too, as we all must. Question is, what to do about them. Maybe you or I can solve all these problems for everybody! Let me know if you have any good ideas!

Sincerely yours,

To: Eric E. Wallace

CC, Emory University
4620 Lelia's Court
Columbia, S.C. 29206

April 27, 1971

Dear Mr. Wallace:

Thank you very much for your letter, and for the very perceptive essay on how you would turn Deliverance into a film.

To answer your questions, Deliverance will begin to be filmed around the 10th of May, although we may have to delay a week. But it will be shot in the late spring and early summer, and the shooting will probably extend into the late summer, or even into the first touch of fall.

You ask me for comments on your comments, and I think you are consistently on target. You have a couple of brilliant strokes of insight which I can only think of as clairvoyant. For example, you say that the scene of the guitar-banjo picking in the filling station might be utilized as the theme music for the entire film, and that is just precisely what we are going to do. The music will be played by two young Portland, Oregon, musicians named Mike Russo and Ron Brentano, and it is an adaptation of an old guitar-banjo piece called, "Duelling Banjos." This music will be tentatively picked out in the filling station scene—which, incidentally, I think is great, too—and then will serve as the music for the climactic end of the film. I won't tell you what this end is, but it is a little different from that in the novel, though the theme and the emphases are not different in the film.

In answer to your other questions, I did the screenplay, though I can't tell you in a relatively short letter how it is structured. I can tell you that I first did a long "treatment" which was then submitted to Warner Brothers. It was very heavily influenced by James Agee, and I thought it was very good, but it turned out to run about seven hours. Of course this wouldn't do, so I cut it down, and we now having a working script that will run about 110 minutes if John Boorman and I can film it as we have set it up to be filmed. As for the cast, we are going to film it with unknowns, except for the lead, Ed Gentry. As it now looks, that part will be played by Warren Beaty. I know that must raise specters of Beaty doing an aquatic version of <u>Bonnie and Clyde</u>, but this need not be the case. Anyway, I will know more about this later, and if you will keep in touch, I will let you know what is going to take place, as soon as Warner Brothers and John Boorman let <u>me</u> know.

The film will include a <u>little</u> material not in the novel. But if I were to show you the names of the people we have turned down for the cast, it would be like a roll-call of all the male actors in Hollywood, because they all want to get into it.

Again, I was very much impressed with the things you had to say about the making of the novel into the film. I quite agree with you that any work of literary art depends very largely on the fact that it <u>is</u> literary: that is that it is written in <u>words</u>. Nevertheless, we have in <u>Deliverance</u>, unlike, say, what we would have if we were attempting to film <u>Moby Dick</u>, a theme which will <u>lend</u> itself to visual interpretation. It is obvious that Ed Gentry is the center of the action, but this can be made obvious by a very primitive device: having him in most of the scenes, and keeping the camera on him most of the time—or, at least, for more time than the camera scrutinizes any of the other people. After all, most of the action footage is about Ed, he resolves the situation, and so on. All this can be carried by such simple devices. The only difficulty from this standpoint, in the writing of the screenplay, is to indicate to the viewer how Ed figures out the manner in which he wishes to ambush the man who is waiting to gun them down. This I think I have solved more or less satisfactorily by having him <u>tell</u> these plans to Bobby before he begins to try to climb the cliff.

If you will keep in touch, it might be possible for you to come up to Clayton, Georgia, where we are filming from, and see some of this happen. I can't guarantee any special attention, or even any accommodations, but if you are as interested in film as your letter and your essay seem to indicate, this would be no problem to you. But it shall be as you wish.

Again, thank you exceedingly for your kindness in writing to me as you have done, and in spending your time in the <u>thinking</u> that underlies your very kind essay. I shall take it with me to Clayton when I meet with Boorman and the cast over there next week, and we will try to put some of your ideas into effect. Again, I can't promise anything, because I don't know how Boorman will react to what you want to do. But believe me, <u>I</u> appreciate your suggestions.

Again, with every best wish, I remain,

Warmly,

To: Patricia Gebhart

CC, Emory University
4620 Lelia's Court
Columbia, S.C. 29206

May 5, 1971

Dear Patricia Gebhart:

Thank you very much for your very kind note. I am very heartened at what you say about the poems, for they certainly cost me blood to write. As to <u>Self-Interviews</u>, I put no great store by the book itself. And yet, like so many other writers, politicians, football coaches, and other <u>soi-biasant</u> notables, I have been interviewed, very nearly, out of my mind. This seems to be the age of the interview, and no one can escape. I thought I would put all the things I keep saying over and over in interviews into a single volume so that people would be able to read it and consequently let me alone. I see now that the making of <u>Self-Interviews</u> has nothing whatever to do with my being let alone; the interviewing is more intensified than ever. But I also thought that it might be of some advantage to writers, particularly younger writers, to see how my particular material got made into poems, and how I sort of backed into the literary life, like most other writers, though in my own way. Poems are explained to death these days, and I thought that it might not be a bad idea if a poet got into his own act, and did a little explaining of his own, though, as I say in the book, I would not dream of substituting my own experience of the writing for someone elses experience, like yours, of the poems.

But the main thing, as you quite rightly say, is the poems themselves. It is often said to poets that their remarks <u>about</u> their poems are better than the poems. I doubt that there is an American poet who hasn't had that said to him not once but several times, and, in some cases, almost all the time. The important thing here is that you <u>don't</u> say that, but go back to the poems, where I intended you to go, anyway. <u>Self-Interviews</u> is a very, very minor book. It might be helpful to some people, including the scholars who constantly write papers, dissertations, and other kinds of things on me, and it might be helpful, in some instances, to young writers. It might be helpful to literary biographers, for I intend to authorize no biography, even should anyone wish to write one. But the main emphasis must be on the poems, and I am very happy that you put it there, and that you have been so kind as to tell me that you have done so.

Again, let me invite you to write in a little more personal vein, and tell me something of yourself. Maybe we could get together, on Riverside Drive or somewhere else, and have a beer or something together, one of these days. I am in and out of New York all the time, and so this would not be unfeasible. But, finally, it shall be as you wish.

Again, thank you so very much for the things you say about the poems. Because of the hullabaloo over <u>Deliverance</u>, the writing of the screenplay, and, now, the filming of the thing, I have had very little chance to write any poetry for the last couple of years. I intend to put the summer in on <u>Deliverance</u>, and then go back to writing poetry in as nearly a full capacity as I am able to manage. I have a desk-full of notes, and I hope you will like some of the new things that I am planning to work out, and some of the new directions I am planning to go in, just as soon as I get time.

Keep in touch. I like your fiery, heartfelt letter. As the blind folksinger, Reverend Gary Davis, says, "when I hear <u>that</u>, I just feel like going on." And go on I will, thanks at least in part to you and your <u>caring</u> enough to write.

Sincerely yours,

To: Ron Brentano

CC, Emory University
4620 Lelia's Court
Columbia, S.C. 29206

May 6, 1971

Dear Ron:

I just got back from a recording studio where I had a dub of yours & Mike's piece "Duelling Banjos" run off for John Boorman. He called from Clayton, where we are staging out of for the movie and requested that I bring this over, and I was only too happy to have it done. The script has been changed around some, but we are still using this piece, as you and Mike do it, as the theme music. The character of Drew, the fellow who plays the guitar, is being played by Ronnie Cox, who plays a little guitar himself, and John wanted to make the scene where he <u>appears</u> to be playing the guitar as authentic as possible. I will check him out when I get up there, tomorrow, and advise John. It may be that you and Mike can play this sequence, particularly the one in the filling station. But even if that doesn't happen, the theme of "Duelling Banjos" comes back in at the very end when the picture is really rising to a climax, and <u>that</u>, you and Mike will play. I have a good dub made of the old concert at Reed, and John will be knocked out about it, I am quite sure.

Meanwhile, should you need to get in touch with me directly, I will be staying at Kingwood Country Club at Clayton, Georgia, for an indefinite period. If, for some reason you can't get in touch with me there, you can call Maxine, here in Columbia, and she will be able to put you in touch with me.

Yes, I have many thoughts of doing as you seem to suggest: taking the money and running. But I was given an option on writing the script, and, since I have been living with the story and the writing of it for such a long time, I could not bear to think of its being butchered by some unfeeling hack. I think John Boorman is a good director, and I think we can make an awfully powerful film. He wants to preserve the basic integrity of the story, and I read that as a good sign. Anyway, I am going ahead and planning to put my spring and summer into the screen version of <u>Deliverance</u>. If we can work it so that you and Mike make the contribution to the film that I <u>know</u> you can make, it will just be that much better. I talked to John on the phone, and there is some static being given us by Warner Brothers about employing <u>their</u> musicians, because there are union difficulties and one thing and another I don't even pretend to understand. But you may be sure that I will hold out for you and Mike in any way I can. The first way is to take this tape I just made this afternoon over to Clayton and let John and the others listen to it. We could <u>not</u> have better theme music for the film. By the way, if it is not difficult or too unusual for him to do so, I would like to have Mike play a twelve-string rather than a six on this piece. I am going to have the guitar that Drew takes into the woods with him be a twelve-string because it has a sound that most people are not familiar with, and, since we are using a banjo also, I think we need a little different sound to keep us from being identified with <u>Bonnie and Clyde</u>, though the stuff they used in that film was ordinary indeed. But the twelve-string sound, if Mike and you can get together on it on that particular piece, is going to be <u>our</u> sound.

Well, we'll see. I'm going over to Clayton tomorrow to try. I'll get back to you whenever I have a chance. Meanwhile, just sit tight and wait to hear from me.

My very best, as always. And it was very good to talk to you the other night. I have <u>got</u> to see your museum!

All yours,

To: Helen Sorrells

CC, Emory University
4620 Lelia's Court
Columbia, S.C. 29206

May 17, 1971

Dear Helen:

I have your very handsome little book, for which I thank you with all that is left of my heart. I am very hard-pressed these days with the film version of <u>Deliverance</u> and a good many other things, but I sat down and read your book straight through. It is quite wonderful, as you surely know. You seem to me to be the finest of all my students, anywhere and everywhere, and believe me, there have been a lot of them, and I see their work all over the place. I am proud of this, and of the people I have helped to become themselves as writers, although, inevitably, there have been some I was a walking disaster for. One must risk that, and one must also risk being enormously heartened by <u>some</u> of the poets. You are foremost of these for me. Your beginnings as a poet were so very modest—I know you won't mind my saying this—and your progress so steady and certain that I feel very much that we got together at the right time and the right place. The proof of all this is in your book, which is one of the finest books of a new writer I have read in a long time. I hope you will rejoice in your quiet triumph as much as I do. I will probably have to come out to Hollywood a few more times in connection with the cutting, editing, publicity, and so on connected with the film of <u>Deliverance</u>, and maybe we could get together once more when this comes about. I do hope so, and will look forward to that as one of the good things in a very hard-pressed life. If you see any of our old people, like Robin Johnson or that strange girl who now spends part of her time in mental institutions, the one they call "Chickie," please remember me to them. I used to get torrential letters from Chickie, though for the life of me I can't even remember her name, as much as I should like to. Also remember me to any of the others you may be in contact with, including Dave Widner, for whom I was initially so bad, and who now tells me that he draws on our class very strongly for the work he is doing, which seems quite good to me.

But none is so good as yours, either from my students at Reid, from Valley State, from the University of Wisconsin, from Georgia Tech, from the University of South Carolina, or Harvard, or anywhere else. As a teacher, I consider you the absolute crown of my <u>experience</u> and effect as a teacher, and I hope you will be as happy as I am.

Whenever the spirit is on you, let me know how you are and what you are writing. But that shall be as you wish.

My very best to your husband, and to all those I know through you.

With every good wish,

To: Willie Morris

CC, Emory University
4620 Lelia's Court
Columbia, S.C. 29206

May 21, 1971

Dear Will:

Thank you so much for your letter, and for your enclosure of the jacket. I meant every word of it, and so, if this means anything, does Maxine. We both read <u>Yazoo</u> for the second time, and we are more convinced than ever that we made the right statement. I see the book reviewed everywhere, as it should be. It is tough to be a Southerner in our time, as you know and as I know. But certain things have to be done for the country, certain wrongs have to be righted, and certain associations have to be made possible and solidified. All this you say, much better than I could do.

Anyway, I hope you will keep in touch, and maybe come down and watch some of the filming of <u>Deliverance</u>, out here on this wild river. I have a private belief that anyone who sees this Chattooga River come up on the Panavision screen, shot for shot, is not going to believe what he sees; is not going to believe that something like this still exists, in these Eastern United States.

I hope we will have a very, very long association, Will. And it pleases me to call you Will as Ben Jonson would have called Shakespeare. It also pleases me that no one else in the whole world calls you Will but me. You say you are proud of our association, and I am doubly proud. I just received this afternoon the notification that "Haunting the Maneuvers" has been chosen one of the best poems of the year, or something like that. It is a source of very great chagrin to me that I will not be publishing under your editorship with <u>Harpers</u>, but the things we have done already should stand by themselves, as all such things <u>should</u> stand.

Anyway, I won't go on and on. You talk about a parallel between your situation now and my situation when I left Atlanta advertising in 1961. Surely such a parallel exists. I hope very much that you will do something that is as personally creative for you as what I did. I went out in my old battered MG, out to the archery range in the early morning, when there could not have possibly been anyone there, and strung up the bow and stepped down to the first shot, which was a thirty-yard shot. I looked around, and listened. A bird was doing his thing, off there to the right. The target was pretty chewed up, but it was there. I began to concentrate. I pulled the arrow back. The shot looked very good. I thought a minute, and I thought maybe I'm a little too high, or maybe a little to the right. I adjusted. Then I let go. And the thing went. It was in. I said to myself, Yes, Lord, I am here where I want to be. That is the feeling that one must have—that one should have—when one leaves a long-standing commitment that was never right to begin with. But the paradox is that I was Atlanta advertising's "Young Man of the year" in 1960, and that you are the best editor that Harper's Magazine has ever had in all its long and venerable history. But these things we put behind us. You are also a wonderful writer, which everyone knows, particularly me. If you need any further vote of confidence or any kind of brotherly assurance, please let me know, and I will do whatever you deem necessary for me to do.

Meanwhile, hang in there. You are one of the best of all of us, and I feel about you as I would about a younger brother who has done it, been done out of it, and will do it again.

Please say hello to Muriel for me. The end is not yet, by God.

All yours,

To: Jacques de Spoelberch

CC, Emory University
4620 Lelia's Court
Columbia, S.C. 29206

June 26, 1971

Dear Jacques:

Thank you very much for your note, and for your kindness in sending along the piece about Willie Morris, which I greatly enjoyed. Like most Southern writers, Willie is inclined to exaggerate a little bit, but what he says is essentially the case, though it sounds a lot better when he tells it. Anyway, thank you again for your thoughtfulness.

I have just got back to Columbia from the set, over in Rayburn County. Yesterday we were filming the part where Ed climbs the rock-face, and if there was ever a harrowing piece of film-making, this was it. Jon Voight did as much of the actual climbing as he was able to, and wanted to do more, but the director, John Boorman, was as frightened for his life as I was, and finally a Hollywood stunt man was used for some of the climbing stuff. But Voight did just as much dangerous climbing as the stunt man did, though at a lower level. Of course we haven't seen the rushes on this sequence yet, but I would bet that it is hair-raising. There are climbing shots that you can fake, but none of these were faked, and when you see it, remember that. Neither is the scene where Burt Reynolds, who plays Lewis, cascades down about ninety feet of hurricane-rushing water. Burt did this, and the shot of him doing it, which I <u>have</u> seen, are hair-raising indeed. If we can just get this gorge sequence out of the way, and the final run down the white water with Lewis in the bottom of the canoe, we will have finished pretty much of the really dangerous footage. We ought to wind up the actual shooting of the film about the first of August, and then John and I will go to Ireland to cut it, edit it, and put it together.

If you have a chance, during the next five weeks or so, come down and watch some of the shooting. I know you would enjoy seeing it, and meeting Boorman and the actors, who are all wonderful people, as the rest of the crew is. If you could let us know beforehand, we would surely fix you up with some nice accommodations.

Failing that, I <u>do</u> want you, as my editor on the novel, to attend one of the premiers with us, which should take place in March. As the plans are now shaping up, we will premier in New York, Atlanta, and Los Angeles at the same time, but the stars, myself, director, and so on will most probably be in Atlanta. It should be a very good occasion, and I would very much like for you to attend, if you can possibly do so.

Ross Claiborne, of Dell, tells me that we are really going to town in the paperback edition, which is fine with me, of course. All of this I owe in a very large measure to you, who worked with me so patiently and diligently and intelligently on the book. I am not inclined to gush; it is not my way, but if a writer ever had the right editor for him on the right book, it was you working with me on <u>Deliverance</u>, and now, look what has come of it! That's what I thought when I gaze up the sides of that rock wall in Tallulah Gorge that Boorman was asking John Voight to see if he could try to get up! I also thought: Lord, Dickey, what kind of horrendous situation have you got all these people—director, cameramen, actors, so on—into! I am deathly afraid that somebody will get hurt on this film, because there is no doubt that it is the most dangerous one ever made. But if we can just get out of the gorge . . .

Anyway, tell me if you might be able to come down either for some of the filming or for the premier. Or, ideally, for both.

Again, my very best. Maxine sends love too.

All yours,

To: Mike Russo   CC, Emory University
                                                  4620 Lelia's Court
                                                  Columbia, S.C. 29206

                                                  July 5, 1971

Dear Mike:

Please excuse the brevity of this letter, but I have to get back over to the set. I'm sure you can understand this, and forgive my seeming to get over, in single, short letter, things I should be taking more time with.

I like the new tape very much; it is the essential Russeau stuff. I talked for a while with my director, John Boorman, and his associates, over in Clayton, where the outdoor stuff is being shot. But I wanted you to know that I voluntarily left the set of my film so that two conditions could be carried out. One of these is that my son, Chris, would be retained as a cameraman and other functionary on the second unit for the remainder of the film. Boorman agreed to this, and has carried it out. The second consideration was that you and Ron would play the final, decisive music. John has not said anything to me about this beyond his promise that it would be carried out. I would like to know, from you, what provision has been made in this matter. I have no knowledge of whether John has sent you a copy of the final shooting script. But if he has, you will know that we have a sequence of visual images depicting the rising of the water over the valley of the Cahulawassee. This then modulates into a dream sequence in which Ed Gentry, the protagonist, played by Jon Voight, imagines himself as captured by the local sheriff—played, God help us, by me—and made to face up to the crimes he has committed. The music comes up very strong here, and I know that you and Ron will do us all credit with it.

Again, please do communicate with me about the situation which you have reached with John Boorman in regard to this music, as it pertains to the film. I have explained to John a number of times, that your music, and Ron's, is what I had in mind when I wrote the screen play, and I will not back up on that. But there is some kind of mysterious question of using musicians that Warner Brothers has contracted to use, and I will try to circumvent this as well as I can. But I might not be able to do it, even so. But understand that your music and Ron's is the music I want for the end of the movie, and I will do the most that is within my power to do to ensure that you are the musicians who play it, and get credit for it.

Meanwhile, thank you very much for sending me the new tape. There is a lot of work to be done with your music in regard to this film, and to a couple of others I will be doing. First, however, we must do <u>this</u> one. Then we can go on to the others.

My very best to your wife and family, and to Ron, if you see him. And I hope you do. But understand that I am trying to swing all the weight I can swing down here for your participation in this film. And, my God, is it ever going to be good! I don't believe the American public will believe, itself, what comes up on that panavision screen, next March. I want you and Ron in on the music, on the good times, and the rest. Let me hear from you, and we will go on from here, wherever that happens to be. And tell Wes Taft, if you see him, that I would like him to come down here too, if he can find a way to do so. He suggested that I should try to find some way to make Warner Brothers finance his trip down, but I have not been able to do that. But if he can come, and find his own way to come, I would be overjoyed to see him, as I will, definitely, you and Ron.

Do you have any notion where Ken Kipnis is, these days? I last saw him at the University of Chicago, where he was in process of becoming a philosophy professor, but I have heard nothing at all of him since that time.

Meanwhile, John Ullman tells me he is trying his desperate best to get back to this country, but I have no idea whatever what he intends to do when he gets back here. I hope you and Ron will keep me posted on these matters.

But the main business at hand is what we do now with the music for our film. I have exacted a promise from John Boorman that he will use you and Ron on the final, all-important sequence. I intend to hold him to that. Perhaps he has found a way to get out of it, and use Warner Brothers musicians, but I will try my very best, you have my word, to cut him off at the pass, if he has any such intentions. Well, we'll see.

All yours,

To: Stewart Richardson

CC, Emory University
4620 Lelia's Court
Columbia, S.C. 29206

July 26, 1971

Dear Sandy:

Thank you for your last letter, and please forgive me for waiting so long to answer it, but I have been over in the north Georgia hills making this blood-thirsty, dangerous movie, and haven't had time for any correspondence at all. But what a film it is going to be! I don't believe the American public—or any-body else, for that matter—is going to believe what they see when it comes up on that panavision screen. I saw part of the rough cut day before yesterday, and it is mighty, mighty frightening. The movie is going to be attacked and defended all over the place. The location was crawling with <u>Life</u> and <u>Time</u> and <u>Newsweek</u> and <u>Esquire</u> and <u>Look</u> people, and they are all going to do stories on it, mostly covers. The actors are exhausted. We did the last stunt today, wherein Burt Reynolds, who plays Lewis, gets catapulted twenty feet up in the air from the back of the canoe and comes down, supposedly, on a rock. The script calls for Burt, a former stunt man, to miss the rock a little bit, just on the other side, but he may not have missed it. Anyway, I am sitting here by the phone waiting to get the news for Boorman that he landed on the rock with his head. Burt himself told me that he waited to do this scene last in case he were to get killed. In other words, if Burt got his brains knocked out, we would still have our footage! I don't think that happened, but I don't know that it didn't. As I say, I'm waiting to hear.

When I get your return letter, I will send you the complete notebook to date. There is three or four times more material down here than you have up there, and you might as well have a look at all of it. Give me your thoughts on the way we should organize the book, which I think, now, we should call, sim-ply, <u>Sorties</u>, instead of <u>Sorties and Returns</u>, as we had tentatively planned. I get tired of "and" titles, and <u>Sorties</u> itself is an unusual enough word to make a better title than it "and" something else. I'd like you to pay particular atten-tion to the long series of entries in Notebook II dealing with the novel that I am now trying to get together in my head, <u>Death's Baby Machine</u>. You can get some kind of idea as to what the novel is going to be about, plus some of the ways in which I hope to go about doing it, plus some of the characters, scenes, and so on. It is coming together slowly, on airplanes, long automobile rides, and all the other things that I have to be doing these days in connection with the film. I know you will give me an awful lot of help on this book, and I am certainly going to need it. But I have written a few notes toward what I think are some very exciting scenes, and I think the book is going to be awfully good, although I have no way of knowing whether it will have the general appeal that <u>Deliverance</u> had; I expect not. However, riding on the publicity we have gotten from <u>Deliverance</u>, the film, and the other things, it may have an enormous initial sale, and that will interest people enough in the <u>quality</u>—or what I hope will be the quality—of the book to carry the day despite the fact that it is not the novel of action such as <u>Deliverance</u> is. But there is a beautiful love story, I think, and this may help things too. After all, <u>Deliverance</u> did without one of those, which isn't supposed to be possible in a best-seller.

Anyway, get back to me in a few days, and let me know whether you are ready for me to send all the material from the journals that I have amassed so far. I remember you told me we were thinking about bringing <u>Sorties</u> out in October, and, as far as I know, that is more or less what you intend to do. Keep me up to date on this, and I will swing with you, whichever way you want to swing.

I'm very, very happy that Genia Yevtushenko liked the translations I did, tried to call me up about them, and so on. Kate Medina has already told me about this, and I am very happy that it all turned out so well.

My very best to Sally and to Ken and all those I know up there. I'll have to come up there in August in connection with the first showing of the work-print of the film, and we'll get together if you're in town. I will sure look forward to that, I can tell you.

All yours,

To: Stanley Burnshaw   **TLS, University of Texas at Austin**

4620 Lelia's Court
Columbia, S.C. 29206
July 29, 1971

Dear Stanley:

Please <u>do</u> forgive me for waiting so long to answer your good letter, but I have been over in the woods, infested with mosquitoes, chiggers, and all manner of bestioles, plus having legs and arms and heads bashed in on rocks on the wild and savage Chattooga River, almost falling off cliffs, and the rest. We are trying to make this movie, and it is going to be something else, I can promise you. I don't believe the American public has ever seen a screen open up on the dreadful and exalting things that we are going to show next March, in New York, Los Angeles, London, and, probably, Atlanta. Anyway, I have been crawling around in the woods and rivers, and have simply not had time to answer any mail, or even be aware of the existence of any mail.

But I am back now, and I will try to answer your questions as best I can. My advice would be to issue a large retrospective volume with the new poems being the first in the book, so that the reviewers would see them first, be impressed by them, as they will damn well have to be, and then go on to the other and older poems, equally good, but not in the same way, in the other parts of the book. I will get the book and review it as soon as it comes out, but I do think that the time has come for a kind of retrospective showing of your work. I think the term New and Selected is a kind of kiss of death, so my advice would simply be to have a book with a new title and have it be a "new and selected" without advertising that on the cover. You are one of the really big, good and deep poets that we have around, and I don't want people to review you as though it were a kind of post-mortem. No; they should review this book as any other that comes out, and I will wager that discerning reviewers will look at your work as that of an ever-vital, developing, exciting writer. I think that a big retrospective volume—again, with the new poems first in the volume to be first read—would be the best way to do this. As I say, I will get it for review, and we will kick it off with the Times, or somewhere equally important. I can't guarantee this, for John Leonard may have other plans, but I will sure try.

Congratulations on your being the judge of the Arts and Letters category of the NBA. I have a new book coming out called Sorties, which may or may not qualify for that category. Again, I don't know.

My very best to you, your lovely wife, and to the whole operation that you form the center of. Let me know what you decide to do about your book, and I will swing with you.

All yours,
Jim

To: Bill Little

CC, Emory University
4620 Lelia's Court
Columbia, S.C. 29206

August 13, 1971

Dear Mr. Little:

Thank you for your very kind letter of July 2, and I hope you will forgive me for waiting so long to answer it, but I have not even been here, but over in the north Georgia mountains making the film version of my novel, <u>Deliverance</u>. I am very much pleased that you are going to do a brief profile of me for your column, and I hardly know how to answer your question as to what my philosophy of life is. I suppose it is essentially religious, though I certainly am not religious in any orthodox sense. I would say that I believe in the basic life force, whatever it is. I think, really, that the key to living a successful human life is in what the French novelist' and essayist Henry de Montherlant calls <u>alternance</u>, or alternation, variety. What I take his point to be is that we should have lots of different <u>kinds</u> of experience. I am surely for that; it is better for us if we have some such life, rather than a humdrum one of routine. Again, as Samuel Johnson once answered to a question much like yours, "Sir, the secret of a man's living a successful human life is for him to know something about everything and everything about one thing."

And that is about as well as I can do, I think, Mr. Little. I ask in return only that you send me a copy of your column, which I am very much looking forward to seeing.

Again, I must apologize for waiting so long, but I have been so hard pressed that I have damn near been pushed right out of the universe itself. God knows where I almost ended up!

Sincerely yours,

To: Stanley Burnshaw   **TLS, University of Texas at Austin**

4620 Lelia's Court
Columbia, S.C. 29206
August 18, 1971

Dear Stanley:

Very good to get your August 10 letter and to know that you are moving forward on the big volume of your work. Again, I can't stand <u>that</u> firm on having the new poems first, but I would surely recommend it, and I am happy that Peter Davison agrees with me. The point is to show <u>different</u> phases of one's writing. Auden once said that the sure test of a minor poet is to look at his poems and see no difference in the poems of different periods. That is, there should be a <u>progression</u>. I want to hit them with the new stuff first, and then let them ease back into the other things, for the various felicities of different periods. That would be my suggestion, for whatever it is worth.

As to the film, I am pretty much in the dark, myself. Now that we have shot all the footage, it looks as though John Boorman, my director, and I will go to

London to cut and edit the film and then bring it back over here and show it to a kind of selected audience around the middle of December. I will sound John out on the possibility of having a few <u>very</u> select friends at the private screening, whenever we get ready to do it. I'll keep you posted on all this, and we will be guided according to what John Boorman and Warner Brothers thinks we ought to do at any given time. But I am fairly sure that I can get you in, and I will proceed with John on that basis, until something else intervenes, if it does—and it almost always does.

<u>Sorties</u> will be out, God willing, in November, at which time I will make sure that you get a copy. It is a strange kind of book—mostly essays in literary criticism interspersed with entries of a kind of undated journal that I have been keeping for the past few years. Anyway, I hope you'll find some things in it to like. And, again, I will be sure to see that you get an early copy, just as soon as the thing is set up in type.

I would love to come up there to Martha's Vineyard, and bring Maxine—<u>without</u> a sprained ankle, this time, Lord willing—and Kevin, but it doesn't look like it will be possible this year. But <u>do</u> know that all of us value our time up there as good lived time, good human time, and when can any of us ever have enough of that?

Please remember us to Luciano, and all the others that we met and remember so warmly from our few days with you a couple of years ago. This will all be renewed, believe me, once the hullabaloo over <u>Deliverance</u>, the making of the film, the publicity, and the rest of it, is all over with. But that will take a little while. I am very happy, though, to wait it out, knowing that you and your wife and Luciano and Martha's Vineyard will be waiting for us when the tumult and the shouting dies.

Believe me, I know very well what you mean about the responsibility of judging a thing like the NBA. Roger Stevens has asked me to be one of the poetry judges, but I have put him off, at least temporarily, by saying that I did not want to jeopardize the chances of <u>Sorties</u> in the Arts and Letters category by being a judge in another category. I don't know how these things are done, really. But <u>Sorties</u> will almost surely be my last book of criticism, and, if any recognition is ever going to be given to the work I have done in criticism, it will have to be for this book. So—I told Mr. Stevens that I would be very happy to serve as a poetry judge if he could more or less assure me that this would not interfere with the chances of <u>Sorties</u> in the Arts and Letters category. What do you advise, on this score?

My very best to you, Stanley, as always. Maxine sends love, and so does my vulnerable boy, Kevin. And when he sends love, he sends <u>love</u>. He tells me to caution Stanley not to go <u>too</u> far out into that cold, cold water, and my God, it is ever <u>cold</u>! Believe me, we don't have any water like <u>that</u> down here in the swamps and pine barrens!

All yours,
Jim

To: Stanley Burnshaw   **TLS, University of Texas at Austin**

4620 Lelia's Court
Columbia, S.C. 29206
27 August, 1971

Dear Stanley:

Well, as they say in South Carolina, that is some kind of good letter. Let me get right to your points about your book. <u>The Terrified Radiance</u> is good. However, you might consider dropping off the article, or changing the phrasing in some kind of way, such as <u>In the Terrified Radiance</u>, or something like that, maybe, or something like <u>Facing the Terrified Radiance</u>. These are just possibilities to fool around with, as I would do if the poems were mine, and the book mine—that is, really, the only way in which I can approach <u>your</u> book, as another poet would be the first to know and recognize. But the idea and the concept—and above all the <u>possibility</u> of the <u>Terrified Radiance</u> is very powerfully <u>taking</u>, as they also say in South Carolina. Question is, how to get a phrase as good as this one to give out with its maximum power. Well, it can be done, and I'll depend on you to tell me what you finally decide. I look at it this way: you've already got very much of a winner as a title.

Now, as to your dilemma about chronology, I can say this: I think you are entirely too worried about such things as "showing progression," and so on. I don't think that the poetry-reading audience cares nearly so much about when poems were published, what collections they first appeared in, or any of that. You are, after all, not presenting something for graduate students to date and write about, but are putting forth a book of living, vital poems. In other words, you are getting in front of the reader a number of <u>good</u> <u>poems</u>, and that matters more than the notion of showing the reader how and by what means the later poems evolved from the earlier—if they did; and that is always questionable. My point is to throw the emphasis on the artistic and imaginative quality of the poems, and not on their historical dating, or anything of that kind. If it were me—and again, that's the only way actual and honest criterion I've got—I would mix the whole business up. I would have only one standard, and that would be this: in what sequence do I want to hit the reader with these poems? How do I want him to go through my work? And I think that historical periods should, ultimately, have very little or nothing to do with it. You think your later poems are your best work. Very well; so do I. Print those first, and then scale the book on down, for a while at least, through poems that you think are good and should be printed, but are not as great as the ones you print first, and then finish the book with another bunch of pieces that you <u>do</u> think are great. There is no substitute for starting strong and finishing strong. <u>Pace</u> the thing, and your readers will go right with you. I not only believe it: I <u>know</u> it.

To get onto something else, I heard from the Warners people yesterday, and it looks as though we'll have some kind of private screening in December, and I'll sure try, by guess and by God—as we used to say of our navigation in the old days of the Air Force—to get you in. Some of the film is so utterly horrifying that the author himself can't even face the screen. But my God, what <u>excitement</u> we've got here! And what dealing with gut issues! I don't think that any of us connected with the film have any real idea of what we're sitting on top of, here. But that's all to see, in the future. I am scared to death that we've got an unbearable masterpiece on our hands. To tell you the truth, I don't know exactly what to feel or how to respond. But the thing is in motion now, and, as the Chinese are supposed to say, he who rides a tiger fears to dismount. Anyway, by God, we'll see what happens.

About the National Book Award jury thing, I am also about as confused as it is possible to be. I wrote to Roger Stevens about the fact that I didn't want to screw up the chances for <u>Sorties</u> by serving as a judge in another category. He wrote back immediately that my serving on the poetry panel would do no such thing: that it would, in fact, have nothing whatever to do with my candidacy in the Arts and Letters category.

But I would rather take your advice than his. But the thing is, that they are leaning on me awfully hard for a decision. So—I'll wait to hear from you on this, and make the decision on the basis of what you tell me. What you said in your other letter about getting good judges, competent judges, for these things, is very important to me. Otherwise we are going to end up with things like the Bly fiasco, or the unspeakable travesty and horror of the Ginsberg performance last year. None of this is good for American letters, or for American poetry, or for poets or the imaginative life. But if you think I shouldn't serve this time, I'll tell Stevens and his boys just that. Again, let me know what you think I should do.

As for your own judgeship—or whatever one might call it—are you the only one doing it, or what? Stevens tells me, for example, that there are now

<u>five</u> judges for poetry. And what the hell do you do with <u>that</u> kind of a thing? If there are other judges in Arts and Letters, who are the other ones? I've been up against some bad juries, as we all have, and I think it's just as well to know what the situation is, in these cases. If you're the guy—the only guy or the main guy—it will sure make a difference. If there are other fellows involved who might, say, swing the thing to Leslie Fiedler, or if there were any of my numerous enemies on the panel, I had just as soon take Stevens' offer and get on the poetry panel and make a stand against the assholes who clutter up and often dominate these things.

Again, I'll wait to hear, and will move when you tell me how.

Love from us,

Jim

And Kevin says you needn't warm up the water at the Vineyard. He likes it like it is, like it was, like he remembers it.

To: John Boorman   CC, Emory University
                                                    4620 Lelia's Court

5 September, 1971
Columbia, S.C.
U.S.A.

Dear John:

Very good indeed to hear from you, and at such length, too! I was in New York last week in connection with the editing I had to do on a new book, and saw Ross Claiborne of Dell. He is on top of the new printing of the paperback, and, if you will coordinate with him and make sure that Warners does, we can easily make the reprinting break to our advantage not approximately but exactly. The Dell people are very excited by the situation. The book has already sold over a million copies, and Ross tells me that it will surely sell another million—or more—as a result of the movie. I talked with him about covers, and I think that the subject deserves a good deal of serious thought. He feels that we should use one of the stills from the movie itself. You feel that we should use the logo we finally decide on. Myself, I'm not sure. My feeling is that if we get a good <u>enough</u> logo, we might go with that. If we don't, it might be of more advantage to use a scene from the film—maybe the one of Burt getting catapulted out of the canoe.

The Falling Man. This could be striking, but it also has a couple of disadvantages. First of all, it may be too much like a good many other such designs that have been used in connection with films (please forgive me if I talk like

Vice President Ed Gentry here!) The other is that it seems to indicate that somebody falls—actually falls, and that isn't the case. In this sense it is kind of misleading, and I don't think that this is a situation we want to get ourselves into. Since I got your letter I have been sitting around thinking of what we might do, here. In our logo, we should certainly play to the strength of our movie, our story. You say that bows and arrows and canoeing are redolent of cowboys and westerns. That might <u>tend</u> to be the case, but, like other things, the effect depends on the <u>way</u> in which the thing is done. I can see a semi-abstract design of a canoe prow, and I can see—or think I can, something with an arrow (that is, a very <u>modern</u>, factory-made, stylish arrow) and I can see an extremely abstract image of of an eye bisected by a bowstring. It could be done in just two or three lines, so that it is not apparent at first—or maybe later, either—what it is. I wouldn't mind at all if there were something of the conversation-piece about it, and a few million sherry-party arguments about what the hell the damned thing is. But, despite my objections, the Falling Man is fine, and if you want to use him, go ahead. I ask only that you consider these other things, and add to these some new ideas of your own.

Another thing occurs to me. Since so much of the heart-stopping part of the movie is Ed's cliff climb, might we not do something with that? That is, not a Falling Man but a Climbing Man? True, it is also equally true that a man climbing a sheer cliff with a bow on his back is at least, shall we say, distinctive. Of course he might be after Dall Sheep or mountain goats or something, but we might be able to make it seem—well, that that's not his aim. Again, I don't know. Ponder it and tell me what you decide. But I do indeed believe that the Climbing Man might serve us better than the Falling Man, in view of what actually does in fact take place in our film. I'll go with you, as I always have.

And to France: sure. I'll talk to Rissient, and we'll work out whatever needs to be worked out. Just let me know what you want me to do. I'd like an excuse to go to Paris, anyway. But just keep me posted. That is vital, as we move through time on this thing.

As to the ending of the film. I agree with you completely on your assessment of the character of Ed, as he comes through the thing and gets to the other side of it. Catharsis and all that—I don't worry about that, nor, indeed, about Aristotle and his ideas. But old Aristotle—and I don't mean Onassis—brings up questions that we probably ought to consider, even so. For example, how would we <u>show</u> catharsis if we <u>wanted</u> to? No, no: your way is better. We should leave it up to the audience. I don't believe in spelling things out. If you want to add "additional dialogue," you should just have Jon ask Burt about his leg, and have Burt say, "It's still stiff, but it"s gonna be all right. It's about a half inch shorter than the other one, but I've got a notion that everything is going to even out, in the end."

Something like that.

But what I want more than anything else is the sense, at the end, of a man with a secret victory. He doesn't have to make a big thing of this, even with himself. In fact, it's better if he doesn't: better even to himself. Just the same, he knows what he's capable of, even though maybe only once. He knows it, and he knows he knows it. When nobody's watching, he smiles, just a little. Catharsis be damned: the thing happens so deep inside, in this case, that it just barely surfaces: again, in secret. The thing is there. It happened, though no one would believe it. It happened, and I did it. (This is Ed talking, if the police question you!)

I long to see you, and look forward to all the good times, controversy, attacks, and so on, that are coming. Also to your letter of fogiveness when I run off with Daisy.

Much love from us,

To: Stanley Burnshaw   RTLS, University of Texas at Austin

4620 Lelia's Court
Columbia, S.C. 29206
September 8, 1971

Dear Stanley:

I have acted on your advice, and declined to participate in the poetry jury for the upcoming National Book Awards. Believe me, I realize that the chance of Sorties is an outside one at best. But, as I said in another letter, it is almost certain to be my last critical book, and I would like to give it the best chance I can to win the award. I know Fred Morgan from being a long-time contributor to Hudson Review. Mr. Lahr I know only from seeing him on the Today Show when his book came out. I was not so moved by his appearance as to go out and buy the book, though I did see his father on opening night in Waiting for Godot. I also ran into the elder Lahr in a bar after the performance, where there were a lot of people milling around and clapping him on the back, and I asked him what the hell the play was about? His answer, as I remember, was, "Believe me, son, I don't know. But I do know that my appearance in it is the best thing that my career has to show, after all these years. But don't ask me what it's about! I don't know what the hell I mean when I say, 'It looks like my shoes are green.'" Anyway, at least I don't feel like I'm up against a stacked deck, as though Robert Bly, Robert Creeley, and other of my numerous enemies were on the jury. No; I will just put <u>Sorties</u> up there, and see what happens. Edmund Wilson will surely be the sentimental favorite, but there is a heartening trend in literary awards these days <u>not</u> to give the award, as though one were giving John Wayne the award for <u>True Grit</u>, on the basis of his having been around a long time. I myself think Edmund Wilson is the most over-rated literary critic I have ever read. Though he is relatively astute, he is, as a critic, exactly as he characterized Stephen Vincent Benêt as a poet: "He writes the kind of criticism that anyone would write if he had gone into the writing of criticism instead of the insurance business." His work is one long tissue of self-indulgent clichés and self-aggrandizement. And when I read the Lowells in the <u>New York Review of Books</u> talk about what a "great writer" he is, I feel the sudden cold touch which indicates the prevelance of literary log-rolling in this country. Edmund Wilson is a great writer to the Lowells and to the <u>New</u> <u>York Review of Books</u> simply because he endorses Lowell as a poet. That's the kind of thing that must be broken down, if we are ever to have a true and free literature in this country. End of sermon.

I am very happy that you have decided to follow my advice and begin with all the new poems. I also think it is a good idea to follow with selections from your three earlier books. And your idea of going in reverse order, after that, is also extremely interesting. I would have to see the manuscript—and I hope you <u>do</u> send it down—to see how this works out. But it surely sounds good. I am looking forward very eagerly to the manuscript, and to the book, too. I have asked Roger Stevens to hold off on my being a member of the jury this year in favor of my being a member of it next year. I have never sat on a five-man jury before, but the fiasco last time, with Ginsberg using the judgeship simply as another platform, and the business a couple of years ago with political-minded friends giving Bly the award for the express purpose of his being able to get up and make a political speech, does not entrance me, to say the least, with the notion of serving as a National Book Award juror in poetry again. But the good thing is that your book will be one of the nominees, and though one man can't do everything there is to be done in a five-man jury, he can sure as hell do <u>something</u>. Carolyn Kaizer—almost a man—swung the jury in favor of Mona Van Duyn last time, which, regrettably, set Ginsberg up for his public pronouncement, but also, on the good side, gave Richard Howard a chance to come back at him, publically in the <u>New York Times</u>, with a very witty put-down of Ginsberg and his ilk. Anyway, I will begin to arrange things with Stevens and these other people about this time next year, if they still want me on the jury. And from their letters to me urging me to serve on this one, I am sure they will. But—we'll see how all that comes out.

Meanwhile, <u>do</u> send me a Xerox of the whole manuscript, and I'll go over it carefully and come back to you with my comments.

I am very happy that <u>some</u> good people are getting into positions of authority. American poetry and American letters generally, are at stake. And nothing can be more important than that.

I'll be here for about three more weeks, so if you need to communicate, just write to me here in Columbia.

My love to all. Maxine and Kevin send love too.

All yours,
Jim

To: Michael Blowen

CC, Emory University
4620 Lelia's Court
Columbia, S.C. 29206

September 15, 1971

Dear Mike:

Thank you very much for the letter, for the box of books, and for all your kindnesses to me. I am sorry that you didn't care much for the Buckley program. Bill tells me that there has been an awful lot of mail on it, some of which I have received. Some liked it, some didn't like it, and so on. But Bill tells me that the response, from <u>both</u> camps, has been larger than that of any Firing Line program he has had since the beginning. I hardly know what to make of all this, myself. But, as you say, I was more or less in Buckley's domain, rather than he being in mine, and that makes a difference, never think otherwise. Anyway, I'm glad the thing is over, and that both Bill and I got a few things said, for better or worse. I'm quite sure that such occasions have a tendency to sink without a trace, and one can only hope that <u>some</u> good was done in some kind of manner. But that shall be as posterity wishes.

I am very happy that you have gone into archery, because it is a breathtakingly beautiful sport. Bear makes a good bow; it is surely the best bow that is mass produced. If you shoot 200 arrows a day, you are probably rapidly approaching a sort of perfection that it has never been mine to attain. Anyway, it is a lovely sport, and I am very happy that you are in it. I have played most sports in my time, except those in which you fasten sliding things to your feet—like skating or skiing—and I can firmly vouch for the fact that nothing

I have ever done has given me more sheer pleasure than shooting arrows. I hope you will like the use of archery in the film version of <u>Deliverance</u>; it is terrifyingly true, and terrifyingly horrible. Also beautiful.

I agree with you about <u>The French Lieutenant's Woman</u>; I could not get through it. It just seemed like a kind of gimmick book, like most of the rest of Fowles' stuff. I don't think I will ever have occasion to read anything of his again.

I am very happy that you are teaching the poems of mine that you say you are teaching in your class. Also, thanks for the comment on the poem in <u>Esquire</u> about Vince Lombardi. If you want to do me and you and other poets a favor, write to the <u>Esquire</u> people—in their letters to the editor column—your feelings about this particular poem. As poetry editor, I am trying to get <u>Esquire</u> to open up its pages and give more space and more <u>authority</u> to the poetry that we print. Like most magazines, <u>Esquire</u> is very letter-to-the-editor-prone, and whatever you write to them will very likely get printed. They run surveys on this sort of thing, and all that sort of business. But you would be doing us all a favor if you wrote to <u>Esquire</u> about the Lombardi poem, because that is the first big one we've had, the first major space we've had, and so on. I want to get the poets I publish out of these little tiny places between the men's deodorant ads and necktie ads and get the poems up there with the exposé articles and the other things that <u>Esquire</u> specializes in. If we could do this, people might see that there is a great deal more in poetry than there is in yet another ephemeral article on the Black Panthers, or whatever. So—if you're of a mind, write to Harold Hays and the other people at <u>Esquire</u> and tell them what you think about the poems, and about the idea of <u>Esquire</u> printing poetry, generally. But that shall be as you wish.

Again, thank you so very much for your letter, and for the things you say. Incidentally, thank you also for the clipping, which is almost as horrible as <u>Deliverance</u>, and for sending your letter to me with two stamps of Emily Dickinson. The fact that the American government would issue stamps under the imprint of Emily Dickinson is a good sign for us all. Again, thanks; thanks for it all. And let me hear from you whenever you have a chance. I must be in New York for a film festival on the 8th of October, and maybe we could get together at that time, though I will only be there for one day. I'll probably be at the St. Moritz, but check this out, either through me here, or through my agent, Theron Raines at 244 Madison Avenue. Theron can tell you where I am going to be and when I am going to be there.

Again, my best, Mike, for your many kindnesses to me.

All yours,

To: Vernon White

CC, Emory University
4620 Lelia's Court
Columbia, S.C. 29206

October 25, 1971

Dear Vernon:

Thank you so very much indeed for the new stills, and for your wonderful letter. Maxine and Kevin and I miss you so very much, we keep trying to invent excuses to get together with you once again.

Meanwhile, I met with John Boorman in New York, and he and I and Joe Hyams went over some of the logos and other publicity devices that Warner Brothers proposed. John and I agreed that one of these might have possibilities, and we are going to explore it a little further. The point is to get an all-encompassing visual _image_ which we would use in publicizing the film, and which would also appear on the cover of the new edition of the paperback, timed to come out at the same time that the movie premiers. This is terribly important, and I would surely, as we used to say in the ad business, like to have your thoughts on this, as well. I think we have _one_ design idea that might work pretty well. This is of four men carrying a canoe, and what appears to be the reflection in the water of their carrying the canoe turns out to be their carrying a human body. That is clever, but I am not sure that it could work, not be over-subtle, and so on. Anyway, get with Hyams and have him show you this and his other projected designs, and let me know what you think. We are still five months out, or practically so, but it is not too soon to begin to coordinate things. Believe me, if I remember anything from American business, it is the fact that if you allow yourself too little time, or allow time to creep up on you, as it always, inevitably does, you are running around from corner to corner trying to patch things up. If you _have_ time, you should use it, to bring the thing up to a smooth consummation. That is what we want to do with _this_ one, and we are damn fools if we don't work it just exactly like that. End of sermon.

Meanwhile, a lot is going on. I have just got a new set of arrows, and a new set of strings on my guitar. I think that it is quite possible that I will go into northern Alberta with Fred Bear at a place called Bella Coola, to hunt the giant grizzly. If you want to declare yourself in, tell me, and I'll tell Fred. Maybe we could end up, or maybe end our lives, up in that virgin territory, with a thousand pound creature coming straight at us and no way to hold him off. You'd have to hit him through the spinal cord, and believe me, under these circumstances, that ain't easy! I think old Kevin and I will go, and, if you want to go too, let me know.

But please <u>do</u> know, in any case, that we think of you very frequently and warmly in our house, Vernon. Let me know what you need from me, and I will surely be guided accordingly. I am delighted that the film is stirring up the interest that it is. I don't think the American public is going to be able to shake it off easily. But—we'll see, in any case.

Can you come and spend time with us one of these mild, winter, South Carolina days? We would surely look forward to it, I can tell you.

Meanwhile, love to all in your house. And send all the pictures and things you can get hold of. They are surely much appreciated at this end.

All yours,

P.S. And thank you again <u>so</u> very much for the newspaper clipping about Jack London. He and I will get into the White Silence yet, believe me! Yes, and bring you with us!

To: Stanley Burnshaw   **TLS, University of Texas at Austin**

4620 Lelia's Court
Columbia, S.C. 29206
27 November, 1971

Dear Stanley:

Some strange things have happened, just in the last couple of days. The main thing is that the French edition of <u>Deliverance</u> has won the Prix Medici, given—or so I was told—for the best foreign language book published in France during the year. This is all quite confusing to me, but I felt that I am more or less obligated to go to Paris today to receive the prize. It is supposed to be a great honor, and all that, but I had <u>so</u> much rather stay here and work on the new poems I have finally been able to start; some kind of new direction, and maybe, with luck, several of them. But, as it is, I'm getting on yet another airplane in a few minutes and going to Paris. At least I'll have Maxine and Kevin with me, and it will be fun to show Kevin what little of Paris I know. I haven't been over there in nine years, and perhaps it is time I went back. Anyway, here we go. I thought it would please you to know that your judgment on my work is vindicated—yes, and in <u>several</u> languages! It is good for me, too, to know that the man who has written the best book ever written on poetry <u>might</u> be pleased at this latest thing.

I'm also very happy that you like <u>Sorties</u>, and I will be indulging in that hope you speak of. I had a copy of the book sent along to Fred Morgan as you suggested. I don't know where in the world Lahr is—that is, is in London, which is a mighty big place. But if you and Fred like it—particularly you—I will be plenty satisfied. And thanks, also, for the backstopping on the typos. I am wretched as a proof-reader. The only only of my books that doesn't have any is <u>Helmets</u>, and that was only because Dick Wilbur was my editor then.

Your questions: Jefferies' <u>Story</u> <u>of</u> <u>My Heart</u> is an old, old book, published sometime in the late nineteenth century. His publisher was Longmans, and, when they published <u>Helmets</u> in England I asked the present editor if I could get any of Jefferies' works. He said they were all out of print, that he no longer had any requests for them. But the Gotham Book Mart might be able to get it for you; that's where I got my copy.

Yes, Lucien Becker is very good; by far the best of the more recent fellows that I, personally, have read. I feel that he has something special for <u>me</u>, which is the way one wants to feel about poets.

My nomination of you was indeed for the National Gold Medal. But not a single one of my candidates was on the final list, which shows you about how much clout <u>I</u> carry around there! Anyway, when one has the chance, one should try. Andy White finally won it, which is a complete mystery to me. He's a nice fellow, but clearly not of that caliber. Well, there'll be other times, and the right man will win it yet.

The business about Epstein I just picked out of a local newspaper column. The gist of it was that Epstein was kept by the FBI for a period of time—a couple of weeks at least—and then emerged from their dungeons to make a statement about the self-aggrandizement that New York intellectuals—he says—indulge themselves in concerning politics. He issued a complete recantation of his own position. I'm not sure where you could look this up, but the <u>New</u> <u>York</u> <u>Review of Books</u> (an organ I simply cannot get through an issue of, myself) is bound to have had a lot about it. Question is: when? I should say about eight months ago.

Maxine and Kevin and I all send the best and deepest love we have. And please <u>do</u> stop by and stay with us when you come through Columbia. I would look forward to such a visit with a lot greater eagerness than I would going to Paris, I can tell you.

All yours,
Jim

To: Stanley Burnshaw   TLS, University of Texas at Austin

4620 Lelia's Court
Columbia, S.C. 29206
9 Decembre, 1971

Dear Stanley:

We just got back from Paris, and I mailed your manuscript back to Seaver right away; he should have it by now. I'm so very sorry that I didn't get a chance to go over it with you page by page, poem by poem, but events have just not allowed it. But it is a wonderful book, full of the most wonderful things, the keenest and deepest insights. You are the only writer of all of us who has found a way to combine what I call the European imagination—the super-sensitive and nuance-filled type of insightfulness and imagination—and the drive and iron of English. It is quite a thing to do, and there's no doubt about that. The world will come to you, because it has to.

The Paris trip was hectic, but exhilirating. AS it turned out, I myself didn't get much a chance to see Paris, for I had a solid week of interviews, nine to five, and sat there hour after hour trying to talk to reporters and critics in broken French—and broken English—until I had quite literally exhausted my entire fund of human knowledge on all subjects. My God, the French really take these prize-things seriously! But I'm glad we had a chance to go, for Kevin took in a lot of the great town, and Maxine, as she dearly loves to do, got in some shopping—and even had an interview or two herself!

But it sure is good to be back, and the prospect of getting together with you later on is the best thing about it. Let me hear from you again when you have a chance; I'll be here in South Carolina until the last of January.

My very best, as always.

All yours,
Jim

To: Christopher Sinclair-Stevenson   CC, Emory University
4620 Lelia's Court
Columbia, S.C. 29206

December 15, 1971

Dear Christopher:

Thank you very much for your note of December 7. Maxine and Kevin and I have just returned from Paris, where the French translation of <u>Deliverance</u> was given the Prix Medicis, which I am told is the highest award that can go to a non-French book. Believe me, the French take these award things seriously! We were over there a week, and, though Maxine and Kevin got to walk around the great city a little bit, I myself was closeted with interviewers, journalists, critics, and so on, from 9 to 5 every day of our time in Paris. Anyway, I hope the award will please you and Jamie and the others. Believe me, it was a hectic time for me, and I hope very much that it will be a good sales-boost for our handsome British edition. The award is given, as you no doubt know, for the best novel not written in French, but translated, and available to French readers. It was said at the beginning that an Italian book and a German book were the leading contenders. But, since Deliverance won, I can have but bewilderment and gratitude. A little lady French journalist crept up to me during the festivities and said, "I am so glad an American book won! But you can believe that it will be a long time before another one wins!"

Well—so be it. But if there is any way that the winning of this award can tie in with our effort, please let me know, and I will be guided accordingly.

The film was originally scheduled for this March, but Warner Brothers now tells me that the computers have spoken, and indicated that it would be better for all concerned if we waited through an elaborately long publicity build-up and released the movie in October. I have nothing to do with this, and will just ride along with what Warner Brothers suggests. They have sunk so much money into the film that I am quite sure that they are looking after their best interests, and I must believe, as is common place in these instances, that their best interests are also mine. Anyway, we'll see.

Meanwhile, what a film we have got! It will be very good to show it to you, or to get your reactions when somebody else shows it to you. I don't believe that anyone who ever walks into the theater to see it will ever walk out quite the same person. I won't say any more, but will just hope that you'll keep in touch with us so that we can bring the whole thing forward: the Hamish Hamilton edition, the Prix Medicis, the movie, and all the personal friendships that otherwise would not have existed. Believe me, these last are the most important; the only kind that endure. As for the other things, these too shall pass away. . . But Maxine and myself and Kevin look forward to seeing you again, under whatever conditions may bring this about. We remember you all with affection and honor.

All yours,

P.S. Tell Joe Hone that I haven't been able to comply with his latest request, but if he will take my letter and get whatever excerpts from it seem to him to further his cause, he is surely welcome to them. I ask only that he let me know what he intends to use, and how he intends to use it.

To: Stanley Burnshaw   TLS, University of Texas at Austin

4620 Lelia's Court
Columbia, S.C. 29206
January 5, 1972

Dear Stanley:

Thank you very much for your lovely Christmas letter. The New York Times book review of Sorties was so inanely silly that it could scarcely bother a ninny, which I ain't—at least most of the time, anyway. I don't know what gets into these Greenwich Village people when they start talking about Southerners. The irony of it is that Boryard is furious with the hayseed Southerner for being taken in by the big city slickers of the East Village, because I wrote an introduction for an anthology—rather a bad one, too—which featured some of their work. The truth of the matter is that I dislike the work of these people very much indeed, and, if I had it to do over again, I would not have done the introduction. The editor sent me the book, and I told him I didn't like the poetry in it, or at least most of it. He then asked me to write a short piece describing the kind of poetry I would like to see come along. This I did, and the result is that ever since the book appeared, I have been bracketed with the very writers I dislike the most. But Boryard would not have it that way, until he says what he says. It is all very stupid and foolish, and I have already forgotten most of the gist of what he's talking about. The other reviews, though, have been awfully good, and the book is selling surprisingly well. It has been out less than a month and has already sold 5,000 copies, and had extremely good notices in the Saturday Review Syndicate, in Cosmopolitan, by Elizabeth Janeway, and best of all, in the Boston Globe by a lady named Manning. My God, if you read that notice and then read the one in the Times you wouldn't know that the reviewers were talking about the same writer! Well, so it goes.

Yes, I remember Tom Goethals, though I didn't get to talk to him very much when I was at Skidmore, since I was only there overnight. I liked him very much, and would be very pleased to renew the acquaintanceship. That's the damn trouble with this traveling: you meet people that you would be absolutely crazy about knowing and then you have to go somewhere else where there's maybe some other good people, or no other good people. Thank God I am able to justify passing up most of these readings because of the fact that I would simply be giving the money to the government. Just in the last few days I have got down to try working out some new poems, and make a tentative start at getting the notes together for what will surely prove to be the only other novel I am ever going to write. I have been running around so much in connection with the film and other matters that I have not really <u>written</u> any poetry to speak of for the last year or so. I have got something strange and new moving now, though, and will send it to you as soon as I get some texts worked out. I got the idea from <u>The Seamless Web</u>, which surely did open up the world of poetry to me, but more especially the world itself. I don't know how you are going to feel about what flowers your seeds have planted in <u>this</u> particular head, but I will show you some of them when they grow a little more.

Keep in touch, from down there in the sunshine country, and we will make plans to get together. I'm sorry you're not going to be in New York or there-abouts in about three weeks, for Yevtushenko and Eugene McCarthy and my-self are going to give a reading up there, and there might be some good times connected with it. It's something my publisher wants me to do, and, since I know Yevtushenko from his reading during my stay at the Library of Con-gress, I thought it no more than courteous to reply in kind with a reading for him—or at least with him. I don't know about McCarthy as a <u>reader</u> of po-etry, but he is certainly no poet. However, he is an old friend, and I linked up with him in his bid to get Lyndon Johnson out. I was there in Washington, and, though I knew little of politics, I am very glad I was in on that particular venture. Gene is going to make another try, but I believe the crest of the wave has already passed over him. Anyway, I need to talk to him, whatever that enigmatic soul plans to do next.

You should have your book back from Seaver by now; I assume that he <u>did</u> receive it, since you say he is trying to place some of the newer poems in mag-azines. Believe me, I'll sure look for <u>those</u>!

Our love to Leda, and to you. Let us know when you arrive down there, and if you get this letter. I have had a lot of important mail lost, and most of this has been because I sent it to a new address for someone who was going there from some place else. I'm sure you've had this experience in Europe. My God, all those American Expresses that have never heard of you! Especially when you expect a check to be awaiting you!

All yours,

Jim

To: Willie Morris

CC, Emory University
4620 Lelia's Court
Columbia, S.C. 29206

January 10, 1972

Dear Willie:

   Thank you very much for your welcome note. In answer to your question about fighter missions in Korea, I can only say that my particular specialty would not be germane, probably, to what you want to write about. My MOS was that of an instrument man, and I never saw the light of day outside the cockpit. We were what was originally called night fighters, but in Korea was called all-weather fighters. The general intention of a night-fighter group is that it "scrambles" and is vectored in by radar on the enemy bent on doing our positions damage. All this worked out fine in World War II. But in Korea the enemy had nothing up at night, and we mainly spent our time banging up and down those ridges doing what is called "night ground support." It was really not much of a war for the kind of thing we did. Most of the fellows with me were retread, like myself, and were just concerned with preserving their lives, putting in their time, and waiting out their orders to go home when the time came for them to be rotated. I looked around for books that you might get something such as you want from, and I'll be damned if I could find more than one or two. The Bridges at Toko-Ri, by Michener, is about fighter missions in the Korean War, but those fellows are flying off a carrier, and I doubt that you'd want to use that aspect of it. Anyway, the book's no good. Oddly enough, the situation that approximated most closely what I remember is the one depicted at the first part of the film of Sayanara. Our base was very much like the one that Marlon Brando flies off, and the command and pilot and crew situation that I remember was substantially similar to the one depicted in that otherwise awful film. If you like, I will browse around some more, and try to find some other stuff for you. I think, though, that you could get everything you need for your book, as you describe it, from a review of the equipment—i.e. the planes—published by the various aircraft industries that turn the planes out, plus various histories of squadrons, all available from the Air Force Historical Section. Also, just talk to the people you know who were flying over there. As I say, my outfit was very largely static, and did little good, though ostensibly doing night ground support work, and patroling, and, as they say, "patroling the area." The day fighter boys, who would be going out as we came in and coming in as we went out, were much different. Those fellows, most of them, had a great thing about going up above or around the

Yalu and running up their scores of kills. I doubt if there were more than five
or six night fighter kills in the whole of the Korean War. World War II was
completely different. I was in the 418th Night Fighter Squadron all the way
from Milne Bay, New Guinea, to Okinawa for the end of the war, up through
the Philippines, and all over. My commanding officer, Carroll Smith, was the
leading night fighter ace of the war, and once knocked down four nips in one
night. The Korean business was a sad anticlimax for all us fellows who were so
gung-ho during the second war. Believe me, I can tell you the <u>psychological</u>
drain that results from being a retread in a no-win war. Then the thing goes
<u>personal</u>: that is you try to run your <u>own</u> score up, and don't bother too much
about what happens to the squadron, the war, or the world. It was greatly different in World War II. I wish I had, as far as wars go, only the memory of that
one, and not the sad, frustrating anti-climax that Korea was to all of us, and
that Viet Nam must be even more of.

Maxine and I must come to New York on the 25th and will stay through
the 29th. I must appear with Yevtushenko and Eugene McCarthy at a reading
at Madison Square Gardens on the 28th. I will be in New York to introduce
James Wright at the Guggenheim Museum on the 25th and then must go to
Choate for a couple of days. I will then come back for the Yevtushenko on the
28th, and maybe Maxine and myself can arrange to stay over a couple of days.
We would both like very much to see you if it can be arranged, though I don't
think it will be possible for us to get out with you on your windy moors. We
will save that for another time. But we <u>do</u> very much hope to see you in the
Big Cave this time, if only for a drink, dinner, or whatever you can allow time
for.

My best to you, my old Will. And love to Muriel, too.

We'll hope to see you in a couple of weeks. Write and let me know whether
or not you will be in the vicinity.

All yours,

To: Geoffrey Hill

CC, Emory University
4620 Lelia's Court
Columbia, S.C. 29206

January 18, 1972

Dear Geoffrey:

Thanks for sending along your book, <u>Mercian Hymns</u>, which I like very
much. You seem to be as mysterious and as gifted as ever, and as obscure a

poet as I have ever read. But you seem to me to be on the right track, and have developed in a way that I think is absolutely unique and amazing. Of course, the question of obscurity is sure to come up with reviewers, as it has with me, and fortunately, or unfortunately—but I think fortunately—I like poetry which I despair of ever getting to the bottom of. And yours is surely that kind. I won't go on and on in this immoderate vein, but do want you to know that I think you are one of the best poets in England today, and that your work is timeless, while the work of others, like Ted Hughes, is already reeling with time.

Meanwhile, whenever you have the time or the inclination, write and let me know how things are with you these days. And if you have anything you'd like for Esquire to have a look at, send that along too. I can't promise anything, of course, since our space is limited to what they can squeeze in between the men's deodorant and underwear ads, but we will have a try at it, all the same. But do communicate, with or without poems.

We hope to get to England either this spring or summer, if all the hullabaloo over Deliverance dies down enough to permit it, and perhaps we can get together at that time. It would be good to see you—and to hear you play the piano.

All yours,

To: Sam Hazo   CC, Emory University
                                            4620 Lelia's Court
                                            Columbia, S.C. 29206

                                            24 January, 1972

Dear Sam:

I have your letter, for which I thank you wholeheartedly. That, together with the phone call, provided me with all the justification for writing Sorties that I will ever need. I have always conceived of myself as writing for one person alone—the one Jacques Riviere termed "the ideal reader," and beside him, who else matters? In the case of Sorties, and perhaps in others, too, you are that reader, and it is profoundly moving to me that you would want to call and write to tell me what you think.

There is a longish review of the book in yesterday's (Sunday the 23rd's) Times that you may want to have a look at. I get so damned tired of these ad hominem reviews, in which the reviewer thinks he knows all about me, personally, has decided that he hates what he thinks he knows, and reviews the book from that viewpoint. I have taken more of that kind of abuse than anyone since Hemingway, and it is an awful bore. If you should choose to write a letter to the Times saying some of the things you say to me, it might serve to redress the balance. But that shall be as you wish.

Meanwhile, Yevtushenko is here this evening (I remember the conversations we had about him while you were driving me into Pittsburgh and the reading at the Forum), and I must spend a couple of hours getting up an introduction. I hope very much that you will be able to get up to Madison Square Garden for the big doings on Friday, for it ought to be some show. Anyway, one way or the other, we'll see each other soon, I am quite sure. That would be good.

Love to all in your house.

All yours,

To: Stanley Burnshaw   TLS, University of Texas at Austin

4620 Lelia's Court
Columbia, S.C. 29206
February 14, 1972

Dear Stanley:

Here is the Boston Globe review of Sorties. Since it appeared, a lot of others have come out, very gratifying and favorable, most of them, except of course, the two New York Times pieces and one that appeared in a small paper in California. The sales have been excellent, and we have gone into a second printing, so the thing is being read.

By now you will have heard of the hideous fiasco we had with Yevtushenko at the Felt Forum a couple of weeks ago. Never on God's earth would I go through something like that again. Wilbur and Kunitz and myself and Senator McCarthy were disgusted with the whole business.

In fact, McCarthy and I spent most of the evening upstairs in the Garden watching the Milrose Games Track Meet. It was infinitely more "poetic" than anything that went on in the Felt Forum. By the time the second program was over—about 2:00 in the morning—I had 103 degrees worth of flu-fever, and went into a long illness, that I am only now recovering from. It was a bad business, and the cause of poetry was not praised.

Not much news here. When you come back up to the City, maybe I can arrange to get you in on one of the private screenings of Deliverance, for there are going to be some beginning the latter part of this month.

But then I hope you'll be coming through to visit us in South Carolina before that.

I have cut down on most of my traveling and other activities, and will almost certainly be in Columbia any time you wish to come through and spend some time with us.

Love to Leda, and to yourself. Let me hear from you whenever you have time.

All yours,
Jim

To: Stanley Burnshaw   TLS, University of Texas at Austin

4620 Lelia's Court
Columbia, S.C. 29206
March 15, 1972

Dear Stanley:

Thank you for your long letter, and for all the tiresome business you have had to put up with on my account at what surely must have been a hellish kind of session. From what you tell me, none of the three judges can agree with another on a single choice. I am indeed surprised at Morgan's actions. Though I don't know him well, I have been a contributor to the Hudson Review for many years, and have recently been on closer terms with him than at any previous time. If he doesn't care for Sorties, that is, of course, his privilege, but it is very odd to learn of his advocacy of his own regular contributors, Haggin and Simon. All these judgings and ring-giving ceremonies are so shot through with personal conflicts, self-aggrandizements, and other such unpleasant things that participating in them is one of those "never again" affairs that one, usually because of other reasons, participates in the next time, even so. I have been trapped into seven or eight of them, including three National Book Awards and three Pulitzer Prizes, and, though I thought each of them a hideous experience—all in different ways—when I thought of what might have happened if I hadn't been on the jury, I approve in retrospect of my participation. I was able to help get some good choices, and was able to prevent some disasters, though most of both types of outcome were effected by compromise. And I expect that if Sorties should happen to win, it will be by some such compromise route. But that kind of win is just as much of a win as a unanimous decision, and that gives us continuing hope. But in any case, do know how very much I appreciate your championship of what will almost certainly be my last critical book.

I am not quite clear on the "announcement" business. I understand that this year there won't be any pre-award announcement of finalists, but I also wonder if there will be an announcement of finalists <u>after</u> the prize is given. There ought to be some way of guaranteeing what is certainly a great plus— in advertizing and publicity—to around fifty books which don't get the prize, many of which are very deserving. In other words, if we don't win, I'd still like to take advantage in some way of being in the finals, particularly since Doubleday very nearly gutted itself trying to get the book out at the time it did. All this has really very little to do with anything but my own situation, of course. Anyway, let me know, when you can, how this is to be handled, and I will be guided accordingly. Meanwhile, I enclose a smashing review from the March 11th <u>Saturday Review</u>, which may even convince Fred Morgan, the small-magazine tycoon, himself.

It was great to have you and Leda with us, even though for just such a very short time. It may very well be that my family and I will be able to come up to the Vineyard, as we all very much wish to do. The house your friend has sounds fine, but Maxine has just rushed in to tell me that if possible we want to try to have my oldest boy and his family come up while we are there, and that this would make three bedrooms almost mandatory. We'll certainly understand, even down through the grandchild, if you can't come up with a house of this sort. But we will tentatively arrange our time so as to be able to come up as you suggest. That would be great, believe me.

And even if we aren't able to make it, I would like very much to work out with you this anthology of "creature poetry." That is surely a great idea. We can talk about it as the format develops in your thinking. You know so much more poetry than I do that I would suggest that you carry most of the load and prestige, though it is my hope that I will be able to suggest some things to you that you may have missed.

Meanwhile, I'll sound out the editors at <u>Esquire</u> to see how much space and backlog we have, for they schedule things a good long time in advance. If we are able to use the one dedicated to me, I think we ought to take off the dedication for reasons that are probably obvious, since I'm the editor, and it would seem almost like self-praise if we retained it. Could you send me a couple of carbons of this one? I'll see what can be done.

Any chance of your coming back through here when you go back to New York for the final Gunfight at the OK Corral? I'll have to be in New York on the 5th of April for the dinner to be given to the inductees of the National Institute, and maybe if you can't come through Columbia, we could arrange it so that our times in New York overlap. That would make that hideous city bearable.

All yours,
Jim

To: Stanley Burnshaw   TLS, University of Texas at Austin

4620 Lelia's Court
Columbia, S.C. 29206
March 23, 1972

Dear Stanley:

Very good to hear from you, with the new news. I also have the proofs of your book, and will hold off on comments until I have gone through the whole thing very carefully. But I <u>can</u> tell you a couple of things. First, the book is <u>great</u>! Second, I am entirely happy with the change of title to <u>In the Terrified Radiance</u>. That is much more provocative and gripping than the former title. I also think that it was a very sound policy to have the later poems come first. The book will have a sudden as well as a deep and lasting impact, I am quite sure. Meanwhile, shall I send "Not to Bereave . . ." on to <u>Esquire</u>? The only possible trouble might be the time-element, because we have already backlogged—and <u>Esquire</u> has scheduled—through the next several issues, and they are very touchy about such matters. I'll wait to hear from you on this, and will be guided by what you say.

I am very happy that you think things look at least fairly good for <u>Sorties</u>. I think that, with a hung jury, we might get the thing. I'm happy you liked the Heyen review. In answer to your question, Heyen is a nice young fellow who teaches at New York University at Brockport. He writes fairly good poetry himself, and does a good deal of reviewing.

Maxine says, with the greatest enthusiasm, that the Dickey family would be delighted for you to serve as our real estate agent on Martha's Vineyard. Just tell us how the situation develops, and we'll swing right with you.

A thought on <u>Sorties</u>. Since you've already mentioned to the committee the business about the notes for the new novel, stressing the uniqueness of this <u>kind</u> of thing, you might also tell them that I published these preliminary notes so that there would be at least one record of a novelist making such information available before the work is actually written; not after the fact, as in the case of Gide's journal of <u>The Counterfeiters</u>. Such things are easy enough to do <u>that</u> way; I'm doing exactly the opposite: letting the reader have a look at the first processes of novel-writing before the thing is accomplished, and not publishing the notes <u>after</u> the book has already appeared.

Another thing: with your stress on giving the award to a creative man rather than, say, to a literary biographer, it may be that a precedent can be established. After all, where are the winners in the Arts & Letters category of yesteryear? Anyway, these are just some suggestions.

Our very best to you, and I'm sorry we won't be seeing you in New York. But you can be damn sure that I'll press your candidacy for the Institute.

All yours,

Jim

P.S. Tell Leda that I received Ed Wallant's book in fine shape. I'm very happy that she was so thoughtful as to send it back. He was a dear friend, and I named the protagonist of <u>Deliverance</u> Ed and had him be an art director because of this.

To: Marian Leith[14]

CC, Emory University
4620 Lelia's Court
Columbia, S.C. 29206

May 23, 1972

Dear Mrs. Leith:

I am currently working on a novel about blind men and airplanes, and although I know a number of blind persons and have talked with them about their personal experiences, I now need to know in more detail about blindness, about becoming blind, about how one learns to live with it, and so on. I wonder if you could help me obtain this information, or if you could direct me to some agency which could. I am particularly interested in the relationship between the blind person and his seeing-eye dog, and how he learns to rely on the dog as he used to rely on his own eyes. Are there schools in North Carolina or here in South Carolina which provide this training to blind people and would it be possible for me to visit one, to learn first-hand what they go through, or at least as nearly as possible without being blind myself?

I would certainly appreciate any help or information you might be able to give me on this.

Sincerely,

14. Librarian for the North Carolina/South Carolina Library for the Blind.

To: John Hollander   CC, Emory University
                                                              4620 Lelia's Court
                                                              Columbia, S.C. 29206

                                                              June 9, 1972
Dear John:

I understand from the people at Farrar Straus that you are doing the re-view of the poems of Trumbull Stickney, long a great favorite of mine, for the <u>New York Times</u>. Two years ago, when the poems were almost impossible to come by, I had them Xeroxed at the Library of Congress and used some of their lines in a kind of latter-day dialogue between Stickney and myself, which finally became the Phi Beta Kappa poem at Harvard for 1970. It is good to know that an enterprising publisher would have sense enough to make Stickney's work generally available, and that you yourself are going to review it for the <u>Times</u>. In case it could be of any help to you in your review—provided, of course, you haven't done it or finished it yet—i'd like you to have a poster of my poem—or rather my and Stickney's poem—from a publication in Berk-eley. You might want to use it in some way in the review, hang it up and throw darts at it, or whatever. In any case, I thought you might like to have it.

My best to you and all your works.

                                                              All yours,

To: Sidney Skolsky   CC, Emory University
                                                              4620 Lelia's Court
                                                              Columbia, S.C. 29206

                                                              September 18, 1972
Dear Mr. Skolsky:

I happened to notice, in the September issue of <u>Show</u>, your column having to do with your liking for the phrase "days of wine and roses," and asking readers to identify the quotation. That I will be happy to do. It comes from a poem by the late 19th century English poet Ernest Dowson. Dowson was given to long Latin titles. This particular one is <u>Vitae summa brevis spem nos vetat incohare longam</u>. It means "the shortness of life prevents us from enter-taining far-off hopes." The poem, which is only eight lines, runs as follows:

They are not long, the weeping and the laughter,
        Love and desire and hate:

I think they have no portion in us after
        We pass the gate.

They are not long, the days of wine and roses:
        Out of a misty dream
Our path emerges for a while, then closes
        Within a dream.

By the way, these eight lines were also quoted by Vincent Price in the film, Laura.

Dowson was a doomed, sick boy, who died of malnutrition and alcoholism at the age of thirty-two. He is an eminently quotable writer, and a fine minor poet. He was a friend of Oscar Wilde, Frank Harris, Bernard Shaw, and the Irish poet William Butler Yeats. His most famous poem, in its third stanza, furnished other famous phrases for our strange 20th century. The first line went to the great all-time best-seller in books and movies, and the last to Cole Porter.

I have forgot much, Cynara! gone with the wind,
Flung roses, roses riotously with the throng,
Dancing, to put thy pale, lost lilies out of mind;
But I was desolate and sick of an old passion,
        Yea, all the time, because the dance was long;
I have been faithful to thee, Cynara! in my fashion.

Dowson was also responsible for the phrase "wine and woman and song," which has been variously corrupted as "wine and women and song."

I hope this will satisfy your creative curiosity.

Incidentally, have you seen my film, Deliverance, now playing at the Cinerama Dome there in Los Angeles?

Anyway, I hope you will go and read Ernest Dowson, for if one likes a single phrase of a poet, there may well be other things in his work equally appealing.

                             Sincerely yours,

To: Armitage Watkins

CC, Emory University
4620 Lelia's Court
Columbia, S.C. 29206

October 2, 1972

Dear Mike:

I have a copy of your letter to Elliott Kastner, for which I thank you very much. I am no expert in matters of finance where literary works are concerned. My own agent, Theron Raines, counsels me not to procede with this particular project. I gather that you have talked with him about it. I understand and admire your continuing function as Allan's agent, concerned now with Joan's interests. That is your business, your line of work. But Allan was my friend as well as yours, and I wanted to do this film as a tribute to what I consider the best of his talent. We are unusually lucky in having Kastner interested in the movie, for Amos Berry is a long-forgotten novel, as you should know better than anyone else. I doubt that the book sold, in all, more than three or four hundred copies. This is a thing that I initiated, took the trouble to bring to Kastner's attention; the film will never be made under the financial conditions that you propose. The possibility of filming Amos Berry is riding on two considerations, and two alone. These are the fact that I have brought the matter to Kastner's attention, and—God forgive me—my name and reputation, and the current success of my own movie, Deliverance. We can make this film, Mike, if you and Joan don't throw financial roadblocks at us. I like and respect Joan, from the one occasion when I got together with her and Allan. But it is a tactical error on your part, and on Joan's part, to ask for the terms you present. On that basis, and on the advice of my agent, I will simply have to walk away from the project. I want to do it, I can do it, and I will do it, and we have the financial backing for it, but you and Joan must go along with our terms. Otherwise, Allan and his fine work—and other films made from it that might be possible in the future—will simply sink deeper into the grave. I don't want that to happen. Neither should you, as his agent—Allan used to speak with great fondness of getting you and me together—and neither should Joan as his wife. As I say, I understand something of the agent's part, but believe me, you are taking the short view here and cutting off possibilities that would be tremendously advantageous for all of us, and for Allan and his reputation, for which he lived and died.

Sincerely,

To: Patricia Gebhart

CC, Emory University
4620 Lelia's Court
Columbia, S.C. 29206

October 3, 1972

Dear Ms. Gebhart:

Thank you very much for your letter, and for the things you say about the poetry. There are a couple of new things coming out—one in the <u>New Yorker</u> and a much longer one in <u>The</u> <u>Atlantic</u>—that I hope you will like also. Have you seen my movie yet? It's at the Tower East.

I'm sorry you didn't like <u>Sorties</u>, but there is nothing I can do about <u>that</u>. Your reaction is so violent that I wonder at it. And the fact that you didn't like Dave Wagoner's edition of Roethke's notebooks also makes me wonder. Dave spent years compiling that book, and I find it fascinating. Roethke's working methods and the knowledge of them that <u>Straw for the Fire</u> gives us, are very precious to me. He was not only a great American poet, he was a very close friend of mine. I can't for the life of me see why <u>anything</u> that concerns a fellow human being to the point that he is willing to note it down would not be of interest to another one of us living here on the blue planet. I have had dozens of letters from people about <u>Sorties</u>. <u>Certainly</u> it is egocentric and perhaps even arrogant. Certainly it is a grab-bag. I am sick of tailor-made literary works. Let us try to get the whole man in, warts and all. Anyway, the book has sustained some people and encouraged others. It was a finalist in the Arts and Letters category of the National Book Award.

So now I can turn to other things. If <u>Sorties</u> struck you so wrongly as you say it did, I maybe should apologize. But only to you. This has to do with the <u>personal</u> relationships between authors and their public, which must always be on a one-to-one basis. I am sorry if I have offended you, or—to you—seemed to make a mistake in publishing the book. But I would do it again, as I must have you know.

I'll hope to meet you when I come to New York again, in about six weeks.

Again, thank you for the things you say about my poetry, and for your fiery thoughts about <u>Sorties</u>.

Sincerely,

To: Dr. John Foster West

CC, Emory University
4620 Lelia's Court
Columbia, S.C. 29206

October 20, 1972

Dear John:

Thank you so very much for your letter, and for the things you are kind enough to say about <u>Deliverance</u>. The movie is out now, and I hope you will like that, too. It is currently in Charlotte, and, if you have a chance, run over and have a look. I'm sure your students would enjoy it, as well. I did the screen play as well as the music, acted in it, and found a good many of the locations. Anyway, tell me what you think.

In answer to your questions: you could say either that the four main characters are <u>more or less</u> based on people I knew—and still know. But it would probably be even more true to say that they are all aspects of myself. For example, I was an art director like Ed, a kind of survival nut and archer like Lewis, a guitarist like Drew, and a weakling like Bobby.

The significance of the model's eye is that the peculiar gold mote in it is what individualizes the unattainable girl to Ed, and this unattainability is what he thinks of when he is with Martha. We all do those things; we all hope that a stranger will deliver us from what we know.

<u>Slowly Toward Hercules</u> is about three-quarters done. I have to finish a couple of long pieces and a long translation from the Dutch.

I much enjoyed the article in <u>Southern Living</u>, and will be looking forward to your next book. No, I don't remember anybody named Judy Credle. I've taught so many hundreds of students since that fine time we had at Hollins that I can't possibly remember all the names. And I don't even try.

And, sure, I'll be very happy to come up some time, and we'll walk around. I'd like that a lot, believe me.

All yours,

To: Christopher Dickey

CC, Emory University
4620 Lelia's Court
Columbia, S.C. 29206

October 23, 1972

Dear Chris,

I have finally finished the letter I talked to you about this morning; this is a kind of second draft. Anyway, I want, first off, to repeat what I said on the phone:

never be in any way intimidated when you write to me. That is just a waste of energy, for I love to read your letters far more, probably, than you like to read mine. For example, I used to wait in a condition of utmost excitement for your letters to come in from France. They were tremendously exciting, and I hope to God that I or your mother had the sense to keep them. And I'm very happy that you should want, now, to begin writing once more on a kind of semi-regular basis. That would please me greatly, I can tell you. Amongst all the official and business correspondence that I have to do . . . well, it is very good to know that there will be letters that I really look forward to getting, and to answering.

Good that you'll be getting the rights to the Supervielle stories. Your schema for their production are fascinating. As to the filmic techniques that they will bring into play, I know very little about those, as you know. But I can see how you can do L'Enfant de la Haute Mer by the joint means of real interiors that look out onto the ocean, models, portions of sets, and so on. At this time of preliminaries, I might venture a couple of suggestions, though only provisionally. First of all, it is important that the architecture, types of interiors and all the other properties belonging to the village that the little girl's father imagines into existence in the middle of the ocean be consistent with one another. I wonder how well, for example, New England fishing towns and the environs of an European city like Amsterdam would dove-tail. Of course there would be ways to make these things consistent, but the important consideration here is that this be a real—or real-seeming—village, with the connotations, so thoroughly European, of security, intimacy with tradesmen, and the whole sense of a unified and familiar locus that such places have and have had for centuries.

The only other thing I can think about at a juncture this early is the title. Literally, as you know, the title means the child of the high sea. But, "high sea," has connotations in English that it does not have in French: to wit, high seas, stormy weather, and things of that nature. Perhaps this is a small point, but I think you should consider calling it, in English, "The Child of the Open Sea," or something to that effect, because one of the most haunting qualities of the story is the calmness of this ocean, at this particular point of latitude and longitude where the father imagines the village as being; it wouldn't be nearly so effective a story if it took place in a hurricane, for instance.

In connection with this project, you and I might find a way to justify a trip to Amsterdam, because I am working on a kind of free adaptation of a long poem by a Dutchman from Amsterdam named Hendrik Marsman. It's even less of a true translation than Lowell's "Imitations," for I really play fast and loose with Marsman's Zodiac, and am ending up by making him an altogether

better poet than he was when he was torpedoed and lost at sea on a refugee
ship bound for England in 1940. I read the poem in a very inferior translation
in a copy of the <u>Sewanee Review</u> back in my college days, and reread it a couple of months ago. It struck me as a possible way of getting my astronomical
interests and education at last energized poetically, and I have been working
away at the poem enthusiastically. It's about a typical European intellectual
poet, lonely and self-analytical to the point of driving the reader mad. He
comes back home, takes a shabby room above a canal, and meditates and self-
analyzes and self-pities and writes. His father, apparently, has been an ama-
teur astronomer, and the poet, surely middle-aged by this time, falls into
meditating on the connection between the zodiac, the imagination, European
history and his own personal situation—not necessarily in that order. Here
are a few tentative last lines, where he seems to have resolved things, at least in
his own mind . . .

> . . . and give this home-come man who listens in his room
>   to the rush and flair of planets through the spin-
>   ning of green oceans.
> the instrument, the tuning fork
> —he'll flick it with his bandless wedding finger—
> which at a touch reveals the form
> of the unbeginning European music
> poetry has never completed,
> whose course involves the heaven-helping sea
> and shall vibrate through the western world
> so long as the spirit hurls on space
> the star-beasts of intellect and madness.

This is just the skelton, the <u>gist</u> of the lines; "the rhythmical component," as
we <u>poets</u> say, hasn't been worked into it yet, but you can get a certain dim idea
of how it's eventually going to sound. If I get deep enough into this thing, I
might find it justifiable to go to Amsterdam and see Marsman's people, if
there are any left. It would be easy to tie this in with your need to go there,
and we might have a fine trip. I'll keep you posted.

Your idea of making <u>Bacchae</u> is an interesting one. It's been years since I've
read it, or indeed any Greek plays, (though Kevin's catching me up on
<u>Antigone</u>, which he's reading in school). I'll read <u>The Bacchae</u> in the next
couple of days. I've seen a few Greek plays, put on by college groups and such,
and a couple of movies. The actors and directors at all levels seem to be so in
awe of the material that the last thing they are capable of doing is to create be-

lievable people. There might be a break-through possible here, and if it will lead to Sparta, I'm all for it.

Your ideas about "The Small Voice" are also very good. I agree quite readily that we should have a cohesive and progressing plot. My original idea was almost exactly the opposite of the one you outline in your last paragraph. My notion was to take an icy and distant aesthetic intellect, a "man alone"—and, he thinks, glad to be so—and by a series of events reduce him to humanity. Some of the events could be funny, some banal, some sad, some even tragic. But the general direction I wanted to go in was up to some kind of provisional regeneration or self-discovery through what happens to our poet in his travels. I still think this has merit, and, if we could find the form for it, might make quite a moving film. Your idea, i.e. "the destruction or near-destruction of a man, an artist, by the image created for him by his admirers," is already, even at this early juncture, risking a disastrous comparison with the career and destruction of Dylan Thomas under just such circumstances as you describe. I would have our man virtually unknown at the beginning; a poet who didn't have enough admirers to destroy an amoeba. Yet he is, perhaps, worshipped by a small, intense coterie. What I wanted to do, beginning with this situation, and at a reading attended by about eight or nine people, would be to build from this situation into one which would depict not only this particular poet's increasing following, but the movement of poetry in my and your time from being the province of such aesthetic coteries toward a much broader human base, a far wider human spectrum. This notion doesn't of course vitiate your plan because he could be destroyed by these increasing numbers of listeners as well as he could be educated and made "sadder and wiser" by them. But we must by all accounts look out for Dylan Thomas.

I'll sign off now, so as to get this in the mail. Please do write again when you have the chance. I long to hear from you on any and all subjects.

Love to all in your house,

P.S. Still no drinking! It's easy! And I have the energy of multitudes! Strange.

To: Bernard Klantzko

CC, Emory University
4620 Lelia's Court
Columbia, S.C. 29206

December 28, 1972

Dear Mr. Klantzko:

Thank you indeed for your Christmas Day letter about the recording that Tony Recupido and I want to do. Yes, as I said before, I will be happy to foot the bill on this, and, if the record turns out as well as the tape that Tony and I have already made, I will consider it among the best money I have ever spent, since I have had any to spend. This is just a kind of whim of mine, because Tony and I have done what amounts to having invented a new kind of Bluegrass sound, where I lay the melody down on the twelve-string and Tony plays the runs. When I get a day or so off from the general hullabaloo arising from the release of Deliverance, I will have a dub of this run off, and send it to you. This was just done on a reel-to-reel home tape recorder, without any rehearsal. We just sat around and played, but it will give you some idea of the kind of thing we have worked out.

The cost of $750 is fine, but I had rather put, say, $1000 into it, and really have something well-done and good-looking. I have been thinking about the cover, and I would like to try a couple of ideas out on you. The trouble is, my great flat-picker, Tony Recupido, is in California, and we would have to make some kind of special arrangement either to fly him in, or for me to go out there. We have a good girl vocalist, nammed Tammy Neufel, though I haven't worked out with her yet. We would have to have some time to rehearse, and all the rest of the stuff that you have to do when you make a record. But all this could be worked out.

As to the cover, since you think, quite rightly, that we should cash in on Deliverance, now the hottest thing in international and U.S. box offices, we might try one of the following ideas. If you have seen the film, you will remember the footbridge that the little mountain banjo player is standing on when the canoes go under. Warner Brothers built the bridge, and, to my knowledge, it is still standing. Tony and Tammy and I could be with our guitars in the middle of that, and a photographer could shoot us from down below with a telephoto lens. That's one possibility. The other is to have us on a rock in the middle of the river, apparently playing, with the white water all around us. If we used this approach, we could call it "Deliverance Country," and of course Tony and I would work up something on the theme music, and probably run that as the first cut on Side A.

I also had the idea of calling the album "News from Lelia's Court," which is the street I live on in Columbia, and where Tony and I have done most of our playing to date for groups, parties, and so on. If we did the album jacket in New York, we could photograph the three of us freezing to death with the vapor coming out of our mouths, down on the East River Drive, amid some grim concrete rubble heap, our guitar cases with us, and our backs, as musicians, absolutely up against the wall. If we did this, we could call it "Far from Lelia's Court," or we could call the album "Out of Work Bluegrass." I know some very good photographers in New York, and also some down here, and my own son is one of the best ones around. So we could work it however it seems to you to be the best. I think, at this particular date, that we probably ought to take the group over into North Georgia and photograph something over there for our cover.

There is no particular rush about any of this. I am working on a new novel, another film, and so on, and our project would have to be sandwiched in between these other projects, but, as opposed to all the things I <u>have</u> to do, this is something that I <u>want</u> to do, and we will put out a good record for you. I don't believe you have ever heard any Bluegrass like it. We'll work up some material with Tammy, where we have three or four vocals, and then Tony and I, and maybe Tammy's husband, George, will play the rest as three-part Bluegrass instrumentals. All that will have to be worked out, but it would please me greatly if the record were to make some dough for you, for I admire your list greatly, and you are making a genuine contribution to early American jazz, blues, and folk music.

Let me hear what you think of all this, whenever you conveniently can. And, if you haven't yet, go see my film and let me know what you think of the use of the music, for which I was responsible, and of the bridge.

Sincerely,

To: John Hollander   CC, Emory University
                                                                              4620 Lelia's Court
                                                                    Columbia, S.C. 29206

December 29, 1972

Dear John:

This is just to keep in touch. I am working on a long, new poem called "The Zodiac." It is kind of loosely based on a poem written around 1940 by a Dutch poet, Henrik Marsman, who was killed on a torpedoed refugee ship in 1940. The only thing I have really taken from Marsman is the basic structure of the narrative; the rest is my own improvisation on his theme. I wonder if <u>Harper's</u> would like to publish this. It's pretty long; about the same length as the poem I have in the current <u>Atlantic</u>.[15] But I believe that, with luck, it will be a major work. One has to believe this, if one writes long poems, and sometimes it turns

---

15. "Reunioning Dialogue," *Atlantic Monthly* 231 (January 1973): 46–49. *Harper's* did not publish the poem, which appeared in 1976 in book format.

out to be true. Anyway, let me know if you'd like to have a look at it, if I should ever be so fortunate as to finish it.

Keep in touch, and let me know what your personal situation is, since Willie and the other good people went out. I saw Marshall Frady the other day, and spent a few good moments with him. But it seems as though you are the only one left of the Big Team at <u>Harper's</u>, and that's got to matter.

And let us have something new for <u>Esquire</u>, for we are trying to do something remarkable for poetry there, among the necktie ads and the plugs for men's deodorants. I would particularly like something long, that will catch the reader up and not let him go. I would also like something with your particular brand of wit, because all the stuff we have been publishing lately is eccentrically heavy-breathing.

Let me hear.

All yours,

To: Steven Spielberg   CC, Emory University
                                                     4620 Lelia's Court
                                                     Columbia, S.C. 29206

January 10, 1973

Dear Mr. Spielberg:

Thank you very much for sending along the script for <u>The Sugarland Express</u>, which I think will be very effective, particularly with such talent as Ben Johnson and Goldie Hawn, and with Vilmos as cinematographer.

Thank you also for the things you say about my work on paper, and, God help us, on screen. As to your kind proposal that I consider the part of either Marvin Dybala or one of the Texas Ranger sharpshooters, I am, of course, quite flattered, not to say delighted. I have put the question to my agent, however, and he advises against it. There are just too many obstacles in the way of such a project, from my point of view, as much as I would like to do the sharpshooter part (but under no condition the other). Anyway, the latter is more or less an academic point, for, as I said, I won't be able to do either one. I have too many half-finished projects with deadlines, too much traveling, too much teaching, too many previously-made commitments. I'm very sorry indeed, but I just can't do it.

My very best to Vilmos, to yourself, and to <u>The Sugarland Express</u>. I'll try to catch a ride on it when it comes through Columbia.

And keep in touch, for maybe we'll be able to do something later on, when life is not so hectic as it is for me right now.

I'm sending the screenplay back under separate cover. And, again, thanks.

Sincerely yours,

To: Minton V. Braddy

CC, Emory University
4620 Lelia's Court
Columbia, S.C. 29206

January 12, 1973

Dear Minton:

It was surely great to see you and the other fellows, after such a long time. In a way, it was like coming back to life, but in another way, in another, older body, and among youthful companions who had somehow been changed by some unknown magician.

It is hard to think of what to say to people under such circumstances. To some, there is nothing to say; to some, there is everything to say, and not enough time to say it. But I will surely tell you this, my old boyhood idol: of all the fellows I talked to, for a good seven or eight hours, the only one whom time seems to be on the side of instead of against is you. Perhaps Jimmy Adams has something of this about him, too; I hope so; I like him a lot. But there is no doubt at all in my mind about Minton Braddy. It seems to me that even thirty-five years ago I could have told you that such would happen; I think I knew it then. In fact, I did know it. It is not myself who is the vindication of the spirit of the Buckhead Boys; it is you. I am just tremendously proud of you, Minton, just as much for what you are as for what you have done. I won't go on and on in this immoderate vein, but must add that one does not practice the craft of writing—particularly of poetry—without knowing people pretty well. There would be no reason for me to carry on in this manner, if these were not my convictions. So many of my people have failed me, failed themselves, failed everything and everybody. You know the names as well as I do. Some I would have bet on in those days, some I would not have. Some I have been right about, some wrong. But I would have bet my soul on you, and by God, I was right. No more.

Keep in touch with a letter every couple of months, telling me about your life, your family, your business. Because if any occasion like the reunion of the Buckhead Boys is anything, it has to be a renewal of certain things, certain relationships. Otherwise, it is just a pretext to get drunk. In my time, I've had too many of the latter. Now I want some renewals.

The acting thing I mentioned is still a ways off, but it is definitely possible. I'll keep you posted.

Love to all in your house.

All yours,

To: Mrs. Hugh Bullock

CC, Emory University
4620 Lelia's Court
Columbia, S.C. 29206

January 15, 1973

Dear Mrs. Bullock:

I will be happy to choose some poems of Edwin Arlington Robinson's. It has been a while since I've done one of your Poetry Pilots for you, and I no longer remember exactly how I submitted the material. If it is customary for the guest editor to submit typed manuscripts of the poems, please let me know, and I'll have my secretary do this. However, if you just want the poems by title, I can give them to you that way now. This is my list of Robinson's seven best short poems, more or less in my order of preference. The edition I am using is The Selected Poems of Edwin Arlington Robinson, which Morton Zabel and I edited several years ago, and for which I wrote a long introduction. The book came out in hard covers from Macmillian in 1965, and was reprinted in paperback by Collier Books in 1966. The page references are the same.

"Veteran Sirens"	page 133
"Eros Turannos"	127
"Hillcrest"	111
"The Sheaves"	209
"Rubin Bright"	16
"Lost Anchors"	196
"The Pity of the Leaves"	12

As to your request for "a few remarks" about Robinson, I would be hard put to find anything to say about him that I haven't said in the introductory essay in Selected Poems, or in a shorter article I did a couple of years ago as the lead piece in the New York Times book section, and which also appears in my latest book, <u>Sorties</u>. You could use any of this material you wish. If you want something different, however, I will endeavor to comply with your desires and requirements in the matter.

With all best wishes,

Sincerely,

To: Arthur Schlesinger, Jr.

CC, Emory University
4620 Lelia's Court
Columbia, S.C. 29206

February 5, 1973

Dear Arthur:

Thank you so very much for your note about the Today Show. You are perfectly right; I have taken a good deal of flack about the program, but it seems to me that Frost and his reputation are better off by being seen and read according to his true achievement. Sentimentality has a way of disappearing, thank God.

And of course you are right about Whitman, too. I love the guy, and the remarks I made on the Today Show were simply in the interest of getting some kind of polarization of <u>kinds</u> of poets suitable to a mass audience. Again, one never knows how these things really merge or what effect such public showings will have. But I am certainly delighted to have your letter. That, at least, I am sure of. I remember sitting on the orange crates with you six or seven years ago when we were supposed to go out and get the National Book Awards. The times spent on the orange crates talking together like human creatures can occasionally do was worth all the public display, and more too.

I have had some people from your school approach me for coming up as a visiting professor for a couple of months, although I don't think I can do it for a couple of years. But maybe I will do it, and we can spend some time together. I would sure like that a lot, I can tell you.

Again, thank you for your letter: for taking the time and for getting your opinions to me. All this is valuable.

All yours,

To: Earl Bradley   CC, Emory University
                                                        4620 Lelia's Court
                                                    Columbia, S.C. 29206

                                                        February 7, 1973
Dear Brad:

Please forgive my waiting so long in answering your March, 1971, letter, but with the making and release of <u>Deliverance</u>, and all the other things I've had to do, I simply have not had the time to keep up the correspondence with those with whom I would most like to keep in touch. With the Academy Awards, this will more or less come to an end, and I can pick up the threads of new projects again.

This note is just to re-establish contact with you, and to make sure I know how to reach you. I am moving on a couple of long novels now, and you can be of enormous help to me in both of them, but particularly the latter, which is a kind of panoramic, tolstoyan novel of the Pacific air war at night. We would need to spend a good deal of time together, and I would be very happy to come over there, or put you up here, which ever you prefer. Anyway, I'll outline all that in a later letter. This is just to make sure that I know where you are and can reach you.

My love to Mildred, and to Doug.

Let me hear.

                                                        As ever,

To: Robert Nathan   CC, Emory University
                                                        4620 Lelia's Court
                                                    Columbia, S.C. 29206

                                                        March 19, 1973
Dear Robert Nathan:

Please accept my deepest congratulations on your eightieth birthday.

I first read <u>Portrait of Jennie</u> as a combat pilot in the Pacific in 1944, and it has never left me. The opening sequence about the desperation and futility of one's artistic strivings has stayed with me for thirty years. You must understand that this impression was made on the mind of a young boy in the most desperate, life-death conditions, who felt that he might eventually become an artist of sorts himself. At any rate, the book has stayed with me, and is with me now.

Your marriage to Anna must surely give you great fulfillment and joy. I know her only slightly, through her contact with my son, who was instructed in horsemanship by Caroline, to whom I once gave a few guitar lessons in the blues.

I don't have all your work, I regret to say. I have just re-read <u>Portrait of Jennie</u> in one of the old Viking Portable series. I have a good many books, but I don't have your poetry, and would like very much to have it. Can you advise as to what you believe to be the best of your work in poetry? If you tell me the name of the book—or books—that you most esteem, I will bend every effort to get hold of them.

But the main purpose of this letter is to let you know how very much I esteem what you have done with your human time in the world. It has surely meant a very great deal to a lonely boy flying night missions over an alien people, and has now come to a fruition of some sort in his own work as a poet and novelist and film-maker.

Sincerely,yours,

To: William Dunlap

CC, Emory University
4620 Lelia's Court
Columbia, S.C. 29206

March 26, 1973

Dear Bill:

It was great to get your wonderful letter, and to know the status of our mask. You are quite right in assuming that I would not want to go through the same experience again, but since I <u>have</u> been through it, I am delighted to know that the impression was a good one. Surely I could not have had a more expert or dedicated artist working on my own perishable head.

The ride over the mountains was absolutely delicious, and, if you feel delicious about a situation in which you don't know whether or not your eyes are going to survive, that is <u>real</u> deliciousness. I wouldn't have missed you, or the experience.

When you come down here for the Carolina Cup, call us a few days before hand, and though I won't be here myself, you can come out to the house, or at least call Maxine. I have told her so much about you that you can be assured of the best of all possible welcomes. You can also get together with her as to the disposition of the various casts of the mask which we want to distribute among the people we love best.

I had planned to send Kevin's shoes up to you by way of my secretary when she goes to Boone this weekend, but if you are coming down here, perhaps you'd rather pick them up yourself. Anyway, let me know.

My best to B.J., to John West, and to all those we met up there, in that strange, mountain place.

And if there's anything I can do for you at the Corcoran Gallery, just let me know. First of all, I need the man's name that you're dealing with. After that, I'll start to move in your behalf. You gave me one name, but I'm not sure that's the right guy. Please inform, and we'll roll.

All yours,

To: John Lehmann   TLS, University of Texas at Austin

4620 Lelia's Court
Columbia, S.C. 29206
April 9, 1973

Dear John Lehmann:

I have just finished <u>In My Own Time</u> for the third time, and I can tell you that it has told me more, not only of the literary life of my time, but of the <u>life</u> of my own time: the history that I have lived through, and also something of the history that is inevitably to come. I am told that I am the major literary influence on the young over here—though in England there has been a good deal of opposition—and it may be that you have even heard of me, despite the jet-lag. Anyway, I simply wanted to record my tremendous enthusiasm for <u>In My Own Time</u>, and pass on. I come to England at infrequent intervals, and maybe the next time you and I can get together, have a drink, or even dinner. I would like that a lot, believe me.

I stand much in favor of your poetry, of your memoirs, and, above all, of your life.

Sincerely yours,
James Dickey

To: Stewart Richardson   CC, Emory University
4620 Lelia's Court
Columbia, S.C. 29206

April 12, 1973

Dear Sandy & Ken:

Every time I get on another airplane I feel that my doom is upon me, and I wanted to leave some instructions about the work I am doing now. I have just about finished a long poem called <u>The Zodiac</u>, and I quite firmly believe that it is a major work, having to do with the human body and its relationship to the universe, as well as treating the artist and the self-destructiveness entailed in creativity. Anyway, I am leaving a kind of garbled draft, which is all I have at this time, here at home. Should anything happen to me, I would like this incorporated into the manuscript of a new book of poems. Theron is very excited about the poem, as is Gordon Lish at Esquire. We want to present this poem, first, as a major piece of writing, which it certainly is. The way to do this, so far as magazine publication, will be up to you and to Theron. I would certainly contact Bob Manning at The Atlantic, and the people at Harpers, as well as the people—Robie Macauley—at Playboy, for example. The point is to raise a good deal of excitement about the poem before it appears in book form. Whether it appears whole in, say, Esquire, I will leave up to you, as my editors, and to Theron. It might be best to print it in sections in different places. Again, I don't know. You might also want to coordinate all of this with Stefan Kanfer and the others at Time Magazine. I'll leave that up to you and Theron.

The main point here is to raise a great deal of excitement about the appearance of the poem, which you and I will then, when the time is right and the excitement is sufficient, issue as a volume of poetry.

I don't really anticipate my demise in a blown-apart aircraft commandeered by some political nut or criminal, but these things do happen, and I wanted to make provision, just in case.

This is just a hasty note to let you know what I'd like in case anything happens. Get The Zodiac publicized as much as may be done, and then issue it with other poems in the new manuscript. Then, a few years later, bring out a big retrospective volume of poems. A man here at the University of South Carolina named Matthew Bruccoli has just brought out a pretty good bibliography, so you could run down all the stuff that hasn't appeared in book form before.

That might make quite a book, you know.

All yours,

To: Malcolm Cowley   CC, Emory University
                                          4620 Lelia's Court
                                          Columbia, S.C. 29206

                                          January 4, 1974

Dear Malcolm:

What a splendid thing you have done in A Second Flowering. Some of the information you make available was known to me, but most of it was not, and I was entirely fascinated by every sentence of the book. I never knew any of these people except Cummings, whom I introduced at what I was later told was his last public reading, at the 92nd Street Y the 1st of February, 1962. Later he and I went to a private party, and he was exactly as you say.

Of course what we must now have is your autobiography. I should like very much to say I could look forward to seeing it; that would be good.

Sincerely yours,

To: Stewart Richardson   CC, Emory University
                                                          4620 Lelia's Court
                                                          Columbia, S.C. 29206

January 4, 1974

Dear Sandy:

I'm sorry that I have been out of communication for a little while, but Maxine has been in terrible shape, with the possibility of having at least four potentially fatal diseases at the same time, and all of my attention has been going to her, and to trying to hold our family situation together financially and emotionally. The last of the tests, the one for cervical cancer, came back yesterday, and the results are favorable to us. I can breathe again, and am once more moving forward on the two novels.

I have an outline and part of the first draft on the first of the two, called Alnilam, and an outline—at least I know what is going to happen through to the end—of the one about the actual war, now called Crux. Neither of these books is highly developed as yet, but they are coming on well, both of them. As you may remember, the first one deals with a newly blind man's search for the identity of his dead son at a primary training base in North Carolina during the first part of World War II. Without going into more detail here, I can say that what happened is that he discovers, by various means, that his boy, whom he has not known since Joel was an infant, has been a figure part Billy Budd, part Rimbeau, part Parcelsus, part Confidence Man, and, maybe, part Hitler and part Jesus. The story of Alnilam is the story of these discoveries. It begins with the blind man and Zack, his seeing-eye dog, coming into the little town where the action takes place at its one and only air base, and ends with his departure.

The second novel, Crux, follows up on this. The key people in the plot, now headed up by a fanatical young officer named Shears, have graduated and are now flying in the Pacific. By various means the plot has spread. Shears is almost as good a pilot as Joel, and he quickly dominates his night fighter squadron and is made operations officer or second in command, and is a great favorite of the general who heads up Fifth Air Force Fighter Command. Most of the story is taken up with the Pacific air night war, with the determination of Shears to turn the mission of the squadron from being night fighters— that is, a defensive unit—into a night intruder force, specializing in preying on enemy shipping and aircraft over or near their own bases. By now the plot, whose purpose I will explain in a later letter, and whose methods I am now working out, dominates not only Shears' squadron but several others as well, including one day-fighter squadron. Anyway, the power fight within the squadron is being waged between the present commander, Conway, and Shears: Conway for patriotic reasons (which Shears makes to seem cowardice) and Shears in order to further the plot. The plot itself is too complicated to explain here, and the working out of its details are very difficult. What I want to do is to show something that might actually have worked under these circumstnaces and produce a kind of general revolt of some sort. I think maybe I will leave the intended end of the revolt deliberately vague, and show something that started as a whim in the mind of a headstrong, brilliant boy as coming to dominate the whole Pacific night air war, and with this, show something of the dangers inherent in a mystique-oriented underground bureaucracy.

The big scene of the second novel is the aftermath of the beheading of two members of the squadron by the Japanese, which Shears takes as a pretext to get the squadron into enemy territory. Meanwhile, Conway, a rather sensitive, intelligent, politically idealistic man, in one scene gets a glimpse of what is going on all around him, why the men have turned against him, why Shears, to all apparent purposes, and with the tacit consent of General Massingale, has taken over the squadron. Shears sets out with all the aircraft in the squadron with him at night for the place where the two squadron members were tortured and beheaded. One of these was an Alnilam plot man, and it is this that most of the other pilots are really going out to avenge. By this time, Conway, a dedicated patriot, conceives that his duty in dying for his country is not to straffe and kill Japanese, but to kill Shears. The raid is a general call to quarters, and as Shears begins to give out with the Alnilam code, to break radio silence, and get the code to naval ships and so on, Conway runs into him.

After this there is a short section on the invasion of Okinawa, as seen through the eyes of the last survivor of the original Alnilam plot, the only one left who actually knew Joel Cahill. He is a simple, sincere Greek boy named

Harbellis, and the second book ends with him at rest and recreation at a commandeered Japanese resort hotel under Fujiama.

That's a very short summary, but I thought I would let you know what I am working on, and see what you thought of it. Please see that Ken gets a copy of this, so I can have his thoughts on it as well. I can let you have a first draft, simply dealing with the events in sequence, and not at all concentrating on style, flow or anything of that nature. Then, if you think we have a workable structure for the first book on that basis, I will go on to the second draft and then to the third and possibly the fourth, all the time working on <u>Crux</u> and bringing it along.

We should issue <u>Alnilam</u> and let the public respond as they will. We should then bring out <u>Crux</u> a couple of years after, which will give me time to polish it and get it like I want it. This procedure will give us double the opportunity for the prizes, the paperback contracts, and all the rest of those things.

I also have about three-quarters of a new book of poems ready, and, when I finish three or four more that are almost finished right now, I can submit it to you. We can consider when to bring it out, following it, as you and Ken suggested, with a big collected poems three or four years later. So you can see that things are moving right along.

What with the energy crisis, I have had to cut down on my travel plans pretty drastically, as everybody has, but would like to invite you and Sally, when you have the leisure time to sit in airport terminals for hours, to come down and visit with us at a place we have just bought down near Pawley's Island. We all could have some time together, and talk these matters out. I'd like that a lot, believe me.

All yours,

To: Robert Penn Warren   TLS, Emory University

4620 Lelia's Court
Columbia, S.C. 29206
January 7, 1974

Dear Red:

I have sent the sections of the new poem on to Gordon Lish in New York, with the strongest recommendations. We still don't have much room, and I don't believe we could possibly do the whole thing as you have it here. I have made some suggestions as to how we might print a part or a couple of parts of the poem, and I have asked Gordon to give me his thoughts on this idea and to come up with suggestions of his own as he wishes. But anyway, the poem is now in the hands of the New York editorial staff, and you will hear either from them or from me on the matter. It is particularly good, Red, and the end is nothing less than smashing, especially the <u>very</u> end.

Well, we'll see.

The pictures we took down at Litchfield came out very well, and we will have reproductions made and send them along to you as a reminder of how human life should be lived and almost never is.

Maxine has been deathly ill. At one time there were indications that she might have as many as four potentially fatal diseases at the same time. It was a dark night not of the soul but of the guts. But one by one the tests came back: the danger of the high blood pressure and coronary problem seem to be overrated, the diabetes suspected aparently either receded or did not exist in the first place, the test for cervical cancer came back blessedly negative (though Maxine had to have a kind of exploratory operation), and now remains only the gravid liver, which she is combatting with a fine mixture of fury and temperance. So we are not as bad off as we thought we might be. But we have been pretty much out of circulation, what with all this medical runaround, and I am only just now getting back to editing and to my own work. I have only been working a few days, but lots of pieces are falling into place, and the new book of poems, <u>Slowly Toward Hercules</u>, is going to be on all counts the best I have done to date.

My warmest love to Eleanor, and keep some for yourself. I hope your flu is better, or, hopefully, now "vanished quite away."

All yours,
Jim

To: The Honorable John C. West

CC, Emory University
4620 Lelia's Court
Columbia, S.C. 29206

February 4, 1974

Dear Governor West:

The other members of the Selection Committee and I agree that without question Ms. Bennie Lee Sinclair (Mrs. Don Lewis) of Campobello is easily the most distinguished poet that came under our scrutiny. I can see no reason, myself, as to why she should not be immediately selected. My personal criteria are as follows. First, I believe wholeheartedly in the improvement of our State's image in the arts. We have, formally, not been strong in the field of poetry. We have had competent versifiers, but few national figures. Ms. Sinclair is, in a small but genuine sense, a national figure. She has published in extremely prestigious magazines, and has had a book of poems introduced by one of the most prominent and acclaimed American poets, critics, and anthologists, Mark Strand. I know Mr. Strand personally—he and I were judges, a few years back, for the giving of the Bollingen Prize, the largest single poetry prize this country bestows—and I can speak freely of Mr. Strand's excellent qualifications to judge all matters pertaining to poetic value. He is most enthusiastic about Ms. Sinclair's qualities, as he makes plain in his introduction. With Ms. Sinclair, South Carolina would attain to a quality in the artistic work of the laureateship that it hitherto has not been able to command. In addition, this candidate is very firmly rooted in our soil. She is partially a mountain woman, and understands the rural ways so deeply associated with South Carolina. On the other hand, she is capable of being extremely sophisticated as to city cultural life, on the national as well as the local literary scene. As a poet, she is absolutely and compellingly direct, and writes with such forthright honesty that any reader who seriously attends her cannot fail to be moved. She has been extremely active in the Poetry in the Schools Program. I have had her in my own classes, talking to my students, and she has a great ability to communicate the human meaning of good poetry. All these are very valuable attributes indeed. As I have said earlier, all the members of the Committee agree that Ms. Sinclair is without question the most distinguished candidate presented to us for examination.

There are, perhaps, one or two slight drawbacks, but I believe these conditions should not seriously be considered drawbacks by anyone interested in getting the best person for this very important post: a post which I think will be capable, if rightly administered, of effecting enormous good among us, and among people who are interested or might become interested in the cultural affairs of our State. Ms. Sinclair is comparatively young; as nearly as I can tell, she is about thirty-six or thirty-seven. But this fact is in reality a plus factor, for, if she turns out as well in the laureatship as I have every reason to believe she would, she could have a long-term effect on all the matters that here concern us. The other slight drawback—if so it may be construed—is that Ms. Sinclair is a diabetic, and must conserve some of her very abundant energies. But neither do I consider this any great hindrance to our selection of Ms. Sinclair. The good qualities in her personality and work so far overshadow these considerations as to make them only of incidental interest.

Finally, it seems to me that the only real consideration here is to have our State represented in the laureateship by as strong and as true a poet as we can possibly get at this time and under these conditions. I am convinced that Bennie Lee Sinclair is just that. She stands forth quite clearly as a genuine poet, a "maker" in the old Greek and original sense of the word <u>poet</u>, and as someone who would give our State an exciting chance to be known for its cultural contributions.

Parenthetically, as a recent electee to the University's Center for Cultural Development, I think that the occasion to change the concept of the laureateship for the better is an extremely fortunate coincidence. It is the kind of contribution I had hoped to be able to make to the office of Senior Fellow of the Center.

Sincerely yours,

To: John Logue[16]

CC, Emory University
4620 Lelia's Court
Columbia, S.C. 29206

February 21, 1974

Dear John and Les:

I enclose the people section for your perusal. I am almost finished with the traditions sections, and will have it to you in a few days. There is no trouble at all about our March 1 deadline, provided you like what I have done so far. I am sending this new material on to you so you can give it as thorough a going-over as may be possible, for we all want this book to be as good as we can humanly make it. Don't hesitate to offer any suggestions that may occur to you. After all, I have been dealing with editors for a long time, and I have never felt more confident than I do with the pair of you.

I am trying to write each of the three main sections approximately the same length. It seems to me that in a book of this kind the reader does not want to have the weight of what is obviously an enormously long text hanging over him. He wishes to read a little here, a little there, to be as unsystematic as my text encourages him to be: to take away one thought, one image at a time. Therefore, as you know, I have discouraged continuity and tried to concentrate on individual scenes and images, to shift from one thing to another with a certain amount of disconcertedness: to blind-side the reader whenever I could. Anyway, let me know what you think. Meanwhile, I will finish up the last section and send it along well in time for the deadline, and also

16. Editorial director of the Book Division of *Southern Living Magazine,* which published several excerpts from *Jericho* in its October 1974 issue.

in time for you to peruse the last section as you are now in the process of doing in the case of this one.

Let me know, in the meantime, what the situation is going to be in Washington: whether you would benefit by my being there at the Book Fair, convention, or whatever the official name for the shindig may be.

The fellow who did the <u>Playboy</u> interview has now become book editor of <u>Playboy</u>, and this will insure us of very good readership and coverage, for he, an Alabamian himself, is very enthusiastic about the <u>idea</u> of the book, and the fact that he and I have worked together before.

Again, let me hear. It all looks good, and I hope you like the new stuff. It strikes me as rather strange and good. But then, <u>you</u> will now tell <u>me</u>!

All yours,

To: Mr. Davis   **CC, Emory University**

23 August, 1974
Columbia, S.C.

Dear Mr Davis, and/or President of Davis Instruments:

I herewith return for repair, under the guarantee, the Mark #12 Master Sextant I purchased from you a couple of months ago. Since the sextant—an outstandingly good one I sorely need to have back as soon as possible—is made of plastic, there is always the chance that things will break off. In this case, it has been the rear housing for the eye-piece and both prongs broke off when I was changing from the regular eye-piece to the three-power scope. If I'd been on the high seas and had that happen I would sure have been sunk, and in more than one sense. I strongly urge you to convert, and make at least that part of the sextant metal, to avert this kind of thing from happening. I will find, I am sure, no better sextant than yours, but I would like a more durable one, so could you put me on to some place that could furnish me with a metal sextant? I'd like to have a couple of them around, just in case. But be assured I'll use the Davis as long as it holds up. There has never been a better, to my knowledge. Get that thing back to me as soon as you can! I <u>need</u> it! Or, if you can't repair it, send me a new one, and I'll be happy to pay for it.

I have bought a good deal of equipment fro, you, including the plot-board, the bino-vision, the range-finger, and the complete celestial navigation course and the Davis Artificial Horizon.

This last is a mighty good aid, but I could make a suggestion or two that might help in the design, if you don't mind. First of all, I think you should have a unit in which the panes—glass and/or plastic—slot into place, or lock in, in some way, so they are not forever sliding off the assembly. It is hard to get a sight on any fairly rough sea, and when your apparatus is continually falling apart, it is well-nigh impossible. Also, the necessity of using water or some other liquid in the basin of the device is terribly awkward. I have had fairly good luck with Duke's Peanut Oil, but even that will not hold a consistent image. And it is terribly messy, necessitating a continual soaping-out of the device. Why could you not simply use a mirror in the bottom og the basin, the main assembly? After all, the liquid which is now used serves exactly the same purpose, and a mirror would not jiggle around as liquid does. If that would work out, and if you could make up a portable package that would, when assembled, lock or slot together firmly in place, you would have done navigation an even greater service that you already have, and can be assured that you have saved many lives, as well as given much pleasure and made much more possible.

The Celestial Navigation Course is the greatest! Even I can understand it1 I'll send you the answers to the first few lessons in a week or ten days. I'm using your material chiefly in connection with a new novel of mine about flying: my first book since Deliverance. There is a mysterious character in it, known only as The Navigator! And I, as the author, have to know what the hell he's talking about!

My best, and do get my Mark #12 Master Sextamt back to me as soon as you can. It's the greatest, and I can't stand to be without it. I take that and my Guitar with me everywhere I go, and those two love each other just as much as I love them.

Sincerely,

To: Daniel Halpern

CC, Emory University
4620 Lelia's Court
Columbia, S.C. 29206

February 21, 1975

Dear Dan:

I think that your idea for presenting tragically neglected books of this century is marvelous. It should be quite a success. God knows, there are thousands of them. My selection is The Journal of a Disappointed Man, by W.N.P. Barbellion. It is a very fine book that has been unfairly neglected in our time.

Thank you for requesting my opinion. My best to you and your associates.

All yours,

To: Charles Fries

CC, Emory University
4620 Lelia's Court
Columbia, S.C. 29206

August 5, 1975

Dear Chuck,

Here is the opening of <u>GENE BULLARD</u>. As to <u>Call of the Wild</u> and the pro-jected series, there are certain difficulties here, but the main one is the strangeness of your dealing with the network on one basis and with me on another. It would appear to me that you sold my script of <u>Call of the Wild</u>—which took me 2 years and a great deal of labor and travel—to the network <u>only</u> on the proviso that there could be a series developed from the pilot. This was never my intention. I was to be paid a flat fee for a script called <u>The Call of the Wild</u>, and was to be involved in nothing other than that. The contracts attest to this fact.

The $40,000.00 you have paid me for <u>The Call of the Wild</u> is an eminently fair sum as you have suggested in your letter, and I have no cavil about this part of things.

But, my man, if you want to do series work, let us do <u>2</u> series instead of just the 1 based on John Thornton! Another on Bullard? As I have said, I enclose our opening for <u>Gene Bullard</u>—though I still think <u>Crownfire</u> is the better title, and, as a title, would get a great many more people into theatres than a film which simply announces itself as a man's name. In order for me to go ahead on schedule, I will need to have a complete typescript of the notes we took at your beach cottage. This procedure will enable me to avoid what I am tempted to call script-slippage.

As soon as the scripts from <u>Call of the Wild</u> come in, please let me have about three copies at my Columbia address. I would like to see how we came out after all of this time. I expect it will be good. I enclose a photo made at MGM. My best to all.

As ever,

To: Christopher Dickey

CC, Emory University
4620 Lelia's Court
Columbia, S.C. 29206

November 11, 1975

My dear boy,

This is by way of congratulations for a twenty-four year old effort well done. I am tremendously proud.

Your mother is bringing along a belt with a buckle made from an original that Tom dug up from the battleground of Cold Harbor, Virginia. He had a casting made from the original, and struck off this bronze buckle from that. It might be a certain amount of fun to use this as a conversation-piece amongst the people who are certain to interview you, and those who are interested in your whole project. It is a buckle from a Mississippi regiment, and you can still see an indentation at the top of the buckle where the entrenching tool wielded by the Demon relic-hunter struck it, "under the pinestraw." The belt inserts to the right, instead of the customary left—comes around (naturally!) and is inserted back under the front part of the belt, where upon the hook is engaged in the proper hole. I am sending along with Mom a prime hole-punch, so that you can adjust things as you wish.

Again, my great boy and marvelous companion, I am overflowing with pride.

Charles Fries is buying back Amos Berry from Elliot Kastner on condition that you and I script it.

Hackman?

Love,

To: Andrew Lytle

CC, Emory University
4620 Lelia's Court
Columbia, S.C. 29206

November 24, 1975

Dear Andrew,

I have <u>A Wake for the Living</u>, and have read it twice with the greatest admiration. The part about the Southern portion of the Revolutionary War is especially interesting, for I have walked over those battlefields of Cowpens and King's Mountain trying to re-create what had gone on there. As well as I can tell, these were the battles that decided America's fate in the war if any two battles could.

This is a remarkable piece of research, and I believe it will be infinitely valuable to historians as well as those who are interested in the drama of warfare and the origin of their country as Americans.

And I'm sure glad they kicked the hell out of Tarleton!

My best to you and yours, after so many years.

Ever,

To: Paul Schmidt

CC, Emory University
4620 Lelia's Court
Columbia, S.C. 29206

August 5, 1976

Dear Mr. Schmidt,

Congratulations on your superb rendition of the works of <u>Arthur Rimbaud</u>. Your translations make available for the first time the marvelous and inspired slap-improvisation of a very great, self-doomed writer. That poor boy! Deluded, but deluded with genius. I would not have missed knowing his work. Nor would I have missed your masterly translations. You have added a cubit to the stature of all of us.

Again, thank you.

Sincerely,

To: Geoffrey Wolff

CC, Emory University
4620 Lelia's Court
Columbia, S.C. 29206

August 5, 1976

Dear Geoffrey,

I have just read your masterly <u>Black Sun</u>. I am an indefatigueable biographee-reader, and feel qualified to judge how much research has been done, how many years spent on the task, as well as the qualities of the biographer's mind. I can tell you without qualification that <u>Black Sun</u> is the best biography I have ever read, among, literally hundreds.

I of course never met Crosby. He was dead when I was no more than six or seven years old. But I do know several people who <u>did</u> know him, among them Malcolm Cowley, Allen Tate, Ernest Hemingway and Archibald MacLeish. and Kay Boyle. Ms. Boyle lent me her home in San Francisco a few years ago when I was speaking at San Francisco State, and she spoke of nothing but Harry Crosby.

Again, congratulations. The book should sweep all the prizes: The National Book Award, the Pulitzer—everything.

But none of these is the true Prize. <u>That</u> prize is the book itself. I am very proud of you Geoffrey. You have done humanity a service.

It might interest you to know that I have a new long poem called, <u>The Zodiac</u>, which you might want to see. It is due from Doubleday in about a month and is said to be—again, I could not say this myself; it would have to be said for me—that it is the most significant significant long poem since <u>The Waste Land</u>. Check out the possibilities of your doing the lead review on this for the New York Times. I am sure that Harvey Shapiro would respond eagerly. It is time—and the current is now running with the poets rather than with the historians and sociologists—toward a new sensiblization of the human head and body.

But the main purpose of this letter is that of simple congratulations. <u>Black Sun</u> is a superb agreement. I cannot <u>imagine</u> how the research was undertaken. But that does not matter; it was, and it won through triumphantly.

All yours,

P.S. Do you still have my Irish cap? I do hope so, for I like to think of your wearing it.

To: Jimmy Carter

CC, Emory University
4620 Lelia's Court
Columbia, S.C. 29206

September 29, 1976

Dear Jimmy,

You're going to win, whether my advice has anything to do with the final outcome or not. Yet I think that after all it may have something to do with it. For I, and the people that will come after you and me, will be more benefited by your winning a landslide victory than they would by a squeak-through win that satisfies no one. Please understand that I, more than most, am cognizant of the undesirability of advice that has not been solicited. Usually advice isn't solicited, but in the political arena it must be. Let me offer a few points to my old friend.

First of all, you <u>will</u> be the President. But as it looks now your margin will be close enough for there to be a certain amount of doubt and dissention among our people. If you were to win on a landslide, there would be that much more of a chance to unify the nation, and get a clear direction as to where we are going. There is no substitute for a great leader of a people, or for one who promises to be of such rare quality. Of this company I firmly believe you to be, but the matter must be proved <u>now</u>, when it counts most.

Let me go on just a bit. The first debate was good enough, but was not inspiring, and, it was I fear, a little dull. In other words, it was not the stuff of which landslide victories are made on either side. I know it, you know it, and the American people know it. The idea of talking to the issues and using a great many statistics that are unassimilable to the TV viewers, as the numbers—including decimals—fly past them, is to the point, but not to the ultimate point. Here, the slide rule and the electronic calculator are of use to a minority of the population only insofar as the election of a candidate is concerned. I should like you to talk about the issues; of course I would.

But this is not the heart of the matter. One can show a relatively low-key sincerity and move no one to the polls in affirmation. It seems to me, Jimmy, that you need in some manner to catch rhetorical fire, to come out louder and stronger with a greater and more emphatic stress on the key words of the key statements. Then people will have your words stay with them, and will vote accordingly. What we need is fire. And we need it now, for timing is imperative. You have two more debates with Ford. If you come out with such phrases—and I am not talking about empty political bombast such as, "We must look forward to greater tomorrows"—but genuinely effective statements that will stay with people and be identified with <u>you</u>, there can be no doubt of your impending victory. I heard none of these in the first debate, though I was straining my ears. You are up against a man who is the prime Wooden-Indian of our time. He cannot rise to the memorable phrase. He is a sitting duck for you. If you come out with fire and memorable statements— whatever these might be—there will be no doubt of the outcome. It will be catastrophic for the Republican Party and a very great thing for the Democratic Party and ultimately for the nation and the world. You have got the future of all of our lives in your pocket, Jimmy.

But you must be capable of saying things that come to be on everyone's lips. If I may be forgiven, statistical surveys slip very quickly off the lips. When John Kennedy said, "Ich bin ein Berliner" international diplomacy was furthered to such an extent that the course of history was changed. Or when Kennedy issued his proclamation stating, "Ask not what your country can do for you . . ." This kind of effectiveness is true throughout national and international, political and philosophical history: the power of words to move people to action. If you were to avail yourself of such <u>words</u> in the last two debates, we could have the nation and the world that you want. If you win a thin and begrudged victory, we cannot have this and will not. Think of Lincoln saying in his second inaugural address, "None of us can escape history." <u>Find</u> your phrases—I don't think you need writers—for you <u>can</u> find them yourself and deliver them at the key points of the next debates, slowly, loudly and emphatically, at moments which will have a devastating effect on the voter. If this happens, as I hope and almost know it will, the next place you and I meet will be the oval office.

All yours,

To: Jimmy Carter   CC, Emory University
                                                4620 Lelia's Court
                                                Columbia, S.C. 29206

                                                October 15, 1976

Dear Jimmy,

We are coming on to the final and crucial debate, and it seems to me that political backbiting can be overpassed by a series of statements having to do not with pettiness concerning Congressional spending and small talk about which politician did what nefarious thing, hoping to win by default because you have proven the other fellow crooked who has not yet proven you crooked.

Crooked you are not, and I know this from the experience of years, <u>but</u> there is a very great difference in what <u>I</u> know and what the American people think and know about you. I don't think you should allow yourself to be put in the position of defending yourself according to this criterion. Ford is trying to do this kind of thing to you, and if you allow yourself to be reduced to his pace he will be able to score points against you. Simply tell him that, "Those who are unable to learn from the past are condemned to repeat it."

But this need not be. This kind of pettiness has come to be identified with Ford and with the current Republican party. On your account, you need not refer to corruption, to Watergate, and to the rest of the things that have formed the matter of the first two debates. Some of this you can do, and I'm sure your aids will furnish you with plenty of ammunition.

But what we want to leave in the American ear and the American heart is something far stronger than the haggling about various funds. Jim, if you come on strong at the very end, and say some things that the American people will remember and identify with you, there is no doubt of the outcome. Do not at the end of the debate be low-key and reasonable.

You might, for example, say something about the recent explorations on Mars which seem conclusively to prove that there is no life on the place where we most hoped it might be discovered. This makes the earth of infinite importance, because here thinking and feeling beings reside, and there is no evidence that they reside anywhere but in <u>our</u> minds and hearts and in <u>our</u> dealings with each other. One of my favorite composers, Kurt Weill, wrote a song titled <u>Lost in the Stars</u>. What we do here on the planet earth is of paramount importance, and I believe that if we conduct ourselves properly and solve our economic and political problems, we shall find ourselves not lost in the stars, but found there.

Ever,

To: Jack Aldridge

CC, Emory University
4620 Lelia's Court
Columbia, S.C. 29206

August 10, 1977

Dear Jack,

Please forgive my waiting so long to answer your very welcome letter of a few months back but a great deal has been happening and I've had very little time for correspondence even with the people I most highly esteem. Maxine, my wife of almost thirty years, died last October. My mother and father also died during this last year, and I have been plunged into various family difficulties which certainly need not concern you, but which may serve to explain why I have not communicated with you earlier as I most assuredly wished to do.

Your desire to come back to the South is very heartening to me, for we need all the good critics and novelists we can get. I myself teach only one semester a year, and am just getting ready for my one term.beginning in September. The year before this last one I was on sabbatical, and so have not been in close touch with English department doings for a good long time now. When school starts, I will see that your case is taken up and will put the full of whatever power I possess behind your suit. God knows I would like to have you come to South Carolina but I must first make a relatively long-range sounding-out of whatever possibilities there may be here. There are also a good many other schools in the South I could investigate for you. My oldest boy went to the University of Virginia, for example, and my youngest is a sophomore at Washington and Lee. If you like' I can try these and some other good schools for you.

I'll wait to hear from you on these matters, and will be guided by your preferences. Know, meanwhile, that I consider you on all counts the best literary critic now writing, especially in that area dealing with the interaction of actual literary works and the intellectual and social climate around them. I have all your books, and teach my students more of your opinions than I do of my own. We Southerners—J. Carter among us—should be getting more of this! As I said at the end of the Inaugural poem I did for Jimmy, I will do what I can.

Yours ever,

To: Louis Simpson

CC, Emory University
4620 Lelia's Court
Columbia, S.C. 29206

August 10, 1977

Dear Louis,

I have just finished <u>Three on the Tower</u> and wanted quickly to write to you and tell you how fine I think it is. It must have been a tremendously difficult job but I don't think such difficulties have ever been dealt with before in such an urbane and readable way. At first I thought your approach—part scholarly, part critical, part biographical, and part personal opinion on the part of the biographer—a little curious but I soon got to like the effect of what I was reading and now I would not wish to go back to perusing more standardized or compartmentalized biographies, especially those of writers.

The section on Eliot, that secretive man, is most enlightening. Like you, I doubt very seriously as to whether any official biography will ever be written on him. As I remember he took some pains to specify that no such <u>Life</u> should be authorized. The only other example of this attitude I can think of is, curiously enough, Matthew Arnold. It seems odd that a man of Eliot's influence should have so little biographical interest. I imagine this fact would have pleased him, but there was something terrible, perhaps unthinkable, underlying all of that scholarly reasonableness. You have certainly fixed my conviction in this matter and it will most probably not waver.

Again, this is only a very brief note to let you know how highly I esteem the book and my acquaintance with you which though reasonably long, has been lamentably infrequent. But I am in and out of New York city a good deal and perhaps it will be possible for us to meet for a drink or even dinner at some time during the upcoming school year. I like to think of that; it would be good human time.

My best to all in your house. Please accept my continuing good wishes for yourself and all your projects.

Yours ever,

To: Lawrence Freundlich[17]   CC, Emory University
                                                4620 Lelia's Court
                                                Columbia, S.C. 29206

                                                August 25, 1977

Dear Larry,
    Thank you so very much for sending along the samples of Marie Angel's projected calligraphy for <u>Tucky</u>. I think, of these three examples, the second—the one with the illustration of the little boy—is the best. The first seems a little too crowded and give the impression that the poem is in a quatrain form

17. Executive director of Crown Publishers.

when actually the whole fun of rhyming is that it is in couplets. Too, I like the spacing of the example I have chosen for it goes more slowly, and a child may presumably be able to savor the words and even the letters better this way. In the third example the letters seem a little too thin physically and might not make the eye-impact a bool like this should have. Let me know what you think about all this and I will be guided accordingly. There are a couple of changes I would like to make while we are at this stage of things. In couplet fourteen, ("He shot the smiling Devil . . .") I would like a comma after dancing in the second line if I don't already have one there. In couplet 23, I would like the first line to read, "And when his mother came for him, before the break of light," instead of "just at the break of light."/ In the second couplet from the end, I would like to change the whole first line form, "They sang of mystic voyages and the rights of man and beast" to read, "They sang in mystic double-tongue, the tongue of man and beast." And I would like to change, in the following line, the word animal to jungle so that the couplet, as recast, will read:

"They sang in mystic double-tongue, the tongue of man and beast,
They sang of Far West buffalo, and the jungles of the East,"

Let me know, at your convenience, how the work is progressing, and do pass onto me everything that Ms. Angel has made available to you. Meanwhile, I am delighted that things are going well at Crown and that there seem to be no difficulties at all in our immediate project. I am very happy indeed that you are my editor and I think we will produce a very good book.

I will be in New York around October 15, to accept a poetry award from the New York Quarterly. I hope that we will be able to have dinner together at that time. That would be good.

All yours,

To: Elizabeth Hardwick   Telegram, University of Texas at Austin
September 13, 1977   Columbia, S.C.

THIS MAN OF WORDS HAS NO WORDS. I LIKE TO THINK THAT CAL WENT IN A GREAT RUSH OF PRIDE IN THE WONDERFUL ACCOM-PLISHMENT OF HIS LIFE AND WORK. I CAN GUARANTEE THAT I WILL HAVE SUCH A FEELING FOR HIM WHEN THE SAME THING

HAPPENS TO ME AND AS I DO NOW. PLEASE KNOW THAT I AM WITH
YOU AND HARRIET ALWAYS, NOW THAT ALL WE CAN DO IS TO LOVE
HIM FOREVER.
   JAMES DICKEY

To: Advisory Board on the Pulitzer Prizes   CC, Emory University
                                                   4620 Lelia's Court
                                                   Columbia, S.C. 29206

                                                   January 5, 1978

Dear Friends:

The Poetry Jury has chosen Howard Nemerov's <u>Collected</u> <u>Poems</u> as the recipient of the Pulitzer Prize for Poetry in 1977. Mr. Nemerov's brilliant career as
a poet has been an outstanding contribution to letters by virtue of the wit and
depth of a large body of work. His poetry, with its tremendously wide variety
of form, its command of language, and its vivid and perceptive use of imagery very particular to Mr. Nemerov's mentality, has seemed to at least two
of us, and perhaps to the third, to merit this award.

I have written to the other members of the jury. Dr. Applewhite and I agree
on Mr. Nemerov's book, while Dr. Vendler appears to favor Robert Lowell's
<u>Day</u> <u>by</u> <u>Day</u>. I have asked her to reconsider her decision, since Dr. Applewhite
and I both wish to honor Mr. Nemerov.

As I say, I have not yet heard from Dr. Vendler, but if you must have a decision
at this time, it is clear that two of us favor Mr. Nemerov. Therefore, it would
be safe to say that he is the winner and should be awarded the prize.

Our second choice would be Allen Tate's <u>Collected</u> <u>Poems</u> <u>1919-1976</u>; other
considerations in our list of the final five were Mr. Lowell's <u>Day</u> <u>by</u> <u>Day</u>, Robert Penn Warren's <u>Selected</u> <u>Poems</u> <u>1923-1975</u>, and John Berryman's <u>Henry's</u>
<u>Fate</u>.

Sincerely yours,

To: Stuart Wright

CC, Emory University
4620 Lelia's Court
Columbia, S.C. 29206

May 24, 1978

Dear Stuart:

You certainly have a knack for coming up with all sorts of projects. Yes—I'll go with your idea on the student poems. I must confess that I can't remember that much about them, but I'm happy that you like them.

How about using a more provocative title, Veteran's Birth, and keeping The Gadfly Poems as a subtitle? Then a little lower on the cover, you could have "The First Published Poems of James Dickey from Vanderbilt University (with the dates)." The rest of your description with the stiff black Arches wrappers with a French Cockerell paper outer wrapper sounds fine.

Your terms of $200 for the four and a percentage of sales is OK, too. I'm ready when you are—send it on down!

Debba and I have no definite plans for the summer. Keep in touch.

One last thing (though certainly not least important)—I am enclosing the prose statement that you requested.

All yours,

To: Herb Yellin[18]

CC, Emory University
4620 Lelia's Court
Columbia, S.C. 29206

June 2, 1978

Dear Herb:

I return The Hemingway Play. I think it is perfectly awful, and I would under no circumstances consider writing an introduction for it. I think you are wasting your very good human and editorial time with such material; there are so many projects that would be more worthy of your efforts than this one is.

18. Editor of Lord John Press.

Meanwhile, I am delighted with your edition of <u>The Enemy from Eden</u>. It is much the handsomest gift book that I have ever done. Everyone I have shown it to is enchanted with it. No less an authority than Matthew Bruccoli pronounced it to be of absolute quality, imaginatively conceived, beautifully illustrated, and generally a first-class example of fine-booking in all respects. Though I was glad to have Matt's opinion, I knew all those things when I first saw the book. I hope you have every success with it, and I will do everything I can to promote it, particularly through readings and interviews. Please let me know what you need, and I will comply.

Please convey my congratulations to Ron Sauter, and tell him that I hope to be fortunate enough to work with him on other projects later on.

All yours,

To: Lawrence Freundlich   CC, Emory University
                                           4620 Lelia's Court
                                           Columbia, S.C. 29206

                                           September 1, 1978

Dear Larry:

I am not one, as you know, to ask favors of editors, but I would like you to have a look at a new manuscript of my old friend Peter Viereck. It is a long poem called <u>Applewood</u>, and if it bowls you over, I would like to think that Crown might consider publishing it. After all, Peter is a Pulitzer Prize winner, and he is a quite considerable poet, as well as being a very good historian and political commentator. If you will write to him, he will send the manuscript of <u>Applewood</u> on to you forthwith. He asks only for a hearing, and from the right party. Have a shot at it. I would appreciate your attention.

Meanwhile, plans for <u>Tucky</u> seem right in line with what I would most like, under absolutely ideal conditions, to happen.

My best, as ever1.

All yours,

To: Peter Vireck

CC, Emory University
4620 Lelia's Court
Columbia, S.C. 29206

September 1, 1978

Dear Peter:

I enclose a copy of a letter to Larry Freundlich, my editor at Crown Publishers, with whom I am bringing out a book next month. I also enclose two copies of the book for your grandchildren. It was written for my own grandson, and is just a kind of jue d'Esprit in doggerel, intended only to amuse. But if there is something beyond mere amusement, I would be pleased to think that you picked up on that quality, if it exists. I drew on Roy[19]—it is odd that you should have sent me his wonderful letter—for some of the bird imagery, which you will easily be able to pick out in those pages illustrated with flamingos and egrets. It is wonderful to recall those conversations we used to have in Firenze, about Roy, and those great wild trips that you and I took to monasteries like Certosa, where you told me about Thomas Merton and his garrulous style. I remember your saying, "Tom Merton became a Trappist, as everyone knows by now. My God, he took the vow of silence seven years ago, and they haven't been able to shut him up since!" Surely he must be the most loquacious Trappist in the history of the Order."

I also remember the time, year after the times in Firenze—too many years then, and too many now—that you and I were together with Muriel Rukeyser on that Sunday morning program called "Camera Three," with that awful fathead of an interlocutor, and I remember your wonderfully losing patience with him and uttering the immortal phrase, "None of that tongue in your chic."

I hope that your dealings with Crown and with Larry Freundlich will be successful for all, for there is no poet writing in my tongue that I more admire or more love. God bless you, Peter, and come down here and give a reading for us in the gloomy, moss-haunted country where I live.

All yours,

19. Roy Campbell.

To: President and Mrs. Jimmy Carter

CC, Emory University
4620 Lelia's Court
Columbia, S.C. 29206

November 27, 1978

Dear Rosalynn and Jimmy,

I am very sorry to miss the December third reception, but I had previously been committed to lecture at the Air Force Academy and some other places, and, therefore, couldn't make it to Washington.

Meanwhile, I thought you might like to have the enclosed folio, on which I collaborated with Robert Penn Warren and Reynolds Price as a present for the seventy-eighth birthday of Aaron Copland, the American composer. My poem of the three is a result of the time that Deborah and I spent in Mexico as your representatives. In one of my speeches, I voiced the hope that Octavio Paz, Mexico's finest poet, would be the next recipient of the Nobel Prize for Literature. Paz and I spent as much time together as we could. I had known him previously, when he served in some diplomatic capacity for his country at the same time I was at the Library of Congress in the Poetry Chair. We thought it might be, as a private matter, interesting to "translate" some of each other's work. The present poem is one of his I did in a free—a _very_ free—adaptation.

My best to you both, and to the good you are doing the world.

As ever,

P.S. Note the middle name of the artist on the woodcut!

To: A. J. Vogl

CC, Emory University
4620 Lelia's Court
Columbia, S.C. 29206

February 14, 1979

Dear A. J. Vogl:

My choices of musical selections for a record to be sent to other worlds are the following:
   1. George Frideric Handel, <u>Water Music Suite</u>
   2. Bix Beiderbecke, "Royal Garden Blues"
   3. Richard Wagner, "Overture" from <u>Rienzi</u>
   4. Bela Bartok, <u>Concerto for Orchestra</u>
   5. "Duellin' Banjoes," recorded by Eric Weissberg and Steve Mandel
   6. Wolfgang Amadeus Mozart, <u>Horn Concerto in D Major</u>
   7. "Ragtime Annie," recorded by Doc and Merle Watson

I am looking forward to receiving Carl Sagan's book as well as a copy of myour magazine.

Sincerely yours,

To: Phoebe Pettingell

CC, Emory University
4620 Lelia's Court
Columbia, S.C. 29206

May 2, 1979

Dear Ms. Pettingell:

I have a copy of your husband's book which you edited, <u>The Critic's Credentials</u>, and recently used it while preparing a lecture on Ezra Pound. Rereading some of his essays prompted me to write you.

I stayed with Stanley sometime after Shirley's death when I read at Bennington, and spent some of the best human time of my life with him and corresponded with him until his death. Ever since I read <u>The Armed Vision</u> while I was a student at Vanderbilt, I have learned continually from Stanley and his example and continue to do so. I would like for you to know that when I delivered the inaugural poem for Jimmy Carter, I owed both the poem and the words with which I prefaced it to an article which Stanley had written that appeared in the Summer 1949 <u>Kenyon Review</u>:

> It is Campbell's contention that all myth is one, "the great myth," "the mono-myth," which can be described as an elaboration of the three stages of Van Gennep's <u>rites de passage</u>, thus: "a separation from the world, a penetration to some source of power, and a life-enhancing return."

This passage was also the prime operative factor in my novel <u>Deliverance</u> as well as in the film made from it.

I thought that you might like to know these things, so I record them, send them to you, and pass on.

Sincerely yours,

To: Jesse Hill Ford

CC, Emory University
4620 Lelia's Court
Columbia, S.C. 29206

May 15, 1979

Dear Jesse:

It's been nearly a year now since we corresponded, so I hope this letter reaches you. I'm sorry that somehow or another I never made it down to Birmingham to give that reading. Maybe the money fell through—I can't even remember now. But I do remember that I've long cherished the idea of working with you on a project, and we can do it. You know I'll back you on anything, and we can write any movie we choose. I just finished a second draft for a television movie that's supposed to be filmed during the summer. You just let me know what you want to do.

What is your connection in the Virgin Islands? Debba and I hope to be there later on in the summer, and maybe we can get together if you go there regularly.

I hope you are still well and happy. We would love to meet Lil.

All yours,

To: Steward Richardson

CC, Emory University
4620 Lelia's Court
Columbia, S.C. 29206

May 29, 1979

Dear Sandy:

How overjoyed Deborah and I were to see you last week in New York! I am tremendously pleased with your reaction to <u>Alnilam</u> and am very grateful for the things you say about it. It's going to be good, no doubt about it. I am also very happy over the success of <u>The Zodiac</u>, and am, needless to say, eagerly looking forward to seeing the new edition. Please make sure to let me know when it will be available in stores, and I will do the utmost I can to promote the sales by personal appearances, television interviews, and so on. For example, you may know that there is a great deal of interest in the arts in South Carolina right now on account of the Spoleto festival in Charleston. There is also a lot of coverage on me at this time resulting from my recent appointment as the first Carolina Professor at the University of South Carolina, and, if possible, we should try to key-in our publication of the new edition of <u>The Zodiac</u> with these conditions. Too, I will be going to Atlanta in a month to finish settling up my parents' estate, and as a hometown boy I can surely do us a great deal of good over there. My target date in Atlanta in 29 June, but I could stay several days on either side of that day in order to promote the fortunes of the book. Do let me know about this, and I will follow through according to whatever you suggest.

Something else extraordinarily fortunate has come up: James Applewhite, a poet who teaches at Duke, has just informed me that he has been made one of the judges for the Pulitzer Prize in Poetry for 1979, to be awarded in the spring of 1980. Jim was one of the two judges under me when I acted as chairman of the selection committee last year, and stood with me in my decision to give the prize to Howard Nemerov instead of to Lowell or to John Berryman, both of whom were preferred by the third judge, Helen Vendler of Boston University. The invariable procedure for the giving of the Pulitzer Prize, at least in poetry—and believe me, I know, for I have been a judge five times and chairman twice—is to appoint the most recent winner and usually the last two winners as judges for the upcoming award. This would mean that not only Applewhite will be on the committee, but certainly Warren, and almost certainly Warren and Nemerov. If Doubleday could move the publication of <u>The Strength of</u>

Fields back a month in order to have the official publication date fall within the calendar year of 1979, we would be an absolute dead-sure certainty to win the prize. Even if either Warren or Nemerov were not to be a judge, one of the two is certain to be, in which case we would also win, though of course I had rather win unanimously. At any rate, this seems just too good a chance to let go by. I remember we did something of the same sort with Sorties, for Stanley Burnshaw was a non-fiction judge—a category I know far less well than I do that of poetry—and, although Stanley fought valiantly for us and we lost, we were still among the five finalists, and that did a good deal to achieve what sales Sorties did finally attain. This situation is completely different, however, for the odds are a great deal better here. Under the present and likely conditions they are sure to be overwhelmingly in our favor. As evidence, I append a note from Warren on the Head-Deep poems, which, as you know, form a part of Strength. I do hope that the publication schedule at Doubleday will not interfere with our capacity to do what on the surface looks as though it would be a relatively simple thing. Do let me know about this, and I will nail the matter air-tight shut with Applewhite, and the others, whoever they turn out to be, will surely follow.

With warmest and best possible regards, I am

All yours,

To: Theron Raines

CC, Emory University
4620 Lelia's Court
Columbia, S.C. 29206

June 5, 1979

Dear Theron:

Since our conversations with Sandy on the last couple of occasions, I had assumed that we would simply ask Rust Hills to send the manuscript of "A Wheedling of Knives" back. Accordingly, I did this, and now get the enclosed note from Hills, which constitutes practically a refusal to turn loose of the manuscript. He seems to think that Esquire would like to publish it if something—some other episode—later on in the novel more or less might "round off" the "Knives" material and so make it more of a self-contained whole than it is. Even if you and Sandy and I had not decided to withdraw the MS., however, I would not consider amending it in any way to fit anybody's magazine policy; if published, the section would simply have to be presented as an "excerpt from" or "episode from" and brought out as it stands. I thought I would run all this late development of things back through you before I actually did give Hills a final no, because it was at your request that I first sent the material to him. It might be that you and Sandy and I might give the possibility of the Esquire publication some further thought, though of course I still stand with the two of you on our last decision, which is to publish nothing else of the book other than the section which Esquire has already printed. Let me know what you think of all this, and I will be guided accordingly.

Meanwhile, the book goes slowly, though it seems to me to be going well. The possibility of magazine publication might have affected very slightly the shape of some of the parts of the book, but I am now proceeding as though no such eventuality existed. If you and Sandy are quite sure that whatever play Esquire might give the book in the way of creating or sustaining or increasing interest in it is overborne by the plans Sandy has for bringing out the limited advance edition he proposes, I'll proceed as I am now doing. Please let me know what you think, and then deal with Hills from your end. If you think it advisable that I write him another letter, I'll do so, but please let me know what you'd like me to do right away.

What is the situation with RKO? Have you heard from Al Korn or gotten in touch with him? I need to know whether I should allot any time for a project with him, so keep me informed on how things stand.

Also, a producer with seemingly good credentials named Bill McCallum has contacted me and asked for your telephone number, so you will be hearing from him in the next few days. Sound him out on his proposition and let me know what you think. I referred him to you rather than to Bobby; if you want to bring Bobby in on the situation for whatever reason, you can let him know from your end.

I have written Sandy about the upcoming Pulitzer Prize for The Strength of Fields. One of the judges will vote for the book—in fact, he already has done so—and another a virtual certainty to do so, and the third a most likely probability. If we can get Doubleday to move the publication back to December, even if publication date is the very last day of December, we will be eligible for the 1979 prize, and we will win it. This seems too good and too sure a thing to pass up, especially considering the fact that I probably will not have another collection for a good long time.

Do check with Sandy on this, and also come to terms with him on the contract for The Strength of Fields and the advance, and let me know what is decided.

Matt Bruccoli says that he has already sent you the money for the Pound lecture edition, so please send it on down here. My tax man is hungry again this month, so I need to make a few appeasements.

Always,

P.S. What do you know and think about Chris's novel, The Colony?

To: James Still   CC, Emory University
                                            4620 Lelia's Court
                                            Columbia, S.C. 29206

                                            June 19, 1979
Dear Mr. Still:

I have just spent a most enjoyable morning, chuckling away as I read some of your stories in the book you were so kind to send me, Pattern of a Man and Other Stories. I do appreciate your giving me a copy, and I think the tales are tremendously good. I am working now on a book on Appalachia, in fact, and your wit is a veritable inspiration for me. You know, my father's people come from north Georgia, so I'm fairly familiar with that particular lifestyle, and you've captured it, no doubt about it.

Please give my regards to Wendell Berry. Perhaps my work on the book will carry me up your way later on in the summer, and I can see both of you then and have a long chat. I'd like that, believe me.

Meanwhile, my best wishes to you,

Sincerely yours,

To: Dwight MacDonald

CC, Emory University
4620 Lelia's Court
Columbia, S.C. 29206

June 26, 1979

Dear Dwight:

Thank you very much for your letter. I am delighted to know that you will go along with me in my proposal of John Simon for the Institute. At this point I don't think he has much of a chance to get in, for he has a great many enemies in the Institute as well as, seemingly, everywhere else. But if some of the people who are in the Institute are in—such as bad jokes like Ginsberg—a man of Simon's quality certainly should be. Along with you, I tried Alfred Kazin and got no support. Also Babette Deutsch, who had asked me to second George Garrett, whom I know and like all right and consequently supported, though he is not much of a writer. She also said no to my request. In advance I had been counting on you, and now that I know from your letter that Harry Levin might be favorable to the cause, I have written to him asking him to act as a second. All this may well turn out to be merely a gesture, but certain gestures ought to be made, and I intend to make this one.

You seem to make a good many unnecessary strictures about Southerners— what they like and don't like, what they are not like and what they are like— and I must point out to you that none of your preconceptions in this line apply to me any more than they did to your friend James Agee, whom incidentally I admire as much as you do, though I never met him.

Thank you very much for the good words about my wife Deborah. She likes you and Gloria very much, as I do, and we hope to see more of you not just at the Institute meetings but at other times she and I come to New York for one reason or another.

As to your comments on my presidential participation, I reject out of hand your opinion. I don't know where the poem I wrote and presented on that occasion would end up in that great Anthology in the sky, but I will stand by what I said in it, and the way I said it; "ghastly doggerel" it is not. The title itself is better than the whole corpus of Agee's work in verse, for example, unfortunate as this may seem to you. As to being soused on that occasion, I was not that either, though I certainly would have had every excuse to be so, in view of the fact that I had had to share a dressing room with Paul Newman and—of all people—John Wayne for four hours previous. As to your opinion of Carter's politics and performance, I can't really say very much, being in no sense as politically oriented as you are. I take my guidance from people who know more about such subjects than I do, and of these you are certainly one of the foremost.

There is a good deal more for us to talk about in agreement, I expect, than in disagreement. Over the years, for example, I have wondered about your admiration for Poe, as evidenced in your little selection of his verse a few years ago. Although you make plain that you don't feel Poe's verse is really much good, mainly, there is a certain grudging admiration for him that shows through, even so, and you have as surely come under Poe's particular spell as Allen Tate ever did. This is odd to me, and yet it is true, as your selection shows better than anywhere else, that there is a poet in Poe, who among various lesser poetasters also therein, is capable of writing lines that quite simply could not have been written by anyone else. I also am astonished at your advocacy of Sidney Lanier, particularly as a foil to Poe. And yet in a way you are quite right to bring this to attention; the level of achievement is probably higher in Lanier than in Poe, though nobody else has noted it.

Well, enough of this. The main business is to put a strong case for John's candidacy. I will see if I can find a copy of <u>Deliverance</u> around here to send you, though I am rather tired of <u>Deliverance</u>, and sometimes wish that I had never written it or gone on those rivers.

I hope you won't mind my bringing Levin into this, but he seems, in relation to his past record in John's behalf, the best choice at this time.

All yours,

To: John Simon

CC, Emory University
4620 Lelia's Court
Columbia, S.C. 29206

July 6, 1979

Dear John:

Thanks for your great letter, and know that both Dwight MacDonald and Harry Levin are seconding our move, and with great enthusiasm. It may be that we won't be able to get you in this first time around, but we shall certainly soften them up, and, if we don't get it this time, we'll try it again next year, when Sontag and Ned Rorem have a little more seniority. It would surely be great to have you in the thing to give it some real class. I'll let you know how things progress, though it is sometimes diffucult to know who votes for whom. For example, I don't know to this day who put me up for membership, who seconded, or what.

Thanks also for your two articles, which I read immediately. I think you are quite right about Elizabeth Hardwick, though I rather like her as an essayist, and I like her, period. But this last thing is surely poor, and should never have been printed at all. As to Eliot, you are even righter. What good that can be done to advance Eliot's cause as a permanently interesting poet has been done as well as it can be by Helen Gardner and F.O. Matthiessen, who seem to me the most helpful of the apologists. But the whole notion of treating The Four Quartets as some sort of sacrosanct revelation of the Holy Mysteries of Religion is manifestly absurd. Like Auden, Eliot is a profoundly unreligious man, interested in the paradoxes and intellectual problematics of theology more than anything else; his pose of humbleness is frightfully false, as it is quite clear that what he called his religion is an emotion compounded of fear and the kind of snobbery that has always been his personal characteristic and stigma. The grave, owlish, pontificating tone is very enervating to me; the qualities I like are drive, purpose, and imaginative energy, and these are nowhere to be found in the fake self-abasement and artificial naivete ("I do not know much about gods . . .") of Four Quartets. To The Wasteland I can give grudging assent—a kind of historical assent—for after all, it did change the way people write poetry, but to the religious Eliot I would pick up Melville's "No in thunder!" and say it again. But enough of this, or the letter would turn into an essay, and I might begin sounding like Robert Graves, which I don't want to do either.

Deborah and I have also been active in getting you set up with the best looking girl in Texas, whom we met on a lecture tour last year. But more about that later. Deborah is writing you a letter.

All is well with us. I am working hard, and have a new book of poems coming out in November. There is lots to be done, and Deborah is working perfectly into the whole scheme of things. My things, anyway. She sends love, and I send everything.

Yours,

To: President Jimmy Carter   RTLS, Emory University
                                              4620 Lelia's Court
                                              Columbia, S.C. 29206

                                              July 16, 1979

Dear Jimmy,

By now you must certainly have gone a great way toward assessing the reactions to your Energy speech, and these certainly should be intensely gratifying to you. I, too, have been doing some assessing, and as I sometimes do, offer forthwith a few comments, which I hope may be helpful in some way.

First of all, you are dead on the center of the central target in <u>focusing</u> on the Energy situation. This very much needed to be done, and it needs continually to be emphasized. Your phrase "War on Energy" is slightly misleading, though, for it seems to imply that Energy itself is the opponent, and is some sort of entity that needs to be defeated instead of the source of continuing well-being and operative autonomy that we need. If the word "war" is desirable in this context, surely it is war <u>for</u> rather than <u>on</u> energy that we are engaged in, with the positive connotations that this shift in perspective implies.

Next, I missed a firm statement as to your stand on nuclear power. The public sorely needs and wants to know what the country intends to do about this, and in your next major address, I think that you should allow consideration to giving this issue an important place. As for myself as a citizen, I believe very much that we must have nuclear power at almost all costs short of atomic holocaust itself, but of course the action followed will be defined by you in the stand you take. In connection with new sources of energy, I think you might also call even more attention to the possibilities of solar power, and step up both your programs and your public espousal of them; everybody is interested in the subject now, and most will support your proposals.

All these things you already know to an extent that I cannot possibly realize, and I bring them forward only as the opinions of a citizen. As a writer and
necessarily therefore a sometime rhetorician, I am as usual chiefly concerned
about the emphases, the slants, the vectors, the rhetorical tactics you command and employ. All of these factors contribute to the image you have at this
time for the American people, and for the rest of the world. I have been most
gratified by the forthrightness and the personal dramatic emphasis you displayed in the last of your debates with Ford, the Inaugural address, and now
the newest declaration; it seems to me that you are presenting the figure of intelligent <u>force</u> that is above all other things needed in a president at this time.
I would like to see more and more of this quality, and I think also that a certain <u>dominance</u> of attitude on your part—outspoken, vigorous, and above all
decisive—would be very helpful to us all. In your last address, you gave the
impression that the nation must take the energy crisis as a kind of renewal-
point for its sense of solidarity and common purpose, but it is difficult to escape the unpleasant association that were we not driven by brute means and
brute forces—the OPEC nations—to affirm this solidarity we would not feel
inclined to do so. Your stern pronouncements about our moral laxity and
selfishness are good points; they should be made, and they are true. But it is
basically difficult to drive, cow and humiliate people to do things that they
ought to have been doing all the time. There is bound to be a certain residue
of resentment in a populace addressed in this manner, and it seems to me that
the whole emphasis could be turned squarely toward the positive by a very
memorably-stated spotlighting of the great resources of intellectual and spiritual power that we as a nation collectively and as individuals do in fact possess: a kind of hidden treasure: enormous, full of power and light and
certainty and even a fierce and renewing kind of joy: above all, a sense of
<u>going</u>-<u>toward</u> rather than <u>escaping</u>-<u>from</u>. It is a great deal better to lead peo-
ple toward a goal, a kind of just city, a "city of the sun," than it is to attempt to
intimidate a nation of sluggards and timorous wastrels into acting for its own
good. I should think that a good way to do this would be to bring to the nation's attention its analogy with the situation at the end of Conrad's short
novel, <u>Youth</u>, when the narrator, Marlowe, attempts, through a long recounting of a shipwreck and the dangerous and painful survival of its crew, to define with exact dramatic force what youth <u>is</u>, exactly. He concludes that youth
for him was in the aftermath of the shipwreck when the crew went into separate lifeboats and attempted to reach the nearest land. I refer you to Conrad's
story for the full impact, but the upshot of it is that the narrator defines youth
as the sense of one's being unconquerable, capable of overcoming any obstacle, any hardship, any uncertainty, and deriving from this situation a fierce

feeling of individual worth, a <u>delight</u>—strong and physical and unique—from overcoming what must be overcome, no matter how formidable. In the story Marlowe puts it up to the other survivors, now old men, as to whether that was not the best time, that time of adversity, danger, vigor, pride, power and joy: silently, they nod in assent.

Something like that feeling, Jimmy, if you could project it as well as at your best moments you have shown yourself able most hearteningly to do, would get us to port, as it did Marlowe and his surviving seamen, and not by just barely making it, but riding in on a great crest of reaffirmation and purpose.

Let me hear from you on this if you conveniently can. Meanwhile, I will be listening and watching.

My wife Deborah sends her love, as I do mine, to all in your great House.

Sincerely yors,
   Jim Dickey

P.S. By the way, my latest collection of poems will be published in November. It is to be called <u>The</u> <u>Strength</u> <u>of</u> <u>Fields</u>, after the Inaugural poem. I'll send you and Rosalynn a copy as soon as it appears.

To: Jean Marie Hamilton[20]   CC, Emory University
                                                4620 Lelia's Court
                                                Columbia, S.C. 29206

                                                August 17, 1979

Dear Ms. Hamilton:

You have asked for my comments as to what I believe the biggest and most unusual changes in life will be during the next decade.

> "I think that during the 80's, people will become increasingly aware of the loss of the natural environment, and the irrevocable changes that are taking place, even as each individual does what he is doing at any given moment. If we could concentrate on an image, it might be that of a man or woman sitting in a convivial company, at a business meeting or a cocktail party, and being struck through with a vision of baby seals clubbed to death, or of the last wandering albatross in mid-ocean, fouled to death with floating oil, never knowing the reason."

20. Editor of *Passages* magazine.

I hope this will be of use to you. Please let me know when the article will appear, and send me tear sheets. If you mention my name, you might also let the readers know that I have a new collection of poetry to be published in December by Doubleday, entitled, <u>The Strength of Fields</u>.

Please let me know how things work out.

Sincerely yours,

To: Ronald Sharp[21]

CC, Emory University
4620 Lelia's Court
Columbia, S.C. 29206

October 19, 1979

Dear Mr. Sharp:

Thank you very much for your consideration in sending me a copy of the <u>"New" Kenyon Review</u>, which looks very good to me, and the format better than ever. I liked very much the piece on Keats, which brings together a good many points about Keats that have not been related before, but which state the case for that fine boy's philosophy in exactly the terms he would I ma sure have wished. Will this essay become part of a larger study of Keats, or another book? Ah yes, I see that it will, and I am delighted also that the University of Georgia Press, where I have some good friends, will do the book; that is good.

Meanwhile, I enclose a new poem, the first in some time. Let me know what you think of it when you can conveniently do so. Some of it is not "Chinese" in spirit or execution, but that I think does not matter as much as some other things.

Sincerely,

21. Editor of *Kenyon Review.*

James Dickey's home, situated on Lake Katherine, at 4620 Lelia's Court in Columbia, South Carolina. (Courtesy of Gordon Van Ness)

Dickey at North Fulton High School in Atlanta, October 1985, addressing the student body in the gymnasium. (Courtesy of Joyce Pair)

Bronwen Dickey in front of the Dickey home in Columbia, 1986. (Courtesy of William Mills)

Dickey at the Buckhead Branch of the Atlanta-Fulton County Libraries, awaiting his introduction by James Taylor, August 1986. (Courtesy of Joyce Pair)

Dickey outside his home, 1987. (Courtesy of Gordon Van Ness)

228

William A. Bake and James Dickey at Oxford Bookstore in Buckhead, October 1988, on a promotional tour for *Wayfarer*. (Courtesy of Joyce Pair)

Willie Morris, Robert Morris, and James Dickey in the Atlanta Hilton during the Southeast Booksellers Association Conference, October 1988. (Courtesy of Joyce Pair)

Dickey at the Atlanta Hilton, October 1988. (Photograph by *Creative Loafing* staff photographer, courtesy of Joyce Pair)

Dickey at the Ritz-Carlton Hotel in Atlanta during a promotional trip for *Wayfarer*, 1988. (Courtesy of Joyce Pair)

Al Braselton, James Dickey, and Joyce Pair at the Hyatt Regency Hotel in Atlanta during the convention of the South Atlantic Modern Language Association, November 1991. (Courtesy of Joyce Pair)

Dickey as keynote speaker giving the general session address at the South Atlantic Modern Language Association meeting, November 1991. (Courtesy of Joyce Pair)

Don Greiner, James Dickey, and Ben Franklin at a "power lunch" outside the Faculty House on the Green Horseshoe of the University of South Carolina, 1993. (Courtesy of Don Greiner)

Dickey with Bronwen and Deborah in the Rare Book Room of the Thomas Cooper Library of the University of South Carolina during the festivities of James Dickey at Seventy: A Tribute, September 18, 1993. (Courtesy of Joyce Pair)

Descent

James Dickey believed that great writers are more important than everybody else; because he had chosen the profession of authorship relatively late in life, or so he felt, and because he wanted to be great, his commitment to literature was authentic and convincing. He did not begin to read poetry systematically until 1944, after he had enlisted in the Army Air Force and was stationed on Okinawa during his Pacific combat service: "I was not introduced to it," he recalled in *Self-Interviews*, "by anybody in my family or any teacher or acquaintance. This has its disadvantages, but it also has one enormous advantage. If you get into poetry in this way, you come to look upon poetry as *your* possession, something that *you* discovered, that belongs to you in a way it could never have belonged to you if it had been forced on you."[1]

Dickey's reading quickly became extensive and eclectic. In one notable letter to his mother dated June 30, 1945, he requested that she order for him almost five dozen books, including works on psychology, philosophy, mythology, music, and literature. He specifically asked for volumes by poets W. H. Auden, C. Day Lewis, Trumbull Stickney, Kenneth Patchen, Richard Aldington, Dylan Thomas, Stephen Spender, Robert Penn Warren, and Randall Jarrell, as well as several poetry anthologies. After the war, Dickey's personal library continued to grow, the working collection of a major author who never stopped reading, discussing, and writing. In the later years of his life, he would sit in his living room surrounded by a castle of books, consisting of approximately a thousand volumes stacked in towers more than four feet high. On the other side of the living room wall were seventeen thousand additional books, all part of his personal library fifty years in the making. A true study of Dickey's career would include a list of the books he read and how he used them. "It is a marvelous thing," he declared in *Sorties*, "this having a house full of books. Something crosses the mind—a flash of light, some connection, some recognition—and one simply rises from one's chair and goes, as though by predestination, to that book, to that poem."[2]

1. *Self-Interviews* (Garden City, N.Y.: Doubleday, 1970), 25.
2. *Sorties* (Garden City, N.Y.: Doubleday, 1971), 5–6.

His career can also be traced in the books he published as well as their critical reception and reputation. Over the course of his life, Dickey published three novels, two books of children's poetry, four volumes of criticism, one book of belles lettres, four volumes of prose, and more than fifteen collections of poetry, in addition to screenplays and specialty volumes. By 1980 he had won the Melville Cane Award, the National Book Award, and the Prix Médicis; served two terms as poetry consultant to the Library of Congress; and been inducted into the National Institute of Arts and Letters. Yet to many that year Dickey's career had stalled. His recent collections of poetry, *The Eye-Beaters, Blood, Victory, Madness, Buckhead and Mercy, The Strength of Fields,* and *The Zodiac,* had been largely dismissed by critics, and earlier volumes had gone out of print. *New Yorker* had allowed its first-read contract with Dickey to lapse. If Dickey's mission during the sixties, what he referred to as his "early motion," had soared, his career in the seventies, his "central motion," had stalled after *Deliverance* and begun to decline. This descent had nothing to do with the absence of publications but rather with their reception. It cannot be understood without taking into account not only Dickey's creation of a public image and the multiple personae, or selves, that inhabit his poems but also the broader historical and cultural currents within which Dickey's work appeared. The attitudes of his personae regarding power, violence, sex, race, and ego, which were at odds with the social and literary climate, were viewed as synonymous with those of Dickey himself. Bothered by Dickey's experimentation with language and techniques that did not repeat his previously successful early forms, critics now intensified their attacks, premised on what they perceived as his lack of political correctness. Moreover, because Dickey did not make public statements against social injustices, critics as well as artists often charged that he lacked a moral conscience.

In his study of the politics of canon, Ernest Suarez has correctly noted that "James Dickey's career provides an especially clear example of the way history alters and informs the reception of a poet's work."[3] As both his poetry and his fiction attest, Dickey believed that violence and volatility are inherent to human nature. The social restraints that generate a civilized facade effectively prohibit the self from becoming fully human by precluding access to the deepest realms of experience, including the imagination. Aggressive and instinctive urges, Dickey contended, were sometimes not only necessary but also desirable. Poems that Dickey published in the mid-to-late sixties, includ-

3. Ernest Suarez, *James Dickey and the Politics of Canon: Assessing the Savage Ideal* (Columbia: University of Missouri Press, 1993), 42.

ing "The Firebombing," "The Fiend," "Slave Quarters," "Falling," and "May Day Sermon," seemed to some reviewers to suggest a preoccupation with violence and power at the very time when social unrest among women and minorities had coalesced and become widespread. Artists such as Robert Lowell, Norman Mailer, and Allen Ginsberg had actively protested against American involvement in southeast Asia. Attacks on Dickey had commenced in 1967 when Robert Bly, upset about what he considered the poet's support of the Vietnam War when he categorically believed all writers should vocally oppose it, reviewed *Buckdancer's Choice.* Bly's critique, largely an ad hominem attack, labeled Dickey "a huge blubbery poet, pulling out southern language in long strings, like taffy, a toady to the government, supporting all movements toward Empire, a sort of Georgia cracker Kipling." It charged that the volume centered on power, particularly a gloating power over others, and concluded by asserting that Dickey increasingly "takes his life and laminates poetry onto it."[4]

The issue, however, went deeper than the principal concern of one book. Dickey identified violence and disorder as part of human history, an attitude that derived from his participation in a world war and from his subsequent readings in anthropology and mythology. Moreover, he rendered this view, originating in the Emersonian tradition, from an almost philosophical or mystical perspective and stressed the fundamental primacy of the individual in any such struggle. Yet with the escalation of the Vietnam War, reviewers valued the didactic over the dialectic and the communal over the individual. Dickey's complex metaphysics collided with a literary establishment whose critical agenda, precipitated by historical particulars—the war, the woman's rights movement, the civil rights movement—would not accommodate the philosophical foundations of Dickey's poetry. As Suarez observed, "The vehement scorn many critics expressed for Dickey and the almost fanatical loyalty of his defenders resulted in a literary civil war that has profoundly affected critics' appraisals of Dickey's place in the post–World War II literary canon."[5] It is a war that did not end with the poet's death.

The objections of Bly and others to Dickey's use of violence generated a widespread reversal of the positive critical reception of Dickey's work and culminated in his being largely dismissed as a reactionary conservative, a phenomenon that failed to acknowledge his early support of the civil rights movement and his support of both Eugene McCarthy and Jimmy Carter. In his essay "Notes on the Decline of Outrage," for example, initially published

4. Bly, "The Collapse of James Dickey," *The Sixties* 9 (Spring 1967): 70–79.
5. Suarez, *Dickey and the Politics of Canon*, 79–80.

in *South: Modern Southern Literature in Its Cultural Setting,* edited by Louis
D. Rubin and Robert D. Jacobs, and later collected in *Babel to Byzantium,*
Dickey unflinchingly examined the condition of blacks in the South from the
perspective of the white southerner:

> He must admit immediately that he has always concurred, or as good as con-
> curred, in the assumptions about Negroes that his forebears and contemporaries
> have had, and have. The unspoken rationale underlying these assumptions is
> that, inexplicably but in perfect keeping with the natural order of things,
> Negroes have been endowed with human shape and certain rudimentary ap-
> proximation of human attitudes, but that they possess these only in a kind of
> secondary or inferior way, and, to the end of having this be readily recogniz-
> able, have also been given a skin pigmentation and a facial bone structure which
> make their entire status apparent at a glance, and even from a very great dis-
> tance. Spoken or unspoken, these are the beliefs that have assigned every Negro,
> from the lowest hod carrier up through the ministry and the medical profes-
> sion, his place in the Southern scheme of things.

Cognizant of the South's history and culture, Dickey challenged the southerner to recognize that "the Negro must become either a permanent enemy or
an equal," that "in one form, one body, unsteadily balanced, live the ex-slave,
the possible foe, and the unknown brother." "It can be a greater thing than the
South has ever done," he concluded, "to see that the last of these does not die
without showing his face."[6] Critics, however, were guided by the subject matter of Dickey's poetry, his southernness, his popularity with the mass media,
and his financial success.

Nowhere were critics and defenders in the eighties and nineties more
deeply divided than over Dickey's depiction of and attitudes toward women.
On the one hand, some critics, including Robert Covel, Robert Kirschten,
Richard Calhoun, Robert Hill, Ernest Suarez, and Joyce Pair, mounted com-
pelling defenses of Dickey's work. Centering their analysis on such poems as
"The Scarred Girl," "Cherrylog Road," "Falling," and "May Day Sermon," they
variously argued that Dickey's poetic portrayal idealized women. Dickey
himself, in a short, overlooked essay first published by *Mademoiselle* in July
1971 and later collected in *Night Hurdling,* had declared: "From going to and
fro in the earth, and from walking up and down in it—the real earth, and not
just the enchanted fragment of it that blazes in the longing mind to furnish

---

6. "Notes on the Decline of Outrage," in *South: Modern Southern Literature in Its Cultural
Setting,* ed. Louis D. Rubin Jr. and Robert D. Jacobs (Garden City, N.Y.: Doubleday and Co.,
1961), 76–94 (quotation at 83–84).

her setting—she becomes a hidden archetype to the beholder rendered god-like by her presence: his possession and promise, soulless and soulful at the same time, receding, flashing up with terrible certainty at the most inopportune times that she then makes opportune."[7] In the literary warfare that had erupted, Robert Kirschten explicitly stated the ground on which defenders would stand: "Dickey's mythopoeic vision has been matriarchal and multi-cultural—even revolutionary feminist—for 25 years," and Joyce Pair asserted that his poetry "views woman as life-giving goddess," a thematic concern that "has been continuous throughout [Dickey's] career."[8]

On the other hand, critics including Robert Bly, Jane Hill, Carolyn Heilbrun, and Sue Walker largely dismissed this analysis, suggesting that Dickey's work reveals a basic prejudice against women either by treating them as objects or by denying them the transcendent experiences enjoyed by male personae. Jane Hill, for example, in a balanced and detailed treatment of the issue, attacked what she labeled "the goddess strain of feminism" and declared: "Dickey's women, as represented in the poems, do not, in general, overcome the obstacles that being female in the world as Dickey renders it presents. They do not, in general, find themselves living the fullest, most intense lives possible; they do not usually come close even to the level of pursuit of those goals that their male counterparts enjoy." Only in *Puella*, Hill asserted, published in 1982, in which Dickey presented the girlhood of his wife, Deborah, "male imagined," did the poet grant the female character "her own voice and her own quest for the full realm of experience." Yet even in this volume, Sue Walker argued, Dickey's presentation is, in effect, "an aggression": "He has made us see what he sees. Only we see more. We see through our own eyes as well as his. We are neither dolls nor toys, playthings that can be manipulated. We see that the difficulty with the *Puella* poems, at least in part, is the fact that they reflect the poet's state. They [re]present where he is in his middle years, at age fifty-three, when he marries a woman less than half his age. The poems that seek to know Deborah, ferret out her identity as she comes into womanhood, mirror the poet's desires more than hers and attend to his need to have 'things of this kind.' "[9] Dickey's death in 1997 did little to effect a cessation of such hostilities; critical opinion remains entrenched.

7. "Complicity," in *Night Hurdling* (Columbia, S.C., and Bloomfield Hills, Mich.: Bruccoli Clark, 1983), 217.

8. See Robert Kirschten's "Introduction" and Joyce Pair's " 'Dancing with God': Totemism in Dickey's 'May Day Sermon,' " in *Critical Essays on James Dickey* (New York: G. K. Hall, 1994), 1–25, 65–76.

9. Hill, "Relinquishing Power and Light: Dickey's Legacy and the Woman Question," *James Dickey Newsletter* 15.2 (Spring 1999): 2–12; and Walker, "Playing with Dolls: Girls Male-Imagined in James Dickey's *Puella*," *James Dickey Newsletter* 15.1 (Fall 1998): 2–9.

While the public image of a macho outdoorsman that Dickey created early in his career enhanced sales of his poems and promoted his reputation, it alienated academics during and after the seventies who, in the midst of a cultural revolution and intense political divisions within academe itself, equated that image with the personae in his poems. These critics, moreover, found themselves being judged by their peers depending on their attitude toward Dickey. As Suarez observes, "The battle between the culturally and theoretically leftist Modern Language Association and the staunchly right-wing National Association of Scholars typifies a profession that has become increasingly doctrinal and disputatious."[10] Affected by literary currents, reviewers faulted Dickey's use of a persona, a tendency that influenced both interpretations and misinterpretations of his political and social attitudes as well as his poetic techniques and themes and that resulted in the flow and ebb of his critical reputation.

As 1980 began, Dickey worked intently on *Alnilam*, though he continually asked for extensions from his editor, Stewart Richardson, delays necessitated in part by an intensive schedule of readings and in part by uncertainty related to the novel's plot and the basic character of the protagonist. In the first five months of the year, he read at William Rainey Harper College, Emory University, the University of North Dakota, the Columbus Cultural Arts Center, and Southern Illinois University. The readings, he explained to Richardson in an unpublished letter dated February 3, owed to his imminent poverty: "I have had to fill up a lot of time between now and May with reading and speaking dates, so that I won't go from the hospital to the alms-house. . . . But the novel is going fine, and now there comes the question of exactly in what stages you want to see it." He proposed sending sections of the work to Richardson every week or two and having his editor react to the narrative "as it unfolds bit by bit, as it would reveal itself to a reader, in his innocence, and—anticipation."[11] Dickey had not yet clarified the motivations and goals of Joel Cahill's Alnilam plot.

The framework for what he referred to as his "big novel about the air" first evidenced itself on page 46 of the fourth of Dickey's early notebooks, a bound ledger containing ninety-five handwritten pages. Dickey dated the initial entry September 29, 1952, and other notations are dated the next day. At the top of page 79 of the ledger, Dickey drew a line with the date August 1956

10. Suarez, *Dickey and the Politics of Canon*, 125.
11. Letters to Richardson are housed in the James Dickey Papers, Special Collections Department, Robert W. Woodruff Library, Emory University, Atlanta (hereafter cited as Dickey Papers).

above it. The novel's original title was "The Romantic," and he intended that the story's three-day time frame possess archetypal significance. Conceived initially as a story and then as a novella, "The Romantic" presents a father, a widowed automobile salesman now employed as a timekeeper in an aircraft factory, who arrives at a primary training base (Dickey planned to use his memories of the base at Camden, South Carolina, where he had been stationed) to interview various individuals about the death of his only son, Joel Mitchell, whom he has neither known very well nor seen for some years. Like Joel Cahill in *Alnilam,* the protagonist in the novella has died in an unobserved plane crash, having inexplicably flown through the turbulence of a fire. Before his death, too, Joel had become obsessed with the poet James Thompson. Although Dickey changed their names, other principal characters in *Alnilam* are also recognizable. For example, the Commanding Officer becomes Colonel Hoccleve in the published novel, and the Commandant of Cadets, Joe Riley, is Colonel Malcolm Shears. Tactical Officer Bean is Lieutenant Spigner. Joel's flight instructor, Willis, becomes McClintock McCaig; his check rider, Broome, is Lieutenant Foy. Dickey does not name the woman with whom Joel Mitchell is having an affair; she becomes Hannah Pelham in *Alnilam.* However, he intended to base her on Matilda Weller, the girl with whom James Thompson was obsessed and whose death at an early age aggravated his tendency toward melancholia and contributed to his imaginative visions. The narrative centers not so much on the use or abuse of power (the entries, for example, do not mention a plot to disrupt the military) as on the archetypal search of a father for his son and on that son's efforts to achieve individuality in the midst of training for a world war.

In a poem entitled "Joel Cahill Dead," published in the summer 1958 issue of *Beloit Poetry Journal,* Dickey offered a poetic interpretation of the crucial scene—Joel's crash into a wildfire and a farmer's effort to rescue him:

> Like a man sent for, he ran,
> Waving his arms, and yelled through his sooty kerchief
> In a curving voice around
> The boy who stood, amazed, beside the plane,
> Exhaled in fire, his shirt at the shoulders smoking,
> Who got then down upon one ragged knee.

The farmer and his wife drag the burning boy to their house, which the fire also threatens, and lay him on "a peacock quilt," where he "dies," "remembering the Colonel, / To whom he must affirm / That he had less than no excuse to lie / Alone." Early drafts of the poem also suggest Joel's rebellious nature, his decision to take the Stearman to "an unauthorized altitude of his own," and his imaginative daring:

> Many, the first time up alone,
> Sing wildly out, and cannot think of other
> Thing to do, become so free near death.
> It was the thing Joel Cahill chose to stretch:
>
> To hands and feet, the body of the air
> Came from the fire, and set him dancing wild
> Within the aircraft body he controlled.
> It was a new becoming, wholly from surprise.

Dickey's conception of the narrative was slow in developing largely because he was about to undertake his poetic career. Two years later, Scribner's would publish his first poetry collection, *Into the Stone.*

By 1971, however, key scenes and characters in *Alnilam* had become established and the novel's focus had expanded, though Dickey remained uncertain about the character of Joel Cahill and the nature of the revolt he plans. In an effort to generate interest in the new work, Dickey included numerous entries in *Sorties* that centered on the novel, including notations that revealed his composition process. "The capacity to think up themes for stories, ideas, conceptions, and so on," he asserted, "depends very much on the *cultivation* of doing so. The more one sets his mind thinking, deliberately, along these lines, the more alert one becomes to possibilities of this sort." Along with the theme of a father's search for his son—with the implications of Dickey's own relationships with his son Chris as well as with his father, Eugene—the novel, now entitled "Death's Baby Machine," attempted to present another concern— "the power of words in a certain order to move men to action." Dickey had not yet worked out either the details of Operation Freeze-Out, the plot his protagonist, now named Joel Cahill, was coordinating, or the nature of the new order that Joel envisioned. That order, he postulated, might suggest that Joel has ideas of becoming "a very special kind of mystical fascist." Although clearly excited in 1971 by the content of the new book, Dickey also expressed reservations about its success: "The basic problem of this novel is to create a character of potentially major dimensions who is never seen, but who is projected by means of his posthumous effect on other people, and whose implications, insofar as they may be known at all, come to rest in his blind father.

This is a terribly difficult undertaking, and must be thought out slowly and in hundreds of details."[12] Dickey would require more than fifteen years to complete those details.

In May 1980, Dickey and Deborah flew to Idaho, where Dickey accepted an honorary degree from the University of Idaho. They then traveled to Seattle, where Dickey underwent major surgery to correct a hiatal hernia. For years Dickey had had difficulty swallowing properly because his intestine was blocking his esophagus; now he was unable to eat solid food. The operation occurred on May 20, two days after Mount St. Helens's spectacular explosion. In letters to Stewart Richardson and others, Dickey seemed to link the two events. In an unpublished letter dated June 30 to Jim Gaston, a friend at the U.S. Air Force Academy who had recently inquired about writing an exposé on Dickey's formative years in the Army Air Force, Dickey declared that while under anesthesia, "I was attempting to fly quite blind—under ether, without even eyesight or consciousness, much less instruments—through the stone snows of Mount St. Helen's. . . . It was all a very strange experience, like a dream of combat where you don't even know whom or what you're fighting, but must be the battleground itself, either on the table or in some manner levitated, where the surgeons must go into action against the Dark Men, with only their short blades."[13] Because he viewed everything as warfare, Dickey described his ordeal as a death and resurrection. On June 8 he returned to Columbia, having been instructed to rest. By the end of the month he was eating enthusiastically and walking for exercise, praising the simple pleasures to friends in his correspondence.

A week later he applied himself to a new book of poems entitled *Deborah Puella*. The poems were originally intended as part of a limited edition entitled "Flowering," a collaborative effort with photographer Bookie Binkley, who had agreed in fall 1977 to pay Dickey $15,000 in two installments to write thirty poems that would accompany his thirty photographs. Early in their collaboration, Binkley would send four or five pictures to Dickey, who would then write the poems that would accompany them, but because he composed slowly, Dickey was relieved when Binkley decided to include only nineteen photographs. He wrote Sidney Stapleton, Binkley's business partner, on September 22, 1979, over a year past the agreed deadline, and in the unpublished letter reviewed his progress: "I have written out complete sketches of the settings, the activities, the attitudes and even the personality of each girl, and

---

12. *Sorties*, 111, 129, 130, 137–38.
13. The letter to Gaston is in the Dickey Papers.

have written the poem to and around these conditions. In addition, I have made the poems sequential, and the presentation of the photographs progresses from dawn to night: from the girls running on the road to the girl asleep with the rose."[14] Dickey was convinced that the limited printing of 2,500 copies would sell out quickly. A cover story on him in the November 1979 issue of *Reader's Digest,* entitled "James Dickey—'Poet of Survival and Hope,'" as well as articles on "Flowering" that appeared in *Southern Living, Vogue, Harper's Bazaar,* and *Cosmopolitan,* would generate large interest. Binkley, however, who had invested large sums of money for studio expenses and materials and who was desperately searching for a publisher to assist with printing and publicity, failed to acquire the necessary funding. When Dickey returned from Seattle following his hernia operation, he wrote Stewart Richardson that he doubted whether Binkley would find a commercial house to publish a book costing $250 a copy. "What I would really like," he declared in his letter of June 17, "is eventually to get the 19 poems released to me so that I can then incorporate them into a new book with Doubleday, for they are surely the best sustained sequence anybody has done since Rilke's <u>Orpheus</u> sonnets." By the end of the summer, he became convinced "Flowering" would not succeed.

Dickey contacted John O'Brien at Deerfield Press to inquire whether he wanted to select several of the *Puella* poems to publish as a chapbook, informing O'Brien that the original publisher, the Golden Chalice Press, had "apparently" returned the nineteen poems to him to publish as a separate book without the photographs. He urged O'Brien to contact Golden Chalice Press and *Atlantic Monthly* (where one of the poems, "The Surround," had appeared) for permission to reprint the poems. On July 28, Dickey informed O'Brien that he had concluded all required arrangements not only with his agent but also with Golden Chalice Press and Doubleday for release of the poems and that O'Brien could now proceed. In December 1980 Deerfield Press published a limited edition entitled *Scion,* despite warnings by Binkley and Sidney Stapleton, his business partner, to Theron Raines and Dickey's lawyer, Kirkman Finlay. Soon after *Puella* was published by Doubleday in 1982, Binkley's lawyer, James Humphrey, browsing in a New York bookstore, discovered a copy and contacted Binkley. Shocked, Binkley hired Vernon Glenn and Kendall Few in Winston-Salem to sue Dickey for breach of contract. In September 1983 the case went to trial; Dickey was eventually ordered to pay Binkley approximately twenty-five thousand dollars.

14. The letter to Stapleton is in the Dickey Papers.

Dickey again served on the Pulitzer Prize committee in 1980, this time as chairman; the other committee members were Nona Balakian, editor for the *New York Times Book Review,* and poet John Ashbery, whose poems Dickey had once described as "a kind of idling arbitrariness, offering their elements as a profound conjunction of secrecies one can't quite define or evaluate."[15] Disagreement immediately followed. Balakian, who had survived Turkey's massacre of Armenians, preferred the darker visions of Mark Strand, Galway Kinnell, and Louise Glück, while Ashbery, who favored avant-garde writing and abstract expressionism, voted to offer the prize to his friend James Schuyler for his collection *The Morning of the Poem.* Dickey preferred Brewster Ghiselin's *Windrose: Poems, 1929-1979,* but because he had listed Schuyler second, he effected a compromise and sided with Ashbery.

Dickey's service on the Pulitzer committee necessitated that he delay publication of *Puella,* which he had originally wanted Doubleday to publish in 1980. He wrote Stewart Richardson on June 17, 1980, that the only reason he had agreed to serve was because the committee included Ashbery, "a kind of clique writer up there, and I thought it best that the award not go to one of his friends." Dickey, however, understood the politics of such awards and committed himself insofar as possible to those whose poetry he himself believed emotionally honest and valid. Because he also recognized that he needed to rehabilitate his own reputation, he corresponded with those in the United States and England whose opinions influenced the literary landscape, including Helen Vendler, whom he had labeled "that dreadful woman 'critic'"[16] in a July 2, 1982, unpublished letter to Stanley Burnshaw and whose antagonistic attitudes about his poetry he wanted to mitigate, and Donald Davie, an important British poet and critic who was a member of The Movement and who had recently accepted a position at Vanderbilt. In his letter to Vendler, Dickey related that he had just read an article in *American Scholar* about her book on George Herbert, declaring that he admired the metaphysical poet and knew about the contemporary state of Herbert criticism. In a flattering letter to Davie dated October 31, 1980, Dickey wrote: "I have been familiar with your work ever since Flannery O'Connor gave me a copy of your <u>Articulate Energy</u> on the front porch of her farm in Millidgeville, Georgia, and have since followed your writing as closely as I was able. In addition to your poetry, which I consider by far the best of the group you are conveniently . . . associated with, your work on Pound is the best that has yet been done, and

15. *Babel to Byzantium: Poets and Poetry Now* (New York: Farrar, Straus and Giroux, 1968), 59.
16. Letters to Burnshaw are in the Henry Ransom Humanities Research Center, the University of Texas at Austin.

despite the mountain of Pound interpretation that will be growing forever, probably, I don't see how your insights into him can easily be surpassed, on whatever mountain." Dickey added, "I hope the strongest warmth of which I am capable will come off this page."[17]

In September, Dickey traveled to England with Deborah for a five-day visit, the primary purpose of which was to participate, along with Auberon Waugh and Robin Maugham, in a series of telecasts by the British Broadcasting Company that William F. Buckley had organized. In witty and often contentious debates, the panel discussed such famous English authors as D. H. Lawrence, Somerset Maugham, and Graham Greene. Dickey also visited famous places in London and made a trip to Sussex to see the grave of Malcolm Lowry, whose *Under the Volcano,* a moving portrayal of alcoholic hallucinations that had influenced Dickey's long poem *The Zodiac,* was one of his favorite novels.

By the end of 1980, Dickey had become involved in writing the screenplay for an epic movie about the Klondike Gold Rush. Jerome Hellman, who had produced *Midnight Cowboy* and *Coming Home,* would make the film. Interested in working with Dickey, Hellman had contacted Theron Raines to discuss his ideas for a Gold Rush film and a few months later visited Dickey in Columbia. They negotiated a contract with United Artists that would pay Dickey $50,000 for a treatment and $200,000 for a script based on the treatment. Dickey, however, was conscious of the precariousness of any Hollywood venture, and while he boasted of the project, he warned Raines not to expect completion. Success depended upon Michael Cimino's *Heaven's Gate,* which promised to be a financial disaster. It was, and Steven Bach, head of United Artists, was deposed because of the millions lost on the movie. When Paula Weinstein and Anthea Sylbert replaced Bach, the future of "Klondike" became precarious. No multi-million-dollar budget materialized, and no screenplay evolved past the treatment stage. Even so, Dickey was slowly advancing on *Alnilam* and readying himself for the publication of *Puella.* Deborah, meanwhile, had informed him that she was pregnant with their first child.

Deborah had become a muse for Dickey, heightening his sensitivity to the physical world and quickening his intuitive responses. She revealed a self that Dickey had not previously discerned, offering him a reality in constant creative motion, a feminine surround of unbelievable intensity, mystery, and possibility. In notebooks Dickey kept during the fifties, he had announced a poetic imperative: "It is the task of poetry to find and articulate the arche-

17. The letter to Davie is in the Dickey Papers.

typal, individual (or possibly racial) vision, examine it, determine (or arrive at a tentative, or even assign one) its meaning, and make this meaning available."[18] Early poems, such as "Into the Stone," "The Rib," "Mary Sheffield," "The Leap," and "The Scarred Girl," had presented this ideal. This attitude had not changed when, in his 1971 essay "Complicity," Dickey had quoted the poet Paul Claudel, "Woman is the promise that cannot be kept," and added: "If she is not the secret of the universe, then there is none."[19] Deborah suggested this ideality, and events from her life, poetically re-created, became the foundation for *Puella*. The book's pointed epigraph, T. Sturge Moore's lines, "I lived in thee, and dreamed, and waked / Twice what I had been," suggests Dickey's continuing belief in Woman as a source of life-enhancing possibilities. Taken together, the poems trace her maturation and reveal her heightened consciousness of the world, including her kinship with the elements of fire, air, earth, and water and her growing knowledge of human relationships. The first-person perspective, in lyric poems that only in composite yield any real sense of "story," along with a technique that offers reality through simultaneous, intuited images or associations, gives the collection a psychological depth and richness not achieved with Dickey's previous narrative methods. In the collection's final poem, "Summons," Deborah urges "With delivery-room patience" a penetration into a power everywhere present, the achievement of "unparalleled rhythm" and "invention unending."

This creativity allowed for a second new muse, his daughter, Bronwen. Her birth on May 17, 1981, provided Dickey with what he declared in an interview the following year to be "a wonderful renewal,"[20] and he celebrated her arrival in a poem entitled simply "Daughter," portraying her as life's true motion: "You are part / Of flowing stone," he asserted, "understand: you are part of the wave, / Of the glacier's irrevocable / Millennial inch." She confirmed for him the existence of a realm of intense mystery, of endless possibility. It is almost as if, in an Aristotelian world, she was proof of a Platonic ideal. In an unpublished letter to Stanley Burnshaw dated September 24, 1982, he called Bronwen "my brand new little female superstar." Growing up, she shared with Dickey a special language. At age eight, as she began to write poetry herself, she would stand with her father looking over Lake Katherine at the rising sun, its glowing light spreading across the sky, bringing shape to the world, and

18. *Striking In: The Early Notebooks of James Dickey,* ed. Gordon Van Ness (Columbia: University of Missouri Press, 1999), 79.

19. *Night Hurdling,* 217.

20. L. Elisabeth Beattie, "James Dickey Rides Again," in *The Voiced Connections of James Dickey,* ed. Ron Baughman (Columbia: University of South Carolina Press, 1989), 187.

they would shout together, "Fireball mail." With her father, she formed an imaginary company, Whitewings Aviation, with her as president and Dickey as chief engineer and test pilot, initially spending hours assembling model airplanes. Later they fashioned planes whose designs they labeled The Highwing, The Cirrus, The Elliptic, and The Dolphin, until gradually they decided to build only experimental models. Dickey taught her how to swim in a neighbor's pool, overcoming her fears (at first she wore an inner tube) until it seemed water was her natural element. In a 1982 interview he declared of fathering Bronwen, "You feel like you're standing in the main cycle of time and nature, part of the great chain of being. You have to be 59 to appreciate how great it really is."[21]

That he should see her this way led him in 1986 to present his daughter in a book-length children's poem, *Bronwen, the Traw, and the Shape-Shifter,* in which a young girl is asked by the King of the Squirrels to defeat the forces of All-Dark. She does, entering nature with an ease that suggests her lack of differentiation from its rhythms and processes, an imaginative integration in it, so that as the flying squirrels return her to her bedroom, she thinks: "The whole land took over her memory, / And they were the same, just about." The scene is reminiscent of Ed Gentry in *Deliverance,* looking down from the perilous cliff onto the terrible brightness of the river, only to realize that he has his eyes closed. When he opens them, he discovers how exact had been the image of his thought. Given Dickey's macho persona in the sixties and seventies, his portrayal of such a transformation in the mind of a little girl indicates that by the eighties he had acquired other visions. "Don't interfere at all, ideally," he asserted in a 1987 interview, "with the way children perceive nature. Don't impose too much explanation, scientific or otherwise, on what they see. Let it be to them what it is to them right then."[22] With Deborah and Bronwen, at least temporarily, Dickey achieved, if not a balance, at least the loss of the restless, unstemming pursuit of the unattainable that characterized most of his personal and creative life. Until Deborah's descent into drugs and the criminal world undermined the situation at home, Dickey's voice seemed comfortable, as if he had accepted the limitations he everywhere felt.

In a letter dated October 5, 1981, film director John Boorman wrote Dickey, asking him to assist Michel Ciment, a distinguished French critic who was writing a book on Boorman's movies. He added, "I am still haunted by 'Looking for the Buckhead Boys.' Why don't you write a film/book about that quest, a

---

21. James Dickey, "In North Carolina: Getting to the Gold with Terry Roberts," *Arts Journal* 7 (May 1982): 12–14; rpt. in *Night Hurdling,* 230–42.

22. Gordon Van Ness, "A Different Kind of Deliverance," *State Magazine,* January 25, 1987, pp. 8–11.

story that would flow back and forth between middle-age and childhood."
Dickey responded on October 22, assuring Boorman of his cooperation with
Ciment but deferring on the proposal, stating that he would need to complete
present projects "before I would ever be able to take the Boys out of moth-
balls and reexamine them." He hoped to make these film efforts good ones
"and then return to the back pages of obscure poetry magazines, which is
where I came from, and where I belonged all the time."[23] One project was
"Klondike," the script to which Dickey returned in early 1982. The other involved Richard Roth, who had sent Dickey a screenplay based on Jon Has-
sler's 1981 novel *The Love Hunter* and asked Dickey to revise the script with
Robert Redford. Redford, who met with Dickey in Columbia, believed that
they could adapt a mediocre novel into something extraordinary; Dickey was
not convinced and did not pursue the endeavor.

Despite informing Boorman that his work schedule was too heavy to involve himself in other films, he traveled to Beaufort, South Carolina, the following month to narrate a PBS documentary on the Depression. Entitled
One-Third of a Nation, the documentary had been written by his colleague
Bernie Williams; Dickey was paid $5,000 for his participation, his interest
spurred partly because the subject intrigued him and partly because he was
tempted by the money. He had lived through the Depression and, in the stories he fabricated for the personal mythology in which he centered himself,
he had suffered from its effects. He was also conscious of James Agee's efforts
to represent the era's hardships on the South in *Let Us Now Praise Famous
Men,* one of his favorite books. Indeed, after learning while in Europe of Agee's
death on May 16, 1955, he somberly wrote in his notebooks, "James Agee is
dead. God keep him, in the depth and trembling of His open shadow," and he
later composed an unpublished poem entitled "In Memory of James Agee." It
concluded:

> Great sorrow, continuing hope
> For the dead, the sun in the pines
> Changing the sea to light,
> Genius gone, and fewer left
> To remember it, with its amazing power
>
> To turn the face of the dead
> to light, and the sun
> To light, of the sea
> Walking between the pines to where you live.

23. The letter to Boorman is in the Dickey Papers.

However, his participation in the project as well as his continued interest in "Klondike" reflect his contradictory attitudes toward money, driving him toward and away from lucrative, but often distracting, movie contracts. On the one hand, Dickey early in his career had sought out Ezra Pound with whose diatribes against capitalism and usury he sympathized as he struggled to establish a career in a culture that, like his parents, measured success economically. In an unpublished letter dated November 2, 1981, to Dana Gioia, who was soliciting information for an essay entitled "Poetry and Business," Dickey responded defensively regarding his years in advertising: "Myself and the others you mention are by no means the only ones of the Brethren who have worked in business, but if these are the ones you want to use, they should be good enough material."[24] Moreover, he was acutely conscious of the effects of wealth on those who have it, declaring in his essay "The Energized Man," first published in 1979,

> The enormous discomfort that settles on Americans as they grow older: the enormous discomfort that settles on them in the midst of all their Comforts, and we can spell that word with a capital, is that their lives—their real lives— seem somehow to have eluded them: to have been taken away from under their very noses. They feel—they *know* their real life, a life of vital concerns, of vivid interest in things, and above all, of *consequence,* was there, someplace: I just laid it down a minute ago . . . and so on.[25]

For Dickey, what mattered most was poetry. On the other hand, the success of his novel *Deliverance* had enabled him to enjoy not only the previously unrealizable comforts of American life, including a second home on Pawleys Island, but also national recognition. In letters during the fifties, he bragged about the money advertising had made him. In February 1982 he proudly announced to friends and family that his short essay "How to Enjoy Poetry," which was sponsored by International Paper in its campaign to improve reading and writing skills, would reach eighty million people and was appearing simultaneously in *Newsweek, Time,* the *New York Times, People, Psychology Today,* and *Rolling Stone.* Dickey would have agreed with W. Somerset Maugham's contention that money was the sixth sense without which the other five senses could not be properly enjoyed.

24. The letter to Gioia is in the Dickey Papers.
25. James Dickey, "The Energized Man," in *The Imagination as Glory: The Poetry of James Dickey,* ed. Bruce Weigl and T. R. Hummer (Urbana and Chicago: University of Illinois Press, 1984), 163–65.

During the summer of 1982, Dickey worked diligently on *Alnilam* and then left for a week and a half of vacation with his family in Paris. Before leaving, however, he sent his editor, Hugh O'Neill, another one hundred pages of the manuscript, which now totaled 474 pages, along with instructions as to how to proceed should he be killed. "In case our aircraft blows up or we are gunned down at a cafe by either Palestinians, Jews, Armenians, Turks, Greeks, or just criminals (that would be a relief, and understandable!)"[26] he wrote in an unpublished letter dated August 13, "publish what you have of the novel." He asked his editor to use his notes and "piece the thing out, as Edmund Wilson did with Fitzgerald's The Last Tycoon. The manuscript of Alnilam is three times longer than Tycoon, and if Fitzgerald-Wilson can edit and publish such a book, so can Dickey-O'Neill." In Paris, the Dickeys stayed at the Hotel du Louvre Concorde and visited such famous sites as the Eiffel Tower, the Louvre, the Jeu de Paume, and the Sorbonne as well as numerous bookstores. Dickey was particularly pleased to see his old friend Marcel Béalu at Le Pont Traversé and tried to visit French writers he admired, including Julien Green, whom he had written two days before his flight. In an unpublished letter dated August 12, he declared: "I think I can truthfully say that your own writing and the example of your life I take from your Journal has had a great and good effect on my own work, and on my standards and values. I learned to read French by reading your Journal."[27] While in Paris, the Dickeys enjoyed a respite from the factiousness and discord of their domestic life together; they considered trying to conceive another child, whose name would be "Galen" if a girl and "Talbot" if a boy.

When they returned to the United States, Dickey confronted the reviews of *Puella*, which had been published on April 29; though he hoped the book would elevate his career, he prepared himself for critical attacks by discussing its method in an address delivered in November to the South Atlantic Modern Language Association convention in Atlanta. The lecture, entitled "The G.I. Can of Beets, the Fox in the Wave, and the Hammers over Open Ground," built upon an entry in the *Notebooks* of Winfield Townley Scott, who had distinguished between two types of poets that Dickey labeled "Magic-Language practitioners" and "literalists." For the former, he declared,

> language itself must be paramount. . . . The words are seen as illuminations mainly of one another; their light of meaning plays back and forth between them, and, though it must by nature refer beyond, outside itself, shimmers

---

26. The letters to O'Neill are in the Dickey Papers.
27. The letter to Green is in the Dickey Papers.

back off the external world in a way whereby the world—or objective reality, or just Reality—serves as a kind of secondary necessity, a non-verbal backdrop to highlight the dance of words and their bemused interplay.

Among the practitioners of this approach, Dickey asserted, were Hopkins, Hart Crane, Stevens, Berryman, Mallarmé, and Valéry and such surrealist or surrealist-influenced poets as Paul Éluard, Federico García Lorca, and Octavio Paz. Dickey, however, had largely sided in his poetry with the latter, whose ranks included Frost, Robinson, Masters, Hardy, Jarrell, and Larkin as well as Francis Ponge and Eugène Guillevic in France, those who believe "words [are] agents which illuminate events and situations that are part of an already given continuum, and which are only *designated* by means of words."[28] For this group, words are supervised by life itself rather than by the poets who erect systems of language. In his address, however, Dickey admitted that lately he had tried to "work out" with the magical side of language, abandoning the anecdote to enter a new linguistic threshold that had opened itself through translating other poets.

Puella, therefore, became a seminal work in Dickey's career. Its involved technique is important, for the images the persona conveys evoke an emotional complex inherent in certain narrative points in time that increasingly seem timeless—that is to say, mythical—presenting the simultaneous penetration of worlds—male and female, present and past, transcendent and physical. Critics such as Peter Balakian, James Applewhite, Ronald Baughman, and Eugene Hollahan discerned in the work a positive advance over Dickey's "central motion." Balakian, for example, argued that the book provided another example of Dickey's search for Otherness whose form indicates a Whitmanesque affirmation and ambitiousness. The poems, he declared, constituted "a large monologue," not simply the outline of an entire mind but also "the pressures of the psyche, body, and spirit striving for transcendence" where the sexes finally unite in "a celebration of marriage" through the procreative powers of the female principle. Baughman believed the book's organization displayed a pattern of imagery that involves the elements as well as images of sound, all of which evoke emotional response and promote reader participation. The thematic conclusion of the volume, he asserted, occurs in "The Surround," spoken to James Wright as he moves from life to death. In addition to depicting Deborah's final incarnation as the environment, the poem unites all the important images: the reflected echo of veer-sounds, the circles and rings that mirror the cycle of life and death, and the unity of fire, air,

28. *Night Hurdling*, 126–27, 131.

water, and earth. *Puella,* he concluded, reveals "new voices and new tones" and completes Dickey's psychological recovery from the Second World War; his tendency to risk language poetically suggests that other effects will follow. *Poetry* editor John Frederick Nims informed Dickey that the five *Puella* poems published in the March issue had won the Levinson Prize. Past winners had included Frost, Stevens, Crane, Cummings, and Dylan Thomas. Other critics, however, met the volume with disdain. Dana Gioia, for example, strongly attacked the collection, labeling it "an unqualified disaster." Specifically, Gioia accused Dickey of meaningless linguistic frivolity—phrasing that consisted of "arbitrarily compounded words ('After-glowing in the hang-time'), hopelessly vague description ('the wide-open collisionless color'), and clumsy wordplay ('All pores cold with cream')." Such strained effects, he asserted, obscured the general sense of many of the poems. "It takes a certain genius to write this badly," Gioia sarcastically declared, and he concluded, "The more one scrutinizes the language of *Puella,* the more it seems improvised and approximate, nothing but pure, old-fashioned southern sound and fury."[29]

Even Donald Hall, at one time Dickey's literary executor, expressed puzzlement, writing the poet on December 16 that he had attempted to read the book four times and had finally given up: "It feels opaque to me, it resists me, it does not let me inside. This could mean that you have done something that fails, that resists me because it has in fact an impenetrable surface. . . . Or on the other hand it could mean that you are doing something new, something that I cannot get to."[30] If Dickey intended *Puella* to present a more sensitive and intuitive self, one that was politically attuned to social reality and that critics would acknowledge as a new direction, he was only partly successful. While the collection had its admirers, reviewers generally failed to discern the book's unique use of language.

Although the poems reflected Deborah's childhood and adolescent experiences, they nevertheless began as responses to Binkley's photographs of numerous girls whom Dickey had never met. He had simply imaginatively unified them under his wife's name. In an undated letter to Shaye Areheart at Doubleday, Dickey endeavored to provide an extensive explication of his sequence in hope that his commentary would assist the publisher in promoting the book. The letter suggests that within the lyric "moments" of Deborah's upbringing, Dickey consciously presented a cyclical journey—the rites of

29. Balakian, "Poets of Empathy," *Literary Review: An International Journal of Contemporary Writing* 27.1 (1983): 135–46; Baughman, *Understanding James Dickey* (Columbia: University of South Carolina Press, 1985), 143; and Gioia, *Can Poetry Matter?* (St. Paul: Graywolf Press, 1992), 190–93.
30. Hart, *Dickey,* 645.

passage—of the mythic hero: "The whole book is intended to be cyclic, or at any rate semicyclic, beginning before dawn and running on through the following midnight." It begins, he wrote, "with a kind of ritual getting-rid-of-the-effects and environments of childhood" in a ceremonial burning of a doll and dollhouse; progresses through experiences in which the narrator "link[s] up with the enormous forces of the universe"; and concludes with an invocation as well as "an affirmation of the imagination, of the mind's associational powers, so that literally the whole universe can result, or build up from, a single thought." In his biography of Dickey, Henry Hart asserts that *Puella*, in its presentation of a woman's coming of age, including menstruation and the growing awareness of temporal cycles, hypocritically "echoes" the poems of Anne Sexton and Sylvia Plath, both of whom Dickey had denounced in *Babel to Byzantium* and *Sorties*. The portrait of Deborah, the "various snapshots, cut up and shuffled as they are," that present her as troubled and destabilized, is itself essentially confessional.[31] Yet Dickey's poetic intent necessitated the treatment of such biological facts; unlike Sexton and Plath, his feminine vision in no way graphically presents a self-exposing and psychologically vulnerable self.

Dickey instructed Shaye Areheart to send *Puella* to Richard Hugo, who was chairing the 1982 Pulitzer Prize committee. With his friend in charge, he hoped to win the major award, but he soon learned that Hugo had died. In an unpublished letter to Dave Smith dated October 29, he declared that he wanted "to go up there to Montana and give a couple of benefit readings, and try to get a plaque or something put up in his memory." Then he expressed a melancholy despair: "Fat lot of good that'll do, though, death being what it is. But we go on, until we can't. Right now, you and I go on." He attempted to have Smith inducted into the National Institute of Arts and Letters, writing Robert Penn Warren on September 15, "God help him, he did his Ph.D. on my work, and has kept in touch for all this time." "I do like his work," Dickey stated, and with a metaphor that suggested his competitiveness, concluded, "I will be more than glad to back his play." In an unpublished letter to Smith dated November 22, he called Smith "My best, my old Pulling Guard," and he urged his other supporters, including Richard Tillinghast and David Bottoms, to "Knock'em down," to continue the game, which he increasingly sensed he was losing but which he remained determined to play. He wrote Tillinghast on October 8 that the *New York Times* might contact him to review *Puella*, stating that it would be good to have him "on the case." "The book is important," Dickey emphasized, "because it marks a shift in my way of going at things, concentrating more on the purely linguistic part of poetry—and es-

31. Ibid., 646.

pecially on the line—and less on the narrative or anecdotal." He also hoped
Tillinghast would do an extensive review of his early work, as the latter had
recently done on Charles Wright, informing him in an unpublished letter
dated December 14 that "if the Times is willing for you to review Wright's old
poems they should be twice as willing to do mine." "There could be a really
interesting possibility, it seems to me of your doing some kind of retrospective, an assessment of some sort, using these books as a base, particularly, in
view of the fact that a kind of new-wave movement, counter to Lowell's con-
fessionalism, seems to be shaping up around the kind of thing that I have
been trying to do over the years." Battered on several fronts, Dickey was nevertheless intent on maintaining new poetic directions, utilizing his friends for
what he clearly understood was needed literary and political "lift." He also
continued to be conscious of the physical debilitation of age. When Norman
German, an English professor at Lamar University, wrote to both praise and
ask questions about an early poem, "Looking for the Buckhead Boys," Dickey
responded on October 18: "Say hello to your class for me, and tell them I'm
alive, though almost sixty. I'm going back to Buckhead next month, though,
and I'll see if Charlie Gates . . . is still around, for I need gas."[32]

In 1983, the year he turned sixty, Dickey was honored by the new governor
of South Carolina, Richard Riley, who asked him to write a poem for his inauguration. In January, Dickey celebrated his state by reading "For a Time
and Place" to assembled politicians and their families. As with his essay "The
Starry Place between the Antlers," the poem celebrated both the abundant
flora and fauna of South Carolina and the geographic diversity, everything
arranged in a rich pattern of natural wealth, a point

> where we best
> Are, and would be: our soil, our soul,
> Our sail, our black horizon simmering like a mainspring,
> Our rocky water falling like a mountain
> Ledge-to-ledge naturally headlong,
> Unstoppable, and our momentum
> In place, overcoming, coming over us
> And from us
> From now on out.

In 1989 Dickey again championed the state's physical beauty—the natural
world as a kind of personal vision—in the foreword he wrote for a coffee-table

32. The letters to Smith, Warren, Tillinghast, and German are all in the Dickey Papers.

book entitled *South Carolina: The Natural Heritage.* "From the mountains of Oconee to the beaches of Pawleys Island," he asserted, "these kinds of original space exist any time we open ourselves to them, and merely *look* without thought of using. . . . We need to substitute instinct for reason, and merely to *behold* what is; and view with primal innocence those parts of creation that have nothing to do with us except to serve as material for contemplation and wonder, born into it as we were, living by means of its processes, part of a mystery, part of a whole scheme, a cosmos, the reason for which will never be known."[33] Throughout his life, Dickey's attitude toward the natural world— South Carolina specifically and the South in general—was one of celebration and reverence at the explicable wonder and mystery of creation.

Riley thanked Dickey in a letter dated January 13, 1983, stating that South Carolina was fortunate to have "someone of your talent who understands both the apparent and the hidden beauty of this great State and who has the capacity to capture this beauty in poetry." Dickey responded in an unpublished letter dated January 19, declaring that the occasion "brought me closer to the things and people I live among, and that cannot be anything but good."[34] He very much believed that being born a southerner constituted the best circumstance that had happened to him, first as a man and then as a writer, and while Dickey never wished to indulge in regional chauvinism, he felt that the history of the South had imparted to him not only a set of values, particularly the sense of the nature of evil, but also a visionary sense of larger modes of existence. He invited the governor to attend the literary birthday party soon to be hosted for him by the University of South Carolina and, among others, Robert Penn Warren, Richard Howard, Norman Mailer, Saul Bellow, John Updike, Harold Bloom, R. W. B. Lewis, and Monroe Spears. The gathering particularly delighted Dickey, whose troubled marriage and declining career threatened his sense of importance. On February 1, his colleague Bernie Dunlap discussed the film *Deliverance;* the following day, former students Franklin Ashley, Ben Greer, and Susan Ludvigson recounted his extraordinary teaching; and later in the afternoon Riley himself hosted a birthday gala at the Governor's Mansion. That night, Bloom and Howard lectured on Dickey's poetry. On February 4, the final day of the symposium, Monroe Spears, Dickey's professor at Vanderbilt, defended his former student's experiments in *The Zodiac* and *Puella,* which he viewed as advancing an exemplary career. Considering the maligned reception these volumes had received, Dickey must

33. Foreword to *South Carolina: The Natural Heritage* (Columbia: University of South Carolina Press, 1989), 9–10.
34. The letter to Riley is in the Dickey Papers.

have been pleased by their defense from so distinguished a scholar. The grand finale of the literary celebration was a banquet hosted by James Holderman, the university's president, who introduced Dickey's reading.

Financial worries engendered by Bookie Binkley's litigation soon caused Dickey to undertake another round of poetry readings. During the winter and spring, he returned to his "barnstorming for poetry," visiting Albright College, the University of North Texas, Savannah College of Art and Design, Fairleigh Dickinson University, New York's West Side YMCA, and the Guggenheim Museum. In late March he also appeared at Clemson for a three-day conference where by chance he ran into his old football coach, Rock Norman, at a Holiday Inn restaurant. Dickey had written a tribute to his coaches in an early poem, "The Bee," first published in the June 1966 issue of *Harper's* magazine, declaring later that "the bad times they gave me come to seem like acts of faith, because they wouldn't have taken the time with me if they didn't think I was worth it."[35] Dickey, always needing to feel self-worth, was pleased that Norman recognized and remembered him.

During the summer of 1983, Dickey focused on several older projects, among them another coffee-table book entitled "The Wilderness of Heaven," whose deadline was in October. Shaye Areheart had mailed him reproductions of paintings by Hubert Shuptrine about which Dickey was supposed to write, but Dickey demurred. "I am proceeding in somewhat the same manner as I did with *Jericho*," he wrote Shuptrine in an unpublished letter dated August 5, "for it seems to me that a kind of double vision of Appalachia—the artist's and the writer's—is better than having one of the interpreters comment on the work of the other, in effect."[36] He informed the painter that he had divided the text into ten sections with two subsections in each. Dickey was more direct with Areheart, stating that Shuptrine's pictures did not afford him enough subject matter and declaring that it was better if he simply worked out his own interpretation of Appalachia. Because such an arrangement risked a fractured book, Shuptrine requested on August 25 that Dickey send him an outline of his narrative to guide his painting. Dickey finished the story quickly, sending a draft to Hugh O'Neill by the end of October and completing revisions in December.

Dickey finished another book in late 1983. On October 15, Bruccoli Clark published *Night Hurdling*, a collection of essays, poems, commencement addresses, interviews, and afterwords that project the self-proclaimed and self-

35. *Self-Interviews*, 171.
36. The letter to Shuptrine is in the Dickey Papers.

proclaiming threads of his identity and continue his exploration of the nature and intent of poetry. In the introduction, Dickey states, "Perhaps in the end the whole possibility of words being able to contain one's identity is illusory; opinions, yes; identity, maybe. Perhaps the whole question of identity itself is illusory. But one must work with such misconceptions for whatever hint of insight—the making of a truth—they may contain: that fragment of existence which could not be seen in any other way and may with great good luck, as in the best poetry, be better than the truth." The readings Dickey offered presented a writer whose identity is eclectic if not contradictory. Dickey himself admitted as much to Stanley Burnshaw in an unpublished letter dated July 28: "Night Hurdling is sure to be mighty controversial, because I say a lot of what I think in there, and, although some of it is self-contradictory—and therefore certain to displease all sides—I mean what I say when I say it, whenever it is." Essays such as "The Water-Bug's Mittens" and "The G.I. Can of Beets, the Fox in the Wave, and the Hammers over Open Ground" constitute Dickey's most intense scrutiny of his own poetry as a means not only of examining himself but also of determining new poetic directions. Indeed, the images Dickey discusses in the latter, Jarrell's "G.I. can of beets," Dylan Thomas's "fox in the wave," and Michael Hamburger's translation of Paul Celan, "the hammers / will swing over open ground," a creative re-creation of the literal wording, "the hammers will swing free," offer a sense of Dickey's critical search for a new poetic ground where images are imaginatively delivered and built upon but held within the poet's imposed limits, which for Dickey involved not so much meter, rhyme, or any such traditional poetic conventions as "the right kind of seeming arbitrariness," the language having the sense of possessing the world. His analyses of other writers, moreover, including Robert Penn Warren's angst, F. Scott Fitzgerald's poetry, Jack London's stylistic vices and narrative virtues, and Vachel Lindsay's suicidal decline, are incisive and convincing.

Dickey returned to his extensive reading tours in October and November 1983, visiting the Governor's School for the Arts in South Carolina, the Folger Shakespeare Library, George Mason University, Northern Virginia Community College, Westchester Community College, Colgate University, and the Alabama School of Fine Arts. Often he assumed the role of the drunken but brilliant bard, alternately offending and mesmerizing audiences with his conversations and readings, acting partly from frustration at the critical inattention his work was receiving and partly from a desire to shock and thereby assure audience attention. As a respite from worries involving both his career and his domestic life, he began to participate in "power lunches" with close friends and colleagues in the English department of the University of South Carolina, a practice that Dickey would continue twice a week until his death. Every Tuesday and Thursday afternoon, he would meet Ben Franklin and Don Greiner for lunch at the Faculty House. Because the tables there seated four people, a "mystery guest," usually a student or another professor whose identity was kept secret, was frequently invited, with Franklin serving as master of ceremonies. Once Henry Taylor joined the group and politely addressed Dickey with the gentle words, "Cher Master." Novelist Frederick Busch, whom Dickey came to like personally and to respect professionally, was the mystery guest at least twice. The conversation was always brisk and high-spirited, with the guest expected to contribute to discussions of music, literature, sports, and movies. These gatherings, in addition to providing one of Dickey's few opportunities for friendly banter and private conversation, also enabled him to unburden himself about his marital difficulties and private fears. With no mask to wear or role to perform and confident that neither colleague would repeat what he said, Dickey's essential voice was readily apparent. His retentive memory, acute critical analysis, and broad disciplinary knowledge as well as an obvious love of great writing all testified to who he was and the value he attributed to his craft. "What came through in the luncheon talk," Greiner stated, "were Jim's astonishing memory for literary matters and his eagerness to talk informally about such things." Matthew Bruccoli agreed. After relating one of their afternoons together at his Columbia home, he asserted: "His literary taste and critical judgment were impeccable. Jim was the best booktalker I have known. Anything he said about literature—drunk or sober— merited careful attention. He was not unnecessarily truthful about himself, but he was trustworthy on literature."[37]

Once, as the three friends seated themselves (they always ate either at the same table inside the Faculty House or in the garden outside), Dickey asked Greiner what he had taught that morning; the latter responded that he was currently teaching Cooper's *The Last of the Mohicans* to a doctoral seminar. Dickey responded with genuine interest, "Do you recall the scene, late in the novel, when Cooper writes about the absolute confidence Natty and Chingachgook have in each other. How do you read that, Don?" The question led to a spirited, serious discussion of the male bonding archetype that Cooper established in American literature and led naturally to *Deliverance*. Similarly, when Dickey heard that Greiner had taught Wallace Stevens in a seminar, focusing the class

37. *Crux: The Letters of James Dickey,* ed. Matthew J. Bruccoli and Judith Baughman (New York: Knopf, 1999), xxi.

on "The Snow Man," he murmured, "Another one of Stevens's innumerable conundrums." The comment sparked an hourlong exchange, with Greiner leading the defense of Stevens.

With movies Dickey would frequently begin the conversation by mentioning a current film he had seen, such as *Platoon* or *The Remains of the Day* (he thought the title "resonant"), but he would reminisce, recalling movies he had admired in his adolescence, such as *Dawn Patrol* and *Gunga Din*. Repeatedly he talked about the impact the original version of *The Four Feathers* had had on him, seeming to relive a moment from his youth. When Greiner inquired about *The Best Years of Our Lives*, Dickey appeared quiet or sad. His favorite scene, he declared, was the one when Dana Andrews visits the "graveyard" of the bombers and climbs into the cockpit. He was less excited about the choices Greiner and Franklin offered for discussion, including *Blowup* and *Claire's Knee*, although he liked such film noir classics as *The Big Sleep, The Maltese Falcon, Criss Cross*, and *Murder My Sweet*.

When the conversation centered on music, Dickey and Franklin took the lead, particularly when discussing jazz. Greiner collected, listened to, and was conversant with "cool jazz" musicians such as Miles Davis and Gerry Mulligan, but Franklin knew all of jazz and could talk enthusiastically when Dickey turned the conversation to his own favorite, Bix Beiderbecke. Greiner remembers, "There was no one-upmanship during these lunch discussions, no showing off—just spirited talk among three friends who trusted one another and who thrived on these twice-a-week meetings." The conversations continued as Greiner and Franklin walked with Dickey from the Faculty House to the classroom where he would meet his seminar.

Dickey's natural generosity came out during these lunches. He would often show up at the table with an inscribed copy of a newly released Dickey reprint, a new Dickey book, or a photocopy of a poem he was drafting. Not only did he offer his two friends bound, inscribed photocopies of the typescript of his novel *To the White Sea*, but he also gave them each inscribed copies of the typescript of "Breaking the Field," the poem he wrote about the Super Bowl for the NFL official program. Even more impressive, Dickey wrote what he termed "a memorial poem" about the power lunches, a parody of eighteenth-century heroic couplets. Ten lines in length and entitled "Some Lines from Samuel Johnson, Slightly Re-Written," it read:

While still my steps the steady staff sustains,
Tho' life still vig'rous revels in my veins,
You grant, Kind Heaven, this indulgent place

Where honesty and sense are no disgrace:
These pleasing bricks where verdant osiers play,
This peaceful vale with nature's paintings gay,
Where Culture's harrass'd Heroes find repose,
And safe in intellect defy our foes:
This secret cell Your gracious Powers give.
Let Don live here, for Don has learned to live.

Dickey substituted the name in the copy he gave Ben Franklin, but he signed both copies, "Samuel Johnson, Esq. J. Dickey, Scribe."

At these lunches, Dickey kept Franklin and Greiner informed on the progress of his projects, including *Alnilam*. He hoped that his friend George Plimpton would publish an excerpt from the novel in the *Paris Review*. He had sent Hugh O'Neill another section of the novel with an unpublished letter dated May 9, 1983; most of this section of the manuscript centered on Frank Cahill and Joel's instructor, McCaig, and their visit to the crash scene of Joel's aircraft and the aftermath of the fire in which he went down. Dickey proposed that the material could be published in either *Playboy* or *Esquire* and suggested it be entitled "The Black Farm." Now that spring semester was over, he declared, he could write with no distractions, citing his only commitment that summer as a two-week Writers' Conference in Aspen. "I'll have the book in to you before I go," he asserted, "barring death or the transmigration of souls." In truth, the novel was nowhere near completion. On December 17, 1984, he signed another amended version of his 1971 contract, extending the deadline to May 1, 1985. Although Dickey made substantive progress on *Alnilam* in 1985, he again needed an extension, which promised the manuscript in August 1985. By mid-May, he had written twelve hundred pages. The August deadline passed, but in October he mailed all fifteen hundred pages to his editor. Dickey variously blamed the delay on Maxine's death, his marriage to Deborah, and the birth of Bronwen and reminded those who inquired or interviewed him that throughout his career poetry had remained his central focus. He asserted, moreover, that the novel would not have the popular appeal of *Deliverance,* telling William Starr in a 1987 interview, "A writer has to go with his imagination. You're not really an artist if you try to give the people what they want. Because most of the time they don't know what they want until they get it."[38] Nostalgic with memories of past success and piqued

38. "*Alnilam:* James Dickey's Novel Explores Father and Son Relationships," in *Voiced Connections,* ed. Baughman, 258–62.

by the recent failures of "Flowering," "Klondike," and his other film treatments, Dickey nevertheless hoped that it would become a best seller. He remained a fighter.

Despite the general critical decline in his reputation, Dickey's prestige remained high in some literary circles. Early in 1985, he was asked to serve on
an international panel of nine judges for the Ritz Paris Hemingway Award,
which Pierre Salinger had conceived and which had been formally established
on January 11. A prize of $50,000 honored the author of the best novel of the
year in English or in English translation. Dickey flew to Paris to join Salinger,
who presided over the judges, and cast his vote for Marguerite Duras's *The
Lover*, which won. While there, Dickey reunited with his friend William Styron. Later that year Ted Koppel invited Dickey to participate in the Fourth of
July edition of his ABC news show *Nightline*. Dickey was usually reticent to
discuss political issues, but when now asked to discuss the significance of
Independence Day, Dickey did so from a poetic perspective, quoting a poem
by Winfield Townley Scott about July Fourth fireworks and remarking on
America's good fortune to have had as its Founding Fathers such statesmen as
Washington, Jefferson, Hamilton, Madison, and Adams. Despite such high-
profile events, however, Dickey's appearances were more and more at small
venue conferences or festivals and largely in the South, a measure of how re-
gionalized the marketplace was to which he appealed. In March 1985, for example, he read at the Writers' Workshop in Asheville, North Carolina, for $1,500,
and in June he accepted $200 to read at the Association of Departments of
English at the University of South Carolina. While he attended a May 9–11
conference on Eastern Comparative Literature at NYU, he received only $400
in payment and $200 for expenses. Indeed, Dickey's gross income from all his
writings in 1986 totaled $27,563, a fraction of what his books had earned
during the seventies when he commanded the literary air.[39]

In 1986 Dickey determined to complete *Alnilam*. Because the novel centers
on the crash of an airplane, he felt a grim coincidence when the *Challenger*
space shuttle exploded on January 28. Gale Combest, who worked with Dan
Rather at CBS, remembered Dickey's accounts of the *Apollo* moon missions
in *Life* and asked him to comment on the disaster. Rather read Dickey's eu-
logy at the end of his special late-night report, "Disaster in Space":

> Put them on the list of men and women who counted, these searchers and
> seekers, these astronauts and teachers who died today in what became the

39. Hart, *Dickey*, 661–62.

spaceship disaster; they died in the blue and silver furnaces of their space-suits. Think about them, who they were and the way they were: dreamers, explorers, adventurers forcing themselves past the point of danger and deep fatigue, to expand our understanding of what is up there and out there. They may never have known the nature of the trouble that killed them. For them, no more cries of "Wow, what a view!"; no more jokes with Mission Control; no more thumbs up for cheering crowds; no more phone calls from the President. They will not see their parents and their wives or husbands and their children meeting them—gone with the rush of the engines and the exploding sky—gone, but theirs were lives that mattered.

The statement, reminiscent in tone of much of A. E. Housman's poetry, reflects Dickey's own desire for heroism, his psychological need for bravery and consequence on which he had first elaborated in his 1973 University of Virginia baccalaureate address entitled "Upthrust and Its Men." That address had celebrated another astronaut, Ed White, the first American to walk in space, who was killed in a training accident. He recollected a photograph in *Life* of White in his space-walking suit, his gold-headed helmet off and a "fun grin" on his face. In the photograph and in the actions of the *Challenger* astronauts, Dickey perceived the bold daring that bespoke essential courage, a stringent and exuberant self-discipline that was not only what was most needed but also what Americans most lacked. "That is really my key word, the possible," he stated. "Possibility, and the openness to it, and the wit to recognize it and the daring to use it."[40] Ironically, perhaps, Dickey could write about such an ideal, could experience it through the illusion of language, but largely could not live it.

In late June 1986 South Carolina inducted Dickey into its Academy of Authors, the first living author to be so honored. The academy, founded several years before by Paul Talmadge, the vice president and academic dean of Anderson College, also honored Julia Peterkin and William Gilmore Simms. Speaking at an Anderson College banquet, Dickey declared, "My real wish is just to put down one word after another until I die," adding, "Every writer is a failed writer. We're all amateurs at this. We don't live long enough to be anything else."[41] The true writer, he suggested, was one who does what he is supposed to do—write—no matter what else is happening around him. With his domestic life upset by Deborah's drug problem and by the physical and verbal

40. "Upthrust and Its Men," in *Night Hurdling,* 175–82.
41. Anne E. Hartung, "Dickey Plays 'Metaphysical Scrabble Game,'" *Anderson Independent-Mail,* June 29, 1986, pp. A1–2.

violence in their household, Dickey had difficulty working and soon developed headaches that he initially believed resulted from eyestrain. However, the headaches became more severe, and after he vomited at dinner he went to the hospital the following day. Physicians at Richland Memorial Hospital administered a CAT scan of his brain and discovered a large blood clot under the skull whose cause was unknown; the subdural hematoma was so threatening they operated that day. He later jokingly told William Starr that, while under anesthesia, "I was consorting with the brothers Sleep and Death, and another fellow named Lazarus. I tried to bring him out with me, but he was waiting for someone else." Dickey had feared that he would die during the operation.

Much of the strength Dickey emotionally needed to recuperate fully from his successful surgery derived from his love for Bronwen and his concern for her psychological well-being should she lose her father. On September 10, 1986, he published *Bronwen, the Traw, and the Shape-Shifter,* presenting a highly idealized version of his daughter as a child of nature who overcomes the force of the "All-Dark" and the monstrous "Shape-Shifter" associated with it with the help of her magical garden tool and a host of strange flying squirrels. As he did in his earlier works, Dickey imposed on the narrative a mythic journey in which Bronwen leaves the warmth and comfort of her home and undergoes an "otherworld" of trials as she experiences an initiation into a source of power before finally returning to her bedroom with lessons learned. Random House and several other publishers had turned the book down before Harcourt Brace Jovanovich agreed to publish it. The publisher offered Dickey a $5,000 advance and printed 20,000 copies. Brisk initial sales elevated Dickey's hopes that the book would sell well—10,000 copies had been sold by December 30—but sales then slackened. The publisher estimated that Dickey would earn about two thousand dollars in royalties by spring 1987. Dickey contacted Richard Jesse Watson, whose illustrations accompanied the poetic text, about a sequel entitled "Bronwen, the Cunicorn, and the Nomain." Bronwen, now living on the plains rather than on a cliff above a river, encounters the Cunicorn, a unicorn-like and equally mythological beast whose main characteristics are its highly stylized horn and its sad eyes. The animal cannot stay in the real world all the time and continually fades away, appearing again to Bronwen when no one else is awake. Dickey's notes state: "The Cunicorn, in other words, is like the unicorn in the poem by Rilke, which 'fed not on grain, but on the possibility of being.'" The only means by which the Cunicorn can remain in "full reality" is by retrieving and listening to the Lost Bell, which lies in Nomain, the land of no shadow. The project never materialized.

As he always did, Dickey fervently promoted the book, signing copies in Columbia and Charleston, South Carolina, and Gainesville and Atlanta, Georgia, and sending a copy to South Carolina's first lady. He also sent copies to Ted Koppel, Tom Brokaw, Barbara Walters, and Johnny Carson, as well as most of the major newspapers, and he wrote Dan Rather in an unpublished letter dated October 10, 1986, that he would be in New York from October 16 through 19 if Rather would like him to appear on a network program where he might discuss the book. "It would be good to be on a program for your network," he stated, "and talk about something cheerful, and not the sad circumstances that had occurred before my other words, the ones about the shuttle explosion, went out over your waves."[42]

The plot of *Bronwen* was more complicated than that of *Tucky the Hunter,* and the meter and rhythms more demanding; Dickey was striving to achieve a more complex children's book than previously. Reviews, however, were mixed. Ann Sporborg's lengthy commentary declared that the "timeless fear of the dark" inspires the book's "powerful echoic verses" and noted that Bronwen's "vision-quest" involves her confrontation with the elements of fire, wind, and water. The changes in tone and cadence, moreover, reflect a deepening despair as the narrative becomes more threatening. Other reviewers, however, were less positive, and their criticism typically centered on Dickey's language. Kathleen D. Whalen spoke for others when she asserted that Bronwen's adventure appears in "excruciatingly lengthy detail," and while Watson's drawings are strong, they do not mitigate the "plodding language" and "dragging action." David Macaulay argued that while Book One succeeds, introducing Bronwen and the All-Dark as the heroine and villain, respectively, and moving from the sunlight and safety of her garden to the menacing shadows in her bedroom as the All-Dark awakens, the story "flattens" as it progresses because imagination yields to mere acceptance. "Conventional fantasy" replaces "the power of suggestion." "The real battle," Macaulay concludes, "is between words and pictures, between the imagined and the unavoidable, the suggested and the concrete" because Dickey's text fights against Watson's illustrations; *Bronwen* therefore is two books whose opposites are not integrated.[43]

After finally sending *Alnilam* to Doubleday, Dickey worked diligently correcting proofs in the early weeks of 1987 so that he could return them by

---

42. The letter to Rather is in the Dickey Papers.

43. Sporborg, "*Bronwen, the Traw, and the Shape-Shifter,*" James Dickey Newsletter 4 (Fall 1987): 25–28; Whalen, "*Bronwen, the Traw, and the Shape-Shifter,*" School Library Journal 33 (October 1986): 173; Macaulay, "*Bronwen, the Traw, and the Shape-Shifter,*" New York Times Book Review, March 8, 1987, p. 31.

February 25. After short visits in January to Clemson University to receive an award and in February to read at McNeese State in Louisiana, where his friend the poet Leon Stokesbury taught, he made a longer trip in March to Washington, D.C., to attend the fortieth anniversary of the poetry consultantship and the inauguration of its replacement, the poet laureateship. He had written Robert Penn Warren to congratulate him on being named the first poet laureate and was disappointed that Warren could not attend because of throat surgery. Many of America's most distinguished poets attended the celebration, including Anthony Hecht, Richard Eberhart, Maxine Kumin, Stanley Kunitz, William Meredith, Howard Nemerov, Karl Shapiro, William Jay Smith, and William Stafford. Stephen Spender commented during the first evening of readings, "We will probably not meet again until we enter Purgatory," to which Dickey responded, "Or Parnassus," adding, "That's where good poets go." Asked what he would call such an august meeting, Dickey said, "I'd call it a Parnassus of poets." The *New York Times* printed his comments the following day.[44]

Doubleday finally published *Alnilam* on June 5, 1987, with a printing of 125,000 copies and a reported six-figure promotional budget. As with *Deliverance,* the novel's genesis lay in a single image, a superstition of World War II aviators, which Dickey later discussed in an essay entitled "LIGHTNINGS, or Visuals."

The novel is about the early days of World War II when the Air Force—in those days it was called the Army Air Corps—was desperately trying to prepare itself to fight a major war in the air. In fact, and probably because of these conditions, the air itself was full of myths and legends. One of these was that if you happen to look through a spinning propeller, on a flight line, say, and on the other side of it another propeller is turning and your look goes through both of them at the same time, the image of a man will be formed in the double-whirling metal, the blades. Whether true or not, that idea and that image appealed to me strongly; there was something about "the ghost in the machine" suggestion that sparked a part of my imagination. . . . As a result of the shadowy figure in the twin propellers, I began to feel that there might be some kind of spirit in the machines that men have made, and that this might be both indifferent to them and superior to them; in short, not so much a ghost in the machine but a God.[45]

---

44. Nan Robertson, "Parnassus-on-Potomac: Poets Celebrate English," *New York Times,* March 31, 1987, p. C13.

45. "LIGHTNINGS, or Visuals," *James Dickey Newsletter* 8.2 (Spring 1992): 2–12.

While teaching at Rice Institute, Dickey originally conceived the plot of a father who has lost his only son early in the Second World War in a training accident, but the narrative developed slowly and its concerns expanded. Because of the novel's massive length and its many layers of meaning, reviewers variously identified its principal theme. Dickey, commenting on the book's composition in 1976, admitted that the conceptualization of the book had grown: "The main thing I want to do with *Alnilam*, is write the ultimate novel of fathers and sons; the mysteries, the frustrations, the revelations, and, at the end, the eventual renunciation and reconciliation." Along with this concern, however, he planned to exhibit both "the dangerousness—the sheer *dangerousness*—of ideas. Their applicability can result in the deaths and mutilations of many" and what he labeled "the concept of the *fabulous* death." He recognized that both *Alnilam* and its intended sequel, "Crux," endeavored to treat so many ideas that their full development and integration remained questionable. While his thematic concerns involved personal, military, artistic, and social relationships, as well as their implications, he asserted, "I think the crux of the matter lies somewhere in the definition of what power does to a man and also charlatanry, and also love." "I mean to show, here," he continued in his summary notes on the works in progress, "the fascination of power and mystery simultaneously. That is, the fascination of power and personal mystery: mystiques. Mystiques, both in their absurdity and their grandeur, and their lending to the personal dramatic significance that human events and human beings so desperately need and respond to." He intended that the two novels "open out from a small incident at a primary training base into a vast Tolstoyian vision of the Pacific night air war."[46]

Following the overwhelming critical and financial accomplishments of *Deliverance,* however, Dickey had declared in 1973 that he would never write a sequel and that his next novel would not achieve such success. "What I want to do now," he asserted, "as far as novels are concerned is to write a resounding and interesting failure. Which I think this [*Alnilam*] is going to be."[47] In an unpublished letter dated January 14, 1974, Dickey had informed Stewart Richardson that the new novel would reach a thousand pages, warning, "it is very important that the style be right, for we are going a very long way, and the style must be right to sustain such a long narrative." Expecting a work similar to his first novel, critics were baffled by the lack of action, the slow pacing, and the stylistic innovation of splitting particular pages into parallel

46. *Pages: The World of Books, Writers, and Writing,* ed. Matthew J. Bruccoli (Detroit: Gale Research, 1976), 11–12, 14, 15.
47. "James Dickey at Drury College," in *Voiced Connections,* ed. Baughman, 107.

columns to suggest the visible world as it is ordinarily perceived and as Frank Cahill, the blind protagonist, mentally envisions it. Reviewers also cited weak characterization and a poetic prose that occasionally yields to overwriting, flaws similar to those noted in *Deliverance*. Carolyn Blakemore, Dickey's latest editor at Doubleday, had expressed reservations in a seventeen-page letter dated January 23, 1986, not only about the length of the manuscript but also about the style. Dickey responded on February 27 with a missive of identical length, largely countering her proposed amendments both to his split-page technique and to his characterization of Frank Cahill, which Blakemore thought insufficiently developed and too much of a cipher.

The novel on which Dickey had labored since the fifties sold reasonably well; critical response was mixed. By October 31, 1987, 52,453 copies had been returned by bookstores to the publisher.[48] Jay Parini's response typified those who criticized the book. Writing in *USA Today*, he termed *Alnilam* disappointing, calling it a "melodrama" that was "windy, often incoherently organized, and—sometimes—downright bad," particularly when Dickey split the narrative into vertical columns to reflect in dark bold type Frank Cahill's subjective impressions. Robert Towers in the *New York Times Book Review*, while praising the novel as ambitious and overreaching, nevertheless asserted that it is alternately pretentious and hindered by windiness and slow pacing. The scrutiny required for the split columns of prose, he asserted, often brings some startling or original play of language, but when the narrative moves "like lava oozing from a fissure" in a work "Melvillean in its aspirations and scope," these sections seem merely digressive. Because Dickey never clearly delineates the mystery of Alnilam, the secret group Joel has created with plans to take over the military, the novel lacks, he concluded, "a white whale to pursue." Gary Kerley and Ron Baughman, however, praised the novel. Kerley asserted that *Alnilam* becomes "essentially a labyrinth of questions about identity," while Baughman argued that the novel displays the many forms of power that radiate from and act on the individual and the need to rise above inconsequence. The danger of an "intensified life," he declared, is its lack of control, such that "its practitioner can become a monomaniac like Captain Ahab in *Moby-Dick* or Lewis Medlock in *Deliverance*."[49]

Ten years before Dickey published *Alnilam*, he had talked about the novel

48. Hart, *Dickey*, 683.
49. Parini, "James Dickey's Massive and Mystifying *Alnilam*," *USA Today*, May 29, 1987, p. 70; Towers, "Prometheus Blind," *New York Times Book Review*, June 21, 1987, p. 7; Kerley, "Dickey Delivers Second Novel," *Gainesville Times*, July 19, 1987, p. 5E; Baughman, "In Dickey's Latest, Blindness Opens a Man's Eyes to Life," *Philadelphia Inquirer*, May 31, 1987, pp. S1, 8.

with his son Christopher, on whom he had based the characterization of Joel Cahill, though he stated in interviews that his son was not as charismatic. Because Joel has died or perhaps only disappeared, Dickey believed that he needed to suggest some vision of the future that informs and motivates the actions of the mystical conspiracy. "The society would depend very heavily on *role-playing*, and on *lying*," he declared. "Joel believes that lying exercises the creative and imaginative faculties, and, when indulged in on either an individual or a group basis, raises the consciousness of the party or parties concerned." In his reminiscence, Chris later related, "It was an idea that Jim Dickey tried to live, but he could never make it work in the novels, and in 1976 it started to fail him and everyone around him in his life." Chris blamed the novel's failure on his father's drinking and his consequent inability to impose discipline on or coherence to the technique of splitting the page into twin columns. "Jim Dickey wouldn't hear of changing them," he remembered, yet he added, "James Dickey's voice was huge, the kind of a voice you don't find in American prose but about once in a generation."[50]

That voice was also the same as it had been when he was teaching at Rice Institute and first conceived the idea for his big novel, which was then entitled "The Romantic," eventually became "Death's Baby Machine," and finally *Alnilam.* It was a voice vulnerable to feelings of inadequacy and that countered real or perceived criticism by assuming a mask, playing whatever role would enable Dickey to command attention. If the illusion he created was sublime enough, he might even feel himself a hero. Often the mask reflected an aspect of Dickey himself; sometimes he invented one because he was curious or because it was appropriate for the moment. It was a voice that wanted to save itself and redeem society, which Dickey believed was sick, frustrated, and defeated. In an entry from an early notebook, he had written, "What I really want to be—or become—a Messiah." He had also declared in the synopsis to "The Spell," "We live in a very affluent society, and we constantly have the feeling of dying of thirst, here at the fountain-side." Yet as his brother Tom, an expert in Civil War munitions, was dying of colon cancer, Dickey wrote Chris on November 20 and expressed the forlornness and inadequacy he felt: "It is a terrible thing, and the utter hopelessness is the worst of it. That, and the way the memory fills up with images of him when he was happy." When Tom died on December 8, 1987, Dickey eventually responded by re-creating the death-watch in a poem entitled "Last Hours," published in the fall 1994 issue of

---

50. *Summer of Deliverance: A Memoir of Father and Son* (New York: Simon and Schuster, 1998), 198–99, 226–27.

Southern Review. In it, Tom is delivered from his fears of dying not by Stone-wall Jackson and James Longstreet, the southern generals whose lives and actions in pursuit of the southern cause had so captivated him, but rather by Ted Bundy, whose serial murders of young women had intrigued Dickey in Seattle when he was preparing for his surgery.

> Brother, take this: your blood kin's last word
>
> Of love: follow not me
> But the murderer. He will kill
> The pain, in the one good act
>
> Long after his execution. Follow. He is helping. Go with him,
>
> Brother; he will cross you over.

Violence, personalized in the figure of Bundy, allows for an escape from the hauntedness of the hospital room and offers a kind of salvation.

With the reality of time and death again assailing him, Dickey pursued new endeavors. From almost twenty years of classes, he gathered the poems of fifty of his former students and published them in an anthology entitled *From the Green Horseshoe.* In the introduction he announced the purposes that had directed his teaching: "to galvanize the associative energies of the individual student, to make him aware of his memory-process, to encourage him to use these with spontaneity and without fear, and secondarily to awaken him to the creative possibilities that reside within the nature of Form itself, and of the resources inherent in particular forms, the whole effort being to embody in words what is stated in Dryden's ringing injunction, where he says that the task of the poet 'is to move the sleeping images of things toward the light.' "[51] Dickey also continued working on the poems he would include in what would be his last collection, *The Eagle's Mile.* Most of his energy, however, went into the film treatment for *Alnilam,* for which Rockingham Productions on August 4 had paid him $10,000. Once again, he hoped the screenplay would generate a blockbuster movie.

Adding to Dickey's sense of optimism was his selection as the 1987 South Carolinian of the Year, an honor previously awarded to notables such as Gen. William C. Westmoreland, Sen. Strom Thurmond, Sen. Ernest "Fritz" Hollings, and Gov. Richard Riley. On January 25, 1988, he attended a luncheon at the

51. Introduction to *From the Green Horseshoe* (Columbia: University of South Carolina Press, 1987), ix–x.

Radisson Hotel in Columbia where Dixon Lovvorn, senior vice president and general manager of WIS Television, introduced him, celebrating Dickey's career and identifying "his contributions to the literary world and the recognition he has brought to our state." On May 18, Dickey received even higher recognition, officially being inducted into the American Academy of Arts and Letters at a ceremony in New York. Also inducted were William Styron and, posthumously, Joseph Campbell. Onstage with Dickey and Styron were 126 distinguished fellows of the academy and its parent organization, the National Institute of Arts and Letters. The academy had been founded in 1904 to honor individuals of the highest distinction in literature, music, and the visual arts, and its first inductees had included William Dean Howells, Henry James, and Mark Twain. The academy was limited to fifty lifetime members, each of whom since 1923 had been assigned to a chair on the back of which was a brass plaque listing the names and dates of its previous occupants. Dickey's chair, #15, had been previously occupied by scholar William Cross, painter Raphael Soyer, and novelist John Steinbeck. In citing Dickey for this honor, Howard Nemerov stated, "James Dickey has done distinguished work in poetry for some 30 years. Original—sometimes to the point of eccentricity—his knowledge and regard for the tradition, as exemplified by his attentive and incisive criticism, of his own work and that of our contemporaries is, nevertheless, unquestionable."[52] John Updike, the academy's chancellor, formally inducted Dickey.

Progress on the screenplay for *Alnilam* was slow. Dickey had sent the director, John Guillermin, whose World War I film *The Blue Max* he admired, a rough draft of act 1 on November 16 and another forty pages on January 20, 1988. Dickey was pleased to be working with Guillermin, who had achieved directorial fame for movies such as *King Kong, Tarzan's Greatest Adventure,* and *The Towering Inferno,* informing him, "My enthusiasm for the project grows, the more I write on it. If we do this film as you and I conceive it, people who watch it will understand that they have never really seen a movie before."[53] Remembering his conflict with John Boorman during the seventies, he anticipated that the director would revise his script, though he urged Guillermin to consider seriously what he had written. Guillermin, however, was unable to acquire the necessary financial backing and abandoned the project by mid-1989. Disheartened after a long struggle to shape the material only to have his effort yield nothing tangible, Dickey nevertheless maintained

52. Dottie Ashley, "Dickey Honored," *The State,* December 4, 1987, p. A16.
53. The letters to Guillermin are in the Dickey Papers.

a survivor's attitude and directed Theron Raines to attempt to secure another Hollywood director.

On May 15, Dickey flew to California to deliver the commencement address at Pitzer College, where he had made a similar address in 1965, when the college concluded its first year of operations. In the earlier talk, entitled "Three Girls Outgoing," Dickey celebrated those rare moments in life when the individual achieves a heightened sense of fulfillment. "Fragile and infinitely enduring," he declared, those moments "explain us and *are* us as we wish to be, as we exist at those times when we seem to ourselves to be existing as we were meant to." He cited passages from Antoine de Saint-Exupéry, W. N. P. Barbellion, and Alun Lewis and urged the graduates to "develop your private brinkmanship, your strategies, your ruses, your delightful and desperate games of inner survival" that would enable them "to live perpetually at the edge, but there very much on your own ground, and to live there with personal *style,* with dash and verve and a distinct and exhilarating sense of existing on your own terms as they develop, or as they become, with time, more and more what they have always been."[54] In the more than two decades that had passed, Dickey's career had soared, stalled, and then descended; friends and family had died; and efforts to push ahead had often failed to energize him or offer elevated moments of existence. Yet in this new address, Dickey again stressed the individual's paramount importance. He now cited Saul Bellow's story "Seize the Day" as an indictment of Americans dying of alcohol, drugs, or boredom, and he emphasized a single antidote to these ills, a simple imperative: "The solution to me is still wonder: amazement, mystery." Dickey intended to pursue his own unique course, his address implied, and he advised the new graduates to do likewise.

The commencement address was delivered shortly after Dickey and Deborah had flown to Japan for a ten-day visit. The previous year he had conceived of another novel involving a tail gunner shot down over the enemy's country during World War II, and he intended to familiarize himself with the land he had first visited in 1945. He needed to imagine not only the destruction of a firebombed Tokyo but also the peaceful countryside of terraced rice fields and contemplative peasants. On August 6, 1987, he had sent Theron Raines a plot outline of a novel entitled "Thalatta," a variant of *Thalassa,* the Greek word for sea, which derived from an account by the Greek general Xenophen in his war against the Persians. After fighting through Persian territory to the Black Sea, the Greeks triumphantly cried "Thalatta!" Figuratively

54. "Three Girls Outgoing," in *Night Hurdling,* 350–55.

retracing the Greek journey, Dickey intended to depict the aviator's bloody trek from the fiery holocaust of Tokyo to the snowy island of Hokkaido in the northern Japanese archipelago. "In the case of my man," he stated to Raines, "Hokkaido signifies the protagonist's coming 'home' to the cold and desolation that are his true *patria*."[55] The novel would eventually become *To the White Sea*.

Because *Alnilam* had been a financial disappointment, Doubleday had little interest in publishing another novel, but Theron Raines had approached Marc Jaffe, an editor at Houghton Mifflin, who was attempting to attract major writers and who viewed the proposal for "Thalatta" as an opportunity to lure Dickey back to the company. Unaffected by financial misgivings, Houghton offered Dickey a $500,000 advance. The sale of foreign rights added to the windfall. The novel also attracted advocates in Hollywood; Richard Roth agreed to produce the movie version for Universal Studios. Although he also would have liked for Houghton Mifflin to publish his poetry, Dickey returned to Wesleyan in August 1988 after consulting Peter Davison.

Dickey completed another project in October when Oxmoor House printed 55,000 copies of his third coffee-table book, *Wayfarer: A Voice from the Southern Mountains*. The book's origin dated to the seventies when, following the success of *Jericho*, Dickey planned to collaborate again with Hubert Shuptrine for another book, whose proposed title was "The Wilderness of Heaven." The original publisher was to have been Doubleday, and the proposed publication date was 1982. However, the new coffee-table book was not a high priority for Dickey; he was working on *Puella* and *Alnilam* as well as various screenplays. He insisted, moreover, on presenting his own vision of Appalachia; when Shuptrine received Dickey's text, he concluded that it was inappropriate because it did not cohere with his paintings. Shuptrine annulled the Doubleday contract by returning his $30,000 advance; when Doubleday insisted that Dickey's contract be canceled and that he repay his advance, he resisted and obtained a new collaborator, William A. Bake, an acclaimed photographer with a doctorate from the University of Georgia who had published three other art books with Oxmoor House and whose work had appeared in such magazines as *Southern Living*, *Life*, and *Audubon*. Without deliberate synchronization, Bake's photographs naturally cohered with Dickey's prose, each portraying gritty, weathered southerners living close to the rugged beauty inherent in the land. In his narrative Dickey returned to his father's heritage in north Georgia, dedicating the book "To the remainder of my father's family—

55. The letter to Raines is in the Dickey Papers.

Fannin County, Mineral Bluff, Georgia" and declaring on the inside dust jacket, "At age 63, I feel I have only arrived at the beginning."

As the book opens, the unnamed narrator greets a wayfarer he encounters. Superstitious and wise, the narrator has lived his life in the Appalachians. When the traveler becomes sick, the narrator uses mountain medicines to restore his health, taking the wayfarer on a figurative journey as he talks about food, geography, customs, handiwork, folklore, and music. He asserts, "We ain't got everything, but we got somethin'." The chance encounter presents a familiar Dickey concern—the confrontation between the individual and a force larger than himself. In *Wayfarer* that Other is the southern mountains and people. While Dickey had treated aspects of this subject before poetically (for example, foxhunting and quilting in "Listening to Foxhounds" and "Chenille," respectively), the narrative framework of *Wayfarer* allowed for a greater breadth of treatment to depict the larger natural inclusiveness Dickey perceived in the world. Consequently, when the speaker asserts, "It don't matter why it comes, but it does; it comes on through, and it's done been put in both of us, don't you see," Dickey moves beyond a discussion of family bloodlines not only into the connections that link all men to the land but also into the human impulse to create and re-create what one sees and hears. Unlike *Jericho* and *God's Images, Wayfarer* avoids inflated or poetic diction; instead, the voice of the main speaker exudes local color and a vitality that embodies a rich identification with the life around him. From late September through mid-December 1988, Dickey and Bake undertook an extensive promotional tour through the South, including visits to Columbia, Atlanta, Greensboro, Charleston, Nashville, Birmingham, Charlotte, Miami, Jacksonville, Memphis, Lexington, and Louisville. Because the economy was mired in a slump, the book sold only about one-fourth as many copies as *Jericho* had. Royalties for the financial year ending on May 31, 1989, totaled only $2,825.[56]

Offers of public appearances continued to arrive largely from the South, reinforcing the claims of some critics that Dickey had, in effect, only a regional audience. Columbia's Ira and Nancy Kroger Center for the Arts, for example, requested his attendance at its January 14, 1989, opening, and Atlanta's Oglethorpe College awarded him an honorary degree in May. That October, Wilmington's Cape Fear Academy asked him to read and to teach some classes. Yet new contracts from Houghton Mifflin and Wesleyan attested that his influence remained large, and other publishers pressed him with proposals, including Birch Lane Press in New Jersey, which that summer offered Dickey $75,000 for a book of childhood reminiscences, though he declined. Indica-

56. Hart, *Dickey,* 695.

tive that northern editors perceived him as a spokesman for southern literature was the contract Dickey signed on July 7 for $1,500 to write an article about the South Carolina "Low Country" for Condé Nast. Moreover, when Robert Penn Warren died on September 15, the *Boston Globe* asked for Dickey's comments; he obliged, calling Warren a great writer whose personal roots lay in the frontier and in folk people but who nevertheless combined primitive instinct with sophisticated intellect.

The most convincing argument that Dickey's influence remained national arrived in July from Yale, the university where Warren had taught. John Ryden, the director of Yale University Press, requested that Dickey judge its annual Younger Poets contest, a task that involved reading forty to fifty manuscripts culled from approximately seven hundred submissions, selecting a winner each year by June 1, and then writing an introduction to each book. For his services Dickey would receive $2,000 a year. In an unpublished letter to Ryden dated July 26, he declared: "the Series is the best of all gateways to the slopes of Parnassus for new American poets, and has been so since its beginning. In other words, as a poet who struggled hard to get onto those slopes years ago, I realize the importance of what I am being asked to do, and can say in response that I will do the best I can, given my abilities and orientation."[57] In becoming the series judge, Dickey joined a group of distinguished writers that included W. H. Auden, James Merrill, and Stanley Kunitz.

Despite a domestic life that continued to be unsettled by Deborah's drug problems, he worked on the new novel, informing Marc Jaffe on February 27, 1990:

A few months ago my wife's narcotic habit increased by geometrical proportions, so that there was not a day—or, especially, a night—when I knew where she was, what people she was among, or whether I and the child [Bronwen] would ever see her again. She abandoned her family all but completely, and entered the dope culture at the very lowest point, where there are only pushers, pimps, whores, hit-men and other murderers, and the rest of an assortment that would make you think Dante was right in consigning all such to the eleventh circle of the Inferno, where everything is frozen solid with vice. There seemed to be nothing I could do, except to try to protect the child and keep her life going, move forward with the teaching as best I could, and write whenever I had a minute amongst all the pity and terror. . . .

But despite all this, I have been moving the book; moving Muldrow. I have another hundred pages, written mainly late at night and just before dawn, but

57. The letter to Ryden is in the Dickey Papers.

written. I have also revised the sequence of events, and now have what I think will give us a straight run out to the end. This is something I value as a novelist: the knowing what happens next, and what that leads to.[58]

Dickey told Jaffe that Jaffe was the best editor he had ever had, a statement he had made to other editors during his career, and promised that *To the White Sea* would be published in 1991.

As the 1980s ended, Dickey's literary fortunes appeared to be again rising. Deborah, however, had been arrested when police had stopped her Volvo and discovered cocaine; she was subsequently sent to a drug rehabilitation center for three weeks and then remanded to Dickey's custody with the stipulation that if she renewed her previous lifestyle, she would be imprisoned. Although the height and success of Dickey's literary mission always depended on the stability of his home life, he was temporarily hopeful that Deborah would recover and domestic life would assume normalcy. At age sixty-seven, however, he was a realist, acknowledging that Deborah was likely to falter. Nevertheless, he believed his creative energies strong enough to bring the new novel to completion. In a 1981 essay, he had written of F. Scott Fitzgerald's poetic ability: "Beneath everything here, even the most trivial, there is the flicker of a fine unmistakable consciousness, and one could do worse."[59] Rather than a mere flicker, he felt his own talents to be a flame living within him, an extraordinary gift that was wasted if not utilized. His personality, in any event, precluded any surrender to the situation. Like the aging protagonist in "False Youth: Spring: The Olympian," published in the summer 1982 issue of *Amicus Journal,* who races a former Olympic gold medalist on a makeshift home obstacle course, Dickey still found himself "ready for the Big One," the knockout literary punch that would restore him to the heralded heights he had known. The persona goes all-out in the race, "lagging lolloping hanging / In there with the best" and

getting the point
At last, sighing like ghosts and like rubber, for fat
And luck, all over the earth, where that day and any and every
Day after it, devil hindmost and Goddamn it

To glory, I lumbered for gold.

In his imagination, where fact and fiction, history and reminiscence and fantasy all melded, Dickey believed such a victory possible.

58. *Crux,* ed. Bruccoli and Baughman, 479–80.
59. "The Unreflecting Shield," in *Night Hurdling,* 56–60.

He needed to believe it, for Deborah's medical, legal, and psychiatric bills threatened his sense of financial security. Extensive reading tours were no longer possible because Dickey lacked the physical stamina and an extended absence from home was not advisable. Feelings of desolation alternated with frustration and anger. Poems such as "Eagles" and "Moon Flock," published in the March/April 1987 and 1988 issues of *American Poetry Review,* respectively, reflect these emotions. "Eagles" insists on the inability of the individual ever to escape the world fully enough to gain an ideal or Platonic understanding of it. While the effort remains doomed, the human need to strive above earthbound limitations is undeniable, necessary, and redemptive, as timeless as Icarus's failed attempt. The speaker imagines himself lifted by the feet of an eagle. The brief flight, which deposits him groveling on the ground among weeds, reveals a larger world, "the circular truth / Of the Void," one whose elements would satisfy any realm but the one where he lives and moves. Now, however, he only asks that the eagle leave "my unstretched weight" and "remember me in your feet." He understands that "The higher rock is / The more it lives," a recognition of human limitation and the need to transcend those restrictions. "Moon Flock" is Dickey's attempt to convey the strength of that impulse and the subsequent frustration at its failure, using the analogy of the moon's effort to create life. Here the imaginative ideal never begins to fulfill the world in which it finds itself. The speaker confesses, "nothing can be put / Up on a wind with no air," and he admonishes the reader not to inquire of his imaginative effort, for the moon remains merely "a wild white world" whose emptiness reflects his own. These poems as well as others on which he was working exposed his true feelings without the bravado that would have previously concealed them. They would become part of his final collection of poems, *The Eagle's Mile,* which would be published in 1990.

In a 1987 interview Dickey commented on the poet's role: "I think a poet is trying, whether he would say this or not, to validate the individual viewpoint. . . . The vision and the true reaction of people to things, the true and if possible imaginative reaction to things, are threatened more and more."[60] In *The Eagle's Mile,* Dickey would undertake his final attempt to establish the presence of the determining personality and in so doing validate his Self both to himself and to the American public. He understood the strides time was making on his track, the physical debilitation and the loss of family and friends, though he believed his imaginative faculties were still capable of godlike flights of creativity that would offer up a renewed sense of the wonder and mystery of the world.

60. Gordon Van Ness, "Living beyond Recall," *James Dickey Newsletter* 3 (Spring 1987): 23.

To: Lia Matera[1]

CC, Emory University
4620 Lelia's Court
Columbia, S.C. 29206

January 5, 1980

Dear Ms. Matera:

Here is the elegy for William O. Douglas. I'm sorry it is three weeks late, but I wanted to get it exactly right, as I conceive right to be; I hope it was worth waiting for. I have concentrated on Douglas's stand on the issue of ecology and wildlife, and have written out of the belief that by his commitment he has thereby entered into the wild creatures—both predators and prey—and the wilderness he protected.

I am not sure whether Douglas lost his eye in a fishing accident in England or Ireland, but (since the syllabication is the same!) we can adjust the locale of the incident according to fact, if you will be so good as to find out for me.

I enjoyed doing this very much, though it took around 130 drafts to get what I wanted. But this is what I want, and I hope it serves your purposes, those of the magazine and the spirit of William Douglas as well.

Let me hear from you on these matters when you can, and please send along the $500 as soon as possible, for tax-time is with me, as well as with everyone else under the law, or under the lightning-splintering of Adam over the Appalachian Trail in North Georgia, where my family comes from, and where I once saw a photograph of Justice Douglas walking, in fall, in a white shirt, as a man.

Sincerely,

---

1. Editor-in-chief of the *Hastings Constitutional Law Quarterly.* The poem mentioned, entitled "The Eagle's Mile," appeared in the fall 1980 issue.

To: George Plimpton

CC, Emory University
4620 Lelia's Court
Columbia, S.C. 29206

January 23, 1980

Dear George:

I was in Washington recently for one of those curious bashes at the White House, and during an interim time, watched some of the television at the hotel where I was staying. I happened to catch your film on the time you spent with the Baltimore Colts, and would gladly have stayed and watched the rest of it rather than attend to the duties I had come to Washington to do. It was a veritable model of the way such things should be done. I don't know what your arrangements for the cameras, crews, and the rest of the equipment and personnel that have been needed to make the film came to, or how you got all that together, but you yourself must certainly have done the script, for it was good enough to certify to such a hand. I thought particularly enthralling the dialogue with Tom Mattee (Mattes?); the things that were said, and the modest way that he chose to tell you about his role as the "fat little half-back," his difficulties in adjusting quickly to the quarterback spot, and the rest of it. I was especially moved by the dramatic buildup for your last play, the quarterback fake pass, and option sneak. The way in which the thing was done, showing the wide open field in front of the stumbling ball carrier, is as heartbreaking as anything in the whole lexicon of sport. In 1942, I played four games for the freshman team at Clemson as quarterback in the T-formation, a system just then gaining credence in college football. I had exactly the same thing happen to me against the University of Georgia, and can still see that wide open field, all those receding stripes I could have crossed, spreading out before my eye after I fell, at that immobile time, almost at eye-level with the stripes. Anyway, I wanted to write to you and tell you how much I enjoyed the piece, even though I didn't get to see all of it, and would like also to applaud your general efforts in doing this kind of thing. There is nothing like an inside view of a subject, and there is nothing even remotely so good as an inside intelligent and creative view of it.

In closing, I would like to inquire about the publication date of Series V of the Paris Review interviews. I naturally have an interest in the number of this series containing my own material. People ask me about it, and I don't know exactly what to tell them, or to do anything but direct tham back to the issue of the magazine where the interview appeared. like to get a line on when the series will come out, or if it already has. Anyway, this shall be as you wish.

Let's try to keep in a little better touch than we have done over the last few years, for I watch you closely, and I think of you and your enterprises and your writing often, believe me.

Sincerely yours,

To: Gretchen Poston   CC, Emory University
                                                              4620 Lelia's Court
                                                        Columbia, S.C. 29206

                                                        February 5, 1980
Dear Ms. Poston:

I have your letter, and the materials you have been kind enough to send along. I have gone over the attendant possibilities and problems very carefully, and now make my report to you on the basis of the situation as I see it.

First of all, since I previously talked to you and Mrs. Mondale, I have had a second conference with my physician, and it has been confirmed that I must have surgery (designated "major," unfortunately and depressingly), and that means that the recuperative period will be, even as such things go, lengthy. This means that, were I to take on the organization of the "poets and Writers for Carter and Mondale (which would also entail my taking on Lenny Bernstein, which I would dearly love to do, believe me!), I would be (surgically) taken out of the midst of the fray just at the time when my participation would be needed most. There is nothing I can do about this, and I would not want to be counted-on for service which I cannot possibly deliver. You should know about this at this time, for it seems likely that you would wish to get someone else to do the job you and Mrs. Mondale and the President have seen fit to offer me. Again, I am not equipped to administer the enormous amount of correspondence that such an assignment calls for. The mission requires, not a man and his wife—both hard-pressed—but a full-time functionary and a staff. I cannot be such, and I do not have such, particularly in view of my physical condition at this time. Perhaps Mr. Nims, who was, I understand, instrumental in organizing the recent affair at the White House, has, with his built-in staff at <u>Poetry</u> magazine, a situation better suited to the job. Again, I don't know.

As things stand now, I think that it would be prudent on your part to seek out some other possibilities for this task than entrusting it to me. My main concern is that the job shall be well done, and effect its ends. You may certainly know that I am entirely with President Carter in his re-election bid, that I think he is by far the best man, and that he will certainly win, with me as "Poets and Writers" organizer or not. Do let me hear from you on these matters. I shall hold these letters and other materials until I have word from you.

Sincerely,

To: Mrs. Paddy Fraser   CC, Emory University
                                                       4620 Lelia's Court
                                                       Columbia, S.C. 29206

                                                            May 5, 1980

Dear Mrs. Fraser,

I send belated condolences for the death of your intelligent and gifted husband. I heard of his death only recently from a young man named Patrick Scott, a former student of your husband's at Leicester, though I don't know whether or not you might possibly remember him. At any rate, your husband's work in poetry and in the criticism of poetry has been with me for many years, and I thought you might like to know this, from this particular American writer. Though I gather that your husband did not care particularly for my writing, I do for his, and have done for the better part of thirty years. I encountered his poetry in an anthology I read when I was on duty with the U.S. Air Force in New Guinea, in 1944 and I immediately wrote home to my mother that she get hold, by any means whatever, of HOMETOWN ELEGY, which I wanted to come home to. As it turned out, she did get it, I did come home, and was most gratified to read your husband's work in more than just one poem, the poem I had seen in the anthology. Over the years, I encountered more and more of your husband's work, and his extremely penetrating reviews and essays became part not only of my literary sensibility, but of the larger human perspective of my life. I always regretted that your husband did not see fit to write more poetry than he did, but if it is any sort of assurance to you of the value of G.S. Fraser's life in literature, you certainly have it from one American writer.

It may be that I shall be coming to England about this time next year, and I would like very much to tell you of these opinions and more of the same sort, looking you straight in the eyes, as such things should be done.

Sincerely,

To: Lt. Col. Jim Gaston   CC, Emory University
                                                4620 Lelia's Court
                                            Columbia, S.C. 29206

                                                    May 8, 1980
Dear Jim:

Thank you, albeit belatedly, for your letter. I am much pleased that you would like to do some biographical work on me, but I feel that I shouldn't encourage you in this. Over the years there has been, really, too much of a tendency on the part of people to focus on my life, my "personality,"—such as it is—and the various events I have moved through and interests and people I have had and been moved by. All this has taken more emphasis off my actual writing than I would like to have taken, and, as I grow older, I see that the tendency is likely to increase with any encouragement I might give to projects such as the one you outline. Oddly enough, I can think of only two writers who refused categorically to have biographies done of them. These were Matthew Arnold and, perhaps not oddly, T.S. Eliot. Though I would not at this time be quite so adamant as those two gentlemen, I would stand somewhere near them, I think; or at least at this time, I would. However, let me think about the matter some more, and maybe we can eventually do something, after all.

But right now I must get through some radical surgery to correct a number of curious developments in my digestive system. The actual Procedure—as the Profession deems it—will take place in Seattle on the 23rd. From now until approximately the middle of June, I will be out there, wrestling with anesthetics and knives. But I am leaving my secretary-assistant here in Columbia to man the fort, and she will always be able to reach me, or to enable you to reach me, should you like.

I am thinking, more and more, of guiding my grandson toward an Air Force career, and of launching him from the Academy. Depending on my degree of strength and rate of recuperation, I am intensely planning to bring him out there as soon as I feel well enough. Needless to say, he is enthusiastic, but no more so than I am. Keep in touch, and I'll tell you how things are progressing. My best to all those I know out there. Remember me especially to those on the famous "Columbia Mission." Everybody including the University president and the Governor are still talking about the show you put on.

My very best to you, Jim. You are the only authentic air-hero I know, now. I used to know some others, but that was long ago, in another war, and almost in another life.

Deborah sends love, too.

Yours,

To: Robert Penn Warren   TLS, Emory University

4620 Lelia's Court
Columbia, S.C. 29206
May 12, 1980

Dear Red,

I am leaving for Seattle in a couple of days for an occasion which involves some "major" surgery, but I wanted to get this off to you before I left on a trip whose outcome may be uncertain. Really, though, this is just to let you know how much your work and your existence mean to me. Rob Cowley has just sent along your <u>Talking</u> book, and I have been going through it, noting points of similarity (so many!) between your background and convictions and mine, and also being rendered absurdly grateful, time after time, for your insights into the creation of poetry, the structure and technique of fiction, and your whole manner of taking life and responding to existence. I seldom write letters to writers; most of my correspondence is of inferior quality in a literary sense, as doubtless this one is, but I wanted to tell you, once more, that whichever writer has been valuable to me is going to have to be identified as you.

One of the fellows who edited your interviews, Floyd Watkins, has approached me as to the possibility of my giving-over my papers, drafts, letters and so on to Emory University in Atlanta, and at the same time spoke of his wish to acquire yours as well. I don't know what I am going to do about this suggestion, but being coupled with you in such a way I take as a good sign, no matter how actuality may eventually resolve things.

Later, when I have more time to dig into comparisons, I will write you at length about the new version of <u>Brothers to Dragons</u>. I haven't time to do the poem justice under the present circumstances, but do know that though I believed the original version to be a classic, I now think that you have made of it a super-classic, and I plan to tell you in detail later on why I think so.

I am happy, also, that you believe <u>Audubon</u> to be one of your best poems. So do I, and from it I chose the end, Section VII, to be read at my wife's funeral. I could think of nothing of my own so fitting, or so likely to last, or to hang longer in the bearded oaks of Waccamaw Cemetery, at Litchfield, where we were all together.

My best to you, always, to Eleanor, and to your children.

Yours,

Jim

To: Mary Hemingway

CC, Emory University
4620 Lelia's Court
Columbia, S.C. 29206

June 11, 1980

Dear Mrs. Hemingway:

It has been years, now, since I've seen you; as a matter of fact, if memory serves, the last time was on some occasion having to do with the Lotus Club there in New York, though I no longer recall what year. At any rate, I wanted to write you and keep the lines of communication open. I have recently undergone some serious surgery, and, lying for weeks in a Seattle hospital under volcano-dust, I began to reflect on the precariousness of all human relationships—how easily lost they are, and in some cases how irrecoverable, and thus began to make certain vows to myself, these having to do with a determination not to let certain things happen, or certain people be lost. That is why I wanted to get in touch with you once more, and to tell you how much the association with you, slight as it has been, means to me, at the Lotus Club or under the pulverized stone of Northwestern mountains. I hope to be in New York after my recovery for a few days, and if you like, and should be in town, perhaps we might meet again for a drink, or even dinner somewhere. In Seattle I reread <u>How</u> <u>It</u> <u>Was</u>, and there are a lot of things in it I would be most pleased to talk with you about, not principally the sections dealing with your life with your husband, but those about your early experiences, and about your career as a journalist. But that shall be as you wish.

If I may presume, on such <u>very</u> slight acquaintance, to ask a kind of favor of you: a young friend of mine named Michael Allin is planning to be in New York at some time during the third week of June. He may already have written you and introduced himself. For my part, I can tell you that he is an unassuming, intelligent, humorous and worshipful person, and I think you would like him very much, should you judge it expedient to meet with him, if only for a few minutes. He is a genuinely sincere and imaginative boy, and such a meeting would mean much to him.

Again, if this letter seems to you to be presuming when I should not presume, I hope you will forgive me. Be assured that I think of you and your work and life often, and was much heartened by your example and the fact of your existence as I lay far off, under the stone snows of Mount St. Helen.

With best wishes and strong admiration, I am

Sincerely,

To: Daniel Hoffman

CC, Emory University
4620 Lelia's Court
Columbia, S.C. 29206

June 11, 1980

Dear Dan:

That was an amazing thing for you to do. Befogged by drugs, lying under the surgical snows and pulverized (almost mythologized) stone of Seattle, I had no adequate words to thank you for the profound grace of your gesture in calling me, there in the hospital, and now, among the familiar birds and huge flowers of South Carolina, I still cannot find any way to tell you how very much I am moved by what you did. Let me just tell you that it helped in those determinative ways in which the recipient responds in ways that he himself

286 of James Dickey

would be the last to understand analytically, but which he knows are there, because their presence and efficacy are increased with every heartbeat. As to the operation itself, it was long, debilitating, and successful. After seven years of taking in terror with every mouthful of food—and, toward the last, every swallow of liquid—it was wonderful to see, in the post-operation tests and on closed-circuit TV, the strange dark mass of barium move through the System as though it had every right to be there, and knew what it was doing.

But I don't mean to describe the doings of doctors and their mystery-machines, but only to communicate with whatever intensity I can muster from the still addled and strung-out head, how much your call meant to me: more than President Carter's, or even (God help us!) Burt Reynolds', who read back to me, as though on cue, some of his lines from Deliverance ("Survival. That's the game. Now you get to play.")

Last spring I used Barbarous Knowledge for the first time in class. The whole thing is terrific, but the section on Graves is even more than that. I was especially interested in your passages on Graves and the folk tradition, for, though no scholar, I have a deep love for folk music and folk poetry, especially ballads, and your insights certainly clarified a great deal about Graves's curious position on such matters. I don't like Graves at all, but if his work can call forth such a lucid and perceptive article as you have written, it must certainly be worth more than I had thought. I intend to take another look at it, but that will not be nearly so much the cause of eagerness as a reading and rereading of your own poems. I think I have most of your books, and now will be with them in depth for some time to come, and probably forever, too.

Thank you so much for your call, for your poetry, and for your existence.

To: Paul Zweig   CC, Emory University
                                                      4620 Lelia's Court
                                                      Columbia, S.C. 29206

                                                      June 11, 1980

Dear Mr. Zweig:

Belatedly, though I am not used to writing to people I don't know, I would like to tell you how much I liked your article in the New York Times Book Review, especially since I have just been severely beset by some grave physical troubles which necessitated a long operation and a lot of hospital-exile. Under those circumstances, it was strange indeed to read your reflections on muscular and other violences and excesses as they occurred in my book, for assuredly I felt no energy at all in the volcanic dust falling on the Seattle hospital where I was when I read your piece. The only energies I encountered—for, as I say, I possessed none of my own—came from your article, which was so hearteningly <u>on</u> to what my work is trying to do, to get at. I am not given to counter-praise, for it always seems a form of conspiracy, but I did want to let you know how strongly your words came to me, in the central place from which my own proceed. It is quite true that the so-called "Improvisations from . . ." are not as good as the original poems. I am glad you saw this and said it, for I have no great need to engage in improvisations, "imitations," or any such, and you have only reaffirmed me in the conviction that my time is better spent on my own productions than in a limbo between them and some other poet whose language I understand by less than half.

Again, thank you for the things you say. Perhaps in the fall, when I must come to New York for a week or so, we may meet and I can tell you of my feelings, looking you straight in the eyes, as such things should really be done.

My best wishes to you in your own work, and with the various reading- and conference-projects to which I see your name appended.

Let me know if you will be in New York in the fall.

With best wishes,

To: Richard Hugo   CC, Emory University
                                                        4620 Lelia's Court
                                                        Columbia, S.C. 29206

                                                        June 13, 1980
Dear Dick,
    I am back now, lying like a stepped-on lizard in the flowery sun down here, with your many phone calls still in the reallest of all inner ears, which are those of the spirit. It may be that you won't believe me—though I hope you do—when I tell you that your messages from Montana were more effective medicine than all the knives, drugs, and radioactive magics of the doctors. You are someone I could always talk to, and your calls to Seattle rank with the

letter I got from you after the poetry-doings at the American Embassy in London, so long ago.

I am busy working on a situation whereby you might come down here for a few days, talk to our kids, and be pretty well paid for it. By the time you get here, you may be sure that they will know your poems as well as the magnificent Triggering Town; the best ones already know these things, but when you come, the worst ones will know them too. It is those "worst ones" that the teacher really exists for, whether he knows it or not. As for me, I had rather be surprised by a student's performance than gratified by one, though both are surely desirable.

The trip back was only a minor nightmare, though when I protested that the film shown on route not be the scheduled Little Miss Marker but a buried classic called Ride a Crooked Road (starring John Agar), I had to be restrained and placed in the seat next to another handcuffed transportee, a fellow named Ted Bundy, who was being returned to Florida.

Again, without jokes, I want to thank you for your calls. I wish it had been possible for you to drive through the stone snows of Mount St. Helen to spend a day or two with us in Seattle, but I surely understand the circumstances and can hope very strongly that we will make up for all these lost years when you come to South Carolina.

My best to Ripley, whom I must meet. You and I must get the new wives together (yours not so new, mine fairly new). It's just as the general said to the admiral in King Kong versus Godzilla after they had outlined the paths of the monsters on a military map and saw that the inevitable was inevitable: "There's no doubt that when they meet, they'll destroy each other." I hope this won't be true of Ripley and Debba; after all, I never did believe in the prophetic powers of Japanese horror mirrors.

Please write soon; I need you still, and always.

Always,

To: Stewart Richardson

CC, Emory University
4620 Lelia's Court
Columbia, S.C. 29206

June 17, 1980

Dear Sandy:

Well, I made it, though I was practically cut in half and stayed under—or out—for a long time. The operation not only entailed a release and dilation of the stricture that was preventing food and even liquid from passing from the esophagus to the stomach, but a kind of reorganization of all my digestive organs, which had been displaced by the stomach rising through the split place in the diaphragm and being in a place where it was never intended to be. There was a thorough check-out of all the organs—not only the digestive ones—for what they were looking for, the doctors later told me, was esophagal cancer and its possible spread to other areas. None was found, however, and the rest of the operation—or the "procedure," as we medical professionals call it—was successful, and I can eat normally, though still slowly. I have been home a week now, just barely moving around, but some strength is coming back, and the soreness is receding enough to give me hope that I will eventually be able to function as before. But my God, it was strange! We left Idaho, where the good folk at the University were foolish enough to give me a degree, and were just <u>over</u> Mount St. Helen when the thing blew. The pilot was so excited by all this he could hardly contain himself from flying into the crater, and he kept yelling to the passengers to get over there and look because "you won't see <u>this</u> every day," as though the eruption were a special service offered exclusively by Eastern Airlines. Then there was the period of uncertainty in Seattle. "The procedure" was scheduled for Friday, and everybody at the Clinic was sweating out the wind, for it was feared that it would shift and blow the ash up into Seattle, which would have clogged up the hospital machinery, the anesthetic paraphenalia, and God knows what else. Luckily the wind off the sea held, and carried the ash back over Idaho, where we had just been, and on into Montana and other places, and, so far as the operation and its aftermath were concerned, everything ended as well as might be. But thank God it is over. <u>All</u> over, and life and work can pick up again.

I am still confused and dismayed about the failure of <u>The Strength</u> of <u>Fields</u> to win the Pulitzer Prize this time. Almost immediately after I got back, Rose Valenstein of the Pulitzer committee called me expressing the same feeling, and asking me if I would <u>please</u> serve as chairman for next year's award. Since this would make the fourth time of performing this particular function, I declined, but she and the other people insisted to the extent that I finally told them I would go ahead with it, particularly since one of the other members of the committee is to be John Ashbery, a kind of clique writer up there, and I thought it best that the award not go to one of his friends. I also asked about the jury for this year. I knew Jim Applewhite was on it, and I suspected that Helen Vendler of Boston University might also be on it, for they were the other two members of the committee the last time I was chairman and Jim and I gave the Prize to Howard Nemerov, over Ms. Vendler's violent objection. She wanted the Prize for Lowell, although he was dead; if I am not mistaken, there was something personal between her and Lowell, though I don't really know or care what. At any rate, I was right about this: Applewhite and Vendler were two of the members of the committee. The great surprise, however, was that Richard Howard was the chairman, and learning that floored me sure enough. Richard Howard's only distinction as a poet was that he received the Pulitzer Prize when I was chairman yet another time, Phyllis McGinley was in the hospital and didn't vote; I suggested that Howard be given the Prize and Auden said only that he "had no objection." And that was that. I dislike extremely these kinds of maneuvering, but they exist. I have no idea how the judges voted, but I do know that Don Justice is a very weak figure indeed, a compromise choice of some sort. I don't ask to be given prizes out of the gratitude of judges; I only ask that the best book win. I am quite convinced that Strength was easily the best book, and if there were any better ones around last year, one of them was certainly not anything by Donald Justice.

All this is past now; we go on. The main thing is that the book was published, and that it is doing so well. Readership, not prizes, is what counts, and I have never had a book of poetry do so well as this one has, or anything like it. I am delighted with the ads that keep appearing and with the generous response of the public, and of the critics whose opinions you send along from time to time. This is very gratifying, indeed. Please keep me posted on everything that happens, regarding Strength, and also of the date of arrival of the mysterious Boxes in which the new edition of The Zodiac will be housed.

Incidentally, as a light note, I might bring in a new joke of Debba's. We watch the political scene pretty closely, and at last count it looks as though Reagan might be the next President. Debba invented a dialogue in which, if this should happen, Reagan might approach me to write an inaugural poem for him, and might say something like:

"Yes, I would like to have you write an inaugural poem for me. Since your poem for President Carter, 'The Strength of Fields,' drew on Carter's background as a farmer, I thought you might do something of the same for me, using, say, my well-known career in films: you might, indeed, consider calling it 'The Strength of Reels.'"

And I am back hard at work on Alnilam. It is moving at about 500 to 750 words a day, and I am having a section typed to send you in the next few days.

In keeping with your suggestion that we light possibly consider another title, Alnilam being too private, I have thought of some other things. There's a section in dialogue where Cahill and another character are talking about the beginnings of radar, and the other person is explaining to Cahill how bats and their "sonar" equipment were tested in labs by having them fly in the dark through entanglements of wire. That is, I think, a good metaphor not only for radar and night-flying, but for the blind man's condition itself, and it occurred to me that the novel might be called Cloud of Wire, or something that would carry the same idea. However, I still hold with Alnilam, or at least at this time I do. After all, it is no more mysterious or private than Hanta Yo, Shogun (which I am convinced many readers read as a misprint for Shotgun), Tunc, Nunquam, or any of Lawrence Durrell's latter-day titles.

Just one or two more items. There is a new poem of mine featured in the July Atlantic, which you might like to have a look at.[2] It is a kind of elegy for the American poet James Wright, a close friend of mine for years, who feared the change from day to night and the coming of the predators, when the whole climate of fighting in the animal world changes to that of prey and predator, in the dark: he used to say that he feared the dark because he feared the change "in the surround." I am telling him in the poem that he is not to fear this any more, for he is the surround; the whole thing good and bad, and that the moon is beautiful on water, and that the tree grows its rings in the dark as well as the light. Anyway, I hope you like it. It is an adaptation of one of the poems in the Flowering book. As to the fate of Flowering, I haven't had any word, but it is my opinion at this stage that the publishers in Winston-Salem won't find a commercial house willing to take it on, for $250 a copy is a lot to ask for a book of photographs by an unknown photographer, even if the poems are by a poet who is not, let us hope, inknown. What I would really like is eventually to get the 19 poems released to me so that I can then incorporate them into a new book with Doubleday, for they are surely the best sustained sequence anybody has done since Rilke's Orpheus sonnets. Again, have a look at the July Atlantic.

Debba and I plan to be in New York at least twice this fall, and one of the visits will be for a whole week. I hope you will be in town then, for there is much to talk about, and I long for your company and the good aura you have about you; have always had for me. There is no way for me to tell you how much I

2. "The Surround."

owe to you as an editor, and as another human being in the world at the same time as I am. I will let all these things be unspoken, but will also reserve the possibility of putting them into words—real words—some time later on. Again, thank you so much, Sandy, for your existence. As long as I can stand up and see lightning and hear thunder (and, now, <u>eat</u>), I will not let you down.

Ever,

To: Jim Applewhite

CC, Emory University
4620 Lelia's Court
Columbia, S.C. 29206

June 20, 1980

Dear Jim,

Well, I am back; I made it. The surgery was long in the doing, but apparently successful, for all sorts of things are now going down into the System, not only as though they belong there but as though they were eager to get there, on down and through. This is a strange feeling. Going under anesthetic was not so very odd, sort of like being half drunk without any elation or sense of social distinction, but coming out was odd. There is some kind of psychic wound that occurs along with the physical one, when the body has been deeply opened and the mind dreamlessly asleep, and that requires a kind of healing, too. During all this, though, and the quite metaphysical terror of the explosion of Mount St. Helen nearby, the people of Seattle and the Pacific Northwest were wonderful to us: the poets flocked in from all over, and the folk musicians, and the painters, and even a few from Indian reservations, particularly the Blackfeet, who did not know that I am honorary Sioux by adoption, though Comanche by birth. I have a Blackfoot name given me by the Great Mystery (no real Indian of <u>any</u> tribe ever mentions or thinks of the "Great Spirit"): the name means "Buffalo-Who-Grows," but whether this refers to stature, numbers, spirit, or weight, I did not ask.

Just after I got back I was asked to chair the Pulitzer committee on poetry again, and I acceded, to keep the bad guys out. Guys like, say, Don Justice. Whatever hapeened up there, anyway? It is really none of my business, though I can't but have a certain interest in such matters. Helen Vendler has always been much against me, largely, I suspect, because you and I gave the Prize to Nemerov instead of Lowell, but also because I took most of Lowell's audience and influence from him, and I suspect there was something personal between her and Lowell, though I don't really care about that. But Richard Howard is no fool, and I can't imagine what turn of events might have prevented The Strength of Fields from getting the Prize, except either that there might have been some misunderstanding as to whether my book was eligible (it was) or that Richard, for some reason, chose to side with Vendler and give the award to a non-entity like Justice instead of to me. Naturally, I'd like to be enlightened on this. But of course, that shall be as you wish. Even when I am the one involved, I hate to see the Southerners lose out to the jerks.

Keep telling me about the progress of your manuscript, for I have the LSU Press alerted to receive it, whenever I can give them a date, or a kind of date.

Sure, I'll give you a quote for promotion. Say this:

James Applewhite's poems are imaginative, lucid, and deep. A moving human voice comes through them with grave and memorable tonality; their resonance is great.

You can do something for me, too, if you wish. I have a new poem, an elegy for Jim Wright, in the July Atlantic. Have a look at it, if you have a chance, and if you like it, write to the editor about it. The poem is a new kind of departure for me, and a strong response by mail from such as yourself would be most helpful.

My love to you, Jan, and all in your house. Write soon, or when you can.

Ever,

To: Peter Viereck

CC, Emory University
4620 Lelia's Court
Columbia, S.C. 29206

June 26, 1980

Dear Peter:

Thank you for the letter about The Strength of Fields. Of all the poets of my time, you have the most integrity and courage; when you say something, you mean it. I am not given to gush, but I do indeed thank you with whatever heart I have. Your letter was especially welcome, since when I got it I was facing major surgery. This was done in Seattle during the very heighth—if that is the word—of the Mount St. Helen's eruption, and I credit your letter and your opinion as being foremost among those agencies that enabled me to arise more or less in one (renewed) piece from under the surgical snows of Seattle and the stone snows of Mount St. Helen's.

Also, your material on the death and "wake" of Georg Heym was most welcome, and vividly interesting. Heym is such a violent writer that he is almost dangerous, and despite my indifferent German, I am very much moved by him, and solidly in his corner. He has not been done any kind of justice in translations. Michael Hamburger has the end of "Judas" as "his feet were small as flies / in the shrill gleam of golden skies." I thought "the golden hysteria of heaven" much better, though it is not really what Heym said. The phrase is neither Heym nor myself, but something in between, and perhaps better than either. The phrase has become a favorite of Red Warren's, incidentally, so he tells me.

Come to think of it, your admiration for Heym and for Roy Campbell indicates very definitely—and has indicated for these many years—that you and I are just as surely mavericks as those two are. I myself count it very good to be a wolf among the sheep that mill complacently around in poetry, these days. There are so many mild-mannered half-talented forgettable people: sheep in sheep's clothing, I call them.

Something you could do for me, if you like. In fact, a couple of things. My literary executor down here, Matthew Bruccoli, has a daughter who is beginning at Mt. Holyoke in the fall, and any help or little kindnesses you might be able to extend to herewould be much appreciated. She is a fine little girl, and I'm sure you won't find any association with her onerous.

The other thing is that I have a new poem, in a completely different style from any of the others in the July Atlantic. It is a kind of elegy for Jim Wright, who died a couple of months ago of cancer of the tongue. If you like it, let the editors of Atlantic know it, for I have a number of other poems written in the same idiom, and I would like as receptive an audience as I can get.

Let me hear from you again soon, and send along as many of those wild offbeat Xeroxes as you care to: they are always welcome here.

My very best to you always, Peter. As I remember, the last time we saw each other was on that strange television show with Muriel Rukeyser. Though I never saw her on more than one occasion other than that one, it is still strange that she is gone. Those left, the best ones, must close ranks; the rest I don't care about. So keep in touch, as you will.

Yours,

To: Andrew Harbelis

CC, Emory University
4620 Lelia's Court
Columbia, S.C. 29206

June 27, 1980

Dear Andy,

It is wonderful of you to write, and to send along the clipping. The whole occasion up there was great, though Debba and I were only able to stay a day. But we'll surely be back, if only to get together with you and your family and spend

When I go back that far in time, and look at the pictures of the Cadet Officers at High Point, I find that I don't remember very much, and have long since completely lost track of the fellows there. One of them, though, either a class before ours or just after, was a boy named Shamburger, and I was surprised to find, through the newspapers, that he was one of the American pilots shot down in the Bay of Pigs fiasco. There was something in the situation where his wife wanted to sue the government either for sending him down there under such conditions or for the cover-up concerning his death and the aftermath.

Smoot called up down here, and I even saw him for a few minutes at one of the North Carolina schools where I was giving a reading, but even of him I don't know much. And, of the others, I know nothing at all.

It is odd that your copilot lived in McAllen, Texas, for I was down in that long-lost border town only last year, and might have been able to look him up, had I known he had any association with you.

Yes, my outfit, the 418th Nightfighter Squadron from the 5th Air Force for the Borneo invasion, assigned to the 13th. We covered the Balikpapen invasion, and Brunei as well. Our skeleton organization flew out of Sanga Sanga, a wretched little place. I lost a very good friend, Bob Baker, over Jolo Island, where he was caught by the Zekes, not after-dark, but after light.

I had better not get started on the war right now; I had better save most of this for the book. I am delighted that I can use your name, for I have been using it through the successive drafts, and can't think of anything about the character without thinking of you. I close with a brief conversation, showing how you talk, or at least how you do early in the book. This takes place in the Cadet Mess.

Cahill is the father of a Cadet killed at the base, which somewhat resembles Camden. He is blind.

> "Here's the best we could get out of the cows around here," Phillipson said, guiding a glass of milk into Cahill's free hand.
> "He's right," Harbelis said from the other side. "No matter how sorry it is, the Air Corps gets the best."

More later! Meanwhile, you might like to look up the opening section of the book, which was the feature piece in the February 1976 issue of <u>Esquire</u>, though you haven't yet come into things.

My best to you, your granddaughters, and everybody else connected with you.

Sending you my very best, Andy, know that I remain

Yours ever,

To: Daniel Hoffman

CC, Emory University
4620 Lelia's Court
Columbia, S.C. 29206

June 30, 1980

Dear Dan,

Thank you very much indeed for your letter. Yes, my condition is improving steadily; now that I can eat, I cannot have enough of that weird condition known as normalcy, and am wolfing down everything including nails, bobby pins, and ground glass. It is good of you to take such an interest in my internal-combustion situation, and, as I say, I am happy to reassure you that I am well on the way back, wherever that is, or is to be.

I hope your discouragement was limited only to the time of your letter, for you of all people have no reason to be discouraged about anything, or at least anything literary. The Poe book is one of the finest achievements in truly creative interpretation that have been in my time, <u>Barbarous Knowledge</u> is just as good, and the poems are just as good as those. As to the latter: is your new book of verse scheduled for 1980? I have a kind of vested interest in this, and would appreciate your letting me know, though the purpose of my asking must for a time be shrouded.

As for my own work, I am beginning slowly to bring out a few things here and there. A new poem is featured in the current (July) issue of the <u>Atlantic</u>. It is a kind of elegy for Jim Wright. I went camping with him a few times, and he used to comment on the change of the "psyche" of the day, at sundown, when the night predators come out, and, as he said, "The surround becomes charged with violence and blood." My poem is an attempt to tell him that he need no longer fear the surround, and its changes and terrors: the surround itself is speaking the poem in a kind of ritual—the ritual of Jim's death—and telling him that, by dying, he is becoming the surround itself: he is now his own surround. Anyway, have a look, and let me know what you think.

In any case, I remain

Yours ever,

To: Liz and John Rosenberg

CC, Emory University
4620 Lelia's Court
Columbia, S.C. 29206

July 3, 1980

Dear Liz and John,

One more note from the grave—or, really, from under the surgical snows of Seattle—very dark down there, and memoryless—and the stone snows of Mount St. Helens. On the way from the University of Idaho, where the good Rocky Mountaineers were foolish enough to give me a degree, we flew over Mount St. Helens at just the very <u>second</u> it blew up like a veritable Krakatoa. The pilot was so excited he could hardly hold the plane in the air, and kept insisting that all the passengers get over to the port windows of the plane with binoculars, cameras, extra-wide eyes, because "This is something you're not going to see every day." And indeed it wasn't, truth to tell.

Anyway, we got the <u>massive</u> surgery done, and it seems to have straightened things out, and I am so busy eating everything in sight for the sheer joy of feeling it go down my gullet unobstructed, that I have added nails, bobby pins, splinters of glass, nuts, bolts, and screws to my diet, and I don't even use ketchup. Believe me, our old friend Epicurus was right: the greatest pleasure is the absence of pain. Amen.

I have a new book of poems finished. It was originally a big picture-book with the poems more or less congruent with photographs of young girls, but the book was slated to cost $250 a copy, subscription couldn't pay for the printing, and no commercial house could afford to bring it out with that price structure being, as they say, part of the package. Various publishers want to print the poems without the pictures, and, since they were originally conceived that way anyway (I am not <u>about</u> to have any verse of mine <u>depend</u> on pictures), I now plan to go ahead, having just obtained the original publisher's permission, to take the book back to Doubleday, rewrite the title, and the titles of the poems, and present the book as though it were really conceived as a cycle of poems about Debba, as in fact it indeed was. It is now called <u>Deborah</u> <u>Puella</u>, and is about girldom in general, but hers in particular.

One of the poems, slightly reworded, appears in the current <u>Atlantic</u>. It is a kind of elegy for Jim Wright. If you have time, have a look. It is different from my other things, and, if you like it, I'd certainly appreciate your letting the editors at the <u>Atlantic</u> know something of your reaction, for they are fanatical mail-assessors, up there, and would greatly appreciate it. Needless to say, so would I.

Speaking of favors—if this can so be considered—I had a phone call from someone on the Chicago paper that you review for, Liz, and had occasion to tell her how highly I regard your acumen and other reviewer-esque qualities. The lady seemed to take me seriously, for the paper seems to have an assessment-system of its own. Anyway, I hope this does you some good in your later traffickings with them.

I haven't time for a really long letter, but will close to get this in the newest outgoing mail. Aside from my convalescence, we are well here, and long to see you. If the reading of which you speak can possibly materialize, please let us know in ample time beforehand, for we would love to see you again, whether all is buried in snow or not.

All yours,

To: Mrs. Paddy Fraser

CC, Emory University
4620 Lelia's Court
Columbia, S.C. 29206

July 10, 1980

Dear Mrs. Fraser,

I have your letter of May 12, and am very happy to have it. It set me to thinking about my own first acquaintance with poetry, the thing I have now spent the largest—and I hope the best—part of my life on. I was looking the other day through some of these books that I retained from that early period. I acquired them in Australia in the early days of the Pacific War, as I may have told you, and I find I have several books of other poets associated with your husband in the "new apocalypse" effort. It was interesting and oddly moving to read through these, after so many years, and to undergo the double effect of a return of those enthusiasms and those conditions and a completely different perspective which depends on the years between, and whatever I have learned therein. Henry Treece is not very good, though I have enjoyed some of his later historical novels. On the other hand, J.F. Hendry is very good, and I would be most interested to know whatever became of him. He is not only a good, though rather erratic, poet, but also a rather good fiction writer and a really first-rate critic. I have a couple of slim (<u>very</u> slim) volumes of his poems, a few essays in magazines, and even a curious book of short stories, based on his experiences in Yugoslavia, called <u>The</u> <u>Blackbird</u> <u>of</u> <u>Ospo</u>. I have an idea that he and your husband were probably friends or at least acquaintances, given the association with Treece and the fact that they were both Scots. If you have any news of his fate, I would welcome knowing about it. But that shall be as you wish.

Let me know how you're coming along with your selection of your husband's work. Do you have an English publisher? Perhaps mine, Hamish Hamilton, would be interested; he would be foolish if he were not. If you need someone to help edit, and perhaps write an introduction, why not Lawrence Durrell?

After all, he and George (if I may make bold to refer to him so) knew each other in the East, and your husband wrote on <u>him</u>.

No, I don't have your husband's <u>Essays on Twentieth Century Poets</u> but would certainly like to. If you could send along a copy, I will certainly reimburse you in one transatlantic flash of money-green. I will also, if you like, send you some of my books.

Perhaps, in a couple of years, when I bring out another novel over there, I will be back in England, and if so, I certainly <u>will</u> come up to see you. That would be something worth looking forward to.

Meanwhile, I remain

Sincerely yours,

To: John C. O'Brien

CC, Emory University
4620 Lelia's Court
Columbia, S.C. 29206

July 17, 1980

Dear Mr. O'Brien:

Thank you very much for your July 14th letter. I am glad that Sidney Stapleton has been gracious to you. It looks as though no publisher will take on the expense of producing the original format of <u>Flowering</u>, nor cares to market the book at the price Sid and his people wish to ask. In keeping with these developments, Sid has <u>apparently</u> turned the 19 poems back over to me, to publish as a separate book without the photographs, and in any format or with any publisher I choose. This is generous and gracious of the Golden Chalice people, I think, for they had great hopes for producing a beautiful as well as an expensive book. But the poems were conceived as autonomous works, which are in no sense dependent on the illustrative material, but which could be read in reference to it. The poems are better—much better—standing alone, and I have changed the titles to allow the cycle to turn around the early girlhood of my wife Deborah, and I think the result will be a revelation to you or anybody else who reads them. The book is now called Deborah <u>Puella</u>, and I expect I will bring it out with Doubleday in a year or so. But the main point at <u>this</u> point is that the poems are in <u>my</u> domain, and as far as I'm am concerned, we can make tentative plans for publication, if you see fit. Since I have

19 poems available, we could easily bypass the difficulties connected with the Wright poem—though I am very happy you think so highly of it—and use some others from the sequence.

I have in mind two possibilities. There are two sets of poems which are paired: that is, each is in a format of I and II. The first of these is called "Ray-Flowers" and the second, "Deborah as Scion." Judging from your format in the Montague and Mahon books, the lengths of either one of these would fit your format, though the Scion poems are a little longer than the others. If you wanted to print one or the other of these two suites, plus the Wright poem, we might be able to do that, and call the book, for example, Ray-Flowers and an Elegy. If you like, I could send you a Xerox of the entire manuscript, and you could perhaps choose for yourself; these are only my initial suggestions.

As to protocol, logistics, or what you will, in addition to your getting a final clearance from Sidney Stapleton, I would like you also to clear the Wright poem with the Atlantic, and the whole idea with my editors at Doubleday. The person to reach there is Blair Brown, my lady editor. Meanwhile I will see to the necessary details with my agent and with the others involved at my end.

I hope very much that we can solve all these problems, for your generosity and interest are of much value to me, as are your kind concern for the state of my health and the way you have voiced it.

I remain

Sincerely yours,

To: Howard Nemerov   TLS, Washington University

4620 Lelia's Court
Columbia, S.C. 29206
29 July 1980

Dear Howard:

I wonder if you would be willing to advance the cause of one of my proposed candidates for election to the Institute? This is M.L. Rosenthal, who is I think a reputable and honest worker for the right things. He would be a valuable addition to the group, I do sincerely believe. Let me know how you feel about this, for as you know the Institute people are sticklers for deadlines.

A couple of months ago I had good news of you from Mona van Duyn, whom I saw briefly at Southern Illinois. It is always good to know you are doing well, and above all, writing, for you are surely the best of us.

Ever,
Jim

To: Richard Wilbur

CC, Emory University
4620 Lelia's Court
Columbia, S.C. 29206

29 July 1980

Dear Dick:

I have the idea that David Wagoner should be invited to join the Institute. He is a hard-working and good poet, and has never really had much recognition. His fiction is also interesting, I think, and for years he has been a first rate editor, out there at <u>Poetry</u> <u>Northwest</u>. Would you consider seconding his candidacy? Do let me know about this, for as you know the Institute is strict about deadlines, especially when it comes to nominations for new candidates.

Meanwhile, my very best to you, as always. They still speak of you here as the best writer we have ever had visit us. Surely it is so; I agree.

Yours,

To: Elizabeth Lasensky

CC, Emory University
4620 Lelia's Court
Columbia, S.C. 29206

30 July 1980

Dear Ms. Lasensky:

Here are the answers to your three questions:

1. Some books that I read as a teenager:

   <u>Baseball Joe and the Silver Stars</u>
   <u>Gary Grayson's Hill Street Eleven</u>
   <u>Poppy Ott and the Stuttering Parrot</u>

<u>Poppy Ott and the Whispering Mummy</u>
<u>The Land of No Shadow</u> by Carl H. Claudy
<u>Tarzan the Terrible</u> by Edgar Rice Burroughs
<u>Bombay the Jungle Boy in the Temple of Vines</u>
<u>Tom Swift in the Caves of Ice</u>
<u>Of Human Bondage</u> by W. Somerset Maugham

2. A book I like very much:

<u>Collected Letters</u> by Rainer Maria Rilke

My favorite writer: James Agee

3. What I would say to encourage teenagers to use the library:

"Every book is a separate new life. I would stress potential, intellectual, and physical excitement, adventure.

I hope these notes will be helpful to you in your display.

Sincerely,

To: William Childress   **CC, Emory University**
4620 Lelia's Court
Columbia, S.C. 26206

7 August 1980

Dear Mr. Childress:

Thank you very much for your letter, your book, but most of all for your enthusiasm. I'm recovering rapidly, and probably will be able to hunt, come October. There is a fabulous place off the coast down here that you would surely like to know about, and where I do most of my serious hunting and fishing. Just after the film of <u>Deliverance</u> came out, <u>Archery</u> magazine sent its editor, Glenn Helgeland, down for a week, and we went out to Bull's and had a great time, and <u>Archery</u> did the cover-story on me and my exploits down there. I don't remember exactly which issue this was, but it would have been in 1973, most likely. Anyway, you could look it up—you can't miss it, for I and my guitar are all over the cover.

Now, if you really want to pursue this thing, you should write to the Refuge Manager, Route 1, Box 191, Awendaw, SC, 29429, and find out when the controlled hunt on Bull's Island will be this year, and also find out how you and I can get our equipment from McClellanville on the mainland out to Bull's, which is about 40 minutes from the continent. Since I was last there, the semi-commercial boat for hunters has not been retained in commission, and the people who manage to get over there have to go by private means. Since I don't have any private means, you and the magazine would have to arrange transportation, though you and I could do the rest of whatever else is required, including the bow-hunting and fishing. Since this is a controlled hunt, you can stalk or tree-stand only during certain hours of the day, which means that the rest of the time everybody surfcasts, which is terrific fishing on a terrific spot; it looks like the earth on the third day of creation, when God was still trying things out, and liking some of what he had dreamed up.

Anyway, if you like, check some of this out, and I will be guided accordingly. I hope we can get together, if not here then in British Columbia, where I have an ex-cowboy buddy who wants me to hunt bear with him, and yet another in Alaska who says he knows a bigger bear. But I'll keep Bull's Island first in mind. I know where the Big One is: he's death-and-resurrection white on his between-islands moonlight swims, and makes noises like a whale; his antlers shine like the arrows I have never shot.

Also, I would have to have a fee. How much can your opulent magazine pay me for doing something I would do anyway, but this time including you and your story?

Sincerely,

To: Robert Penn Warren   **TLS, Emory University**

4620 Lelia's Court
Columbia, S.C. 29206
11 August 1980

Dear Red,

Thank you so very much for the book and for the inscription, which Debba and I will prize for as long as we can stand up and see lightning and hear thunder; yes, and longer than that, too. As it happens, I have just reviewed the book for the <u>Saturday Review</u>, and I believe on my honor it is the best piece I have ever done, in all my reviewing: surely the closest to my intent, and to what I really do feel about a writer.[3] The kind of criticism I do is closer to Ruskin or Walter Pater than it is to Eliot or somebody like William Empson; I am a very <u>emotional</u> critic, and am as likely to be talking about myself as about the poet I'm supposed to be dealing with. But I believe that in this piece, I subordinate my own reaction to your work (which is intense) to the work itself, and I believe I have got pretty close to the heart of it. I haven't seen the printed article yet, but am told it is in the August issue, so have a look and let me know what you think.

Debba sends her love, and I do mine. Please remember us with great fondness to Eleanor.

Ever,
Jim

To: Truman Capote

CC, Emory University
4620 Lelia's Court
Columbia, S.C. 29206

11 August 1980

Dear Mr. Capote:

Would you like to come down here to South Carolina and speak to us some-time next spring? If your schedule might permit such an occasion, and you were inclined to it, I can get back to you on the details—including the finan-cial—once I hear from you.

When you can, do let me hear from you on this. Needless to say, I hope very much you can come. When I first moved here from the Library of Congress twelve years ago, I asked the President of the college what might be the ad-vantages of living in South Carolina, which I as a Georgian had always thought of as a depressed area, full of pellagra and prejudice, and he answered, simply,

---

3. Dickey reviewed Warren's *Being Here: 1977–1980* in "Robert Penn Warren's Courage," *Saturday Review* 7 (August 1980): 56–57. The article was collected as "The Weathered Hand and Silent Space" in *Night Hurdling*.

"Flowers and birds." They were here—and are—and so am I. You come too. (Though I hate to quote that super-jerk Robert Frost to end a letter intended as friendly, and as at least a mild enticement.)

With best wishes,

To: President Jimmy Carter   CC, Emory University
4620 Lelia's Court
Columbia, S.C. 29206

August 12, 1980

Dear Jimmy,

I have just watched your win over Senator Kennedy on TV, and as a result I have great hopes, as many (or probably most) Americans do now. I send this to let you know that I stand ready to help in any way I can at this time, which is of such vital importance, and will not come again. Timing is crucial in politics, as in most other things; what is done now will be what is done, and will have the results that it will have. This is platitudinous, maybe, but it is also basic, and as the late Mr. Justice Holmes said, basics are of some importance.

Whatever assistance I may have been to you in our correspondence before and during your debates with Gerald Ford, or as a poet at your Inauguration, or as your personal representative in Mexico, I now offer again. Let me know whatever I might be able to do in any capacity in your campaign, and I will do my best to help. My area is words, and in making them effective and memorable. That I can do, and make bold to assert that I can do it better than anyone else. I can stay clear of the inside of the campaign, and just look on with the rest of the populace by television and newspaper, or I can be part-way into the actual workings of it, or I can give it, with your permission and direction, a full, all-out commitment; in any case, that shall be as you wish, and as you indicate. I will wait to hear from you on these matters; but meanwhile remember that, as I am told a poet once said, I will do what I can. The fields are still here, and still strong.

Debba sends love to you and Rosalynn, and so do I.

Ever,

To: John C. O'Brien

CC, Emory University
4620 Lelia's Court
Columbia, S.C. 29206

August 27, 1980

Dear Mr. O'Brien:

Thank you indeed for your most welcome letter. I am delighted that you like the poems, and especially that you like the "Scion" one, which is a particular favorite of mine. As regards the title of the book, my wife and I have talked it over and have decided that the book should simply be called SCION, and should have, inside, a simple "To Deborah" as the dedication. And as to the actual presentation of the poems themselves, let's also make it "Scion" instead of "Deborah as Scion." We both like one-word titles, for they are dramatic, and have a starkness that is arresting. However, if your type has already been set, leave it as it is. That would be fine too. So, unless I hear otherwise from you, I will tell people that SCION is the name of the book, and we'll all go on that basis. Concerning your question about the spaces between the words "logic" and "fretted," please leave the two spaces there.

I'll be looking forward to getting the pages for signing, and will try to return them to you within whatever deadline you suggest. According to your schedule, when will the book appear? How many author's copies will I be allowed? How will the distribution be handled? Will there be an actual contract for the book? I must let my agent know about this, and also about the manner in which payment and/or royalties will be forthcoming. Please excuse all this crass kind of palaver, but if I don't furnish my agent and his IRS pursuers with exact figures, he will nail me to the nearest thorn-bush.

And sure, I'd like very much to meet with you, and would not be at all averse to spending the whole of the advance on a trip up there for that purpose. I like that area, anyway, and would thus have a chance to see my grandson, some of my Harvard acquaintances, the <u>Atlantic</u> <u>Monthly</u> people, John Updike, and some others. Let me know your situation as to time, and maybe we can bring something together. I'd like that a lot, believe me.

Sincerely,

To: Paul Rifkin

CC, Emory University
4620 Lelia's Court
Columbia, S.C. 29206

September 22, 1980

Dear Paul,

Thank you very much for your letter.

In answer to your question—do I believe in God—I would say this: whatever made what is, from the sand grain to the galaxy, is worthy of my worship. Whether such a force as we call God knows anything about me or not, I don't know. I would say to God what the angels say to him in Goethe's <u>Faust</u>:

> Thine aspect cheers the hosts of heaven
> Though what Thine essence, none can say.

Sincerely,

To: President Jimmy Carter

CC, Emory University
4620 Lelia's Court
Columbia, S.C. 29206

October 24, 1980

Dear Jimmy:

Since I haven't heard from Jody Powell, and since time is getting short, I thought I had better send you what thoughts I have on the points you might want to emphasize in your debate with Reagan—if this reaches you in ti e—and in any other statements you make between now and the election.

I can put my suggestions very succinctly. I am reasoning here first from the standpoint of a voting citizen and second from that of a writer, a rhetorician, or what Santayana called himself, "an ignorant man, almost a poet." Though questions of an economic nature are of great concern, the issue of over-whelming importance is that of war, particularly of precipitious, foolishly-provoked and unnecessary war. The belief in the minds of many more than half the voters is that the election of Reagan would make such an eventuality much more likely, as I myself believe. In connection with this situation, and in furtherance of your own re-election, you need two things: the first of these is a simple, graspable, widely applicable and memorable metaphor to describe your position. This figure of speech should or might be the familiar one, urged on all citizens of driving as well as voting age, of <u>driving</u> <u>defensively</u>. The implications of operating an automobile so as not to <u>allow</u> any accidents to happen to one's own vehicle are obvious, and instantly applicable to any individual's own case. If you can use this approach together with continued references to your record in office as evidence of your having done just this— driven this nation defensively—and can also link these assertions up with a key phrase—I think that the essential message will be effectively conveyed. If I am right, the phrase would be "A passion for peace."

Again, please accept my best wishes for everything concerning you and your family. Debba sends love, and so do I.

Ever,

To: Tim Engelland

CC, Emory University
4620 Lelia's Court
Columbia, S.C. 29206

October 29, 1980

Dear Tim Engelland:

Thank you so very much for sending along the dummy of <u>Scion</u> with your extremely striking, original and effective illustrations. I have gone through the text very carefully, and I much admire the way you have set it up. There is only one request I would like to make, if I may. The spacing between words is very important to the way I write poetry, and I would like it very much if you could open up some more space in the second line of the first of the two poems, so that it would read

   Lace: white logic   fretted cloud-cloth.

If you could do that for us, things would be absolutely perfect. Believe me, I am impressed. This is my seventh or eighth small-press book, and it is by far the best of them, already (and I like the others, too). I am grateful for your enormous care with this project, your experimentation with colors, the daring and originality of your designs, the choice of hand-coloring as well as the execution of it, the extra time and effort you have given all-round. Thanks for all these, and for the things you say about <u>Scion</u>. I was at the big gala for Poets & Writers last week in New York and no fewer than six or seven people, including Norman Mailer, William Styron, John Updike (a devoted small-press man) and George Plimpton, came up to me and told me, in various ways, that the rumor was out that "some small press" (I quickly told them Deerfield) is getting ready to "bring out the best Dickey poetry in ten years." So you will have no trouble with sales, I can guarantee. In addition to the word-of-mouth, I have a very heavy reading schedule from now on through the summer, and I am quite sure we will be able to sell just as many copies as Deerfield can produce.

Again, thanks for everything. I love woodcuts and other graphics of that sort and am a great admirer of the Greats in that field (in addition to Engelland!) like Kirchner and Nolde.

If you like, I'd like to see successive stages of the production of <u>Scion</u>, if it were possible for you to send them. But that shall be as you wish.

Yours,

To: Helen Vendler

CC, Emory University
4620 Lelia's Court
Columbia, S.C. 29206

October 30, 1980

Dear Ms. Vendler:

I know only your work on Wallace Stevens, plus a couple of short phone conversations connected with the Pulitzer Prize of a few years ago, but I notice from a recent issue of <u>The American Scholar</u> that you have also written on George Herbert, and I would like to get hold of this. Though Herbert is much respected, his commentators, with a few exceptions, have not been as good as I would like to see, though I remember an essay of L. C. Knights which I thought good, and Rosamund Tuve is good, and the long Empson gloss on "The Sacrifice" is good, though I don't commonly like Empson. I have a big <u>Works</u> of Herbert edited by F. E. Hutchinson, and have gone through that from time to time with much interest. But for Hutchinson's edition I would not have known of the <u>Jacula Prudentum</u>, to which I frequently return with much wonder and instruction. "A Scab'd Horse Cannot Abide the Comb." That is good, is it not? Especially for the comb'd and the combing among the poets and critics.

Please forgive this intrusion, and come off this letter with my best intentions and wishes.

Sincerely,

To: Dave Smith   CC, Emory University
                                                                                4620 Lelia's Court
                                                                      Columbia, S.C. 29206

November 17, 1980

Dear Dave:

Thank you indeed for sending along the review,[4] Please be completely at rest as to my reaction, for whatever I might take exception to would be completely lost in the strong wonderment and gratitude I feel. Your whole stance on the work, the whole <u>motion</u> of your mind over it, is so hearteningly favorable that there is very little the poet can say to express his gratitude to the critic. The man of words, in <u>other</u> words, has no words.

Yet a few, even so. I am delighted at your attitude toward <u>The Zodiac</u>, which of <u>course</u> is a failure; there is no way that any poem which attempts to be a projection of booziness and confusion is ever going to be the kind of hand-fitted-together sort of "success" that, say, <u>The Waste Land</u> is. <u>The Zodiac</u> is trying to get at one of the central concerns of the act of composing poetry: the feeling that one has, or can have: that many have had, are having, will have. The difficult magic that the mind engages on with self-delusion and alcohol is <u>necessarily</u> grandiose and foolish, and mostly empty. But what the Eliots of the world do not seem to understand is that the great, universal visions, such as this poor Dutchman is trying to have, are intermittently akin, in just fits and starts—the combination of a couple of words here, an association there, a rhythm, a line-break—are sometimes very close to <u>real</u> vision, and the real <u>saying</u> of something extraordinary that could not even be guessed at under any other conditions. That you have seen this is important,

4. "The Strength of James Dickey," *Poetry* 137 (March 1981): 349–58.

and I would put my cold coin on the possibility that the future will see the poem as you have done.

As to the cavils, you are probably right, though there may be some extenuation, too. The marathon poem you don't seem to like because of what you interpret as an unnecessarily cheery ending, which is maybe true. But it struck me, looking at footage of these strange races through the city, that the whole point of almost anyone's participation in them is the participation—for any one of that rag-tag mob could run as much as he wanted to, by himself, at any time—and above all in the finishing, the actual finishing, of the thing. Not more than ten of the contestants have any chance of winning the race, or even think they have, so the brute finishing, in each individual case, is the message, as Mr. McLuhan might say. Otherwise, I thought there were a couple of humorous things in it, particularly those about the reflections of the runners going by the stores where the mannequins and dummies are looking out at them. Anyway, that's my defense (if that's what this is!) As for the Lombardi poem, you seem to condemn it, also, for unearned "uplift" at the end, when what I intended was precisely the opposite of this. If you like, you can imagine the last line as being savagely and ironically muttered (or savagely and ironically mutter it yourself) by someone who feels bitter, cheapened and cheated by football, and by its irresponsible and self-righteous Satan, Lombardi and what he stands for. I intended to write about the baleful entrapment that football is—or of all sports—and the lifelong ambiguity it contains. The key to my attitude is in the one overt passage of abstraction, to the effect that "love-hate is stronger / Than either love or hate." I think that is true not only of Lombardi, football players, ex-football players and fans, but of people and situations, generally. In fact I cannot think of a single case in my own life that it has not been true. But please don't think I approve wholeheartedly of the Vince Lombardis and George Pattons of the world. They are there, though, and their eternal fascination is that for some situations they are useful (if not indispensable), that they are spectacular, and that they do win. Myself, I was the boy who wrapped his head in the red jersey and crammed it into the rusty locker. That's the side of football I know best.

I won't go on and on in this immoderate vein, but will just close to tell you of my extreme gratitude, and of my great hope and expectation concerning your own work. The wave of the future will be of the poets of your type, and not that of the followers of Lowell and his scab-picking lady cohorts. When you can take a poem of mine like "Camden Town" and see what is really in the thing, when without exception everybody else missed it, you are certainly the right (the rightest) commentator on my poetry, and are the best fitted to carry on the kind of orientation toward experience that I represent. You have got the essential of what I am trying to do, and the vindication of my effort, for whatever it may be worth, is in your own poetry, and I will go with that.

As for my own, I can surely tell you that I feel what any poet feels on reading commentary on his work of the penetration and sympathy of your article: no matter what happens to me, there is this single thing: out of all the critics, well-wishers, detractors, members of any and all audiences, there was one who truly understood the inmost.

One. Just one, but sufficient. And better than that.

                                                                    Yours,

To: Eliot Wigginton   CC, Emory University
                                                            4620 Lelia's Court
                                                          Columbia, S.C. 29206

                                                          November 25, 1980

Dear Eliot Wigginton:

Since the time, now so long ago, that you—or someone who represented the Foxfire project, who I like to think I remember as being you—came to the Poetry office at the Library of Congress in connection with the Foxfire project, I have followed with avid and increasing interest the progress of Foxfire, and have drawn on your material for a great many things I have attempted to do in my writing and thinking. I am now engaged in a strange—and, to me, exciting—endeavor: a book on Appalachia in collaboration with the artist Hubert Shuptrine, with whom I did a previous book on the South called Jericho. The Appalachia book will be called The Wilderness of Heaven, and will be brought out by Doubleday as soon as Hubert can finish the pictures to his satisfaction and I can complete my part of the book to mine. By this letter I hope to establish a new contact with you, so that I may be able to get together with you at some undefined time between now and the completion of the book, and perhaps take advantage of your knowledge of the various forms of Appalachian life and culture, its people, folkways, legends, and other facts and aspects of it. Beyond the book, I have a very real interest in the region, since my father's people came from there, about forty miles west of where we filmed Deliverance, in fact. There is a certain yearning for place, for custom.

I would be most pleased if we could get together on this or indeed any other basis, for I not only admire greatly what you have done to make the uniqueness of "the wilderness of heaven" known and appreciated by people who don't live there, but I feel that to some extent, by blood and natural affinity, I belong to the region, and thus to your cause.

Let me hear from you when you can conveniently do so, and if you like, we will make some plans.

Sincerely yours,

To: Dave Smith

CC, Emory University
4620 Lelia's Court
Columbia, S.C. 29206

November 26, 1980

Dear Dave:

Well, as we say down here, that is some kind of good letter.

That you would want to write a book on my work gives me the most intense gratification, whether you actually end up writing it or not. A young poet named Bruce Weigl in Arkansas has asked me if it would be all right for him to write a book, and, as I remember, mentioned you as a possible collaborator. I am not sure whether or not that is the book you are referring to, or whether you wish to undertake one on your own. Either way is fine with me, because I like what little I know of Weigl, and would certainly help and encourage him in any way I could. But if you intend to undertake the book alone, I could probably be of more help than I could in the other case, for at such a suggestion on your part there is a quick draw of affirmation on my vitals, as from somewhere down deep in a well. Let me know what you need, and I will surely comply.

As the first step, here is the new book, <u>Puella</u>, more or less exactly as it will appear, word for word. Five of these will be in the issue of <u>Poetry</u> which carries your essay, and it will be interesting to me, as a kind of game between us, as to which ones you would be inclined to pick—that is, if you like any of them. However, that may be, these poems are quite different from any I have ever done. If the sort of linguistic search Mallarme instituted has something to do with this approach, I would not be surprised, though certainly none of them sound like him or are as tenuous as his. I have tried to get a very intense and densely-packed line, going for the static quiet at the meridian point of insight, a uniform level of intensity, the most intense I could get, with no relaxing relapsing. The poems are an imagination of various aspects of a mid-adolescent girl's life—Deborah's life, or perhaps any girl's life—male-imagined. There are almost no sexual references, and these only by inference. Except for one or two exceptions, the sequence of the poems is from morning through until night, beginning with the third poem, about being at dawn, "open-browed on the blood-road," and going on through to the last piece, which is a kind of free-floating invocation, a kind of spell cast as consciousness fades, that ends on a note of daring—of "go for it"—and the unending invention of creativity itself. Though the poems are written around Debba, this copy is for you, as I have signed. When you can, let me know what you think of this strangeness.

Yours ever,

P.S. I'm glad you have got to know Red Warren. You might like to have a look at the review I did of his last book in the <u>Saturday</u> <u>Review</u> a couple of issues ago. I think it is the September issue, but if it is not that it is either August or October.

To: Shaye Areheart

CC, Emory University
4620 Lelia's Court
Columbia, S.C. 29206

December 1, 1980

Dear Shaye:

Hubert Shuptrine and his sky-bound brother came here last week, and we spent a day being photographed by the people from the Atlanta paper, all this to culminate in a cover-story for the Sunday magazine section in a couple of weeks. Hubert had carefully-wrapped pictures, which he unwrapped for the photographer, and I spent some time being interviewed by a rather intelligent young red-headed reporter. I also had some time to talk out a possible format with Hubert, give him some ideas about landscape, which we strongly need in a book which has a title like this one, and since then I have attempted to get my mind into some kind of relation to Hubert's material which would provide us with a reasonable modus. His idea now, if we decide to make the pictures and the text interdependent is simply for me to write the text around Hubert's pictures, which means that I will be forced to find some way of bending this way and that to accord with what are essentially Hubert's whims and the "art" that chance has given him. This cannot possibly be satisfactory to me, for in undertaking this project, as I do in the case of any project, I want to hold out at least the illusion that I have an outside chance of creating something of permanent value, and that I am not nailed into a situation in which I must do nothing but furnish fancy footnotes to some ambitious and quite mediocre artist's efforts. I don't mean to be high-handed about this, but you and I must find some way of guaranteeing my creative autonomy. I don't wish to offend anybody, but I certainly do not wish to be put in a position where I can't do what I would like to do, and can do. I'd like for you to think on these matters, and give me your ideas, before I sink a lot of time into the venture, time that I had much rather be putting into Alnilam. Everybody seems to like the "Stranger" idea, and since it was mine to begin with, I think I can do something with it, but whether that something has anything to do with Hubert's pictures I very much doubt. Again, let me know about this. Perhaps you could kick around some ideas for a subtitle which would open up an approach that would be satisfactory to us both, and to Hugh, and Hubert could then make his peace with that. So far I have "Annals of the Stranger," but I am not all that sold on "Annals"; something else might be better; something involving the word Stranger in some way.

As to Alnilam, I am working well on it, and just over 1000 words a day, which I then polish and retype. I will be sending you a batch of this new material in a week or so. Do you have your own copy of the text to date? If not, please make sure that Hugh gives you one, so that we can work directly.

Please keep leaning on Theron about the contract and the other stuff he needs to coordinate, particularly the business with Bookie. Kirk says we are free to go ahead without paying Bookie anything, since Theron did not have a copy of the contract I signed, and it was part of the original agreement that he be consulted. Anyway, see what Theron has done, and meanwhile, continue to keep the wheels in motion toward a publication date for Puella. Two of the poems will come out as Scion from Deerfield Press in Massachusetts, the Paris Review will run "The Lyric Beasts" in their 25th anniversary number, and Poetry magazine will give the entire April issue to five of the poems,[5] plus a long essay by Dave Smith on my work since the last big Wesleyan book; that

---

5. "Five Poems from Puella," *Poetry* 137 (March 1981): 313–20. The poems were "Deborah Burning a Doll Made of House-Wood," "Deborah, Moon, Mirror, Right Hand Rising," "Veer-Voices: Two Sisters under Crows," "Heraldic: Deborah and Horse in Morning Forest," and "Springhouse, Menses, Held Apple, House and Beyond."

is, all the poems I have done with Doubleday. You will like what he says, I can surely tell you.

So—let's keep the whole thing going. Write and tell me your news, and also please give me the latest sales figures on Strength of Fields.

We are well here, and working hard and with some joy. Debba sends her best, and so do I. Let us hear.

Yours ever,

To: Donna Martinelli   **CC, Emory University**
4620 Lelia's Court
Columbia, S.C. 29206

December 11, 1980

Dear Ms. Martinelli:

Here is the final exam for the Davis Celestian Navigation Course, which for the last 6 years I have enjoyed working on to an extent it would be difficult to explain. If this final "voyage" is all right, and really does get my mythical vessel to Honolulu—or part way, at least, and on course—I would appreciate very much your sending along my certificate. In fact, I would appreciate it even more if you would send two of them, for I would like a duplicate for my office. Nobody believes I have done this thing, and I'd like a lot of proof, which I will be most happy to pay for.

Please remember me to the others there who have given me such good instruction and vicarious pleasure. And send me your latest catalog, too.

Sincerely,

P.S. By the way, there will be a feature article in the April issue of Esquire which has to do in part with navigation, so have a look, if you can remember that far ahead.[6]

---

6. "Why I Live Where I Live," *Esquire* 95 (April 1981): 62–64.

To: Stanley Burnshaw   RTLS, University of Texas at Austin

4620 Lelia's Court
Columbia, S.C. 29206
January 7, 1981

Dear Stanley,

It is great to hear from you, and to be back in a contact I have never really been out of, except for actual news of your movements, writings, current situations.

I was as dumbfounded as everyone else by Sandy Richardson's dismissal at Doubleday. He had handled my stuff for the last ten years, was in charge of all the new material that I am developing, had various duties relating to my work delegated to other functionaries placed in various positions around Doubleday, so that when Sandy left, all these other people either left at the same time or were fired, and where my whole team of people had been, there was nothing at all. I am most distressed about the fate of The Refusers, and hardly know what to say, except that I felt that Richardson would be a conscientious and good editor for you since I felt at the time that he was such for me. But now—I don't know what to think.

Yet one thing does occur to me. My literary executor, soi-disant, is a man named Matthew Bruccoli, the biographer of John O'Hara and also, in a book forthcoming in June, of Scott Fitzgerald. He has his own imprint, connected in some way which I don't fully understand with Harcourt Brace, and if you like I'll talk to him about The Refusers. Let me know if you would like me to do this, and I will swing right with you.

Did you drive down to Miami? If so, I wish you had been able to stop by here, for I welcome any and every chance I have to get together with you. When you go back up to the Vineyard, please do plan to come by here, or perhaps meet with Debba and me at Pawley's Island, where we have another home that I think you'd like. Keep me posted as to your plans, and we'll get together somewhere, some way, at some time.

Much has happened, meanwhile. I had really massive surgery last May, but I have almost fully recovered now, and have a great many projects going at the same time. I'll tell you about these in the next letter, as soon as I learn that you are at your Miami address.

My best to you. Do let me hear from you, and everything about you.

Ever,

Jim

To: John Hay

CC, Emory University
4620 Lelia's Court
Columbia, S.C. 29206

January 8, 1981

Dear John:

Thank you very much for sending your two books. I have already read them, and they are just as impressive as the others. I like writing about beaches to begin with, and have read around in the field to some extent, though I have by no means read all that has been written, I can assure you. One of my main favorites before I encountered your work was Charlton Ogburn's The Winter Beach, which I liked mainly for the ending, where the author stands there and watches a bird with a good many of its flight-feathers shot away, trying to keep itself in the air, and even fly upwind. It is a sad and beautiful image, I think, and stands for a great deal of what is going on, that you and I and a few others stand against.

Yes I do agree with you largely about Peter Matthiessen, though I like and read most of what he does. One of the main things about him is that he either gets financed or finances himself to go to these remote places like New Guinea and the Himalayas that are inaccessible to almost any writers but him. There should be somebody like that, I think, and, as I say, I read most of what he brings back, for I doubt I will ever know any other snow leopards but his.

And yes I do think your work on the Cape is better than Henry Beston's, though I like The Outermost House pretty well, even so. I was put onto it by reading some of the miscellaneous work of Winfield Townley Scott, who evidently knew Beston over a number of years, and admired him. Did you know Scott, incidentally? I never met him, though I had some correspondence with him toward the end of his life. Incidentally, if you want to read a true horror story of a talented American poet, read Scott Donaldson's life of Winfield Townley Scott, called Poet in America. It is truer to the facts of what happens in the decline, despair and death of gifted American poets than the stories of all the other excessive people like John Berryman, Delmore Schwartz, Sylvia Plath and the other determinedly unbalanced and self-destruct case-histories people make so much over.

I can't make this the long letter I'd like to, but will just cut it short here and get it in the mail. Thank you again for your fine books, and for the poems, which I like very much. For God's sake don't sell that side of things short. For God's sake, and for my sake.

Yours,

To: Bruce Weigl   CC, Emory University
                                                  4620 Lelia's Court
                                                  Columbia, S.C. 29206

                                                  January 9, 1981

Dear Bruce,

It is good to have your letter and the joyful news of the birth of Andrew Kondo Weigl. A new baby is a marvelous creature indeed, and even more marvelous— and frightening—when one has never had one before. But, as you say, life certainly does change around the new child, and you come to find that he is the perfect center for the life you always wanted to live, but had never encountered before.

In keeping with all these good tidings, our child will be born the last week of May, and will be named Talbot, regardless of whether boy or girl. Talbot is a family name that goes far back in my father's line; as far at least as Shakespeare, where Talbot, in the Henry VI play, is one of the few characters in his plays that Shakespeare seems to approve of. Anyway, we're excited here, and everyone is amazed at the genealogy that will result. Talbot will be the uncle of my grandson—and how does one figure that?

I am very happy that Hummer and you and Dave are making progress on the book; however it comes out, it will be fine with me.[7] I like Dave's piece; it and

---

7. *The Imagination as Glory*, ed. Weigl and Hummer.

five of the new poems from <u>Puella</u> will take care of most of the March issue of <u>Poetry</u>—the book itself will come out in the fall.

Meanwhile there is for some reason a great run on my work right now. All of the earlier poems, beginning with the Scribner's book, <u>Into the Stone</u>, will be reissued in new formats. <u>Drowning with Others</u> and <u>Helmets</u> will come out as a single volume called <u>The Early Motion</u>. <u>Falling</u> and the other poems in the last section of the 1957–67 volume will be issued separately, there will be a new edition of <u>Babel to Byzantium</u>, the original screenplay-treatment of <u>Deliverance</u> will be out with a blistering introduction, and there are more and <u>more</u> projects, new books, articles, interviews, movies, picture-books—and just God knows what all in the works. It is almost impossible for me to keep on top of all this stuff, but I am doing my best, and I hope you will like at least some of it.

Yes, as I may have said, Dick Hugo was here for a couple of days, and we had a good reunion. I'm surprised at what you say about his abusing his body, though; he gave evidence here that he considered himself more or less free of alcohol, if that's the abuse you mean. He is a mighty good man, though, and I have never known anyone more dedicated to poetry. I hope he will come out of his troubles all right. Certainly he is one of the ones most worth saving.

I'll close this now and get it in the mail. Write again when you feel free to do so, and tell me how the book is going, what I can do, and what satisfactions there are.

Yours,

To: Robin Kuzen[8]

CC, Emory University
4620 Lelia's Court
Columbia, S.C. 29206

January 9, 1981

Dear Ms. Kuzen:

I have talked to both John Ashbery and Nona Balakian by phone, and also have from them letters confirming the information I send on here. The winner of the Pulitzer Prize for Poetry for 1980 is, by the ballot of this group, <u>The Morning of the Poem</u> by James Schuyler, published by Farrar, Straus and Giroux.

8. Assistant to the administrator of the Pulitzer prizes.

The breakdown of the original voting runs as follows, with the candidates listed according to the preferences of the individual judges.

Dickey

1. Windrose—Brewster Ghiselin
2. The Morning of the Poem—James Schuyler
3. The Right Madness on Skye—Richard Hugo

Ashbery
1. The Morning of the Poem—James Schuyler
2. Selected Poems—Mark Strand
3. A Part of Speech—Joseph Brodsky

Balakian
1. Selected Poems—Mark Strand
2. Mortal Acts, Mortal Words—Galway Kinnell
3. Descending Figure—Louise Gluck

On revising the initial vote, I found that, since my first choice, Ghiselin, had no chance, I would be willing to vote in accord with Mr. Ashbery and award the Prize to James Schuyler. On rereading all the work in question, I feel that the Committee has made a sound and good choice, and I hope that you and the others at Columbia will agree.

There remain only the official announcements, and of course the payments to me and the other judges for our part in the enterprise. Please send this along as soon as you can conveniently do so. And, for the three of us, thanks in advance.

Sincerely,

To: Richard Finholt

CC, Emory University
4620 Lelia's Court
Columbia, S.C. 29206

January 14, 1981

Dear Rick Finholt:

Thank you indeed for your generosity in sending me the book and the article, both of which I have just read with great interest and even a certain amazement. Your reading of <u>Deliverance</u> is certainly among the very best of the good many that have been done, and I am much beholden to you for a number of insights into my own proceedings. I had no idea that I have been attacked by the Marxists (yet!), but I much appreciate your defense. Those people like Mr. Jameson and like better critics such as Christopher Caudwell, in reducing all human motivations to questions of economic priority and the "class struggle" are leaving out a great many of the deeper and more dramatic aspects of the human creature, I believe. If it were possible that Ivan or Dmitri, instead of toiling in the slag-pits of Bethlehem Steel, or in the oakum-picking tin sheds of the Gulag could by some ideological and economic sleight-of-hand all have nice houses, nice lawns, nice cars, nice labor-saving devices, all equally and there be no more money-enmity or class war, the problems inherent in <u>Deliverance</u> would still exist; these have to do not with the problem of having but with that of being. Ed Gentry's dilemma, as Lewis points out, is that he has everything the society promises. But there is still something in him deeply dissatisfied, as my epigraph from Bataille has it: there exists at the base of human life a principle of insufficiency. That principle is to be dealt with not by the acquisition of goods but by something other, something inner. These things you have seen, and again I am most grateful to you for sending along the articles in which you say them.

I will be in your area, speaking at Kenyon in Gambier, on January 27th, and maybe you could come over for the evening. I'd like that very much, believe me; it would be good to see you.

Sincerely,

To: Paul Christensen

CC, Emory University
4620 Lelia's Court
Columbia, S.C. 29206

January 16, 1981

Dear Paul Christensen:

I have gone over Joe's manuscript, which brings back many affectionate images of my association with him. He was a demon correspondent, though I
only met him once. At that time out in El Paso, though, I spent several days,
and I have seldom felt such warmth and kinship for another American writer,
nor been so sure that this good man, this enthusiast and poet, was going to
play in hard luck for the rest of his life, and that he was not going to live very
long. In late years I had lost track of Joe, and it was a truly strong shock to me
when his son wrote me that he had died. In those few days in El Paso, when I
was given the key to the city and a date with Miss El Paso—and very pretty
she was, too—I stayed with Joe and remember his son only as a little boy who
was there, as Joe and I with our two-man combo—guitar and drums—played
hour after hour of blues and bluegrass with Jes as our only audience. These
things have got to matter.

As to the manuscript: I would like to work with it, but I cannot in all conscience do the job with it I would like to. That would amount to my rewriting
the poem, and I would feel queasy about doing such, and that, coupled with
the fact that I have no time, either, makes it necessary that I try to find some
other way to help you, and to help Joe's work. I will keep the Xerox you've
sent, but what I'd like you to do is, as editor, work on it yourself and send me
a version that in your opinion as publisher you want to put before the public:
one that would do the most for Joe's reputation, and would eliminate the
needless repetitiousness and irrelevancies of a great deal of this version. Joe's
chief virtue is energy, and his best secondary virtue is daring. His greatest
weakness is diffuseness and lack of concentration. Judging from what I have
read of your work, by your book on Olson, and by the recent interview in Long
Star Review, you would be the man to give Joe Simmons his best shot at immortality. If you will get these poems into shape, I will write an introduction.

Meanwhile, my best to you. Perhaps we may meet some day. It'd like that, you
may believe.

Sincerely,

To: Christopher Dickey

TLS, Emory University
Litchfield Plantation
Pawleys Island, S.C.

January 16, 1981

My dear son,

It has been years since I have written you an actual <u>letter</u>, for we usually talk on the phone or face to face, but I had the impulse to write you this one, particularly after Carol's phone call of the other night and the news of the events down there. Last night, reporting the wounding of the <u>Newsweek</u> guy Rebbot, John Chancellor concluded with saying, ". . . and this makes El Salvador the most dangerous country in the world for foreign journalists." Well, I thought with numbness but also some other emotion too, I've got a son down there, and he is a journalist, and he is certainly foreign; he never grew up in El Salvador in his life; he is the gringo of gringos, there in his flak vest and talent, with his uncompromising blue eyes and steadiness of purpose, with his very great courage, and with all those memories that I have, going back through many years, not only to the beginning of him but to the beginning of me, and before that too, back to the caves and before, to the creation of the life-chemicals themselves, which the physicist Urey, who died the other day, said were fused and/or created by lightning. All that, I thought, and this guy who is myself as well as my son—the latter by far the more prominent and better of the two—is down there among all that high-speed random lead, and there's nothing I can do about it except to pray that none of it hits him, and to pray especially that none of it even comes close. Since you told me about your girl stringer in Salvador, I have been wondering whether the woman blown up by the Claymore last night might be the same, and whether in consequence it might have been you in the car instead of her. How may I resolve this?

The most dreadful thing about war is the unexpectedness with which things happen. Given any chance at all, any forewarning, I have strong hopes for your safety, and these may even be reasonable, based on your ability to read a situation, your resourcefulness and your coolness, but the trouble is that some of the time there is no way to assess all the elements. For example, Rebbot was hit by a sniper, flak-vest and all, and this means that someone—someone hidden—was shooting specifically at <u>him</u>, and that bothers me. It bothers me particularly because I can't give you any advice which might enable you to deal with it, except to say that when there is firing—<u>any</u> firing, no matter how distant—to stay low, and take whatever cover there is.

You needn't answer this at any length, or even at all if you don't have time or if things are too hectic; I just wanted to write it to tell you how very precious you are to me, and how proud I am of you and of the stand you are making in that war. You are in a crucial area not only of geography and politics but of history. Hemingway or Malraux or Tolstoy or anybody else was never more central to a crucial situation than you are now. When you come out of this, a legend will come with you: the legend of what you write, which will be also what you have lived and what you have dared and surmounted and made possible in the way of understanding. That is heroic, son; nothing else. Believe me, my blood and your mother's must be good, for it is in you and has produced you. Just don't spill any of it. Keep your head down and your vest on; keep your cool and your good sense, and your talent will do the rest.

Things are well here, though many projects must constantly be attended to. Kevin was accepted into medical school at Charleston, we are back in the house at Litchfield, and Debba and I are feeling okay. I am on sabbatical, but with the work-load life is more strenuous than when I had the relief—maybe comic relief—of teaching. Stephen Spender is filling in for me this semester, and seems to like it here well enough.

I'll sign off, and send more love and pride.

Yours,
Dad

P.S. I enclose a picture of me + Tucky the Hunter on that illustrious occasion when we went after Bigfoot, here in the back yard.

To: Paul Hemphill   CC, Emory University
                                      Litchfield Plantation
                                      Pawleys Island, S.C.

January 16, 1981

Dear Paul:

Your book just came, and I read the whole thing straing through last night. Some of it is quite marvelous, especially the war pieces and the piece on Wallenda. A compilation of journal and magazine pieces depends for its effec-tiveness largely on variety, and you have plenty of that. I am interested in this not only because you wrote it and because it is good, but because two other things are also true. The first of these is that some of my friends—close friends like Mailer and George Plimpton and Willie Morris, and acquaintance-friends like Marshall Frady and Harry Crews—are always hammering at me and at everybody else who will listen on their main philosophical thought regarding what they do, which is the "higher journalism," the journalism of sensibility. Another of these, Tom Wolfe, was here last year and stayed with us a few days, and he is quite convinced that the real literature of our time is in this form. He may be right, for he is an exciting writer, as are all these others, and as you are, who belong right up there with the best of them. The second considera-tion I mentioned is that my oldest son is a journalist, doing exactly the same thing; he is in El Salvador, right in the middle of all that high-speed random lead, and he feels the same way as Mailer and the others do. The form has de-veloped its own set of standards and techniques. The danger of the "journalism of high sensibility" is that it is already tending to run to a formula in which the main ingredients are over-heavy and obvious irony and self-consciously colloquial diction. Too much of either one of these, or both of them at the same time, wear out very quickly, and the formulaic quality tends to sub-merge the individual sensitivity that brings this genre, at its best, close to the art that Plimpton and Wolfe and the others want to make of it. Among these writers, you are certainly among the top-flight, if not indeed the best of all of them already, or surely potentially so. But the dangers of any literary ap-proach, any literary form, are real dangers and are peculiar to that form. The avoidance of them or the turning of them into virtues are the main tasks that must be faced. And that's the end to <u>that</u> catechism!

I also return the poem you sent over a few weeks ago, with some tentative edits and suggestions. Keep me informed as to the progress of the thing; I feel I have a stake now.

My best to everyone in your house: or houses, maybe I should say: your pub-lishing house and your real house.

Yours,

To: Stuart Woods   CC, Emory University
                                                         4620 Lelia's Court
                                                         Columbia, S.C. 29206

                                                         January 26, 1981

Dear Mr. Woods:

I have been in communication with your editor, and I also have your own letter of January 21st. I am sorry to be so churlish about all this, but your op-
portunism did seem extreme, as does your self-abasement now. There is no
need for any of this. Though I was not able to give your book a publicity
quote, I do feel that I have some sort of stake in it, and will be interested to
know what happens to it. But you really should not go to strangers asking for
favors, and you should not name-drop, particularly when there is any chance
of there being sexual inferences. On the other hand, anyone who can sail
across the ocean by himself has got some of the human qualities I most admire; I have often wanted to do such myself, but never will be able to, I am
quite sure.

Anyway, don't be bothered by anything concerning me. If your book is good—
and your editor thinks it is—it will make its way without my endorsement.
                                                         Sincerely,

To: Shaye Areheart   CC, Emory University
                                                         4620 Lelia's Court
                                                         Columbia, S.C. 29206

                                                         February 5, 1981

Dear Shaye:

I send along some Atlanta publicity about the <u>Wilderness</u> book. It seems to
me fairly mediocre as an article and seems to give the reader the idea that if he
doesn't like local genre painting, he won't like the book. But this is something
Hubert insisted on doing, largely in his own self-interest and with some
string-pulling involved, I suspect, and I guess it is all right, and to the general
good of the book. At any rate, it's too late to do anything about it now except
to hope that the article will stir some sort of curiosity in the venture, and sell
something besides Hubert's pictures. As to my part, I am going ahead and

writing the book much in the style of <u>Jericho</u>: incidents, scenes, people, and so on. I think my part of it will be pretty good, but of course I don't know how others will react to it. The novel is coming along well. I just finished a long section dealing with Cahill's early life. It is called "The Air-Frame," and I'll send it to you in a few days. Would you coordinate with Theron and Hugh as to the advisability of publishing this and maybe some other sections of the novel in magazines? People are asking, and I'd like to know what you and Theron think.

There is a favor you can do for me, if you would. A blind writer from Illinois named Gary Adelman is a friend of mine, and has a manuscript somewhere at Doubleday. He is a very deserving guy, blind, with terrible diabetes, and in addition to all that has just had a kidney transplant given to him by his 65-year-old <u>mother</u>, of all things. He has played in gruesome luck all his life; the worst I know, in fact. He has a manuscript there called <u>Smiler</u>, and it is in the hands, or maybe <u>was</u> in the hands, of an editor there named Roy Wandelmaier. I would much appreciate it if you would run this manuscript down and have a look at it. I can't of course recommend publication or anything of that sort, for I have not even seen the manuscript. But I would like to assure Adelman that someone up there has at least read the material. That is really all I can ask you to do, but I do hope that you will be able to do it, and write him, at the University of Illinois English Department at Urbana, what you think of it. That would be a great service to me, since I drew heavily on Gary's diabetic history and his blindness for details in <u>Alnilam</u>; in fact, it was he who suggested the business about the gold lines going across the occluding vision of Cahill, which device is now, by the way, actually being used by doctors (two of them anyway!) in their diagnosis of some kinds of diabetic blindness! Anyway, please <u>do</u> run down the manuscript of <u>Smiler</u>, see what you think, and drop Gary a note about it. That would be good.

Work is progressing well here, though we have had to travel some to defray expenses in the summer, when I am not on salary. Most of the March issue of <u>Poetry</u> will be devoted to five poems from <u>Puella</u>, together with a long essay by Dave Smith on the work I have done since coming with Doubleday in 1970. The <u>Paris Review</u> will print "The Lyric Beasts" in its 25th anniversary number, and I will probably bring out some of the others with <u>The New Yorker</u>, <u>Harper's</u>, <u>The Atlantic</u>, and maybe some other places. So publicity should be good. A couple of books about my work should appear about the same time as <u>Puella</u>, and all this should contribute to the interest.

Incidentally, thank you for whatever part you played in getting the first royalty check for The Strength of Fields to me. Since I never did get an advance, it was good to have royalty payment from copy one. The sales are quite gratifying, and I am most pleased at the way in which Doubleday handled the distribution and publicity.

What is the story on the boxed Zodiac? Is that project still on? Or what? Do let me know about this because since the announcement collectors and other weird folk have been asking.

One other thing: The Esquire April issue will carry an article of mine about why I live in South Carolina. It is harmless enough, and some of it is funny, I think. Matt's Harcourt Brace—BC Books is going to make a little gift book out of it, and I'll see that you get one when it is printed.

Let me know about these matters as soon as you can. I'd like that a lot.

Ever,

To: Bruce Weigl   CC, Emory University
                                                    4620 Lelia's Court
                                                    Columbia, S.C. 29206

March 4, 1981

Dear Bruce:

Thank you for your letter, and for the exceptional news about the book. Yes, I like the title very much, and I congratulate you and Terry and Dave—any or all responsible—for thinking it up. It is exactly what I intend, and what my writing intends, and you could not have put the whole thing better. As to format, I think THE IMAGINATION AS GLORY should be presented starkly as the title, and "Essays on the Poetry," etc. should be printed as kind of a bold but smaller subtitle. Presented that way, the book would jump out at the prospective buyer more quickly, I think, in all those bookstores, or at least in whichever ones end up selling it. Believe me, I look forward to all this with the greatest interest, and I hope that you will keep me posted as to plans, dates, and any and all information about publication.

You ask for some pages of autobiography, to enable you to complete the biographical note. I can't think of anything I could say beyond what I have already said in <u>Self-Interviews</u>, in the biographical information in <u>Babel to Byzantium</u> and <u>Sorties</u>, and in the various things that have been written about me by Dave, Lieberman, and others. If it will be of any use to you in this connection, I enclose a standard vita sheet, to supplement what information you may already have.

Again, thank you for all the things you have done. This should be a smashing volume, even if I do say so myself, and will be most helpful to many people. It is coming at a good time, too, for various publishers are arranging to reissue all of my previous books, including the earliest, in new formats, <u>Puella</u> will appear in the fall, and there will be a lot of publicity, opinions pro and con (but all, assuredly, loud), and other attendant ruckus. Our book will be part of this, and I am delighted that this will be so.

Let me hear from you when you have a chance. Debba sends love, and so do I.

Ever,

To: James Atlas

CC, Emory University
4620 Lelia's Court
Columbia, S.C. 29206

March 6, 1981

Dear Mr. Atlas:

I should like to ask some curious advice of you, and inquire as to whether you might like to help out in some way with a project which will either come to a great deal of something or a great deal of nothing, but which will come, either way.

The point is this. The producer Jerome Hellman, who did <u>Midnight Cowboy</u> and <u>Coming Home</u> among other films, wishes me to write a huge film for him and United Artists, and preliminary discussion has already taken place. The reason I am in on this is not <u>Deliverance</u>, as one might well suppose it to be, but the fact that I did an adaptation for NBC a few years ago of Jack London's <u>Call of the Wild</u>, which received some prizes and other such notice, and because Hellman is fascinated by the Yukon, the Klondike, the era and the atmosphere of that time. Though this is not grammatical, you may grasp what I mean when I say that such is the fascination of the period for him, that Hellman is willing to devote literally years of his time to bringing the project to completion.

Early on, the question of the motivation of the central character came into play: why would a certain person, a protagonist, want to go up there with the thousands of others who did? The motivation, as we see it at this point, is that this motivation is provided by a young fellow he meets in Seattle while he is there on a lumber transaction. This second character is the pivot of the story, and he is based to a large if not exclusive extent on Delmore Schwartz, even to the point of calling him Delmore. From what you know of the Schwartz family, of his literary executors, and of the other conditions and people pertaining to him, do you think there would be any objection to our doing the story this way? Though I met Schwartz only once, when he was very far gone, I have been as much fascinated by him as Bellow has, or Dwight MacDonald has, or many others have. His super-intelligent, enthusiastic, creatively crazy personality is just right for this part, and if I were to tell you the actors ("stars") we have already turned down for the part you would accuse me of fantasy. Anyway I would much appreciate your letting me know if you can think of any objection to my going ahead with the project on these terms: of anyone who might object, or any grounds. Believe me, the thing as I am writing it is intended entirely as a tribute, you may well believe.

Let me know what you think of all this, and if you might also be interested in giving me a little advice on Schwartz from time to time. I don't know whether I could get you paid for this, for it is a little early to determine such things, but I probably could. Anyway, we'll see, if you like.

My best to you, and to whatever work you are doing.

Sincerely,

To: Saul Bellow

CC, Emory University
4620 Lelia's Court
Columbia, S.C. 29206

March 6, 1981

Dear Mr. Bellow:

Though all I remember of you personally—and doubtless more than you remember of me—occurred a good many years back when we were both on some sort of Rockefeller committee to give money to other writers, I like many others have followed your work with great interest, fascination, and joy, and on the basis of these general credentials would like to ask some running advice of you, if you have time.

I have entered into an arrangement with United Artists, and with the director and producer Jerome Hellman, to write what the trade papers call an "epic" film, this one dealing with the Yukon and the Klondike gold rush. United Artists has given Hellman and me the money to go ahead with this, and it will be done, one way or the other.

Where you come into this is that I am quite intentionally basing one of the characters on Delmore Schwartz, and if you want to see how Delmore would influence and perhaps dominate the Klondike in 1898-99, you will have to see my movie, which is scheduled for 1983. As the author of <u>Humbolt's Gift</u>, which is surely the best book ever written by a writer about another writer, and quite possibly your best book as well (if I may judge), I wonder if I might ask you from time to time for some information about Schwartz's personality, his kind of imagination, characteristic attitudes, and sayings of his? This is only a preliminary sort of venture, here, a preliminary sort of letter, but I thought I might as well lay it on you early, for I am drawing heavily, even in the first stages, on your version of Delmore. I hope this is all right, for if it works out as I intend, the film will be the second-best tribute to Schwartz that anybody has yet conceived, and with luck may even be in the same class with the first-best.

Let me know what you think of all this, and I will be guided accordingly. Meanwhile, thank you for your work, and your existence.

Sincerely,

To: Stanley Burnshaw   **TLS, University of Texas at Austin**

4620 Lelia's Court
Columbia, S.C. 29206
March 10, 1981

Dear Stanley,

It is wonderful to hear from you, and know that your big book has a good publisher. As to the baffling business of Sandy Richardson and his demise and the probability of his being at present here or there, anywhere or nowhere, I am as confused as anybody. I hear rumors that he is setting up his own imprint, but I have no details, and I don't even know whether this is true or not. But I like what I know about Horizon Press. I have a whole row of books of Herbert Read's that they did, and I have been most grateful for many years that the people there were so intelligent and responsible as to issue these and keep them in print. I'll look forward eagerly to your book, and will say what I can about it anywhere and everywhere, you may be sure.

It is good of you to inquire about the surgery I had done in Seattle last May. This was a seventeen-hour thoracic "correction" for enlarged hiatal hernia, which means that the diaphragm closing off my lower internal organs from the upper ones had split, with the consequence that three quarters of my stomach was up in my chest, narrowing down the passage from my lower esophagus into my stomach, so that food could not pass through—and right at the end, not even liquids—and I was starving to death and experiencing very great and increasing pain. I labored as I could to finish the semester, for I didn't want to leave my kids hanging, and finally did finish the semester, went out to Idaho for an honorary degree not so much for the degree but because the University of Idaho paid for the trip, and then gravitated on out to Seattle for the operation just as Mount St. Helens exploded. Regarding this last, the mountain blew, quite literally, when our plane was right <u>over</u> it, nonplussing the pilot, who said, in a shaken, exalted voice over the speaker, "Come on over to the left side of the airplane, folks! Bring your cameras! You won't see <u>this</u> every day!" Anyway, after all that and many other things, and after ten months of recuperation and many tests, the operation seems to have been successful, and now I'm eating at a great rate and working at various new and old projects, which I'll tell you about later on, if you like.

I'm sorry you won't be able to get by Columbia on your way to the Vineyard, but we'll catch up with each other sooner or later, and I hope sooner.

Meanwhile, we are well. Debba is expecting a baby in May, and we are delighted with the new life, the new world, the new human race.

Love,

Jim

To: Adrien Stoutenburg

CC, Emory University
4620 Lelia's Court
Columbia, S.C. 29206

March 10, 1981

Dear Ms. Stoutenburg:

Twelve years ago, when I was one of the judges for the Pulitzer Prize, along with W.H. Auden and Phyllis McGinley, your name and your book came up. Or at least they came up between Auden and myself, for Miss McGinley was in the hospital with a broken jaw, having fallen in a bathtub accident. Though Richard Howard was finally decided upon as the recipient of the prize, I have been over your poems many times since those days, and hardly ever over Mr. Howard's, and I thought I should write a note to you and tell you how much pleasure your work has given and gives me, and how very fine I think it is. For my money, the best women poets writing now are yourself, Mary Oliver of Provincetown, and Margaret Atwood from Canada. Your vehement interest in the natural world is extremely powerful, appealing, and imaginative; just what is needed right now. I won't go on and on, for I am not given to gush, but will simply get this in the mail hoping that it will establish relations with one who feels as you do, and writes some things himself.

Let me hear from you if you are inclined. But that shall be as you wish.

Sincerely,

To: Claire Curtin

CC, Emory University
4620 Lelia's Court
Columbia, S.C. 29206

March 19, 1981

Dear Claire Curtin:

Thank you for your letter, for the information about the royalties, and for the royalties themselves, which I look forward to getting with the greatest of all pleasures.

Could you send me seven of the tapes at the artists' price of $3 apiece, and bill me for them? I'll send a check back right away.

Sure, I'll do anything I can to help sell the tape, or indeed to help sell any and all of your other poets, as well. Since I do a good many readings, it strikes me that you might want to contact the booksellers and record outlets in the various localities where I read, for my publishers usually have plentiful stocks of my books on hand, and I keep busy signing them. If you could have tapes and records at these places, I could sell just as many of them as I do books, and perhaps even more. If you think this is a good idea, let me know, and I will swing with you, in whatever direction.

I have written a lot of stuff since my last recording with you, and we could make a very lively new record, I have no doubt. The new book of poems, Puella, is due from Doubleday next fall. These are about and dedicated to my wife Deborah, and are subtitled "Her girlhood, male-imagined." There is already a good deal of interest in and controversy about these, and we may want to tap in on the situation as it develops further. Incidentally, five of the poems are featured in the current (March) issue of Poetry, and you might want to have a look. Also, there is a piece in the April Esquire which has been published, already, by Harcourt Brace and sold out in the first three days. This could also be part of a new recording, and if we make it, and if you will furnish me with the name and sales figures of your other bestselling poets (Dylan Thomas excepted! With him it might take a little longer!) I will guarantee to break them within six months. Now that's arrogance, is it not? But then, I was never a believer in false modesty. Or even in true modesty, if the truth were known.

Get back to me on all this as soon as you can, and we'll swing.

Best,

To: Ron Sharp[9]

CC, Emory University
4620 Lelia's Court
Columbia, S.C. 29206

May 6, 1981

Dear Ron:

Thanks so much for the note. My editor was here last week, and I talked to him about the possibility of publishing some of the sections from the novel in

9. Editor of Kenyon Review.

magazines, and he said he would talk it over with <u>his</u> superiors at Doubleday, and with my agent, and with God knows how many other people as to the advisability of bringing some of these things out. When these people give me some kind of reading on the situation, I will let you know. One of the difficulties, though, of printing a long section of the book like "A Wheedling of Knives" is that the page has to be split into two sections, one to represent how the blind protagonist interprets—or "visualizes"—the scene he is in, and the column down the right side of the page showing what really is there. This is a curious format, I know, but it is the way I want to present the story. As I say, the format might present some difficulties with one of the longer sections, but there are a couple of shorter ones that don't use the split-page "system." There is one, especially, called "The Air-Frame," that might be suitable, and if you like I'll try to shake it loose for you.

As to some possible poetry, everything I have in the way of poetry is part of <u>Puella</u>, which Doubleday will do in the fall. If you could arrange to print one or two of these before the book comes out, I could let you have them, or I am almost dead certain that I could. Let me know if your publication schedule could accommodate this, and I will be guided by what you tell me.

Meanwhile, my very best to you, and to Fred and Perry and the others we met when we were up there. Debba and I remember the visit very fondly, and even are thinking seriously about naming the <u>second</u> child Kenyon, if it is a boy, though this first one will be named Talbot, regardless of sex. We'll let you know about the baby in a couple of weeks, when it is due to be here.

Debba sends love, and so do I.

                                             Ever,

To: Adrien Stoutenburg   CC, Emory University
                                              4620 Lelia's Court
                                              Columbia, S.C. 29206

                                              April 1, 1981

Dear Ms. Stoutenburg:

Thank you indeed for your letter, and for the things you say about my work. Most of the poems you mention were written long ago, and it is good to see that they still seem to have life, at least in the minds of a few people.

Though I had no notion you knew him, I have had some letters from David Slavitt, who also admires your work as you no doubt know, and who tells me that you have been ill, have been operated on, and now seem to be recovered. Believe me, I know the grisliness of operations, for I had a huge one last May, under the stone snows of Mount St. Helens, and am only just now getting back to full strength, or something like it. I hope you are all right, for we must have more poems from you; a lot. In my opinion the three best women poets these days are yourself, the Canadian gal Margaret Atwood, and a strange lady recessed in Provincetown named Mary Oliver, and of these three you are by far the best. Anyone who can say that she rode in a red tire on a post "as in the rings of Saturn" can do anything. As I say, we must have more, or at least I must.

Sure, I'd love to have your Greenwich Mean Time, as well as Heroes, Advise Us, if you have an extra copy. It is odd, this dual interest in astronomy, for that has been a lifelong passion of mine, and I enclose a little offprint of a current article in Esquire which tells of the connection between the stars, GMT, and where I live. I hope you enjoy it, and I hope you can visit here sometime and participate in some of this. I'd like that a lot, believe me.

Write again when you feel like it. But that shall be as you wish.

                                                             Sincerely,

P.S. I enclose also a recent publicity photo, showing how I appear when I read my animal and military poems.

To: William Pritchard   CC, Emory University
                                                        4620 Lelia's Court
                                                     Columbia, S.C. 29206

                                                              May 1, 1981

Dear Mr. Pritchard:

Oxford Press recently sent me a load of books, among which was your Lives of the Modern Poets. I read through these with not much interest, though some of the other names were more familiar to me than yours, but when I came to your book I developed interest fast, and plenty of it. This is one of the very few letters I have ever written to an author I don't know personally, but I did want to register with you how very good—how useful, how insightful, how much the kind of book we need, the kind of approach to poetry we need—this is. I note in passing, also, your remarks on my Robinson introduction, and am glad to see that you find me mostly right. I would point out, though, that you are confusing two entirely different issues when you talk about my insistence on Robinson's "speculation upon possibilities," which is an <u>attitude</u> of Robinson's, and then turn around and say that "the poems' rhythms show no such uncertainty," and so on. There is no point in my belaboring this, but surely you see the difference between <u>what</u> is being said and the prosodic means by <u>which</u> it is said.

But this is all mere carping on my part, which is not at all in keeping with the real purpose of the letter, which is to give you my purest vote of confidence. You really do care deeply about poetry, and though I disagree—healthily, I hope—on a good many points, I had rather posterity listened to you talk about these poets than to me, for I change opinions fast and often, and posterity needs more steadiness than I can give or want to give.

One final thing that might interest you. I note the reference to Groucho Marx on the bottom of page 99, and felt how odd it was—truly odd indeed: crazy, unforeseeable—that I once asked the great Original Witness of modern poetry—no, of <u>all</u> poetry—what Robinson was like. Louis Untermeyer replied, without hesitation, "Well, he was like Groucho Marx, only taller. And drunker, or just as."

Accept my sincere congratulations on your book. I hope some day to be able to tell you this looking you straight in the eyes, as such things should be done.
                                                            Sincerely,

To: Stanley Burnshaw   **TLS, University of Texas at Austin**

                                            4620 Lelia's Court
                                            Columbia, S.C. 29206
                                            May 13, 1981
Dear Stanley,

It is wonderful to hear from you, and especially to hear the details about <u>The Refusers</u>. I am studying out, now, what I might do to be helpful, and I guess the first thing I need to do is to read it. At this point the difficulty that presents itself is not whether I will furnish you with a jacket quote, for I will certainly do that, but whether I have the background and the knowledge of your subject matter to make it the supremely effective quote that I would like it to be, that it <u>must</u> be. As soon as I get the galleys I will read straight through them and take notes, and maybe I will be able to come up with something worthy of being used in connection with the "capstone" of the writing career of one such as you. Well, we'll see what can be done. But know that you can count on me. I'll do my best.

The subject of <u>The Refusers</u> is of great interest to me right now for other reasons, even, than that you wrote it. I am writing a new film—one with a huge budget and almost infinite resources—and as I have conceived the story, one of the two main characters, the one on whom the main events turn, is a young Jewish fellow from the Bronx: a wild-eyed, enthusiastic, likable, exasperating and very Jewish <u>tummler</u> very much like what I remember—but mostly what I have heard—of Delmore Schwartz. My producer is Jerome Hellman, who did the much-awarded-to <u>Coming Home</u>, <u>Midnight Cowboy</u>, and other films of note, and he is much taken with this character, and wants to build the film almost exclusively around him. I don't know how the final balance will come out, but I do know that in developing this character I must delve more deeply than I have ever had occasion to do into the Jewish experience in this country, particularly that of the Jewish immigrants of the late nineteenth and early twentieth centuries. To this end I am not only reading all of Delmore, some of which is extremely good and some not so good, but historical work like Irving Howe's <u>World of Our Fathers</u>, which has certainly been a revelation to me, especially about the first-generation of Eastern European Jews transplanted to New York City. I don't want to bore you with all this, but would only like to indicate that I may well draw on your knowledge of Judaism, particularly the conditions and attitudes of the Jewish intellectual inclining to poetry, whether he is a <u>tummler</u> like Delmore—or like my character—or not. I'll let you know how the project goes forward as it develops. I went out to Hollywood in February and Hellman and I spent two weeks, 9 to 5 every day—and sometimes longer—working out a story that suited us both. We have 1000 pages of transcribed notes, and still the story is at least to some degree nebulous, though the possibilities are exciting, or at least I think so. I'll tell you more about this later on, but right now there is a big Writers' Strike on and not much further can be done until all that is settled. But we have begun the thing, and eventually you'll see it.

Debba and I are now within two weeks of changing the human race by adding to it the element it has lacked from the beginning: namely, a child consisting of us. The target date is the 27th of this month, and everything is ready. Biology itself is in the final stages of readiness, and the Little Hero will come forth, as they say, "on or around" that date. Believe me, we'll let you know.

My love to Leda, and keep plenty for yourself. Keep in touch, and we'll bring all projects to great climaxes. Keep well, my old friend.

Ever,
Jim

P.S. I enclose a recent publicity photograph showing how I appear when I read my animal and military poems.

To: Meg Stocks

CC, Emory University
4620 Lelia's Court
Columbia, S.C. 29206

May 25, 1981

Dear Ms. Stocks:

Thank you indeed for your unexpected and most welcome letter concerning my old nurse Mamie Doster. As I remember—and I have only a very few images of Miss Mamie that I remember—she was an old lady who had spent much of her life working in textile mills. She was the only servant around our place who was white; as you know, my mother was an invalid, or a semi-invalid, with an acute heart condition, and this necessitated hiring other people to do the work around the place, even though the Depression hit when I was six years old, and we had to scramble in order to pay wages. The main thing I remember about Miss Mamie Doster was that she rocked—and rocked us—my younger brother Tom and me—with a peculiar motion the likes of which I had never experienced before and have not seen since, either. I was later told that this was inculcated by the work she did for years in the mills, and that may well have been, for even when she was not rocking us she was rocking herself in the same manner. She was a very kindly woman, and loved us very much, as we did her.

As for my mother, she was a gentle, affectionate, humorous woman who lived for her children and would do anything for them, give them anything, live for them, suffer for them, die for them. She was very proud of all of us, and worried continually about us. I left the family in my late teens, and went away to school and then into the Air Force, and never really lived in it again from the age of 17 or 18, always coming back as a kind of visitor. But one's early years are strong in the memory, and my mother's kindness not only to the members of our family but to other people—her imaginative and very caring and also very practical kindness—remains with me as the best example that I possess of unqualified and continuous human goodness.

Please tell your friend Dorris that I am glad to hear of her, and that I hope she is well and living happily in life. I also hope that you are, also, for your thoughtfulness in writing to me.

Sincerely,

To: William Childress

CC, Emory University
4620 Lelia's Court
Columbia, S.C. 29206

May 27, 1981

Dear Chilly,

Thank you so much for your letter, and for your good wishes for Bronwen. She is ten days old—today, the 27th, is the date on which she was actually <u>supposed</u> to be born—and she is lively and lovely, and much a credit to Debba's and my astrological mix of stars and genes; you'll like her.

Before I chat anymore, let me get to your "business" question, having to do with your <u>Sports Afield</u> project. The longer rattlesnake piece was not a poem but an article which I did for the <u>Esquire Super Sports</u> issue of October 1974. It was then called "Blowjob on a Rattlesnake," and starts on page 177 of that issue. If I had a better machine and if the print were not so small, I would Xerox it for you, but it may be too long for your purposes to begin with, and if you want to have a look at it, any library would have the issue in its back file. The piece was also printed as a small gift edition with the original title, which is <u>The Enemy from Eden</u>, restored. This is obtainable still, I think, from the Lord John Press in Northridge, California. The one man operation's name is Herb Yellin*, and I think he has a few copies left. I'd like to send you one of my own, but I only have one, and it is inscribed to Debba. The other possibility is a poem I did a long time ago, back in the early sixties, and published in the Texas Quarterly for autumn, 1963, pages 158-160. I no longer have a copy of this and only vaguely remember it, but if you like, you can have a look, and if you think it is worth reprinting you are certainly welcome to it. It is called "Blowgun and Rattlesnake."

As to payment, get in touch with my agent, Theron Raines, 475 Fifth Avenue, NYC, 10017, or (212) 684-5160. He is always ready to take money, being of that breed.

One more personal note. Though I am not familiar with the format of Sports Afield, I am with the work of Theodore Roethke, particularly the poems in his last—and posthumous—book called The Far Field. I remember suggesting that he call it by that title when we were sitting in a bar in Seattle on the way to one of his periodic incarcerations in the sanitarium there. As I recall, the manuscript was then going by the title of Dance On, Dance On, Dance On, and I told Ted that the poems were some of his best, but that he really should call the book The Far Field, which I thought was much more echt (sp?) Roethke. At the time he seemed to dissent, and then died. But the story has a happy ending, for when the book appeared it was indeed called The Far Field, and won the National Book Award. I know, because my own book, Helmets, was one of the defeated contenders. Ted would have liked that a lot, and I like it too. I'll close now, so as to get this in the mail.

My love to all your people, and, since I haven't gotten
Ever,

I enclose a new photograph, taken at Kenyon by a man named J. Phil Samuell, for whatever publicity or personal use, including target practice, it may serve.

*Herb Yellin, 19073 Los Alamos, Northridge, California

To: Richard Blessing   **CC, Emory University**
                                                   4620 Lelia's Court
                                                   Columbia, S.C. 29206

May 29, 1981

Dear Mr. Blessing:

Your book on Roethke came in here a few days ago with a lot of other books on the same and similar subjects—poetry, biographies of poets, anthologies, this and that. I read some of these without much interest, but when I got to your book I had <u>plenty</u> of interest, for I developed it fast. I knew Ted pretty well during the last year of his life, and I thought a great deal of him. I also knew Allen Seager for the last few years of <u>his</u> life, when he was working on Ted's biography and dying of lung cancer. I wrote a couple of articles about Ted, and one about Ted and Allen, but I haven't had much use for most of the stuff that is written about Ted's poetry, or about his curious, loveable and exasperating personality. And now along comes your book. Surely it is the most sensible as well as the most imaginative thing I have ever read not only about Ted's actual poems but about the attitudes that went into them. As I have been saying in recent articles, I think that the path of instinctualism and an "unthinking" approach to experience is going to be the best of the directions being offered now; much better, for damn sure, than the mundane cigarette butts and scraping-the-dried-egg-off-the-plate school of naturalism and nullity that so many people are enrolling in, in the name of "reality," and what is." The difference between Lowell on one hand and Roethke on the other is striking; everything in Lowell closes down on the solipsistic person of the poet, and everything in Roethke opens out into the world. Well, I won't go on and on, but will just register with you how much I enjoyed your book, and how good it is.

Incidentally, the latest issue of <u>Poetry Northwest</u> has just come in, and I immediately read your two contributions, which are good indeed. Let me register <u>that</u>, too!

I can't write on and on in this immoderate vein, as I'd like to do, but I did want to let you know how your work—in both critical prose and poetry—"strikes a contemporary."

My very best to you. Keep on!

                                                   Sincerely yours,

To: Shaye Areheart

CC, Emory University
4620 Lelia's Court
Columbia, S.C. 29206

June 2, 1981

Dear Shaye,

Just to catch you up. I had an awfully nice visit with Hugh down here a couple of weeks ago. I am much impressed with his grasp of the situation regarding the novel. The important thing at this stage, where I am able to work on it more or less uninterruptedly, is to make sure that the scaffolding, the skeleton, the armature of the story is right, for I dislike the prospect of spending a great deal of time trying to work out a story line that might not be as good as another one I might have used, and might have come on if I had considered a sufficient number of alternatives. To be specific: I am limiting the action to an exact week, Monday to Monday. I have itemized the events of each day's action, so that I have a clear working knowledge of a progression, of something going <u>from</u> something <u>to</u> something. I recommend this to any novelist, by the way; there is a great deal of assurance that one gets from knowing in advance that something will work out. I am proceeding in this way to a far greater degree than I did with <u>Deliverance</u>, though it was only after I had begun to structure the novel in a similar fashion—after I got down here to Columbia, actually—that <u>Deliverance</u> began to take on the sense of the inevitability of the events that it needed. At any rate, I am writing, at the rate of about 4000 words a day, a kind of summation of all the action, all the days, all the scenes of the novel. I will be through doing this in about a week, or certainly within two, and I will then lay copies of this extended prospectus, which itself will run to a couple of hundred pages, on you and Hugh and Ken, and when I have your comments, and we are all satisfied, I will then proceed to draft the novel in what will be virtually its final form. As you know, I already have about 250 pages that I have sent to you, but some— I hope not a great deal, but surely some—of this will need to be recast to fit in with what I am doing in the chapters that I am in the process of drafting. This seems a good modus to me, for all interested parties will know how the story is set up, and will be able to offer suggestions before I put in a lot of time writing something that might have been disagreed with earlier, and that time saved.

Let me know what you think of this, and I'll do what I can to swing with you.

Meanwhile I have this invoice from Doubleday having to do with the boxed copies of <u>The Zodiac</u>—which, incidentally, I am very much pleased with and very happy to have. But I should think that these should be author's copies; certainly it seems odd to be charged for a new edition of one's book, and apparently charged at the gift price, too! I stayed up all one night in New York signing these for Sandy because he said that there was a big rush for the signatures. I was glad to do this, though it was exhausting, and now, a couple of years later, the books and boxes come in, together with a bill. Again, as I say, this is rather odd, don't you think? It is especially odd to me, considering that Franklin Mint paid me $2 a signature for signing their edition of <u>Deliverance</u>, and I have been told that it is the going rate for gift editions. Looked at that way, it might be supposed that Doubleday in fact owes me $1000, and if that is true, I would be amenable to your taking out the $150 from that sum, and sending the rest on to me. That is absurd, of course, but so, it seems to me, is the present charge. See what you can find out about this, and if the company still thinks I should pay for the books—and boxes—I will be happy to do so, though this would not seem to me to be correct. See what you can find out, and also let me know how this gift edition is being offered, what the marketing plans are, and the rest of the logistical part of this particular operation.

Otherwise I couldn't be more pleased with Doubleday and the people there I am working with. All seems good, and I think it is a first rate idea of yours to bring out <u>Puella</u> on Bronwen's birthday, the 17th of May. That is just fine; better than fine. The added time will also give me a chance to publish the remaining poems in various periodicals. The July issue of a new, brash large-circulation outfit in Texas called <u>The Lone Star Review</u>, is doing the "Tapestry and Sail" poem, together with a long interview. <u>The Kenyon Review</u> wants to print the remaining few poems that have not yet been spoken for, and I am relieved to be able to tell these people there to go ahead, without so much rush.

The personal news here is still very good. Bronwen is almost three weeks into the mission now, and all the signs and doctors say that she is doing just great. She is a very pretty little girl, and almost no trouble. People have been very interested and kind, but no one more so than your mother. I hope you will find your own way to tell her how much we appreciate her presence.

Sorry to make this so long, but do get back to me in a few days and cover the points I make here. Meanwhile, I'll be going forward on the basis I outlined above.

                                        Ever,

To: Katie Pauley

CC, Emory University
4620 Lelia's Court
Columbia, S.C. 29206

June 4, 1981

Dear Ms. Pauley:

Thank you for your letter, and for sending along the poems, which I like. The "Roughneck" one is the best by far, though that is not the right title for it, being too self-assertive and emancipated, which is to say class-conscious. There is plenty wrong with it. The second line of the second stanza is first-rate, though, and the evocation of the piston of the oil rig as the male organ, a comparison which ordinarily would be obvious and trite, is not, here. In the last line, the word "liquid" is wrong for lightning, but pure is not; it is just exactly right, and good, and better than good.

It seems to me that you have the seeds of grace as a poet, or some of them anyway, and I'm glad you like Emily Dickinson, for there are some things that one can learn from her. Personally I never learned anything from her except to do something other than what she does. It is odd about her: no poet shows better in a single piece, or loses more when read in bulk. Yet, even when she is read in bulk, she always gives _something_; even in the weakest, most self-imitative poems there is always something inimitable and inevitable, something no one but she could have thought of. So you should read all of her, and the letters too. They are all worth a lot, because she is worth a lot.

Yes, that is good news about my daughter. She has been here for three weeks now, and it is wonderful to have a child in the house, after so many years. Her name is Bronwen, which is Gaelic (Welsh Gaelic) for White-breasted, which she certainly is. Thus the White Goddess comes among us, thank God without Robert Graves.

Write when you feel like it, and tell Siegel that I wish him good luck when he meets the Whale of Light, known as the Great American Critical Judgment— or maybe the Whale of Light is the public. I don't know. Anyway, wish him luck, and keep some for yourself.

Sincerely,

To: Radcliffe Squires   **TLS, Washington University Library**

4620 Lelia's Court
Columbia, S.C. 29206
June 9, 1981

Dear Jim,

How good the stuff is! I am so very sorry that I have waited even this long
to write you about <u>Gardens of the World</u>. I don't know of any poetry anywhere—Lord how these generations struggle with the Word! Many are called
. . .—that is any better than "Men and horses: Wyoming" or that is as good as
"The first day out from Troy." It seems to me that you are totally remarkable,
and Anne Stevenson is fairly right, but has missed the essential gist, in what
she says on the jacket. I think that the conjunction of the American western
wilderness and the great classical themes of Europe that gets into your poems
is the most totally remarkable thing I know, not only in the poetry that is
being written now, but in that which has already been written, or could be
written, even. The poet who could say <u>When you are cold and wet enough</u>
<u>that / The weight of clothes proves nakedness . . .</u> could say anything, and also
<u>would</u> say anything. I won't go on and on, because I am not given to gush, but
I did want you to know how your poems, your new poems, come over to, get
down into and stay with one who defers to no man—or woman or child or
animal—in his admiration, and in his gratitude for the states of spirit you
have made available.

My best to you, my old friend.

                                        Ever,
                                        Jim

P.S. I wonder if you have news of Frederic Prokosch? I lose these things, these
people. If he is still alive, and if you are in communication with him, please
say hello for me.

To: Senator and Mrs. Strom Thurmond   CC, Emory University
                                                4620 Lelia's Court
                                                Columbia, S.C. 29206

                                                              June 12, 1981
Dear Senator and Mrs. Thurmond:

Thank you very much for the good wishes on the birth of our daughter Bronwen Elaine. This was a considerate and kind human act, an individual act beyond politics and the public arena and simply between people, and that is the
feeling Deborah and I most respond to. Again, you have our warmest thanks,
and Bronwen sends hers too: after her personal thanks to God for being born,
which has to be the first order of business in her new language-noises that
precede language itself, and are better than language, I can assure you—for I
am one of the few who can truly translate those Sounds—that Bronwen also
sends her thanks into the exceedingly bright warmth of your letters to us, and
especially of the one to her—as they say—herself.

Again, thank you both for your good wishes, and we'll hope to see you soon,
under whatever lucky circumstances there may be.

                                                With best wishes,

To: Stanley Burnshaw   TLS, University of Texas at Austin

                                              4620 Lelia's Court
                                              Columbia, S.C. 29206
                                              July 13, 1981

Dear Stanley,

Since Ben Raeburn was not able to get in touch with me in time, I'm glad you
went ahead and edited my quotation yourself. I am very happy with the way
you have set things up. If this pleases you, let's go ahead with it just this way.

I haven't time for the long letter I'd like to write, but just wanted to get this in
the mail so that you and Raeburn will have my final okay on the quotation.
When is publication set for, by the way? You may be sure that I'll be looking
forward to the appearance and reception of The Refusers with the greatest interest in the world.

I want to thank you, Stanley, from the best place in me, for all of the digging you've done for me about the East Side, the Jewish immigrations, the various Jewish practices, names, and all the other materials you've made available. Now if the damned writers' strike would come to some kind of resolution, Hellman and I could move forward on the film. The money and everything else is just sitting there, waiting for the producers and the writers to get some kind of contract agreement on the residual-rates to be paid writers for their part of the home TV market: videotapes, cassettes, discs and all the new stuff. The writers are getting systematically swindled about this, and though I am only tangential to the film industry, I, like the rest of them, would like to get what can be got, so I support the strike, though it won't make any difference in the final outcome whether I did or didn't. Anyway, thank you very much for your help in this first part of The Golgotha Claim, which is my working title for the thing as it is now, and which will doubtless be changed a thousand times before Delmore hits the gold fields.

Please remember me to Helen and Tom Maley, and tell Tom that the sound of his flute is still with me.

Ever,
Jim

To: Richard Howard

CC, Emory University
4620 Lelia's Court
Columbia, S.C. 29206

July 15, 1981

Dear Tex,

It is great to hear from you, and to know of your new plans. I cannot imagine you without thinking of you hard at work on something, interested in something, researching something, bringing something out, or about. I notice a good deal of attention being paid to the new update on Proust, and I remember that at one time you envisioned doing the whole huge thing over again, by yourself. That would have been good, for, though I was raised on the Scott-Moncrieff approach, I have always believed that Moncrieff gave away entirely too much of his notion of Proust's interest in Ruskin, for from what I can make out of the French the sentence-structure of the original is not nearly as involuted as Moncrieff makes it into, or as Ruskin is. Well, this is just byplay on my part, and is meant as a tribute to your energies, for you are the only person I have ever known who not only had the audacity to conceive such a project, but would also have done it, and done it better—much better—than anyone else who attempted it.

But Baudelaire is better for you, even, than Proust would have been. Being a poet, Baudelaire is linear, and this gives another poet a chance to talk about the exquisite inner mechanics of his work. When I was in advertising I read a lot of French at night, and I can say that Baudelaire is one of the only—perhaps the only—poet(s) of whom I have read every word, including the voluminous ones in the Pleiade edition. In keeping with your new project, since I last wrote you, I have gone back and read Enid Starkie's biography (how can biographers dig up all that intimate stuff, such as the fact that B. was attempting to brush his teeth when his last seizure hit him?), and even Sartre's curious evaluation, and an odd new thing called Prince of Clouds. Well, I envy your real involvement with the guy: an involvement that can have a real result, as opposed to my own well-meaning dilettantism. But I look forward with great pleasure to seeing what you do with Baudelaire, and I'll keep reading around to see if I can come up with something that might be of help to you. That would certainly give me what the lay psychiatrists call an outside interest; something to get me away from the endless struggle with my own words, which I understand less and less, but which are more and more exciting, or at least to me.

I checked my back correspondence with David Wevill and his big terrific milkmaid of a wife, and I find that, though they sent Debba and I a congratulatory telegram about Bronnie, they were leaving for Spain almost immediately, on a Guggenheim I am glad to say I helped him get. So I guess you won't be able to see him this trip, after all, but later on, surely. He is worth a lot, I think.

And now something else. I will be in New York for the National Institute meeting on November 12, and at that time I would like, with your permission, to, as they say, "put your name forward." Would this be all right with you? The Institute is full of lesser people than you, and it is hard for me to imagine anyone of my generation who would give the organization more distinction. Let me know if you agree with this idea and later on we can talk about who might best serve as co-sponsors. I remember in the palaver about the Pulitzer Prize the year you got it, that Mr. Auden wanted to make it a provision that the person we selected "be someone who will continue, who will persevere and keep on adding." He asked me if I thought you would do this, and when I told him I certainly did think so, he nodded immediately, and that was it. Auden never made a better choice, and neither did I. All that should be coming into a period for you where you get the recognition you deserve, and the Institute is only one place where this should happen. Let me see what I can do.

My best, as always, and let me hear.

                                                        Ever,

To: John Paul II   CC, Emory University
                                                      4620 Lelia's Court
                                                      Columbia, S.C. 29206

                                                      July 20, 1981

To His Holiness John Paul II:

Though I am not a Catholic, my wife is, and very devout. We have a new little girl, Bronwen, whom we want to raise as a Catholic. We also have a close friend, Michael Allin, whom we would like to he godfather to our daughter. I am quite convinced that, with his sincerity and love of our family, he would be ideal in this role, and for the rest of his life. But our main difficulty is that Michael Allin has never been baptized, and the local priest, here in Columbia, South Carolina, tells us that he cannot be our daughter's godfather because of this. From our standpoint this is regrettable, for if we looked the world over we could, I am sure, find no one so well qualified for this responsible position as Mr. Allin is. If in some way you could find a means by which Mr. Allin might become godfather to my daughter, I would be most grateful. Not knowing the Church doctrines, I am yet convinced that the precepts of Christ—kindness, forbearance and love—which Mr. Allin so perfectly embodies, may move you to intercede on his behalf against those forces which seem determined to keep the lives of my daughter and her proposed godfather from uniting in love, mutual responsibility and delight.

                                                Most sincerely,

To: Walter Clemons

CC, Emory University
4620 Lelia's Court
Columbia, S.C. 29206

July 21, 1981

Dear Walter:

I have been meaning to write to you for some time to tell you how very good I think your reviews are, and the piece you did on Dumas Malone's Jefferson biography gives me a pretext, though really I feel I don't need one, for after all you write a lot of reviews, and I have read them all, or just about, I think. If you'll allow me an unsolicited comment or two, I do just want to say that it seems to me that the best thing about your approach to criticism and reviewing is the largeness and receptiveness of your mind, or what I would be more inclined to call your "spirit." This willingness to meet the books you review on their own terms—or at least what they think their own terms are—is quite remarkable in our age of smallmindedness, and though you have plenty of reservations about some aspects of the works you deal with, the general effect of your writing is that of intelligent friendliness. This is a very great plus, and it is for this quality that I always turn to the book section of <u>Newsweek</u> first. I have read only a few biographies of the length of Malone's Jefferson, but on your recommendation I will certainly try this one. To me, admittedly deficient in my knowledge of American history, and having been accused of lacking "the historical sense," Jefferson has always been the great man of all our times, the hero of American history. He stood out in an age which had plenty of outstanding statesmen and political thinkers, and it has always seemed to me remarkable that this country had John Adams and Hamilton—with his economic and financial genius, despite what Malone says of him—as well as Jefferson, just when it needed them. Most remarkable, I say. In fact, it would maybe not be too much to believe that Providence of some sort seems to have been involved. I sent my oldest son to the University of Virginia largely because it was Jefferson's school, and when I went to visit him there I would wander around Monticello, as part of the visit. I know little about sculpture, but the object which seems to me to have the most sculpturesque beauty and interest that I have ever seen is a wooden ploughshare that Jefferson designed, and is in one of the basement rooms. It is more beautiful to me than anything I have ever seen in a museum, and I have been in lots of museums. But is it not a curious fact that, with all his gadgetry and labor-and time-saving devices and preoccupations, Jefferson never saw the transforming effect that machinery and its encampment, industrialism, would have on this country, and indeed on the world. His dream of an agrarian America, a nation of yeoman farmers, was just that, the proverbial impossible dream, though one views an age like his, which believed that such a thing was or would be possible, as though looking backward toward the lost paradise itself.

Well, I've gone on long enough, and maybe too long. But I did want to write to you and give you this vote of confidence, if you need such, or would like to have it. My wife and I will be in New York for a week in November, centering around the Institute meeting on the 12th, and perhaps at some time during the visit you and I might have a drink or even dinner, so that I can tell you these things looking you right in the eyes, as such should always be done. I think of you and your example with great warmth and pride, and of those old days in Rome when Blackmur was still alive, Elizabeth Taylor and Burton were getting together, and you were playing the piano at Bricktop's, so long ago.

With best wishes,

To: Christopher Dickey

CC, Emory University
4620 Lelia's Court
Columbia, S.C. 29206

July 21, 1981

My dear son,

We have just had a good note from Carol, and I wanted to write immediately and tell you how proud I am of your award. That is truly a very great distinction, and the competition is tough. I think this distinction is just super, but there will be plenty more distinctions for you, because you have the ability and the will and the talent that are given to very few, and these things will be apparent to more and more people, as you continue to write. I am much looking forward to your <u>Playboy</u> piece, and I hope that the editors there will give you the best possible space, for there are a great many readers who not only want to know about the situation in El Salvadore, but want to know what <u>you</u>, Chris Dickey, have to say about it. You have your finger on the very nerve-ending—an exposed nerve, too—of what is very probably the most crucial and prophetic situation in the world today. You are right <u>there</u>, and what you say will very likely be the definitive word on the subject. As I may have indicated, one of your readers in Columbia, South Carolina, is certainly waiting to read anything and everything that comes from you.

As for us, we are all well. Bronnie is fat and getting to be a lot of fun. She is red-headed and good-natured, and very little trouble.

Kevin is fine, and is working in a pizzeria at Murrell's Inlet before he goes to Emory Medical School in the fall. We went down to visit him a couple of weeks ago, and the one exciting event was that I killed a 6 1/2 foot water moccasin with a blow-gun, whose picture I enclose. The orange bead of the blow-dart you see sticking out of his head was not the shot that I got him with, but the back-up shot that finished him off after the wildlife ranger and I got him out of the water and onto the bank. The ranger, who moonlights as a grounds-keeper on the Plantation, saw the snake in the water back of our house, and was going to try to kill him with a stick. But, sensing an opportunity not to be missed, I brought the blow-gun out, missed one shot, and then blew through him from just under the chin up through the back of his head about seven or eight inches worth. After I took his picture, the ranger took him off and skinned him, and then <u>ate</u> him, or so he told me later. He is (like Lewis, King and Medlock) a survival freak, and I expect he will survive, if anyone can. What price longevity, eh?

I also enclose a piece I did for the April issue of <u>Esquire</u>. Matt Bruccoli picked it up and made a little pamphlet out of it, which I hope you will enjoy. Surely you'll recognize a good many of the references in it.

That is good news about Tucky: that he is well, and that you had a good time with him. I write to him now and then, but he has answered only one of my letters. Do you think he would still be interested in going to the Air Force Academy with me? If you think he is seriously interested I'll try to arrange to take him out there next spring.

Debba sends love, and so do I, and plenty of it.

Let me hear from you when you have a chance. I would surely like that a lot.

Ever,

To: David Dodson

CC, Emory University
4620 Lelia's Court
Columbia, S.C. 29206

July 22, 1981

Dear David,

Thank you indeed for your letter of a month ago. It is awfully good to know that you will be in this area, down here with us, and that we will be seeing more of you. That will be good. The best, in fact.

I am much taken with your attitude toward the law. My father had much the same sort of position, being more interested in the philosophical and ethical approach to it than in the technical legalisms, which he referred to as "barbed wire tangled up like spaghetti." I think your having a kind of overview of the profession will be nothing but good, the only danger being that there really is a very great deal of that frustrating and blood-letting spaghetti connected with it. But I also remember another thing my father said, earlier on in my life, when as a little boy I asked, as children will do of their father, why he was a lawyer. He said, "Because, Jimbo, the law is the only thing that stands between men and the jungle." He was at the farthest possible remove from Rousseau, and also disliked what he knew of Plato. His favorite was Thomas Hobbes, whose doctrine of the social contract he admired, and whose belief in the limitations of men and their self-serving egotism he also endorsed. His more recent idols were Clarence Darrow, another atheist, and Darrow's predecessor and teacher, Robert Ingersoll, who used to go around debating preachers in their own churches and challenging God, if He (or he) existed, to strike him dead where he stood. My father was not all that dramatic, but like Ingersoll and Darrow and Hobbes and Chief Justice Holmes, he believed that a philosophical overview of the law was not only desirable but necessary to anyone who practiced it. I am much pleased that you have this approach, and I hope you will keep it, for it will sustain you through a lot of frustration, and battling with barbed wire.

Debba is well, and so is Bronnie, who is growing fat and fun at a great rate. We all send love.

Ever,

P.S. If you ever happen to be out toward that navigation place, that nautical supply store we visited when I first got out of the hospital, I'd much appreciate it if you would pick up a couple of pads of Universal Plotting Sheets for me. I'll be glad to reimburse.

To: Ashley Walker

CC, Emory University
4620 Lelia's Court
Columbia, S.C. 29206

July 22, 1981

Dear Ashley,

Thank you so very much for your note about the flowers. I am terribly sorry about your mother's death. She was a noble, intelligent, kind and loving woman. When my father died, she came into the hospital room where I was playing the guitar as a kind of last of all last requests for my father, at the exact moment he drew his last breath (you can tell; there is a change: something goes; is gone). She stood there for a time, as I remember, and nobody said anything. Then she and I just went off, and went to a restaurant she knew about, somewhere over on Piedmont Road. I don't remember the occasion as being at all grim, and it was not, because of your mother. She told me about her own coming blindness, and I took a few notes which I later wrote into the first chapter of a novel I am still working on. At any rate, she gave the most imaginative and interesting account of how it feels to go blind from diabetes that you can imagine. She was completely devoid of any form of self-pity, and the whole occasion was full of intelligent, memorable and caring talk. Believe me, after the hopeless dead weight of grief closed in, I was grateful to remember that incident, and I still am.

I know how great your loss is, Ashley. I can offer no words of condolence, for those things are never any good. But you have my full sympathy, and you must know that the best of your mother is in you, and that is a very great thing to possess.

I go through Augusta occasionally, and perhaps I could drop in at one of the times when I do. I'd like that a lot, believe me. I'd like to meet your husband, and to see what your life is like.

Meanwhile, let me hear from you on whatever subject, whenever you like. That shall be as you wish, of course, but do remember that whatever your needs may be, I am here for you.

My best to you, and to all those you care for.

Ever,

To: Robert Penn Warren   **TLS, Emory University**

4620 Lelia's Court
Columbia, S.C. 29206
July 24, 1981

Dear Red,

Thank you for your letter. I am glad you like Ghiselin, for he is a deserving fellow, from what I know of him, and an altogether better poet than William Jay Smith, who is amiable and rather skillful and charming, but strikes me as disastrously thin and almost totally unmemorable. Ghiselin does really have hold of something, or makes significant grabs at it, I think. He is good with the ocean, especially, and with deserts and bare hills. He is less good in writing erotically, though even here, not at his best, he is better than Bill Smith at <u>his</u> best. So I think we should go ahead and give the prize to him, for despite what Stern may come up with as a judgement, there has never been a time in the history of the race, or of mathematics, that two could not out-vote one. If you are firm on Ghiselin, so am I, and if you like—as you seem to suggest you would—I can assume the pose of "chairman" and convey these determinations to the committee, so that they can go ahead and announce Ghiselin as the winner and pay us the pittance they owe us for reading all these unrewarding and well-meaning books.

We are well here, and Bronnie, in her third month, is thriving. Life when it is this new is certainly a wonder. I don't know how I could have gone so long without a child in the house.

Please convey my love to Eleanor. Debba sends hers too. We'll hope you can make the fall Institute meeting, for we will almost definitely be there, and would sure like to see you.

Ever,

Jim

To: Corinne M. Titus

CC, Emory University
4620 Lelia's Court
Columbia, S.C. 29206

July 29, 1981

Dear Ms. Titus:

Thank you indeed for your letter, and for the instruction sheet on the B-301 artificial horizon. Everything works fine, except that I am not able to adjust the instrument, since there was no Allen key with it when it came to me, nor was there the shade glass you mention in Item #2 of the instruction sheet you were kind enough to enclose. It would be of great service to me if you were able to send me a key, so that I can calibrate the scope. On second thought, send two—or even three—Allen keys, for those things are very easily lost.

A couple of things you might also clear up for me, if you care to. First of all, since you only mention using the instrument for stars, I need to know what to do in the case of the sun and moon. By trial and error, and since the operator is bringing the observed body to the center of the bubble, I would assume that, in the case of the sun, for example, one would have to subtract 15' from the observed height to get an accurate reading of the center of the body. What, then, to do about the Main Correction? Since the Main Correction figures in the Almanac are given for the lower limb of the sun, I also assume that this figure would also have to be halved. Is this correct? In the case of the moon, since its appearance is about the same diameter as the sun, I would think that 15' would also have to be subtracted from the HS observation and the various moon corrections also would need to be halved. But would this apply to all the moon corrections, including the HP? Or how, exactly, does one work with the moon? I would much appreciate the answers to these questions, for I am a celestial navigation nut, a real freak, and I do love this bubble set-up. So please do send me three Allen keys that will fit this thing, and I'll be happy to pay for them. Also send a shade glass, if you can.

With best wishes,

To: Dugan Barr   CC, Emory University
                                                   4620 Lelia's Court
                                              Columbia, S.C. 29206

                                                       July 29, 1981

Dear Dugan:

Well, it is wonderful to hear from you, over the confusing, sad silence of the years! I remember talking to Rian Cooney about you, and asking him to remember me to you, but I'm damned if I can remember when or where this may have been. Could this have been at Hilton Head, down in the islands, here?

I must come to California, now that the writer's strike is over, for I am doing a new movie with Jerome Hellman, who produced "Midnight Cowboy" and "Coming Home," among other deathless products of celluloid, and it may well be that we could get together, on some kind of basis. I'd like that a lot, believe me. But I'll have to pass up the drinking, I'm afraid. I came to the end of the string on that activity about five years ago. I was beginning to have memory lapses because of it, and so I quit. But I crash-quit, which was a mistake, for I immediately went into withdrawal shock, which is like a form of induced epilepsy, bit off part of my tongue and damn near bled to death. So that is enough of <u>that</u>, pleasant as it used to be.

Especially at Reed. My two years out there were some of the best I ever had. In memory the place and everything about it seems entirely remarkable. Nowhere else have I had such good students, or such interest in the subjects I taught. And the whole atmosphere of learning, creativity, folk music and politics was one exactly suited to my (perhaps peculiar) temperament. Since I left I have not been back, though occasionally I hear from a few of the people I knew there. One of these told me that Lloyd Reynolds, from whom my whole family learned calligraphy, is dead, and God knows who else may be—no; must be—dead by now after almost 20 years. But in memory the place is very bright and warm. I expect I will not ever cease to be able to draw on what I gained there.

Thanks very much for your comments on my "performance" in "Deliverance," which novel, incidentally, was written while I was at Reed, or at least most of it was. Though the press was surprisingly kind about my all of three minutes and two scenes I really feel that I can take but very little credit for what I did, because I was only in the picture because the others, particularly Burt, insisted; actually, all I did was play myself, dressed up in a sheriff's uniform. But I do appreciate what you say, and very much, too.

But your connection with the film goes a lot deeper than just eating popcorn and watching me. It was the tape of the Russo-Brentano concert that you dubbed for me when I was at the University of Chicago that was the basis for the use of the "Dueling Banjos" sequence in the film. I played it for my director, John Boorman, and he liked it, and Ronnie Cox, who played Drew in the film, could play it (or play at it, maybe I should say), and we went right along with it. It has become, due exclusively to the film, a bluegrass fixture, even a "classic" by now, as you know. Flatt and Scruggs have an album built around it, and I even heard it the other day used as the music for the floor-exercise routine of someone in a gymnastics meet. But, damn it, someone made off with the original tape of that concert. It was most likely Burt, though it might have been Ronnie Cox, or even Boorman. But the point is, I don't have it, and I would like to. If you still have the tape, I would be most pleased if you could run off another dub, because that thing has been part of my life ever since I first heard Mike and Ron Brentano play it in 1963.

I must close now, but do let me tell you again how delighted I am to hear from you. Since you were at the University of Chicago with him, it occurred to me that you might possibly know where Ken Kipnis might be. Or how about Ruthie Meyers? It was in hearing the three of you play and sing at a faculty get-together that first drew me into music in a serious way, and it is one of the best things that ever happened to me.

When you can, write and tell me your news, and what your life is like.

Ever,

To: Robert Penn Warren   **TLS, Emory University**

4620 Lelia's Court
Columbia, S.C. 29206
July 31, 1981

Dear Red,

You can see by the enclosed Xerox that I have already wrapped up the matter of the Williams Prize, conferred with Gerald Stern, and have done everything

I can think of to see that the matter is closed out, with the only remaining ball, which is payment to us, squarely in the Poetry Society's court. I feel good about giving the thing to Ghiselin, for I think a good deal of some of his work, the best of which is kind of like Robinson Jeffers', with more sensitivity and less violence, and I like him personally, too, though my acquaintance with him has been limited to just two or three visits out there to his writers' conference in Salt Lake. Now we can sit back and let him enjoy his award, for whatever there may be in it for him.

Yes, Debba and I will be most happy to see you and Eleanor as soon as this might be. That would be good. Tell Eleanor that, though I saw a review of her latest book, I haven't read it, and don't have a copy. If she has an extra copy around, I'd sure like to see it, so I'll have something more to talk to her about, in my state of general and deep admiration.

We are well, and Bronnie is now almost three months old. A daughter is a great thing, as you say. It is all true.

Ever,

Jim

To: Dannye Romine

CC, Emory University
4620 Lelia's Court
Columbia, S.C. 29206

August 18, 1981

Dear Dannye:

Thank you very much for your letter, and for enclosing the copies of your article,[10] which I look on with some favor and some disfavor, I regret to say. The whole emphasis on the "bad boy" aspect of either my real or imagined personality is exactly what I asked not to be brought out, much less made the subject of the headline of the article. As to this usage, I can assume only that you wrote the headline, and thereby set the essential tone of the piece, or that this was forced on you. I would prefer to believe the latter, for you seem to me to have more intelligence and linguistic tact than to come up, and as a headline, yet, with the ponderous attempt at elephantine levity that that headline

10. "Bad Boy Writer Provides More Poetry, Less Puff," *Charlotte Observer,* August 2, 1981, pp. E1, 6.

is. The whole effect of what you seem to be trying to say is that I was once, as you seem to delight in assuming that just <u>everybody</u> knows, a kind of drunken Southern blowhard, and that I have now, thanks to good Christians like the readers of the Charlotte Observer, truly seen the error of my ways—I was surprised not to see God and Jesus brought in—with a corresponding diminishment of interest. As you must know, this is all foolish in the extreme. You speak in your letter of the "changes" you now think you see. This seems to be given as an opinion stemming from a long acquaintance with me, which in fact you do not have. Like many other reporters, some greatly inferior to yourself, you put a great deal of credence in hearsay. This is unfortunate, for it takes the emphasis off what I have written and am now trying to write and puts it exactly where it should not be put, on my personal life and characteristics, none of them really known to you, but superficial and largely erroneous. This cannot be welcomed with any real warmth by the subject of such articles as you write, or indeed of any article. My wife and son were deeply offended by your piece, for they know me as you do not, and they would not have recognized, they tell me, the image that you project, whatever your reasons. As for myself, I have less resentment than they, though some.

You are a very good writer, and I enjoyed talking to you. There was some favorable reaction to the piece, I understand; Ervin Jackson of Ivey's wrote a nice letter, for example, so it may be that some people took your article differently than I and my family. As for my own feelings, such things are pretty much a matter of indifference to me, I have been through so many of them pro and con. But I hate to see my people hurt, and I don't like to see them filled with dislike for someone we welcomed openly. I hope you will continue as a journalist, for you have a good eye and a good style, and that you will find subjects to engage you and interest you and bring out what you can do. But not me.

Sincerely,

To: Walter R. Stone

CC, Emory University
4620 Lelia's Court
Columbia, S.C. 29206

August 28, 1981

Dear Walter:

Well, the article on the development of navigation is most welcome. I enjoyed it greatly, and do thank you so much for your considerateness in sending it along. I was mainly struck by the ancients' difficulty in establishing longitude, which of course depends on having an accurate method of measuring time and a central point to which the time is related. My Lord, how those old boys would have relished having a modern quartz digital watch, now selling for as little as four dollars, which displays <u>seconds</u>! Anyway, thanks a whole lot; I am most grateful.

I'm glad you like the article on poetry; it is what I want to say. Bill Fuess is not only a good account executive, but an excellent editor as well; truly first rate, and I've had a lot of them, not only in regard to poetry, novels, literary criticism, essays and advertising, but movies also. Bill is certainly among the very top editors I have known, and I hope you will find your own way to tell him my feelings, here.

One thing. Bill seems to want to keep the title <u>How To Enjoy Poetry</u>, mainly, I think, because it fits in with the previous titles in the series.[11] But from my point of view <u>Poetry: Being and Saying</u> is a good deal more evocative and less off-putting in the sense of a kind of do-it-yourself manual or the "invitation" of a Sunday School teacher or scoutmaster to do something you don't really want to do, which is exactly the effect we want to avoid. If it is not already too late, see if you can prevail on Bill to do things this way. If he insists, however, on sticking with the previous format, it is all right with me, and you can go ahead with the project under those conditions. I simply wished to record this sentiment with you, and pass on.

My best to you, and, again, thanks for the article on navigation. Incidentally—pursuant to this, I guess, in a way—I spoke in New Mexico last week and after the reading a fellow from my squadron came up to me. At first I didn't recognize him as the brave adventurous young guy of 35 years ago. He was shrunken and apologetic, and—somewhat furtively, I thought—pressed a business card into my hand. Afterwards I looked at it, and he is a sanitation engineer for the city of Santa Fe. Thus the eagles of the night go underground, in their old (or late middle) age!

Yours by Polaris,

11. The Power of the Printed Word Series distributed gratis by the International Paper Company. *How to Enjoy Poetry* was published in 1982.

To: Lewis Turco

CC, Emory University
4620 Lelia's Court
Columbia, S.C. 29206

September 1, 1981

Dear Lewis:

Thank you so very much for your new book. I have gone through it several times, and it is certainly one of the best things to come out of our time. "Fire and knives and the dark weather" . . . well, anybody who could say that could do anything. And it is kind indeed of you to think of me, and send your book, which, together with the inscription, I will value with the other things I value.

This afternoon I am beginning my fourteenth year of teaching at the University of South Carolina. All fourteen years I have used, in the main class I teach here, your Book of Forms. I train poets, the ones that have the capacity, and everyone that has been through my Verse Composition class—"been through the fire," as some or perhaps all of them would say—has been through your book, forward, backward, upside down and inside out. It may please you to know that some of these people have gone from poetry into other forms of writing, including the movies. Pat Conroy, author of Conrack, The Great Santini, and the novel and forthcoming movie The Lords of Discipline, cut his uneven teeth on your book, and so did Ben Greer, who eventually became the author of Halloween.

So today I'm starting the Sisyphean rock up the hill again, with a new class, and the same book. It is the best book—the most sheerly useful, helpful and practiceably interesting book—in the field, far better than the age-old Brooks and Warren Understanding Poetry, which, incidentally, I first encountered when I picked it up out of a hole of mud and coral slime on Okinawa after the island library blew away in the great post-War hurricane of October, 1949. Your book is far more interesting and less prejudiced, and, as I say, much more usable.

Well, I won't go on and on in this immoderate fashion, but will just close with another thanks. Perhaps one day we'll meet, and I can tell you these things correctly, looking you straight in the eyes, as such things should be done.

Cordially,

To: Jim Elledge   CC, Emory University
                                                                 4620 Lelia's Court
                                                              Columbia, S.C. 29206

                                                              September 23, 1981

Dear Jim Elledge:

I have your two-part supplement to the bibliography, and it would be hard
for me to tell you how deeply indebted I feel for all your labors on behalf of
my words. Some of this stuff I don't even remember having written, though
thanks to you I have looked it up in a few cases, and was at least reasonably
happy at what I had done, even though I didn't know what I was doing. I am
most grateful to you for the work you have done, and the interest—no; it
must be devotion—you have shown, are showing. Surely, if my work survives,
much of the credit will be due to you, your finding and keeping.

Let me know how you are doing, and how your own work is moving.

                                                              Ever,

To: Stanley Burnshaw   TLS, University of Texas at Austin

                                                              4620 Lelia's Court
                                                              Columbia, S.C. 29206
                                                              September 24, 1981

Dear Stanley,

Thank you so much for your letter, and your advice. The writer's strike has
now ended, and I can go back to work on the Yukon project, the material for
which is sitting around the house in bales, whose assimilation into a coherent
story is very slow. My situation is this. The producer with whom I am doing
this, Jerome Hellman, is very prestigious and rich; at least he is rich now, and
although wealth and affluence come and go very quickly in Hollywood, at
this time he has or can get as much money as he wants to spend on any project he comes up with. It is the kind of situation that used to be called a
"dream of a lifetime." The dream of a producer's lifetime is to produce and
direct a movie about a subject which has had a lifetime fascination for him. In
this case, the fascination is the Yukon and the Klondike gold rush. Jerry is a
Jewish fellow from the lower East Side of New York, very conscious of his an-
cestry on the one hand and drawn to wildernesses and mountains and forests

as only a city person can be. He came to me with this project a year or so ago not because of <u>Deliverance</u>, but because I had done Jack London's <u>Call of the Wild</u> for NBC a few years ago. He wished me to invent a story which would be interesting and unusual in itself as to the delineation of characters, and would also "tell the real truth" about the "Klondike experience." Also, without knowing very much about the story—even <u>I</u> don't know much, at this stage, about the story—Dustin Hoffman expressed, as they say, a desire to play in the movie. I don't know Hoffman at all well, but he is a Delmore Schwartz fanatic, and his obsession with Delmore, his identification with him, and so on, gradually got to be part of the story we were concocting. It now appears that Jerry doesn't <u>want</u> Dustin Hoffman to be in the picture, can't pay his price, doesn't like him any more, or some damn thing. At any rate, by this time Jerry <u>himself</u> has fallen in love with the Delmore—or Delmore-like—character and wants the whole picture to be built around him. I have to go out to Hollywood next week and thrash some of this out with Jerry and his people, for everybody is bound up contractually with everybody else, and now there is no getting out of it, for I have taken the dollar from the drumhead, or at least part of the dollar. But I still don't know exactly where things stand. But if I have any kind of orientation at all, it is the one you have given me, for I know almost nothing, except that, about either Delmore's background or Jerry's, or about the Jewish immigrations into New York, the customs, mores, language, or anything of that sort. But I do have the flicker of a feeling that this might just turn out to be an extraordinary film, for Jerry Hellman is no fool, and what I have seen of his directing abilities convinces me that he is not bad at that, either. Well, we'll see.

But I did want to write and thank you for your help. In connection with all this, I too have reread <u>Humbolt's Gift</u> and I don't like it as much as I did, either. Bellow is rather too much addicted to trivia—details of dress, women's make-up, and so on—for my taste. But you needn't worry that I am taking more than should be taken for my character from either the actual Delmore Schwartz or "Humbolt von Fleisher." As the character has evolved, he is really not much like either one of them.

Keep me informed about <u>The Refusers</u> because it is a book that is going to matter very greatly to a very great number of people. Let me know what more I can do to help out.

Meanwhile, you are almost a kind of folk hero down here with <u>The Seamless Web</u>. Among others the head of the department, who sits in on my classes, is presently deep in the thrall of it (and even, as is the wont of professors, in the bibliography as well!).

All three of us send love, and Chris and Kevin too.

Ever,

Jim

To: Margaret Mills

CC, Emory University
4620 Lelia's Court
Columbia, S.C. 29206

November 30, 1981

Dear Ms. Mills:

Debba and I most enjoyed seeing you at the last meeting, and look forward to the spring occasion as well. I'm sorry we'll miss the winter get-together, but much work must be done, as well as travel to places I enjoy far less than I do the Institute.

A couple of things. As the recent meeting we were told that the Nobel Prize people wish the Academy and Institute to suggest a candidate for the Noble Prize in Literature. Would it be forward of me if I were to <u>put</u> forward the name of Robert Penn Warren for this? If it is all right for me to make this suggestion, I'd appreciate your letting me know what the <u>official</u> steps are by which I may do so.

As to the Institute's current question about nominating someone outside the Institute for the Award for Distinguished Service to the Arts, I would like to suggest Stanley Burnshaw for this. He is a distinguished poet, a fine editor, and his approach to translation is the most important in my time. I can't think of a better candidate, or anyone who would better fill your description of the kind of person to whom we should give the award.

Let me hear from you on these matters, and if you could also send along a couple more lapel-rosettes, those very valuable but easily losable insignia of our proud House, I would wear them, and even both at the same time, for I have very few coats with only one lapel!

Sincerely,

To: Weems & Plath, Inc.

CC, Emory University
Litchfield Plantation
Pawleys Island, S.C.

December 9, 1981

Dear Sirs:

Though not a sailor, I have an intense interest in celestial navigation, have graduated from and am certified by the Davis Instruments correspondence course, and have acquired a Plath Navistar and the bubble attachment. I enjoy using your equipment very much, for it is surely the best in the world. But, though I have had the bubble attachment for a year, do what I may I cannot seem to calibrate it correctly so that the nautical almanac and the 249 sight reduction tables give me a consistent answer on my sights. The trouble is that there was no operating manual sent with the bubble attachment, and I even had to acquire the Allen wrench needed to adjust the instrument from another source. But since I have no horizon here at this island location, I don't have the correct means of trueing-up the bubble. I could get around that by other means, I think, but I still have the problem of relating the bubble reading to the tables in the almanac and 249. If you put out a manual in connection with this instrument, I would surely like to have it. If there's not one, I'd like to be in contact with one of your staff there who could answer these questions.

Please let me hear from you at your convenience.

Sincerely,

To: Philip Lader

CC, Emory University
4620 Lelia's Court
Columbia, S.C. 29206

January 7, 1982

Dear Mr. Lader:

Thank you for the invitation to join Senator Edward M. Kennedy and other Democrats on January 14th.

While I am interested in lending my support to the South Carolina Democratic Party in connection with Senator Kennedy's visit, I would prefer to do so in a more intimate atmosphere than the breakfast at the Carolina Inn will afford. I was close to Jimmy Carter throughout his campaign and administration and would be willing to meet with Senator Kennedy to discuss any ways in which I might be of help. If this is agreeable with you, and if you have sufficient preliminary contact with Senator Kennedy to inform him of my availability on a less public basis than your announcement suggests, please let me know far enough in advance for me to be able to meet with him either privately or with a selected few others.

Again, thank you for your communication.

Sincerely,

To: Thomas G. Hart   **CC, Emory University**

4620 Lelia's Court
Columbia, S.C. 29206

January 15, 1982

Dear Mr. Hart:

Thank you indeed for your unexpected and very welcome letter, as well as for your comments on Jericho, which I think—if I do say so myself—is one of the better and more original books of the sort. Hubert and I are doing another book together, this one on Appalachia, called The Wilderness of Heaven, though when either of us will get the time to finish it is hard to say.

It is quite extraordinary that you are with Bowater, for in a sense so was I, about twenty years ago, or a little more. The advertising agency I was then working for, Liller, Neal, Battle and Lindsey, was handling the account of Bowater Board, and I developed the advertising, including the logo of the twisted "board" that showed it to be "smooth on both sides," and which was supposed to be used extensively with the product that Bowater's was putting into the field to compete with Masonite, which as you know has only one smooth side, the other being a grid. At any rate, I paid several visits to the huge plant that Bowater's was then building in Rock Hill to produce the Board. I engaged in endless planning sessions with the sales manager, Joe (Hines? or Joe something), about the possible markets, prospected volume sales, and various other strategies we hoped to initiate and implement. But at the time I left the agency, the mill—conceived as a twenty-four hour, incessant or perhaps interminable operation—had not worked, was not working, and seemed not able to be made to work. And there my association with Bo- water's ended, though I have often wondered if the mill ever did get going; if it ever produced the fabulous smooth-on-both-sides Board I and my art di- rector, Bob Hiers, had expended so much ingenuity to advertise. Ah well, maybe you could catch me up on some of this, being so high up on the Board (one kind of Board or another) as you seem to be.

And, sure, the invitation for a drink is still open; wide open, in fact. Keep me informed of your whereabouts, and I'll do the same with you about mine, and we'll get together somewhere, some way or other.

Again, thanks so much for your letter. Good things can happen.

With best wishes,

To: Dana Gioia

CC, Emory University
4620 Lelia's Court
Columbia, S.C. 29206

January 20, 1982

Dear Mr. Gioia:

Thank you indeed for your letter, your poem, and the news of yourself. I liked all three, and your review as well. I am glad to see Jim Squires get some recog- nition. I see him only every few years, but have always liked and encouraged his work, and his critical activities as well. He wrote very good books on Frost and Tate, and took up the cudgels for a hyper-romantic, out-of-fashion poet and novelist named Frederick Prokosch, who was one of my earliest influ- ences, beginning way back when I was in New Guinea in the early forties. Anyway, I am sure Jim is most pleased at your notice, but he could scarcely be more pleased than I am.

You ask about my advertising years. No, I was not ever officially on the ac- count side of things, though in the case of several businesses I worked with, I might as well have been. I started as a copywriter in the spring of 1956 with McCann-Erickson, which had just taken over the Coca-Cola account from Darcy, of Saint Louis, which had had it for thirty-odd years. I did some print work, and then moved into the radio-television end of it, my main function being to develop TV commercials for Eddie Fisher and his announcer, Fred Robbins, on a fifteen-minute, three-times-a-week program called "Coke Time," which had the lowest Nielsen ever recorded on television, or one of them, surely. The program folded, and the radio-TV part of Coke went from New York to Atlanta, and I went with it as senior writer. I worked there, developing material for various local bottlers, for the next three years, and then went to a smaller, Atlanta-based agency called Liller, Neal, Battle and Lindsay as copy chief. I also began some design work there, and worked closely with the art department; these are the offices described in the beginning chapter of Deliverance. My main accounts there were for Armour products—mainly fertilizer—a couple of non-competing banks, Bowater's paper and hardboard, and some industrial holdings accounts. After about two years there I jumped agencies again, and went with the largest Atlanta agency, Burke Dowling Adams, as Creative Director (how ad people like titles!), having charge of both copy and art departments, and engineering the campaigns for the principal accounts, chief among which was Delta Airlines. In a way this suited me fine; I had some good people working under me, and Delta had just been awarded the East-West transcontinental route, and it was up to me to make as much of this as I could, publicly. But I was tired of the business life by that time, so that when I got the first and main part of the new campaign for Delta done, I left, and for a couple of months, before I took up a Guggenheim Fellowship I had been given, I lived on relief, on Georgia unemployment compensation, and by giving guitar lessons, and moonlighting (with dark glasses at night, yet!) at a coffee house in the hippie-and-dope section of town called The Fourteenth Gate. After that, I went to Europe, and the only time I looked back at advertising was when I gave the keynote speech at the annual congress of the four-As at White Sulphur Springs, West Virginia. Billy Friedkin was on the same program, and we talked about communications, as I remember. He had just finished making The French Connection, and was working on The Exorcist, and I had published Deliverance, and was working on the movie.

I hope that all this will help you in some way. But whether it does or not, thank you for your communication, and for sending me your work. It is certainly good to have it. And you may be sure that I shall look forward to reading your article in The Hudson Review.

With best wishes,

To: Lee Bartlett

CC, Emory University
4620 Lelia's Court
Columbia, S.C. 29206

January 25, 1982

Dear Mr. Bartlett:

Thank you very much for your letter. I am delighted that you have done the work you have on my correspondence with Pound. It is years since all this happened, and I have little recollection of what is in the letters, except at the time it seemed to me that his letters could be published as new Cantos, not with a little alteration, but with <u>no</u> alteration at all. I am happy that you find my letters "sane and interesting"; most if not all of them were written at the last part of the time I was at the University of Florida, which I think would place them between January and April, 1955, though a few of them may be a little prior to that, or a little after. Let me get to your questions:

1. Bill Pratt is a professor of English at Miami University of Ohio. He was a colleague of mine at Vanderbilt, and is a poet, translator, literary critic and historian. At the time we visited Pound at St. Elizabeth's Bill was in the Navy, on duty somewhere in or around Washington.

2. Yes, my wife, Maxine, who died five years ago, did knit a sweater for Pound. I'm not sure, but I don't think the famous Gaudier sketch was worked into it, though that was the original plan. I remember Ezra's asking that he "be left open in front," so Maxine did that, and made a sweater that buttoned.

3. There was a confusion on Ezra's part about the organization I spoke to down there. Ezra thought it was the PEN bunch, when it was actually a much less formidable—and I dare say, less interesting—group called the Pen Women of America, which is hardly more than a large garden club. As I remember, I read some poetry to them, none of it mine, and then at their in-sistence read part of a poem called "The Father's Body," which I had in my pocket and was working on. This had some sexual references that the (Pen) Women didn't like, and they made complaint. I refused to apologize, left the University, and went to work in New York for McCann-Erickson, on the Coca-Cola account. The poem was later published in <u>Poetry</u>, though I never collected it.

4. I wrote many hundreds of catch phrases for Coke, though not "the pause that refreshes," unfortunately; or fortunately: that particular bit of verbal immortality was written before I was born. "Things go better with Coke" may have been based on an idea I had and turned in, but whether this was unearthed and used, or whether somebody else later came up with the notion independently, I don't have any idea. As Thurbert says, I just don't think about those things any more.

Again, keep me posted as to how all this goes, for you may be sure I am most interested. The year before last I gave the annual Pound lecture at the University of Idaho, and this was later published as The Water-Bug's Mittens: Ezra Pound: What We Can Use. If you like, I'll send you a copy.

I was in New Mexico last August, oddly enough, giving the Witter Bynner lecture under the auspices of the Foundation of that name in Santa Fe. Even more oddly, I will be back out that way around the middle of May, when Arizona State is giving me a degree, and the combined arts forces—if that is the way to put it—of the school are giving a kind of multi-media "premier" of a new book of poems of mine called Puella. It strikes me that, since I am going to be in that neck of the woods anyway, with my expenses paid by Arizona State, I might be able to come by your school and give a reading there, if you have some dough. Let me know about this, and I will be guided accordingly. See if you can work this out, for it would be good to meet a fellow Poundian—especially down there in the D. H. Lawrence country!

Sincerely,

To: Howard Moss

CC, Emory University
4620 Lelia's Court
Columbia, S.C. 29206

March 1, 1982

Dear Howard:

Here, at last, is a new poem.[12] It is the last in a series of four poems, all variations on the "false youth" theme, two of which—the winter and fall sections—

---

12. "False Youth: Spring: The Olympian" was printed in the summer 1982 issue of *Amicus Journal.*

The New Yorker did a few years back; The Atlantic, as I remember, printed the summer part. Anyway, this is the longest and I think the best of them: a kind of satire and tragi-comedy about athleticism, aging, California, smog, the American Dream of a swimming pool culture in which one eats and drinks anything one wants, and does it all the time. This seems funny and sad to me and needless to say, I hope you will like it. It came out of a situation when I did live in California, in a set-up pretty much like the one described in the poem. The Olympian himself is based on Mike Larabee, who did in fact win the 400-meters in the Tokyo Olympics, and was a high school math and physics teacher in the San Fernando Valley, where my oldest boy, Chris, went to school. Other than the existence and the Olympic victory of Mike, the situation in the poem is invented, though it came to seem very real to me as I wrote about it. Again, let me know what you think when you have a chance.

It was good indeed to see you in New York last fall, and I hope very much that we'll be able to get together again soon. I'd like that a lot.

Jim Mann has written me a couple of postcards from New York, though without an address. Have you seen him? If you do see him, tell him to send me an address, so that I can answer his cards and letters, which I feel guilty about not doing.

My best, as always.

Ever,

To: Peter Borrelli[13]

CC, Emory University
4620 Lelia's Court
Columbia, S.C. 29206

March 29, 1982

Dear Mr. Borrelli:

I have now had another idea about the poem for you, and have gone ahead and completed it. This is an odd twist for an ecology poem, but I think it will have more impact and a great deal more reader-interest, than a poem dealing with ecology and conservation having more obvious designs on the reader's

13. Editor of *Amicus Journal*.

sympathies. This is about athletics, and what might well be called the pollution center—or city—of the world, Los Angeles, where the freeway smog is so thick that it turns the crow grey in the air, and only rats seem really to belong there; it is their domain: they seem the very symbols of the conditions. Anyway, I hope you like "The Olympian," whose narrative framework deals with a kind of beer-drinking gag-race on Sunday afternoon between a real Olympic champion and a fat middleaged out-of-shape guy in the latter's back yard, around the inevitable Southern California swimming pool; which even the tract-houses out there have.

"The Olympian" is part of a new book to be published in the fall, so it could appear in your summer issue preceding the book publication. The book itself is called False Youth: Four Seasons; the other three "seasons" and the prologue have appeared in The New Yorker, The Atlantic, Harper's, and The Nation, so, if you like "The Olympian,"—which is the best of the lot—you will be in good company so far as publishing stable-mates go.

Get back to me on this as soon as you can, and we'll move according to your wish.

With all best regards, I am

Sincerely yours,

To: Hugh O'Neill

CC, Emory University
4620 Lelia's Court
Columbia, S.C. 29206

April 27, 1982

Dear Hugh,

Here are some more pages (202–255); not as many as I would have liked, but all I have been able to get into shape with all the activities that are going on right now. The rest of the book is in several hundred pages of notes, and when I get through the end of school and doing what I can do for the cause of Puella, I will be able to work steadily on it, all of every day—and the nights too, if need be—until I can put the whole thing in your hands and you and I can sit down and see what we've got.

As to these pages, I'm not sure what you'll think. It may be that the scene at the waterfall is not convincing, though I like the idea of it, and it might work out in another treatment, if you don't like this one. I wanted something in which water and air would mix, and the body, while standing on the earth—or a rock, in this case—would seem to fly. The book is about the air, and the relation of the human body to it, and to motion through it and experience in it, detached from the ground. This is the element in which the disappeared—or dead—boy has been supreme. To project this idea, I have amended somewhat the relationship of Joel to the air, and I now think it is better—a great deal better—that Joel has in a sense found his metier only after he has come to the Peckover field, the training base: that the air, and the airplane, have in a sense created him, and he has been quick to pick up on what everyone acknowledges as his superiority in this area to found a youth-mystique based on elements he has come upon since he has been at the Base. It is the retracing of the Alnilam plot through what Cahill finds out from the other people at the Base who have—most of them inadvertently—been parts of the creation of the Plot that forms the structure of the novel. So we don't bring on Joel as someone who is already a fully-formed, tough and mystical young fellow when he gets to the Base, and simply starts putting his ideas into effect when he arrives. It is the Base itself, and his entry into skills that he himself had no idea he had, that engender the Plot, and one of the larger denouements of the story is Cahill's coming to be made aware that his own appearance is the key piece of the puzzle ("When the father comes, Orion will leap free"). Anyway, see if you think the present pages are beginning to get this idea across.

Meanwhile, I'll keep pushing, and will try to handle the Puella commitment as well as I can. The Arizona publicity is staggering in the extent of its involvement with us, and its coverage, and I don't see how we can fail to do well out there. Can you not come?

I'll be in Florida from May 1st to the 21st, in residence at the Atlantic Center for the Arts at New Smyrna Beach, where I hope to hole up and drive ahead on the book. Let me hear when you have time.

Cordially,

To: Paul S. Patterson

CC, Emory University
4620 Lelia's Court
Columbia, S.C. 29206

May 28, 1982

Dear Pat:

Well, it is certainly very good to hear from you, after all these years. And thanks so much for your thoughtfulness in sending along the clipping, too. It is good to have such accurate remembrance of a time so long ago, which I remember with a clear affection. But believe me I had no idea that you and I and our dinosaur promotion had such an earthquaking effect on the formation of Frito-Lay, Pepsico and such huge combines: so huge, in fact, that they resemble octopi more than pterodactyls!

It was all so long ago, and yet I still feel that I must get up early to make Bill Neal's Monday morning meeting, though I can't for the life of me remember a damn thing that went on in any of them. Al Braselton, my best friend of that time and still close, and now fighting a fearful battle with alcoholism, told me that Bill died the death of a true ad-man, in his office, his last words being "the client'll like that." A few years ago I saw Howard Axelberg and Dick Hodges at the 4As meeting at White Sulphur Springs, West Virginia, when I made the keynote speech there. This must have been around 1972 or 1973. Since I never had anything much to do with them at the agency, there wasn't much to do on that occasion except to shake hands, acknowledge, and pass on.

As to what I might be able to do about the nuclear arms race, I can't really promise much. But it does seem to me that if there were no means of inducing Russia to reduce or eliminate nuclear arms, this country would be very foolish to do any such. I shouldn't think we would want to put ourselves in the position of Percy in Belloc's wicked little epigram.

Pacific Percy thought it wrong to fight,
But Roaring Bill, who killed him, thought it right.

Again, thanks so much for writing, Pat. You were the best in that agency: the most intelligent, the most responsive, and the most imaginative. These things must count, in memory as well as reality. Surely they do, with me. Keep in

touch, and perhaps we can have a drink together, at some time or other. I'd
like that a lot, believe me.

                                                With best wishes,

To: Stephen Berg[14]   CC, Emory University
                                            4620 Lelia's Court
                                            Columbia, S.C. 29206

                                                June 16, 1982

Dear Steve:

Thank you for your note. Though I wish it had been more personal, I understand something of the logistical problems of editors, and what may be your
shortage of help.

As to your project, I would be interested in trying to help you, and might be
able to with a little more information. If you will pick the poem of mine, I
would be more likely to consider doing as you request, although five pages of
prose is a whole lot for one to write about his own verse. I would also have to
know what other 29 poets would be included. I'm afraid I must be center stage
in some way, for there is no point, things being what they are, in my being lost
in a miscellany of other people, and there are definitely some on the scene
with whom I would not want to appear.

Also, can you let me know something about payment? I am in such a rush of
work that I must weigh time against money, as I am sure you can understand.

You say that you must receive 20 written commitments to the book before the
publisher will go ahead with it. You may (tentatively) consider this one of
them, not because of any feeling of opportunity I have, but because you are the
poet who wrote the Akhmatova poems, which are the best my generation has
done.

My best to you, as always. Do more writing and less editing. But I will go with
you on this one, certain things being made clear.

                                                Warmly,

14. Editor of *American Poetry Review*.

To: Edward Abbey   CC, Emory University
                                                4620 Lelia's Court
                                                Columbia, S.C. 29206

                                                July 2, 1982

Dear Edward Abbey:

I have just read <u>Down the River</u>—I have an especial interest in rivers—and I thought I would write you and tell you that, for whatever it's worth, I am solidly with you as an ecologist and a human being, but most especially as a writer. You not only say things that I profoundly agree with, but you say the hell out of them, and the quality of recklessness and abandon, without bluff—my own is largely bluff—is one I esteem above almost any other, love not excepted—if love is a quality; to tell the truth, I don't know what it is. My own ecological battles are nothing like so strenuous or eloquent as yours, though I did what I could to get the Chattooga River put on the Wild and Scenic Rivers list, and so not damned up, as was the river in <u>Deliverance</u>, and I have taken a few public stabs against various mill and other "development" projects in the area where I live. My youngest son, who started as a marine biologist and ended up in medical school, engaged in some political activity in Ecuador over the fate of the Galapagos Islands; my oldest boy, Chris, is in El Salvador, trying to save <u>himself</u> from extinction. Anyway, though my credentials as a conservationist are not really impressive, I am with you a thousand percent in spirit, for what, as I said earlier, it may be worth.

As far as I know, the only time our tracks ever crossed was that I visited Western Carolina College at Cullowhee a few years ago, and was put up in a room—a small apartment, rather, as I remember—where you had lived some time before. I have no idea, really, as to what your stay may have been like, but opinion was strong, mainly in favor, though I did get the impression that you were disgruntled with the place, as well you might have been. Anyway, you were there, and so was I, and the main point is that we should make some effort to get together in the same place at the same time, before the lights go out for everybody. I'd like that a lot, believe me.

Write and tell me what your life is like, and what satisfactions there are.

                                                Sincerely,

To: William Dunlap

CC, Emory University
4620 Lelia's Court
Columbia, S.C. 29206

August 27, 1982

Dear Bill,

Debba and I have just got back from Paris, and I had a moment to check in with you and let you know how things are going.

Most of the time we were in Paris we were looking at pictures, particularly the Louvre, next to the hotel where we lived, and the Jeu de Paume. Debba is keenly interested in graphics, and especially in drawing, as I, conversely, and rather on the team of Baudelaire, favor color, particularly dramatic color as in Delacroix. Anyway, while she was looking at Ingres and I at Delacroix, we were both thinking of you, our very most favorite painter friend, and how wonderful it would have been to have you with us, making your inside comments in loud, excited whispers. Maybe we will all be there together one day; I like to think of that.

I was most interested in your new approach—narrative painting—and I feel that the Civil War has never yielded anything in that area nearly so powerful and deep as lies there waiting for the right hand to bring it forth. Let me mention something to you, for what there might be in the way of subject matter. I am thinking of the scene in <u>The</u> <u>Killer</u> <u>Angels</u> before Pickett's charge, when the Confederate boys are all lined up, ready to go, across the roads and fields toward Little Round Top. There is a feeling about this scene that would be devastating on canvas, done by the right person. The atmosphere is something like that before a crucial football game, where these Southern boys are saying things to each other like "J.C., you never looked so good. I've just got to tell you; you look real good." It is all a matter of family and intimacy and pride, and masculine tenderness before walking straight into the fire. I am sure there is something beautiful here, in the early light.

Well, I won't go on and on, but will just close to get this in the mail.

Debba and I long to see you, and I hope you will tell us where you are, what you're doing, when we'll see more of your work, and when we can get together.

Ever,

P.S. You can take a look at Debba and me and Bronnie in the current—Robert Wagner/Jill St. John—issue of <u>People</u> magazine, if you like. Strange piece![15]

To: Jeffrey Meyers   CC, Emory University
                                                4620 Lelia's Court
                                                Columbia, S.C. 29206

                                                September 3, 1982

Dear Jeffrey Meyers:

Thanks indeed for the Jarrell offprint. As I told you when you were here, I suspected that these things were so, but until now I had no proof. I'm not sure how all this makes me feel because Randall's example is so strong in my thinking and responding to things that it is a shock to me—this late, even— to find that, yes, it is true: he did throw all that away—all that sensibility, all that intelligence, all that responsiveness. Even at this late date it is too dreadful to believe. I suppose that all that can be done is to profit by the example of what he wrote, for the man is there, or he is nowhere.

I hope you are doing well with your biography, and that you will get a copy to me when it appears.

One thing about the death: you don't touch on the possibility of <u>impulse</u> suicide, which is strong in everyone—it certainly is in me—and, though the impulse may have been the culmination of various preceding circumstances, it still may have <u>occurred</u> spontaneously. There is no way to know that, of course. But it does seem that a suicide as <u>deliberate</u> as you seem to think this one was, would not have used this particular means. Again, it might have, but deliberation seems not quite to fit the circumstances. Or so it strikes me, at any rate.

My best to you on your (many) projects. Keep me posted on your doings, for I have you in view and want to keep you there.

                                                Warmly,

15. Dolly Landon, "James Dickey's Wife, Deborah, Says Deliverance Is Escape from Her Poet Husband's Shadow," *People* 18 (August 30, 1982): 37–38, 41.

To: Stanley Burnshaw   TLS, University of Texas at Austin

4620 Lelia's Court
Columbia, S.C. 29206
September 10, 1982

Dear Stanley,

Debba and I managed a trip to Paris for a couple of weeks, and so I have sort
of been out of things, and am just now getting back to teaching, and being
able to answer your letter of July 13th, which was long, good and most welcome.

I am back working on the long novel, and some other things. The Hollywood
business is being phased out, for I don't really like Hellman personally, and he
has such a conventional mind that it is impossible to get anything over to him
that is even in the least unusual. All he wants to do is to screen old movies and
try to pick up suggestions from them that he might be able to use. He wants
everything to be like every other movie that everyone has ever seen. I don't
have time for that kind of thing, so I am taking the last payment on the preliminary part of the film-making and getting out, for I have a good many projects I had rather put my time on.

Puella is doing well, and has sold out the first printing of five thousand, which
is rather heartening. However, the fellow in North Carolina who originally
commissioned the poems for use in another book he was never able to publish, now wants his money back, or at least some of it. I consider the fifteen
thousand dollars he paid me as payment for a year and a half he took out of
my life, when I suspended work on the novel, turned down a good many
readings, and went through multiple other vicissitudes to complete the project, only to find out that he could not find any way to bring the book out. The
poems were written independently of his photographs, however, because
under no circumstances would I ever have any poem of mine depend on an
illustration, and I brought them out in magazines, and, eventually, as Puella.
The lawyers are going round and round about all this, and I may eventually have
to give the guy a little money. This is only a minor irritation, but it will resolve
itself fairly soon, or so my lawyer tells me. Anyway, we'll see.

Red Warren and I finished the film we were doing for CBS-Cable; even the
editing has been done, I am told. I don't know when the thing will screen, but

the producer called yesterday and said that it was being put through the final stages, and is just about ready to go for an October date. Again, I'll let you know.

And, yes, Warren does like and esteem your work very much. I'll sound him out as to the possibility of his seconding my nomination for you at the Institute.

About the matter of honorary degrees: my God, you should have a whole <u>wall</u> of them! I have been asked to be on some committees in connection with these things, and I will certainly militate strongly for you, in any case in which I am a participant. I'll also see what I can do with the Boston outfit.

Odd you should mention Helen Vendler, who was at Kenyon last May with Wiesel and myself. For some reason or other, the college had mixed up my hood and hers, and she came into my room at the college guest house with what turned out to be my garment in her hands. "Is this your academic hood?" she asked.

"Madam," I answered gravely, sweaty and unshaven as I was from traveling, "I <u>am</u> the academic hood." And that's about the extent of my association with her, though she is certainly a very poor writer, who writes a kind of jargonish substitute-poetry—and very unimaginative, too—which she passes off as "criticism." And I don't like her main subject, Wallace Stevens, either. If all poetry were like his, I would have no interest in the subject, or certainly not enough to write it.

I have just finished the second week of teaching, and most of the time spent in the composition class has been concerned with <u>The Seamless Web</u>. In preparation, I read through the whole thing again, plus my notes, and came to the same conclusion, all over again, that my class came to for the first time: that it <u>states</u> and <u>documents</u> what the whole sentient human race has been waiting to hear, but didn't know it: that we are bodily linked with natural process, with <u>rerum natura</u>. Incidentally, my class liked especially the section illustrating the connection of the body with the rotation of the earth, with day and night, sun and moon. Man, <u>that's</u> the stuff to give the troops! I became an instant hero in about ten minutes! Thanks so much for this, Stanley, as for all the other things I have to thank you for.

I must close now, but will be in closer and better touch from now on.

My love to Leda. To her, first, and then to Stan Hart, Tom Maley, and all my other friends on the Vineyard.

Ever,
Jim

To: Constance Urdang   TLS, Washington University

4620 Lelia's Court
Columbia, S.C. 29206
October 1, 1982

Dear Constance Urdang:

I saw somewhere that you have a new book, and I'd appreciate it a lot if you'd let me have the name of it, because I am writing an article on contemporary American women poets, among whom it seems to me that you are certainly among the best. I admire greatly your "Moon Tree" poems, and have drawn heavily on them. I have a recent book about (young) women called Puella, and what I consider one of the best poems in it, about a generation of girls falling from the air like dandelion-seed into a field, was directly suggested by your phrase "you make their weather"; there is even a fountain in the poem that is partly your fountain.

Anyway, please do let me know the name of your book, and I'll carry on from there. It seems a long time since I was in St. Louis, but I remember the period with great affection. Please give my regards to those I know, and those who, perhaps by chance, recall the time.

With best wishes for your work and life,
James Dickey

To: Donald Hall   TLS, University of New Hampshire

4620 Lelia's Court
Columbia, S.C. 29206
November 19, 1982

Dear Don:

It was certainly good to see you again, after all this time. All the way from Cannon Bay! I'm sorry I didn't get to talk with you more, down in Jack Kennedy's Dallas, but the re-connection meant a lot to me, and I'm glad I went down there if for just the reason that it occurred, though the people were certainly generous and enjoyable, too; I hope you had as good a time as I did, and didn't get as tired.

I have just reread your <u>Remembering Poets</u>, which I think is an absolute glowing model of what such a book ought to be. Especially the part on Dylan Thomas is good. I knew all the others you write about, including Sylvia Plath—the ultimate poetry-groupie—and knew Anne Sexton particularly well; there is a large correspondence with her that I hope to God never gets printed. Anyway, the business about the "fashion" of suicide is right on the nail, though I'm surprised you didn't include Randall Jarrell, who was more valuable than all the rest of them put together, though I liked Berryman as a person very much, too. I was surprised to find, after his death, that he had written a poem to me about late-night phone calls, entitled "Damn it, Jim D., You Woke Me Up," though it was John B. who used to do all the calling, usually collect. But your book is just great; my kids here eat it up.

A thought occurs to me: have you been put up for the American Institute and Academy? You ought to be in it, being more deserving than most of the people that <u>are</u> in it. Let me know about this, and if you like I will try to get something moving.

And send me <u>Kicking the Leaves</u> and sign it. I would like to have such a book. Also, I'll send you some of my new stuff, if you like.

My best to you, and to all in your—getting-cold-now, I bet—house, which I hope one day to visit.

Debba says Hello without knowing you, and hopes to meet. She's great; you'll like her.

                                                                    Jim

To: Donald Hall   **TLS, University of New Hampshire**

4620 Lelia's Court
Columbia, S.C. 29206
November 26, 1982

Dear Don:

Thanks so much for the book, the inscription, the letter, and the meeting in Dallas. All are very moving to me, and mark at least as far as I am concerned the prospect of something very good happening from here on out.

The book is by far your best; it is one of the few books of poetry I have ever seen regarding which the comments on the jacket are true—I doubt if you could have done better yourself, being modest! Anyway, I have read <u>Kicking the Leaves</u> twice-through, and it seems to me that everything you have written leads up to it. Not only that, but there are many profitable avenues—or perhaps dirt roads—leading out from it and up from it, and that kind of situation, on-going and mysterious, is what we all want.

How you will take <u>Puella</u> I don't of course know, but for me it is my kind of on-go at this point. I have reached a place where the versified anecdote does not seem to me capable of doing some of the things—linguistic things—that are possible, and so with <u>Puella</u> I have tried to keep the situation minimal—though in most cases it is there—and the language, particularly as regards the <u>line</u>, maximal, whenever I could get it to what I consider such a point. Anyway, here the thing is, for however it strikes you.

About visits, nothing is impossible. You and Jane could come down here to the low country, and we could spend some time down among the live-oaks and Spanish moss. I have a house on a refurbished rice plantation, and it is quiet and beautiful. We could do some fishing and other kinds of loafing, which is a (non-) occupation I like a lot. Then, too, I travel around a lot, more or less out of necessity, and am in and around Boston a good deal. My twelve-year-old grandson lives near there, on a horse farm at South Westport, and he and I are going out to the Air Force Academy this spring. We'll probably leave from Boston, and maybe we could swing by your place in some manner. Well, we'll see.

Please remember me to Jane, whom I have met only that once in The White House—of all places!—but tell her that I look forward to a continued acquaintance, and to getting the families together on whatever basis. My best to you, your people, and your surroundings.

Jim

To: Shaye Areheart   **CC, Emory University**

4620 Lelia's Court
Columbia, S.C. 29206
December 13, 1982

Dear Shaye:

It is good to know the recent news about <u>Puella</u>, its sales, nominations for awards, and so on. Since you tell me that we are in a fair way toward going for a second printing, I enclose here the full text of "Summons" as it should appear in the book. I take this from the first carbon, which is the one I read in public from. You will notice that the fourth stanza—the one with four lines plus the refrain-line is the one that has for some reason been left out. The mistake was not made at this end, for the original of which my copy is the first carbon is the text as it went in to you at Doubleday. As I remember, I never did get to see actual proofs on these, for if I had this omission would not have occurred. Well, not matter; the thing to do is to make sure it's right the next time around.

Another thing: in the first of the "Ray-Flowers" poems, it is not only desirable but necessary that the units presented in opposition to each other "true-up" on the page as they do in the manuscript I sent. Some of the effect of <u>balance</u> I intended is undone by displaying the poem as it appears in the Doubleday version. There should not have been any difficulty as to typography here, for there was none when the poem was printed as desired in the <u>Kenyon Review</u>, nor was there any trouble in the gift edition that our friend out in Arizona, Janet McHughes, had done for the occasion last May. If indeed we do go for a second printing, please handle these two things for me, for I like, as any author would, to have things exactly right in the versions of the poems that people will actually buy and read. Please keep me informed as to the possible new edition, and I will be guided accordingly.

I talked to Jeannette Hopkins at Wesleyan and told her the news about Wesleyan's acquisition of the rights to the out-of-print Doubleday books.

She assumed that, in addition to <u>The Eye-Beaters</u>, <u>The Zodiac</u>, and <u>The Strength of Fields</u>, <u>Puella</u>, as soon as the first edition goes out of print, would also be part of the package. I told her no: that from what you had told me it is likely that Doubleday will reprint <u>Puella</u>, and if so I would keep the book with Doubleday, plus publishing successive volumes of poetry in hardback with Doubleday, as I write them. However, if Doubleday does not plan to keep <u>Puella</u> in print, I will indeed give the book to them, as well as the later volumes, for that will solve, if it happens, all this continuing transferring of rights and the rest of the red tape that goes with changing houses back and forth. I don't mean to make the continuation of my publishing poetry with Doubleday contingent on whether or not <u>Puella</u> is reprinted; that will happen one way or the other. But it <u>is</u> important that you let me know <u>as soon as possible</u> whether you intend to reprint, so that I can keep Wesleyan informed as to the status of the book. They plan to get the other Doubleday books together in one volume, the tentative title of which is <u>The Central Motion</u>, and will eventually bring out, whenever I am dead—or near it!—a collected poems to be called <u>The Whole Motion</u>.

That, at least, is the starry-eyed plan, which I may live—or die!—to accomplish. But the main thing right <u>now</u> is to effect some way by which all the poems I have written are in the public domain. People keep asking for <u>The Zodiac</u> and the others, and send in beat-up copies of the Doubleday books to be signed, and it will be a relief when they can buy these straight-out, and order them from any bookstore, wherever the people live.

There are three books on me coming out in the next six months. University of Illinois Press is doing one that Dave Smith and some other people got together, and in conversation with one of the editors there I was somewhat surprised to learn that Ted Roethke's Doubleday books, all but one of which have gone out-of-print, are now being offered around to various university presses. I suggested that Illinois pick up <u>The Lost Son</u> and <u>The Far Field</u>, which I expect they will do. The dead, too, want to be in print!

Let me know how things stand, and, if we go to a new printing with <u>Puella</u>, please do get the formats of the "Summons" and the first past of "Ray-Flowers" corrected for me.

Our best, and we look forward greatly to seeing you in a few days.

Love,

To: Theodore Weiss

CC, Emory University
4620 Lelia's Court
Columbia, S.C. 29206

February 1, 1983

Dear Ted:

I have prevailed on the Princeton Press to send me a copy of <u>The Man From Porlock</u> for review, and have not only read through the whole thing twice, but have used it extensively in class, with the result that my kids are so enamoured of Lucretius that I cannot get them to jump the fence between the ancient world and the medieval; Dante must wait in the wings for another week because of Lucretius' grim beauties, and because the case you make out for him is the best that the centuries have yet made. But, then, the whole book is remarkable, Ted. The part on Pound is better than the whole corpus of Hugh Kenner's exhaustive—and exhausting—would-be-ness about Pound, and your statement about Pound's attempt to weld a whole lot of imagistic fragments into an epic is what somebody should have made a long time ago, and didn't; it is the definitive statement about that sometimes amazing but frequently stupefying would-be epic, <u>The Cantos</u>.

You are also right about Larkin, and his foolishness. John Betjeman, indeed! Larkin himself, as a poet, is fairish, but only just so. He lacks open excitement, and most of the other qualities that I esteem.

But you have said all this better than I could possibly do. I mean only to congratulate you, here. I always feel wonderful when one of my close and old friends <u>proves</u> <u>out</u>, as they say in the South: is as good as you want him to be. I want to help you feel as entirely good as this book—and your recent poetry—should make you do; I would be glad if I had a hand in that. But really you don't need me for such. The sturdiness and deep flash of your talent, together with your incorruptibility, should give you all the self-esteem you need. Please accept my congratulations, though, for your extraordinary work, and for your extraordinary life.

Let me know on what basis we might meet again, the sooner the better. Meanwhile, I enclose an invitation that comes out of my current—regrettable, but not as yet fatal—sixtieth birthday. Though the invitation arrives maybe a little too late for you to come down, I will hope for you in spirit. That is <u>some</u> spirit.

Ever,

To: Martin H. Greenberg

CC, Emory University
4620 Lelia's Court
Columbia, S.C. 29206

March 2, 1983

Dear Mr. Greenberg:

Thank you for both your letters, and please forgive me for being late in answering them, but I have been out of town, and have only recently got back and looked through the mail that had come in. Again, please forgive. The best short story I have ever read is one called "A Distant Episode," by someone named Frederick Brantley. I read the story in an issue of <u>The Partisan Review</u> years ago, and have not been able to forget it. At this late date, around thirty years late, I am not absolutely sure that that is the name of the story, though I am almost positive it is. I believe the author's first name is Frederick, and I am certain that his last name is Brantley. Beyond that, I can't tell you anything. But it is a super short story, about occupation duty on one of the Pacific islands, and the showing of pornographic photographs to a starved Japanese prisoner who has been flushed out of the caves, and doesn't know that the war is over. Believe me, you would be doing me a very great favor in looking up the story. I am dead certain it appeared in <u>The Partisan Review</u> during the time I was at Vanderbilt, from 1946-1950; that's when I would have read it.[16]

If you can't find the Brantley, story, my next candidate would be James Stern's "Two Men," about an African outpost, and the third choice would be "Passion" by Sean O'Faolain, which is not about sex but a funeral.

That's what I have in my head, in the way of great stories. As for your part, do send along the $100 as soon as you can, and thanks, in advance.

Sincerely,

16. Frederick Brantley, "A Distant Victory," *Partisan Review* 15.7 (1948): 794–806.

To: Robert Penn Warren   **TLS, Emory University**

4620 Lelia's Court
Columbia, S.C. 29206
April 28, 1983

Dear Red:

I have just been sent the book version of <u>Chief Joseph</u>, and have read through it again, full of praise for the extraordinary power of the thing, and with gratitude at your dedication. There is not much else I can say, except that I think the poem is extraordinary—the pulse of it, in its urgency, and also in what Parkman used to call manliness—is unforgettable, and lives not only in the blood but in whatever it is in the body that makes the blood—the marrow, maybe. As for the gratitude, there is no way to measure it, except to think of it as part of whatever human life has given us to do together, and in acknowledgment of each other. The film is one part of this, and the poems—especially this one—are another. Again, thanks for the words and the conjuring-up of the name you set at the head of this extraordinary piece of human imagination and tragic valor.

Let me hear from you when you have time. And remember me to Eleanor with great warmth and regard.

Ever,
Jim

To: Robert Penn Warren   **TLS, Emory University**

4620 Lelia's Court
Columbia, S.C. 29206
June 1, 1983

Dear Red:

Thanks a whole lot for your letter and card. Though I hate to turn loose of the card, I am sending it back, as you request. Thanks for the things you say on it, which I will keep with me for good.

Mark Brugnoni, the fellow who directed the film we made, called yesterday and tell me that he hasn't placed the film yet, but that he has some good prospects. He sent me a print of it, which I have played several times, mainly to friends, and I must say that any network that picks up on the thing will be getting something unusual, and quite unlike the ordinary fare on T.V. For me, it is enough that we made the thing, for there is nothing about the making of it that I don't remember with great satisfaction and nostalgia. It is a kind of record, and I can't think that other people—and later generations—won't benefit from it, or learn from it in ways that will be valuable to at least a few. Well, we'll see.

I have a bunch of new books—and reissues of old books—coming out in the next few months, and I'll send them along to you as I get hold of them. The first of them, which will be out in a couple of weeks and is called <u>Night</u> <u>Hurdling</u>, has the essay I did on you for the <u>Saturday</u> <u>Review</u>, which I hope is all right with you; it's what I think, as I told you.

We are well here. My oldest boy won a journalistic grant, which will get him out of the jungles of El Salvador come September, and I'm grateful for that. My second boy is halfway through medical school at Emory, in Atlanta, and Bronnie has just passed her second birthday, never stops talking, and can climb up on anything.

That is awfully good news about your <u>New</u> <u>and</u> <u>Selected</u> <u>Poems</u>, which should be the best of our century, by an American. Let me know if I can help in any way, advise about selections—anything at all. Whatever I can have to do with such a project, I will be glad to do.

Debba sends her best to you and Eleanor, and you have mine, beyond these or any other words.

Ever,
Jim

To: James Tuckerman Dickey   **RTLS, Emory University**

4620 Lelia's Court
Columbia, S.C. 29206
December 13, 1983

Dear Tucky,

I hope you have got your Christmas present by now, but if you haven't you should in a couple of days. It's one that I think, with your current camping and woods activities, you'll like a lot, though I probably shouldn't say any more about it, knowing you'll probably want to keep it packaged up until Christmas morning; that's what I'd do, anyway. But I <u>do</u> hope you'll like it, because it has to do with finding out where you are, and with getting to wherever it is you want to go. In other words, when you get your navigation on water down really well, with this new equipment you will also be able to navigate on land— in the woods, on mountains, or anywhere—and can be sure that you'll always come out where you want to, which is a thing that most people never master.

I'm glad you saw your father in New York. I saw him there, too, about a month ago, and we had a wonderful afternoon walking in the streets of the city together. I wouldn't take anything in the world for that afternoon, and I hope that when you see your father—for your English trip with him, or any other time—you will find your own way to tell him how much I love him, and how proud I am of him. I am maybe a little shy about this, myself, but do tell him, the first chance you get.

Things are going pretty well with us, though there is a lot of work to do. I just finished a couple of new books, and am pushing on with the long novel. One of the new books is another children's book, called <u>Bronwen, The Traw, and the Shape-Shifter</u>, and I'll send you a copy, if you like, as soon as it comes out. There are some good fight scenes in it, and some nice stuff about flying, too, as a little girl flies with some flying squirrels.

I wonder if we can figure out some way to get together. I haven't seen you since that one canoeing Christmas, that now seems such a very long time ago. I have a sail-boat now, a Sunfish, and, since the water is back in the lake, you could show me how to sail, because I really don't know much about it, at all. But what I do know I like a lot, and am game to learn more, and maybe we'll get a bigger boat later if I can get to where I can do pretty well with the Sunfish.

Please remember me to your mother, and to <u>her</u> mother, and to everyone I met up there. Or just to anyone you like.

Much love for the holidays, and after. And write soon.

Yours,
Fun-Man

To: Richard Calhoun

CC, Emory University
4620 Lelia's Court
Columbia, S.C. 29206

December 15, 1983

Dear Dick:

I have waited a while to write you and Bob about your book,[17] because I wanted to live with it a while, so that I could say what I have to say after a period of immersion, and maybe some degree of osmosis. Having satisfied these conditions, I can come up with only one judgment after all, and this emotional rather than intellectual.

It is simple gratitude, coupled with a resurgence of confidence that is an awfully good thing to have at the age of sixty. If I have done, in all these forms, what you and Bob say—and some would maintain, prove—then I have not wasted my life, and that is a good thing to know, believe me. I look back over the material you deal with, and can remember how almost every word of the poems, say, came to me: where they were written, the technical problems I had in connection with them, even the food and the weather associated with them. The same is true, though not having quite the same intensity, of the writing of the articles, critical essays, and the novel (Alnilam, by the way, is almost finished, and is so painful I can hardly bring myself to reread parts of it). But the way you and Bob have handled the whole of the work—am I correct in assuming that you did Chapter 8, mainly on the criticism and the speculative work, such as "The Self as Agent"? If so, you can be assured that I am particularly grateful—is remarkable: the overall structure of the book is fine, and works, and the individual sections are impressive not only in the degree of personal commitment to the various subjects, but in the quality of insight brought to them.

All this makes the poet in question think only one thing: is my work really worth all their work? If he can answer yes with all truth, he can believe that he has not wasted his life trying to do something impossible to do, or that he was not equipped to do. Part of the value to the poet of a work like yours and Bob's is that it gives him that lift of hope to go on and work more, write more, think more, and live more. That you and Bob have given me, and you not only have my thanks now, but have it for good.

With a warm hand,

17. Richard J. Calhoun and Robert W. Hill, *James Dickey* (Boston: Twayne, 1983).

To: David Havird   **TLS, Property of David Havird**

4620 Lelia's Court
Columbia, S.C. 29206
December 21, 1983

Dear David:

Thanks indeed for your letter, and for the things you say about <u>Night</u> <u>Hurd-</u><u>ling</u> and my other work. I'm especially pleased by your response to "The Eagle's Mile," which is one of the last serious poems I have written, and is different from most of the others. The phrase—and the image—of "Adam in lightning" just alludes to the fact that a bolt of lightning, with all its off-branchings, looks something like an anatomical chart, a map of veins, a kind of instantaneous sketch of a human (because upright) vascular system, and it seems to me a much more dramatic and unexpected way of "creating" Adam than the relatively commonplace traditional one, the matter of the molded clay into which God breathed life. If you come by here, I have a large poster featuring the poem, and if you'll remind me I will be happy to give you one. I would also give you a copy of <u>The</u> <u>Central</u> <u>Motion</u>, if I had more than one, and certainly will if the author's copies reach me by the time you do. If not, I'll get one to you as soon as Wesleyan sends them.

I am most happy that your students have been responding to the poetry. Since I am almost sixty-one now, the vague shape of life-after-death—at least for the work—begins to loom, and it is gratifying to learn that the poems in that book have moved your students.

As far as I know, I will be here the week after Christmas, for it looks like I will have some surgery done on my upper jaw—nothing serious—and that should keep me in town. If you could give me an exact date for your visit, I'll put it on the calendar, to make sure we don't miss.

Our love to Ashley, and to everyone you love and work with. We'll see you in a few days.

Ever,
Jim

To: Willis Barnstone

CC, Emory University
4620 Lelia's Court
Columbia, S.C. 29206

February 20, 1984

Dear Mr. Barnstone:

I have been reading your renditions of the poems of Vicente Aleixandre, and have been much impressed; I like what you and Mr. Garrison have done, having tried a free-ranging version of one of Aleixandre's poems: this was in a little book called Head-Deep in Strange Sounds, later collected in The Strength of Fields.[18] Encouraged by your (and Aleixandre's!) A Bird of Paper, which Ohio University Press was generous enough to send me, I thought I might try some renditions—very free ones—of several of these poems, drawing on your interpretations at least somewhat. Would you mind this? Needless to say, if the poems turn out well I will be more than happy—I would be pleased—to acknowledge the help that you and Mr. Garrison will have given me. As I see things now, the group will be of about thirteen or fourteen poems, the whole thing being (tentatively) called Transfigurations.

Do let me know about this, and I will be guided accordingly. And thanks, in advance, for whatever interest you might have, and for your translations, your original poetry, and your presence on the general scene.

Sincerely, yours,

To: Robert Fitzgerald

CC, Emory University

4620 Lelia's Court
Columbia, S.C. 29206
March 28, 1984

Dear Robert Fitzgerald:

Again, we have missed connection; indeed, what I have come to consider, over the years a kind of essential connection, at least from my point of view. I must be out of town while you are speaking, and that is a circumstance I wish I could have done something about, but, as it turns out, could not. But I did

---

18. "Undersea Fragment in Colons."

want to send you this, and to reiterate my great and entire admiration for you, and most especially for your original work. Though I am no real judge of the famous translations, since I simply tend to read them as poetry rather than as poetry coupled with scholarship, I think you have done extraordinary service here in bringing the ancient world forward in time, in the way the ancients intended it, as profound and moving art. Nevertheless, I send with my secretary for your signing only copies of your own poems, for these are the contributions that mean the most to me. I have carried the two Arrow Edition books with me since the war, and have never failed to have the life-force and the sharpening ingredient of classicism renewed by means of them. I would be most honored if you would sign your books for me. But that shall be as you wish, of course.

I hope you will have a good experience of us here at Carolina, and will come back whenever you can, or whenever you like.

With a warm hand,

To: William Page[19]

CC, Emory University
4620 Lelia's Court
Columbia, S.C. 29206

May 14, 1984

Dear Bill:

Thanks indeed for the letter, for the things you say about the various readings—and for your good news on several fronts. To answer your request, I enclose three short poems in a kind of odd hybrid form I've been working in lately, where I take off from original poems in other languages, translate them, then retranslate them back into the original, composing and changing as I go along, and then finally bring them back over into English, still changing, altering, inventing, ordering and disordering. The result doesn't sound like anything I've ever written before, and that is what I like. Aleixandre would surely never recognize these, and neither would any literal translator, for by the time the poem is finished it is a long way from the launch-pad. All kinds of things have come in; for example, the last line of "Word" is not from Aleixandre but from the notebooks of William Blake.

---

19. Editor of *Memphis State Review.* The interview appeared in the fall 1984 issue, though none of the poems were included, and was later collected in *The Voiced Connections of James Dickey.*

Anyway, I hope you like these. According to your space requirements you're free to use all of them, or two, or one—or of course none. But do let me know if you like them as soon as you have a chance; I must keep an eye on things, though I have never really been very good at doing so, I can tell you.

I look forward to hearing from you on this or indeed any matter, and to seeing the interview in the Fall; those are the best questions I ever got asked.

My best to Nancy; she makes things around her good—where one would want to be.

Cordially,

To: Louis D. Rubin, Jr.   **CC, Emory University**
4620 Lelia's Court
Columbia, S.C. 29206

June 19, 1984

Dear Louis:

Well, that was a fine shower of golden weather you invited me to stand under in The New York Times. I don't know, myself, if I am worth all that much, but if somebody of your ability and record says so, there must be something in it. Anyway, thanks a whole lot, from now in the present, and for all the years going back into the past, from the time I first knew you, and understood a little of your concern and your dedication, all of which have now been proved by time, which—or who—is the only reliable arbiter in these matters.

Incidentally, I just picked up in a bookstore your book on the Fugitives, which is by far the best that has been done, including Louise Cowan's. I felt like I was coming home to my past. Dan Young, who is quoted on the cover, was a couple of classes ahead of me at Vanderbilt, about at the same time as Louise and Elizabeth Spencer. Davidson was the only one of the original group still there, if you except Walter Curry, and he was not up to his full potential as a teacher because of his unfortunate involvement with various right-wing political groups, some of them pretty dubious. Later, I was Andrew Lytle's assistant at the University of Florida, I knew Allen Tate fairly well off and on, I made a film last year with Warren, and he dedicated his last book to me, and William Yandell Elliott was my ex-mother-in-law's (unsuccessful) suitor. I also knew Carolyn Gordon, though not well, and did my thesis—dreadful it was, too—

under Richmond Beatty. So I felt more or less at home with the characters and attitudes you dealt with, and am much in your debt for clearing up a good many matters that have puzzled me since those days, such as Warren's particular angle in his contribution to I'll Take My Stand.

Well, I won't go on and on in this immoderate fashion, but will close now with continued thanks. As the blues player Blind Gary Davis says, "I just feel like goin' on." Where I'll go I'm not entirely sure, but there are some new things that I hope you will like when they come out.

One more thing. My secretary-assistant, Rebecca LaClair, is coming up to Chapel Hill to graduate school, and I hope you will get to know her and develop a personal interest in her academic functioning and career. She is a brightly intelligent, industrious and worthy person, the best I have ever worked with, and I am sure that she will do well up there. She wants to come up in a week or so to talk over her curriculum, and if you're in town I'd appreciate your arranging an interview. If you'll drop me a note letting me know what your situation is, she can arrange a visit at a time when you'll be there.

Once again, thanks for the golden weather; in such a climate I might amount to something yet. If I don't it won't be your fault.

Ever,

To: Miller Williams[20]

CC, Emory University
4620 Lelia's Court
Columbia, S.C. 29206

July 16, 1984

Dear Miller:

Well! I have pondered the weekend on exactly how to answer your letter concerning Immortals, and I think I can do that, though I could never answer the tenacious solicitude of your Reader, who knows more about my work and the phases of my "career"—to say nothing of my "public image"—than I do by far. If I knew who he is—she is?—I would thank him/her for all this attention, and for the good will that seems to be evident. I realize that it is sup-

20. Director of the University of Arkansas Press.

posed to be bad form, or something to reveal who these invisible Readers may acutally be, but I would certainly like to find out who this one is, if it is within your conscience. If it is not, please convey my very great thanks to this person, finding your own way to make my gratitude clear. I'd appreciate that a lot.

Needless to say, I'm glad you approve of the poems, and would like to publish them if I can do more. I probably could, or can, though of course I have no idea whatsoever of how any of these may turn out. Yesterday I went through Aleixandre's Poesias Completas, and found some more things of his I would like to try my hand at—or, according to the way I approach the task, to take off from. This is, I realize, an odd method, but for me a very exciting source of revelations and counter-directions. But "thirty or so" poems is a whole lot of poetry, especially at my amoeba-like speed, and all the other commitments I have. It would be a while before I could turn in that number of pieces. Could you not consider lowering the figure a bit? See what you can do about fixing a more or less exact count on the number of poems that you think a volume—an ideal volume—of this kind should carry, and I'll try to temper my wind to your sail. But remember, I am slow, though mostly diligent. In my groping way, I have to invent around the phrases and ideas of Aleixandre's that I like—even though some are either inadvertent or deliberate mis-readings—and adjust all these elements into something that sounds like, and therefore is another side of me. A kind of slow and frustrating excitement is in this, but please don't set any exact deadline on the rest of the manuscript, for God knows when I will be done with it.

Another thing bothers me somewhat. Doubleday has a lien on all my future original poetry, and I intend these to be read as originals, as I did The Zodiac and some others; there are only a few hints from Aleixandre in these poems; he would never recognize them. So in all conscience, if we make this a full-size book, the people at Doubleday may get disgruntled, or want to publish it themselves, and, since you've seen it first, I feel obligated to you for this reason—and for others including friendship—and naturally I don't want to cause anyone trouble. I thought that if Arkansas offered the book simply as a small gift edition, as Palaemon Press did with Head-Deep in Strange Sounds, later incorporated into The Strength of Fields, it wouldn't make all that much difference. But if I do a whole book, it might be a source of contention, for, as I say, I offer Immortals as original poetry.

So let me know what you think of all this. Meanwhile, I'll begin working through some of these new things, and see what happens. In other words, I'll go ahead on the premise that we will do <u>Immortals</u>, if the new poems turn out well, and meantime will wait for you to get back to me.

With the greatest affection.

Ever,

To: Christopher Dickey

CC, Emory University
4620 Lelia's Court
Columbia, S.C. 29206

25 July 84

Dear Chris:

Here are a couple of pictures I took of Tucky down at Kevin's wedding, and thought you might like to have them. He and I spent most of the afternoon talking, and it was revealed that I have been given the grandson that I most wanted, but wouldn't have known about if he hadn't appeared. He is full of plans, and I want to do whatever I can to help him carry through on whichever ones are most obsessive and magical—he is at a good age for magic—and those for which he is best suited. I hope all of us will be able to keep in a little closer communication than we have been doing, for timing might turn out to be crucial in one way or another, or might yield us rewards which we couldn't have by any other means. So, do keep in touch, and Tucky and I will keep in touch.

Let us know about your plans for coming down to Litchfield, and we'll swing right with you. Debra and Bronnie and I will go down next week and get the place cleaned up, and we will have some keys made for you. One of the air-conditioners—the one for the ground-floor—is on the blink, but I'll try to scare up a thousand dollars somewhere and have it fixed. But the upper floor should be all right, and the middle floor should be <u>sort</u> of all right, even if we're not able to get the machinery put in good order. Let us know your plans, and we'll bring it all together.

Love to Carol. And do let us hear as soon as you can.

Love,

To: James Anderson[21]

CC, Emory University
4620 Lelia's Court
Columbia, S.C. 29206

July 26, 1984

Dear Jim A.:

Thanks very much for your letter, and your good news. It is good to know that Breitenbush has a chance for survival; certainly publishers like yourself are the cream of whatever milk the literary profession has in this country, and I want to encourage your particular enterprise for a good many reasons. One of these is that you make very good-looking books, and you publish the people that an outfit like yours ought to publish. That is, you have some literary sense as well as book-design sense. All these things are good, and I hope you <u>can</u> keep going.

And I hope also that Rice's book will do as well as you hope for. Again, let me know what I can do. And, yes, I have read the book, and it is just as good as you say it is. And I said it is; keep using the quote.

As for <u>Immortals</u>, the University of Arkansas Press, under the direction of Miller Williams, a good poet, and so very poetry oriented, wants to do it, but, since there are only fifteen poems in the present manuscript, wants me to do about fifteen or twenty more, which takes some work, at my pace. However, if for some other reason or other Arkansas and I can't get together—if, for example, I can't find the time to write the other poems, or if I can't produce any that please me as the first ones do—Breitenbush still has first option, if you remain in existence, and if you would take on the publication of a small gift-type book, which I would not collect in a larger volume, as, for example, I did with the poems originally brought out as <u>Head</u>-<u>Deep</u> <u>in</u> <u>Strange</u> <u>Sounds</u>, which later became part of <u>The</u> <u>Strength</u> <u>of</u> <u>Fields</u>. So keep the door open, up there, among the firs and the down timber; you and I may make it yet.

Is Milwaukie Avenue near Milwaukie, Oregon? I ask, because I lived in Milwaukie for two years, when I taught at Reed in 1963-65. My house was at 1200 Lava Lane, on the Wilamette River, next to the golf course of the country club. I liked it a lot; my dog Frieda is buried there. As I say, the place is full of memories.

My best to you.

21. Publisher of Breitenbush Publications.

To: Wade Hall[22]

CC, Emory University
4620 Lelia's Court
Columbia, S.C. 29206

September 13, 1984

Dear Wade:

Here are the three poems I promised you, and I hope you and your readers will like them. They represent a kind of new line of attack for me, for they result from improvising on—really, just taking off from—a line or image that has struck me. These are not like Lowell's Imitations, for they are in no sense translations, and come out baring no resemblance to the original lines that formed the inceptions. Anyway, here they are, and as I judge they come out somewhere short of the sixty-line limit you mention. I'll look forward to seeing these in your Spring issue. There is no danger of a conflict with the book publication, for the volume these will appear in, Strong Horses Circling, won't come out for a year or two.

Please give my love, and Deborah's, to all we met when we awere there. And thanks once more, belatedly, for your hospitality when we were with you. The grey Bellarmine jacket with the red-striped sleeves has become my favorite autumnal outfit! I hope the publicity around this school is good for your school.

Cordially,

To: Eugene J. Woods

CC, Emory University
4620 Lelia's Court
Columbia, S.C. 29206

September 28, 1984

Dear Mr. Woods:

Thank you for your letter, and your offer of $50.00, which I will be happy to have from you in response to this communication. Thanks also for your rather full explanation of your royalty arrangement, which, I agree, is quite fair and suits me fine.

22. Editor of Kentucky Poetry Review.

There are a lot of things that I wish I had written, but the one about which I wish this the most is the short poem by James Agee which appears in the Ballantine paperback of his <u>Collected</u> <u>Poems</u> on page 68 in a section called "Theme with Variations", and is "Variation IV". Though it is only twelve lines long, it is the best I know. If you can't find this, tell me and I'll type it up for you.

Again, let me know what else I might be able to do.

Sincerely,

To: Scott Donaldson

CC, Emory University
4620 Lelia's Court
Columbia, S.C. 29206

January 1, 1985

Dear Scott:

Good to get your letter, and to know that you're working on a biography of Cheever. I didn't know him well, but he did read at the Library of Congress when I was there, and as his host I spent several days with him. He was, as I remember, a modest little guy, and his reading went well. He was not someone you could get close to on short acquaintance, but he was very well-mannered and gentlemanly. In his demeanor, though, was something of the decor, if you know what I mean, of the aging homosexual. I was surprised to find that he was married, though I shouldn't have been, for I have a couple of similar cases as relatives, and, though they have the same fastidious, slightly aggrieved manner, they also are married. You could feel some suppression in him, some kind of withdrawn and secretive thing, though this was not, at least to me, bothersome. Toward the end of his visit he grew very friendly, and at a party we gave before he left I was sitting on the floor talking to Reynolds Price, and I felt a hand on my head, and, when I looked up and saw that it was Cheever's I was surprised; and then I was not surprised. But I liked Cheever, and like his memory, and at times I think he is a very good writer indeed.

Well, how are things up there? Did you get to know a mad Irish friend of mine, Joe Hone? He's a trial to some people, but an awfully good fellow, I've always thought.

Something strikes me: why don't you in your distinguished professorship, and all, get me an honorary degree from William and Mary? I have nine of these, but would much welcome one from a Virginia school, especially yours. I have always had good vibes about the place; though he didn't go there, my youngest son was recruited as a basketball player by William and Mary; the coach came down here and stayed with us for a few days.

Let me know what you think of all this, and meanwhile I'll go back through my notes on Cheever's visit and see if I can find anything else that'll help you.

My best, as always,

To: Gary Kerley   TLS, Property of Gary Kerley

4620 Lelia's Court
Columbia, S.C. 29206
July 23, 1985

Dear Gary Kerley:

Thank you very much indeed for your letter, and for the things you say about the telephone session last week. I, too, enjoyed the occasion immensely, and was struck by the seriousness and intelligence of the students. I have had letters from several of them, and read them with a strong feeling of certitude that such occasions are worth the doing. Too, it was very good for a writer to hear from whatever readers he may have; as with the telegraph operator, he is gratified to know that he is not sending with a dead key. Please tell your students how much I appreciate their interests and concern.

And, sure, it will be fine with me if you transcribe the interview and do an article for the Newsletter. Joyce Pair, the editor, tells me that they are going from a letter to a magazine format in the next issue or so. Such popularity is a mystery to me, though as you can imagine I am most interested. I'd appreciate your letting me have a copy of the transcript after you edit it, so that we can both get it exactly as we want. I'll be looking for it, when you're ready.

And do send along the check as soon as you can. My tax man is after me to keep his records straight, and I don't want to get into trouble with him!

Cordially,
Jim D.

To: Mary B. Jones

CC, Emory University
4620 Lelia's Court
Columbia, S.C. 29206

August 9, 1985

Dear Mary,

Forget your physical Being? Never!

I was happy to hear from you, my Mary, and to have a look at the pictures. And thanks for the clipping. My assistant tells me she heard on her car radio that the blind pilot made her flight successfully. Paul Harvey, the commentatior, led off by saying that Karen Pendergast waited until she was thirty-six to learn to fly, described the flight, including a successful landing in a crosswind, and then capped the story off by saying, "She enjoyed everything about flying but the scenery; Karen Pendergast is blind."

It surely would be good to see you. I should be up that way from time to time. Maybe we could get together. I'll keep you informed of my travel plans, and we'll make it happen. I'd like to meet your friend Robert. I'll look for the next man I meet that matches the photograph: a man with no head and no feet— and the solution to acid rain!

I send along my best wishes to you in your new place. And do keep in touch.

Ever,

To: Kendrick Smithyman

CC, Emory University
4620 Lelia's Court
Columbia, S.C. 29206

August 29, 1985

Dear Kendrick Smithyman,

It is wonderful to get your letter, across all those seas and all those years! Surely I remember my time down there with great delight and honor, especially the afternoon with you and Allen Curnow and the others on Allen's porch there, near the harbor. There are not many such times, and I certainly cherish that one among the very best the Lord has ever given me. If you see any of the others that were there, please remember me to them with as much warmth as you, as my envoy, can endow me with. I hope you will keep in touch, for I have every intention of coming back down there if I can find any excuse, or a way, or both. Can you think of any possibilities that might lead to a visit? It would be a good inducement for me to live a little longer, and those are always welcome at the age of sixty-two.

I don't wish to close without telling you that, whether you know it or not—how could you know it?—your work was the largest single influence on my own sense of the possibility of form, back in the war years and just after. Your "Double Sonnet" in an old issue of <u>Angry Penquins</u> gave me the clue I needed. When I got your letter I looked the poem up in that magical issue; I still have it, and the poem is still good. I do thank you, and God bless.

Cordially,

p.s. Send me your books, and I will send you some of mine. And that's a promise.

To: Bruce Beans

CC, Emory University
4620 Lelia's Court
Columbia, S.C. 29206

November 29, 1985

Dear Bruce Beans:

Thank you very much indeed for your letter, for your preliminary questions about the interview, and most especially for your comments on the Bronwen poem, together with your suggestion about one of the lines. I knew the business about sills, of course, but couldn't resist the rhyme, which seemed of its own accord to want to be there. Thank you very much for the suggestion about the sash, so that we can change the line to read "Bronwen lifted the sash from the sill." How's that? Pencil the change into your copy, read it to Carolyn again, and tell her you contributed that line, which you damn well did. And thanks again, too.

About the interview. I can answer your questions easily, but want to make some comments following. No, I have not done any flying since World War II in military aircraft. I do not have a pilot's license; my main interest now is in navigation; I have a Navigator's certificate and diploma from the school run by Davis Instruments, in California.

If you do the interview I want to stress at the outside that I want as little biographical emphasis as can possibly be arranged. In connection with <u>Deliverance</u> I was foolish enough to give out a good deal more biographical information that was needed, with the result that the focus came to be on me rather than on the book I had written, and I have no wish to let that happen again. Thanks to my generousity—or garrulousness, it may be—the press built me up into some kind of Hemingwayesque character, a real Natty Bumppo—or even Chingachgook—of the wilderness, a guitar player in the same league with Chet Atkins, an archer comparable to Howard Hill, and a number of other things that I emphatically am not. This time I want the focus on the book, and the book alone. If the interviewer can't do it this way, I don't want to be interviewed.

But I'm sure this won't happen in your case, for I feel a good rapport, and I'm sure we can work together to get something we are both enthusiastic about.

As to your being sent an advance copy—a copy of the typescript rather—of <u>Alnilam</u>, I will leave that to my editor at Doubleday, Carolyn Blakemore, whom you might like to write in connection with your request. Tell I said it would be O.K.

Meanwhile, keep letting me hear from you. And get together with <u>your</u> Carolyn again, in your own time, and hers. Tell her that her father has now become a poet, which he needed to find out about, for the poet is the best part of any writer. And any father.

Cordially,

To: Carolyn Blakemore   CC, Emory University
                                                4620 Lelia's Court
                                               Columbia, S.C. 29206

                                                 January 27, 1986

Dear Carolyn:

Thanks for your close reading and for the things you say about the book. I am most pleased and gratified.

Let us now get to your comments, one by one. First a suggestion about the DARK/LIGHT sections. Let me offer what may be at least a partial solution, in the way that I have shown in the revised manuscript, where I suggest printing the sections in which there are now large blanks on either side of the page as regular presentations of dialogue. As to the key sections—for example, the Flight Sequence, which you find "staggering"—is staggering just as it is. And the scene where Cahill makes it through the propellers and Zack is killed cannot be done in any other way, with the simultaneous happenings to the blind man and the cadets in the demolition-derby of aircraft. You speak of inventing "a design that would cause the eye to stop and jump from DARK to LIGHT and back again," on which point I would welcome your suggestions, but I see no difficulty at all in asking the reader to read down one side of the page and then down the other, and have his perceptions altered thereby. As to this being a "designer's and a typesetter's nightmare," that is not my concern, nor is the "cover price of the finished book." I suggest you have a look at the Complete Poems of e. e. cummings if you have any doubts about this; strike in anywhere. Alnilam is nothing in difficulty beside what Harcourt Brace produced in the case of cummings.

Your comments on the DARK/LIGHT motif is good editorial counsel. My desire in using it in certain places is to focus on and dramatize the situations in which it can be most effective. You say "In a short piece, the parallels might be considered brilliant." Perhaps; I am not, employing this approach, however, in a short piece, but as a device in an action which is a complete novel. It is used at the points of maximum intensity, and I can see no way in which this quality can be enhanced. In passing, it ought to be apparent, also, that the split page will be much commented on; much attacked and at least somewhat praised, though this is not any part of the reason I choose to employ it. The reason is that it seems to me—who must be accorded some credence in the matter—to work, and to work in a new way, and the fact that it will immediately be much imitated—which it will—is irrelevant from my point of view, though it is of some interest, I think, and should be noted. I might add, here, too, that none of the other six editors I have had at Doubleday—Sandy Richardson, Randy Green, the Brown girl, who worked with me on Puella, Hugh O'Neill, or Kate Medina and Shaye—have objected to this feature, but have encouraged it, in some cases vehemently, so I went ahead with it in good faith, natural to do.

Next, you say that "Cahill is too much of a cipher." If you think more background on him is desirable, I might consider implementing the information about his earlier life. There could be some other things, as many as we want, though I had rather keep the action in the present, and not give the reader a great deal of case-history information about him. What I had intended to do was to give just a few incidents in his early life, incidents which are as mysterious to him as they are to the reader, such as the bull-like sprinter with the gold-trimmed shorts, which the reader is intended to feel as an off-set to and precursor of Cahill's notion of a static and concentrated strength—his "centrality"—his only bodily prowess as a blind man. To go at great length into his childhood, his upbringing, his school-time, his early sex life, or whatever else the novelist might envision, is to take the focus off where the action should be, which is the snowed-in military field where the blind man come with his dog. I can't say that "the more mystery about Cahill the better"; that is maybe too extreme, but not irrelevant. I do, however, maintain that too much about his former life is destructive of the atmosphere of suddenness and accountability in which he appears.

You ask me who Cahill's friends are, beyond the lifeguard and Ruiz, and his women. You ask what he does with himself. The notion here is that he remains essentially at a loose end. He has little to occupy himself with, but this is something a self-centered person will not admit. He gets along, and what he does is nobody else's business. If he wants to walk for hours in Piedmont Park, that is his business. If he wants to work on his amusement park, if he wants to balance accounts with Ruiz, if he wants to sit in his tower and look out over the suburbs, these things are his business. He needs no one and he wants no one. If you have never known a person like this, I hope you will not. But Cahill is one of them; his insistence on autonomy is absolute, and with his blindness it becomes obsessive, almost maniacal. But impressive it is; it comes to the beholder like something from another world, as Joel Cahill's equal mysteriousness seemed to come.

As to what Cahill does when he shuts down the entertainment park, or what he does with himself during the winter months, aside from what I have already said, I have no very clearcut notion, and would welcome suggestions. He is so self-centered, and so much determined to be a law unto himself, a kind of king, that I should think it would follow, that, combined with his drive to build things, change them around, add to them, and so on, he would spend most of his time working on his own property, in one way or the other. An amusement park takes as much work as farming; the intensity with which the equipment is used during the season necessitates a long session of work during the off-season to get everything ready to be town down again, when the crowds come back. But, as I say, there could be other things, though I don't want to go on overly much about these. There should be a few activities, scenes, people, which register strongly, and epitomize the rest, rather than a long recounting of incidents.

Yes, it is true; there are the discrepancies you note, and these I have corrected by hand. The events of the book were written over such a long time-span, and under such different circumstances, all of them, that I find I had forgotten, a few hundred pages and several years later, what I said at the earlier times. But as to his association with his wife, I do want her to be a florist, and the conversation with her over the phone to be essentially as it is. You like the version of the marriage where his wife left him because he had a "mistress who was a florist," which is fine, but I don't think we should have two florists. A mistress should not be hard to find, though, and she would have the same function; that is, as having to do with Cahill's wife leaving him. We can find a mistress almost anywhere (don't ask me how I know!). Anyway, as you can see, I have made the mistress an employee in a loan office.

Cahill had never shown any interest in his son simply because he doesn't have any. The reader should see that he is a man who never should have married, and is, as he feels himself to be, someone so entirely intent on self-sufficiency and autonomy as to be a kind of monster. It is the breaking-down of this shell, which in its way is responsible for many of Cahill's better qualities—his courage, for example, and his stoicism, his self-reliance and even his creativity—that is the true subject of the story, as he realizes, very dimly at first and then mysteriously and strongly, what it involves to have a son, even though a dead—or disappeared—one. The whole idea, here, is the drawing together of the dead son and the blind father by means of the dead boy's arrangements and the Alnilam plot, which may possibly, as is said by Major Ianonne late in the story, to have been either an unconscious or a conscious scheme to bring the father into the son's scope of action, and to place him at the center of it, as the star Alnilam is the center of Orion.

Cahill comes to Peckover, ostensibly, because his son has named him next-of-kin. But this is no more than a pre-text, at least at the beginning. It in fact represents an out-of-the-blue development for Cahill's new life as a blind man. Whether or not he would say so, this will constitute his first big challenge: to take on this situation with no human help, nothing but himself and the extension of himself, his dog. The occasion has simply been given to him. It is legitimate; his boy for some reason not known to him did name him his next-of-kin, and he feels ready to take on the test: the travel, the people he will meet, and whatever happens as a result. That is the situation and state of mind in which we bring him to Peckover, and, given the character and the circumstances, should be quite clear to anyone who assesses these.

And as to the military personnel taking time with Cahill, extending every courtesy to him, at least at first, I can assure you that this is exactly what they would have done. I saw something very similar to this happen at the Primary base where I trained. Peckover (Latham Field) is a new base; there has never been a trainee death before. There is really no precedent for handling such a case, and when the next-of-kin parent shows up, and is a blind man into the bargain, there is an extra element to the bending-over-backward of which the military in such cases is quite capable of displaying. There is no difficulty at all about this; I have seen similar things happen more than once.

Now to your specific points. Most of them have been taken care of by my alterations of the text, but I'd like to go over them item by item as you have listed them, so that you can check the manuscript and see if we agree, in each instance, as to the effectiveness of the way in which your points have been handled.

p. 23. See amended text.

p. 50. I have taken out the whole memory scene of the hunting trip and the strange quilts. It didn't seem to add anything, and I had already used a similar situation in a poem years ago.

p. 79. I have specified the gamy or "green" taste as something Zack has never had "from anything that was wild," which should leave out the horses.

79-89. You suggest cuts here, but don't specify which. I have left the pages in, with some changes, though we can discuss this later, if you like. It seems of some importance to record Cahill's first physical experience of the Colonel, and the Colonel's first impression of Cahill, as given on page 88.

92. "Missing, presumed dead" is standard procedure for military personnel whose bodies cannot be found within a certain time limit. There is every reason to assume that Joel has not survived the fire. I think you are not fully onto the point about the father's being listed as next-of-kin, in that it surely is a mystery to everyone concerned. It is this having given the father's name on the part of the son which precipitates the whole action of the book, and the slow revelation as to why he did so, and the speculations by various people, mainly the Flight Surgeon, as to these matters, are of the greatest importance. They indicate, among other things, that Joel had been—had always been—yearning for a father, his father, and either unconsciously or consciously had sought this curious way to summon him. In the earlier part of the letter I have commented on this, and you can have a look back, a couple of pages, if you need to.

94. Helmet has been eliminated; there's no longer any reference to it. (See 99. below. left out.)

109. See earlier part of letter.

113. I don't know what you mean by "dense." There are two sections of the book where Cahill listens to "official" speeches and his thoughts at certain words of these are counterpointed against what the speaker is saying. This section is one of them, and the scene at the graduation is another. When you say this "doesn't work," I disagree with you, simply. If you have suggestions as to how this might be improved, I'd be happy to have them.

117. "Neutral" has been eliminated all the way through. Also, since I haven't scratched DARK/LIGHT passages in all the 1271 pages of the book, you may consider them eliminated wherever you should find them.

99. Have changed in text. The "questions" refer to those that he has asked the Colonel, which should be clear now.

118. As to his sense of smell. In another section, which you'll come on as you read back through the manuscript, it is explained that Cahill's sense of smell

is not the best, but that he is attempting to improve it, or let it improve with his blindness, as his hearing did. In other words, on 118, it is all right if he smells the chicken.

118-19. Don't know what you mean; please explain.

122. Line has been cut.

131. Have changed reference to pools, which see in latest text.

129-32. Yes, I would like to keep this material about Ruiz, or most of it, for Ruiz is the nearest Cahill has ever had to a son, and his image, as it keeps re-curring to Cahill, should be evidence of his unconscious longings for a son. Also, the business about Ruiz's voice echoing from the empty swimming pool is like the voice of the dead, singing from underground, and also constituting a kind of summons.

134. Which symbols? If you mean the prosodic notations I have put in from time to time, those are only notations to myself for the way I want the rhythm to go in those places, and from which I went onward in the narrative until I could find the right word and go back and put it in. All these occasions have been taken care of in the present text. I don't find any of these on 134, though, so you may mean something else.

136. "Mistake" substituted for "treason."

137. Earlier mistress is now an employee of a loan office. Also, prosodic nota-tions ("symbols") taken out.

137ff. You say that somehow you don't believe this information about his marriage, and find it "unreal." Perhaps. Let's leave this for the moment, so that you can suggest something else. Otherwise we will just be trying this thing and that thing, and we won't get anywhere.

146. Pregnancy. I should think that what I say on 146 should be in line with Cahill's general indifference to other people, which extends to his unborn child. In another place in the manuscript—as amended—it is established that Cahill's wife left him before the child was born. What has this to do with making his visit to the base "all the more inexplicable"?

134-159. You say these pages don't work for you, that they hold the story up and don't add to our knowledge of Cahill. Perhaps other material would add to the knowledge in a way that would please you more, but I have not the slightest inking of what form this would take, unless you tell me. You say repeatedly that Cahill is too much of a cipher, that we don't know enough about him, his former life, his interests, and so on, and then you propose taking out most of the material dealing with this that I have given. I can only conclude that you don't think this material does what is needed, but it is what I have envisioned, and we either go with it, perhaps implemented in some way according to your suggestions, or we interpolate a whole lot of new material, which I invent, which you might also not like, either. That way, we just go round and round in the dark, which neither of us wants to do. So let me know what you think. But the part about the model airplane must stay in; that I am sure of. The novel's chief character is the air itself, and this is Cahill's first true apprehension of it; it must stay. Some of the material on the kites, which is a kind of pre-figuring of this, might come out, but this must remain.

162-63. Again, I don't follow you in your feeling that these pages are too hard for the reader. They have to do with the first encounter with Malcolm Shears, the inheritor of leadership from Joel, which is quite necessary to the story. Explain what you mean; I'd appreciate it.

170-73. You're quite right; I had just as soon drop all the business about the boxing brother, if you like. I haven't indicated this cut in the text, but if you'll tell me what you think judicious, I will make the changes in my copy. I would still like to keep the frosted window, and something he might remember as having seen through a space rubbed clear on such a window in his childhood. It seems a good device, and especially in this part of the story. It is not bad, though, is it, to have the blind man shadow-boxing in the room by himself? That strikes me as being rather a good touch, and as saying something about Cahill's belligerency and his helplessness, at the same time. Let's see if there might be a way we could keep this.

176. Taken care of in new text.

177. See previous reference in this letter to Cahill's sense of smell.

178-80. Check what I have done in the current text, and see if there is an effective way we could do this part in regular format, which I am quite willing to do.

200. Give me your suggestions, here.

205-06. Ditto.

211. See earlier part of letter.

212. Are you referring to McCaig's feeling in the LIGHT section? Again, I am not certain as to what you mean, in your reference to this page.

224ff. You say that LIGHT could follow DARK, here. Though I haven't indicated this in the text, we could try it that way, if you feel sure, now, in what you said. Consider, though, that this leads into the sequence about the twin waterfall, and the connection is made between the waterfall of the Colonel's AT-6 and the memory of the twin falls. I would like this to register as strongly as possible.

229. Cahill's general indifference to other people is what was wrong with the marriage; his willed sense of autonomy and supremacy, his bed-rock egocentricity. He is the kind of man who needs this feeling about himself, as I said earlier, more than he needs food. No marriage could withstand such an outlook on the part of one of its members; and blindness has raised it to the status of fanaticism. Or lowered it, as the case may be.

229. Again, I am open to suggestions.

235. McCaig has simply found that he can touch Cahill, now that he knows him a little better.

238. Changed to a week.

264. Taken care of; see changes in text.

270ff. Good; recast in regular font.

277. Changed "his face" to "him."

It seems to me that there are a sufficient number of references to the failure of recovering the body. There are some of these later, which you may have noted after working forward from the point where you make this observation.

301 and earlier. I think the gas lecture is pretty good, myself, although, if you suggest cuts, we may be able to make them. The reason the gas lecture is in ordinary format and the one on principles of flight is in the split rendition is that the one about flight concerns aircraft and the air, and it is Cahill's increasing recognition of the properties and mysteries of the air that is one of the important feature of the book.

242,3. Taken care of in present text.

346-7. I am willing to go with this just as it stands, just as it was printed in Partisan Review's 50th anniversary number. The reason for the density is the fact that the physical conditions are extreme and unusual, and the heightening and telescoping of Cahill's memories require such treatment. As I say, I will go with this as it is.

372. Both the Bombardier's story and the Navigator's story are in a sense set pieces, and require their own uninterrupted development. They are stories within stories, and are important because they deal with actual warfare from the standpoint of participants. Monologues are monologues, and to break these things up simply for the sake of breaking them up, is not to the purpose. It is my hope, and belief, that the reader will be just as absorbed in the account of these early raids in Europe and the South Pacific as in the rest of the story; certainly the audiences where I have read these sections have registered their receptiveness on this basis.

384. Cahill hasn't reacted because he is interested in the same way. He can but listen. What could he contribute? These are the stories of other men.

385. The confusion—real, enough, I see as I go back through these portions—as to which officer flew from where, is cleared up in the current version, which see.

397. I am unable to find earlier reference mentioned. Please clarify.

397. The long scene is meant to convey what it does in fact convey, the sense of participation in aerial warfare by those who have been involved in it. You ask for cuts, and I am willing to listen to your suggestions, if you choose to make them. There is no point in cutting just for the sake of cutting. In other words, convince me.

402. The drinks are now Jack Daniels and Four Roses (see p. 352). I don't know if Southern Comfort was made then, though it is awful enough for any-body.

403-05. You ask what this adds, and I answer that it is simply a scene, the Cadet Club, together with what is in it and who is in it; from 405-408, as you'll see, I suggest changing to a regular format.

437. You suggest that this information should come much earlier. Again, tell me where. As to the rest of your comment here, see the first part of the letter. And I'm not certain what you mean by "Has McCaig been speaking this way all along?" What way is it that you refer to?

442. The material about cockfighting is a fill-in on McCaig's character and personality, and it also brings in the country man's mystique of "blood" in the genetic sense, which bears on the father-son blood tie, or is meant to, though I hope this is not overly obvious.

459. Farmer is now named Rabun, throughout.

467. Debris was left of the plane, and what was towed away. I imagine the ribs and the undercarriage were towed.

469. The military brass believe—they must believe, since they have failed to find the body—that Joel is dead. As is plain later, the Alnilam plotters don't believe it; they believe he will come back when he judges the time is right.

476. Again, I am open to suggestions. What narrative do you mean?

482. Correct; this is the first time the possibility of Joel's being alive has been broached. That's the way I want it.

522-23. See additions to the text.

530. See current text.

543. Neither would Cahill know it. What is the difficulty?

569-71. Please advise as to re-casting this. Adler has not come in before.

577. He might ask the boys about the initials on the goggles, though he has already asked the Colonel. This comes out later, when it is more important.

583. I imagine we could re-cast this material to alternate DARK and LIGHT, though it was not conceived in this way. Show me what you mean.

589. Please clarify. I don't understand what the antecedent of "him" might be. Cahill? Or Joel?

591-594. Yes, let's cut the whole parrot story; that helps us. Check the new version and you'll see what I've done here.

609. There is nothing unusual about this. Many—if not most—operators of simulator and mock-up equipment didn't fly, either having no interest in it or being a little apprehensive about the real thing. As I say, not unusual.

610. Correct. This is an item which registers Cahill's deepening involvement with the son he was quite sure he had never cared anything about. No, Cahill has never seen Joel. I want to keep Joel's comments to the cadets about his father to a minimum, just a few aphoristic things that come out later. No, Joel's mother is not dead. I'm surprised you should ask this, since the text makes such things quite clear. And the point is that Joel did know where his father was; that it mattered to him to find out. See earlier part of letter.

623. Again, I don't agree. To show the effect of the dog fight on a blind man and at the same time to show the actual fight as it takes place under the streetlights is, if I do say so myself, something of a tour de force. Let the reader shuttle back and forth on the page. Let him join in the confusion.

Cahill's sex life before he was blind needn't be gone into. Suffice it to say, as is said, that he likes women, and that his mistress from the loan office was one of the causes of the breakup of his marriage.

685. See amended text.

734-35. See amended text, with addition at bottom of page.

735. Cahill wouldn't know. Shears assumes Cahill knows, but he doesn't. See amended text.

738. What do you mean by reference to Joel's theory? Please explain.

759. Again, it seems of advantage to have Shears talk the blind man through the flight in the chair, and have Cahill's reaction, and what goes on in his mind, happen at the same time. If the structure here, as you say, fights the reader too much, then let it fight him, and let the reader fight back. And as for the setting problems and the cover price, I must say—I hope without sounding lofty— that that is not my concern. My business is to produce as good a novel as I can, using what means I feel would be conducive to this end.

774-5. I'm not sure we should drop the reference to bowling, though as the edited text indicates, we should put it in regular format. I want to give an in- dication, now and then, and increasingly as the book goes on, that Cahill is searching for things that he can do, later on in life; that despite his solipsistic attitude, he is looking for new ways to operate; that he is capable of growth.

The code scene is explained as much as it needs to be, I think. The code itself is simple enough, and is as Shears says it is. Cahill doesn't respond much be- cause he must take on faith what he is being told. It is mystifying to him, and it would not be any less mystifying if Shears went into more detail.

788. Zack doesn't need to be doing anything here; there is no reason to bring him up. Dogs spend a good deal of their time lying around when people are talking.

795. Joel did not <u>know</u> that his father was coming; this was at least partly bluff, at which he is good. He hoped, though, that his scheme would draw his father in, would draw his father to him. Throughout the book there is, or at least should be, the suspicion that Joel has intended to set up a situation of mystery and disappearance so that he can come back, but has miscalculated, gone down and injured himself, but has still tried to pull off the disappearance.

As to things in Joel's book being too many and too long, I was afraid there were not enough of them. There are plenty more, believe me. Suggest what you think would be of advantage here.

800. As I say, dogs lie around. There is nothing for him to do in this section.

845. On p. 841 McCaig tells Cahill he has "a surprise for him," which surprise is that he intends to take Cahill in the Stearman back from the auxiliary field;

there being no way to bring Zack back in the aircraft, McCaig insists on Cahill leaving the dog behind, with Hannah, as it turns out.

859. See amended text.

867-68. See amended text. I added something, and now it does track.

873ff. Yes, the flight section could go to a magazine—I'm thinking either Esquire or Plimpton's Paris Review, which has asked for anything we wished to excerpt.

891. See amended text.

I'm not sure what you mean about the "out-size capital letter," but it sounds good even if I don't know what you mean. Tell me what you intend and maybe we can make a major innovation in fictional technique!

918. See text, as changed.

924ff. Tell me what changes you think would help.

951. Farmer named Rabun, all the way through the text. We don't explain how the Colonel knows these things, or who "squealed." Or who the Judas figure is, or will be.

995. In the amended text we have changed things around as to the dispensation of Zack, where he is at what times, and so forth. Whether I have done this adequately, I don't know, but you're quite right; I hadn't taken sufficient care about this. See if you think what I have done is all right.

The Colonel could have got Joel's mother's name from this form 1-A, which lists living parents. Again, Joel would have made it his private business to know his father's whereabouts.

1017. He knows that she doesn't know about his blindness, but finds himself believing that somehow she might have. He sees that this is wrong and explains.

1018. You suggest a small cut here. Suggest what it might be, and maybe we can do it.

1019. Book now standardized on one week, if you think that's all right.

1020. We might have the phone call earlier, but I would prefer not. This, too, coming when it does, is further evidence of his increasing involvement with Joel. Previously he would not be interested enough to call Florence. Explain further about your suggestions in regard to the Colonel.

1021. The point is that Florence <u>knows</u> that Cahill hasn't got any pictures because she hasn't sent them; nor has he asked for them; she is holding this against him.

1028. I think the part about the magazines, the old horror pulps, is good, and even a little funny. Certainly it is in line with Joel's sexual sadism, though this latter is unknown to Florence. Cahill has an idea what it is about, though; there can't be any mistake about that.

And, yes, Cahill did have a mistress, the aforesaid employee of the loan office. But the main reason for the breakup of the marriage has been Cahill's indifference, his autonomy, his lack of real concern for other people.

1030. I don't find the turn the conversation takes so difficult to accept. Florence has not re-married; she is lonely, and wants to talk as much as she does, or is now finding that he does. And she is talkative by nature, as I have heard some women are. She likes to bend whatever ear she can find, even Frank's, when she has a chance.

1045. She has been helping McLendon move Cahill's things to the shed, as will become clear.

1063. We can cut some of this, if you like, except that some important revelations about personality are made during the conversation, and by means of it. You suggest cuts. Again, specifics.

The next reference, I must confess, bewilders me. What do you mean, "Cahill's life after Hannah left is a big gap"? When Hannah doesn't get on the bus with him is quite literally the end of the book, which is a big gap indeed! The biggest! Do you mean when <u>Florence</u> leaves? Do fill me in on this; until you do I will assume Florence and not Hannah, as you mean Rabun when you say Raben, for the farmer.

1066. Zack is around. Again, there is not much for him to do. Why should we have him do something.

1071. See edited text. We now have one split-bottom chair.

1093. For one reason, he doesn't know where to start, with a bunch of boys so intent on doing their own thing. He is afraid of seeming foolish, which he is not the kind of man to do. He has plenty of curiosity, but figures that they are into something that must run its course without interruption, and in this he is right.

1102. Please specify "small cut."

1128 and earlier. I'm not sure what you mean about the figure of Parris Gilbeau. I need someone to present the "black" side of Joel, the evil side, and I also need someone else besides Cahill who claims to have heard Joel's voice in the wind, in this case the "wind-tunnel hallway between the Flight Surgeon's office and sickbay. Tell me what you think I should do to give Gilbeau more reality than you think he has, for we need someone to do what he does in the story.

1139ff. Difficult, perhaps, but the counterpoint between the boys who see the film and what is working in Cahill's mind at the same time benefits greatly by being set up in this manner, it seems to me. The ironies are must stronger with the simultaneous presentation. If you can think of a more effective way to do this part, please let me know.

1148-49. See new text, that now tracks.

1170. As you will note from the edited text, the material from 1162 to 1192 can be changed to regular format. As to the Colonel's calmness, it is his business to be calm. He is essentially a man of reason; everything he says is reasonable.

1177. Most of what Cahill has heard from almost all sources can either be fact or rumor. A lot of the information about Joel, about the Colonel and Lucille Wick, about Knocker Nicholson and the Chinese villages, and so on, could as easily be rumors, their pervasiveness in service life, and so on.

If the reader doesn't know what happened physically on the field, I can't tell him. We have both Cahill's experience of it and Harbelis', with a good deal of description, physical description, of the wrecking of the aircraft in the parking area. What else is needed?

1194. <u>Does</u> Cahill know McCaig is already gone? He knew he was planning to leave, but did not know when. I should think Cahill would ask this.

What was supposed to have happened <u>did</u> happen. The "plan," as indicated in the Code scene, was for the Alnilam group to destroy all aircraft at Peckover as an initial show of power. The only hitch has been the death of Faulstick. None of this happened because Cahill was on the field, but as it turns out, and as Shears says later, this turns into yet another plus for the plotters.

1205. No; certainly not to kill him. But Shears and the others saw him as a weak link; that he was unsure of himself, and would panic. The callousness of the boys about his death is meant to be chilling, since they are enthralled by the working-out of the plan they have set up. I have known young men like this, in the grip of a terrible illusion, and they are frightening people.

Zack comes up, but these other things have to be talked about first, and they would be.

1212. Loved it? Maybe; love-hate might be a little more like it. Anyway there will be no occasion for him to do it again.

Not sure what you mean about Joel writing the book. He had a standard college English anthology in which he wrote a number of aphorisms, these are all the written material he left. The rest of the quotations are from writers in the anthology. The part about the charioteers in from Shelley, the most wide- and wild-eyed of youthful idealistic poets, and the quotations used in the ceremony with the film projector are from James Thomson ("B.V."), a nihilistic and pessimistic late Victorian poet from whose poem, <u>The City of Dreadful Night</u>, the quotations are taken.

1213. Suggest cuts here. I don't feel that I understand what you mean. Cahill knew that the boys planned some kind of disturbance during the graduation ceremony, and when he found himself literally in the middle of a kind of demolition derby of aircraft, he would certainly know what was going on. Again, I don't know what you mean by "inferences from what he overheard."

He just never has tried to get in touch with him, for reasons of his own. Why should this be explained? It is obvious that Joel has a strong imagination, and is given to fantasizing. It may well be that he has built his father into a figure that a real father could not possibly satisfy, and would prefer to relate to him through some elaborate scheme of his own devising, such as has happened.

The Colonel would certainly have told the Flight Surgeon about Joel's not knowing his father, especially since, later, there is strong evidence that the Colonel and the other officers, perhaps even including Whitehall, are making an effort to gather evidence against Shears and the plotters, and have been trying to pump Cahill to this end.

1218. The major would have been able to get this much information, especially since Whitehall has talked to Joel, and makes no secret of the subject. As to Judas, there isn't one yet, but the indication is that there will be.

1223ff. I agree; there is too much talk and over-simplification, and I'd appreciate your telling me how much is needed, and which part should go out. Some of it is needed, I'm quite sure, because there are going to be conventional people trying to explain what has happened in a conventional way. I tried to indicate this in the section following, after the Major has left, and Whitehall says that what the Major has been talking about is "just conventional . . . a preview of what other conventional folks are going to be saying when the investigation comes up." Nevertheless, we can cut some here.

1243. It's not immortality Shears and Cahill are talking about, but the possibility of Joel's still being alive. If you mean the sentence where Shears says "This is going to be your immortality, if you want one," he is not talking about life after death in the religious sense, but surviving in history, in the sense, say, of Abraham Lincoln.

1250. I have heard people say "Take care" all my life. If you like we could change it to something like "Watch out for yourself" or "Take care of yourself."

Are you asking for more irony in Cahill's being the instrument, or as you say, "the blind instrument"? He is that, but I am not sure what your reference to irony signifies. Again, you say that Cahill is "too much of a cypher." How would it suit you to make him less of one? The main characteristics of Cahill are his iron monomaniacal will, his determination to control everything that concerns him. It seems to me that this is projected quite fully, if not over-insisted on. What are your suggestions here?

I just talked to Theron this morning, and he seems pleased that I am sending the book back to you, with all these weeks of going through it inch by inch and word by word, and what I trust the labor will yield in the way of clarification, of bringing us significantly closer to a final version. Believe me, I am most grateful for your close reading of the manuscript, and your comments and suggestions.

As to your ideas on magazine publication, here is a list of possibilities. I don't think all of these are self-contained enough, but some of them are, and you can't really tell what editors will consider to be so; I am continually surprised by the kind of excerpts people print. Anyway, here are some candidates, together with tentative titles.

1. The Bonbadier's—Faulstick's—story, "The Creation."

2. Whitehall's story of the New Britain Raid, "The Rising of Algol."

3. Or, both of these monologues combined, and called "The Captains."

4. The sequence at the crash site, called either "The Black Farm" or "Honey and Well-Water: The Black Farm."

5. The sex-with-dulcimer, as you suggest, called "Broomstraws."

6. The Flight Sequence, "A Wheedling of Knives."

7. The dog-fight scene, called, maybe, "A Field of Dogs," or "The Dog of Peace," which last I like better.

8. The film sequence in the shed, called "Son on the Wall."

9. The last big scene between Cahill and the Colonel, when Cahill threatens him with Zack, called Face-Off."

10. The Link Trainer sequence, called either "The Link," or "In the Link," or "Riding the Link," or, simply, "Link." I thought also of calling this "Stone Flight," since the Link doesn't really do the flying it simulates, but is stationary.

To: Robert Penn Warren   **TLS, Emory University**

4620 Lelia's Court
Columbia, S.C. 29206
March 13, 1986

Dear Red:

Thanks for your letter, and please forgive me for waiting so long to answer, but a great deal has been going on, and I have had to scramble as I could. Meanwhile, I have been reading about you in the various places where such news is reported. I am glad that you are Poet Laureate, whatever the duties may be, and I am sorry that you have been in the hospital, for whatever illness, whatever surgery you had. I have been in so many hospitals myself, in my time, mainly military hospitals, but some civilian too, and I know the life of the wards, believe me. I am glad you are out, and maybe headed for another rendezvous with me, when we can sit down and talk and read to one another the things that we love. I would like that a lot, believe me.

As for your suggestion that I serve as a seconder for Peter Davison, sure, I will be glad to do it. Just set the wheels in motion, and I will follow through with whatever rotation I can effect. And, as for these things, would you be willing to second George Plimpton if I were to be the original sponsor? Let me know how you feel about these matters, and I will be guided accordingly.

It all seems so long ago, when the cameras were grinding away and you and I were sitting among the yellow flowers of your yard, or wandering among the stones of Gabe's hanging Stonehenge, out in your backyard. I remember all that time, and the time under the moss at Litchfield, as good human life; in fact, I have had no better, and I am happy to wake up, during the darkest part of the night, and remember this as being recorded, as a record of what you and I had a chance to do, and did.

Let me know what I might do in any direction for your life on earth, for I will step right into it, as I can. My best to Eleanor, and the jumping-open glass doors of The Bitter Box.

You ask for my news, and I hope for yours, too.

Ever,

Jim

To: Pamela Susan Tehrani[23]   CC, Emory University
4620 Lelia's Court
Columbia, S.C. 29206

March 13, 1986

Dear Susan Tehrani:

It is great to hear from you, and with such good news! I hope you will tell Rich Watson—I will tell him myself, too—how very happy I am with his illustrations. He has got the exact feel of the story, and has added to it some qualities that I myself do not have, but am pleased to recognize; he gives to his part of things that element of strangeness without which, as Francis Bacon says, "there is no excellent beauty." If I were to cavil at anything at all, I would question the inclusion of the Teddy bear in two of the illustrations. As it seems to me, the Teddy bear is so much a part of children's literature, particularly as sentimentalized by adults, that the appearance of such an element in our story cuts down on the wild strangeness of it by bringing in an expectable symbol. In other words, we don't really need the Teddy bear, though if you and Rich want to keep him, we can do so. Let me know how you feel about this, and I will abide by your decision. This is a small point, I realize, and should not be allowed to take any sort of precedence over the stunning positive qualities of the art Rich has given us.

One more thing, though. As to your use of the fountain scene, very good indeed, in its way, on the cover of the catalog, I wonder if we might not want to reconsider about this, if it's not too late. It seems to me that the essence of the story is much more to be grasped from the scene with Bronwen in the darkness, battling with what she is battling with, the traw shining in her hand like

23. Associate editor of children's books for Harcourt Brace Jovanovich.

some kind of garden-tool Excalibur. That has much more of the sweep and excitement and drama of the story than the fountain scene, charming and imaginative as the latter is. Again, tell me what you think. But whatever you think, I'm with you.

From what you tell me, things are beginning to steamroll, with sales conferences, catalogs, the reps getting out of their various routes, and so on. All this is good, and I hope you will let me know, down to the smallest detail, what I might be able to do for the project.

Meanwhile, understand how pleased I am at how everything is going. Believe me, an author could not possibly be happier with the situation in which he finds his character and his story. What we all need to do is just keep doing what we're doing, and not let down. The current is with is. All we need to do is sail.

With every good wish, with thanks for the books you sent Bronnie, I am

Yours sincerely,

To: Robert L. Woodrum   CC, Emory University
                                                        4620 Lelia's Court
                                                        Columbia, S.C. 29206

March 14, 1986

Dear Mr. Woodrum:

I have read the three novels which are candidates for the Hemingway Prize this year. They are all good, with the result that I read each of them a second time, and came to the following conclusion. Jamaica Kincaid's <u>Annie John</u> is a sincere and honest piece of work, and the projection of the central character is extremely well-done, the character and her Carribean <u>milieu</u> are engaging to read about, but in the end, considering this novel in comparison with the other two, I felt it to be the least qualified of the three for the prize.

<u>The Old Gringo</u> has real rawness and power. Ambrose Bierce is a fascinating personage, and though I don't believe in Fuentes' Bierce as much as I do in the real one, this depiction of him in the Villa campaigns is highly imagina-

tive and dramatically effective, though the drawing of the American woman, Harriet Winslow, is not completely convincing, at least to me. As to the judging itself, I weighed The Old Gringo strongly against the Duras novel, and finally decided for the latter.

The Lover is a strange kind of book, and in some ways can hardly be called a novel at all. There is hardly any character delineation; for example, one knows almost nothing about the lover himself, except that he is Chinese, has a chauffeur-driven limosine and plenty of febrile sexuality, and weeps a lot. The protagonist's mother is also hard to grasp. She is presented alternately as being poverty-stricken, and later on, back in France, she has acquired an entire chateau for the purpose, insofar as one can tell, of providing the narrator's hated older brother with a fitting habitat in which to ruin himself. As I say, mysterious.

But the book is haunting indeed. The terrible dream-like doomed and enthralled passion of the girl, the sense of hope being destroyed by the very thing—the new thing—that one wants, and above all the the depiction of the sick colonialism, the Mekong Delta and River, the crowds moving around the afternoon streets of Cholon while the lovers are weeping and desperately trying to do the ultimate for each other, the thing that was never possible—all these qualities are parts of a true experience which the reader has with him as a disturbing addition to his life, something he would not have had except as given him by a real artist. It would be difficult for me to understand it if the other members of the jury do not perceive these qualities. But that shall be as they wish and decide, of course. As things are from my standpoint, I will go with Marguerite Duras' The Lover, and I will hope that you'd convey my sentiments and reasons to her, with my best wishes.

Meanwhile, let me know what else I might be able to do in connection with the prize, and remember me to the other members of the jury. when you see them or communicate with them. I'd appreciate that a lot, believe me.

Sincerely yours,

The One Voice of James Dickey

To: Monroe Spears

CC, Emory University
4620 Lelia's Court
Columbia, S.C. 29206

April 8, 1986

Dear Monroe and Betty,

I have just got back here, tired as always, full of new memories and a sense of having had a couple of days as I would wish to have them, among old friends who have turned out to be remarkable, and a place to remember from the old days, when I taught Composition and Report Writing for Technical Students, and went upstairs to a freshman class one morning and announced the death of Dylan Thomas. None of the students had ever heard of him, but maybe a couple of them will still remember that something extraordinary—an extraordinary death—had happened to them and the rest of the human race. It was good indeed to be down there. I don't know whether I will ever be back again, but I took some pictures you might like to have, and will send them along when they are developed.

But do know how much I enjoyed being there for just that short time, to see you both again, to know how well Monroe is working, to learn of the new book from Johns Hopkins, and of the continuation in poetry. I remember the one batch of poems you sent me, Monroe, with extreme favor. There is the quality of imaginative wit in them that is almost lost in our time. Nemerov has some—a little—Wilbur has some, Hollander has some. But you have a chance to have more than any, it seems to me. That is the way to go. I wish I had some of the element, myself, but I don't, and must take things out in my appreciation of those that do. Send me what you write, and I will ride with you. But that shall be as you wish, of course.

Meanwhile, remember me to all those I met down there, and find your own way of telling them how much I enjoyed the occasion; how fine it all was.

Ever,

To: Paul Carroll

CC, Emory University
4620 Lelia's Court
Columbia, S.C. 29206

September 18, 1986

My Dear Old Paul:

Thank you so much for your good book; it is certainly wonderful to have it, to hear your poetic voice as well as the human, humorous, one I heard last Christmas in Chicago, on that iron night when we walked across the bridge of snow to get to your van—I swear there was no concrete or metal of girders involved; just snow itself, holding us up by miracle—and we went out past Al Capone's pad to <u>your</u> pad, spiralled up the stairs, and entered into the best time of all, with the atmosphere you and Maryrose created, there within the still tension of the absolute cold outside. For a long time I have been wanting to write you about that night. I lay in the hospital after brain surgery, with my draining head-fluids mixing with the sick body-sweat of hospital nights, thinking how, if I could get out of the grasp of the blind brothers, Sleep and Death, I would write you as I am now doing, and tell you these things. After all, there is no in-depth communication like those of people whose very being is geared to what they can invent, what they can imagine. And you are the best imaginer I know. My God, anybody who could compare fountains to empty beehives could do anything! Keep <u>on</u>!

I send you a couple of books, one a kind of coffee-table affair where this Appalachian photographer tries to catch some things in my early work by;means of flying nightshirts and deer-skulls, and tha other a curious big effort I made at the time Maxine died, ten years ago, that nobody seems to like but everybody keeps writing about. Anyway, I wanted you to have these things, for whatever might be in them for you.

My greatest love, my old remarkable Paul. Give my best to Maryrose, and tell her that she creates the kind of atmosphere for a home in which a man would wish to live, and not die.

Ever,

To: Rust Hills   CC, Emory University
                                                  4620 Lelia's Court
                                                  Columbia, S.C. 29206

                                                  December 10, 1986

Dear Rust Hills:

Here is the edited manuscript, with some notations of my own. First of all, thanks a very great deal for your helpful work on this material. I had thought, when you made some general suggestions over the phone, that it would be difficult to create a convincing dialogue by putting words in the mouths of characters who were not—in the original—the people who were speaking them. But it turned out fine, I think, and again I render my thanks.

A couple of things. I have rewritten the opening paragraph to give a little more expository information, and this I have put on a separate sheet.

The whole thing should end with Whitehall's sentence, "My star is Vega, from now on and for good." I have read these two stories around in various colleges a good deal, and this is the ending I always use. It is exactly the right ending, I think, for it concludes and doesn't tail off into something else. I have indicated this as being the ending, as you can see from the manuscript.

I also offer some other possible titles, though I am quite willing to go with the original title, and simply call it "The Captains." However, something you said on the phone got me to thinking about a different possibility, which is to call it something like "Spark and Star," and maybe subtitle it either "A Dialogue" or "Two Monologues." When I read the latter section, the navigator's story, I usually call it "The Rise of the Falling Vulture," and, if we wanted to consider that idea, and include the bombadier's story about the flash from the 109's nose cannon, we might call the whole thing "The Spark, (or A Spark or One Spark), and The Rise of the Falling Vulture," or, since the bombadier attaches so much significance to the flash that almost killed him, we might be slightly more complicated and call it "Death, Creation, and the Ride of the Falling Vulture (or Buzzard)," if you like.

I have told Herman Gollob and the other Doubleday people that we are shooting for your April issue, which I think will work out fine. Do you plan for there to be illustrations, as there were when Esquire published the first part of the novel a few years back? If you can manage this I think it would work admirably, as it did before.

Again, will I get to see proofs when you have set the material up? I would like for this to be the case, as with most writers I usually benefit from having a last look, and fine-tuning, as need may dictate.

Let me know anything else I might do in connection with this presentation and I'll jump right on it. And again, thanks for your good help. I think your readers will respond to the results.

With best wishes,

To: Joyce Pair   **TLS, Property of Joyce Pair**

4620 Lelia's Court
Columbia, S.C. 29206
July 17, 1989

Dear Joyce:

I went over your long letter three or four times, each time with greater gratitude, and am very happy to have your detailed explanations of the various questions I had about the <u>Newsletter</u>, and the other things. To have someone like yourself doing all this work on my behalf makes for a certain shyness on the part of the person being written about, especially if he is myself, with all the attendant fears and doubts to the effect that he may very well not be worth it. But as long as you think I <u>am</u> worth it, I am only too happy to cooperate with you in any and all endeavors concerning the <u>Newsletter</u>, and indeed anything else you are engaged upon.

Here, there is some good news and some bad news. The good news is that the poems I am writing now are by far the best I have ever done; are so good, in fact, that I am quite literally in awe of them. The two long poems in question are the last two I need for the complete manuscript of <u>Real God, Roll</u>, which I would like to turn in to Wesleyan at the end of next month, God willing, for Spring publication. The bad news is that we have struck a snag on the plans for filming <u>Alnilam</u>. Though I have finished the script and my director, John Guillermin, and I have gone over it in detail, he doesn't seem able to get the cast or the money he wants; he is one of these megalomaniacal directors who have to be given the gates of Heaven before they consider doing a project. Since he has had the material a year and hasn't started rolling on the film, we can now, if we like—my agent and I—have the rights revert to us. Theron and I are thinking of taking the project elsewhere, though Guillermin says he has one more good prospect in mind, and it is probable that we will see how this turns out before we make any further moves. All this is very disconcerting, as well as disappointing, but there is not much I can do about it except to hope for the best. It is a pretty good screenplay, if I do say so myself, and I'd like to see the thing done and not shelved. In due time we'll see, I suppose.

Please remember me with warmth to Bob Covel, who is really hanging in there on his projects, and to the others I know in Atlanta. I very seldom get over there any more, and haven't any immediate plans to do so, but you may be sure I will let you know if there's any need for me to come. It would be good to see you again, sure enough; such occasions are always of the very best.

Let me know what I might be able to do to further your aims, and I'll make every effort to swing with you.

Ever,

Jim

To: Diane Wood Middlebrook   CC, Emory University
                                                        4620 Lelia's Court
                                                        Columbia, S.C. 29206

July 24, 1989

Dear Ms. Middlebrook:

Thank you for your letter, and for your remarks on my work; they were gracious indeed.

As to using some of the letters I wrote to poor Anne Sexton, I don't mind at all. I only saw her on a couple or three occasions, and, as you say, we wrote back and forth a few times. You may, however, want to correct one or two points, or add to what you already have. The occasion on which I spent the most time with Anne was at Syracuse University, where I had given a reading and then gone to bed, staying clear of the almost obligatory party that follows such affairs. I was stopping at the home of the college President, Dr. Piskor, and Anne woke me up over the phone to see if we could not meet for at least a little while. I got up and she came by, in a big black coat that looked like it had come from a gorilla, and we walked up and down the suburban road a few times, during which, as I remember, she told me about various episodes of her childhood, particularly in relation to her mother. I remember asking her what her maiden name was, and she told me it was Harvey. Have I got that right?

The last time I saw her was at Towson, Maryland, where I had lectured, and we lunched together and had a couple of drinks. At that time I remember she told me she had once caught her arm in a laundry mangle, though it seemed difficult to me to understand how this might be possible. Do you have documentation on this? Even if untrue, it is an interesting thing to invent, don't you think?

Well, I won't go on and on. I remember Anne with some affection, though her continual pushiness in literary circles was irksome to me, I'm afraid I must say. The only other person I have ever encountered who put such store on literary reputation and literary politicking was Robert Lowell, and, since she studied with him, maybe that came over as an influence. May she rest where she is now, and as they say happens to writers when they go to Heaven, may she have nothing to do again for the rest of eternity but read favorable reviews.

Again, if there's anything else I can do to help out, I'll do my best to comply.

Sincerely yours,

Ground Control

In a letter dated January 24, 1990, to Gordon Van Ness, who was then editing his early notebooks, James Dickey stated that his situation on all fronts,
literary and otherwise, was going well—*The Eagle's Mile* had just been copy-
edited by Wesleyan University Press, and Robert Kirschten was editing a critical
study about his work. While his creative efforts were proceeding, however,
and while he declared to others that he had never been so much written about,
he told Van Ness that "there is always a sense of pressure." Nevertheless, he declared, "I was born for combat, for the struggle, and would be lost without it.
He who ever strives upward, Goethe says: Ah! Him can we save."[1] Despite such
optimistic bravado, Dickey was largely uncertain as the nineties commenced
whether his artistic mission would ever again achieve the heights it had
known and whether he would be able to control not only the literary career
he had managed to manipulate since his early correspondence with Andrew
Lytle, James Wright, and others, but also an increasingly disruptive domestic
life that precluded any sustained writing. With the publication of *The Eagle's
Mile* in 1990, *The Whole Motion: Collected Poems, 1945–1992* in 1992, and *To
the White Sea* in 1993, Dickey's creative mission ended; he would develop hepatitis the following year and, two years later, fibrosis of the lungs, which would
result in his death in 1997.

Critics such as R. S. Gwynn have argued that Dickey's career had effectively
ended after the appearance of *Deliverance* and his acting debut in the film
version. "Today," Gwynn wrote in a 1994 essay in *Sewanee Review*, "the mere
mention of his name summons up sniffy dismissals," and he asserted, "If a
poet does not publish any work of unquestioned merit in a whole quarter of
a century, no amount of spin control can save his reputation from a down-
ward spiral." Even Dickey's son Christopher believes that his father's creative
talents diminished after the novel. "It seemed to me then," he wrote in his
memoir, "and for a long time afterward that forces of self-indulgence and
self-destruction, which were always there in my father but held in check, were

1. The letter is the private papers of Van Ness.

now cut loose. And worse." *Deliverance*, he declared, was "a line of demarcation," and while his statement refers partly to what happened in the lives of both Dickey and his family, it also constitutes the measure by which to view his career, for his father's best poetry, Christopher has noted, resides in *Poems 1957–1967*, "the single best and most consistent volume of his work."[2] In 1990, however, Dickey himself remained unwilling to cede the literary skies to any rival or to acknowledge openly that his best work was behind him; he was committed to making the truth, not telling it, and he defended his poetic and fictional techniques against hostile reviewers and critics.

Dickey felt that those whose roles dictated that they merely observe and evaluate writers, that they track and criticize, did not understand either what he was doing or his emphatic need to explore "New thresholds! New anatomies!"[3] Ensconced in comfortable offices, grounded in academe or the literary establishment, they wanted to control him from their safe positions. It is not surprising, then, that he had angrily declared to Dana Gioia in 1987 at the Library of Congress's fiftieth anniversary reunion of consultants, "You're all the same. I gotta grow, gotta try new things. All you want is the same damn thing."[4] Creatively and personally restless, unwilling simply to continue writing what had previously been successful, he determined to fly solo. He would not participate in any literary movement or group assault; he would not be boxed in. And he said so in a loud voice.

If it is true that there is no such thing as reality, only perception, it is also true that one's perceptions are what they are; they are true for that individual. So, too, is a writer's choice of material. Dickey believed in the creative possibilities of the lie, and these fabrications were not limited to his poetry. As Matthew Bruccoli admits, Dickey "deliberately promoted and exaggerated his various reputations—genius, drinker, woodsman, athlete—until the legends took over after *Deliverance*."[5] Dickey's voice, in its largest sense, was always a creative one. Monroe Spears, his professor and literary mentor at Vanderbilt University, had suggested to him in the context of discussing how to improve a particular poem that an artist is not restricted by factual truth. The statement was a revelation to Dickey, and he had later seen the same lesson in

2. Gwynn, "Runaway Cannons: At War with Dickey and Bly," *Sewanee Review* (Winter 1994): 152–60; *Summer of Deliverance: A Memoir of Father and Son* (New York: Simon and Schuster, 1998), 14, 275.

3. *Sorties* (Garden City, N.Y.: Doubleday, 1971), 118.

4. Gioia, " 'How Nice to Meet You, Mr. Dickey,' " *American Scholar* 72.1 (Winter 2003): 83–88.

5. *Crux: The Letters of James Dickey*, ed. Matthew J. Bruccoli and Judith Baughman (New York: Knopf, 1999), xxii.

Nietzsche. He told his son, "No true artist will tolerate for one minute the world as it is."[6] In his poetry, therefore, Dickey reimagined the world as he wanted it to be in an effort both to validate his self-identity and to impart to his life the sense of consequence he felt did not exist. However, he never confused the truth of fact for the truth of his fictions.

The Pacific air campaign during World War II had, in some sense, confirmed an early need for such illusion. Adolescent insecurities and the perceived failure to satisfy parental and social expectations had led a young Dickey to imagine himself as such pulp fiction action heroes as Tarzan and Doc Savage. He wanted to be a superman who made himself superior to everyone else through sheer self-discipline and a stubbornness of will. The war's brutality ironically enhanced his imagination, providing the necessary impetus for Dickey to escape into the literature he requested from his mother or that he himself procured on Okinawa. As a twenty-two-year-old second lieutenant, he had encamped in July 1945 in an area that proved to be, as he wrote in the squadron history, "in the middle of one of the biggest battlefields of the war. Everywhere were helmets, canteens, rifles, gasmasks and Japs in various stages of decomposition." The grimness of the scene, bad as it was, fractured the naïveté of a parochial childhood and worsened when he saw firsthand in the coral caves of Okinawa, as he declared in a 1987 interview, "Japanese guys sitting up there in what must have been a machine-gun emplacement just incinerated. Just black."[7]

Such brutality encouraged a Romantic idealism that critics occasionally condemned as unbelievable and escapist in his poems. These critics were analogous to the officers during the war who had manned Ground Control. In what Samuel Hynes, himself an aviator during the conflict, describes as "a dark, cave-like" room, they viewed the aerial combat from a distance: "This was where all planes in the air over Okinawa and to the north were tracked, where enemy raids were first noted, and fighters sent against them." While the controller's job was "simply to see that his man wasn't shot down, he could watch the drama of fighter interception on the screen before him and follow the action on his earphones." It was vicarious participation, and Dickey himself always needed and wanted direct involvement. Dickey's correspondence during the nineties, however, suggests that while he remained committed to his mission—

6. *Summer of Deliverance*, 26.
7. See "History of the 418th NFS," typescript, Andrews Air Force Base, 109; and Gordon Van Ness, "Living beyond Recall: An Interview with James Dickey," in *The Voiced Connections of James Dickey,* ed. Ron Baughman (Columbia: University of South Carolina Press, 1989), 247–57.

that is to say, relentless in his pursuit of new techniques or the revitalization of old forms—the deterioration of his health and the instability of his domestic life mitigated his active participation and partly confined him, as it were, in Ground Control, in what Hynes terms "the visual part of this show,"[8] where he watched the drama unfold apart from his actions.

In the midst of his marital discord, Dickey assembled the poems that would compose his last collection, *The Eagle's Mile,* which Wesleyan published in October 1990 and which he dedicated to his children and grandchildren. Its title derived from Blake's "Auguries of Innocence"—"The Emmet's Inch & Eagle's Mile / Make Lame Philosophy to smile. / He who Doubts from what he sees / Will ne'er believe, do what you please"—lines that emphasize the variety of approaches to experience. Dickey's collection is dominated by two contrasting perspectives: the ideal, dispassionate, and inclusive gaze of the eagle in high flight and the restricted, anxious, and exclusive stare of a man walking on the ground. The speaker, both as he imaginatively rises with the bird in "Eagles," "receiving overlook," and as he stands on a beach in "Circuit," "foreseeing / Around a curve," recognizes these points of view as essential to knowing "the circular truth / Of the void." Each poem in the volume captures a singular experience or stance, an emotional and physical complex addressing one of the perspectives that reveals a moment of acceptance, celebration, or even transcendence. Each captures a still point in time, Frost's "momentary stay against confusion," that increasingly links each poem to others by patterns of imagery. Taken together, these poems and images reveal the principled physical relevance of things and the vital and redemptive role of the imagination.

The series of opposite propositions or contraries become unified or reconciled in the volume's title poem. In "The Eagle's Mile," celebrating with Whitmanesque affirmation the godlike creative impulse, the speaker demands that William Douglas, who in life was blind in one eye, now "step out of grass-bed sleep" and possess the world anew, "drawing life / From growth / from flow." If he will "catch into this / With everything you have," Douglas can enter again into the multiplicity of physical reality, the endless and marvelously varied creation, because potential form once again becomes actual. Here Dickey suggests the interrelationship of all things, all natural forces, all individualities merging in their motions to render an eternal Idea—"The whole thing is worth." In a world of continual Becoming, the individual can "Splinter

8. Samuel Hynes, *Flights of Passage: Reflections of a World War II Aviator* (New York and Annapolis: Frederic C. Beil and Naval Institute Press, 1988), 225.

uncontrollably whole" because death constitutes part of life's headlong, un-stoppable momentum, part of the very great hand of contraries dealt every-one. Life's circularity will bring death, actuality will become potentiality, but the process, enhanced here by the artistic impulse, extends one into the many, which nevertheless always remain the One.

Dickey's persona intuits life, the dynamic and mysterious process of cre-ation, as well as the immobility and anonymity of death, an intuition that provides a double vision. The earthbound persona understands that the two perspectives, metaphorically rendered as the eagle's mile and the emmet's inch, encompass human truth and the artistic impulse as manifested in physical reality. The book's poetic arrangement, moreover, reflects this larger compre-hension of perspective and traces the speaker's own physical and spiritual journey through his understanding of what he sees or intuits. In "Expanses," the collection's final poem, Dickey endeavors to establish the importance of the individual personality when the narrator becomes the eagle and now sees with the bird's sweeping gaze but without loss of his human perspective, a perspective that unites opposites. Grounding oneself only in and on the phys-ical world, Dickey suggests, limits the individual to an Aristotelian concep-tion of reality that does not visualize the Platonic or ideal. As he views himself from the air walking on the beach, the persona experiences in his earthbound perceptions "all you want— / Joy like short grass," an image alluding to the cemetery but recognizing that life and death are both one and not one. The human voice will fail, Dickey understands, will finally lose its heat and be-come cold, but for an instant will break like lightning against the emptiness of space. When he declares in "For a Time and Place" that we "begin with our-selves / Underfoot and rising," he presents his philosophical awareness of the elemental human condition and the beginning of the imaginative process that validates and resurrects the individual presence.

Technically and thematically, *The Eagle's Mile* constitutes a culmination of Dickey's poetic journey, an extension of *Puella* in one sense and a return to poetic elements apparent in the early motion in another. In his essay "Meta-phor as Pure Adventure," Dickey had clearly stated the nature and function of poetry: "I think of the poem," he declared,

> as a kind of action in which, if the poet can participate *enough*, other people cannot help participating as well. I am against all marmoreal, closed, to-be-contemplated kinds of poems and conceive of the poem as a minute part of the Heraclitean flux, and of the object of the poem as not to slow or fix or limit the flux at all but to try as it can to preserve and implement the "fluxness," the flow,

and show this moving through the poem, coming in at the beginning and going back out, after the end, into the larger, nonverbal universe whence it came.[9]

In his last collection, Dickey searches for the basic human act and the proper net or form by which the poet allows the experience to show itself. The making of this net, the use of metaphor and image to hold the experience and reveal its essential wonder, became a primary intent. In the process, Dickey returned to elements present in earlier poems. The poems not only offer a narrative situation reminiscent of his early work, although the action usually remains static, but they also exhibit the spacings or interstices of the split-line technique. Dickey utilizes the block format only in "The Olympian," and this is slightly modified. Frequently the poems appear balanced on the page with the lines symmetrically branching off a central idea. Yet in *The Eagle's Mile,* unlike any previous volume, Dickey thematically relates the poems through a series of interconnected images that thread through the work. While *Puella* captures the individual moments in a girl's life as she matures, uniting the poems that depict her emotional and physical states through their narrative chronology and emphasizing her elemental connections, *The Eagle's Mile* links many separate images, including those of grass or weeds; graves; footprints; rocks; birds; the elements of air, water, and earth; curves or curving; and climatic heat and cold. All life, Dickey implies, is fundamentally connected at all times.

Reviews were generally positive. John Updike praised the volume; others, including Herbert Mitgang and Fred Chappell, while admiring the collection, cited occasional problems with language. Updike had contributed a dust jacket statement, which declared, "James Dickey is the high flier of contemporary American poets. In *The Eagle's Mile* he is flying higher than ever." Mitgang's review saw the collection as a continuation of Dickey's examination of man's connection with nature, a relationship that included "many nuances about myth and machismo." Mitgang, however, seemed to qualify his analysis by asserting that the language "meanders down the page in rivulets," although they finally merge in "a rushing mainstream" that includes linked words and startling phrases that, taken together, extend Dickey's vision. Chappell also praised the volume, citing it as representative of an idiom he referred to as "the High Bardic, the vatic, the transcendent—the Pindaric Grandiose, if you will," which he then defined: "It is the poetic attitude that sets for itself heroic

9. *Sorties,* 173–74.

visionary ambitions marching out to trample the limitations of ordinary poetic diction." Yet Chappell also asserted that in the "intoxicated grandeur" of
these tall flights, the collection suffered from a variety of flaws, including
overstated language, banality, bathos, slang, far-fetched tropes, disingenuous
direct address, the overuse of certain words, and an insistence on gerunds. He
concluded, however, that Dickey "has put everything on the line and has
come off, on balance, a winner. He has suffered some pretty steep losses, but
overall the book is a victory. If in some places he has not succeeded, there are
others in which he has advanced beyond what he has done before and has
done so in a new and unexpected fashion."[10]

In his biography of Dickey, Henry Hart notes that the book, not counting
the section entitled "Double-Tongue: Collaborations and Rewrites," offered
only twenty-six poems, many short and written in the eighties (*Buckdancer's
Choice*, which won the National Book Award, contained twenty-one poems).
Hart suggested that Dickey's "dependence" on translations and his use of
older poems constituted "one sign of his struggle to find new inspiration."
Dickey, however, had used older poems in previous collections, and his interest in reworking poems written in other languages, what he variously referred
to as rewrites, collaborations, or improvisations, dated back at least to *The
Zodiac* and constituted part of his effort to enlarge his "voice." In an unpublished letter to the *Memphis State Review,* he insisted that his rewrites were
not translations: "I don't want these poems to be presented as translations or
adaptations of other translations, which they are not. They are original poems—
and much better than the originals, I can tell you."[11] He had published several
of these poems, including "Heads" (with Lucien Becker), "Attempted Departure" (with André du Bouchet), "Lakes of Varmland" (with André Frénaud), "Farmers" (with André Frénaud), and "Craters" (with Michel Leiris)
in the March/April 1983 issue of *American Poetry Review,* and James Anderson of Breitenbush Publications had expressed interest in publishing a collection of such poems to be entitled "Immortals." Dickey discussed his methods
of translation in a January 19, 1987, letter to Ben Belitt, declaring:

> [T]he whole question of translation and the cross-pollinization of cultures by
> means of translation, is very large and important, and will be more so. People
> are not only coming forth with more translations, but with theories of transla-
> tion, which is to say defenses of the kind they themselves practice. Since Pound

10. Mitgang, "Man, Nature and Everyday Activities in Verse," *New York Times,* October 27,
1990, p. 16; Chappell, "Vatic Poesy," *The State,* December 9, 1990, p. 5F.
11. Henry Hart, *James Dickey: The World as a Lie* (New York: Picador, 2000), 706.

at least, a new kind of curious form, which I try to experiment with myself, has come into existence. This is neither a translation or a completely original poem, but a kind of hybrid which for want of a better name I am tempted to call "the rewrite." Such an approach may seem on the surface of it contemptible, but it is not, and I think more and more people, either those who don't know the foreign language very well or those who <u>do</u> know it well but want to do something <u>different</u> in English, will be the ones to watch.[12]

Poets such as Robert Lowell and Robert Bly had also reworked poems in this form.

While Deborah's addictions remained a continual source of concern to Dickey, so too did personal medical ailments. He wrote Marc Jaffe, his editor at Houghton Mifflin, on June 18, 1991, that he had a "semi-gangrenous situation" in his foot that would likely require partial amputation of his toe, a problem that resulted from a toenail fungus contracted during his combat in the Philippines. He also complained that he would likely require further surgery on his esophagus to improve his digestion. Nevertheless, on August 1 he promised to complete the new novel, though he would not detail his present difficulties, "so disheartening, so endlessly complicated with legalities, with medical solutions that don't work, with lawyers, doctors, psychiatrists, policemen, judges, probation officers, and God knows who or what else, that to lay all this on you would be an extreme unkindness, so I won't." He apologized again on December 18, this time citing the delay as resulting from the task of collecting his poems for *The Whole Motion*.[13]

Other distractions, however, had complicated his creative efforts. On July 30 he had accepted an invitation from Cleanth Brooks to judge the Hanes Poetry Prize along with Fred Chappell. The award was given by the Fellowship of Southern Writers. In October he published his fourth coffee-table book, *Southern Light,* which presented a circular journey that sectioned a day into dawn, morning, noon, afternoon, and evening and examined the world as light defined it during those times. Dickey's text was accompanied by 188 glossy photographs of southern landscapes by Jim Valentine. Publication was followed by a two-month tour of book signings in Atlanta, Nashville, Birmingham, Charlotte, and Columbia. Additionally, he spoke at the University of Arkansas in Monticello, Lee College in Texas, the Harbour Front in Toronto, DeKalb Community College, and the Book Fair in Miami. On November 13

12. *Crux,* ed. Bruccoli and Baughman, 441.
13. The letters to Jaffe are in the James Dickey Papers, Special Collections Department, Robert W. Woodruff Library, Emory University, Atlanta (hereafter cited as Dickey Papers).

he addressed the South Atlantic Modern Language Association in Atlanta; the paper, entitled "LIGHTNINGS, or Visuals," described how images act to produce fully involved stories.

In the introduction of *Southern Light,* Dickey urged the reader to undertake the imaginative connection, a surrender similar to ones critics had faulted in his other oversize books. "Enter light," Dickey demands, "as though you were part of it, as though you were pure spirit—or pure beholding human creature, which is the same thing—to become part of light in many places and intensities, to make it something like a dream of itself with you in it; that way you will be seeing by human light, as well as by the light shining since Genesis." In contrast to his previous mixed-media works, in *Southern Light* the prose text anticipates rather than complements Valentine's photographs. Their subtle textures and startling vibrancy demand confrontation, while Dickey's descriptions establish the uniqueness of the moments captured by the camera. When the dawn light, for example, causes the things of the world to come into themselves, Dickey invites participation by singling out what one might personally hold in perspective: "In all remoteness and closeness you have a hand; a quickening hand, as everything sharpens, attunes: sharpens *toward.* If you want more leaves, beckon, and they come." At evening, he asks how successful the encounters have been and reminds the reader of the special quality that the light makes possible: "Nothing like it ever given, except by means of Time. This time, this day." The artistic intent is to deliver a physical and emotional confrontation by having the words defer to the photographs and yet prepare one to experience them. Dickey establishes this collaborative dependency when, speaking of the creative impulse present throughout all human history, he states in the introduction: "The cave artist and the photographer, standing for all others, want to see not through but into: want you to stay with and *in* the work, and for it to stay with you, for it is in its very essence a form of ritual magic." When Dickey guides the reader's journey through the twenty-four hours *Southern Light* captures in word and pictures, he paradoxically remains less tangible a presence than in *Wayfarer,* despite his use of the imperative and despite the latter's narrative, which often subsumes Dickey's voice. However, as in all his efforts, his principal concern is the sense of consequence derived from human connection with the world.

Throughout his career, Dickey always declared that poetry was the center of his creative wheel and that all other artistic efforts were secondary. In 1992 he published *The Whole Motion: Collected Poems, 1942–1992.* Wanting the poems to speak for themselves, Dickey offered no introduction or preface that would establish his perspective on the half-century of poems that he believed defined his career. "When you look at all of it gathered there," he told

William Starr, "475 pages, almost 50 years, then you do have some trepidation. And when you open up the book, you know the blood in your stomach sinks. You think you're going to read those poems and say, 'You know, this is not as good as I thought.' Luckily, that didn't happen when I read through them again. I have to say in all honesty, this is better than I thought—sometimes a lot better." The collection underscored the diversity of techniques Dickey had attempted. "I've never forgotten the great lesson of Picasso," he declared, "which is that he never allowed himself to be trapped in a single style. When I start to explore some area of language or experience, I start with the question of 'What would happen if I did such and such,' and for me that invariably leads to, 'Well, let's try it and see what happens.'" He emphasized, however, that despite collecting his life's work, he was not finished. "I don't stop here," he asserted, "I try to explore new directions. I want to make each book I write different. I don't believe in repeating myself. I think the worst thing about so many American writers is that they're afraid to make a mistake. They're afraid one mistake, one book people don't like, will blow away everything else they've done."[14]

Dickey hoped for a large critical response, but it never came. David Biespel in the *Washington Post Book World* typified the feelings of the critical community, praising the poems from Dickey's early motion and lamenting those published later: "By the 1970s Dickey's work had declined, and it's hard to find anyone who doesn't agree that his poetry is now uneven; the grace and control of that remarkable decade [1957–1967] reveal themselves only here and there in poems that retain, to paraphrase the poet, a one-drink-too-many tone and energy." He asserted that Dickey's best poems derive from the guilt and joy he experienced during the Second World War and his feelings of being a survivor, which resulted in a "unified vision" compromised by a quarter-century of failed experiments.[15] Reviews from southern editors such as Starr, however, praised the book, referring to Dickey as a commanding poet of engulfing intelligence whose gigantic stature derived from his refusal to remain above the fight. Sales of *The Whole Motion* typified the critical conflict in which Dickey himself was mired. By April 1994 Wesleyan had sold out the hardback copies of the volume, but sales of the paperback had fallen off. Wesleyan had paid Dickey an advance of $4,500, a high figure for a university press, and decided not to reprint the hardback. The absence of critical attention and the failure of the book to win any awards revealed how low Dickey's star seemed to have fallen. Although his voice remained loud, few were listening. Those that were,

14. Starr, "James Dickey," *The State,* July 12, 1992, p. F1.
15. Biespel, "Poetry: James Dickey," *Washington Post Book World,* November 8, 1992, p. 8.

including the students in his poetry courses, increasingly heard him talk about a poet's need to repudiate fame and fortune. What mattered, he emphasized, was creating poems that endured.

Dickey determined at the beginning of 1993 that he would complete his third novel, *To the White Sea*. Early in the summer he met with Marc Jaffe in New York to go over revisions. Jaffe urged Dickey to excise a scene in which Muldrow strangles a child he has entertained with string tricks as well as one in which he kills a young girl and sticks her head on a waterwheel. Dickey spared the child in the former and substituted an old woman for the decapitated girl. Houghton Mifflin published the novel in September amid a gala of publicity, and Dickey, who was on sabbatical, was optimistic about the book's marketability. He had simplified the heroic quest that had dominated his earlier novels, suggesting that Muldrow's journey returns him to his beginnings; he parachutes into Tokyo and travels to northern Japan, where the ice and snow parallel his childhood in northern Alaska. Dickey also abandoned the fictional technique that reviewers had so criticized in *Alnilam* in favor of the straightforward interior narrative of the protagonist. Central to the story is Dickey's conviction that life exemplifies Darwin's principle that the strongest endure. Muldrow, who has murdered a college girl from Kansas whom he met in Point Barrow, Alaska, has honed his survival skills; he is fascinated with disguise, priding himself on his ability to blend into a crowd or a landscape. Although he initially kills Japanese out of necessity, his killing quickly becomes pathological, satisfying sadistic whims. As he travels into the cold wasteland, he becomes his surroundings, embodying the amoral universe. In a September 21, 1993, interview with Alex Chadwick on National Public Radio's *Morning Edition,* Dickey declared that he wanted readers at first to ally themselves with Muldrow—he is, after all, an American in the enemy's country—but then slowly realize that his actions are barbarous and that "the American military has loosed on the Japanese civilian population the equivalent of Ted Bundy." Asked if he had ever known someone like Muldrow or whether the character was completely imagined, Dickey responded, "No, it's completely imaginary, but, like the characters of any author, there are certain parts of your own personality that come to the fore and you just maybe kind of exaggerate those. As the German poet Goethe says, 'The strength of my own imagination as a poet and a novelist is the fact that I cannot imagine any crime of which I myself would not be capable.' "[16] Creating the character of

16. Typescript of NPR interview with James Dickey, September 21, 1993, pp. 21–22, Andrews Air Force Base, Maryland.

Muldrow, Dickey suggested, a figure whose brutality is so heinous and alien as to fascinate, was a creative exercise that validated the imagination.

As Dickey anticipated, the reactions of reviewers depended on their attitudes toward Muldrow. John Skow in his October 4, 1993, *Time* magazine review stated that Dickey had intentionally created "a strange airlessness to this brooding, mannered tale—part adventure story, part death chant," related in a first-person meditation by a powerfully intuitive man. However, despite being a "primitive marvel," Muldrow remains incomplete, not fully human, because, while he would be a sociopath in society, "out of it, for all his interior monologue, he is simply a doomed predator." John Logue praised the novel in *Southern Living*, citing not only the originality of a point of view that compels reader involvement first for and then against Muldrow, but also Dickey's "great language," that "voice, the poet's instinctive voice, [which] sings all the pages in *To the White Sea*." In the *New York Times*, Christopher Lehmann-Haupt faulted the book's lack of dramatic tension, which he argued results from Muldrow's indiscriminate killings; unlike the horror of *Deliverance*, where circumstance forces four canoeists to commit and conceal murder, Muldrow murders "so mechanically that his acts lack any moral resonance." In one of the most negative reviews, Jonathan Yardley in the *Washington Post* asserted, "since so little happens along the way, and since the wayfarer is in all respects unengaging . . . one is hard pressed to say anything more urgent than, 'Who cares.' "[17] Rather than scrutinize *To the White Sea* on its own merits, critics generally compared the novel to *Deliverance*, a tendency also evident when they reviewed Dickey's poetry after *Buckdancer's Choice*.

To the White Sea did not become a best seller in the U.S. market, but German, French, and Japanese publishers paid large advances and secured healthy sales. Moreover, Dell paid Dickey a substantial fee for paperback rights, and Universal Studies, which had paid Dickey $500,000 for the movie rights, proceeded with its plan to film the novel. On June 13, 1993, Emory University confirmed its purchase of Dickey's personal papers for a sum in excess of $100,000. In addition to these monies, Dickey earned $5,000 from Audio Productions to tape-record *To the White Sea*, $9,000 from *Architectural Digest* to write an article on Shinto models, and substantial fees from several readings.[18] Financially, Dickey was once again successful even if his critical reputation fell short of its former heights.

17. Skow, "Alone and on the Run," *Time*, October 11, 1993, p. 88; Logue, "Books about the South," *Southern Living*, October 1993, p. 78; Lehmann-Haupt, "From Man to Beast of Prey," *New York Times*, September 13, p. C17; Yardley, "The Great Escape," *Washington Post Book World*, August 29, 1993, p. 3.

18. Hart, *Dickey*, 721–22.

On September 17, 1993, the University of South Carolina honored its Carolina Professor writer in residence with a lavish, three-day tribute that celebrated Dickey's seventieth year, his quarter century of teaching at the university, and his publication that month of *To the White Sea.* The school announced that Dickey would now hold the honorary title of "distinguished professor." The tributes began with a dinner and reception at the Capital City Club; as master of ceremonies, George Plimpton delivered a humorous narration of Dickey's life. John Palms, the university's new president, hailed Dickey's intellect and passion. Other tributes followed, and the evening closed with Dickey reading from his new novel. On Saturday, a series of lectures and panels discussed Dickey's career. Richard Howard chaired the opening session on Dickey's criticism and teaching; Joyce Pair and Gordon Van Ness contributed. R. W. B. Lewis sat on a panel with Richard Calhoun and Robert Hill to explore Dickey's fiction, and on Sunday morning Robert Kirschten moderated a roundtable assessment of Dickey's career. That afternoon, Monroe Spears chaired a panel that discussed his former student's poetry and included Susan Ludvigson and Elizabeth Adams. As Spears reminisced in the Richland County Library auditorium about getting to know Dickey at Vanderbilt, Dickey, Deborah, and Bronwen listened in the front row.

In January 1994 Dickey's poem "Breaking the Field" appeared in the program for the Super Bowl. Several months earlier, an NFL representative had offered Dickey $3,000 to contribute a poem about returning a punted football. In his December 4, 1993, letter to Phil Barber,[19] who had commissioned the poem, Dickey explained that he wanted "a sense of balanced chaos, which corresponds to the field in the last part of a punting situation. . . . What I have tried to do is to give the essential fluidity and anarchy of the punt-return situation, as opposed to the rigidity, the straight-line formulations of the scrimmage, the rehearsed formations, and so on." In the poem, Dickey addressed his own literary situation. The persona sees "In the midst / One good block out of nowhere. Chaos field-breaking— / Closing jerseys, all wrong. Not many friends / But the right ones" and decides that importance lies in the "Green daylight . . . Beyond friends and enemies." He had long used football as a metaphor for life, beginning with a Hemingwayesque essay he wrote in college entitled "Practice at Clemson" and later in poems such as "In the Pocket" and "For the Death of Lombardi."

Spring 1994 saw Dickey engaged in a variety of small duties. From May 11 to 13 he served in a Virginia Center for the Book Writing Life Residency in Richmond, where he was honored at an authors' luncheon. His responsibili-

19. The letter is in the Dickey Papers.

ties included a public reading, during which he discussed the creative process and the writing craft; signing copies of his books at the Virginia State Library and Archives; and teaching a local high school class. "Teaching," he told a local reporter, Sibella Connor, "is an interchange and all that the human being has got is to interchange with other human beings. And the teacher and the learning experience is the height of it." His own writing process, Dickey asserted, was not patterned:

> My whole house is booby-trapped with typewriters. If anybody wants to give me a Christmas present, a birthday present, a Father's Day present, just give me another cheap Japanese typewriter that runs on batteries. Six D batteries. So I can put another project in one. And in some weird way they all cross-pollinate with one another. It can be a screenplay, a poem, a children's book, a novel.
>
> I'm a very peripatetic person. The only thing I dislike about the writer's life is the sedentary aspect. I'm a restless person. I'm always moving around. And at any hour, if I move, I'm going to pass by a typewriter. I might start reading what's in it and think again, "I don't like this paragraph." I sit down and fool with it until I get restless with it and move around and do something else.[20]

He posed for a picture at the Poe Museum, sitting at a desk as if penning a poem with a stuffed raven perched on his shoulder.

On May 14, Dickey visited Appalachian State University in North Carolina, where he was awarded an honorary degree and gave the commencement address. Entitled "The Eyes of the Egg," the lecture revealed agrarian influences and warned about the devastating effects that science had inflicted on the environment. Opening with references to the atomic device exploded at Los Alamos, Dickey read a two-page account of the site by John Hay, which described the old, adobe Native American hut—which for Hay and Dickey represented the primitive, mysterious forces that had created the world—being obscured by modern houses and clipped lawns. The atomic blast, figuratively representing modern culture, had completely destroyed almost all signs of life's essential mystery. Deborah appeared in the address as an Indian earth mother tending the élan vital by the adobe hearth, and Bronwen became the thirteen-year-old girl who hung on her wall a copy of *The Egg* by the nineteenth-century French presurrealist painter Odilon Redon, whose symbolic works, often depicting a dream world, are related to those of writers such as Poe, Baudelaire, and Mallarmé. For Dickey, eggs were fertility symbols in the modern wasteland. The sterility of the modern condition demanded a

20. Sibella Connor, "James Dickey: Riding the Flood Tide," *Richmond Times-Dispatch,* May 8, 1994, pp. G1, 4.

deliberate, concerted response, and Dickey's voice clearly announced it: "We must take on faith, which is religious faith, that it will be given, for what we are attempting to connect with is nothing less than the Universe: something beyond those geometric premises, the tract houses, those quick-plotted human dwellings."[21]

The seriousness of Dickey's medical problems became more evident in late October 1994 at one of his "power lunches" with Don Greiner and Ben Franklin, neither of whom suspected his deteriorating health. As they sat in the garden section by the fountain of the university's Faculty House and waited for Dickey, who was late, to arrive, they saw him hobbling across the shaded lawn. It took him five minutes to arrive, and when he did, he grasped the tables for support, his eyes yellow and sweat pouring off him in large droplets. He asked his colleagues for help. Once seated, however, he declined offers to drive him to the student health center or the hospital, declaring that the university paid him to teach and that was what he was going to do. Later, Deborah drove her husband to Richland Hospital, where doctors discovered that his liver had stopped functioning, the result of years of alcoholism, and that he had a severe case of hepatitis. Bile had flooded his bloodstream, causing jaundice. Deborah called Christopher and left a message on his answering machine: "Chris, you better do something. Your father is in the *hospital,* and he's yellow, yellow, yellow—yellow as the Yangtze River." Thinking that Deborah was playing what he called "another of her fantasy games," Chris downplayed her communication. However, when Bronwen faxed a brief handwritten note that said simply, "Dad is in bad shape," he recognized the severity of the situation. "I knew it was real," he later said.[22] Dickey sufficiently recovered within ten days to return home, but by November 14 he had suffered a relapse and was readmitted to the hospital. Doctors in Columbia treated his hepatitis for another five days.

At home Deborah was unable to care for her husband properly; she lacked medical training and was taking methadone to cure her heroin addiction. Mayrie MacLamore, the housekeeper who had cooked, cleaned, and cared for the Dickey household since 1987, administered his medications—Duphalac, Colace, and Prilosec—and gently harassed him into eating vanilla pudding and drinking Ensure. Deeply devoted to Dickey, she had visited him daily in the hospital and now continually teased him to lighten his mood. When he had regained strength enough to play his guitar, Dickey sang "The Cacklin'

21. From the typescript of "The Eyes of the Egg," Dickey Papers.
22. *Summer of Deliverance,* 244–45.

Head." "Oh, you don't like my Blues," he intoned, to which she would respond with feigned irritation, "Sing whatever you want to sing." Dickey continued to sing, and she continued to needle.

On November 28, however, he suffered another setback and was admitted to Providence Hospital; the effects of the hepatitis continued to assault him. He related to Henry Hart in an interview on August 5, 1996, that the condition "just depletes your system so much, it takes you years to recover from it. The main thing it did to me was take all the calcium out of my system, or almost all of it. I had enormous dental bills. It cost me ten thousand dollars to keep my teeth in my head. I lost fifty pounds in a week. I wasn't supposed to live. I was supposed to die. In fact, I did die at Richland County Hospital, twice. I flat-lined on the monitor, watching the monitor with the doctor. The second time I went under, the last I heard was the doctor say, 'We've lost him.'" Dying, he later related, was not terrifying. "It's not at all frightening. You have a sense of relief. . . . Everything just sort of goes, and that's it."[23] Finally sober, he now determined to set his life aright.

By mid-January 1995, Dickey's health was enough restored for him to teach one class of ten students at his home. They gathered together on the glassed-in porch that Dickey had added to the house several years previously from which they could see Lake Katherine. On April 12–14 he participated in a conference on World War II, "The Last Good War," organized by his University of South Carolina colleagues George Geckle and Bill Fox. Prominent writers, including Joseph Heller, William Styron, Paul Fussell, Mickey Spillane, and William Manchester, spoke on topics such as "America, Then and Now" and "Revisionist History and World War II." On April 13 in the Business School auditorium Dickey read from *To the White Sea*, later commenting to Michael Sponhour, a *State* reporter, not only about his contempt for revisionists and his semester at Clemson, "which at that time meant the grueling discipline of a military school plus the demands of Coach Frank Howard," but also about the men killed in the war. "We felt like we were going to die," he declared. "We had seen so much, we had lost so many friends."[24]

While his convalescence proceeded, Dickey usually sat in the large stuffed armchair in his living room, where he read during the day and watched old movies at night. At the end of the summer, Deborah suffered another relapse to heroin. With her addiction now seeming incurable and with his health failing, Dickey signed his official Last Will and Testament on August 22, 1995. He

23. Hart, *Dickey*, 729–30.
24. Sponhour, "Literary Veterans of World War II Revile Revisionists," *The State*, April 14, 1995, p. A1.

divided his personal property among his children, appointed NationsBank as his personal representative and Matthew Bruccoli as his literary and personal representative with "full and complete authority" over his literary estate. Christopher and Kevin were named as Bronwen's guardians. Despite the fact that Dickey still loved Deborah and wanted to keep the family together, he eliminated his wife from the estate and attempted to resolve the marital discord by proceeding with a divorce.

Emory University opened its James Dickey Archive on October 11. An honorary banquet at the Houston Mill House featured William Chace, the president of Emory, as well as family and friends. Al Braselton, Lewis King, and Inman Mays, all former advertising colleagues, offered tributes to a friendship that began in the fifties; Tom Dickey Jr., Kevin, and Bronwen (Chris, who worked for *Newsweek,* was on assignment in Bosnia) also spoke. Confined to his wheelchair, an exhausted but grateful Dickey made a few unrehearsed comments. Steve Ennis, head of special collections, and Joan Gotwals, the vice provost of Emory, then presented Dickey with an award. The following day Dickey talked informally to students gathered at Woodruff Library, asking his audience to identify the top poets of the twentieth century and chatting about the film version of *To the White Sea.* In the evening he read at Emory's Michael C. Carlos Museum and signed books in the special collections department.

That fall the University of South Carolina also honored Dickey, assigning *Deliverance* to all first-year students and showing the film several times at the university theater. On November 3, Dickey read from the novel to several hundred students assembled at the Kroger Center. Wearing a sports coat and turtleneck, clearly frail and short of breath, he cautiously climbed the steps to the stage, greeted by whistles and shouts from the students, and answered questions about whether he could have written the novel without the strong language and the violence. "No, I don't think so," he said. He declared that the characters were derived from bits and pieces of individuals he knew in real life and that Lewis "is in many respects based on me." There have been few movies, he asserted, "which followed their source as closely as this one did," and added, to laughter from the students, "The book is better." The program closed with Dickey reading for fifteen minutes from the final whitewater journey in the last section of the novel, his voice growing stronger and more animated as he proceeded. Appreciative students applauded when he rose to leave. "I've enjoyed this," he said in closing, "thank you,"[25] though Dickey qui-

25. William Starr, "Dickey Delves into *Deliverance,*" *The State,* November 4, 1995, B3.

etly told Gordon Van Ness and Keen Butterworth, who had made testimonial speeches, that the students merely felt sorry for him.

On December 13, he signed an agreement with the University of South Carolina Press that established a James Dickey poetry series. William Wadsworth, the director of the Academy of American Poets, had assisted the press by suggesting possible editors for the series. Richard Howard agreed to serve as the series editor, and a grant of $9,000 a year from the academy enabled the series to begin the following spring.

On December 18, Dickey delivered the commencement address at the Carolina Coliseum. In "The Weather of the Valley: Reflections on the Soul and Its Making," he adopted Keats's definition of life as a "vale of soul-making" as he reflected on his career and his values. He had committed his life, he declared, to the works of the imagination and to the teaching of subjects related to them. What he frequently told his students in class, he now reiterated: "I have always believed that teaching is the second greatest occupation that the human mind and energy can undertake. . . . the *most* important preoccupation . . . is learning." He reminisced about how, while stationed on Okinawa, he had read the poems of Trumbull Stickney and discovered the line "his island shivered into flowers," which acted as an epiphany and determined his course to be a poet. His injunction to the graduates was clear and emphatic:

> We need the plural mind that the individual mind contains: the plural mind in the plural universe. We need to be occupied with the eternal problem of language, language expanding consciousness and then consciousness expanding language, in circular or spiral ascent, perhaps. This is exactly what makes the creative mind so inestimably precious, the one thing to which one must undeviatingly devote oneself, if only because in this one can fully realize that joyful dance, the delightful—and delighted—wisdom of being. Everything is included in one expanding synthesis.[26]

Although they were aware of Deborah's drug problems and the tumult they were causing at home, Don Greiner and Ben Franklin never seriously believed Dickey would follow through with a divorce; he remained stubbornly faithful to romantic ideals about marriage. On January 18, 1996, however, Dickey filed the requisite papers with the Richland County Court. An "Obligations of Each Party" agreement gave custody of Bronwen to Dickey, while Deborah would receive a $213 monthly payment as beneficiary of his retirement

---

26. "The Weather of the Valley," in *All the Rights and Privileges* (Columbia: University of South Carolina Press, 1998), 37.

plan, $25,316 as her portion of the property, and $40,000 in death benefits from his life insurance. Additionally, she would receive 10 percent of future movie rights for *To the White Sea* and $8,333 in alimony payments each year. A financial declaration filed as part of the divorce estimated Dickey's assets at $800,000 and his income for the year at $187,000.[27] Legal maneuverings postponed the agreement on final terms until November 8. By early January the divorce was ready to be finalized because Deborah had vacated the house for over a year.

In February 1996 Dickey was diagnosed with fibrosis of the lungs. Kevin, now a physician at Yale University Medical Center, announced to Christopher after examining their father's X-rays that this was the condition that would finally kill him. It had developed independently of the liver cirrhosis and established itself to the point that Dickey could not breathe for more than a few minutes without the assistance of oxygen. Having undergone brain surgery and defeated his liver problems, Dickey seemed surprised at the diagnosis of this new medical problem. Depending on his mood, his attitude toward his health vacillated from witty denial to stoic resignation to melancholic reflection. In discussions with friends, he often appeared generous and kindhearted, desirous of reconciliation and renewal, always interested in the projects of colleagues, the apprentice poems of his students, and the careers of struggling writers. In an unpublished letter dated June 3, 1996, to Michael Hanson, who was attempting to become published, he wrote of his own early efforts to lift himself into the literary air:

> [T]here were periods when there didn't seem to be any hope at all. But during that night of the soul I discovered one thing that has never betrayed me, and has gotten me through such periods, and everything else. It is this. A writer with standards can only go on and produce a life-work on one basis, and that is love. If you love words, and if you love writing, you will do it. If you don't then you won't, because there are many other more lucrative, and maybe involving, occupations. But they are not more involving to the real writer: he already has the terms of his appeal. Speaking from my own case, I wrote for years without publication and without <u>thought</u> of publication. I was just fascinated with what I was doing, and if that fascination ever leaves me I will not write any more. It is a very simple situation, but these are the facts about it, and they can't and won't change.[28]

Debilitated by medical problems, Dickey nevertheless maintained the empathy and generosity that were always characteristic of who he essentially was.

27. Hart, *Dickey,* 738.
28. The letter is in the Dickey Papers.

Small literary reviews and magazines had sustained Dickey early in his career; late in his life, he returned to their pages. While this owed partly to the fact that larger venues such as the *New Yorker* had abandoned him, it was also partly because Dickey felt a strong allegiance to the publications that had initially given his own poetic mission height. In the eighties and nineties, his poems appeared in such places as *Graham House Review, Amicus Journal, Clockwatch Review, Corona, Southern Magazine,* and *Southpoint.* Dickey was pleased, therefore, when Philip Gossett, dean of humanities at the University of Chicago, announced that he had won the Harriet Monroe Poetry Prize, a $1,000 award judged that year by poet James Reiss, who had helped edit *Self-Interviews.* Previous recipients of the prize, named after the founder of *Poetry* magazine, included John Berryman, Robert Penn Warren, and Elizabeth Bishop. Because his health precluded extended travel, Dickey graciously accepted the honor by mail.

Dickey's writing now focused on the screenplay for *To the White Sea,* which was being written by David and Janet Peoples, and on "Crux," the sequel to *Alnilam.* He had drafted brief scenes for the screenplay and mailed them on December 28, 1995, to Richard Roth, who was going to produce the movie for Universal Studios; several months later he received a draft of the script. On July 23, 1996, he responded with several suggestions, declaring, "These observations and suggestions are offered in one connection only, and that is toward the making of as good a film as is possible. Emphasize that my intention is not to interfere, or to supersede the Peoples' screenplay in any way, but simply to be of whatever service I can in the furtherance of their already superior script."[29] He insisted that Muldrow hide in the sewer pipe at the opening of the film, the pipe itself acting as a kind of movie screen, and offered to write the scene himself. He also complained that minor events were being dwelled on while major scenes were truncated. Muldrow's dialogue, moreover, needed to be shortened into basic statements with nothing added to render them more personal or human. If his communication became enigmatic, Dickey declared, that would be fine because it was indicative of his character. The film's conclusion, he stated, should have the posse wandering futilely over the frozen snow, unable to discover any trace of Muldrow, finding no blood and only its own tracks. He suggested the possible use of a voice-over as the credits were brought up: "When I tell you this, just say it came from a voice in the wind." Like Joel Cahill in *Alnilam,* Muldrow was to remain complex and mysterious.

29. *Crux,* ed. Bruccoli and Baughman, 506.

Dickey in his final months attempted to become closer to his children, opening himself to them as if needing the continuity they provided. He doted on Bronwen, who now attended Choate and was home on vacation, and conducted long taped interviews with Christopher, who had flown in from Paris to gather information for what would become his memoir, *Summer of Deliverance*. On September 24, he participated in a conference celebrating F. Scott Fitzgerald's one-hundredth birthday, including a one-hour televised discussion with Joseph Heller. He wrote two tributes, a poem entitled "Entering Scott's Night," in which he imagined himself joining Fitzgerald in death— where "in the paper-lit garden / A dark-glowing field of folk, the dead, the celebrants / Making company as Scott would, / Who brought their time / Through time"—and an essay entitled "The Slow Surprise and the Deepening of Art," which praised Fitzgerald's high aesthetic standards.

Dickey felt better in November when doctors took him off steroids, writing Marc Jaffe that he was proceeding with "Crux" and had completed a publishable section entitled "Vines." Jaffe requested a proposal for the new novel. Although Dickey never complied, he did mail his editor the twenty-five-typed-page opening section of "Crux" at the end of the year. The pages open with Andrew Harbelis watching flying fish sail over the waves after he has embarked on a troopship for the Pacific, a scene that Dickey himself had experienced a half-century previously on the USS *Anderson*. Henry Hart has asserted that the opening pages of the typescript "read like a thinly veiled memoir of Dickey's World War II experiences. . . . Unwilling to forget his failure to become a decorated war pilot, at the end of his life he was more prepared to write about it realistically." Christopher Dickey, moreover, asserts in his memoir, "Harbelis is nothing but Intercept Officer Jim Dickey."[30] It is indeed possible to see in Harbelis's comments about pilots and radar observers, on the one hand, and his recollections about aerial gunnery school and P-61s, on the other, specific parallels with Dickey's training experiences. However, nothing in Dickey's early correspondence supports the contention that Dickey shared Harbelis's attitudes.

Dickey completed only twenty-nine pages of notes on "Crux," though he had fully elaborated his plans for the novel in 1976 when he detailed both *Alnilam* and its intended sequel, in which "the full diabolical scope of the Alnilam plot takes place, and culminates in a holocaust somewhere in the Pacific." At the conclusion of "Crux," Harbelis, who is "the decent guy" and who always carries his E6B flight computer with him, has emerged from the war

30. Hart, *Dickey* 743; *Summer of Deliverance*, 47.

terribly burned. He is on rest leave in Japan, has played in a Ping-Pong tournament, and has visited a Japanese school where the children dance and sing around him and give him American flags. He decides to decode Alnilam's final message, hidden on the inner strap of his goggles, which Joel had ordered never decoded unless Joel were dead or unless he gave the word. It is a single word—"nothing." Harbelis then goes out into the cold and with binoculars looks toward Mount Fuji, whose brightness blinds him. Swinging the binoculars toward the bottom of a tree, he moves up it, wanting it to be the right tree, the one whose beautiful and logical form complemented the mountain. The novel was then to read: "It drew what it needed from the earth, so the movement of life was in it." The last sentence of "Crux" was to be a statement of affirmation: "it was not impossible, like the mountain."[31]

In notes dated August 8, 1994, however, Dickey altered the conclusion. Harbelis looks at Mount Fuji and decides he will let Alnilam go, will turn away and not look back: "This is the perfect mountain, the organization, the beautiful and logical form. Demented with rigidity and perfection, and he turned to the trees. The wind blew. They would die, but here they were alive, and they moved." Dickey no longer believed he would finish his sequel, but the language, the voice of Harbelis, in the opening section that he did complete is among the strongest prose he ever wrote. Harbelis watches the flying fish as they leap free of the water:

> They broke; there just enough. Now he would add one thing to them, each time they rose. One thing. They flattened into their pattern, the sun catching everywhere on it, one spark to a fish. Or it could be a contest of some kind: not to get somewhere first but to go farthest, stay, hold out for most time in the air? Was the same one always in front? Yes, it must be, it must be that way, Harbelis thought.[32]

Dickey had always wanted to go the farthest, to commit himself to the air at the front of the group, to fly point. Once he had done so, but now he was flying by words.

Despite his deteriorating health, labored breathing, and lack of stamina, Dickey remained determined to fulfill his teaching commitment. Like the high school geometry teacher in his 1965 poem "Mangham," who suffers a heart attack in class but continues to instruct his students in "Identities," in "those

---

31. *Pages: The World of Books, Writers, and Writing,* ed. Matthew J. Bruccoli (Detroit: Gale Research, 1976), 14–19.

32. *The James Dickey Reader,* ed. Henry Hart (New York: Simon and Schuster, 1999), 212.

things that, once / Established, cannot be changed by angels, / Devils, light-ning, ice or indifference," Dickey was fiercely unwavering in his desire to reveal to his students the connections that poetry made possible. He had, however, informed the English department that he would take a sabbatical and a med-ical leave of absence for the 1997–1998 academic year and that the spring 1997 term would constitute his last. Realizing that his close friend was near-ing death, Matthew Bruccoli arranged with Instructional Services to tape-record Dickey's last classes. On January 14, 1997, Dickey met his first group of students for the new term, coughing and retching for a few minutes until he was able to breathe. His lecture—too formal a term, really, for the personal atmosphere, the climate of camaraderie that he always established with his students—ranged over a wide landscape of topics, including the poet's use of the unconscious, the necessity for imaginative lying, the nature of God, and the poet's role as a secondary creator. The students listened as if hypnotized to a voice that sounded weak. "Poetry is a matter of luck," he declared,

> you can't teach it. You can point it out when it occurs, but you can't teach it. Verse, however, you can teach. . . . This is a class in verse hoping to become po-etry, with luck.
>
> I teach this semester what I call "creature poetry." Poetry written with the whole, the whole, the *whole* of the sentient organism. Mind, body, guts, blood flow, breath. Everything that enables you to be a living human being, we have a resource. So we start with dreams. And with automatic writing. Anything to break through the barrier that leads from the conscious mind to the uncon-scious and to the dream life.
>
> I have the dream, the most terrible dream, of pursuit. . . . I am always mov-ing against a terrific wind. Which doesn't bother my pursuer at all, but I have to grab the grass and try to inch forward, you know? And something is just gain-ing on me in leaps and bounds. It is some sort of guilt, I guess. If I were a post-Freudian, I am sure I would have to admit to it. But in the dream it is only the terrible pursuit.
>
> Invent. Invent the guts of it. To invent, you can say as much as you like with stuff you know. But don't be confined to it. Don't think about honesty. Don't think about telling the truth. Because poets are not trying to tell the truth, are they? . . . They are trying to show God a few things he maybe didn't think of. It takes us to supply that. We are not trying to tell the truth. We are trying to make it so that when we sit down to write we are absolute lords over our material. We can say anything we want to, any way we want to. The question is to find the right way. This is what we are going to be looking for.

Dickey informed his students that, given his physical condition, this would undoubtedly be his last class. Yet he urged them forward, stating, "What we start here I would like you to continue on your own regardless of what the course or the person teaching the course would have you do. . . . When we get started, I want you to fight this thing through . . . with your own unconscious, with your own dreams, and see where it comes out. That is the excitement and the fun of it—deep discovery, deep adventure. It is the most dangerous game, and the best." He concluded by telling his students about how society views its poets: "The world doesn't esteem the poet very much. They don't understand where we are coming from. They don't understand the use for us. They don't understand, or if there is any use. They don't really value us very much. We are the masters of the superior secret, not they. Remember that when you write."[33]

The day after teaching his class, Dickey succumbed to feverish chills, shaking uncontrollably, and was rushed by ambulance to Providence Hospital. Doctors diagnosed a chest infection they believed curable with antibiotics. Dickey, always viewing his medical problems as a kind of warfare, remained unfazed, believing he would be home by Monday. Although he had trouble breathing Thursday night, the following morning brought renewed strength. Don Greiner visited, and together they recited Frost's "After Apple-Picking," alternating lines until they reached the conclusion: "One can see what will trouble / This sleep of mine, whatever sleep it is. / Were he not gone, / The woodchuck could say whether it's like his / Long sleep, as I describe its coming on, / Or just some human sleep." Moved by his favorite Frost poem, Dickey reached out and hugged his close friend and colleague, saying that he loved him. Other friends also visited. In the evening, however, Dickey weakened. He fought for breath and continued to lose weight. Notified of his decline, Christopher, Kevin, and Bronwen made arrangements to fly to Columbia.

On Sunday, Ben Franklin saw Kevin and Bronwen beside their father's bed and decided not to intrude. Matthew Bruccoli shortened his visit later, agonized by his friend's physical state. That night, Mayrie MacLamore attended him. She temporarily left the room when she received a call from one of her children who wanted to know how Dickey was doing, but returned around 11:00 p.m. He lay serene, as if sleeping, then suddenly gripped her hand. She said, "Mr. Dickey?" He gasped and said, "Don't leave me." He was afraid of being alone but not of dying. Then she watched him stop breathing.

The first announcements of Dickey's death summarized his life and career, noting his Rabelaisian lifestyle and the critical controversy surrounding his work. Almost all the articles linked him to *Deliverance*. The *Washington Post*,

33. Typescript of James Dickey's verse composition class, January 14, 1997, private papers of Christopher Dickey.

for example, observed, "He loved life and lived it with a macho swagger," and the *Richmond Times-Dispatch* declared that he "achieved his greatest fame for his novel and Oscar-nominated movie *Deliverance.*" More personal tributes soon followed. Sibella Giorello in a January 24 article asserted: "The essential Dickey was pure poet. As a writer, he didn't so much pen his poems as wrestle words until their meaning hit the ground; didn't so much employ phrases as bite them off of life, spit them onto the page. . . . Dickey steered away from inconsequence both in literary terms and real life, gravitating toward the edge. He lived hard, until his 6-foot-four-inch frame finally gave out." Describing an interview she had had with Dickey, she remembered: "For several hours, we talked about books. He would reach into the paper tower and extract one level, read a portion aloud. Each piece was unlike the last. Poems, reminiscences, love stories. Yet each had a continuing thread: conflict. Conflict provided the thread of his own work—man against man, man against woman, man against nature, man against science." The most moving statements came from Dickey's daughter, Bronwen, in *Newsweek*. Describing her father as he lay in the hospital, "nothing more than a pained skeleton" whose "chest heaved as though every breath was a last valiant effort" and whose "fingers were purple from lack of oxygen," she nevertheless remembered his greatness: "Not the greatness of the writer but the greatness of the father and the teacher." "My father was not physically recognizable," she wrote, "but his essence was still strong in the room. His books were strategically arranged nearby, and he still wore two watches, his Citizen Wingman and his Ironman Triathlon." Against the onslaught of time and the prejudice of critics, Dickey pitted himself, armed with books and a poetic imagination. In an extended defense of Dickey against the inadequacy of his critics, Jeffrey Meyers declared: "he knew the tears of things." Rodney Welch admitted Dickey's problems. "For most of his final years," he stated, "Dickey's life was in free fall. Professionally, his stock had dropped, the prices for books and readings fluctuated, and there was always the looming threat that his old lies would be exposed. That was the least of it. His home life was a nightmare: he was a hardened alcoholic and an incurable womanizer, and his much younger wife Deborah was a heroin addict who often took out her rage on him." "Always at the forefront," he then declared, "was Dickey's expansive personality, easily eloquent on subjects both literary and domestic, his conversation peppered with brilliant judgments, well-remembered quotes, tall tales, and statements guaranteed to shock all but the most jaded."[34] Even in death, Dickey remained controversial.

34. Richard Pearson, "James Dickey Dies; Author of Deliverance," *Washington Post,* January 21, 1997, p. B5; "James Dickey Dies at 73," *Richmond Times-Dispatch,* January 21, 1997, p. B2;

Dickey was buried next to Maxine in the All Saints Waccamaw graveyard on Pawleys Island. The funeral was held on the afternoon of Friday, January 24, the service limited to family and close friends. Ben Franklin, Matthew Bruccoli, Michael Allin, Don Greiner, Al Braselton, Lewis King, and Christopher's son were pallbearers. Dickey had instructed that his gravestone read, "James Dickey, 1923– , Poet, Father of Bronwen, Kevin and Christopher." His children decided in addition to inscribe an eye like the one on the first edition of *Deliverance* as well as the words "I move at the heart of the world," from his 1961 poem "In the Tree House at Night." On Monday the University of South Carolina held a memorial tribute on the green lawn of the Horseshoe near where Dickey, Don Greiner, and Ben Franklin had enjoyed the good conversations of so many "power lunches." The Capital City Chorale sang "Sweet Chariot," "Amazing Grace," and "Shall We Gather at the River," and Julie Bloemeke, one of Dickey's students, read "The Heaven of Animals." Ward Briggs and Matthew Bruccoli offered remarks, and Pat Conroy, the principal speaker, told of Dickey's complicated life, declaring, "A whole city of men lived in that vivid, restless country behind Dickey's transfixing eyes." Robert Newman, the English department chair, concluded the ceremony as "Dueling Banjoes" was played. Later, on November 14, 1998, at 11 a.m. in Thomas Cooper Library, the university would announce the dedication of the James Dickey Poetry Seminar Room and the acquisition of Dickey's personal library.

Giorello, "Seeking His 'Deliverance,'" *Richmond Times-Dispatch*, January 24, 1997, pp. C1, 3; Dickey, "He Caught the Dream," *Newsweek*, March 24, 1997, p. 19; Meyers, "What the Monsters Know," *New Criterion* 18.9 (May 2000); Welch, "The Haggard Heroes Recall Their Lost Pal," *Free Times*, April 19–25, 2000, pp. 25, 28–34.

To: Mary Bly

CC, Emory University
4620 Lelia's Court
Columbia, S.C. 29206

January 19, 1990

Dear Mary Bly,

Thank you for your letter, and for listing the lines from the poems that your father wants to use. As I said, I will be happy to allow you to use these lines in the anthology your father is doing, which I will be very interested in seeing when it appears. You might want to check the next-to-last item as you list it, for I have written no poem called "Treebombing." It may be that you have in mind "The Firebombing," to which your father has, I am told, made reference in the past.

But that too is all right. It would help me if you could give me some notion of how these 173 lines will be used. I will be happy to waive my fee, but I would like some assurance that the quotation from my poems in <u>American Poetry: Wildness and Domesticity,</u> will not be used as material for a personal attack. My talk with your father the other day seemed to indicate that his intentions are otherwise, and that his anthology would deal with other matters than the personal. That seems to me to be the best course, but I would like to communicate as to this.

You may assure your father that I miss the thirty years of friendship that we could have had. But you may also tell him that the end is not yet, and much is still possible on the positive rather than the negative side: that there can be good human time.

And as for yourself, Miss Mary Bly, I remember when you were born. At that time I had young children of my own, and, as I felt then, it seemed that my closest friends should also get into the Great Chain: not the great chain of buying, but the Great Chain of Being. By whatever circumstance, your father followed up, and you were the result. Never have I had such fine letters from a new father than from your own father to me, about you.

I am very happy you are working with him, and I hope to see you both on any conceivable occasion.

Again, thanks for your letter, and for the things you say. As I done said, the end is not yet, and may even be far off. We'll see, all of us.

With best wishes,

To: Al Poulin, Jr.[1]

CC, Emory University
4620 Lelia's Court
Columbia, S.C. 29206

January 23, 1990

Dear Al:

Thank you very much for your letter, and for the invitation to do a Foreward to John Logan's <u>Collected Fiction</u>. I doubt whether I could do this, for my schedule is so jammed that I don't know when I might be able to read John's pieces. When would you need this, by the way? Let me know, for it is important.

No, I didn't get a copy of John's <u>Collected Poems</u>, and would like to have one if you don't mind sending it.

I remember the early part of my association with John with favor, this having been when he was at Notre Dame. The latter part I had just as soon forget, after he had become involved with Bly and with many another questionable character, and had become so demoralized with drink and his incessant affairs that I lost track of any merit I might ever have seen in him.

But he did have merit; some, though not a great deal, or at least this is my opinion. I realize that you have a stake in his particular game, such as it is, and I will help in some modest way if I can. But taking a great deal of time with the work of John Logan, or his life, is something I am not prepared to do, since I have too many things of my own to attend to.

Let me know what you think about all this, and I will be guided accordingly. But it strikes me that you should try to find someone more enthusiastic about Logan than I am, who could give you the Foreward you desire.

My best to you. Your translations of Rilke's French are the best there is, I am convinced. Keep on with your life, and your work.

Sincerely,

---

1. President of BOA Editions Ltd.

To: Gordon Van Ness   **TLS, Property of Gordon Van Ness**

4620 Lelia's Court
Columbia, S.C. 29206
January 24, 1990

Dear Van:

Thank you for your letter, and, again, for the things you say. I return the paper on my early notebooks that you sent Matt Bruccoli with just a few pencilled changes, indications of misspelled words, and so on. But on the whole I am most pleased, and look forward to your editing of these notebooks, and to reading back through the years to what I thought I was doing in those days. You can see how hard it was for me to articulate anything, but you can also see how hard I tried, and how I did not fool myself about what I was doing. I think that those who are interested in my work will enjoy seeing this part of the development of it, and I have gone from what was at first a mild interest in your project to a positive enthusiasm for it. So go ahead, and tell me how the going goes.

It is also wonderful news that you will be contributing to Bob Kirschten's new book. I am also glad that Romy Heilen is reading <u>Puella</u>. I met her briefly when she was here interviewing for a job she didn't get—they took on someone in Women's Studies, Black Studies, or something equally foolish urged on them, or demanded, by Affirmative Action—and I thought her very impressive. So . . . we'll see what happens.

<u>The Eagle's Mile</u> has just been copy-edited by the people at Wesleyan. I have sent back the manuscript as approved, and they have moved into the next stage, which is, I guess, to set type. But the management up there shifts with such bewildering rapidity that I hardly know to whom you should write for a look at the manuscript. My present editor has taken another job, so that the person for you to write is the incoming director, Eliza Childs. If Wesleyan has no objection to your looking over the book, <u>I</u> sure don't! If Wesleyan can't furnish you with a Xerox, let me know, and I'll have one made for you down here.

Meanwhile my best, as always. Things go well here, though there is always a sense of pressure. But I was born for combat, for the struggle, and would be lost without it. He who ever strives upward, Goethe says: Ah! Him can we save!

Ever,

Jim

To: William Phillips

CC, Emory University
4620 Lelia's Court
Columbia, S.C. 29206

March 19, 1990

Dear William Phillips:

Thank you very much indeed for your letter—or two letters, really—and your kind invitation to publish something with you. What I have now are parts of a long poem and about 135 pages of a new novel. I don't know when either of these will be finished, for I make whatever haste is possible to me very slowly, among much doubt and confusion. But if you would like to look at these things I will be happy to send them to you. The long poem, in two parts, is called <u>Two Poems on the Survival of the Male Body</u>, and of these I have a few pages I am satisfied with, and am willing let stand as they are. I don't know if just printing a page or two of an unfinished poem would appeal to you, so I must wait to be guided by your feelings in such a matter. The novel, called <u>To the White Sea</u>, might yield more latitude, for there may be more than one episode from it that is capable of being excerpted. If you like, I'll send you the whole hundred and thirty-odd pages, and you can decide for yourself. A couple of other magazines are offering to print something from the manuscript, and if <u>Partisan</u> would like to examine what I have done to date, there might result a situation where you could print part of the book and some other magazine another part, depending on what is decided between you and other editors and me. But there should be enough to go around, and, as I say, I'll be happy to send you what I've done as soon as you indicate that I should.

Do let me know about these matters when you have time. And know, also, how pleased I am to hear from you. I remember my association with <u>Partisan Review</u>, and the things I have published with you, in the clearest and warmest light. Forty-five years ago, when I was at Vanderbilt, I read one of the issues of that time from cover to cover; it was the first intellectual magazine I had ever read, and, though I didn't understand a lot of it, the experience was a revelation to me. Among the articles was one of your own on Dostoyevsky's Underground Man. I remember it well; I still have the copy.

And speaking of copies, I'd appreciate your telling Ms. Edith Kurzweil that I will be most happy to receive a complimentary subscription to the magazine. Nothing out of the blue has ever been so welcome here.

Sincerely yours,

To: Charles Grench[2]   CC, Emory University
                                               4620 Lelia's Court
                                               Columbia, S.C. 29206

                                               March 21, 1990

Dear Mr. Grench:

Thanks very much for your letter, the copy of the rules, and the general cast of intelligence and helpfulness your words give off. I don't have any changes to make in procedures. I <u>would</u> like to see the complete list of entrants, just to go through it and register anyone I might have read and liked in another connection.

Though I'd like to, I don't think it will be possible for me to come to Yale and go through the boxes, since I have many commitments this spring. I shall be very glad to accept the judgement of yourself and your screening crew, and concentrate on the books that you and they have decided upon. Will you send the manuscripts all at the same time, or at intervals? When can I expect them? It would help me if I had this information, because I must ration my time in order to do the best possible job of which I am capable.

But there doesn't seem to be any difficulty at this stage, at all. I am very eager to get into the assignment, and await your phone call, further correspondence with you, and the manuscripts, whenever they may be forthcoming.

Again, thanks for your thoroughness, and the light that comes off your words. Everything is going to be good.

                                               Cordially,

To: Heather Schafroth   CC, Emory University
                                               4620 Lelia's Court
                                               Columbia, S.C. 29206

                                               March 27, 1990

Dear Ms. Schafroth:

Well! Over the years I have received a lot of mail, some favorable and some not, but I have never been more pleased than on reading you letter and your paper on my wolverine poem, which I think is remarkably acute and imaginative for one so young to have written—or, indeed, for anyone to have written. The theme of the poem, extinction, is one that has long haunted me, and when, years ago, I saw in the paper that the wolverine—which is kind of the

---

2. Executive editor of Yale University Press.

ultimate wild animal, and along with the peregrine falcon and the barracuda is one of my totem creatures—had been put on the endangered species list, I knew I must write something about it. Again, I am very happy that the poem moved and touched you.

I was in Ames once, during the spring of 1966, when I gave a reading at the university. I remember that I was domiciled with the wrestling team, and that during the visit I managed to stick a metal guitar fingerpick into one of my fingers, which then became infected and almost resulted in my losing the finger, which would have been very bad news for this guitar player! However, despite that bad luck, I remember Ames with much favor, and would like to come back there some time, if conditions favor. Though my finger healed all right, there still is one bad condition in Ames, however, that as far as I know is still a feature—if that is the word—of the local landscape. It takes the form of a teacher at the university named Neal Bowers, who once wrote an attack on me in the form of a very bad book. You might like to contact him and tell him the same thing you tell me about the effect my work has had on you. You needn't really do this, of course; but you might, if the notion takes you. Anyhow, it shall be as you wish.

The eleventh grade should make you about 16 or 17, I should think, which is a good age for a young writer—and a young pianist, and a voracious young reader: all the things, in fact, you tell me about. Believe me, I hope you realize your dreams of joining the Cricket magazine editorial board. If the other writers on the Cricket can write as well as you do, that particular insect will make quite a distinctive chirp!

Believe me, my best to you, Heather Schafroth. Write again when you feel like it. Meanwhile I send along a picture, if you'd like to have it. If not, tear it up and scatter it for the crows over the Iowas cornfields.

Cordially,

To: William H. Pritchard[3]

CC, Emory University
4620 Lelia's Court
Columbia, S.C. 29206

March 29, 1990

Dear Pritchard:

Thanks so much for sending along the Jarrell books. Your biography is very good indeed; Randall would have been pleased and I'm sure Mary is. I

---

3. A member of the English department at Amherst College whose biography of Randall Jarrell was published in 1990.

realize how difficult it must have been for you to deal with the question of suicide. As for myself, I don't doubt in the least that Randall killed himself; after all, he was down there at Chapel Hill at the Hand Clinic because he had already made one attempt. The hard thing is to figure out why a person with so many gifts should want to do such a thing, but that whole generation of poets—most or all of the best ones—were caves of self-destruction. Barryman, Randall, Win Scott, and Weldon Kees were actual suicides, and Roethke, Delmore, Lowell, Paul Goodman and Elizabeth Bishop were virtual suicides from drink and the kind of living—or dying—they did. I knew them all—some pretty well and others only slightly—and their example is both exhilarating (temporarily) and dangerous (permanently). I think Randall's case was the saddest of the lot, with a possible competition—in that grim category—being Jim Agee, who in my opinion was the most talented of them all. Well, what to do? Read their work, I guess, is the only thing, for we will not see them any more, except in dreams, where, for me at least, they keep coming back, Randall with particular dimensionality, and with more meaning than the others.

Again, thanks so much for your considerateness. You are surely among the best biographers and critics around. What I'd like most is to see some original work of yours. After all, if Edmund Wilson can shut Mary McCarthy off in a room and tell her to write fiction, and have the result turn out as well as it did, I feel I can tell you the same thing, and get you to write poetry. Give it a shot. I would bet cold coin (also gold) on your ability to do it.

My best surely.

To: Marc Jaffee

CC, Emory University
4620 Lelia's Court
Columbia, S.C. 29206

May 15, 1990

Dear Marc,

Surely there have been but few letters written from an editor to an author which have been so heartening as your note to me. In fact, it came at a very dark time indeed; the darkest of all. You seem to understand, even from that distance, the unrelieved difficulty that obtains here, though there would have to be a great deal of description for me to be able to make you understand just how bad it has been. Things seem a little better now, though there is still much trafficking with legality, with police, magistrates, counselors and other supervisory agencies. In a matter of days it will be decided as to whether my wife goes on trial, but we have reason to hope that she will be given something called pre-trial intervention, and if she satisfies the conditions over a period of time, she—and the family—will be able to resume at least the semblance of a normal life. All of us involved hope for this, but it is not yet an established fact. As I say, we will know in a few days, and I will keep you posted.

Amongst all this confusion and uncertainty, I have managed to do another fifty pages of the book, which I will send as soon as my secretary types them. Even this much was hard to manage; the section was accomplished mainly in police stations and waiting rooms and other places not generally thought conducive to creative writing. However, I think that what I do in these places is pretty good, now that I read it over, and I hope that you will, too.

There is also some other good news, to counterbalance all the other. One of my students, a young middle-aged man named Tim Williams, turns out to be a professional researcher, and will find out everything I need to know about Air Force equipment and wartime Japan without even asking a fee. He went straight to the Smithsonian, for example, and dug up a great deal of material about the B-29 that I needed. This will make it possible for me to go over the initial section and get the facts exactly right. Most of them, which I had previously guessed at, turn out to have been essentially right, so I won't have to do much rewriting on the part you have already read. Nevertheless, I plan, now, to use research more than I have in this draft of the novel, so that I won't need to go back and change the parts I've done earlier.

Meanwhile, word has gotten around, and Rust Hills at Esquire called the other night about printing a section of the book he had asked to read. George Plimpton at Paris Review will also do something from the 150 pages I've done, as will William Phillips of Partisan Review, and there are several other magazines, as well, that are asking to see the manuscript.

But we can handle all that later. I have a good chance now, I think, to get back to working full time on the book, for I do believe my wife's situation is stabilizing, I have a good new secretary, and look forward with confidence to finishing the book before school opens September 1st. When I have time, and am more or less free of worry, I work hard, and by now I know the story episode by episode very well. I know what is going to happen, and I know how to connect the events so that they flow from one to the other with plausibility, and yet with some surprise, which I like to spring when I can.

But, the main purpose of this letter, Marc, is to let you know how profoundly grateful I am for your words, and for the renewed confidence you have given me in what I am doing. I am not prone to gush, but I hope you can tell what lies behind what I say. And I will not fail you; I wanted to make sure you know that.

My best to your wife, and to those who work with you at Houghton.

Ever,

To: Charles Grench   **CC, Emory University**
                                                              4620 Lelia's Court
                                                              Columbia, S.C. 29206

May 20, 1990

Dear Mr. Grench:

I got the batch of manuscripts the other day, and have been looking them over. This is a heavy load of stuff! It'll take a little time to come up with a clear-cut winner, which I would like to do. I go slow about these things, because to these contestants it will mean a lot, and it is much to the purpose that I make the right choice. Meanwhile, I have gone back over the list of previous winners and have wondered what happened to a good many of them. I wish I had all the books of the people who have won, for it might be possible for me to "rescue" some of them, like Joan Murray, whom Auden picked as his first selection, and who I think is just terrific, as is Robert Horan. This last is surely a remarkable talent. Could you tell me something about him? I think he is probably dead, now, but I don't really know. Someone should collect everything of his that can be found and publish a memorial volume.

Well, I won't go on and on, though I thought I would throw these possibilities at you for whatever they might be worth.

But the main business at hand is—well, the main business at hand, which is to pick a winner from the manuscripts you have sent. I don't see any difficulty with any of your requests, and will try to have a winner for you within a week. After you and I—and the others involved—decide upon a winner, I'll go ahead and write the introduction, and we will proceed as you have outlined. Again, no problem.

It is great to look into the minds and imaginations of the people who have written these poems; rather like dipping your hand in new blood, some of which becomes your own.

Let me know what you need, and meanwhile I will go ahead with things at this end.

My best to you, surely.

Cordially,

To: John Logue

CC, Emory University
4620 Lelia's Court
Columbia, S.C. 29206

May 21, 1990

Dear John,

Thanks very much for your note, and for the things you say. But your comments on my work are not the main thing here.

The main thing is your poem. I have just been made judge of the Yale Series of Younger Poets, which gave James Agee birth, among others. But there is nothing in them to compare with your pages. This is not bullshit. Bullshit is not easy for me, for in matters of imagination, I must level. The ultimate tribute I could possibly make regarding your poem is that it draws me in, and makes me want to meddle with it, for the quality of imagination is high. As I say, that is the main thing. The skill is less, and there could be some cutting and rearranging, all in the service of <u>staging</u> the drama of which you write.

Believe me, I am astonished, and can do no less than urge you to write more poetry. If we can go back and forth on this thing, I would like to submit it either to <u>The</u> <u>New</u> <u>Yorker</u>, or, what might be better, to Dave Smith, who has just taken over the editorship of the <u>Southern</u> <u>Review</u>, out of Baton Rouge. If we can get rid of a certain sense of scatter, here, we can bind together a remarkable piece of rhetoric. Again, let me know if you'd like me to work and edit, to the best of myuability.

But have no doubt that your imagination is remarkable. I have no axe to grind, but savor the imagination where I find it, in whatever form.

Do get back to me on this, and we will go somewhere with your work, either to <u>The</u> <u>New</u> <u>Yorker</u> or to Dave at Baton Rouge, or to the Arts of Kingdom Come, wherever she might be found.

Ever,

To: Christiane Jacox Kyle[4]   CC, Emory University
                                                      4620 Lelia's Court
                                                     Columbia, S.C. 29206

                                                        June 12, 1990

Dear Ms. Kyle,

I write in congratulation for your having been chosen the winner of the Yale Series of Younger Poets for this year. There were some unusually strong manuscripts in a variety of styles, but yours had a human dimension that the other did not even approach—many of them being long-winded reminiscences of childhood fishing trips or equally long recountings of love-hate family situations—never before have I encountered people with so many grandparents!— and a clarity that most of the others lacked. Yours is a very clear depth, and your dramatic sense, particularly in poems like the first one, is remarkable and completely convincing. I won't go on and on, but as judge of this contest for the first time, I want you to know that I am very happy indeed that you are the winner. And I would say this, also. Not only was your manuscript the best of the current batch, but except for a few rare exceptions—Robert Horan, whom Auden chose—none of the previous winners that I have read are as distinctive and memorable as you are. I thought you might like to know these things, so I pass them on, for what they might be worth to you.

The editors at Yale suggest that I might like to make some suggestions to you about your book, but I hesitate to do this, since you have chosen the work just as you wanted to present it.

However, I do have a couple of very slight suggestions, if I may make them. You might want to reconsider the title, for example. It is a good enough title as it stands, but there are many books of poems with similar names, and for this reason another might be preferable; something about human beings, among whom you move with such grace and imaginative understanding, rather than animals.

I like to look at all aspects of a book's appearance, and I am most interested in your name. I assume that Jacox is your maiden surname, but it is such an interesting word—sound—that I wonder if it might be possible for you to use it as a Christian name, and publish the book as Jacox Kyle. The chances are that for reasons of your own you would not want to do this, but I thought I would suggest it, because the possibility fascinates me, and I think the strangeness of the name, thus put, would not be lost on the possible audience, either,

---

4. Kyle lived in Spokane, Washington. Her book, *Bears Dancing in the Northern Air,* was published in the Yale Series of Younger Poets in 1991.

and might prove a real, though minor, sales factor. I do know that when I was on the Awards Board of the National Institute, and was given a number of poetry books to read, I read, first off, one by a poet named McKeel McBride, because I wanted to know—as quickly as possible!—what someone with a name like that would <u>write</u>! Turns out she was pretty good, too.

But not so good as you. And I want to close by saying, just once more, how pleased I am with what you have done; how happy I am that you are my first choice, my first winner.

Cordially,

To: Gary Kerley   **TLS, Property of Gary Kerley**

4620 Lelia's Court
Columbia, S.C. 29206
November 8, 1990

Dear Gary,

Thank you very much indeed for your letter, for the review and other material you send along, and for what you say in them. I am not given to gush, but I would like again to tell you how much I appreciate your feelings and insights, and your kindness in sending them to me.

And, sure, we could talk about <u>The Eagle's Mile</u> in a phone interview, if you like. Call any morning, for I am always at this number then. (803) 787-9962.

If I possibly could, I would arrange to come to Brenau, my mother's old school, in whatever manner might be arranged, and at whatever time I can manage. I like that area very much, and always have. When I was in high school I used to play football against the Gainesville team, which was always good, and one of the best friends I had at Clemson was from there; his name is Esco Shaw. I believe he is in the automobile business in Gainesville still. And he was some kind of a hell of a football player, I can tell you. If you happen to know him—or know <u>of</u> him—please remember me to him with all favor.

And do keep in touch. I am very proud indeed of what you have done since we were in class together—as <u>I</u> see it—and look forward with great interest to what you are doing, and will do.

Ever,

James Dickey

James Dickey

To: Cleanth Brooks   RTL, Emory University
December 14, 1990   4620 Lelia's Court
                                                  Columbia, S.C. 29206

Dear Cleanth,

Thanks for the note outlining the Hanes Poetry prize. Sure; I'll be happy to
help you out, but I must know what money is involved, for I belong to a ra-
pacious agent who does not allow me to do such services without payment. I
am sure you can understand that, and be guided accordingly.

But believe that I will help if I can, though poor Fred Chappell is hardly the
collaborator I myself would choose. Maybe it will work out, regardless. Anyway, I will try, and see what can be done.

My best to you, as always. Your notion of paradox threw the key block for
me, and I will never cease to be grateful. Whatever work I do is in that particular debt.

Let me hear.

                                                            Ever,

To: Joyce Pair   TLS, Property of Joyce Pair

                                                     4620 Lelia's Court
                                                  Columbia, S.C. 29206
                                                      January 31, 1991

Dear Joyce,

A very hasty note to suggest a couple of other possibilities for the panel
at SAMLA. (Incidentally, when is the conference, anyway?) There are a couple of people in Missouri who know my work pretty well. One of them is
Beverly Jarrett, who is now head of the University of Missouri Press, and
the other is her husband, Billy Mills, also a poet, and a very good one. I have
written Beverly about this, and find out that both she and Billy will be at the
conference, so they could easily serve. She seems to think that, if only one of
the two were chosen, Billy, as a working poet, might be the better. Myself, I
don't know, but in any case you might want to write both of them in care of
the University of Missouri Press. They are enthusiastic and good people,
and I think you'd enjoy connecting up with them on this basis, or on any
other.

To keep you abreast of things: I finished two more books over the holidays,
and they are set to come out, one in about six months and the other in a year.
The first-mentioned is another coffee-table book for Oxmoor House, called

<u>Southern Light</u>. It should be a stunningly handsome piece of work, and I think my text not unworthy of the format, if I do say so myself. The second book is an edition of my early notebooks and journals, culled from various ledgers I kept during the time I was starting out, back in the war years and the few following them. Van Ness will be the editor on these, for the Press people here were much impressed with his article in the JDNL, and have immediately engaged him. The provisional title is <u>Striking In</u>, though I hope some unkind reviewer won't take this as an opportunity to say that the real title should <u>Striking Out</u>! I don't mean to give you any ideas, but don't <u>you</u> do it!

Let me know how things are shaping up. Here, we are driving forward as best we can, though I am much worried by my correspondent son in Jordan, subject to all those aerial attacks from both sides. Meanwhile, my second son, Kevin, has just presented me with a third grandchild, another girl, this one named Molly. We are all happy.

Write when you can.

Much love,
Jim

To: Joyce Pair

TLS, Property of Joyce Pair

4620 Lelia's Court
Columbia, S.C. 29206
April 26, 1991

Dear Joyce,

I have just sent in my acceptance of the role of General Session speaker at SAMLA together with a brief prospectus of the subject, the title of which is VISUALS, having to do with the mind's eye, as it pertains to poetry. It is an interesting subject, or so I believe, and working with it will afford considerable reach and, possibly, some insight into what the poetic imagination is like. Anyway, we'll see.

Young Wayne Cox tells me that he has been rejected for the Panel and it is difficult for me to deal with his situation, since he was originally one of my choices. If you could give me a run-down on who the panelists will be, it would help, at this end. And if you could bring Wayne Cox, a fine young poet, serious and dedicated, into the situation it would be good from my standpoint, to say nothing of his.

See if you can do this, and I will be guided accordingly.

Meanwhile, I have the latest <u>Newsletter,</u> and have read it, as always, avidly. What a jerk Robert Peters is! He is a big fat faggot who had me to read at San Diego, when I lived in California, and then pursued me to the University of Utah the following summer where there was a poetry conference at which I spoke. His animus against me is due to the fact that I rejected his blubbery advances, and he never got over it. His kind does what it can to play the literary game and become power brokers because they can't write. Helen Vendler is another such. And there are many.

But not us. Let me hear from you when you have a moment. And <u>do</u> re-think on Wayne Cox, if you can. I'd appreciate it.

Ever,
Jim

To: Charles McNair

RTL, Emory University
4620 Lelia's Court
Columbia, S.C. 29206

May 2, 1991

Dear Red,

Thank you so very much for sending along the Robert Johnson tapes, which are the very essence of the Delta Blues. Although I am not much on bottle-necking, I like the sound, and may pick up on some of it. Not a hard style, but one which requires some attention.

In exchange I enclose a tape I made in 1967 in El Paso, Texas, where I did some numbers at a dive called The Gutter, at which everybody and his brother was sitting on the floor, drunk and enthusiastic. I did some blues, some bluegrass, a good many rags, some hymns; you name it! Anyway, it was an enjoyable evening, and I hope you will get some good listening from it. It was made with just a portable tape recorder, and the bass over-recorded and was out of balance. But you can get some notion of the kind of thing I was doing twenty-four years ago. I no longer play that three-finger style, although it is a good enough style of its kind. But I wanted to go on to "spread the whole board," and get in some classical chords, and not limit the instrument to just three tones.

Well, you can see, from this tape. So listen to what I was doing in that long lost Texas night, when everybody had such a good time. Believe me, I did!

Again, thank you so much for the Robert Johnson tapes. And understand that it is my severe intention to sit down and play some music with you, till it come death or morning.

Thanks so much. And I hope you will like this tape, and pick up from it. Some of the stuff is easy to copy, but for the other things I might have to re-record, or tab off for you. Whichever, I will be glad to do. A guitar player is a gift from heaven, and one who is also a fine writer is a treasure indeed.

Thanks for your generosity. And I hope you like this tape, full of mistakes, where I was dropping half the notes. But on that <u>kind</u> of night it don't matter all that much.

Cordially,

To: Theron Raines

CC, Emory University
4620 Lelia's Court
Columbia, S.C. 29206

May 10, 1991

Dear Theron,

Here are the signed contracts, which I am very happy to participate in, since they constitute a dealing with the whole of my writing life. It is a strange feeling, believe me, to have the whole of one's work between single covers, and a little frightening. I hope to write more poetry, but it will not be given to me to write <u>this</u> much again, ever. But a writer must stand on what he has produced, and I am willing to stand on the poetry in this book. As I say, I must, but I am also willing, and that is not a bad feeling. I am ready to lay it on the line.

One of my editors, Gordon Van Ness, has assembled the manuscript, and is in contact with the new editor at Wesleyan, Terry Cochran. The only possible question about the book has to do with the number of early poems I wish to include, and which they may be. I read through these the other day and, my God!, the young guy was good! So, we ought to let him have his say. Anyway, I am waiting to hear the decision about these early poems, for I thought I should stand aside to some extent and let Gordon and Terry have their own opinions, and then we can go back and forth about a final selection.

Let me know what else I need to do in this situation, or in whatever others come up.

My love to Joan, and to all in your house.

Ever,

To: Theron Raines   **RTL, Emory University**

4620 Lelia's Court
Columbia, S.C. 29206
August 2, 1991

Dear Theron,

I have sent a large package to Marc Jaffe; it went out at noon. Since you tell me that he has only the first hundred pages, I made up a big manuscript that includes the first hundred plus a little over a hundred more, the latter part of which I now send you. Let me know what you think.

Meanwhile, the current Partisan Review is running a section taken from the early part, and the editors tell me that it is already creating a sensation; I take this as a good sign, surely! Another good indication, I think, is that despite the maelstrom of misfortune down here I have found a way to produce ten pages a day—3,000 words—and that is a lot, as you know. At this rate I will be able to lay the whole manuscript on Marc by the end of this month, unless the story elongates more than I plan it to. As I send pages to him I will send them to you, probably at the rate of fifty at a time, so do your best to keep things together, that we may know where we are at all times.

As I say, I sent Marc the big manuscript with everything up to page 203, and a copy of Partisan, which I also enclose here. I sent as well a piece of Japanese calligraphy, the ideogram for snow, which I suggested we might consider for the cover. I'm sorry I don't have another one of these to give you, but that was my only one; maybe you and Marc could get together for lunch and look it over. I do think it would be quite a striking design element.

How about more magazine publications? I have asked Marc about this, and I will be guided by whatever you and he say. Rust Hills wants something—anything—and I have so many solicitations that I think we could publish about anywhere we wanted to, according to my feeling about the various places and editors and your advice. Do let me know, and I'll follow through.

Meanwhile, the Collected Poems is coming well. Everyone seems very enthusiastic, and I just filled out a long intricate questionnaire for publicity purposes. As to this, are you and Gordon Van Ness in contact? He has worked very hard toward shaping up a final manuscript for The Whole Motion, and it strikes me that it might be profitable if you and he were to coordinate with each other as well as the publisher on the final format, the publicity plans, and the rest of the things we will be doing.

I hear from the Oxmoor people that we should have bound copies of Southern Light in October, which is good. If I can introduce and maintain some kind of stability in the home situation, and get Bronnie taken care of, I will go out on some of the tours that Oxmoor usually has me do. Let me know how much of this kind of thing I should be prepared for, and I will try to comply.

One more thing. Bob Kirschten, who wrote a pretty good book on me and has film connections, tells me he has an offer for me to make a one-hour video aimed at ETV for which there will be, he says, a pretty good amount of money. I told him I would run the idea by you, and you can probably expect to hear from him fairly soon.

Well, enough. Let me know what you think about all these matters, and in the meantime I will strike ahead with the novel, hoping for the best from page to page. I do think it is extraordinarily good, though, if I do say so myself. The central character is a real enigma, and what happens to him when he achieves the perfect camouflage of himself in the elements of sleet, fog and snow, and becomes the invisible spirit of these, the "heart of heartlessness," is something I thought you'd like to see: this is what we are going toward through the pages you already have, these new ones, and the others I am writing. And we won't miss, I can tell you right now.

My best to Joan, and to all you know and work with.

Ever,

To: Mary Crittendon[5]

RTL, Emory University
4620 Lelia's Court
Columbia, S.C. 29206

January 3, 1992

Dear Ms. Crittendon:

Heavens! What a job! As many books as I've written, it is a little different, dealing with one's _life_! But for better or worse, here it is, and I hope I have explained with sufficient care my responses to the various questions that you and your compositors have been kind and patient enough to ask. Please let me know whatever else I may need to do, and I will comply.

A couple of things. As to the earliest poems, those in the _Summons_ section, I have made a whole separate little book of them, retyping some and re-grouping the pieces according to subject. I think this is a very effective way to present these poems, and I hope you will approve.

Again, since one of my books, _Puella_, is not represented in the present format, I am taking the liberty of including the six best pieces from that volume, these to be presented just before _The Eagle's Mile_ under the overall title of "Six from _Puella_." I hope this is not too much trouble, but a good many people value these poems, and would like to have them. I fought a savage lawsuit over the right to publish them, and would do it again. As I say, I would like these included. I enclose a copy of the book with the six poems designated, plus a re-written ending for one of them.

I have sent a copy of the _Summons_ poems to Terry Cochran, so you may want to cross-check with him on any details that need consideration.

But we should be able to move now, and wing into the next stage of things. Let me know what you need.

And, again, thank you for your meticulous attention. I cannot keep the word _love_ out of the situation. There _is_ that, you know, going into the (green!) marks on a page.

Cordially,

5. Managing editor of the University Press of New England.

To: David Havird   **TLS, Property of David Havird**

4620 Lelia's Court
Columbia, S.C. 29206
June 9, 1992

Dear David,

Thanks so much for your letter, and all your information, and bird-dogging the various small points in my <u>Collected</u> <u>Poems</u>. My God! I should have had you as my copy-editor! No! As my <u>real</u> editor! Some more commentary a little later on.

I have read Scott Donaldson's <u>MacLeish,</u> a good enough biography, though he surely overrates MacLeish, both as a poet and as an influence and an intellectual Power. I know Scott pretty well, and think a lot of him; I find myself quoted all over the cover of his biography of Winfield Townley Scott, which I recommend to anyone interested in the point-by-point demise of an American poet; as so many are, a weak, good, talented man done in by over-ambition in the literary scene. As to the <u>MacLeish</u>, I found a good deal of interest, for I knew Archie slightly, both here, when we had him to read, and at the Academy in New York. It is fashionable for people like Edmund Wilson and Randall Jarrell to put him down, but what they don't seem to recognize is that MacLeish is one of the few American poets who ever really <u>had</u> a voice. His is a kind of Anglo-Saxon elegiac Americanized voice, very sad and nostalgic and very masculine: the kind of poetry Hemingway might have written if Hemingway had been able to write poetry. Well, you will do your own review; but these are my notions, for whatever they might be worth.

Back to my own work. It is maybe regrettable that there are a few typos in the long book, and perhaps your comments on indentation and capitalization should be observed in the next edition, if there is one. To answer your questions, I included only those poems from <u>Puella</u> that I liked best: those that won the Levinson Prize given by <u>Poetry</u>, previously received by Eliot, Frost, Hart Crane, Dylan Thomas, and other notables. Again, the Doubleday edition left out a complete stanza from the last poem in the book, and there was no time to re-type. Rather than ask for a delay, I simply went with the six I thought most representative, for better or worse. In reference to the "You bet" inclusion in "From Time," I will stand with that; it is exactly what I want. This is exactly what one feels, at long last, in regard to a discipline, music or otherwise. I'm sorry I didn't include "The Surround," but one can't have everything, and since Jim Wright's wife and estate took umbrage at my long review of his <u>Collected Poems</u> in the <u>Southern Review</u>, I decided I wouldn't include it this time, though maybe later.

In your review, I hope there will not be too much emphasis placed on typographical errors, for that is not the real purpose, ever. It seems to me that my intention, over 475 pages, is clear enough, for better or worse, and I hope you will deal with that, as I am confident you will.

Let me know when you are coming to town, and we'll spend some time together. There is no one I'd rather spend time with; now that I am coming up on seventy it is important where the time goes, and with whom it is spent. So do keep me up to date as to your movements and plans, and I will try to be here for you when you are able to make the connection.

My best to Ashley, and to yourself and your work.

Ever,

Jim

To: Jody Gladding   RTL, Emory University
31 July 1992   4620 Lelia's Court
                                         Columbia, S.C. 29206

Dear ms. Gladding:

So . . . it's official, and a very fine choice all around. Resulting from our conversation the other day, I'll move ahead with the introduction, and let you see it when I'm finished. If you would like to tell me—in a letter—some of the ideas you might have about your own work, it may be that I can incorporate some of these in the essay. If you would like me to make any suggestions about the book, I will be happy to do so. As I said on the phone, your new title is much better than tte first one, and in the section where you group a number of poems as "Pieces for Mouth Organ," I would suggest that you change this also, for the poems really have nothing to do with a mouth organ, which is a silly instrument to begin with—though I play one myself—and is so redolent of ethnic folk music that your reader will be deceived into thinking that this has something to do with your poems. I had rather see you call this section something general, like "Variations," or maybe something with a local reference, having to do with your community or geography. But that shall be as you wish, of course.

Again, congratulations. You fully deserve the award, and your book is good; very good.

And we'll go on from here.

Sincerely yours,

To: John T. Casteen[6]   **RTL, Emory University**

                                                    4620 Lelia's Court
                                                    Columbia, S.C. 29206
                                                    August 11, 1992

Dear President Casteen:

Thanks very much for your letter, and the things you say about my taking part in the Virginia Festival of American Film, in which I will be glad to participate, if certain matters can be worked out. I am in communication with Ms. Corry, and have informed her of the conditions under which this might be possible. I hope it can come about, believe me.

Thanks, too, for telling me about Chris. I only see him every few years, so it is always good to have news. As you know, Chris was the first graduate in film from U. Va., and his movie, War Under the Pinestraw, about the cultists who dig up shells and bullets from Civil War battlefields, won the first Prize for Documentary in the Atlanta International Film festival in its initial year. I told Ms. Corry I would bring a print of the film with me, should I come. I think it would interest many on a lot of counts, prominent among which would be to indicate how well University of Virginia is capable of doing in the film world. And the first time out, too!

Have we met? Perhaps when I spoke there, at graduation, the year Chris finished? I remember that Bill Buckley was the other speaker. Or the second time, when Lady Bird was?

Sincerely yours,

6. President of the University of Virginia.

To: David Havird   **TLS, Property of David Havird**

> October 21, 1992
> James Dickey
> 4620 Lelia's Court
> Columbia, South
> Carolina 29206

Dear David:

Thank you indeed for your letter, and for the tendering of the Corrington Award, which I accept with pleasure. If you name a date, I'll be glad to come out there whenever in the Spring it turns out to be, and we will do the things you so invitingly propose, such as visiting Leadbelly's grave and walking down Fannin Street in <u>short</u> pants! I knew Corrington slightly, when he and Miller Williams were editing the <u>Loyola</u> <u>Review</u> in New Orleans. I published some things with them, and then went down and gave a benefit reading for the magazine. It was a good and strange event, the only one I know in which there was a full pitcher of beer on the speaker's podium; again, Corrington's doing. After the reading we all went out to lunch together, and Walker Percy came along. He was then writing <u>The</u> <u>Last</u> <u>Gentleman</u>, and we talked over some of the problems. I never saw him or Corrington again, but, as I say, I remember the occasion with great favor, and I am glad to be able to renew it, in a sense, with being able to accept the Award in Bill's name.

I am very happy that your own work is going well, and that you are writing poetry as good as the piece you sent me—especially the last part is good, when you and Uncle Paul actually get on the water. You are one of the few young poets who tend naturally toward the longer kind of organization, and this is good because it makes for a certain kind of fictional—even novelistic—progression in the poem, and a certain kind of reader will always pick up on this and enjoy following it.

And don't worry about the lapse of time between now and whenever your material on <u>The</u> <u>Whole</u> <u>Motion</u> happens to appear; I'll be delighted to see it whenever it comes.

Please remember me to Ashley. And say hello to Chase Crossingham for me, too. He was great friend of mine when he was here; I call him The Linebacker.

Let me hear from you when you can spare the time, and we'll bring all these things forward.

Ever,
    Jim

To: John Palms[7]

RTL, Emory University
4620 Lelia's Court
Columbia, S.C. 29206

October 23, 1992

Dear Dr. Palms:

Thank you very much for your letter, and for the increase in salary. This is a real vote of confidence, expressed in concrete terms, and I appreciate it. I will continue to do my work here to the best of my abilities, and will also hope to see soemthing of you, personally, whenever you have the time and the inclination.

Please remember me to your wife, with warm regards.

Sincerely yours,

To: Pat Conroy

RTL, Emory University
Early 1993?
4620 Lelia's Court
Columbia, S.C. 29206

Dear Pat,
    I have your letter, and believe me I am deeply involved in every implication—down to the last and least one—of what you say. Without dwelling unduly on my own situation, which is that of a writer nearing seventy, and every day coming up against the possibility that all the things he has played his life on might very well have been wrong, it is gratifying indeed to get your paragraphs.

7. President of the University of South Carolina, who had approved an 11 percent salary increase for Dickey as of October 1, 1992.

Understand me: there is no student of mine of whom I am more proud. And understand this also: the pride is not for the public acclaim, the novels, the movies, and all those things, but for a certain integrity of spirit that you showed from the beginning, and which I was sure would not be lost. There are few people who come into the classroom of a teacher and exhibit the twin characteristics of language-love and go-for-it that are yours by natural endowment. The Word is important to you—that fascination—and so is the power and terror of letting go: to see what happens, no matter what. All this is good, and can produce extraordinary things: as, in order to see, you need only to look at your own works.

This, though. You and I are both creatures of the Word. We want this word, rather than this word's second cousin twice removed. And that exclusiveness will save us, I do believe. Therefore, I want you to continue with your poetry, because if you and I hold that center of the creative wheel, nothing can violate us. If we submit honestly to the discipline of poetry in its mania to say the most possible thing that can be said by means of the human tongue, then everything we do partakes of that, and will draw energy and courage from it.

Now: I can only espress extreme gratitude for your letter and for the things you say. Time is maybe getting fairly short for me, and the Dark Man may not be too far from paying me a visit. But I will say one thing, and make a promise. There will come a time before the Dark Visit in which you and I will sit down in the dead-low and middle of the night and talk as we have never talked before about the things that mean the most to us: the things we love—and those we hate: talk as the earth turns, till it come death or morning.

Ever,

To: Mike Russo   TLS, Emory University

4620 Lelia's Court
Columbia, SC 29206
June 11, 1993

Dear Mike:

Thanks so much for your letter, address, phone number and all. I send along a photograph of Leadbelly's grave, which is about twenty miles out from Shreveport in a little country graveyard. It was a good trip there, and good to see these things. The people at the church gave me some Leadbelly tapes, all tunes I had heard you play.

I also enclose a copy of the new book, which I hope you will like. It is full of typographical errors, but you can follow the story pretty well even so, I think. I just signed the film contract yesterday, so when Hollywood gets around to making the movie, it will be made. I can never tell about the people out there, for they operate in more mysterious ways than the human mind can comprehend. But when Universal gets around to shooting, I will come back into things with some suggestions about the music, though whether they will be acted on is not known to me. But I think the public would respond strongly to the sound of the twelve-string guitar, for it is not familiar to most people, and is very powerful and dramatically effective. I can't promise anything, except that I will put your name forward first, and insist as strongly as the writer can do, against all the Los Angeles bureaucracy. But this is a little way down the road, and I will certainly let you know how things develop, as they do.

I don't have time to write the long letter I would like to, but will just enclose the picture and the novel, and hope to hear from you again soon.

My best to all in your house, and to your instruments and fingers.

Ever,
Jim D.

To: Will McIntyre

CC, Emory University
4620 Lelia's Court
Columbia, S.C. 29206

November 4, 1993

Dear will:

Thanks so much for your letter, and for enclosing the contact prints. The general quality of the photographic work—if not the subject—is so high that it is hard to choose among them. I have gone over all the sheets with my family and my assistant, and have let each of them, as well as myself, pick out preferences. As you can see, there are a good many of these, and I'd like 8 X 10's of all of them; whatever the cost, let me know and I'll pay you by return mail. Then, after all of us have settled on one, I will order a whole lot of prints of it, give them out to friends and autograph hunters, and use it on my next book, due out nest year. I hope all this is clear to you and that you will be able to comply as soon as possible. I would appreciate it a lot, believe me.

I'm glad you're getting some use out of the guitar pick. At first, it is a little hard to get accustomed to picking off the thumb alone, but it has many advantages. If you will get used to letting the side of the thumb itself brush the next-lower string than the one you're playing on, doing things this way guarantees that the pick will always engage the string at the same depth, so that your playing is automatically a lot cleaner, and, when you've done it for a while, a lot faster as well. You can experiment with how much of the pick you want to have engage the string, and if you want the pick shorter all you have to do is take some scissors and cut it off to the length you want. I myself like to use as little pick as possible, but as you say, experiment to find out what is best for you and your style, and the kind of music you want to play.

Well, enough for now. But do keep in touch, for there will be more good times. There always are when good people are involved.

Ever,

To: Dave Smith[8]

CC, Emory University
4620 Lelia's Court
Columbia, S.C. 29206

December 4, 1993

Dear Dave,

Thanks so much for your letter. You ask for a poem, and I offer one of three possibilities, I think. The first is the poem I enclose, which is a fragment from a much longer effort called "Two Poems on the Survival of the Male Body." The printing of this, as you see it, was part of the 70th Celebration last September, and the poem has not come out anywhere else. Princeton has asked for it, but whether or not they have actually contracted to do it is not known to me, for I have no return correspondence with the Princeton people. So it seems to me that if you want to print "The Drift-Spell" as I send it along, you can.

Another possibility is that I might be able to excerpt a section from the two long poems, as I did with "The Drift-Spell," and submit it for your perusal.

Yet another possibility would be my being able to finish a savage poem about my brother's death from colon cancer, in which, in his delirium—and owing to his oxygen-starved brain—he turned from his life-long preoccupation with the Civil War to the terrible career of Ted Bundy. His daughter read to him from the Bundy Chronicles, and I want to envision the death-bed situa-

---

8. Editor of *Southern Review*.

tion in which the dying father, in his delirium, sees his own daughter as the murderer's victim. This may take some working-out, for I never know how far down the road the poem is going to end.

So, if you're in a bind about deadlines, go ahead and print "The Drift-Spell," which I think is pretty good. The other two alternatives will take some time, but maybe when you have published this issue, I will be able to send you these other things, as they have come along.

Let me know what else I may be able to do, and I will try my best to comply. You and I have always been good at double-teaming. A pulling guard is indispensable to my offensive strategy—the veer!

Ever,

To: Pat Conroy

CC, Emory University
4620 Lelia's Court
Columbia, S.C. 29206

December 30, 1993

Dear Pat:

Thank you so much for your last letter, and for the things you say about the new book. I never had any idea that the story would be so universally received, with the film studios clamoring for it, and all <u>that</u>. This is just another one of those things that startles you—by which I mean <u>me</u>—an essentially obscure person whose main public life, such as it is, has been conducted in the back pages of little-known poetry magazines, which pay nothing, or next to it. That is the magma out of which I arose, and which I aspire to go back to, with luck and poverty. But that shall be as fate has it.

There is some news, other than news of movie-making, high finance, and the rest. I just did a new poem for the SuperBowl printed program, which I enjoyed doing, and which deals with the split-second decision-making of the punt returner, who, when he gets the ball, must do <u>something</u>. It is called "Breaking the Field," and I hope you will like it when you see it.

Meanwhile, is it at all possible that you might come here to speak? All sides would be in favor of it, but especially myself, because it would allow us one of those rare meeting-times that give a transfusion to life. Let me know what might be possible, if anything is, and I will be guided accordingly. But come if you can.

Understand, too, that you are frequently if not always in my thoughts as a validation of what I have tried to do as a poet and teacher.

Don't give down. Play it bold. Bold and not cautious, but not foolhardy. That is what makes soldiers, and wins wars.

Ever,

To: William Maxwell

CC, Emory University
4620 Lelia's Court
Columbia, S.C. 29206

March 9, 1994

Dear Mr. Maxwell:

I have just re-read all your fiction as well as the essays and critical pieces I can find, and I want to offer you the foremost vote of confidence that can come out of the blue sky of South Carolina. I have known your work since I was a (belated) undergraduate at Vanderbilt, and it has always sustained and encouraged me, first as a beginning writer and then as one who picked up (some) momentum. I am now seventy-one, and can truthfully tell you that you have been the one writer I could always trust, and that the truth you made available to me was not only the truth of fact (as important as that is) but the truth of the imagination.

And there is more. You are an authentically <u>feeling</u> person, and this is a quality I have tried to get into my own work; whether or not I have always succeeded is a different matter. But I did want to let you know these things, for whatever might be in it for you.

The scene in <u>Time Will Darken It</u> where the guy tells the other people how the men crawled into the carcass of a cow to keep from freezing to death is one of the great scenes in fiction. And if you think that my current novel, <u>To the White Sea</u>, does not bear a debt to this you would be wrong, and the world would be wrong.

Again, I hope you will accept my best wishes for your work and for your life. I will hope also that I'll see you on some future meeting of the Academy, where I shall tell you what I say here, looking you straight in the eye, as such things should be done.

Sincerely,

To: Charlie Byrd

CC, Emory University
4620 Lelia's Court
Columbia, S.C. 29206

June 7, 1994

Dear Charlie

I am so very sorry I missed your visit here, but I was out of town and there was no way I could make it back in time. But I have great hopes that we can get together later on, for I would surely love to jam with you. Although, I must add, whatever jamming I might be able to do at my level would not be much in comparison to yours. As I may have told you, I first came to your playing through my wife Maxine, years ago when I lived in Atlanta and was just getting serious about the guitar. She insisted on calling me away from the writing I was trying to do to come to the television to watch you and Herb Ellis play on the <u>Today</u> <u>Show</u>. Ellis is good, but he has nothing like your originality, and I became a convert on the spot. Then, when we moved to Los Angeles, I heard you play an evening at Shelly's Manhole, and was even more impressed. Years later I acquired your tapes from Guitarists' Workshop and had great instruction from you. The tapes, including the Christmas songs, were difficult for a folk player not used to complicated chord formations, but, as I say, I got great learning, not only about the guitar, but about music in general, of which my knowledge is very sketchy. In addition to being the guitarist that you are, you are a very fine teacher, patient and helpful.

And I <u>do</u> thank you for everything. I am sure we will get together again, somewhere down the road. I have just learned that I can use the university airplane any time I want to go to Washington; so, since I have a great deal of business in Washington, that opens up a lot.

If you will keep in touch we can plan some things. I would like that a lot, believe me. <u>Do</u> write, when you can or when you want to. But that shall be as you wish, of course.

With all best wishes,

To: Paul Carroll

CC, Emory University
4620 Lelia's Court
Columbia, S.C. 29206

July 4, 1994

Dear old Paul,

Thanks so much for your new book, and for the things you say about my work. I like your book a lot, as I have always liked your energy and imagination and your forthrightness in dealing with people. And I also like very much the fact that you are living in the South, and especially that you are in the mountains, which is my own turf and the domain of my father's family. I am very sorry that we didn't get together when I was at ASU, but I plan to come back up that way within the next few months and we will surely get together. I want <u>very</u> much to see your new spread. I blame the missed letter on my own excessive and misplaced desire to be more right than right when it comes to details like addresses. I do live on Lake Katherine, but it is not a place that has a separate post office; you still have to put Columbia, SC after it; the zip is 29206.

Your account of a poetry reading of Elizabeth Bishop and Richard Howard is hilarious. I introduced her when she was here; she didn't raise much of a crowd, and her work did not seem to go over very well. I have never been partial to it, myself, perhaps because of all the Roman candles sent up by Lowell and Randall Jarrell. Anyway, when the reading was over, I went downtown, where my wife was in the hospital; she died that night. I will never be able to think of Elizabeth Bishop without that coming to mind, even though the memory is based on just a coincidence.

I'll get this in the mail to make sure that the lines of communication are open, and we'll start writing back and forth again. I'd like that a lot, believe me.

Meanwhile, my love to you and Maryrose.

Ever,

To: Theron Raines

TL, Emory University
4620 Lelia's Court
Columbia, S.C. 29206

August 19, 1994

Dear Theron:

I am sending along this permission request from Gale Research; please assess and advise.

Meanwhile, the paperback of <u>White</u> <u>Sea</u> is being printed and will appear in the stores in October. Sharon Zimmerman, Foreign Rights Manager with Houghton Mifflin, calls and asks me if I will grant some interviews with our Finnish publisher, which I am happy to do. Please keep me informed as to the various countries and languages that are involved with us. I also need to know how far along we are toward defraying the advance, so that I can look forward to whatever royalties there may be.

Again, let me know the plans for the movie. It seems that David Peeples has been "just about to finish" his current script for at least the last eighteen months. Let us see if he cannot terminate what he is doing, and turn to our effort. Please do look into this. I would appreciate it a lot, I can tell you.

The play, <u>May</u> <u>Day</u> <u>Sermon</u>, is going to town in Edinburgh, and we will probably be bringing it off Broadway in a few months. Broadway should see it.[9]

Ever,

To: John Updike

RTL, Emory University
4620 Lelia's Court
Columbia, S.C. 29206

August 22, 1994

Dear John:

First off, it was good to see you at the Ceremonial, because it is a long time between visits, and I wish there were more of them.

---

9. Directed by John Gallogly, who had credentials as a screenwriter and actor, the play was a dramatic resurrection of Dickey's poem and starred Bridget Hanley as the Baptist preacher.

So I propose something. Matthew Bruccoli may already have written you with the invitation to come down here and speak at the centenary of Scott Fitzgerald on September the twenty-four upcoming, at a lunch or dinner given by the Thomas Cooper Society, which is the most prestigious organization we have here. I would be more than delighted if you could come and stay with us, or we could put you up at one of the VIP guest suites; whichever you'd like. If you feel amenable to this, work ou the details—and payment— with Matt, and if there is a possibility you could follow through on the project, we'll bring everything together. But do let me know, and I'll be guided accordingly.

One thing more: I do want to thank you with all my gratitude for the things you say about <u>The Eagle's Mile</u>. That is above and beyond the call, if you know what I mean. <u>I</u> mean <u>above</u>. Up there on the mile! Again, thanks so much.

Ever,

To: Stanley Burnshaw   **TLS, Emory University**

4620 Lelia's Court
Columbia, S.C. 29206
December 16, 1995

Dear Stanley,

Please forgive me for waiting so long to write, but with the process of recovery from severe jaundice and the amount of teaching and literary work I have had to keep up with, I haven't had time to stay in close touch with those I most esteem and love. I hope to do better now, though, and will be writing more often; especially since I get some time off from the school these days.

Everything is going pretty well with me, except that recovery from jaundice is such a long period that one gets extremely restive. I have always been very active physically, and this sitting still and being told constantly to rest, relax, refrain from worry, gets on my nerves and makes me more neurotic than I am used to being. But this, too, shall pass away, or so my doctors say. Needless to add, I hope to prove them right.

This spring I have a new book coming out composed of journal and notebook entries I wrote during the time I was in my late twenties and early thirties, plus the poems I was writing at the time. The title is <u>Striking In</u>, and I hope that some unfriendly reviewer doesn't rechristen it Striking Out, though

I suppose I must be reconciled to that. Anyway, I'll send you a copy when it comes out.

The White Sea movie is on track; the screenplay is finished and we are now looking at directors and actors. This week I should know more about the project when I talk to my producer. Believe me, I'll let you know.

I'll cut this short and turn it loose into the mail as a kind of test letter to determine where you are currently in residence. If you get it write back as quickly as you can, let me know where you are, and we'll pick up where we left off. That will be good.

Love,

Jim

To: Gwen Walti[10]

RTL, Emory University
4620 Lelia's Court
Columbia, S.C. 29206

December 26, 1995

Dear Gwendl:

Maibelle tells me that in your yearly letter to her you mentioned the fact that some curious literary biographer named Henry Hart has been asking you for information about you and me. As far as I am concerned, you can tell him anything you like, or remember; or tell him nothing; whatever you like. Such people are everywhere these days; I suppose it is because that I am 73, have been fairly sick, and figure they had better get as many books and articles written about me as they can before I croak. However, my recovery has been

10. The married name of Gwen Leege, whom Dickey dated and with whom he fell in love shortly before being shipped to the Pacific on December 31, 1944. Following the war, she introduced him to the Gotham Book Mart in New York City, where he purchased dozens of literary books.

pretty good, so the doctors tell me, though very slow. I am about 80% now; a little short of breath, but gradually coming back. I hope that I'll be around for at least a few years more; I have a fourteen year-old daughter I'd like to take as far through her education as I can manage. Up into college, maybe; that would be good.

Meanwhile, I send a copy of my latest novel, out a couple of years ago. We are making a movie from it and the script and pre-production tribulations are finished, though we haven't cast it yet. If all goes well we should be able to produce it in a year or so. Needless to say, I hope you will like it when it comes out. Meanwhile, tell me what you think of the book.

Tell me, also, your news. Maibelle was not able to fill me in on very much, so that I would much welcome whatever information you might be able to give. I gather that Rudi is not well, and that concerns me. What is the situation? He is a very noble fellow, as I remember, and deserves the best.

Which is certainly you. Send me some recent photographs, and long letters—at least one—like you used to write when I was in Fresno, or overseas. Fresno was a true high point for me: I was young, I had discovered poetry, I was going to a war, and I was in love. That's a combination that can't be beat; of that I'm sure: as they say, "from experience."

Do let me hear from you. It has been a long time since Madison. Those were great days also; maybe the greatest of all.

                                                                                Ever,

To: Dave and Jan Peoples   RTL, Emory University
                                                        4620 Lelia's Court
                                                  Columbia, S.C. 29206

                                                       February 26, 1996
Dear Dave and Jan:

Thank you indeed for your letter, and for the good news about the screenplay. I look forward to seeing what you have done any time you choose to send along your draft, or any part of it. Please be assured that I stand ready to help in any way I can, at whatever time seems best. I, too, am a great believer in successive drafts of things, whether screenplays, poems, novels, essays or any other form of writing. I suppose there is a kind of difference in artists like Mozart who can, say, write out whole movements of symphonies and even scenes from operas in their head, and simply transcribe them to paper, and the other sort, like Beethoven, who began with an idea, a phrase, and then work beyond it through successive attempts until the final form is reached. I myself am pretty much in the latter category. I sometimes get a flash of something, but it is never a <u>whole</u> flash, never a complete work; therefore, I envy people like Mozart and Auden who work fast, knowing that the stuff will come and bring its own form with it out of the blue, so to speak.

As I say, I look forward very much toward the end of March, when I may be of some actual help to you. I will stand at the right distance from the material, as you tell me what the distance is; and we'll go on.

Meanwhile, my health is somewhat better, though jaundice takes a long time to heal up, and I am not completely back to full normality as yet. I can see it off in the future, though; and, better still, can feel it in the present. If you like, I'll tell you how things go.

My best to you, not just on our mutual project but generally. I hope to know you better as time passes. But that shall be as you wish, of course.

Sincerely,

To: Hubert Shuptrine   CC, Emory University
                                            4620 Lelia's Court
                                        Columbia, S.C. 29206

March 29, 1996

Dear Hubert and Phyllis:

Thank you indeed for the letter, and for the good wishes. It is true that I have been a little bit under-average physically for the last year and a half, since jaundice moved in. I was supposed to die, and, I think, <u>did</u> die at least once or maybe twice, when the hospital monitor flat-lined. From that time on, though, I have been convalescing, and now, except for shortness of breath and a comparative lack of appetite, I am more or less okay again. During the down-period I kept on functioning, and only missed a month or so of classes, when the disease was doing its worse. But the recovery is, I believe, good news, though I am not all the way back again yet. But the signs are good. Again, thanks for your concern.

Deborah and I have had to split up because of her dreadful addiction to hard drugs. The story is long and sordid, and I won't bother you with it. At present she is in a rehabilitation center in Georgia, but with such a history as hers it is doubtful that anything can be done. I am very much on her side, but my efforts on her behalf have never resulted in her improvement, and I am extremely doubtful as to whether the intervention of yet another group of professionals will prove beneficial, either. All this is terribly sad, for she has a number of outstandingly positive qualities. If she would bring these more into play, things would be better; better for us all.

Meanwhile, my oldest son is head of the European division of *Newsweek*, specializing in Middle Eastern affairs, my second son is a staff surgeon at Yale Medical, and my fifteen-year-old daughter is going to school at Choate in Connecticut, and dancing with the New Haven Ballet. As for myself, I am much involved with the movie version of my last novel, To The White Sea, and this requires a lot of time as well as the usual Hollywood version of agony. But with good luck we will make a good film, I do believe. I have an outstanding producer and a good budget. Anyway, we'll see what we can do.

I remember both of you with great affection, and would much welcome seeing you at any time, under whatever conditions there may be. I hope your work is going well, Hubert, and that if you have a few sketches that otherwise might be thrown away, you might send them to me. As you know, I am a great admirer of your work, and remember with great favor the time we spent together on Jericho. We did the right book at the right time. The world knew it, and continues to know it.

I signed and sent the book to your friend in North Carolina, so all that is taken care of.

My best to you. Communicate when you can, and when you feel like it. But that shall be as you wish, of course.

Ever,

To: Pat Conroy   **CC, Emory University**

4620 Lelia's Court
Columbia, S.C. 29206
April 8, 1996

Dear Pat:

I finally got the inscribed copy of <u>Beach Music</u> you had left with Bill Starr, and I wanted to write and tell you how pleased I was, and am, that I could have befriended and been in any way beneficial to a writer of your caliber. This is indeed heartening; I feel, as they say on shipboard, that I haven't been sending with a dead key. Anyway, thanks again for the book, which I enjoyed very much; the emergency scene in the boat and its aftermath is particularly good. Again, thanks for your thoughtfulness.

And for your life and example. I only regret that I don't get to see more of you, so that we could sit and talk about the things that interest us. For example, Catherine Fry[11] has shown me the extraordinary jacket design for Jonathan Green's <u>Gullah Images</u>. Since I have been living in South Carolina—and even before that, for I used to range up and down the Georgia coastal islands when I was a teenager—I have had a strong interest in the Gullah culture, but have never known much about the history or the real meaning of it, and for years have intended to inquire further. Their music is wonderful, and the <u>sound</u> of that strange language is enough to involve anyone who is fascinated with old things that are new to him.

My news is pretty good, except for the after-effects of the jaundice I contracted a year and a half ago. I am mending very slowly, but the attack was so catastrophic I lost eighty pounds in two weeks, and my system was so depleted that recovery, especially at my age, takes a lot of patience, as well as hard work. The main trouble is shortness of breath; my stamina was just about completely knocked out, and I have had to bring it back bit by bit, with much frustration and many set-backs and delays. But I will win out, yet. If I can get twenty minutes of real wind—matter-of-fact natural breath—I will have what I want. For this year, at least.

Meanwhile, the various projects are doing well. <u>To The White Sea</u> is going into production at Universal, and another story of mine called <u>The Sentence</u>—

11. Director of the University of South Carolina Press.

a film about a prison—has also been requested. As a rule, I don't much like movie work, but I do it in order to keep some other person from messing up what I think is good enough not to be messed up. Well, we'll see.

A new book of my early journals, and the poems I wrote concurrently with them, will be out in a couple of weeks; I'll send you a copy on the publication date.

I'd like to make this a longer letter, but will quit now to get it in the mail. Keep doing what you're doing, and include a letter to me somewhere in there.

Ever,

To: Lance Morrow

CC, Emory University
4620 Lelia's Court
Columbia, S.C. 29206

April 26, 1996

Dear Lance:

I have your letter, for which I thank you very much. I, too, enjoyed the time we had, and will cheerfully renew it by any means I have available. Will you get down this way any time soon? As you know, I am somewhat limited as to travel, for my doctors tell me I must stay here and carry out their schedule. I feel I should do this, as much to the letter as I am able, for I am heartily sick of this particular species of semi-invalidism. The signs are a little better, though, and I am hopeful. I had a good report from the doctor a couple of days ago, and he tells me that my liver is back to normal, and that the only thing I need to work on is my stamina. Believe me, it is a real trial not to have much of that! I'll let you know how things come along, if you like.

Sure; we can talk out your novel at whatever length you'd like, though I don't know much about the history and politics of the time in which—you tell me—the story is set. I ought to be able to help you, though, on things that concern the novel-form, generally. Except for Alnilam my novels are not very complicated as to plot, but I did manage a lot of characters in Alnilam, and I think I am fairly competent in the aspects of fiction which deal with pace, interpersonal relations, incident, and so on. Let me see whatever you have— or project—and we'll go on from there.

I'll write at greater length later on, but now I'll close to get this in the mail, hoping that you understand how much I enjoyed meeting you, and contemplating the start of what I hope will be a long relationship. It is good to think of such things.

My best to you,

To: Gray Banks

RTL, Emory University
4620 Lelia's Court
Columbia, S.C. 29206

April 29, 1996

Dear Mr. Banks:

Please forgive my belatedness in answering your letter, and acknowledging your kindness in sending me the tape and the various materials you included. I have been rather ill for the past year and a half, though, and that fact has made it impossible for me to handle all the correspondence that has come in. Your letter is unique, however, and I would like, here, to pay attention—more attention—to your passion, and your stand for Southern values. It is true that the Leviathan has won, is winning more and more with every new mill that locates among us. It is also true that we had and still to some extent have a way of life with more to recommend it than any yet instituted in the New World. But one thing is certain. Once industry is in we can't throw it out. Once the city is instituted it will remain and grow, and the land and its traditions will die. Whatever preservation we may hope for will be only in music, in museums and a few books, for the stuff that is in Southern blood and at the heart of our region will in a few generations die out. The rest will be history—and history books. But you and I and a number of others have known what the South at its best was capable of being. The worst we know only too well, but amputations are supposed to cure the patient and not kill him. You and I can watch, and remember. And write. Remember what Faulkner, Agee, Walker Percy and others have done. They have proved what you and I know: that the South accomplished something that no other region or body of people could have done. That, too, is history.

I haven't played the tape you sent, but on looking at Samuel Barber's adaptation of James Agee's pieces I noticed that the one printed as a poem is actually a composite of several poems from his first book, <u>Permit Me Voyage</u>. These lines are often given in this manner, but it is not as Jim would have them, which you can easily verify if you will refer to the book. Why Barber chose to do things in this way is not known to me, but I don't much like the setting of poems to music to begin with; Barber's gruesome rendition of Agee's rhapsody about Knoxville is a good case in point.

Well, I won't go on and on, but will close to get this in the mail, with my gratitude and good wishes. Let me hear from you again, if you are of a mind, because I would like to keep up with such an impassioned and forthright mind. As I say, let me hear. But that shall be as you wish, of course.

Sincerely,

To: Vance Morgan   RTLS, Emory University
                                                 4620 Lelia's Court
                                                Columbia, S.C. 29206

                                                    May 2, 1996
Dear Mr. Morgan:

I sent your signed book, which I hope you will get right away.

Let me tell you in this note how much moved I am by the things you say about <u>Alnilam</u>. It is far and away my best novel, despite anybody else's opinion; it does more and <u>is</u> more than the other two; although, naturally enough, I like them also. For some, <u>Alnilam</u>—incidentally the word is pronounced Al-ni-LAM—was difficult to read, not only because of the split-page format that some of it uses, but in that it has so many characters, and is as long as it is. But good readers will take the time, and—<u>I</u> believe—will not feel they have wasted it. As a study in the psychology of power, and as a treatment of a new kind of human orientation occasioned, say, by blindness, the novel makes its points in a way that I am quite willing to assert is unique and memorable. That you have seen these qualities also is highly gratifying; once more I thank you for your comments.

As to the inscription in the book, remember that <u>Alnilam</u> is about air: the air we breathe and live in, and can fly in. You might say that it is about air as <u>Moby Dick</u> is about water.

The emblem of the snake is not intended to have any profound philosophical importance; only that wrong—or evil—sometimes comes in disguise. The disguises are usually on the outside, but Buster's is on the inside. In other words, the rattlesnake in this case works on springs and buzzers, but he is still a snake.

If you like, let me hear from you again, and tell me what your life is like. And watch for the new movies coming out in the next year or two, for we are filming To The White Sea. The screenplay is finished, and we will move onward from there. Give us what blessing you can muster.

Sincerely,
    J.D.

To: Eric Halpern[12]   CC, Emory University

                                                   4620 Lelia's Court
                                                   Columbia, S.C. 29206
                                                   May 7, 1996

Dear Mr. Halpern:

Thank you very much for sending the copy of David Slavitt's *Odes and Dithyrambs of Bacchylides*. I am quite familiar with Mr. Slavitt's translations from Latin and other classical languages, and think highly of them. I particularly esteem the rather free renderings from Virgil, who is, through Slavitt in, say, the Georgics, is both the familiar poet and one we had not quite known before. Mr. Slavitt has an astonishing knack for making classical poetry readable and, above all, experienceable. It may be that stickler-scholars might back off a little from Mr. Slavitt's extreme use of colloquialism, but he certainly does write a living contemporary language, and makes—or allows—Virgil to speak one. Since your numbered questionnaire seems to concern scholars rather than creative writers or creative translators, I find that I can eliminate many of the subjects and approaches you cite. But I certainly do believe that the author's reasons for thinking this book is needed are completely justified, that his writing style is excellent, that the material is well organized and the length appropriate to the subject matter. Doubtless because of my indifferent Latin and nonexistent Greek I am not really qualified to speak of the accuracy involved in these translations between languages; I speak of the works as living

12. Director of the University of Pennsylvania Press.

poetry. Mr. Slavitt seems to have a free and easy—and very personal—conversance with the ancient world, and this is refreshing indeed; it makes that whole world available to us in ways it has not been before. When Mr. Slavitt refers to ancient gods, we not only understand how and why the people of previous times believed in them, but we are more than half-inclined to believe in them, also. When he tells us that

> "With arrogant shouts, Trojan horsemen
> charged the dark-eyed ships to turn them away
> and send them homeward again so that their god-built
> city would have dancing and feasts
> to celebrate their salvation.
> But they were doomed nonetheless
> to die and to dye the whirling
> Scamander crimson with their blood,
> at the hands of the tower-destroying
> Achilles and Ajax,"

we not only get the very good Bacchylides (and Slavitt) but also the force of Homer coming through them. This is all very good, very readable, very exciting.

As must be apparent, I am much in favor of Slavitt's translation work. He has such an easy, tolerant, <u>believable</u> relationship with the ancient world and its authors that making the changeover from that world to ours is less a leap than an enjoyable stroll. The reader feels a continual sense of gratitude, and keeps asking "Why hasn't this been done before?" Well, it has been done before, or at least tried, but to my knowledge with nowhere near the success that Mr. Slavitt has achieved. I not only recommend the publication of this work; I recommend the hell out of it.

That's my opinion. If there is anything else you require of me, please let me know and I will do my best to comply.

With best wishes,

P.s. I prefer payment in cash, and thus enclose the W-9 tax form, completed as you request.

To: Kregg Spivey   CC, Emory University

4620 Lelia's Court
Columbia, S.C. 29206
May 8, 1996

Dear Mr. Spivey:

I much appreciate your letter, and your sending me the photograph. It was a good occasion and a good class, and I am delighted that you were able to participate. Come back any time, and we'll take up where we left off. That would be good.

Thanks, too, for the things you say about To The White Sea. The movies were after it before it was even completed, when a section of it came out in *Playboy.* Universal put in the best bid and we went with them. The screenplay is now finished, and when we fine-tune it we will cast and shoot. The budget is good; if we don't make a good film it is our own fault. But the signs are quite favorable, and I believe that, baring unforseen circumstances, the film will be made within a year. White Sea is a strong book; strange enough for anybody. I am glad you like the part about Muldrow's freeing the bear, even though he kills the man who saved his life to do it. "One is enough," Muldrow says; I think so, too. Needless to say, I am eager to see what comes up on the screen; my main ambition is just to pay my $6.00 and go in and watch it with the rest of the public, knowing that I no longer have to worry about script changes, actors, producers, studios, or budgets. That will be a great day! The day of Jubilo, sure enough!

As to your designating the work of my students in *New Review,* I myself had rather they'd just appear with the other contributors with no special designation except their names and their poems. Which ones will you be printing, by the way?

I look forward, also, to your essay on Monroe Spears and myself. As you know, I much esteem Monroe, and owe a very great deal to his example.

Keep in close touch, and we'll see what we can put together, together. I am much in favor of your effort, your taste, and your methods. Good things can come of all this. And will, I am sure.

Cordially,

To: Sam Tomlinson   CC, Emory University

4620 Lelia's Court
Columbia, S.C. 29206
May 20, 1996

Dear Sam:

Thank you indeed for your letter and invitation. I'm afraid it won't be possible for me to join you in June in Las Vegas, though I would much like to see some of our old boys again after fifty years. Would it be possible for you to provide me with a roster of the remaining squadron members? I know that Racy Porter died or was killed some years back, but I haven't heard from any of the others since I was recalled in 1951 and ran into Black George Kamajian and a couple of others in the Training Command. Other than that I draw a complete blank and would much appreciate your bringing me up to date as to which of us are still around, ready to take off again.

Don Armstrong and Jim Lalley were beheaded by the Japanese on Panay in the spring of 1945. The poem I wrote about Don is called *The Performance*, and is in my collected poems, The Whole Motion, as well as some others I wrote about the squadron, such as *The Enclosure, The Jewel, The Wedding, Between Two Prisoners,* as well as the much-anthologized *The Firebombing*. I enclose the book so that you can look this up. There may be others you can find; I'm sure there are.

Thanks for sending the page from our squadron History. And if you could possibly get me a copy of the whole History I would be most grateful. I wrote all of it between the time Carroll Smith went home—his RO was the Historian before me—until we went up to Japan on occupation duty. I am writing a novel in which this information would be very helpful, and, since I didn't preserve a copy of the History for myself, I would be very grateful indeed to have another one.

Try as I may, I don't remember you from those days. Were you in the outfit before I came, or afterwards? Some of the Old boys were going home just as I joined the squadron, and it may be that you were one of those whom I never really got to know.

In some ways, horrible though the events were, those were great times. We had a wonderful squadron: fine, intrepid, courageous young guys, all very close to each other. We were by far the ranking night fighter squadron in the war; any-body would tell you that; the rest of them looked up to us, and that is good to remember.

I close with my warmest greetings, hoping to see you soon. Since you live in Hartsville, could you not come by? Let me know, and I will make provision.

Cordially,

To: Jim Applewhite   RTL, Emory University
                                                   4620 Lelia's Court
                                                   Columbia, S.C. 29206

                                                      May 29, 1996

Dear Jim:

Thanks very much for your letter, and for the things you say about my work; I appreciate them greatly, I can tell you.

And it was also good to know that you are in Rome, my favorite city over there. I took my wife and daughter to Italy a couple of years ago when Mondadori published the Italian version of To The White Sea. We stayed a week, and the only crisis—a continual one—was whether, that day, the girls would visit historical sites or window shop (and more!) the stores along the Via Veneto. I didn't get to see very much myself, because I was too busy giving out with interviews and being on television, all the stuff that the publisher gets his money for when he pays your travel and expenses.

But I *did* notice one thing I hadn't recalled from the time when I used to live there. In the Keats-Shelley Museum, there at the foot of the Spanish Steps in the house where Keats died, there is a portrait of Byron by Géricault that I had never remembered seeing. As I looked at it I said "That is *my* Byron! All the other portraits are not really him." So . . . if you have a chance to be around the foot of the Spanish Steps, take a minute to climb the stairs going the other way—the couple of flights up to the Museum—and check out the Géricault portrait. Ask the curator if they have any reproductions of the picture, or if they know where I might get one. I didn't have time to do this when I was in Rome, but *you* are in Rome now, and might be able to do it. Let me know if you can, and I'll appreciate it either way.

Again, thanks for your remarks on my poetry. I am afraid I am not far from the end now, and it is good to know that someone of your stature believes that I have not wasted my life, or, as they say on shipboard, that I haven't been sending with a dead key.

Ever,

To: Michael Jasper

CC, Emory University
4620 Lelia's Court
Columbia, S.C. 29206

May 29, 1996

Dear Mike:

It is good to have news of you and to know that the sorrows of Priapus are still going on, with an occasional (furtive) joy. As for me, I am about the same, very short of breath, and in out and out of the hospital to get my gullet opened up so that I can eat and drink things. All this is a wretched situation, I can tell you, but I take some positive content in that I've not let anything slip that I would otherwise have done, although it's harder to do things this way. The film version of *To the White Sea* is going forward. The screenplay is finished, and as soon as various things are signed we will go ahead and make the movie. I haven't yet been told who will play in it or direct, but I imagine my producer will let me know when he wishes.

As to the Suarez book, I agree with you entirely. Suarez seems quite well-intentioned, but I need no such defense as he offers; it is foolish to bring up such a thing. I have never been so much written-about or sought after. This is the best time of all, and I don't need people like Suarez to seem to find me neglected, or any such, for I certainly am not. What you say I much appreciate. It seems to me that readers like yourself are my audience, and bring to the work just as much as I do. Those are the readers I wish to reach, and, really, no others.

Your account of the customs there, the curfews and so on, are most entertaining. It is natural to seek pleasure, and this is as much true of Turkish girls as it is of any others. I do worry, however, that the laws over there may be set against you, and I don't like to think of you being hauled up in some Turkish court for whatever innocent—or not innocent—activities you may have been engaged upon. My son, who is head of *Newsweek*'s European division and conversant with Near- and Middle-Eastern affairs, tells me that the laws and customs down there are strange and very hostile to Anglos. Though my father was a lawyer, I have what amounts to an almost instinctual hatred and dread of due process, and what passes for such in a foreign country, especially an Arabic or Semitic one, is something that I don't even want to contemplate. So . . . watch out what you're doing, and don't get those folks down on you; they're likely to bury you in their wretched sand. Keep up with your writing, and, if you have anything you'd like me to see, send it along.

Ward is well, and the people who know you here all send their best, as do I. Write when you can.

Ever,

To: Saul Bellow   **TLS, Emory University**

4620 Lelia's Court
Columbia, S.C. 29206
June 13, 1996

Dear Saul Bellow:

Thank you indeed for your letter, and for the things you say about <u>Deliverance</u>. It was written so long ago that, on re-reading it, I have not always been sure what I intended in certain places, but your remarks convince me that, in the case of the character Lewis, I actually got what I was driving at. In the movie version I was saddled with an actor who did not grasp the part as I conceived it. If Burt Reynolds is not dumber than an ox, he is not any smarter than one, either, and insisted on playing Lewis as an over-bearing bully, when the whole point is that the others follow him because of his mystiques, which they think may supply some of the answers they seek, only half-knowing that they do. Anyway, I thought we made at least a fairish try with the movie, and *did* follow the essential story, which doesn't happen in the case of most novels made into films.

By the way, a couple of years ago I saw on television your story, <u>Seize The Day</u>, which is a great favorite of mine; I have, ever since I first read it, wanted to find Tamkin and get counsel from him! I thought the film was a very credible try, and as evidence I adduce the fact that Robin Williams was pretty good in it, or so I thought. Ordinarily, I don't much like him, but I thought the scene with the adamant father was very moving, and as true to *my* version of your intent as could be got. By the way, did I not catch a glimpse of you in one of the hotel scenes? I could've sworn it.

I won't go on and on, but just acknowledge once more how grateful I am for your generous letter. And I am also very happy to know that you are moving among the fields and mountains of New England, as you describe them in your essay in It All Adds Up. If you like soft mountains you must come down here and see some of mine, at the tag end of Appalachia. I was born there, and I know a lot of good places. Once I was walking a trail and I came on a young man sitting on a rock writing, and said to myself, "He must be a poet! At last things are right!" I made bold to ask him what he was doing, certain, really, that he was working on his taxes or composing a protest letter to a newspaper, but he said, "I'm writing poetry," and I went on. Right is right.

Thanks again, and communicate when you like, or if you want to.

Cordially,

Jim D.

To: Henry Hart

RTL, Emory University
4620 Lelia's Court
Columbia, S.C. 29206

June 24, 1996

Dear Henry:

I enclose some forms and requests that went through the Atlanta school-records mill, for you to use as you see fit. Let me know whatever else you may need, and I will be happy to provide it, if I can.

It is nice to know that my track-mates at Vanderbilt remember me so warmly; I certainly recall the time with affection, though I was a little old for a sprinter and hurdler, being in my mid-twenties because of the war. That was a good bunch of kids, and we had a fairly good team. Did you talk to John North or Charlie Hoover, by the way? They were teammates I liked. Also Tony Corcoran and Lee Nally, and a sprinter named Fuqua (I think it was Bill), and a high jumper named Ford, that we called Flicky. As I say, quite a team. My best was at the Cotton Carnival at Memphis, where I won, though not in the best time. Well, enough of <u>that</u>!

Jane Pepperdene I see occasionally around Atlanta. She retired from Agnes Scott and now teaches in an exclusive prep school.

Sure, come on by here in August, and stay with me here, if you like. I live by myself, and have lots of room.

Let me hear, when you can, and when you like.

My best, from the Escarpment,

Bolgani[13]

To: Jay Semel[14]

CC, Emory University
4620 Lelia's Court
Columbia, S.C. 29206

June 25, 1996

Dear Mr. Semel:

I much appreciate your letter with the information of what you're doing; what has become of you. Thank you also for the things you say about my work; it is

13. In Edgar Rice Burroughs's *Tarzan the Untamed,* bolgani are the gorillas that, along with the great apes, contend with Tarzan.
14. Director of the Center for Advanced Studies at the University of Iowa and an English graduate student at the University of South Carolina in the late sixties.

good to know that, as they say on shipboard, I haven't been sending with a dead key. I too think of "The Sheep Child" with affection. It was the only poem I wrote during the frozen-in winter at the University of Wisconsin in Madison. Since I didn't have any carbon paper in my little apartment I used the carbon from the grade-sheets so that I would have a copy of my own after I sent it to be published. The poem seems to have an astonishing resonance for some people—in keeping, you should have seen the faces of the audiences when I read it in New Zealand! Australia too!—resonance that I can only partly account for. Despite the Down-Under reaction I intended no blasphemy, but only to indicate the need for contact that runs through all of sentient nature, and will have its way, even when it produces monsters that have no place.

It is good to have news of Ken Kipnis, whom I remember with great fondness. He taught me to fingerpick, and what repertoire I still have is due largely to him. Have you ever heard him play? He is truly gifted; a real natural. In spite of all the years between I still cannot play like he does; or did, at least back in 1963 when I first met him. Incidentally, do you have an address for Ken? I would like to write and tell him some of these things, for he gave me a very pleasant part of my life, as well as a good deal of imagery for poetry and fiction. If you have a location for him please send it along. I would be more than grateful if you would.

Keep in touch. As one of Ken's songs has it, Let the Circle Be Unbroken.

Cordially,

To: Bill Carroll   RTL, Emory University
                                                                  4620 Lelia's Court
                                                            Columbia, S.C. 29206

                                                                       July 2, 1996
Dear Bill:

Well! Believe me, I never in a thousand years would have expected the Subic Slasher to show up here! I do thank you so very much. I have a modest knife collection, but certainly nothing like this! It is a beautiful piece of work, and I am happy to know that there is at least one knife maker in Olongapo who is a real professional. If there is any way you can write to him—and to his son, who made me a sheath from part of a forest—and tell him how grateful I am to hold his work in my hand—though I haven't as yet slashed with it: that comes later, when the critics speak—I would also be grateful. Again, thanks a lot for your accurate kindness. Sharp, too!

In response I enclose my latest, a book of early reflections, comments, and poems I did about fifty years ago, when I was in school and just out of it. Some of the material still seems good, and I hope that you will be able to find out, on your own, which parts those are. Anyway, read the book and tell me what you think.

As to blowguns. There is a quite good outfit in Provo, Utah, called the House of Weapons, that makes guns and darts. They are surprisingly cheap; under ten dollars, the last I heard. Their gun is very stylish, and you can cut the darts— of spring steel—to the lengths you want. The House also furnishes beads for the near end of the darts; all you have to do is cut the darts to length, sharpen the needles, and heat the other end of the darts so that the beads will fuse with them. The outfit furnishes as many darts and beads as you want; it is really a very good deal. I don't have the address, but you could look it up; the people there are very accommodating. As to hunting, it is better that there be two of you so that the snake will concentrate on one and the other can shoot. Try to hit him in the head with the first shot; a needle through the body causes the snake to writhe and twist about so much that it makes a head shot difficult. But a blowgun up to a certain range is as accurate as a rifle. There is no torque, which means that the gun will shoot exactly where you are aiming. By the way, when my article first came out, in *Esquire,* it was called "Blowjob on a Rattlesnake," which title I saw fit to change for book publication, because of, as they say, reasons of my own!

A thought. If you can get free, why not come down here and stay for a day or two? I live by myself, I have a house on a lake, and plenty of room. For you, believe me, the latch-string is always on the outside.

Again, thanks so much for the knife. So damn thoughtful! And from Subic Bay, too! We out-staged from there for the invasion of Okinawa in the spring of 1945. I remember that the Base even had an orchestra! Well!

Ever,

To: Richard Roth   CC, Emory University

                                                    4620 Lelia's Court
                                                    Columbia, S.C. 29206
                                                    31 July, 1996

Dear Richard:

As I write this it is quite likely that you are having lunch with my son, and I like to think of that. If you agree, I believe he can be of very great help to us in a good many ways. He is experienced in film, being the first graduate in that subject ever allowed by the University of Virginia, and did his graduate work at Boston University, where he wrote and directed a documentary about Civil War relic-hunters called War Under The Pinestraw. It won first prize in the documentary field, this given by the Atlanta International Film Festival, which at that time was quite prominent. He was also full-time on the making of Deliverance, where he served as John Boorman's assistant. He is now writing a book called The Summer of Deliverance, which should be good. I tell you these things on the possibility that he might not have gone into them, or at least not sufficiently, and I wanted you to be certain of his qualifications, and that he is an awfully good man to have with us. I, of course, don't know what you might wish him to *do,* but he is capable of a lot of positive input. As I say, I have great faith in the guy! I've known him a long time! Knew his parents, too—strange people; no others like them.

A few more remarks about the Peoples' script. I would like to have the later segment about Muldrow's "R & R" at the waterfall, where he fishes, rests, and gets himself together for the final push over the strait and on up into the mountains of Hokkaido. I think the scene should be in, for it fills out yet another side of Muldrow's personality: it would be good, after the savagery and callousness that he has shown, to see him here in the most idyllic circumstances, leaping down the rocks in the middle of a creek, running races with leaves, and doing other things that are truly child-like: no faking; really *enjoying.* Also, the night fishing scene there could also be effective, and have its own kind of suspense in a very strange atmospheric way: all moonlight, all silver. The waterfall itself could be a really nice visual touch: the purity of it, the inevitability.

I would also like to see the train sequence handled a *little* differently, beginning with his listening for the train on the tracks in the manner of a hunter who is *stalking* the train, this culminating in his falling on the train from above. Otherwise, the Peoples have handled this scene in quite a wonderful way. If it is filmed as they suggest it will be unforgettable.

Since there is very little actual dialogue in the film, it is doubly important for us to characterize Muldrow, at times through his very idiosyncrasies, by this means. The two main areas are the talk with the other crewmen in the Quonset hut before the mission, and the conversation with the American Zen monk in the monastery. In that section there should be the monk's reference to "Keeping on the good side of the army," which is the index to his betraying Muldrow. In other words, the audience should have the after-thought of "So *that's* what he meant!"

I would like to cut out entirely Muldrow's talking to himself, except when Muldrow kills the man over the remaining sacrificial bear and says, "One is enough."

Examine very carefully the use of the Voice Over. I don't as a rule like this device at all. I can see some advantage of using it, such as at the very beginning and end, but during most of the rest of the script I feel there is too much reliance on it. Too many times the same point is made, and we seem to be spelling things out more than we should. Our use of the V. O. should be very sparing, and when it is used it should *count*, and count strongly, and not have its effects blurred by repetition. We want to keep the V. O. from interfering with the story, the flow of action.

The most important thing in this letter, and the most important I will make in regard to the script, is the need for the beheading scene at the water wheel. This is absolutely crucial. Without it we have hardly more than the adventure story of a downed flier, raised in cold latitudes, trying to make his way to the mountains of northern Japan, where he feels that he will not only be able to survive but can dominate. Without the water wheel scene, as I say, we have a good adventure story, but it lacks the dimension we most want, which is the deadly ambiguousness of Muldrow's *character*. It is this scene that will bring the audience up short, and cause its members to take sides. The realization will begin to dawn on them that the American military has turned loose on the Japanese civilian population the equivalent of Ted Bundy—or worse. The beheading of the woman is so gratuitous, so unnecessary, so chillingly callous that the audience will be blindsided, and on this incident the main dramatic unfolding will thus depend, and the riveted and continuing attention of the audience: what is this man going to do next? What is he capable of? What is he *not* capable of? On this scene depend other important details, such as the episode with the children at the food-cache. Also, coupled with the material about the Kansas girl, Muldrow's character will be seen more clearly as that of a sociopath. But this will not register *enough* with only the references to the Kansas girl. We must *see* Muldrow do something, and it must be unexpected, gratuitous and horrible. Then we will be set to deliver the full impact of the story, with the audience confused, involved, and hanging on Muldrow's next situation, his next move, his next violence, playfulness, or even tenderness. *This* is our means of engaging the watchers of these things, and will more than make up for the lack of interaction between characters that most movies—indeed most stories—depend on.

These are the main points, except to mention briefly that the Colorado sequence really does not need to include a carnival scene. That is really a little *too* mechanical a contrast to the Brooks Range. Freeways and neon and traffic would be much more characteristic, and would horrify Muldrow and his father even more than the carnival, for they are the *ordinary* civilized world, where they would have to live if they moved to the States: not in a carnival but in and around malls, with continual noise, machinery, smells, and perpetual meaningless agitation.

Say! I would sure like to have Kevin Spacey play the Zen monk! I can see him sitting in a hood in the snow, telling Muldrow that God is in every flake. And Muldrow replies ". . . . ."

Ever,

To: Kenneth Kipnis   CC, Emory University
                                                                        4620 Lelia's Court
                                                                    Columbia, S.C. 29206

                                                                        August 13, 1996
Dear Ken:

I have your address from your friend Jay at Cedar Rapids, Iowa, and wanted to write and tell you how much I have enjoyed the guitar ever since I knew you at Reed, so long ago. Much has happened during that time, but I have never ceased to play, and the basis of everything I do is pretty much based on what you taught me at that time. You were a good teacher indeed, very explicit and patient, and I have no doubt that these are also the qualities of your teaching philosophy. It was my undergraduate major at Vanderbilt, and I would be most interested to know what aspects of it you deal with in your classes.

Meanwhile, after I finished my term at Reed I taught for a year in residence at Cal State at Northridge, then at the University of Wisconsin at Madison, from which I went to Washington as Consultant in Poetry to the Library of Congress, now called Laureate, from whence I came down here to South Carolina in 1968. My wife, Maxine, who was very fond of you, died in 1976. I remarried and had a daughter, and she and the boys are doing well. Chris is head of the European division of *Newsweek,* and Kevin is a staff doctor at Yale Medical in New Haven. Bronwen goes to Choate, and dances with the New Haven Ballet.

I don't mean to bore you with all this information, but simply to let you know how perpetually grateful I am to you for giving me what has been a constant pleasure in my life. I love music, and I love guitar music most of all. You are at the center of it, and will always be. As I think I once told you, you have gotten into my hands.

If you like, write and tell me what your life is like. But that shall be as you wish, of course.

Cordially,

To: Henry Hart   CC, Emory University

                                                        4620 Lelia's Court
                                                        Columbia, S.C. 29206
                                                        August 26, 1996

Dear Henry:

Yes, I too, would like to extend your visit so that interesting—and, I hope, important—matters could continue to be in the local air rather than the tiresome duty-language that fills it up these days. Come back, soon. *Do.*

In answer to your questions:

1. The novel begins on March 8 on Tinian Island because that is the date before the great fire-bomb raid on Tokyo March 9. It has come to be known as "The night Tokyo burned," and there is a book of that title. Tinian was where a large part of the 20th Air Force was based, including the planes that participated in that raid and those that dropped the atomic bombs.

2. I don't know when I actually did start writing the novel, but it was a long time after I finished <u>Alnilam</u>, and has nothing to do with it. It will be the burden of <u>Crux</u> to carry on from <u>Alnilam</u>.

3. The high school football coach here is named Eddie Muldrow. Somehow, I don't think our man is named Eddie.

4. Sure, you can look at my correspondence with my parents during the war. Gordon Van Ness is the man to contact. Also, see Matt Bruccoli, who has copies of <u>everything</u>, believe me. I have also unearthed some of the letters I wrote to my mother when I was playing football at Clemson; you may want to see these, too. Anyway, I'll hold them for you.

Meanwhile, things go well here, though sometimes confusedly. Clint Eastwood looks like the best bet to direct <u>White Sea</u>. What do you think?

Write again when you can, or call. Or both. Yes; both.

Ever,

To: George Plimpton   RTL, Emory University
                                                       4620 Lelia's Court
                                                       Columbia, S.C. 29206

                                                       September 5, 1996
Dear George:

Just touching base. I have to do it from a single position, not walking around as I usually write. I am (temporarily, I hope) on a life-support system, for apparently my aging apparatus, for some years posing as a body, needs more oxygen than the Universe will give it on its own. As I say, though, there are better prospects, and I hope to be free and walking around before too much longer. All this just by way of catching you up.

Meanwhile, how are *you*? I keep getting glances at you in various movies on TV, some of them where I would *never* expect to see you, though the sight is always welcome. Let me know beforehand about some of this, and I'll try not to be so surprised next time, though that is fun, too. Speaking of movies, we are at work making a film version of <u>To The White Sea</u>, now at the stage where we must choose a director. Do you think Ridley Scott would be good? Or Clint Eastwood? The people at Universal want him, and I have no objection. My input at this stage is, as you may imagine, rather slight, and I expect will not really be much of a factor. Still, I have been asked by my producer to render a judgment, so I am doing my best in a field of which I know but little. If you have any suggestions about a director—or main actor, either, for that matter—let me know. You have been in a lot more movies that I have!

Write when you can. And, before I forget, if you have a couple of copies of Poets At Work lying around, or can tell me where I might get them, I would appreciate having them. And how about the *rest* of the Series? It is a godsend for teachers, to say nothing of the students and what they get from the opinions of all those writers. What is the status of the Series, anyway? I would like to give a full set to my oldest boy, who is Chief of Newsweek's European Division, and wants to be a . . . a . . . well, a *serious* writer. I'd like to read what he might be able to write, with your help, and all those others.

My best, as always.

Ever,

To: Elizabeth Spencer   TLS, Emory University

4620 Lelia's Court
Columbia, S.C. 29206
October 7, 1996

Dear Elizabeth:

It is good indeed to hear from you, and to know that you are connected with the people down in Shreveport. They give something called the Corrington Award, are very hospitable, and show you around Shreveport, where they *insist* on you eating all the crawfish that have been dredged out of the bayous the previous week—I think that I myself had at least two weeks' worth, which called for their dredging at night, but that was all right with them, because I went out in a pirogue and played Cajun music with them, with which they seemed to be familiar—though not with my bluegrass variations! Only a little of this is true, except the part that might induce you to go down there and enjoy that place and those people; I guarantee you will, should you go.

Sure, I remember the old days on the Awards Committee, and Ginsberg trying to get Academy money for his queer cohorts and other crazies, and what we did to prevent it. I also recall Irving Howe's obtuse opposition to Shelby Foote's Civil War trilogy, which I guarantee he had not read in full. I have, not once but twice, mainly because my brother, Tom, was the leading authority on Civil War projectiles, and I have gone over those battlefields with him and a metal-detector many times. Shelby is dead right on the terrain, as to the ones I have researched, and to have Howe dismiss that whole monumental work with a noncommittal "too many battles" I took as a personal affront, or at least partially did. That is too bad, because I liked Irving and otherwise thought he was a good chairman for our committee. Didn't you? Except, of course, for the fact that he didn't kick Ginsberg off, and one or two other oversights which I remembered then but have forgotten now.

Well, enough of committee work. I think we did some good, but it has long been time to turn back to our own fields, and this time I don't mean battle-fields.

Know that I think of you often, and wish life had given me the chance to know you better. But what I do know is good indeed, and I hope you will continue writing, and writing to *me*. Though I am still struggling with the aftermath of jaundice and have some lung problems, I will be around for a while, yet. I hope to write more, for I have lots of plans. Right now I am making a movie of my last novel, To The White Sea; Universal is doing it. The screenplay is completed, and we are settling on a director and cast. I'll let you know what happens when the West Coast people tell me; sometimes they do, and sometimes they don't. But it will be a big production, no matter what. We have a good budget, and I hope we can get the most out of it. As I say, more later.

Keep writing to me, because, since I am on a life-support system, I can't move around as much as I'd like to, and mail means a ot. In my case, the sedentary life of a writer has become *really* sedentary, and I am driven back almost exclusively on the mind and imagination. And on friends, of whom I count you among the most valuable as well as most talented. You bet.

                                                    Ever,
                                                    Jim

To: Alan Stephens   RTL, Emory University
                                              4620 Lelia's Court
                                           Columbia, S.C. 29206

                                              October 23, 1996
Dear Alan:
    It has been a while since I have communicated, but I thought I would write once more and tell you how much your work means to me, and to my stu-

dents. What I said on the back of your collected poems I meant entirely, and the more I read you the more I mean it; I wish you would write as many poems as Southey.

As for myself, I have been pretty much knocked out of action by a ferocious attack of jaundice which hit me two years ago, and since then I have been on a life-support system (oxygen) which limits my mobility and energy a good bit. I don't know exactly how far I am from the shadow-line, but, not taking any chances, I wanted to write to those among the poets whose work has meant the most to me, and among those you are very high; very high indeed.

It strikes me that, since very little is heard of you, you may sometimes become discouraged, but if this is true, I hope that what I say will alleviate the condition. There is not a single poem of yours which is not distinctive; each of them has a combination of truthfulness and imagination that I have seldom seen in any poetry, in any language. I won't go on and on. But just refer you to what I have already said.

Please keep in touch as much as you might desire, and I will respond as I can. But above all, keep writing poetry. You not only have a great supporter in me, but my students are also very enthusiastic, and when it comes to my commissioning sonnet sequences from them, I have only to refer them to your Hendry poems, and to George Meredith's *Modern Love* (sixteen lines and all!).

My very best. Keep doing what you are doing; what you *must* do, as our best man.

Ever,

To: Phoebe Pettingell Hyman

RTL, Emory University
4620 Lelia's Court
Columbia, S.C. 29206

November 13, 1996

Dear Ms Hyman:

I hope this will not surprise you to the point of shock, even minor, but I was reading over some of Stanley's work and I almost automatically thought of you, and the very short time I spent with Stanley, Ben Belitt, Malamud, Howard Nemerov, and the others who were there when I came through Bennington. In all my travels I don't believe I was ever more satisfied and gratified than I was by that occasion, and I sat here, convalescing from jaundice, remembering. I recall—also from your Introduction to one of his books—that you were a student of his, and that you married after Shirley died, as I did a student of mine after my own first wife died. I *believe* I have a description of you in my mind, though I may be wrong. Anyway, I wish you to know certain things, some about Stanley and one or two about yourself. I like to believe that Stanley would be pleased that when I spoke at the Presidential Inauguration of Jimmy Carter I used Van Gennep's *rite de passage* concerning the journey of the mythical hero, which I had got in college from an article on myth and ritual that Stanley did for the <u>Kenyon</u> <u>Review</u>, and which I read at Vanderbilt and never forgot. I intended this, as I tell you belatedly now, at least partly as a tribute to Stanley for the tremendous influence he was—and is—on my life and work. The fact, also, that he liked the blues, that we talked a lot about them when I was there, was also good; I wish I had had my guitar, and we could have swapped out on some stuff; I like to think it might have been so.

Some years ago I published a book of poems called <u>Puella</u> about female adolescence—"male-imagined" as I had it—over which I had had to fight a hard and debilitating legal battle. The book did not get much attention, though since it has attracted a good deal, and I read only a few of the reviews. Among those, however, was yours, and it was onto—and *into*—the thing I was trying to do more than any of the other commentators were. Again, belatedly, I wish to thank you for this: for your insight and the other human qualities you brought to bear on my words. I won't go on and on, but just make sure you know that the book was an important one to me, for it marked a sharp change in my style; sharp, indeed, almost enough to have been written by someone other than myself. Whether the turn I made then was right or wrong is not up to me to judge, but whatever it was happened in that book, and your comments were most valuable, especially now since so many of the younger poets have picked up on what I did then, and keep writing to me about it. So to speak, in the words of the blind street-singer, the Reverend Gary Davis—one of the best of the bluesmen: Stanley liked him—"Lord, I feel just like goin' on." I did then, and I do now, and will write more in that vein. But to tell you these things is more important.

Let me hear from you if you like. Much can be done.

Cordially,

To: Alan Stephens

RTL, Emory University
4620 Lelia's Court
Columbia, S.C. 29206

November 15, 1996

Dear Alan Stephens:

Thanks indeed for your note. This is a correspondence I won't press, but would like to have, if that's all right with you. The poetry you have written is a constant reminder to me of what disciplined art can do, and that is plenty. I was just teaching the sonnet in class last week, and I used some of your Hendry material. I had the class write a sequence, much shorter than yours, but the idea of linked poems fascinated some of them, and they produced quite good work based on yours. This was in some part due to the fact that I had the means to *prove* that a long sequence of sonnets could be written about running on a beach (where *is* Hendry's, anyway? I would like to know this, truly; I feel I have spent so much time there. It may even get me into better shape!)

You talk about my life in a very positive way, for which I certainly thank you. Though lively, it was not all that noble; I have my demons, and a lot of them. But if I can shake off the aftermath of this jaundice I will stir them up again, and we'll see what gives out.

I know about you only what you tell me, but your writing is so good that what it comes from is more or less eclipsed, except as human association; friendship, say. You speak of the prose you are writing, but you must *not* give up poetry. Feeling as I do, that would be more tragic for me than it would for you. Mind what I say.

Your way of going shows me quite a lot. I was pretty hard on Yvor Winters in print, and would be so again. But there are some virtues which he espoused that are real virtues, though not the only ones. He must have been very exacting as a teacher, but he has a way of fixing on small details to the exclusion of everything else that bothers me. Yet I continue to read him (Winters himself is the weakest poet of all his students) and the people associated with him, and there are certainly fine things to be found.

This is maybe not the time to go into all that, but I had a moment at the end of the day, and thought I would get this letter in the mail, hoping to get one back. If I am disturbing you, let me know, and I'll desist. You have the thing I wish to tell you, though not in much detail, and I will be content with that. But I hope I will hear from you again. Old age is lonely, but the consolation is that there is a lot to talk about when one reaches it; could you still field-strip a .50-calibre? All I remember, and could find them in my sleep, are the two little springs that are almost the same size but won't fit in each other's holes.

Forgive all this run-on; it is well-meant, I can tell you. Good things have happened to you and your talent, and so to me. That is enough. But we could go on a little, if you like. Let me know one way or the other, and we'll do whatever it is.

Cordially,

To: Maryrose Carroll   RTL, Emory University
                                                         4620 Lelia's Court
                                                      Columbia, S.C. 29206

                                                        November 15, 1996
Dear Maryrose:
     Thank you very much for sending me the program of Paul's funeral service. If I had not been laid low myself I would have been right there, but in my lungs enough air could not be contained for a journey, and sometimes I think that there is not enough in the world for it, either. But I did want to tell you how gratifying it is to me that Paul spent his last years in my territory, the mountains of the South, where my father's people come from and my true roots are, and to imagine what surrounds Paul now that he is lying where he is. That is the true World, as it was made by something other than men. The trees and the creeks and the round rocks of them are as real as anything God could have given reality to, and the mountain *space* is real, and Paul is there with the things I am sure he had come to love.
     As he may have told you, Paul and I first met in New York when we read at the Poetry Center of the YMHA in 1959. It was my first New York audience, and when I looked out and saw Norman Mailer in the first row and my venerable (new) editor at Scribner's, John Hall Wheelock, I felt that I was in the right place, and when I talked to Paul, a few minutes before the reading, I knew I was.
     Over the years we met at various places, and I used to stay with him at his highrise on Lake Shore Drive in Chicago. One of these times was in connec-

tion with a reading, and Paul had a party. I stayed over the next day and it snowed, and I sat in a chair with my feet next to the window, drinking a martini and the snow falling a few inches from my feet, and I do sincerely believe that was the happiest I ever was in my life. The happiest.

I won't go on and on, but will just say once more how much Paul meant to me. He was as true a friend as I have ever had, and that matters. I hope you will continue to stay in touch, so that we may be with Paul on both sides of the shadow-line. One can do such things, as you know.

I can see Paul now, and feel the steadiness of his warmth and his imagination: something that was always there, and still is.

Ever,

To: Susan Brind Morrow

CC, Emory University
4620 Lelia's Court
Columbia, S.C. 29206

November 19, 1996

Dear Susan:

I must say I have never read anything quite like it: animal signs into writing, scratch into script; well, that is something. No; it is *something*! The reminiscences are extraordinary; sometimes I think that Freya Stark is coming at me from one direction and Robert Graves from another, and that when they meet a new third thing will be born. But that doesn't happen; what happens is that I concentrate on you instead of them, and you are better than either—or both together. I must go over the whole thing again because it is so original I could not possibly have thought of it, or anything like it, if I hadn't seen it. For a book dealing with all that heavy-aired country the tone is unexpectedly light: I don't mean funny but buoyant. I have been editing a new edition of the best of Stephen Crane, and your work in some regards is like his in that it makes use of the instantaneous penetration, the laser *glance*. I won't go on and on, but just tell you all over again how much I appreciate your sending your book along. When will the actual publication be? I would like to know, for I plan to be the first in line at the book store. That will be a good day.

I loved having you and Lance here; surely it was the best human time I have spent in a *long* time. I hope we can visit some more under any circumstances possible. Let me know where you are and how you move, and we will bring things together, somewhere. That, too, will be a good day.

Lance, I must report that Chris is headed for Africa, to cover an African summit meeting. This morning he gave me a rundown on the refugees, and the political situation behind them is far more complex that I would have thought simply looking at television footage of all those people, those children with the most beautiful eyes in the world, starving and left at roadside to wait for someone who will never come back, being dead. It is all so dreadful that if it were not happening to real people it would be inconceivable. However, it is happening to real people, and is conceivable, just barely. Anyway, Chris is going down there. Do you think he might be in any real danger? Chris does not always level with me on this factor, not wishing to cause worry, though I worry enough on other grounds to make up for that and many other such sources. One human life. True, but it is his. And *that's* what worries me the most of all.

I don't mean to inflict all this on you, but I think of you so often—and now Susan, too—that it is hard for me to realize that I have not known you for years. Your empathy is so instantaneous that it would be impossible not to feel thus. Tell me what I might need to know about Africa, and what, as a reporter, Chris may be prepared to expect. Will he be with soldiers, "peace keepers," and such? More worry, and again, I don't want to lay all this on you. But *do* tell me what you can.

As to news at this end, my producer, Richard Roth, meets with the Coen brothers, the studio people, and various lawyers, agents, and other functionaries on the 23rd. By the time you get this I should know more than I do now, and I'll tell you right off.

My best, and keep in (close) touch,
Ever,

To: David Bottoms[15]   RTL, Emory University
                                             4620 Lelia's Court
                                             Columbia, S.C. 29206

                                             December 2, 1996
Dear David:

Here is something for you, if you like it. The next time William Tecumseh Sherman comes after us, all the (Southern) forces of nature are going to com-

---

15. English professor at Georgia State University and editor of *Five Points* magazine. Dickey submitted a poem entitled "The Confederate Line at Ogeechee Creek."

bine against him, as well as the domestic and farming implements, and we'll see what happens *then*!

Anyway, let me know if you can use this, and I'll be guided accordingly.

I'll cut the letter short to get it in the mail. Let me hear from you as soon as you can, by phone if you like.

Ever,

To: Hal Wooten

CC, Emory University
4620 Lelia's Court
Columbia, S.C. 29206

December 12, 1996

Dear Mr. Wooden:

I appreciate greatly your letter, and the things you say. I have no idea where you may have read the information about my life, but I am glad that you found something in the account that was of value to you.

I send a picture of myself, taken some years ago.

Again, thanks for telling me about seeing *Deliverance* on TV. It might interest you to know that my latest novel, To The White Sea, is now being made into a movie, and I hope you will like that one, too.

As to my "heroics," I have nothing further to say that my life has not already said. I consider myself a survivor; luck has been with me on land and sea, and in the air. And as to the handshake, I would be glad to offer it actually, as I do now, invisibly. Anytime.

Cordially,

To: Betty Spears

CC, Emory University
December 1996
4620 Lelia's Court
Columbia, S.C. 29206

Dear Betty:

Thank you very much for your card and your news. Believe me, I know what this immobility is all about, since I am still hooked up to a life-support system myself. I hope to work free of it by some means, and thus regain at least a small measure of outside movement. But, as much as I have traveled, it doesn't look as though I will be taking any long-range trips. So much of my life has been occupied with movement that I am not really sorry, and am pretty much content to sit here and do what I should do, which is to write, and take advantage of the last part of my mind, before the whole thing goes. I take confidence from the fact that Monroe is working; it would be impossible to believe that anything he says wouldn't be good. I just want to read it, when it comes out.

Bronwen is well, and will be home for a month over Christmas. Her school-work is challenging, but she likes that, and is very deeply into it. She reads a lot, and talks endlessly, and I sit and serve as a sounding-board. It is quite good time, between us.

I'll close by wishing you the best of all Christmases, and hoping for more. We must all be together the next time. I would like that a lot. I mean, a *whole* lot.

If you see him tell your local poet—Prunty, is his name?—hello for me, and have him send me some of his work. The little I have seen is very good indeed.

Ever,

Debriefings

Despite proceedings to the contrary, Dickey's marriage to Deborah legally continued; the divorce was never finalized. Ill and at times uncertain as to whether he really wanted a divorce, Dickey never signed the final papers. On August 15, 1997, all parties finally agreed to a settlement. Christopher, Kevin, and Bronwen became the beneficiaries of the estate, while Deborah received Dickey's retirement benefits, which totaled approximately $170,000.

In July 1998 the editorial board of Modern Library, which had been publishing classic English literature at affordable prices since 1917 and which was now a division of Random House, selected the top one hundred novels of the twentieth century. The board members making the selection were Christopher Cerf, Gore Vidal, Daniel J. Boorstin, Shelby Foote, Vartan Gregorian, A. S. Byatt, Edmund Morris, John Richardson, Arthur M. Schlesinger Jr., and William Styron. Heading the list was Joyce's *Ulysses,* followed by Fitzgerald's *The Great Gatsby* and Joyce's *A Portrait of the Artist as a Young Man.* Writers such as Flannery O'Connor and Nobel laureate Toni Morrison were not included, nor were Eudora Welty, Thomas Pynchon, John Updike, and Doris Lessing. James Dickey's *Deliverance* was forty-second, a fact that would not have pleased Dickey; he would have viewed the entire selection process either as a fraud or a marketing gimmick. The German publishing conglomerate Bertelsmann, which owned Random House, was then publishing fifty-nine of the one hundred novels, and nine of the ten board members were published by the group. Dickey, in any event, maintained until the end of his life that *Alnilam* was his best novel.

At his death Dickey was working on a collection of poems entitled "Death, and the Day's Light." One of the poems, "The Drift-Spell," presented a trip Dickey and Kevin took to visit Maxine's grave. Beneath the Spanish moss in the old cemetery, Dickey imagined joining her in death:

. . . Without words, we shall know
That we have her forever: are learning to the full
What we have: death, and the day's light,

The three of us in love. Moss,
Your mother's eyes, and an owl in stone.

Love, and the day's light?

No, she is honest with us
Anywhere, son. Death and the day's light

With us here, full of the drift-spell.

Two other poems were grouped together under the collective title "Two Poems on the Survival of the Male Body"—"Show Us the Sea," a long expansion of a poem Dickey had written years before, "Giving a Son to the Sea," about an aging father watching with binoculars his lifeguard son and other young men on the beach as they bodysurf and strike poses like weight lifters, and "For Jules Bacon," which depicts a flier in the Pacific during World War II who attempts to emulate Mr. America by fashioning a set of weights from discarded war materiel and exercising rigorously. In the former, Dickey, who is "invisible with sand," addresses what he calls "Real God," asking that the magnified physicality and male camaraderie be brought forward for him to witness. In "For Jules Bacon," the persona affirms the human body in and of itself, its essential structure of muscles and blood, as a counterstatement against the destructiveness of combat, against death itself: "I rose. War, Jules, and nothing else / Jules, but death / But body. War. I rose. War, war, Jules, / War. War roared with life, and you saved me." If he can perfect his body, enter a mystique of perfection, the narrator believes, he will inexplicably achieve a state of invulnerability that time and circumstance cannot affect.

James Dickey had been a Buckhead Boy, born in 1923 on West Wesley Road in a monied section on the edge of Atlanta that resembled an enclave more than a neighborhood. Even though Dickey himself believed that his academic and athletic accomplishments had disappointed his parents and that he was generally a failure, growing up in Buckhead during the decade before World War II conveyed an attitude of uniqueness. Buckhead Boys viewed themselves as entitled, representing "the best that privilege offered, a kind of monied hypermasculinity that strutted with confidence of a time and place that viewed itself as manifestly special." The area was "its own nation-state, with its own rituals, manners and rites of passage. For the boys who grew up there, the principle [sic] rites involved cars, women, and football." Anne Rivers Siddons, whose novel *Peachtree Road* is largely set in Buckhead, has asserted, "They were like a brood of royal cousins running around. They were the perfect match of creature and habitat; it's what made them so supremely comfortable in their skins."[1] Dickey had graduated from North Fulton High School in 1941, played football and run track, and his 1969 poem, "Looking for the Buckhead Boys," revealed his emotional need to recapture that youth, a need derived from and driven by his experiences growing up in Buckhead. The past held him; returning to it, even in poetry, was irresistible.

In his 1986 essay "Cosmic Deliverance," he reveled in what the universe had given him. "Toward where you are," he wrote, "the whole of it, alive with angles and exact, is pointing, and it will find you where you stand, and will— yet always with its wilderness arrogance—confirm you as surely as it does the lion and the comet, and bear you out, and on."[2] Yet Dickey's heightened sensitivity to the promises of life, to its wild and inexplicable wonder and mystery, necessitated that he re-create that past if for no other reason than that he wanted to be larger, better than he felt he was. He admitted in an interview four years later that because he was essentially fainthearted and lacked self-assurance, he deliberately embraced force and vigor, an "assumed personality" that he characterized as "big, strong, hard drinking, hard fighting." "Nothing could be less characteristic of the true James Dickey," he asserted, "who is a timid, cowardly person." Although the public perception was otherwise, Dickey said, "you can't fool yourself, so you spend your life fooling yourself. The self that you fool yourself into is the one that functions."[3] Dickey's personality, then, contained this diversity, or contradiction, and his poetic voice often suggested it, which is the dilemma Peter Davison confronted when he examined Dickey's poetry in 1969.

Davison argued that the world for Dickey was not a classical social structure that formulated a city governed by law, with anarchy, like a terrible ocean, ever nibbling at its shores. The world for Dickey had depth and dimension that demanded exploration by a sensibility that would penetrate ever more deeply into its guises of reality. His poetry, then, constituted, in a line from "Buckdancer's Choice," "the thousand variations of one song." From a linguistic standpoint, Dickey's problem became how to express his mystical intentions in concrete images—that is, how to discover a bridge between the flesh and the spirit, the Aristotelian and the Platonic—because his poetry is "a search, in a sense, for heaven on earth." Ironically, Davison asserted, the ultimate way of becoming more than the self is to die. Dickey's technique, however,

1. Drew Jubera, "The Buckhead Boys," *Atlanta Constitution*, December 20, 1990, pp. G1, 3.
2. "Cosmic Deliverance," in *Halley's Comet*, Commemorative Issue (Prestige Publications, 1986), 8–9.
3. Suarez, "An Interview with James Dickey," *Contemporary Literature* 31.2 (1990): 117–32.

still lagged behind his aspirations because he arrived at his craft late, knowing what he wanted to say but not how to say it, not, as it were, how to fly with words. Davison worried that in straining to reach the universal, Dickey would overstep the abilities of language, suggesting that such writing "requires a vast fire to keep the cauldron boiling. If he were to encounter a slight recession of energy, such as that which seems lately to have overtaken Robert Lowell, Dickey's value as a poet might easily enter into a decline just at the moment when his reputation, like Lowell's today, has reached its apogee."[4]

It is possible to argue that with the financial success three years later of his novel *Deliverance* and his ever-increasing use of alcohol to "keep the cauldron boiling," Dickey lost both the motivation and the creativity to explore more deeply into reality. Moreover, the central motion of his creative wheel assumed a new direction in the seventies just at the time society itself assumed new political directions. The public persona that Dickey had created in the sixties (and that he largely continued to assume into the eighties) in order to promote himself in particular and poetry in general now seemed to work against him.

In one of his early published poems, "The Call," which later became part of "The Owl King," the speaker wanders the woods at night, searching for his blind, lost son:

I hear the king of the owls sing.
I did not awaken that sound,
And yet it is coming back,

In touching every tree upon the hill.
The breath falls out of my voice,
And yet the singing keeps on.

In January 1997 the breath in Dickey's voice was indeed "falling out." He knew this but accepted it with difficulty. Because he had declared six years previously, "We're all aviators of the word,"[5] staying with language literally necessitated continued survival. Yet he also recognized that the body, that breath, would give out; surrender was an inevitability. In the final poem of *The Whole Motion,* he had offered that recognition and the possibility of something more:

4. Davison, "The Difficulties of Being Major," *Atlantic Monthly* 220 (October 1967): 116–21.

5. Robert Morris, "Dueling Dickeys: James Dickey's Odyssey Home," *Creative Loafing,* December 14, 1991, p. 29.

Heat makes this, heat makes any
Word: human lungs,
Human lips. Not like eternity, which, naked, every time
Will call on lightning
To say it all: No after
Or before. We try for that

And fail. Our voice
Fails, but for an instant
Is like the other; breath alone
That came as though humanly panting
From far back, in unspeakably beautiful

Empty space

And struck: at just this moment
Found the word "golden."

Stepping out of convention, Dickey undertook a mission to re-create the world in order to rediscover it, recognizing that the higher he flew, the better his chance to discern the "golden" language necessary not merely to relate the facts of the earth but also to possess and offer a world now rendered uncontrollably whole. There was, however, always the problem of time, a concern he recognized in an unpublished poem written in the fifties, "At My Family's Burial Plot." "Soon," it opens,

What shall be told
To tell the half-old bones,
Come walking here, no mother
No father, not a child
Would come,
And my bones half-wish to lie down

Here, in this marble place.
Shook up, the grass is yet,
One day a week, almost long enough to mow.
It is the wind of time
Shakes them, and I
In my trousers, sit on a marble bench,
Enveloped, on fire with Time.
Who would believe it is this?

His voice was human, he knew, and so would fail, but needing to possess the sky, courting public opinion and the dangers of absurdity, he might yet win. "I can sit on my grave," he wrote, "In the sun, and feel both life and death / Outlined, and waiting / And the sun on the heart / Dare the skin to die." Unlike Whitman, whose poetry he had always admired, he could not at the end of his life rest peacefully on the waters of the past. He wanted to "feel the fires / Of the sun and the earth, / When they were one, burning plotless, un-equalled, from the stone." It was who he was.

Index